THE ISRAEL–ARAB READER

Walter Laqueur was born in Breslau (then in
Germany) in 1921. He is Director of the Institute
of Contemporary History and the Wiener Library
in London and Professor of the History of Ideas
and Politics at Brandeis University in America.
He is also co-editor of the *Journal of Contemporary
History*. His books are about Central and Eastern
Europe and the Middle East; those on the Middle
East are *Communism and Nationalism in the
Middle East*, *The Middle East in Transition*, *The
Road to War* (also published in Penguins), and
The Struggle for the Middle East (to be published
in Penguins).

The Israel–Arab Reader

A DOCUMENTARY HISTORY OF
THE MIDDLE EAST CONFLICT

Edited by Walter Laqueur

PENGUIN BOOKS

Penguin Books Ltd, Harmondsworth,
Middlesex, England
Penguin Books Australia Ltd, Ringwood,
Victoria, Australia

First published in the U.S.A. 1969
Published in Great Britain by Weidenfeld & Nicolson 1969
Revised Edition published in Pelican Books 1970

Copyright © B. L. Mazel, Inc., 1969, 1970

Made and printed in Great Britain by
C. Nicholls & Company Ltd
Set in Linotype Pilgrim

Contents

Introduction

This collection of documents and comment aims to provide a
better understanding of the background of the Arab–Jewish
conflict, which has led to three wars within two decades. There
is no certainty that war will not break out again, nor can it be
taken for granted that it will always be possible to localize it.

Zionism and the Arab national movement appeared on the
political scene at about the same time. When Britain received
the Mandate for Palestine on behalf of the League of Nations,
the total population of the country was less than a million. It
was widely believed at the time that the aspirations of Jews
and Arabs could be combined. By 1937, a British Commission
of Inquiry found that an 'irrepressible conflict' had arisen between two national communities within the narrow boundaries of one small country. Jewish immigration grew by leaps
and bounds following the rise of Nazism in Europe ; the Arabs,
supported by public opinion in the neighbouring countries, demanded that no more Jews should be permitted to enter Palestine.

In this collection, the story of the unfolding crisis is traced on
the basis of Zionist and Arab declarations, and of the findings
and recommendations of the various commissions of inquiry
during the nineteen thirties and forties. The partition of Palestine, decided by the United Nations in 1947, was rejected by the
Arabs ; it led to the establishment of the State of Israel and the
first Arab–Israeli war in 1948. As a result of the war, new problems were created – such as the refugee question – which made
a reconciliation between the two peoples even more difficult.
Arab guerrillas carried the war into Israel even after the armistice agreements had been signed and Israel retaliated by raids
beyond its borders. The neighbouring Arab states refused to

recognize the existence of the Jewish state which, in their view, was illegitimate; they boycotted Israeli goods, blocked the Suez Canal and the Gulf of Aqaba. The war of 1956 ensued, and after a decade of uneasy truce, there was a new escalation culminating in the Six Day War in 1967.

The selection of documents has been made with an eye to the interests of the general reader, not the expert in international law. The armistice agreements of 1949, whatever their intrinsic importance, are mainly of a technical character and therefore of no great relevance in the present context. In many cases, substantial cuts in the documents were necessary; such deletions are indicated in the text. The historian always dislikes such procedure, for it opens him to charges of suppression of evidence, however careful and impartial his selection. But there was no other choice, for it is the aim of the present collection to present pertinent documents, viewpoints and opinions; it is not a legal source book. No useful purpose would have been served, for example, by reprinting the whole of Herzl's *The Jewish State* or the unabridged text of Nasser's speeches.

The editor has refrained (not without a struggle) from commenting in detail on the documents. A reader of this kind includes by necessity not only views with which he disagrees, but also statements which are factually untrue. But this is well nigh inevitable in polemics on a subject which is so highly charged with emotion; those claiming to speak with detachment and objectivity are not necessarily nearer to truth and justice than the self-avowed partisans. The discussions of the merits and demerits of the Jewish and the Arab case will continue for a long time and there will be no lack of involvement on the part of the participants. The task of a reader is more modest: to present a survey of representative views, past and present, on the Arab–Israeli conflict, but not to pass judgement on their intrinsic value.

I would like to record my gratitude to the Middle Eastern Document Section at the Institute of Contemporary History (The Wiener Library) in London and in particular to Mrs Christa

Wichmann and Mr Ze'ev Ben Shlomo in assisting me to collect the documents, as well as to B. L. Mazel for his help during this entire project.

Walter Laqueur

N

Occupied by Israel after the 1967 War

0   50
m.

Mediterranean

Sea

Beirut

Sidon

LEBANON

Damascus

Tyre

Quneitra

Haifa

Sea of
Galilee

Jenin

I S R A E L

S Y R I A

Nablus

Irbid

R. Jordan

Tel Aviv

Jerusalem

Gaza

Hébron

Amman

Port
Said

El
Arish

Dead
Sea

J O R D A N

Qantara

Ismailia

Cairo

MITLA
PASS

Maan

Suez

Kuntilla

R. Nile

Eilat

Aqaba

U N I T E D

Gulf of Suez

Gulf of Aqaba

S A U D I

A R A B

A R A B I A

R E P U B L I C

Sharm al
Shaikh

Straits of Tiran

(EGYPT)

Red   Sea

Part 1

From the Bilu to the British Mandate

Part 1 of the Reader covers the period from the
first stirrings of the Jewish and Arab national
movements to 1917, the date of the Balfour
Declaration. The tie between the Jewish communities
in what was still commonly defined as the diaspora
had been submerged but never entirely severed ;
it survived, for instance, in the traditional prayer
('Next year in Jerusalem') and found its political
expression in the emergence of the Zionist movement
in the last decade of the nineteenth century.
There was no specific Arab Palestinian national
consciousness, but among the leaders of the Arab
population of the Ottoman Empire the demand for
national self-determination gained ground.
After the defeat of the Turks in 1918, this movement
quickly gathered momentum.

Document 1

The Manifesto of the Bilu

BILU are the first letters of a passage in Isaiah, chapter ii, verse 5: 'House of Jacob, come, let us go.' The Biluim, about five hundred young people mainly from the Kharkov region, were part of the wider movement of the 'Lovers of Zion' (*Hovevei Zion*) which had developed in Russia in the early eighteen-eighties mainly under the impact of the pogroms of 1881. This manifesto was issued by a Bilu group in Constantinople in 1882.

*

To our brothers and sisters in Exile!

'If I help not myself, who will help me?'

Nearly two thousand years have elapsed since, in an evil hour, after a heroic struggle, the glory of our Temple vanished in fire and our kings and chieftains changed their crowns and diadems for the chains of exile. We lost our country where dwelt our beloved sires. Into the Exile we took with us, of all our glories, only a spark of the fire by which our Temple, the abode of our Great One, was engirdled, and this little spark kept us alive while the towers of our enemies crumbled into dust, and this spark leapt into celestial flame and shed light on the heroes of our race and inspired them to endure the horrors of the dance of death and the tortures of the *autos-da-fé*. And this spark is again kindling and will shine for us, a true pillar of fire going before us on the road to Zion, while behind us is a pillar of cloud, the pillar of oppression threatening to destroy us. Sleepest thou, O our nation? What hast thou been doing until 1882? Sleeping, and dreaming the false dream of Assimilation. Now, thank God, thou art awakened from thy slothful slumber. The Pogroms have awakened thee from thy charmed sleep. Thine eyes are open to recognize the cloudy delusive hopes. Canst thou listen silently to the taunts and mockeries of thine enemies? ... Where is thy ancient pride, thine olden spirit? Remember that thou wast a nation possessing a wise religion, a law, a constitution, a celestial Temple whose wall[1] is still a silent witness to the glories of the past; that thy sons dwelt in palaces and towers, and thy cities flourished in the splendour of civilization, while these enemies of thine dwelt like beasts in the muddy marshes of their dark woods. While thy children were clad in purple and fine linen, they wore the rough skins of the wolf and the bear. Art thou not ashamed?

Hopeless is your state in the West; the star of your future is gleaming in the East. Deeply conscious of all this, and inspired by the true teaching of our great master, Hillel, 'If I help not myself, who will help me?' we propose to form the following society for national ends.

The Society will be named 'BILU' according to the motto 'House of Jacob, come, let us go'. It will be divided into local branches according to the numbers of its members.

2. The seat of the Committee shall be Jerusalem.

3. Donations and contributions shall be unfixed and unlimited.

WE WANT

1. A home in our country. It was given us by the mercy of God; it is ours as registered in the archives of history.

2. To beg it of the Sultan himself, and if it be impossible to obtain this, to beg that we may at least possess it as a state within a larger state; the internal administration to be ours, to have our civil and political rights, and to act with the Turkish Empire only in foreign affairs, so as to help our brother Ishmael in the time of his need.

We hope that the interests of our glorious nation will rouse the national spirit in rich and powerful men, and that everyone, rich or poor, will give his best labours to the holy cause.

Greetings, dear brothers and sisters!

HEAR, O ISRAEL! The Lord our God, the Lord is one, and our land Zion is our one hope.

GOD be with us! THE PIONEERS OF BILU.

---

1. The Wailing Wall.

Document 2

*Negib Azouri: Programme of the League of the Arab Fatherland**

N. Azouri, a Christian Arab, edited the journal *L'Indépendance Arabe* in Paris before the First World War. His *'Réveil de la Nation Arabe dans l'Asie Turque* ... (1905) from which this excerpt is drawn was the 'first open demand for the secession of the Arab lands from the Ottoman empire' (Sylvia G. Haim: *Arab Nationalism*).

*

... There is nothing more liberal than the league's programme. The league wants, before anything else, to separate the civil and the religious power, in the interest of Islam and the Arab nation, and to form an Arab empire stretching from the Tigris and the Euphrates to the Suez Isthmus, and from the Mediterranean to the Arabian Sea.

The mode of government will be a constitutional sultanate based on the freedom of all the religions and the equality of all the citizens before the law. It will respect the interests of Europe, all the concessions and all the privileges which had been granted to her up to now by the Turks. It will also respect the autonomy of the Lebanon, and the independence of the principalities of Yemen, Nejd, and Iraq.

The league offers the throne of the Arab Empire to that prince of the Khedivial family of Egypt who will openly declare himself in its favour and who will devote his energy and his resources to this end.

It rejects the idea of unifying Egypt and the Arab Empire under the same monarchy, because the Egyptians do not belong to the Arab race; they are of the African Berber family and the language which they spoke before Islam bears no similarity to Arabic. There exists, moreover, between Egypt and the Arab Empire a natural frontier which must be respected in order to avoid the introduction, in the new state, of the germs

---

* Translated by Sylvia G. Haim.

of discord and destruction. Never, as a matter of fact, have the ancient Arab caliphs succeeded for any length of time in controlling the two countries at the same time ...

Document 3
Theodor Herzl: 'The Jewish State'

Theodor Herzl (1860-1904) was the founder of modern political Zionism. In the preface to *Der Judenstaat* (published in 1896) he says: 'The idea which I have developed in this pamphlet is a very old one: it is the restoration of the Jewish State.'

*

...The Jewish question still exists. It would be foolish to deny it. It is a remnant of the Middle Ages, which civilized nations do not even yet seem able to shake off, try as they will. They certainly showed a generous desire to do so when they emancipated us. The Jewish question exists wherever Jews live in perceptible numbers. Where it does not exist, it is carried by Jews in the course of their migrations. We naturally move to those places where we are not persecuted, and there our presence produces persecution. This is the case in every country, and will remain so, even in those highly civilized – for instance, France – until the Jewish question finds a solution on a political basis. The unfortunate Jews are now carrying the seeds of anti-Semitism into England; they have already introduced it into America.

I believe that I understand anti-Semitism, which is really a highly complex movement. I consider it from a Jewish standpoint, yet without fear or hatred. I believe that I can see what elements there are in it of vulgar sport, of common trade jealousy, of inherited prejudice, of religious intolerance, and also of pretended self-defence. I think the Jewish question is no more a social than a religious one, notwithstanding that it sometimes takes these and other forms. It is a national question, which can only be solved by making it a political world-question to be discussed and settled by the civilized nations of the world in council.

We are a people – one people.

We have honestly endeavoured everywhere to merge ourselves in the social life of surrounding communities and to preserve the faith of our fathers. We are not permitted to do so. In vain are we loyal patriots, our loyalty in some places running to extremes; in vain do we make the same sacrifices of life and property as our fellow-citizens ; in vain do we strive to increase the fame of our native land in science and art, or her wealth by trade and commerce. In countries where we have lived for centuries we are still cried down as strangers, and often by those whose ancestors were not yet domiciled in the land where Jews had already had experience of suffering. The majority may decide which are the strangers; for this, as indeed every point which arises in the relations between nations, is a question of might. I do not here surrender any portion of our prescriptive right, when I make this statement merely in my own name as an individual. In the world as it now is and for an indefinite period will probably remain, might precedes right. It is useless, therefore, for us to be loyal patriots, as were the Huguenots who were forced to emigrate. If we could only be left in peace . . .

But I think we shall not be left in peace.

Oppression and persecution cannot exterminate us. No nation on earth has survived such struggles and sufferings as we have gone through. Jew-baiting has merely stripped off our weaklings ; the strong among us were invariably true to their race when persecution broke out against them. This attitude was most clearly apparent in the period immediately following the emancipation of the Jews. Those Jews who were advanced intellectually and materially entirely lost the feeling of belonging to their race. Wherever our political well-being has lasted for any length of time, we have assimilated with our surroundings. I think this is not discreditable. Hence, the statesman who would wish to see a Jewish strain in his nation would have to provide for the duration of our political well-being ; and even a Bismarck could not do that.

For old prejudices against us still lie deep in the hearts of the people. He who would have proofs of this need only listen to the people where they speak with frankness and simplicity: proverb and fairy-tale are both anti-Semitic. A nation is everywhere a great child, which can certainly be educated; but its education would, even in most favourable circumstances, occupy such a vast amount of time that we could, as already mentioned, remove our own difficulties by other means long before the process was accomplished.

Assimilation, by which I understood not only external conformity in dress, habits, customs, and language, but also identity of feeling and manner – assimilation of Jews could be effected only by intermarriage. But the need for mixed marriages would have to be felt by the majority; their mere recognition by law would certainly not suffice . . .

No one can deny the gravity of the situation of the Jews. Wherever they live in perceptible numbers, they are more or less persecuted. Their equality before the law, granted by statute, has become practically a dead letter. They are debarred from filling even moderately high positions, either in the army, or in any public or private capacity. And attempts are made to thrust them out of business also: 'Don't buy from Jews!'

Attacks in parliaments, in assemblies, in the press, in the pulpit, in the street, on journeys – for example, their exclusion from certain hotels – even in places of recreation, become daily more numerous. The forms of persecutions varying according to the countries and social circles in which they occur. In Russia, imposts are levied on Jewish villages; in Rumania, a few persons are put to death; in Germany, they get a good beating occasionally; in Austria, anti-Semites exercise terrorism over all public life; in Algeria, there are travelling agitators; in Paris, the Jews are shut out of the so-called best social circles and excluded from clubs. Shades of anti-Jewish feeling are innumerable. But this is not to be an attempt to make out a doleful category of Jewish hardships.

I do not intend to arouse sympathetic emotions on our behalf. That would be foolish, futile, and an undignified proceeding. I shall content myself with putting the following questions to the Jews: Is it not true that, in countries where we live in perceptible numbers, the position of Jewish lawyers, doctors, technicians, teachers, and employees of all descriptions becomes daily more intolerable? Is it not true, that the Jewish middle classes are seriously threatened? Is it not true, that the passions of the mob are incited against our wealthy people? Is it not true, that our poor endure greater sufferings than any other proletariat? I think that this external pressure makes itself felt everywhere. In our economically upper classes it causes discomfort, in our middle classes continual and grave anxieties, in our lower classes absolute despair.

Everything tends, in fact, to one and the same conclusion, which is clearly enunciated in that classic Berlin phrase: '*Juden Raus!*' (Out with the Jews!)

I shall now put the question in the briefest possible form: Are we to 'get out' now and where to?

Or, may we yet remain? And, how long?

Let us first settle the point of staying where we are. Can we hope for better days, can we possess our souls in patience, can we wait in pious resignation till the princes and peoples of this earth are more mercifully disposed towards us? I say that we cannot hope for a change in the current of feeling. And why not? Even if we were as near to the hearts of princes as are their other subjects, they could not protect us. They would only feel popular hatred by showing us too much favour. By 'too much', I really mean less than is claimed as a right by every ordinary citizen, or by every race. The nations in whose midst Jews live are all either covertly or openly anti-Semitic.

The common people have not, and indeed cannot have, any historic comprehension. They do not know that the sins of the Middle Ages are now being visited on the nations of Europe. We are what the Ghetto made us. We have attained pre-eminence in finance, because medieval conditions drove us to it. The same process is now being repeated. We are again being forced into finance, now it is the stock exchange, by being kept out of other branches of economic activity. Being on the stock exchange, we are consequently exposed afresh to contempt. At

the same time we continue to produce an abundance of mediocre intellects who find no outlet, and this endangers our social
position as much as does our increasing wealth. Educated Jews
without means are now rapidly becoming Socialists. Hence we
are certain to suffer very severely in the struggle between
classes, because we stand in the most exposed position in the
camps of both Socialists and capitalists ...

The Plan

The whole plan is in its essence perfectly simple, as it must
necessarily be if it is to come within the comprehension of
all.

Let the sovereignty be granted us over a portion of the globe
large enough to satisfy the rightful requirements of a nation;
the rest we shall manage for ourselves.

The creation of a new state is neither ridiculous nor impossible. We have in our day witnessed the process in connexion
with nations which were not largely members of the middle
class, but poorer, less educated, and consequently weaker than
ourselves. The governments of all countries scourged by anti-
Semitism will be keenly interested in assisting us to obtain the
sovereignty we want.

The plan, simple in design, but complicated in execution,
will be carried out by two agencies: The Society of Jews and
the Jewish Company.

The Society of Jews will do the preparatory work in the
domains of science and politics, which the Jewish Company
will afterwards apply practically.

The Jewish Company will be the liquidating agent of the
business interests of departing Jews, and will organize commerce and trade in the new country.

We must not imagine the departure of the Jews to be a sudden one. It will be gradual, continuous, and will cover many
decades. The poorest will go first to cultivate the soil. In accordance with a preconceived plan, they will construct roads,
bridges, railways and telegraph installations; regulate rivers;

and build their own dwellings ; their labour will create trade, trade will create markets and markets will attract new settlers, for every man will go voluntarily, at his own expense and his own risk. The labour expended on the land will enhance its value, and the Jews will soon perceive that a new and permanent sphere of operation is opening here for that spirit of enterprise which has heretofore met only with hatred and obloquy.

If we wish to found a state today, we shall not do it in the way which would have been the only possible one a thousand years ago. It is foolish to revert to old stages of civilization, as many Zionists would like to do. Supposing, for example, we were obliged to clear a country of wild beasts, we should not set about the task in the fashion of Europeans of the fifth century. We should not take spear and lance and go out singly in pursuit of bears ; we would organize a large and active hunting party, drive the animals together, and throw a melinite bomb into their midst.

If we wish to conduct building operations, we shall not plant a mass of stakes and piles on the shore of a lake, but we shall build as men build now. Indeed, we shall build in a bolder and more stately style than was ever adopted before, for we now possess means which men never yet possessed.

The emigrants standing lowest in the economic scale will be slowly followed by those of a higher grade. Those who at this moment are living in despair will go first. They will be led by the mediocre intellects which we produce so superabundantly and which are persecuted everywhere.

This pamphlet will open a general discussion on the Jewish Question, but that does not mean that there will be any voting on it. Such a result would ruin the cause from the outset, and dissidents must remember that allegiance or opposition is entirely voluntary. He who will not come with us should remain behind.

Let all who are willing to join us, fall in behind our banner and fight for our cause with voice and pen and deed.

Those Jews who agree with our idea of a state will attach themselves to the Society, which will thereby be authorized to confer and treat with governments in the name of our people.

The Society will thus be acknowledged in its relations with governments as a state-creating power. This acknowledgement will practically create the state.

Should the powers declare themselves willing to admit our sovereignty over a neutral piece of land, then the Society will enter into negotiations for the possession of this land. Here two territories come under consideration, Palestine and Argentine. In both countries important experiments in colonization have been made, though on the mistaken principle of a gradual infiltration of Jews. An infiltration is bound to end badly. It continues till the inevitable moment when the native population feels itself threatened, and forces the government to stop a further influx of Jews. Immigration is consequently futile unless we have the sovereign right to continue such immigration.

The Society of Jews will treat with the present masters of the land, putting itself under the protectorate of the European Powers, if they prove friendly to the plan. We could offer the present possessors of the land enormous advantages, assume part of the public debt, build new roads for traffic, which our presence in the country would render necessary, and do many other things. The creation of our state would be beneficial to adjacent countries, because the cultivation of a strip of land increases the value of its surrounding districts in innumerable ways.

Document 4

The Basle Declaration

This official statement of Zionist purpose was adopted by the first Zionist Congress in Basle in August 1897.

*

The aim of Zionism is to create for the Jewish people a home in Palestine secured by public law.

The Congress contemplates the following means to the attainment of this end:

1. The promotion, on suitable lines, of the colonization of Palestine by Jewish agricultural and industrial workers.

2. The organization and binding together of the whole of Jewry by means of appropriate institutions, local and international, in accordance with the laws of each country.

3. The strengthening and fostering of Jewish national sentiment and consciousness.

4. Preparatory steps towards obtaining government consent, where necessary, to the attainment of the aim of Zionism.

Document 5

The Sykes–Picot Agreement

Sir Mark Sykes (1873-1919), a distinguished British orientalist, and Charles Georges-Picot, formerly French Consul in Beirut, prepared a draft agreement in 1915–16 about the post-war division of the Middle East, which was also approved in principle by Russia.

*

1. Sir Edward Grey to Paul Cambon, 15 May 1916

I shall have the honour to reply fully in a further note to your Excellency's note of the 9th instant, relative to the creation of an Arab State, but I should meanwhile be grateful if your Excellency could assure me that in those regions which, under the conditions recorded in that communication, become entirely French, or in which French interests are recognized as predominant, any existing British concessions, rights of navigation or development, and the rights and privileges of any British religious, scholastic, or medical institutions will be maintained.

His Majesty's Government are, of course, ready to give a reciprocal assurance in regard to the British area.

2. Grey to Cambon, 16 May 1916

I have the honour to acknowledge the receipt of your Excellency's note of the 9th instant, stating that the French Government accept the limits of a future Arab State, or Confederation of States, and of those parts of Syria where French interests predominate, together with certain conditions attached thereto, such as they result from recent discussions in London and Petrograd on the subject.

I have the honour to inform your Excellency in reply that the acceptance of the whole project, as it now stands, will involve the abdication of considerable British interests, but, since His Majesty's Government recognize the advantage to the general cause of the Allies entailed in producing a more favourable internal political situation in Turkey, they are ready to accept the arrangement now arrived at, provided that the co-operation of the Arabs is secured, and that the Arabs fulfil the conditions and obtain the towns of Homs, Hama, Damascus, and Aleppo.

It is accordingly understood between the French and British Governments:

1. That France and Great Britain are prepared to recognize and protect an independent Arab State or a Confederation of Arab States in the areas (A) and (B) marked on the annexed map [*map not reproduced: Ed.*], under the suzerainty of an Arab chief. That in area (A) France, and in area (B) Great Britain, shall have priority of right of enterprise and local loans. That in area (A) France, and in area (B) Great Britain, shall alone supply advisers or foreign functionaries at the request of the Arab State or Confederation of Arab States.

2. That in the blue area France, and in the red area Great Britain, shall be allowed to establish such direct or indirect administration or control as they desire and as they may think fit to arrange with the Arab State or Confederation of Arab States.

3. That in the brown area there shall be established an international administration, the form of which is to be decided upon after consultation with Russia, and subsequently in con-

sultation with the other Allies, and the representatives of the
Sharif of Mecca.

4. That Great Britain be accorded (1) the ports of Haifa and
Acre, (2) guarantee of a given supply of water from the Tigris
and Euphrates in area (A) for area (B). His Majesty's Government, on their part, undertake that they will at no time enter
into negotiations for the cession of Cyprus to any third Power
without the previous consent of the French Government.

5. That Alexandretta shall be a free port as regards the trade
of the British Empire, and that there shall be no discrimination
in port charges or facilities as regards British shipping and
British goods; that there shall be freedom of transit for British
goods through Alexandretta and by railway through the blue
area, whether those goods are intended for or originate in the
red area, or (B) area, or area (A); and there shall be no discrimination, direct or indirect, against British goods on any railway
or against British goods or ships at any port serving the areas
mentioned.

That Haifa shall be a free port as regards the trade of France,
her dominions and protectorates, and there shall be no discrimination in port charges or facilities as regards French shipping and French goods. There shall be freedom of transit for
French goods through Haifa and by the British railway through
the brown area, whether those goods are intended for or originate in the blue area, area (A), or area (B), and there shall be no
discrimination, direct or indirect, against French goods on any
railway, or against French goods or ships at any port serving
the areas mentioned.

6. That in area (A) the Baghdad Railway shall not be extended southwards beyond Mosul, and in area (B) northwards
beyond Samarra, until a railway connecting Baghdad with
Aleppo via the Euphrates Valley has been completed, and then
only with the concurrence of the two Governments.

7. That Great Britain has the right to build, administer, and
be sole owner of a railway connecting Haifa with area (B),
and shall have a perpetual right to transport troops along such
a line at all times.

It is to be understood by both Governments that this railway is to facilitate the connexion of Baghdad with Haifa by rail, and it is further understood that, if the engineering difficulties and expense entailed by keeping this connecting line in the brown area only make the project unfeasible, that the French Government shall be prepared to consider that the line in question may also traverse the polygon Banias-Keis Marib-Salkhab Tell Otsda-Mesmie before reaching area (B).

8. For a period of twenty years the existing Turkish customs tariff shall remain in force throughout the whole of the blue and red areas, as well as in areas (A) and (B), and no increase in the rates of duty or conversion from *ad valorem* to specific rates shall be made except by agreement between the two Powers.

There shall be no interior customs barriers between any of the above-mentioned areas. The customs duties leviable on goods destined for the interior shall be collected at the port of entry and handed over to the administration of the area of destination.

9. It shall be agreed that the French Government will at no time enter into any negotiations for the cession of their rights and will not cede such rights in the blue area to any third Power, except the Arab State or Confederation of Arab States, without the previous agreement of His Majesty's Government, who, on their part, will give a similar undertaking to the French Government regarding the red area.

10. The British and French Governments, as the protectors of the Arab State, shall agree that they will not themselves acquire and will not consent to a third Power acquiring territorial possessions in the Arabian peninsula, nor consent to a third Power installing a naval base either on the east coast, or on the islands, of the Red Sea. This, however, shall not prevent such adjustment of the Aden frontier as may be necessary in consequence of recent Turkish aggression.

11. The negotiations with the Arabs as to the boundaries of the Arab State or Confederation of Arab States shall be continued through the same channel as heretofore on behalf of the two Powers.

12. It is agreed that measures to control the importation of

arms into the Arab territories will be considered by the two Governments.

I have further the honour to state that, in order to make the agreement complete, His Majesty's Government are proposing to the Russian Government to exchange notes analogous to those exchanged by the latter and your Excellency's Government on 26 April last. Copies of these notes will be communicated to your Excellency as soon as exchanged.

I would also venture to remind your Excellency that the conclusion of the present agreement raises, for practical consideration, the question of the claims of Italy to a share in any partition or rearrangement of Turkey in Asia, as formulated in Article 9 of the agreement of 26 April 1915 between Italy and the Allies.

His Majesty's Government further consider that the Japanese Government should be informed of the arrangement now concluded.

Document 6

The McMahon Letter

Sir Henry McMahon (1862-1949), British High Commissioner in Cairo, negotiated in 1915-16 with Hussain ibn Ali, the Sharif of Mecca. The British government promised to support his bid for the restoration of the Caliphate (and leadership in the Arab world) if Hussain supported the British war effort against Turkey. Palestine was not mentioned by name in this exchange: the Arabs subsequently claimed that it had been included in the promise of an independent Arab state. The British denied this – as evidenced by McMahon's letter published in *The Times* in 1937.

*

24 October 1915

I have received your letter of 29 Shawal 1333, with much pleasure and your expression of friendliness and sincerity have given me the greatest satisfaction.

I regret that you should have received from my last letter the impression that I regarded the question of limits and boundaries with coldness and hesitation; such was not the case, but it appeared to me that the time had not yet come when that question could be discussed in a conclusive manner.

I have realized, however, from your last letter that you regard this question as one of vital and urgent importance. I have, therefore, lost no time in informing the Government of Great Britain of the contents of your letter, and it is with great pleasure that I communicate to you on their behalf the following statement, which I am confident you will receive with satisfaction.

The two districts of Mersina and Alexandretta and portions of Syria lying to the west of the districts of Damascus, Homs, Hama and Aleppo cannot be said to be purely Arab, and should be excluded from the limits demanded.

With the above modification, and without prejudice to our existing treaties with Arab chiefs, we accept those limits.

As for those regions lying within those frontiers wherein Great Britain is free to act without detriment to the interests of her ally, France, I am empowered in the name of the Government of Great Britain to give the following assurances and make the following reply to your letter:

(1) Subject to the above modifications, Great Britain is prepared to recognize and support the independence of the Arabs in all the regions within the limits demanded by the Sharif of Mecca.

(2) Great Britain will guarantee the Holy Places against all external aggression and will recognize their inviolability.

(3) When the situation admits, Great Britain will give to the Arabs her advice and will assist them to establish what may appear to be the most suitable forms of government in those various territories.

(4) On the other hand, it is understood that the Arabs have decided to seek the advice and guidance of Great Britain only, and that such European advisers and officials as may be required for the formation of a sound form of administration will be British.

(5) With regard to the *vilayets* of Baghdad and Basra, the Arabs will recognize that the established position and interests

of Great Britain necessitate special administrative arrangements in order to secure these territories from foreign aggression, to promote the welfare of the local populations and to safeguard our mutual economic interests.

I am convinced that this declaration will assure you beyond all possible doubt of the sympathy of Great Britain towards the aspirations of her friends the Arabs and will result in a firm and lasting alliance, the immediate results of which will be the expulsion of the Turks from the Arab countries and the freeing of the Arab peoples from the Turkish yoke, which for so many years has pressed heavily upon them.

I have confined myself in this letter to the more vital and important questions, and if there are any other matters dealt with in your letters which I have omitted to mention, we may discuss them at some convenient date in the future.

It was with very great relief and satisfaction that I heard of the safe arrival of the Holy Carpet and the accompanying offerings which, thanks to the clearness of your directions and the excellence of your arrangements, were landed without trouble or mishap in spite of the dangers and difficulties occasioned by the present sad war. May God soon bring a lasting peace and freedom of all peoples.

I am sending this letter by the hand of your trusted and excellent messenger, Sheikh Mohammed ibn Arif ibn Uraifan, and he will inform you of the various matters of interest, but of less vital importance, which I have not mentioned in this letter.

(Compliments)
A. Henry McMahon.

Document 7

The Balfour Declaration

British policy during the war years became gradually committed to the idea of the establishment of a Jewish home in Palestine. After discussions at cabinet level and consultation with Jewish leaders, the decision was made known in the form of a letter by Arthur James Lord Balfour (1848-1930) to Lord Rothschild.

Foreign Office
2 November 1917

Dear Lord Rothschild,

I have much pleasure in conveying to you, on behalf of His Majesty's Government, the following declaration of sympathy with Jewish Zionist aspirations which has been submitted to, and approved by, the Cabinet.

'His Majesty's Government view with favour the establishment in Palestine of a national home for the Jewish people, and will use their best endeavours to facilitate the achievement of this object, it being clearly understood that nothing shall be done which may prejudice the civil and religious rights of existing non-Jewish communities in Palestine, or the rights and political status enjoyed by Jews in any other country.'

I should be grateful if you would bring this declaration to the knowledge of the Zionist Federation.

Yours sincerely,
Arthur James Balfour.

Document 8

The Faisal–Weizmann Agreement and Faisal–Frankfurter Letters

During the peace conference Emir Faisal (1855-1933), the son of Hussain, the Sharif of Mecca, met various Jewish leaders and signed an agreement with Dr Chaim Weizmann (1877-1952), leader of the Zionist movement. Faisal, who in 1921 became King of Iraq, had it announced ten years later that 'His Majesty does not remember having written anything of that kind with his knowledge'.

*

Agreement between Emir Faisal and Dr Weizmann, 3 January 1919

His Royal Highness the Emir Faisal, representing and acting on behalf of the Arab Kingdom of Hejaz, and Dr Chaim Weizmann, representing and acting on behalf of the Zionist Organization, mindful of the racial kinship and ancient bonds existing

between the Arabs and the Jewish people, and realizing that
the surest means of working out the consummation of their
national aspirations is through the closest possible collaboration in the development of the Arab State and Palestine, and
being desirous further of confirming the good understanding
which exists between them, have agreed upon the following
Articles:

Article 1. The Arab State and Palestine in all their relations
and undertakings shall be controlled by the most cordial goodwill and understanding, and to this end Arab and Jewish duly
accredited agents shall be established and maintained in the
respective territories.

Article 2. Immediately following the completion of the de-
liberations of the Peace Conference, the definite boundaries
between the Arab State and Palestine shall be determined by a
commission to be agreed upon by the parties hereto.

Article 3. In the establishment of the Constitution and Administration of Palestine all such measures shall be adopted as
will afford the fullest guarantees for carrying into effect the
British Government's Declaration of 2 November 1917.

Article 4. All necessary measures shall be taken to encourage
and stimulate immigration of Jews into Palestine on a large
scale, and as quickly as possible to settle Jewish immigrants
upon the land through closer settlement and intensive cultivation of the soil. In taking such measures the Arab peasant and
tenant farmers shall be protected in their rights, and shall be
assisted in forwarding their economic development.

Article 5. No regulation nor law shall be made prohibiting or
interfering in any way with the free exercise of religion; and
further the free exercise and enjoyment of religious profession
and worship without discrimination or reference shall forever
be allowed. No religious test shall ever be required for the exercise of civil or political rights.

Article 6. The Mohammedan Holy Places shall be under Mohammedan control.

Article 7. The Zionist Organization proposes to send to Palestine a Commission of experts to make a survey of the economic
possibilities of the country, and to report upon the best means

for its development. The Zionist Organization will place the aforementioned Commission at the disposal of the Arab State for the purpose of a survey of the economic possibilities of the Arab State and to report upon the best means for its development. The Zionist Organization will use its best efforts to assist the Arab State in providing the means for developing the natural resources and economic possibilities thereof.

Article 8. The parties hereto agree to act in complete accord and harmony on all matters embraced herein before the Peace Congress.

Article 9. Any matters of dispute which may arise between the contracting parties shall be referred to the British Government for arbitration.

Given under our hand at London, England, the third day of January, one thousand nine hundred and nineteen.

Chaim Weizmann
Faisal ibn Hussain

Reservation by the Emir Faisal

If the Arabs are established as I have asked in my manifesto of 4 January addressed to the British Secretary of State for Foreign Affairs, I will carry out what is written in this agreement. If changes are made, I cannot be answerable for failing to carry out this agreement.

Faisal ibn Hussain

Faisal–Frankfurter Correspondence

Delegation Hedjazienne, Paris, 3 March 1919

Dear Mr Frankfurter,

I want to take this opportunity of my first contact with American Zionists to tell you what I have often been able to say to Dr Weizmann in Arabia and Europe.

We feel that the Arabs and Jews are cousins in race, having suffered similar oppressions at the hands of powers stronger than themselves, and by a happy coincidence have been able to take the first step towards the attainment of their national ideals together.

We Arabs, especially the educated among us, look with the deepest sympathy on the Zionist movement. Our deputation here in Paris is fully acquainted with the proposals submitted yesterday by the Zionist Organization to the Peace Conference, and we regard them as moderate and proper. We will do our best, in so far as we are concerned, to help them through: we will wish the Jews a most hearty welcome home.

With the chiefs of your movement, especially with Dr Weizmann, we have had and continue to have the closest relations. He has been a great helper of our cause, and I hope the Arabs may soon be in a position to make the Jews some return for their kindness. We are working together for a reformed and revived Near East, and our two movements complete one another. The Jewish movement is national and not imperialist. Our movement is national and not imperialist, and there is room in Syria for us both. Indeed I think that neither can be a real success without the other.

People less informed and less responsible than our leaders and yours, ignoring the need for cooperation of the Arabs and Zionists, have been trying to exploit the local difficulties that must necessarily arise in Palestine in the early stages of our movements. Some of them have, I am afraid, misrepresented your aims to the Arab peasantry, and our aims to the Jewish peasantry, with the result that interested parties have been able to make capital out of what they call our differences.

I wish to give you my firm conviction that these differences are not on questions of principle, but on matters of detail such as must inevitably occur in every contact of neighbouring peoples, and as are easily adjusted by mutual goodwill. Indeed nearly all of them will disappear with fuller knowledge.

I look forward, and my people with me look forward, to a future in which we will help you and you will help us, so that the countries in which we are mutually interested may once again take their places in the community of civilized peoples of the world.

> Believe me,
> Yours sincerely,
> Faisal

5 March 1919

Royal Highness,

Allow me, on behalf of the Zionist Organization, to acknowledge your recent letter with deep appreciation.

Those of us who come from the United States have already been gratified by the friendly relations and the active cooperation maintained between you and the Zionist leaders, particularly Dr Weizmann. We knew it could not be otherwise; we knew that the aspirations of the Arab and the Jewish peoples were parallel, that each aspired to reestablish its nationality in its own homeland, each making its own distinctive contribution to civilization, each seeking its own peaceful mode of life.

The Zionist leaders and the Jewish people for whom they speak have watched with satisfaction the spiritual vigour of the Arab movement. Themselves seeking justice, they are anxious that the just national aims of the Arab people be confirmed and safeguarded by the Peace Conference.

We knew from your acts and your past utterances that the Zionist movement – in other words the national aims of the Jewish people – had your support and the support of the Arab people for whom you speak. These aims are now before the Peace Conference as definite proposals by the Zionist Organization. We are happy indeed that you consider these proposals 'moderate and proper', and that we have in you a staunch supporter for their realization. For both the Arab and the Jewish peoples there are difficulties ahead – difficulties that challenge the united statesmanship of Arab and Jewish leaders. For it is no easy task to rebuild two great civilizations that have been suffering oppression and misrule for centuries. We each have our difficulties we shall work out as friends, friends who are animated by similar purposes, seeking a free and full development for the two neighbouring peoples. The Arabs and Jews are neighbours in territory; we cannot but live side by side as friends.

Very respectfully,
Felix Frankfurter

Document 9

Recommendations of the King–Crane Commission

The King–Crane Commission was appointed by President Wilson, following a suggestion by Dr Howard Bliss, President of the American University in Beirut and a sympathizer with the Arab cause. Its main function was to determine which of the Western nations should act as the mandatory power for Palestine.

*

28 August 1919

The Commissioners make to the Peace Conference the following recommendations for the treatment of Syria:

1. We recommend, as most important of all, and in strict harmony with our instructions, that whatever foreign administration (whether of one or more powers) is brought into Syria, should come in, not at all as a colonization power in the old sense of that term, but as a Mandatory under the League of Nations, with the clear consciousness that 'the well-being and development' of the Syrian people form for it a 'sacred trust'.

(1) To this end the mandate should have a limited term, the time of expiration to be determined by the League of Nations, in the light of all the facts as brought out from year to year, in the annual reports of the Mandatory to the League or in other ways.

(2) The Mandatory Administration should have, however, a period and power sufficient to ensure the success of the new state; and especially to make possible carrying through

important educational and economic undertakings, essential to
secure founding of the state.

(3) The Mandatory Administration should be characterized
from the beginning by a strong and vital educational emphasis
in clear recognition of the imperative necessity of education
for the citizens of a democratic state, and the development of
a sound national spirit. This systematic cultivation of national
spirit is particularly required in a country like Syria, which has
only recently come to self-consciousness.

(4) The Mandatory should definitely seek, from the beginning of its trusteeship, to train the Syrian people to independent self-government as rapidly as conditions allow, by setting
up all the institutions of a democratic state, and by sharing
with them increasingly the work of administration and so forming gradually an intelligent citizenship, interested unselfishly in
the progress of the country, and forming at the same time a
large group of disciplined civil servants.

(5) The period of 'tutelage' should not be unduly prolonged,
but independent self-government should be granted as soon as
it can safely be done; remembering that the primary business
of government is not the accomplishment of certain things, but
the development of citizens.

(6) It is peculiarly the duty of the Mandatory in a country
like Syria, and in this modern age, to see that complete religious
liberty is ensured, both in the constitution and in the practice
of the state, and that a jealous care is exercised for the rights
of all minorities. Nothing is more vital than this for the enduring success of the new Arab state.

(7) In the economic development of Syria, a dangerous
amount of indebtedness on the part of the new state should
be avoided, as well as any entanglements financially with the
affairs of the Mandatory Power. On the other hand the legitimate established privileges of foreigners such as rights to maintain schools, commercial concessions, etc., should be preserved,
but subject to review and modification under the authority of
the League of Nations in the interest of Syria. The Mandatory
Power should not take advantage of its position to force a
monopolistic control at any point to the detriment either of

Syria or of other nations; but it should seek to bring the new State as rapidly as possible to economic independence as well as to political independence. Whatever is done concerning the further recommendations of the Commission, the fulfilment of at least the conditions now named should be assured, if the Peace Conference and the League of Nations are true to the policy of mandatories already embodied in 'The Covenant of the League of Nations'. This should effectively guard the most essential interests of Syria, however the machinery of administration is finally organized. The Damascus Congress betrayed in many ways their intense fear that their country would become, though under some other name, simply a colonial possession of some other power. That fear must be completely allayed.

2. We recommend, in the second place, that the unity of Syria be preserved, in accordance with the earnest petition of the great majority of the people of Syria.

(1) The territory concerned is too limited, the population too small, and the economic, geographic, racial and language unity too manifest to make the setting up of independent states within its boundaries desirable, if such division can possibly be avoided. The country is very largely Arab in language, culture, traditions, and customs.

(2) This recommendation is in line with important 'general considerations' already urged, and with the principles of the League of Nations, as well as in answer to the desires of the majority of the population concerned.

(3) The precise boundaries of Syria should be determined by a special commission on boundaries, after the Syrian territory has been in general allotted. The Commissioners believe, however, that the claim of the Damascus Conference to include Cilicia in Syria is not justified, either historically or by commercial or language relations. The line between the Arabic-speaking and the Turkish-speaking populations would quite certainly class Cilicia with Asia Minor rather than with Syria. Syria, too, has no such need of further sea coast as the large interior sections of Asia Minor.

(4) In standing thus for the recognition of the unity of Syria,

the natural desires of regions like the Lebanon, which have already had a measure of independence, should not be forgotten. It will make for real unity, undoubtedly, to give a large measure of local autonomy, and especially in the case of strongly unified groups. Even the 'Damascus Programme' which presses so earnestly the unity of Syria, itself urges a government 'on broad decentralization principles'.

Lebanon has achieved a considerable degree of prosperity and autonomy within the Turkish Empire. She certainly should not find her legitimate aspirations less possible within a Syrian national state. On the contrary, it may be confidently expected that both her economic and political relations with the rest of Syria would be better if she were a constituent member of the state, rather than entirely independent of it.

As a predominantly Christian country, too, Lebanon naturally fears Muslim domination in a unified Syria. But against such domination she would have a four-fold safeguard : her own large autonomy; the presence of a strong Mandatory for the considerable period in which the constitution and practice of the new state would be forming; the oversight of the League of Nations, with its insistence upon religious liberty and the rights of minorities; and the certainty that the Arab Government would feel the necessity of such a state, if it were to commend itself to the League of Nations. Moreover, there would be less danger of reactionary Muslim attitude, if Christians were present in the state in considerable numbers, rather than largely segregated outside the state, as experience of the relations of different religious faiths in India suggests.

As a predominantly Christian country, it is also to be noted that Lebanon would be in a position to exert a stronger and more helpful influence if she were within the Syrian state, feeling its problems and needs, and sharing all its life, instead of outside it, absorbed simply in her own narrow concerns. For the sake of the larger interests, both of Lebanon and of Syria, then, the unity of Syria is to be urged. It is certain that many of the more thoughtful Lebanese themselves hold this view. A similar statement might be made for Palestine; though, as 'the Holy Land' for Jews and Christians and Muslims alike, its situation is unique, and might more readily justify unique treatment, if such treatment were justified anywhere. This will be discussed more particularly in connexion with the recommendation concerning Zionism.

3. We recommend, in the third place, that Syria be placed under a Mandatory Power, as the natural way to secure real and efficient unity.

(1) To divide the administration of the provinces of Syria among several mandatories, even if existing national unity were recognized; or to attempt a joint mandatory of the whole on the commission plan: – neither of these courses would be naturally suggested as the best way to secure and promote the unity of the new state, or even the general unity of the whole people. It is conceivable that circumstances might drive the Peace Conference to some such form of divided mandate; but it is not a solution to be voluntarily chosen, from the point of view of the larger interests of the people, as considerations already urged indicate.

(2) It is not to be forgotten, either, that, however they are handled politically, the people of Syria are there, forced to get on together in some fashion. They are obliged to live with one another – the Arabs of the East and the people of the Coast, the Muslims and the Christians. Will they be helped or hindered, in establishing tolerable and finally cordial relations, by a single mandatory? No doubt the quick mechanical solution of the problem of different relations is to split the people up into little independent fragments. And sometimes, undoubtedly, as in the case of the Turks and Armenians, the relations are so intolerable as to make some division imperative and inevitable. But in general, to attempt complete separation only accentuates the differences and increases the antagonism. The whole lesson of the modern social consciousness points to the necessity of understanding 'the other half', as it can be understood only by close and living relations. Granting reasonable local autonomy to reduce friction among groups, a single mandatory ought to form a constant and increasingly effective help to unity of feeling throughout the state, and ought to steadily improve group relations.

The people of Syria, in our hearings, have themselves often insisted that, so far as unpleasant relations have hitherto prevailed among various groups, it has been very largely due to the direct instigation of the Turkish Government. When justice is done impartially to all; when it becomes plain that the aim of the common government is the service of all classes alike, not their exploitation, decent human relations are pretty certain to prevail, and a permanent foundation for such relations to be secured – a foundation which could not be obtained by dividing men off from one another in antagonistic groups.

The Commissioners urge, therefore, for the largest future good of all groups and regions alike, the placing of the whole of Syria under a single mandate.

4. We recommend, in the fourth place, that Emir Faisal be made the head of the new united Syrian state.

(1) This is expressly and unanimously asked for by the representative Damascus Congress in the name of the Syrian people, and there seems to be no reason to doubt that the great majority of the population of Syria sincerely desire to have Emir Faisal as ruler.

(2) A constitutional monarchy along democratic lines, seems naturally adapted to the Arabs, with their long training under tribal conditions, and with their traditional respect for their chiefs. They seem to need, more than most people, a king as the personal symbol of the power of the state.

(3) Emir Faisal has come, too, naturally into his present place of power, and there is no one else who could well replace him. He had the great advantage of being the son of the Sharif of Mecca, and as such honoured throughout the Muslim world. He was one of the prominent Arab leaders who assumed responsibility for the Arab uprising against the Turks, and so shared in the complete deliverance of the Arab-speaking portions of the Turkish Empire. He was consequently hailed by the 'Damascus Congress' as having 'merited their full confidence and entire reliance'. He was taken up and supported by the British as the most promising candidate for the headship of the new Arab state – as Arab of the Arabs, but with a position of wide appeal through his Sharifian connexion, and through

his broad sympathies with the best in the Occident. His relations with the Arabs to the East of Syria are friendly, and his kingdom would not be threatened from that side. He undoubtedly does not make so strong an appeal to the Christians of the West Coast, as to the Arabs of the East; but no man can be named who would have a stronger general appeal. He is tolerant and wise, skilful in dealing with men, winning in manner, a man of sincerity, insight, and power. Whether he has the full strength needed for his difficult task it is too early to say; but certainly no other Arab leader combines so many elements of power as he, and he will have invaluable help throughout the mandatory period.

The Peace Conference may take genuine satisfaction in the fact that an Arab of such qualities is available for the headship of this new state in the Near East.

5. We recommend, in the fifth place, serious modification of the extreme Zionist programme for Palestine of unlimited immigration of Jews, looking finally to making Palestine distinctly a Jewish state.

(1) The Commissioners began their study of Zionism with minds predisposed in its favour, but the actual facts in Palestine, coupled with the force of the general principles proclaimed by the Allies and accepted by the Syrians, have driven them to the recommendation here made.

(2) The Commission was abundantly supplied with literature on the Zionist programme by the Zionist Commission to Palestine; heard in conferences much concerning the Zionist colonies and their claims and personally saw something of what had been accomplished. They found much to approve in the aspirations and plans of the Zionists, and had warm appreciation for the devotion of many of the colonists, and for their success, by modern methods, in overcoming great natural obstacles.

(3) The Commission recognized also that definite encouragement had been given to the Zionists by the Allies in Mr Balfour's often-quoted statement, in its approval by other representatives of the Allies. If, however, the strict terms of the Balfour Statement are adhered to – favouring 'the establishment in Palestine of a national home for the Jewish people', 'it being clearly

understood that nothing shall be done which may prejudice
the civil and religious rights of existing non-Jewish communities
in Palestine' – it can hardly be doubted that the extreme Zionist programme must be greatly modified. For 'a national home
for the Jewish people' is not equivalent to making Palestine
into a Jewish state; nor can the erection of such a Jewish state
be accomplished without the gravest trespass upon the 'civil
and religious rights of existing non-Jewish communities in
Palestine'. The fact came out repeatedly, in the Commission's
conference with Jewish representatives, that the Zionists looked
forward to a practically complete dispossession of the present
non-Jewish inhabitants of Palestine, by various forms of purchase.

In his address of 4 July 1918 President Wilson laid down the
following principle as one of the four great 'ends for which
the associated peoples of the world were fighting': 'The settlement of every question, whether of territory, of sovereignty,
of economic arrangement, or of political relationship upon the
basis of the free acceptance of that settlement by the people
immediately concerned, and not upon the basis of the material
interest or advantage of any other nation or people which may
desire a different settlement for the sake of its own exterior
influence or mastery.' If that principle is to rule, and so the
wishes of Palestine's population are to be decisive as to what
is to be done with Palestine, then it is to be remembered that
the non-Jewish population of Palestine – nearly nine tenths of
the whole – are emphatically against the entire Zionist programme. The tables show that there was no one thing upon
which the population of Palestine were more agreed than
upon this. To subject a people so minded to unlimited Jewish
immigration, and to steady financial and social pressure to
surrender the land, would be a gross violation of the principle
just quoted, and of the peoples' rights, though it kept within
the forms of law.

It is to be noted also that the feeling against the Zionist programme is not confined to Palestine, but shared very generally
by the people throughout Syria, as our conferences clearly
showed. More than 72 per cent – 1350 in all – of all the petitions

in the whole of Syria were directed against the Zionist programme. Only two requests – those for a united Syria and for
independence – had a larger support. This general feeling was
only voiced by the 'General Syrian Congress', in the seventh,
eighth and tenth resolutions of their statement.

The Peace Conference should not shut its eyes to the fact
that the anti-Zionist feeling in Palestine and Syria is intense
and not lightly to be flouted. No British officer, consulted by
the Commissioners, believed that the Zionist programme could
be carried out except by force of arms. The officers generally
thought that a force of not less than fifty thousand soldiers
would be required even to initiate the programme. That of itself is evidence of a strong sense of the injustice of the Zionist
programme, on the part of the non-Jewish populations of Palestine and Syria. Decisions, requiring armies to carry them out,
are sometimes necessary, but they are surely not gratuitously
to be taken in the interests of a serious injustice. For the initial
claim, often submitted by Zionist representatives, that they
have a 'right' to Palestine, based on an occupation of two
thousand years ago, can hardly be seriously considered.

There is a further consideration that cannot justly be ignored, if the world is to look forward to Palestine becoming a
definitely Jewish state, however gradually that may take place.
That consideration grows out of the fact that Palestine is 'the
Holy Land' for Jews, Christians, and Muslims alike. Millions
of Christians and Muslims all over the world are quite as much
concerned as the Jews with conditions in Palestine, especially
with those conditions which touch upon religious feelings and
rights. The relations in these matters in Palestine are most delicate and difficult. With the best possible intentions, it may be
doubted whether the Jews could possibly seem to either Christians or Muslims proper guardians of the holy places, or custodians of the Holy Land as a whole. The reason is this: the
places which are most sacred to Christians – those having to
do with Jesus – and which are also sacred to Muslims, are not
only not sacred to Jews, but abhorrent to them. It is simply impossible, under those circumstances, for Muslims and Christians
to feel satisfied to have these places in Jewish hands, or under

the custody of Jews. There are still other places about which Muslims must have the same feeling. In fact, from this point of view, the Muslims, just because the sacred places of all three religions are sacred to them, have made very naturally much more satisfactory custodians of the holy places than the Jews could be. It must be believed that the precise meaning, in this respect, of the complete Jewish occupation of Palestine has not been fully sensed by those who urge the extreme Zionist programme. For it would intensify, with a certainty like fate, the anti-Jewish feeling both in Palestine and in all other portions of the world which look to Palestine as 'the Holy Land'.

In view of all these considerations, and with a deep sense of sympathy for the Jewish cause, the Commissioners feel bound to recommend that only a greatly reduced Zionist programme be attempted by the Peace Conference and even that, only very gradually initiated. This would have to mean that Jewish immigration should be definitely limited, and that the project for making Palestine distinctly a Jewish commonwealth should be given up.

There would then be no reason why Palestine could not be included in a united Syrian state, just as other portions of the country, the holy places being cared for by an International and Inter-religious Commission, somewhat as at present, under the oversight and approval of the Mandatory and of the League of Nations. The Jews, of course, would have representation upon this Commission.

[The remaining part of this document recommended that the United States be asked to undertake the single Mandate for all Syria. Ed.]

Document 10

Memorandum Presented to the King–Crane Commission by the General Syrian Congress

This is one of the first Arab statements on record opposing Jewish migration to Palestine.

*

2 July 1919

We the undersigned members of the General Syrian Congress, meeting in Damascus on Wednesday, 2 July 1919, made up of representatives from the three Zones, viz., the Southern, Eastern, and Western, provided with credentials and authorizations by the inhabitants of our various districts, Muslims, Christians, and Jews, have agreed upon the following statement of the desires of the people of the country who have elected us to present them to the American Section of the International Commission ; the fifth article was passed by a very large majority; all the other articles were accepted unanimously.

1. We ask absolutely complete political independence for Syria within these boundaries : the Taurus System on the North ; Rafah and a line running from Al Jauf to the south of the Syrian and the Hejazian line to Aqaba on the south ; the Euphrates and Khabur Rivers and a line extending east of Abu Kamal to the east of Al Jauf on the east ; and the Mediterranean on the west.

2. We ask that the government of this Syrian country should be a democratic civil constitutional Monarchy on broad decentralization principles, safeguarding the rights of minorities, and that the King be the Emir Faisal, who carried on a glorious struggle in the cause of our liberation and merited our full confidence and entire reliance.

3. Considering the fact that the Arabs inhabiting the Syrian area are not naturally less gifted than other more advanced races and that they are by no means less developed than the

Bulgarians, Serbians, Greeks, and Roumanians at the beginning of their independence, we protest against Article 22 of the Covenant of the League of Nations, placing us among the nations in their middle stage of development which stand in need of a mandatory power.

4. In the event of the rejection by the Peace Conference of this just protest for certain considerations that we may not understand, we, relying on the declarations of President Wilson that his object in waging war was to put an end to the ambition of conquest and colonization, can only regard the Mandate mentioned in the Covenant of the League of Nations as equivalent to the rendering of economical and technical assistance that does not prejudice our complete independence. And desiring that our country should not fall a prey to colonization, and believing that the United States is farthest from any thought of colonization and has no political ambition in our country, we will seek the technical and economical assistance from the United States of America, provided that such assistance does not exceed twenty years.

5. In the event of America not finding herself in a position to accept our desire for assistance, we will seek this assistance from Great Britain, also provided that such assistance does not infringe the complete independence and unity of our country and that the duration of such assistance does not exceed that mentioned in the previous article.

6. We do not acknowledge any right claimed by the French Government in any part whatever of our Syrian country and refuse that she should assist us or have a hand in our country under any circumstances and in any place.

7. We oppose the pretensions of the Zionists to create a Jewish commonwealth in the southern part of Syria, known as Palestine, and oppose Zionist migration to any part of our country; for we do not acknowledge their title but consider them a grave peril to our people from the national, economical, and political points of view. Our Jewish compatriots shall enjoy our common rights and assume the common responsibilities.

8. We ask that there should be no separation of the southern part of Syria, known as Palestine, nor of the littoral western

zone, which includes Lebanon, from the Syrian country. We desire that the unity of the country should be guaranteed against partition under whatever circumstances.

9. We ask complete independence for emancipated Mesopotamia and that there should be no economical barriers between the two countries.

10. The fundamental principles laid down by President Wilson in condemnation of secret treaties impel us to protest most emphatically against any treaty that stipulates the partition of our Syrian country and against any private engagement aiming at the establishment of Zionism in the southern part of Syria; therefore we ask the complete annulment of these conventions and agreements.

The noble principles enunciated by President Wilson strengthen our confidence that our desires, emanating from the depths of our hearts, shall be the decisive factor in determining our future; and that President Wilson and the free American people will be our supporters for the realization of our hopes thereby proving their sincerity and noble sympathy with the aspiration of the weaker nations in general and our Arab people in particular.

We also have the fullest confidence that the Peace Conference will realize that we would not have risen against the Turks, with whom we had participated in all civil, political, and representative privileges, but for their violation of our national rights, and so will grant us our desires in full in order that our political rights may not be less after the war than they were before, since we have shed so much blood in the cause of our liberty and independence.

We request to be allowed to send a delegation to represent us at the Peace Conference to defend our rights and secure the realization of our aspirations.

Document 11

The British Mandate

The San Remo Conference decided on 24 April 1920 to assign the
Mandate under the League of Nations to Britain. The terms of the
Mandate were also discussed with the United States which was not
a member of the League. An agreed text was confirmed by the
Council of the League of Nations on 24 July 1922, and it came into
operation in September 1923.

*

The Council of the League of Nations:

Whereas the Principal Allied Powers have agreed, for the
purpose of giving effect to the provisions of Article 22 of the
Covenant of the League of Nations, to entrust to a Mandatory
selected by the said Powers the administration of the territory
of Palestine, which formerly belonged to the Turkish Empire,
within such boundaries as may be fixed by them; and

Whereas the Principal Allied Powers have also agreed that
the Mandatory should be responsible for putting into effect the
declaration originally made on 2 November 1917 by the Government of His Britannic Majesty, and adopted by the said
Powers, in favour of the establishment in Palestine of a national home for the Jewish people, it being clearly understood
that nothing should be done which might prejudice the civil
and religious rights of existing non-Jewish communities in Palestine, or the rights and political status enjoyed by Jews in any
other country; and

Whereas recognition has thereby been given to the historical
connexion of the Jewish people with Palestine and to the
grounds for reconstituting their national home in that country;
and

Whereas the Principal Allied Powers have selected His Britannic Majesty as the Mandatory for Palestine; and

Whereas the mandate in respect of Palestine has been formulated in the following terms and submitted to the Council
of the League for approval; and

Whereas His Britannic Majesty has accepted the mandate in respect of Palestine and undertaken to exercise it on behalf of the League of Nations in conformity with the following provisions ; and

Whereas by the aforementioned Article 22 (paragraph 8), it is provided that the degree of authority, control or administration to be exercised by the Mandatory, not having been previously agreed upon by the Members of the League, shall be explicitly defined by the Council of the League of Nations ;

Confirming the said Mandate, defines its terms as follows :

Article 1. The Mandatory shall have full powers of legislation and of administration, save as they may be limited by the terms of this mandate.

Article 2. The Mandatory shall be responsible for placing the country under such political, administrative and economic conditions as will secure the establishment of the Jewish national home, as laid down in the preamble, and the development of self-governing institutions, and also for safeguarding the civil and religious rights of all the inhabitants of Palestine, irrespective of race and religion.

Article 3. The Mandatory shall, so far as circumstances permit, encourage local autonomy.

Article 4. An appropriate Jewish agency shall be recognized as a public body for the purpose of advising and cooperating with the Administration of Palestine in such economic, social and other matters as may affect the establishment of the Jewish national home and the interests of the Jewish population in Palestine, and, subject always to the control of the Administration, to assist and take part in the development of the country.

The Zionist Organization, so long as its organization and constitution are in the opinion of the Mandatory appropriate, shall be recognized as such agency. It shall take steps in consultation with His Britannic Majesty's Government to secure the cooperation of all Jews who are willing to assist in the establishment of the Jewish national home.

Article 5. The Mandatory shall be responsible for seeing that no Palestine territory shall be ceded or leased to, or in any way placed under the control of, the Government of any foreign Power.

Article 6. The Administration of Palestine, while ensuring that the rights and position of other sections of the population are not prejudiced, shall facilitate Jewish immigration under suitable conditions and shall encourage, in cooperation with the Jewish agency referred to in Article 4, close settlement by Jews on the land, including State lands and waste lands not required for public purposes.

Article 7. The Administration of Palestine shall be responsible for enacting a nationality law. There shall be included in this law provisions framed so as to facilitate the acquisition of Palestinian citizenship by Jews who take up their permanent residence in Palestine.

Article 8. The privileges and immunities of foreigners, including the benefits of consular jurisdiction and protection as formerly enjoyed by Capitulation or usage in the Ottoman Empire, shall not be applicable in Palestine.

Unless the Powers whose nationals enjoyed the aforementioned privileges and immunities on 1 August 1914 shall have previously renounced the right to their re-establishment, or shall have agreed to their non-application for a specified period, these privileges and immunities shall, at the expiration of the mandate, be immediately re-established in their entirety or with such modifications as may have been agreed upon between the Powers concerned.

Article 9. The Mandatory shall be responsible for seeing that the judicial system established in Palestine shall assure to foreigners, as well as to natives, a complete guarantee of their rights.

Respect for the personal status of the various peoples and communities and for their religious interests shall be fully guaranteed. In particular, the control and administration of Waqfs shall be exercised in accordance with religious law and the dispositions of the founders.

Article 10. Pending the making of special extradition agreements relating to Palestine, the extradition treaties in force between the Mandatory and other foreign Powers shall apply to Palestine.

Article 11. The Administration of Palestine shall take all necessary measures to safeguard the interests of the community in connexion with the development of the country, and, subject to any international obligations accepted by the Mandatory, shall have full power to provide for public ownership or control of any of the natural resources of the country or of the public works, services and utilities established or to be established therein. It shall introduce a land system appropriate to the needs of the country having regard, among other things, to the desirability of promoting the close settlement and intensive cultivation of the land.

The Administration may arrange with the Jewish agency mentioned in Article 4 to construct or operate, upon fair and equitable terms, any public works, services and utilities, and to develop any of the natural resources of the country, in so far as these matters are not directly undertaken by the Administration. Any such arrangements shall provide that no profits distributed by such agency, directly or indirectly, shall exceed a reasonable rate of interest on the capital, and any further profits shall be utilized by it for the benefit of the country in a manner approved by the Administration.

Article 12. The Mandatory shall be entrusted with the control of the foreign relations of Palestine, and the right to issue exequaturs to consuls appointed by foreign Powers. He shall also be entitled to afford diplomatic and consular protection to citizens of Palestine when outside its territorial limits.

Article 13. All responsibility in connexion with the Holy Places and religious buildings or sites in Palestine, including that of preserving existing rights and of securing free access to the Holy Places, religious buildings and sites and the free exercise of worship, while ensuring the requirements of public order and decorum, is assumed by the Mandatory, who shall be responsible solely to the League of Nations in all matters connected herewith, provided that nothing in this article shall prevent the Mandatory from entering into such arrangements as he may deem reasonable with the Administration for the purpose of carrying the provisions of this article into effect; and provided also that nothing in this Mandate shall be construed as conferring upon the Mandatory authority to interfere with the fabric or the management of purely Muslim sacred shrines, the immunities of which are guaranteed.

Article 14. A special Commission shall be appointed by the Mandatory to study, define and determine the rights and claims in connexion with the Holy Places and the rights and claims relating to the different religious communities in Palestine. The method of nomination, the composition and the functions of this Commission shall be submitted to the Council of the League for its approval, and the Commission shall not be appointed or enter upon its functions without the approval of the Council.

Article 15. The Mandatory shall see that complete freedom of conscience and the free exercise of all forms of worship, subject only to the maintenance of public order and morals, are ensured to all. No discrimination of any kind shall be made between the inhabitants of Palestine on the ground of race, religion or language. No person shall be excluded from Palestine on the sole ground of his religious belief.

The right of each community to maintain its own schools for the education of its own members in its own language, while conforming to such educational requirements of a general nature as the Administration may impose, shall not be denied or impaired.

Article 16. The Mandatory shall be responsible for exercising such supervision over religious or eleemosynary bodies of all faiths in Palestine as may be required for the maintenance of public order and good government. Subject to such supervision, no measures shall be taken in Palestine to obstruct or interfere with the enterprise of such bodies or to discriminate against any representative or member of them on the ground of his religion or nationality.

Article 17. The Administration of Palestine may organize on a voluntary basis the forces necessary for the preservation of peace and order, and also for the defence of the country, subject, however, to the supervision of the Mandatory, but shall not use them for purposes other than those above specified

save with the consent of the Mandatory. Except for such purposes, no military, naval or air forces shall be raised or maintained by the Administration of Palestine.

Nothing in this article shall preclude the Administration of
Palestine from contributing to the cost of the maintenance of
the forces of the Mandatory in Palestine.

The Mandatory shall be entitled at all times to use the roads,
railways and ports of Palestine for the movement of armed
forces and the carriage of fuel and supplies.

Article 18. The Mandatory shall see that there is no discrimination in Palestine against the nationals of any State Member
of the League of Nations (including companies incorporated
under its laws) as compared with those of the Mandatory or of
any foreign State in matters concerning taxation, commerce
or navigation, the exercise of industries or professions, or in
the treatment of merchant vessels or civil aircraft. Similarly,
there shall be no discrimination in Palestine against goods
originating in or destined for any of the said States, and there
shall be freedom of transit under equitable conditions across
the mandated area.

Subject as aforesaid and to the other provisions of this mandate, the Administration of Palestine may, on the advice of the
Mandatory, impose such taxes and customs duties as it may
consider necessary, and take such steps as it may think best to
promote the development of the natural resources of the country and to safeguard the interests of the population. It may
also, on the advice of the Mandatory, conclude a special customs agreement with any State the territory of which in 1914
was wholly included in Asiatic Turkey or Arabia.

Article 19. The Mandatory shall adhere on behalf of the Administration of Palestine to any general international conventions already existing, or which may be concluded hereafter
with the approval of the League of Nations, respecting the slave
traffic, the traffic in arms and ammunition, or the traffic in
drugs, or relating to commercial equality, freedom of transit
and navigation, aerial navigation and postal, telegraphic and
wireless communication or literary, artistic or industrial property.

Article 20. The Mandatory shall cooperate on behalf of the Administration of Palestine, so far as religious, social and other conditions may permit, in the execution of any common policy adopted by the League of Nations for preventing and combating disease, including diseases of plants and animals.

Article 21. The Mandatory shall secure the enactment within twelve months from this date, and shall ensure the execution of a Law of Antiquities based on the following rules. This law shall ensure equality of treatment in the matter of excavations and archaeological research to the nationals of all States Members of the League of Nations ...

Article 22. English, Arabic and Hebrew shall be the official languages of Palestine. Any statement or inscription in Arabic on stamps or money in Palestine shall be repeated in Hebrew and any statement or inscription in Hebrew shall be repeated in Arabic.

Article 23. The Administration of Palestine shall recognize the holy days of the respective communities in Palestine as legal days of rest for the members of such communities.

Article 24. The Mandatory shall make to the Council of the League of Nations an annual report to the satisfaction of the Council as to the measures taken during the year to carry out the provisions of the mandate. Copies of all laws and regulations promulgated or issued during the year shall be communicated with the report.

Article 25. In the territories lying between the Jordan and the eastern boundary of Palestine as ultimately determined, the Mandatory shall be entitled, with the consent of the Council of the League of Nations, to postpone or withhold application of such provisions of this mandate as he may consider inapplicable to the existing local conditions, and to make such provision for the administration of the territories as he may consider suitable to those conditions, provided that no action shall be taken which is inconsistent with the provision of Articles 15, 16 and 18.

Article 26. The Mandatory agrees that if any dispute whatever should arise between the Mandatory and another Member of the League of Nations relating to the interpretation or the application of the provisions of the mandate, such dispute, if it cannot be settled by negotiation, shall be submitted to the Permanent Court of International Justice provided for by Article 14 of the Covenant of the League of Nations.

Article 27. The consent of the Council of the League of Nations is required for any modification of the terms of this mandate.

Article 28. In the event of the termination of the mandate hereby conferred upon the Mandatory, the Council of the League of Nations shall make such arrangements as may be deemed necessary for safeguarding in perpetuity, under guarantee of the League, the rights secured by Articles 13 and 14, and shall use its influence for securing, under the guarantee of the League, that the Government of Palestine will fully honour the financial obligations legitimately incurred by the Administration of Palestine during the period of the mandate, including the rights of public servants to pensions or gratuities.

The present instrument shall be deposited in original in the archives of the League of Nations and certified copies shall be forwarded by the Secretary General of the League of Nations to all Members of the League.

DONE AT LONDON the twenty-fourth day of July, one thousand nine hundred and twenty-two.

Part 2

Palestine 1920-47

Part 2 of the Reader deals with the unhappy history of the British Mandate, from the Balfour Declaration promising the establishment of a Jewish Home in Palestine to the British decision to return the mandate to the United Nations, and the UN Resolution about partition and the establishment of an Arab and a Jewish state in Palestine. During this period Arab opposition grew against Jewish colonization and immigration; there was frequent unrest (in 1920–21, 1928, 1933, 1936–39) and the various suggestions for a solution to the conflict were rejected as impractical.

Document 12

The Churchill White Paper, 1922

In view of growing opposition to Zionism, a new statement of policy was drafted in 1922 by the then British Colonial Secretary, which, while not explicitly opposing the idea of a Jewish state, 'redeemed the Balfour promise in depreciated currency' to quote a contemporary British source.

*

Statement of British Policy in Palestine
Issued by Mr Churchill in June 1922

The Secretary of State for the Colonies has given renewed consideration to the existing political situation in Palestine, with a very earnest desire to arrive at a settlement of the outstanding questions which have given rise to uncertainty and unrest among certain sections of the population. After consultation with the High Commissioner for Palestine the following statement has been drawn up. It summarizes the essential parts of the correspondence that has already taken place between the Secretary of State and a Delegation from the Muslim Christian Society of Palestine, which has been for some time in England, and it states the further conclusions which have since been reached.

The tension which has prevailed from time to time in Palestine is mainly due to apprehensions, which are entertained both by sections of the Arab and by sections of the Jewish population. These apprehensions, so far as the Arabs are concerned, are partly based upon exaggerated interpretations of the meaning of the Declaration favouring the establishment of a Jewish National Home in Palestine, made on behalf of

His Majesty's Government on 2 November 1917. Unauthorized statements have been made to the effect that the purpose in view is to create a wholly Jewish Palestine. Phrases have been used such as that Palestine is to become 'as Jewish as England is English'. His Majesty's Government regard any such expectation as impracticable and have no such aim in view. Nor have they at any time contemplated, as appears to be feared by the Arab Delegation, the disappearance or the subordination of the Arabic population, language, or culture in Palestine. They would draw attention to the fact that the terms of the Declaration referred to do not contemplate that Palestine as a whole should be converted into a Jewish National Home, but that such a Home should be founded *in Palestine*. In this connexion it has been observed with satisfaction that at the meeting of the Zionist Congress, the supreme governing body of the Zionist Organization, held at Carlsbad in September 1921, a resolution was passed expressing as the official statement of Zionist aims 'the determination of the Jewish people to live with the Arab people on terms of unity and mutual respect, and together with them to make the common home into a flourishing community, the upbuilding of which may assure to each of its peoples an undisturbed national development'.

It is also necessary to point out that the Zionist Commission in Palestine, now termed the Palestine Zionist Executive, has not desired to possess, and does not possess, any share in the general administration of the country. Nor does the special position assigned to the Zionist Organization in Article 4 of the Draft Mandate for Palestine imply any such functions. That special position relates to the measures to be taken in Palestine affecting the Jewish population, and contemplates that the Organization may assist in the general development of the country, but does not entitle it to share in any degree in its Government.

Further, it is contemplated that the status of all citizens of Palestine in the eyes of the law shall be Palestinian, and it has never been intended that they, or any section of them, should possess any other juridical status.

So far as the Jewish population of Palestine are concerned

it appears that some among them are apprehensive that His Majesty's Government may depart from the policy embodied in the Declaration of 1917. It is necessary, therefore, once more to affirm that these fears are unfounded, and that that Declaration, re-affirmed by the Conference of the Principal Allied Powers at San Remo and again in the Treaty of Sèvres, is not susceptible of change.

During the last two or three generations the Jews have re-created in Palestine a community, now numbering 80,000, of whom about one fourth are farmers or workers upon the land. This community has its own political organs; an elected assembly for the direction of its domestic concerns; elected councils in the towns; and an organization for the control of its schools. It has its elected Chief Rabbinate and Rabbinical Council for the direction of its religious affairs. Its business is conducted in Hebrew as a vernacular language, and a Hebrew press serves its needs. It has its distinctive intellectual life and displays considerable economic activity. This community, then, with its town and country population, its political, religious, and social organizations, its own language, its own customs, its own life, has in fact 'national' characteristics. When it is asked what is meant by the development of the Jewish National Home in Palestine it may be answered that it is not the imposition of a Jewish nationality upon the inhabitants of Palestine as a whole, but the further development of the existing Jewish community, with the assistance of Jews in other parts of the world, in order that it may become a centre in which the Jewish people as a whole may take, on grounds of religion and race, an interest and a pride. But in order that this community should have the best prospect of free development and provide a full opportunity for the Jewish people to display its capacities, it is essential that it should know that it is in Palestine as of right and not on sufferance. That is the reason why it is necessary that the existence of a Jewish National Home in Palestine should be internationally guaranteed, and that it should be formally recognized to rest upon ancient historic connexion.

This, then, is the interpretation which His Majesty's Government place upon the Declaration of 1917, and, so understood, the Secretary of State is of the opinion that it does not contain or imply anything which need cause either alarm to the Arab population of Palestine or disappointment to the Jews.

For the fulfilment of this policy it is necessary that the Jewish community in Palestine should be able to increase its numbers by immigration. This immigration cannot be so great in volume as to exceed whatever may be the economic capacity of the country at the time to absorb new arrivals. It is essential to ensure that the immigrants should not be a burden upon the people of Palestine as a whole, and that they should not deprive any section of the present population of their employment. Hitherto the immigration has fulfilled these conditions. The number of immigrants since the British occupation has been about 25,000.

It is necessary also to ensure that persons who are politically undesirable are excluded from Palestine, and every precaution has been and will be taken by the Administration to that end.

It is intended that a special committee should be established in Palestine, consisting entirely of members of the new Legislative Council elected by the people, to confer with the administration upon matters relating to the regulation of immigration. Should any difference of opinion arise between this committee and the Administration the matter will be referred to His Majesty's Government, who will give it special consideration. In addition, under Article 81 of the draft Palestine Order in Council, any religious community or considerable section of the population of Palestine will have a general right to appeal, through the High Commissioner and the Secretary of State, to the League of Nations on any matter on which they may consider that the terms of the Mandate are not being fulfilled by the Government of Palestine.

With reference to the Constitution which it is now intended to establish in Palestine, the draft of which has already been published, it is desirable to make certain points clear. In the first place, it is not the case, as has been represented by the Arab Delegation, that during the war His Majesty's Government gave an undertaking that an independent national gov-

ernment should be at once established in Palestine. This representation mainly rests upon a letter dated 24 October 1915
from Sir Henry McMahon, then His Majesty's High Commissioner in Egypt, to the Sharif of Mecca, now King Hussain of
the Kingdom of the Hejaz. That letter is quoted as conveying
the promise to the Sharif of Mecca to recognize and support the
independence of the Arabs within the territories proposed by
him. But this promise was given subject to a reservation made
in the same letter, which excluded from its scope, among other
territories, the portions of Syria lying to the west of the district
of Damascus. This reservation has always been regarded by
His Majesty's Government as covering the vilayet of Beirut
and the independent Sanjak of Jerusalem. The whole of Palestine west of the Jordan was thus excluded from Sir H. Mc-
Mahon's pledge.

Nevertheless, it is the intention of His Majesty's Government
to foster the establishment of a full measure of self-government
in Palestine. But they are of opinion that, in the special circumstances of that country, this should be accomplished by
gradual stages and not suddenly. The first step was taken when,
on the institution of a Civil Administration, the nominated Advisory Council, which now exists, was established. It was stated
at the time by the High Commissioner that this was the first
step in the development of self-government institutions, and it
is now proposed to take a second step by the establishment of a
Legislative Council containing a large proportion of members
elected on a wide franchise. It was proposed in the published
draft that three of the members of this Council should be non-
official persons nominated by the High Commissioner, but rep-
resentations having been made in opposition to this provision,
based on cogent considerations, the Secretary of State is prepared to omit it. The Legislative Council would then consist of
the High Commissioner as President and twelve elected and
ten official members. The Secretary of State is of opinion that
before a further measure of self-government is extended to
Palestine and the Assembly placed in control over the Executive, it would be wise to allow some time to elapse. During
this period the institutions of the country will have become

well established; it financial credit will be based on firm foundations, and the Palestinian officials will have been enabled to gain experience of sound methods of government. After a few years the situation will be again reviewed, and if the experience of the working of the constitution now to be established so warranted, a larger share of authority would then be extended to the elected representatives of the people.

The Secretary of State would point out that already the present Administration has transferred to a Supreme Council elected by the Muslim community of Palestine the entire control of Muslim religious endowments (Waqfs), and of the Muslim religious Courts. To this Council the Administration has also voluntarily restored considerable revenues derived from ancient endowments which had been sequestrated by the Turkish Government. The Education Department is also advised by a committee representative of all sections of the population, and the Department of Commerce and Industry has the benefit of the cooperation of the Chambers of Commerce which have been established in the principal centres. It is the intention of the Administration to associate in an increased degree similar representative committees with the various Departments of the Government.

The Secretary of State believes that a policy upon these lines, coupled with the maintenance of the fullest religious liberty in Palestine and with scrupulous regard for the rights of each community with reference to its Holy Places, cannot but commend itself to the various sections of the population, and that upon this basis may be built up that spirit of cooperation upon which the future progress and prosperity of the Holy Land must largely depend.

Document 13

The MacDonald Letter

Following the Arab riots of 1929, the British Labour government
published a new statement of policy (the Passfield White Paper),
which urged the restriction of immigration and of land sales to
Jews. It was bitterly denounced by Zionist leaders as a violation of
the letter and the spirit of the Mandate. The MacDonald letter, while
not openly repudiating the Passfield report, gave assurances that
the terms of the Mandate would be fulfilled. It was rejected by
the Arabs as the 'Black Letter'. James Ramsay MacDonald (1866–
1937) was Prime Minister in 1931; Lord Passfield (Sidney Webb,
1859–1947) was Colonial Secretary in the Labour cabinet.

*

13 February 1931

Dear Dr Weizmann,

In order to remove certain misconceptions and misunderstandings which have arisen as to the policy of His Majesty's
Government with regard to Palestine, as set forth in the White
Paper of October 1930, and which were the subject of a debate
in the House of Commons on 17 November, and also to meet
certain criticisms put forward by the Jewish Agency, I have
pleasure in forwarding you the following statement of our
position, which will fall to be read as the authoritative interpretation of the White Paper on the matters with which this
letter deals.

It has been said that the policy of His Majesty's Government
involves a serious departure from the obligations of the mandate as hitherto understood ; that it misconceives the mandatory
obligations, and that it foreshadows a policy which is inconsistent with the obligations of the Mandatory to the Jewish
people.

His Majesty's Government did not regard it as necessary to
quote *in extenso* the declarations of policy which have been
previously made, but attention is drawn to the fact that, not
only does the White Paper of 1930 refer to and endorse the

White Paper of 1922, which has been accepted by the Jewish Agency, but it recognizes that the undertaking of the Mandate is an undertaking to the Jewish people and not only to the Jewish population of Palestine. The White Paper places in the foreground of its statement my speech in the House of Commons on 3 April 1930 in which I announced, in words that could not have been made more plain, that it was the intention of His Majesty's Government to continue to administer Palestine in accordance with the terms of the Mandate as approved by the Council of the League of Nations. That position has been reaffirmed and again made plain by my speech in the House of Commons on 17 November. In my speech on 3 April, I used the following language:

> His Majesty's Government will continue to administer Palestine in accordance with the terms of the Mandate as approved by the Council of the League of Nations. This is an international obligation from which there can be no question of receding.
>
> Under the terms of the Mandate His Majesty's Government are responsible for promoting the establishment of a national home for the Jewish people, it being clearly understood that nothing shall be done which might prejudice the civil and religious rights of existing non-Jewish communities in Palestine or the rights and political status enjoyed by Jews in any other country.
>
> A double undertaking is involved, to the Jewish people on the one hand and to the non-Jewish population of Palestine on the other; and it is the firm resolve of His Majesty's Government to give effect, in equal measure, to both parts of the declaration and to do equal justice to all sections of the population of Palestine. That is a duty from which they will not shrink and to the discharge of which they will apply all the resources at their command.

That declaration is in conformity not only with the articles but also with the preamble of the Mandate, which is hereby explicitly reaffirmed.

In carrying out the policy of the Mandate the Mandatory cannot ignore the existence of the differing interests and viewpoints. These, indeed, are not in themselves irreconcilable, but they can only be reconciled if there is a proper realization that the full solution of the problem depends upon an understanding between the Jews and the Arabs. Until that is reached, considerations of balance must inevitably enter into the definition of policy.

A good deal of criticism has been directed to the White Paper upon the assertion that it contains injurious allegations against the Jewish people and Jewish labour organizations. Any such intention on the part of His Majesty's Government is expressly disavowed. It is recognized that the Jewish Agency have all along given willing cooperation in carrying out the policy of the Mandate and that the constructive work done by the Jewish people in Palestine has had beneficial effects on the development and well-being of the country as a whole. His Majesty's Government also recognizes the value of the services of labour and trades union organizations in Palestine, to which they desire to give every encouragement.

A question has arisen as to the meaning to be attached to the words 'safeguarding the civil and religious rights of all inhabitants of Palestine irrespective of race and religion' occurring in Article 2, and the words, 'ensuring that the rights and position of other sections of the population are not prejudiced' occurring in Article 6 of the Mandate. The words 'safeguarding the civil and religious rights' occurring in Article 2 cannot be read as meaning that the civil and religious rights of individual citizens are unalterable. In the case of Suleiman Murra, to which reference has been made, the Privy Council, in construing these words of Article 2 said 'It does not mean ... that all the civil rights of every inhabitant of Palestine which existed at the date of the Mandate are to remain unaltered throughout its duration ; for if that were to be a condition of the Mandatory jurisdiction, no effective legislation would be possible.' The words, accordingly, must be read in another sense, and the key to the true purpose and meaning of the sentence is to be found in the concluding words of the article, 'irrespective of race and religion'. These words indicate that in respect of civil and religious rights the Mandatory is not to discriminate between persons on the ground of religion or race, and this protective provision applies equally to Jews, Arabs and all sections of the population.

The words 'rights and position of other sections of the population', occurring in Article 6, plainly refer to the non-Jewish community. These rights and position are not to be prejudiced ; that is, are not to be impaired or made worse. The effect of the policy of immigration and settlement on the economic position of the non-Jewish community cannot be excluded from consideration. But the words are not to be read as implying that existing economic conditions in Palestine should be crystallized. On the contrary, the obligation to facilitate Jewish immigration and to encourage close settlement by Jews on the land remains a positive obligation of the Mandate and it can be fulfilled without prejudice to the rights and position of other sections of the population of Palestine.

We may proceed to the contention that the Mandate has been interpreted in a manner highly prejudicial to Jewish interests in the vital matters of land settlement and immigration. It has been said that the policy of the White Paper would place an embargo on immigration and would suspend, if not indeed terminate, the close settlement of the Jews on the land, which is a primary purpose of the Mandate. In support of this contention particular stress has been laid upon the passage referring to State lands in the White Paper, which says that 'it would not be possible to make available for Jewish settlement in view of their actual occupation by Arab cultivators and of the importance of making available suitable land on which to place the Arab cultivators who are now landless'.

The language of this passage needs to be read in the light of the policy as a whole. It is desirable to make it clear that the landless Arabs, to whom it was intended to refer in the passage quoted, were such Arabs as can be shown to have been displaced from the lands which they occupied in consequence of the land passing into Jewish hands, and who have not obtained other holdings on which they can establish themselves, or other equally satisfactory occupation. The number of such displaced Arabs must be a matter for careful inquiry. It is to landless Arabs within this category that His Majesty's Government feels itself under an obligation to facilitate their settlement upon the land. The recognition of this obligation in no way detracts from the larger purposes of development which His Majesty's Government regards as the most effectual means of furthering the establishment of a national home for the Jews ..

Further, the statement of policy of His Majesty's Government did not imply a prohibition of acquisition of additional land by Jews. It contains no such prohibition, nor is any such intended. What it does contemplate is such temporary control of land disposition and transfers as may be necessary not to impair the harmony and effectiveness of the scheme of land settlement to be undertaken. His Majesty's Government feels bound to point out that it alone of the governments which have been responsible for the administration of Palestine since the acceptance of the Mandate has declared its definite intention to initiate an active policy of development, which it is believed will result in a substantial and lasting benefit to both Jews and Arabs.

Cognate to this question is the control of immigration. It must first of all be pointed out that such control is not in any sense a departure from previous policy. From 1920 onward, when the original immigration ordinance came into force, regulations for the control of immigration have been issued from time to time, directed to prevent illicit entry and to define and facilitate authorized entry. This right of regulation has at no time been challenged.

But the intention of His Majesty's Government appears to have been represented as being that 'no further immigration of Jews is to be permitted so long as it might prevent any Arab from obtaining employment'. His Majesty's Government never proposed to pursue such a policy. They were concerned to state that, in the regulation of Jewish immigration, the following principles should apply : viz., that 'it is essential to ensure that the immigrants should not be a burden on the people of Palestine as a whole, and that they should not deprive any section of the present population as a whole, and that they should not deprive any section of the present population of their employment' (White Paper 1922).

In one aspect, His Majesty's Government have to be mindful of their obligations to facilitate Jewish immigration under suitable conditions, and to encourage close settlement by Jews on the land; in the other aspect, they have to be equally mindful of their duty to ensure that no prejudice results to the rights and position of the non-Jewish community. It is because of this apparent conflict of obligations that His Majesty's Government have felt bound to emphasize the necessity of the proper application of the absorptive principle.

That principle is vital to any scheme of development, the primary purpose of which must be the settlement both of Jews and of displaced Arabs on the land. It is for that reason that His Majesty's Government have insisted, and are compelled to insist, that government immigration regulations must be properly applied. The considerations relevant to the limits of absorptive capacity are purely economic considerations.

His Majesty's Government did not prescribe and do not contemplate any stoppage or prohibition of Jewish immigration in any of its categories. The practice of sanctioning a labour schedule of wage-earning immigrants will continue. In each case consideration will be given to anticipated labour requirements for works which, being dependent upon Jewish or mainly Jewish capital, would not be or would not have been undertaken unless Jewish labour was available. With regard to public and municipal works failing to be financed out of public funds, the claim of Jewish labour to a due share of the employment available, taking into account Jewish contributions to public revenue, shall be taken into consideration. As regards other kinds of employment, it will be necessary in each case to take into account the factors bearing upon the demand for labour, including the factor of unemployment among both the Jews and the Arabs.

Immigrants with prospects of employment other than employment of a purely ephemeral character will not be excluded on the sole ground that the employment cannot be guaranteed to be of unlimited duration.

In determining the extent to which immigration at any time may be permitted it is necessary also to have regard to the declared policy of the Jewish Agency to the effect that 'in all the works or undertakings carried out or furthered by the

Agency it shall be deemed to be a matter of principle that Jewish labour shall be employed'. His Majesty's Government do not in any way challenge the right of the Agency to formulate or approve and endorse this policy. The principle of preferential, and indeed exclusive, employment of Jewish labour by Jewish organizations is a principle which the Jewish Agency are entitled to affirm. But it must be pointed out that if in consequence of this policy Arab labour is displaced or existing unemployment becomes aggravated, that is a factor in the situation to which the Mandatory is bound to have regard.

His Majesty's Government desire to say, finally, as they have repeatedly and unequivocally affirmed, that the obligations imposed upon the Mandatory by its acceptance of the Mandate are solemn international obligations from which there is not now, nor has there been at any time, any intention to depart. To the tasks imposed by the Mandate, His Majesty's Government have set their hand, and they will not withdraw it. But if their efforts are to be successful, there is need for cooperation, confidence, readiness on all sides to appreciate the difficulties and complexities of the problem, and, above all, there must be a full and unqualified recognition that no solution can be satisfactory or permanent which is not based upon justice, both to the Jewish people and to the non-Jewish communities of Palestine.

Ramsay MacDonald

Document 14

From the Report of the Palestine Royal Commission (Peel Commission), 1937

A Royal Commission headed by Lord Peel was appointed in 1936, following the outbreak of fresh Arab riots earlier that year. Its report, published in July 1937, stated that the desire of the Arabs for national independence and their hatred and fear of the establishment of the Jewish National Home were the underlying causes of the disturbances. It found that Arab and Jewish interests could not be reconciled under the Mandate and it suggested, therefore, the partition of Palestine. The Jewish state was to comprise Galilee, the Yezreel Valley and the Coastal Plain to a point midway between Gaza and Jaffa, altogether about twenty per cent of the area of the country. The rest, Arab Palestine, was to be united with Transjordan. Jerusalem, Bethlehem, a corridor linking them to the Sea, and, possibly, Nazareth and the Sea of Genezareth would remain a British mandatory zone. The Arab leadership rejected the plan, the Zionist Congress accepted it with qualifications – against the wish of a substantial minority. The British government which had initially favoured partition eventually rejected it in November 1938. (Document 16.)

*

... To foster Jewish immigration in the hope that it might ultimately lead to the creation of a Jewish majority and the establishment of a Jewish state with the consent or at least the acquiescence of the Arabs was one thing. It was quite another to contemplate, however remotely, the forcible conversion of Palestine into a Jewish state against the will of the Arabs. For that would clearly violate the spirit and intention of the Mandate System. It would mean that national self-determination had been withheld when the Arabs were a majority in Palestine and only conceded when the Jews were a majority. It would mean that the Arabs had been denied the opportunity of standing by themselves: that they had, in fact, after an interval of conflict, been bartered about from Turkish sovereignty to Jewish sovereignty. It is true that in the light of history Jewish rule over Palestine could not be regarded as foreign rule in the same sense as Turkish; but the international recognition of the right of the Jews to return to their old homeland did not involve the recognition of the right of the Jews to govern the Arabs in it against their will. The case stated by Lord Milner against an Arab control of Palestine applies equally to a Jewish control ...

An irrepressible conflict has arisen between two national communities within the narrow bounds of one small country. About 1,000,000 Arabs are in strife, open or latent, with some 400,000 Jews. There is no common ground between them. The

Arab community is predominantly Asiatic in character, the Jewish community predominantly European. They differ in religion and in language. Their cultural and social life, their ways of thought and conduct, are as incompatible as their national aspirations. These last are the greatest bar to peace. Arabs and Jews might possibly learn to live and work together in Palestine if they would make a genuine effort to reconcile and combine their national ideals and so build up in time a joint or dual nationality. But this they cannot do. The war and its sequel have inspired all Arabs with the hope of reviving in a free and united Arab world the traditions of the Arab golden age. The Jews similarly are inspired by their historic past. They mean to show what the Jewish nation can achieve when restored to the land of its birth. National assimilation between Arabs and Jews is thus ruled out. In the Arab picture the Jews could only occupy the place they occupied in Arab Egypt or Arab Spain. The Arabs would be as much outside the Jewish picture as the Canaanites in the old land of Israel. The National Home, as we have said before, cannot be half-national. In these circumstances to maintain that Palestinian citizenship has any moral meaning is a mischievous pretence. Neither Arab nor Jew has any sense of service to a single state. . .

Document 15

V. Jabotinsky: 'A Jewish State Now': Evidence Submitted to the Palestine Royal Comission*

Vladimir Ze'ev Jabotinsky (1880-1940) was the leader of the Zionist Revisionists advocating the establishment of a Jewish state in its historic borders.

*

The conception of Zionism which I have the honour to represent here is based on what I should call the humanitarian aspect. By that I do not mean to say that we do not respect the other,

---

* V. Jabotinsky, House of Lords, London, 11 February 1937.

the purely spiritual aspects of Jewish nationalism, such as the
desire for self-expression, the rebuilding of a Hebrew culture, or
creating some 'model community of which the Jewish people
could be proud'. All that, of course, is most important; but as
compared with our actual needs and our real position in the
world today, all that has rather the character of luxury. The
Commission have already heard a description of the situation
of World Jewry especially in Eastern Europe, and I am not
going to repeat any details, but you will allow me to quote a
recent reference in the *New York Times* describing the position
of Jewry in Eastern Europe as 'a disaster of historic magnitude'.
I only wish to add that it would be very naïve, and although
many Jews make this mistake I disapprove of it – it would be
very naïve to ascribe that state of disaster, permanent disaster,
only to the guilt of men, whether it be crowds and multitudes,
or whether it be governments. The thing goes much deeper than
that. I am very much afraid that what I am going to say will not
be popular with many among my co-religionists, and I regret
that, but the truth is the truth. We are facing an elemental
calamity, a kind of social earthquake. Three generations of
Jewish thinkers and Zionists among whom there were many
great minds – I am not going to fatigue you by quoting them –
three generations have given much thought to analysing the
Jewish position and have come to the conclusion that the cause
of our suffering is the very fact of the 'Diaspora', the bedrock
fact that we are everywhere a minority. It is not the anti-
Semitism of men; it is, above all, the anti-Semitism of things,
the inherent xenophobia of the body social or the body economic under which we suffer. Of course, there are ups and
downs; but there are moments, there are whole periods in history when this 'xenophobia of Life itself' takes dimensions
which no people can stand, and that is what we are facing now.
I do not mean to suggest that I would recognize that all the
governments concerned have done all they ought to have done;
I wolud be the last man to concede that. I think many governments, East and West, ought to do much more to protect the
Jews than they do; but the best of governments could perhaps
only soften the calamity to quite an insignificant extent, but the

core of the calamity is an earthquake which stands and remains.
I want to mention here that, since one of those governments
(the Polish Government) has recently tried what amounts to
bringing to the notice of the League of Nations and the whole of
humanity that it is humanity's duty to provide the Jews with an
area where they could build up their own body social undisturbed by anyone, I think the sincerity of the Polish Government, and of any other governments who, I hope, will follow,
should not be suspected, but on the contrary it should be recognized and acknowledged with due gratitude. – Perhaps the greatest gap in all I am going to say and in all the Commission have
heard up to now is the impossibility of really going to the root
of the problem, really bringing before you a picture of what
that Jewish hell looks like, and I feel I cannot do it. I do hope
that the day may come when some Jewish representatives may
be allowed to appear at the Bar of one of these two Houses just
to tell them what it really is, and to ask the English people :
'What are you going to advise us ? Where is the way out ?' Or,
standing up and facing God, say that there is no way out and
that we Jews have just to go under. But unfortunately I cannot
do it, so I will simply assume that the Royal Commission are
sufficiently informed of all this situation, and then I want you
to realize this : the phenomenon called Zionism may include all
kinds of dreams – a 'model community', Hebrew culture, perhaps even a second edition of the Bible – but all this longing for
wonderful toys of velvet and silver is nothing in comparison
with that tangible momentum of irresistible distress and need
by which we are propelled and borne. We are not free agents.
We cannot 'concede' anything. Whenever I hear the Zionist,
most often my own party, accused of asking for too much –
gentlemen, I really cannot understand it. Yes, we do want a
state; every nation on earth, every normal nation, beginning
with the smallest and the humblest who do not claim any merit,
any role in humanity's development, they all have states of their
own. That is the normal condition for a people. Yet, when we,
the most abnormal of peoples and therefore the most unfortunate, ask only for the same condition as the Albanians enjoy, to
say nothing of the French and the English, then it is called too

much. I should understand it if the answer were, 'It is impossible', but when the answer is, 'It is too much' I cannot understand it. I would remind you (excuse me for quoting an example known to every one of you) of the commotion which was produced in that famous institution when Oliver Twist came and asked for 'more'. He said 'more' because he did not know how to express it; what Oliver Twist really meant was this: 'Will you just give me that normal portion which is necessary for a boy of my age to be able to live.' I assure you that you face here today, in the Jewish people with its demands, an Oliver Twist who has, unfortunately, no concessions to make. What can be the concessions? We have got to save millions, many *millions*. I do not know whether it is a question of re-housing one third of the Jewish race, half of the Jewish race, or a quarter of the Jewish race; I do not know; but it is a question of millions. Certainly the way out is to evacuate those portions of the Diaspora which have become no good, which hold no promise of any possibility of a livelihood, and to concentrate all those refugees in some place which should *not* be Diaspora, not a repetition of the position where the Jews are an unabsorbed minority within a foreign social, or economic, or political organism. Naturally, if that process of evacuation is allowed to develop, as it ought to be allowed to develop, there will very soon be reached a moment when the Jews will become a majority in Palestine. I am going to make a 'terrible' confession. Our demand for a Jewish majority is not our maximum – it is our minimum: it is just an inevitable stage if only we are allowed to go on salvaging our people. The point when the Jews will reach a majority in that country will not be the point of saturation yet – because with 1,000,000 more Jews in Palestine today you could already have a Jewish majority, but there are certainly 3,000,000 or 4,000,000 in the East who are virtually knocking at the door asking for admission, i.e., for salvation.

I have the profoundest feeling for the Arab case, in so far as that Arab case is not exaggerated. This Commission have already been able to make up their minds as to whether there is any individual hardship to the Arabs of Palestine as men,

deriving from the Jewish colonization. We maintain unanimously that the economic position of the Palestinian Arabs,
under the Jewish colonization and owing to the Jewish colonization, has become the object of envy in all the surrounding
Arab countries, so that the Arabs from those countries show
a clear tendency to immigrate into Palestine. I have also shown
to you already that, in our submission, there is no question of
ousting the Arabs. On the contrary, the idea is that Palestine
on both sides of the Jordan should hold the Arabs, their pro-
geny, *and* many millions of Jews. What I do not deny is that
in that process the Arabs of Palestine will necessarily become a
minority in the country of Palestine. What I do deny is that *that*
is a hardship. It is not a hardship on any race, any nation, possessing so many national states now and so many more national states in the future. One fraction, one branch of that
race, and not a big one, will have to live in someone else's
state: well, that is the case with all the mightiest nations of
the world. I could hardly mention one of the big nations,
having their states, mighty and powerful, who had not one
branch living in someone else's state. That is only normal and
there is no 'hardship' attached to that. So when we heard the
Arab claim confronted with the Jewish claim; I fully understand that any minority would prefer to be a majority, it is
quite understandable that the Arabs of Palestine would also
prefer Palestine to be the Arab state No. 4, No. 5, or No. 6 –
that I quite understand; but when the Arab claim is confronted with our Jewish demand to be saved, it is like the claims of
appetite versus the claims of starvation. No tribunal has ever
had the luck of trying a case where all the justice was on the
side of one party and the other party had no case whatsoever.
Usually in human affairs any tribunal, including this tribunal,
in trying two cases, has to concede that both sides have a case
on their side and, in order to do justice, they must take into
consideration what should constitute the basic justification of
all human demands, individual or mass demands – the decisive
terrible balance of Need. I think it is clear.

Document 16

*Against Partition: British Statement of
Policy, November 1938*

. . . 3. His Majesty's Government have now received the report
of the Palestine Partition Commission who have carried out
their investigations with great thoroughness and efficiency,
and have collected material which will be very valuable in the
further consideration of policy. Their report is now published,
together with a summary of their conclusions. It will be noted
that the four members of the Commission advise unanimously
against the adoption of the scheme of partition outlined by the
Royal Commission. In addition to the Royal Commission's
scheme, two other schemes described as plans B and C are
examined in the report. One member prefers plan B. Two other
members, including the Chairman, consider that plan C is the
best scheme of partition which, under the terms of reference,
can be devised. A fourth member, while agreeing that plan C
is the best that can be devised under the terms of reference,
regards both plans as impracticable. The report points out that
under either plan, while the budget of the Jewish State is likely
to show a substantial surplus, the budgets of the Arab State
(including Transjordan) and of the Mandated Territories
are likely to show substantial deficits. The Commission reject
as impracticable the Royal Commission's recommendation for
a direct subvention from the Jewish State to the Arab State.
They think that, on economic grounds, a customs union between the States and the Mandated Territories is essential and
they examine the possibility of finding the solution for the
financial and economic problems of partition by means of a
scheme based upon such a union. They consider that any such
scheme would be inconsistent with the grant of fiscal independence to the Arab and Jewish States. Their conclusion is that,
on a strict interpretation of their terms of reference, they have
no alternative but to report that they are unable to recommend boundaries for the proposed areas which will afford a

reasonable prospect of the eventual establishment of self-supporting Arab and Jewish States.

4. His Majesty's Government, after careful study of the Partition Commissioner's report, have reached the conclusion that this further examination has shown that the political, administrative and financial difficulties involved in the proposal to create independent Arab and Jewish States inside Palestine are so great that this solution of the problem is impracticable.

5. His Majesty's Government will therefore continue their responsibility for the government of the whole of Palestine. They are now faced with the problem of finding alternative means of meeting the needs of the difficult situation described by the Royal Commission which will be consistent with their obligations to the Arabs and the Jews. His Majesty's Government believe that it is possible to find these alternative means. They have already given much thought to the problem in the light of the reports of the Royal Commission and of the Partition Commission. It is clear that the surest foundation for peace and progress in Palestine would be an understanding between the Arabs and the Jews, and His Majesty's Government are prepared in the first instance to make a determined effort to promote such an understanding. With this end in view, they propose immediately to invite representatives of the Palestinian Arabs and of neighbouring States on the one hand and of the Jewish Agency on the other, to confer with them as soon as possible in London regarding future policy, including the question of immigration into Palestine. As regards the representation of the Palestinian Arabs, His Majesty's Government must reserve the right to refuse to receive those leaders whom they regard as responsible for the campaign of assassination and violence.

6. His Majesty's Government hope that these discussions in London may help to promote agreement as to future policy regarding Palestine. They attach great importance, however, to a decision being reached at an early date. Therefore, if the London discussions should not produce agreement within a reasonable period of time, they will take their own decision in the light of their examination of the problem and of the

discussions in London, and announce the policy which they propose to pursue.

7. In considering and settling their policy His Majesty's Government will keep constantly in mind the international character of the Mandate with which they have been entrusted and their obligations in that respect.

Document 17

The White Paper of 1939

After the failure of the partition scheme and a subsequent attempt to work out an agreed solution at a Conference in London (February–March 1939), the British government announced its new policy in a White Paper published on 17 May 1939. The Arab demands were largely met: Jewish immigration was to continue at a maximum rate of 15,000 for another five years. After that it was to cease altogether unless the Arabs would accept it. Purchase of land by Jews would be prohibited in some areas, restricted in others. Jewish reaction was bitterly hostile (Document 18), but the Arab leaders also rejected the White Paper: according to the demands, Palestine was to become an Arab state immediately, no more Jewish immigrants were to enter the country, the status of every Jew who had immigrated since 1918 was to be reviewed.

*

17 May 1939

In the Statement on Palestine, issued on 9 November 1938 His Majesty's Government announced their intention to invite representatives of the Arabs of Palestine, of certain neighbouring countries and of the Jewish Agency to confer with them in London regarding future policy. It was their sincere hope that, as a result of full, free and frank discussion, some understanding might be reached. Conferences recently took place with Arab and Jewish delegations, lasting for a period of several weeks, and served the purpose of a complete exchange of views between British Ministers and the Arab and Jewish representatives. In the light of the discussions as well as of the situation in Palestine and of the Reports of the Royal Commission and the Partition Commission, certain proposals were formulated by His Majesty's Government and were laid before the Arab and Jewish delegations as the basis of an agreed settlement. Neither the Arab nor the Jewish delegation felt able to accept these proposals, and the conferences therefore did not result in an agreement. Accordingly His Majesty's Government are free to formulate their own policy, and after careful consideration they have decided to adhere generally to the proposals which were finally submitted to, and discussed with, the Arab and Jewish delegations.

2. The Mandate for Palestine, the terms of which were confirmed by the Council of the League of Nations in 1922, has governed the policy of successive British Governments for nearly twenty years. It embodies the Balfour Declaration and imposes on the Mandatory four main obligations. These obligations are set out in Articles 2, 6 and 13 of the Mandate. There is no dispute regarding the interpretation of one of these obligations, that touching the protection of and access to the Holy Places and religious building or sites. The other three main obligations are generally as follows:

(i) To place the country under such political, administrative and economic conditions as will secure the establishment in Palestine of a national home for the Jewish people, to facilitate Jewish immigration under suitable conditions, and to encourage, in cooperation with the Jewish Agency, close settlement by Jews on the land.

(ii) To safeguard the civil and religious rights of all the inhabitants of Palestine irrespective of race and religion, and, whilst facilitating Jewish immigration and settlement, to ensure that the rights and position of other sections of the population are not prejudiced.

(iii) To place the country under such political, administrative and economic conditions as will secure the development of self-governing institutions.

3. The Royal Commission and previous Commissions of Enquiry have drawn attention to the ambiguity of certain expressions in the Mandate, such as the expression 'a national home

for the Jewish people', and they have found in this ambiguity and the resulting uncertainty as to the objectives of policy a fundamental cause of unrest and hostility between Arabs and Jews. His Majesty's Government are convinced that in the interests of the peace and well-being of the whole people of Palestine a clear definition of policy and objectives is essential. The proposal of partition recommended by the Royal Commission would have afforded such clarity, but the establishment of self-supporting independent Arab and Jewish States within Palestine has been found to be impracticable. It has therefore been necessary for His Majesty's Government to devise an alternative policy which will, consistently with their obligations to Arabs and Jews, meet the needs of the situation in Palestine. Their views and proposals are set forth below under the three heads, (1) The Constitution, (2) Immigration, and (3) Land.

1. The Constitution

4. It has been urged that the expression 'a national home for the Jewish people' offered a prospect that Palestine might in due course become a Jewish State or Commonwealth. His Majesty's Government do not wish to contest the view, which was expressed by the Royal Commission, that the Zionist leaders at the time of the issue of the Balfour Declaration recognized that an ultimate Jewish State was not precluded by the terms of the Declaration. But, with the Royal Commission, His Majesty's Government believe that the framers of the Mandate in which the Balfour Declaration was embodied could not have intended that Palestine should be converted into a Jewish State against the will of the Arab population of the country. That Palestine was not to be converted into a Jewish State might be held to be implied in the passage from the Command Paper of 1922 which reads as follows:

Unauthorized statements have been made to the effect that the purpose in view is to create a wholly Jewish Palestine. Phrases have been used such as that 'Palestine is to become as Jewish as England is English.' His Majesty's Government regard any such expectation as impracticable and have no such aim in view. Nor have they at any time contemplated ... the disappearance or the subordination of the Arabic population, language or culture in Palestine. They would draw attention to the fact that the terms of the [Balfour] Declaration referred to do not contemplate that Palestine as a whole should be converted into a Jewish National Home, but that such a home should be founded *in Palestine*.

But this statement has not removed doubts, and His Majesty's Government therefore now declare unequivocally that it is not part of their policy that Palestine should become a Jewish State. They would indeed regard it as contrary to their obligations to the Arabs under the Mandate, as well as to the assurances which have been given to the Arab people in the past, that the Arab population of Palestine should be made the subjects of a Jewish State against their will.

5. The nature of the Jewish National Home in Palestine was further described in the Command Paper of 1922 as follows:

During the last two or three generations the Jews have re-created in Palestine a community, now numbering 80,000, of whom about one fourth are farmers or workers upon the land. This community has its own political organs; an elected assembly for the direction of its domestic concerns; elected councils in the towns; and an organization for the control of its schools. It has its elected Chief Rabbinate and Rabbinical Council for the direction of its religious affairs. Its business is conducted in Hebrew as a vernacular language, and a Hebrew press serves its needs. It has its distinctive intellectual life and displays considerable economic activity. This community, then, with its town and country population, its political, religious and social organizations, its own language, its own customs, its own life, has in fact 'national' characteristics. When it is asked what is meant by the development of the Jewish National Home in Palestine, it may be answered that it is not the imposition of the Jewish nationality upon the inhabitants of Palestine as a whole, but the further development of the existing Jewish community, with the assistance of Jews in other parts of the world, in order that it may become a centre in which the Jewish people as a whole may take, on grounds of religion and race, an interest and a pride. But in order that this community should have the best prospect of free development and provide

a full opportunity for the Jewish people to display its capacities,
it is essential that it should know that it is in Palestine as of right
and not on sufferance. That is the reason why it is necessary that
the existence of the Jewish National Home in Palestine should be
internationally guaranteed, and that it should be formerly recognized to rest upon ancient historic connexion.

6. His Majesty's Government adhere to this interpretation
of the Declaration of 1917 and regard it as an authoritative
and comprehensive description of the character of the Jewish
National Home in Palestine. It envisaged the further development of the existing Jewish community with the assistance of
Jews in other parts of the world. Evidence that His Majesty's
Government have been carrying out their obligation in this
respect is to be found in the facts that, since the statement of
1922 was published, more than 300,000 Jews have immigrated
to Palestine, and that the population of the National Home
has risen to some 450,000, or approaching a third of the entire
population of the country. Nor has the Jewish community
failed to take full advantage of the opportunities given to it.
The growth of the Jewish National Home and its achievements
in many fields are a remarkable constructive effort which
must command the admiration of the world and must be, in
particular, a source of pride to the Jewish people.

7. In the recent discussions the Arab delegations have repeated the contention that Palestine was included within the
area in which Sir Henry McMahon, on behalf of the British
Government, in October 1915, undertook to recognize and support Arab independence. The validity of this claim, based on
the terms of the correspondence which passed between Sir
Henry McMahon and the Sharif of Mecca, was thoroughly and
carefully investigated by British and Arab representatives during the recent conferences in London. Their Report, which has
been published, states that both the Arab and the British representatives endeavoured to understand the point of view of the
other party but that they were unable to reach agreement upon
an interpretation of the correspondence. There is no need to
summarize here the arguments presented by each side. His
Majesty's Government regret the misunderstandings which

have arisen as regards some of the phrases used. For their part they can only adhere, for the reasons given by their representatives in the Report, to the view that the whole of Palestine west of Jordan was excluded from Sir Henry McMahon's pledge, and they therefore cannot agree that the McMahon correspondence forms a just basis for the claim that Palestine should be converted into an Arab State.

8. His Majesty's Government are charged as the Mandatory authority 'to secure the development of self-governing institutions' in Palestine. Apart from this specific obligation, they would regard it as contrary to the whole spirit of the Mandate system that the population of Palestine should remain forever under Mandatory tutelage. It is proper that the people of the country should as early as possible enjoy the rights of self-government which are exercised by the people of neighbouring countries. His Majesty's Government are unable at present to foresee the exact constitutional forms which government in Palestine will eventually take, but their objective is self-government, and they desire to see established ultimately an independent Palestine State. It should be a State in which the two peoples in Palestine, Arabs and Jews, share authority in government in such a way that the essential interests of each are secured.

9. The establishment of an independent State and the complete relinquishment of Mandatory control in Palestine would require such relations between the Arabs and the Jews as would make good government possible. Moreover, the growth of self-governing institutions in Palestine, as in other countries, must be an evolutionary process. A transitional period will be required before independence is achieved, throughout which ultimate responsibility for the Government of the country will be retained by His Majesty's Government as the Mandatory authority, while the people of the country are taking an increasing share in the Government, and understanding and co-operation amongst them are growing. It will be the constant endeavour of His Majesty's Government to promote good relations between the Arabs and the Jews.

10. In the light of these considerations His Majesty's

Government make the following declaration of their intentions regarding the future government of Palestine:

(i) The objective of His Majesty's Government is the establishment within ten years of an independent Palestine State in such treaty relations with the United Kingdom as will provide satisfactorily for the commercial and strategic requirements of both countries in the future. The proposal for the establishment of the independent State would involve consultation with the Council of the League of Nations with a view to the termination of the Mandate.

(ii) The independent State should be one in which Arabs and Jews share in government in such a way as to ensure that the essential interests of each community are safeguarded.

(iii) The establishment of the independent State will be preceded by a transitional period throughout which His Majesty's Government will retain responsibility for the government of the country. During the transitional period the people of Palestine will be given an increasing part in the government of their country. Both sections of the population will have an opportunity to participate in the machinery of government, and the process will be carried on whether or not they both avail themselves of it.

(iv) A soon as peace and order have been sufficiently restored in Palestine steps will be taken to carry out this policy of giving the people of Palestine an increasing part in the government of their country, the objective being to place Palestinians in charge of all the Departments of Government, with the assistance of British advisers and subject to the control of the High Commissioner. With this object in view His Majesty's Government will be prepared immediately to arrange that Palestinians shall be placed in charge of certain Departments, with British advisers. The Palestinian heads of Departments will sit on the Executive Council which advises the High Commissioner. Arab and Jewish representatives will be invited to serve as heads of Departments approximately in proportion to their respective populations. The number of Palestinians in charge of Departments will be increased as circumstances permit until all heads of Departments are Palestinians, exercising the administrative and advisory functions which are at present performed by British officials. When that stage is reached consideration will be given to the question of converting the Executive Council into a Council of Ministers with a consequential change in the status and functions of the Palestinian heads of Departments.

(v) His Majesty's Government make no proposals at this stage regarding the establishment of an elective legislature. Nevertheless they would regard this as an appropriate constitutional development, and, should public opinion in Palestine hereafter show itself in favour of such a development, they will be prepared, provided that local conditions permit, to establish the necessary machinery.

(vi) At the end of five years from the restoration of peace and order, an appropriate body representative of the people of Palestine and of His Majesty's Government will be set up to review the working of the constitutional arrangements during the transitional period and to consider and make recommendations regarding the constitution of the independent Palestine State.

(vii) His Majesty's Government will require to be satisfied that in the treaty contemplated by sub-paragraph (i) or in the constitution contemplated by sub-paragraph (vi) adequate provision has been made for:

(a) the security of, and freedom of access to, the Holy Places, and the protection of the interests and property of the various religious bodies.

(b) the protection of the different communities in Palestine in accordance with the obligations of His Majesty's Government to both Arabs and Jews and for the special position in Palestine of the Jewish National Home.

(c) such requirements to meet the strategic situation as may be regarded as necessary by His Majesty's Government in the light of the circumstances then existing.

His Majesty's Government will also require to be satisfied that the interests of certain foreign countries in Palestine, for the preservation of which they are at present responsible, are adequately safeguarded.

(viii) His Majesty's Government will do everything in their power to create conditions which will enable the independent Palestine State to come into being within ten years. If, at the end of ten years, it appears to His Majesty's Government that, contrary to their hope, circumstances require the postponement of the establishment of the independent State, they will consult with representatives of the people of Palestine, the Council of the League of Nations and the neighbouring Arab States before deciding on such a postponement. If His Majesty's Government come to the conclusion that postponement is unavoidable, they will invite the cooperation of these parties in framing plans for the future with a view to achieving the desired objective at the earliest possible date.

11. During the transitional period steps will be taken to increase the powers and responsibilities of municipal corporations and local councils.

2. Immigration

12. Under Article 6 of the Mandate, the Administration of Palestine, 'while ensuring that the rights and position of other sections of the population are not prejudiced', is required to 'facilitate Jewish immigration under suitable conditions'. Beyond this, the extent to which Jewish immigration into Palestine is to be permitted is nowhere defined in the Mandate. But in the Command Paper of 1922 it was laid down that for the fulfilment of the policy of establishing a Jewish National Home

it is necessary that the Jewish community in Palestine should be able to increase its numbers by immigration. This immigration cannot be so great in volume as to exceed whatever may be the economic capacity of the country at the time to absorb new arrivals. It is essential to ensure that the immigrants should not be a burden upon the people of Palestine as a whole, and that they should not deprive any section of the present population of their employment.

In practice, from that date onwards until recent times, the economic absorptive capacity of the country has been treated as the sole limiting factor, and in the letter which Mr Ramsay MacDonald, as Prime Minister, sent to Dr Weizmann in February 1931 it was laid down as a matter of policy that economic absorptive capacity was the sole criterion. This interpretation has been supported by resolutions of the Permanent Mandates Commission. But His Majesty's Government do not read either the Statement of Policy of 1922 or the letter of 1931 as implying that the Mandate requires them, for all time and in all circumstances, to facilitate the immigration of Jews into Palestine subject only to consideration of the country's economic absorptive capacity. Nor do they find anything in the Mandate or in subsequent Statements of Policy to support the view that the establishment of a Jewish National Home in Palestine cannot be effected unless immigration is allowed to continue indefinitely. If immigration has an adverse effect on the economic position in the country, it should clearly be restricted; and equally, if it has a seriously damaging effect on the political position in the country, that is a factor that should not be ignored. Although it is not difficult to contend that the large number of Jewish immigrants who have been admitted so far have been absorbed economically, the fear of the Arabs that this influx will continue indefinitely until the Jewish population is in a position to dominate them has produced consequences which are extremely grave for Jews and Arabs alike and for the peace and prosperity of Palestine. The lamentable disturbances of the past three years are only the latest and most sustained manifestation of this intense Arab apprehension. The methods employed by Arab terrorists against fellow-Arabs and Jews alike must receive unqualified condemnation. But it cannot be denied that fear of indefinite Jewish immigration is widespread amongst the Arab population and that this fear has made possible disturbances which have given a serious setback to economic progress, depleted the Palestine exchequer, rendered life and property insecure, and produced a bitterness between the Arab and Jewish populations which is deplorable between citizens of the same country. If in these circumstances immigration is continued up to the economic absorptive capacity of the country, regardless of all other considerations, a fatal enmity between the two peoples will be perpetuated and the situation in Palestine may become a permanent source of friction amongst all peoples in the Near and Middle East. His Majesty's Government cannot take the view that either their obligations under the Mandate, or considerations of common sense and justice, require that they should ignore these circumstances in framing immigration policy.

13. In the view of the Royal Commission the association of the policy of the Balfour Declaration with the Mandate system implied the belief that Arab hostility to the former would sooner or later be overcome. It has been the hope of British Governments ever since the Balfour Declaration was issued that in time the Arab population, recognizing the advantages to be derived from Jewish settlement and development in Palestine, would become reconciled to the further growth of the Jewish National Home. This hope has not been fulfilled. The alternatives before His Majesty's Government are either (i) to seek to expand the Jewish National Home indefinitely by immigration, against the strongly expressed will of the Arab people of the country; or (ii) to permit further expansion of the Jewish National Home by immigration only if the Arabs are prepared to acquiesce in it. The former policy means rule by force. Apart from other considerations, such a policy seems to His Majesty's Government to be contrary to the whole spirit of Article 22 of the Covenant of the League of Nations, as well as to their specific obligations to the Arabs in the Palestine Mandate. Moreover, the relations between the Arabs and the Jews in Palestine must be based sooner or later on mutual tolerance and goodwill; the peace, security and progress of the Jewish National Home itself require this. Therefore His Majesty's Government, after earnest consideration, and taking into account the extent to which the growth of the Jewish National Home has been facilitated over the last twenty years, have decided that the time has come to adopt in principle the second of the alternatives referred to above.

14. It has been urged that all further Jewish immigration into Palestine should be stopped forthwith. His Majesty's Government cannot accept such a proposal. It would damage the

whole of the financial and economic system of Palestine and thus affect adversely the interests of Arabs and Jews alike. Moreover, in the view of His Majesty's Government, abruptly to stop further immigration would be unjust to the Jewish National Home. But, above all, His Majesty's Government are conscious of the present unhappy plight of large numbers of Jews who seek a refuge from certain European countries, and they believe that Palestine can and should make a further contribution to the solution of this pressing world problem. In all these circumstances, they believe that they will be acting consistently with their Mandatory obligations to both Arabs and Jews, and in the manner best calculated to serve the interests of the whole people of Palestine, by adopting the following proposals regarding immigration:

(1) Jewish immigration during the next five years will be at a rate which, if economic absorptive capacity permits, will bring the Jewish population up to approximately one third of the total population of the country. Taking into account the expected natural increase of the Arab and Jewish populations, and the number of illegal Jewish immigrants now in the country, this would allow of the admission, as from the beginning of April this year, of some 75,000 immigrants over the next five years. These immigrants would, subject to the criterion of economic absorptive capacity, be admitted as follows:

(*a*) For each of the next five years a quota of 10,000 Jewish immigrants will be allowed on the understanding that a shortage in any one year may be added to the quotas for subsequent years, within the five-year period, if economic absorptive capacity permits.

(*b*) In addition, as a contribution towards the solution of the Jewish refugee problem, 25,000 refugees will be admitted as soon as the High Commissioner is satisfied that adequate provision for their maintenance is ensured, special consideration being given to refugee children and dependants.

(2) The existing machinery for ascertaining economic absorptive capacity will be retained, and the High Commissioner will have the ultimate responsibility for deciding the limits of

economic capacity. Before each periodic decision is taken, Jewish and Arab representatives will be consulted.

(3) After the period of five years no further Jewish immigration will be permitted unless the Arabs of Palestine are prepared to acquiesce in it.

(4) His Majesty's Government are determined to check illegal immigration, and further preventive measures are being adopted. The numbers of any Jewish illegal immigrants who, despite these measures, may succeed in coming into the country and cannot be deported will be deducted from the yearly quotas.

15. His Majesty's Government are satisfied that, when the immigration over five years which is now contemplated has taken place, they will not be justified in facilitating, nor will they be under any obligation to facilitate, the further development of the Jewish National Home by immigration regardless of the wishes of the Jewish population.

3. Land

16. The Administration of Palestine is required, under Article 6 of the Mandate, 'while ensuring that the rights and position of other sections of the population are not prejudiced', to encourage 'close settlement by Jews on the land', and no restriction has been imposed hitherto on the transfer of land from Arabs to Jews. The Reports of several expert Commissions have indicated that, owing to the natural growth of the Arab population and the steady sale in recent years of Arab land to Jews, there is now in certain areas no room for further transfers of Arab land, whilst in some other areas such transfers of land must be restricted if Arab cultivators are to maintain their existing standard of life and a considerable landless Arab population is not soon to be created. In these circumstances, the High Commissioner will be given general powers to prohibit and regulate transfers of land. These powers will date from the publication of this statement of policy and the High Commissioner will retain them throughout the transitional period.

17. The policy of the Government will be directed towards the development of the land and the improvement, where possible, of methods of cultivation. In the light of such development it will be open to the High Commissioner, should he be satisfied that the 'rights and position' of the Arab population will be duly preserved, to review and modify any orders passed relating to the prohibition or restriction of the transfer of land.

18. In framing these proposals His Majesty's Government have sincerely endeavoured to act in strict accordance with their obligations under the Mandate to both the Arabs and the Jews. The vagueness of the phrases employed in some instances to describe these obligations has led to controversy and has made the task of interpretation difficult. His Majesty's Government cannot hope to satisfy the partisans of one party or the other in such controversy as the Mandate has aroused. Their purpose is to be just as between the two peoples in Palestine whose destinies in that country have been affected by the great events of recent years, and who, since they live side by side, must learn to practise mutual tolerance, goodwill and cooperation. In looking to the future, His Majesty's Government are not blind to the fact that some events of the past make the task of creating these relations difficult; but they are encouraged by the knowledge that at many times and in many places in Palestine during recent years the Arab and Jewish inhabitants have lived in friendship together. Each community has much to contribute to the welfare of their common land, and each must earnestly desire peace in which to assist in increasing the well-being of the whole people of the country. The responsibility which falls on them, no less than upon His Majesty's Government, to cooperate together to ensure peace is all the more solemn because their country is revered by many millions of Muslims, Jews and Christians throughout the word who pray for peace in Palestine and for the happiness of her people.

Document 18

*The Zionist Reaction to the White Paper:
Statement by the Jewish Agency for
Palestine (1939)*

1. The new policy for Palestine laid down by the Mandatory in
the White Paper now issued denies to the Jewish people the right
to rebuild their national home in their ancestral country. It
transfers the authority over Palestine to the present Arab majority and puts the Jewish population at the mercy of that majority. It decrees the stoppage of Jewish immigration as soon as
the Jews form a third of the total population. It puts up a territorial ghetto for Jews in their own homeland.

2. The Jewish people regard this policy as a breach of faith
and a surrender to Arab terrorism. It delivers Britain's friends
into the hands of those who are biting her and must lead to a
complete breach between Jews and Arabs which will banish
every prospect of peace in Palestine. It is a policy in which the
Jewish people will not acquiesce. The new regime now announced will be devoid of any moral basis and contrary to international law. Such a regime can only be established and
maintained by force.

3. The Royal Commission invoked by the White Paper indicated the perils of such a policy, saying it was convinced that
an Arab Government would mean the frustration of all their
[Jews'] efforts and ideals and would convert the national home
into one more cramped and dangerous ghetto. It seems only
too probable that the Jews would fight rather than submit to
Arab rule. And repressing a Jewish rebellion against British
policy would be as unpleasant a task as the repression of the
Arab rebellion has been. The Government has disregarded this
warning.

4. The Jewish people have no quarrel with the Arab people.
Jewish work in Palestine has not had an adverse effect upon
the life and progress of the Arab people. The Arabs are not
landless or homeless as are the Jews. They are not in need of

emigration. Jewish colonization has benefited Palestine and all
its inhabitants. Insofar as the Balfour Declaration contributed
to British victory in the Great War, it contributed also, as was
pointed out by the Royal Commission, to the liberation of the
Arab peoples. The Jewish people has shown its will to peace
even during the years of disturbances. It has not given way to
temptation and has not retaliated to Arab violence. But neither
have the Jews submitted to terror nor will they submit to it
even after the Mandatory has decided to reward the terrorists
by surrendering the Jewish National Home.

5. It is in the darkest hour of Jewish history that the British
Government proposes to deprive the Jews of their last hope and
to close the road back to their Homeland. It is a cruel blow,
doubly cruel because it comes from the government of a great
nation which has extended a helping hand to the Jews, and
whose position must rest on foundations of moral authority
and international good faith. This blow will not subdue the
Jewish people. The historic bond between the people and the
land of Israel cannot be broken. The Jews will never accept the
closing to them of the gates of Palestine nor let their national
home be converted into a ghetto. The Jewish pioneers who, during the past three generations, have shown their strength in
the upbuilding of a derelict country, will from now on display
the same strength in defending Jewish immigration, the Jewish
home and Jewish freedom.

Document 19

Towards a Jewish State:
The Biltmore Programme (1942)

During a visit to the United States by David Ben Gurion, Chairman
of the Executive of the Jewish Agency, Zionist policy was reformu-
lated. At a conference at the Biltmore Hotel in New York, in May
1942, the establishment of a Jewish state was envisaged to open the
doors of Palestine to Jewish refugees escaping from Nazi terror and
to lay the foundations for the establishment of a Jewish majority.

*

Declaration Adopted by the Extraordinary
Zionist Conference, Biltmore Hotel, New York
City, 11 May 1942

1. American Zionists assembled in this Extraordinary Conference reaffirm their unequivocal devotion to the cause of democratic freedom and international justice to which the people
of the United States, allied with the other United Nations, have
dedicated themselves, and give expression to their faith in the
ultimate victory of humanity and justice over lawlessness and
brute force.

2. This Conference offers a message of hope and encouragement to their fellow Jews in the Ghettos and concentration
camps of Hitler-dominated Europe and prays that their hour
of liberation may not be far distant.

3. The Conference sends its warmest greetings to the Jewish
Agency Executive in Jerusalem, to the Va'ad Leumi, and to
the whole Yishuv in Palestine, and expresses its profound admiration for their steadfastness and achievements in the face
of peril and great difficulties. The Jewish men and women in
field and factory, and the thousands of Jewish soldiers of Palestine in the Near East who have acquitted themselves with
honour and distinction in Greece, Ethiopia, Syria, Libya and
on other battlefields, have shown themselves worthy of their
people and ready to assume the rights and responsibilities of
nationhood.

4. In our generation, and in particular in the course of the
past twenty years, the Jewish people have awakened and
transformed their ancient homeland; from 50,000 at the end
of the last war their numbers have increased to more than
500,000. They have made the waste places to bear fruit and
the desert to blossom. Their pioneering achievements in agriculture and in industry, embodying new patterns of cooperative endeavour, have written a notable page in the history of
colonization.

5. In the new values thus created, their Arab neighbours in
Palestine have shared. The Jewish people in its own work of

national redemption welcomes the economic, agricultural and national development of the Arab peoples and states. The Conference reaffirms the stand previously adopted at Congresses of the World Zionist Organization, expressing the readiness and the desire of the Jewish people for full cooperation with their Arab neighbours.

6. The Conference calls for the fulfilment of the original purpose of the Balfour Declaration and the Mandate which 'recognizing the historical connexion of the Jewish people with Palestine' was to afford them the opportunity, as stated by President Wilson, to found there a Jewish Commonwealth.

The Conference affirms its unalterable rejection of the White Paper of May 1939 and denies its moral or legal validity. The White Paper seeks to limit, and in fact to nullify Jewish rights to immigration and settlement in Palestine, and, as stated by Mr Winston Churchill in the House of Commons in May 1939, constitutes 'a breach and repudiation of the Balfour Declaration'. The policy of the White Paper is cruel and indefensible in its denial of sanctuary to Jews fleeing from Nazi persecution; and at a time when Palestine has become a focal point in the war front of the United Nations, and Palestine Jewry must provide all available manpower for farm and factory and camp, it is in direct conflict with the interests of the allied war effort.

7. In the struggle against the forces of aggression and tyranny, of which Jews were the earliest victims, and which now menace the Jewish National Home, recognition must be given to the right of the Jews of Palestine to play their full part in the war effort and in the defence of their country, through a Jewish military force fighting under its own flag and under the high command of the United Nations.

8. The Conference declares that the new world order that will follow victory cannot be established on foundations of peace, justice and equality, unless the problem of Jewish homelessness is finally solved.

The Conference urges that the gates of Palestine be opened; that the Jewish Agency be vested with control of immigration into Palestine and with the necessary authority for upbuilding the country, including the development of its unoccupied and

uncultivated lands ; and that Palestine be established as a Jewish Commonwealth integrated in the structure of the new
democratic world.

Then and only then will the age-old wrong to the Jewish
people be righted.

Document 20

*Adolf Hitler, Zionism and the Arab Cause**

Haj Amin al Hussaini, the most influential leader of Palestinian
Arabs, lived in Germany during the Second World War. He met
Hitler, Ribbentrop and other Nazi leaders on various occasions and
attempted to coordinate Nazi and Arab policies in the Middle East.

*

Berlin, 30 November 1941

Record of the Conversation between the Führer
and the Grand Mufti of Jerusalem on 28 November
1941, in the Presence of the Reich Foreign
Minister and Minister Grobba in Berlin

The Grand Mufti began by thanking the Führer for the great
honour he had bestowed by receiving him. He wished to seize
the opportunity to convey to the Führer of the Greater German
Reich, admired by the entire Arab world, his thanks for the
sympathy which he had always shown for the Arab and especially the Palestinian cause, and to which he had given clear
expression in his public speeches. The Arab countries were
firmly convinced that Germany would win the war and that
the Arab cause would then prosper. The Arabs were Germany's
natural friends because they had the same enemies as had Germany, namely the English, the Jews, and the Communists. They
were therefore prepared to cooperate with Germany with all

Documents on German Foreign Policy 1918–45, Series D, Vol.
XIII, London, 1964, pp. 881 ff.

their hearts and stood ready to participate in the war, not only negatively by the commission of acts of sabotage and the instigation of revolutions, but also positively by the formation of an Arab Legion. The Arabs could be more useful to Germany as allies than might be apparent at first glance, both for geographical reasons and because of the suffering inflicted upon them by the English and the Jews. Furthermore, they had had close relations with all Muslim nations, of which they could make use in behalf of the common cause. The Arab Legion would be quite easy to raise. An appeal by the Mufti to the Arab countries and the prisoners of Arab, Algerian, Tunisian, and Moroccan nationality in Germany would produce a great number of volunteers eager to fight. Of Germany's victory the Arab world was firmly convinced, not only because the Reich possessed a large army, brave soldiers, and military leaders of genius, but also because the Almighty could never award the victory to an unjust cause.

In this struggle, the Arabs were striving for the independence and unity of Palestine, Syria, and Iraq. They had the fullest confidence in the Führer and looked to his hand for the balm on their wounds which had been inflicted upon them by the enemies of Germany.

The Mufti then mentioned the letter he had received from Germany, which stated that Germany was holding no Arab territories and understood and recognized the aspirations to independence and freedom of the Arabs, just as she supported the elimination of the Jewish national home.

A public declaration in this sense would be very useful for its propagandistic effect on the Arab peoples at this moment. It would rouse the Arabs from their momentary lethargy and give them new courage. It would also ease the Mufti's work of secretly organizing the Arabs against the moment when they could strike. At the same time, he could give the assurance that the Arabs would in strict discipline patiently wait for the right moment and only strike upon an order from Berlin.

With regard to the events in Iraq, the Mufti observed that the Arabs in that country certainly had by no means been incited by Germany to attack England, but solely had acted in reaction to a direct English assault upon their honour.

The Turks, he believed, would welcome the establishment of an Arab government in the neighbouring territories because they would prefer weaker Arab to strong European governments in the neighbouring countries, and, being themselves a nation of 7 millions, they had moreover nothing to fear from the 1,700,000 Arabs inhabiting Syria, Transjordan, Iraq, and Palestine.

France likewise would have no objections to the unification plan because she had conceded independence to Syria as early as 1936 and had given her approval to the unification of Iraq and Syria under King Faisal as early as 1933.

In these circumstances he was renewing his request that the Führer make a public declaration so that the Arabs would not lose hope, which is so powerful a force in the life of nations. With such hope in their hearts the Arabs, as he had said, were willing to wait. They were not pressing for immediate realization of their aspirations; they could easily wait half a year or a whole year. But if they were not inspired with such a hope by a declaration of this sort, it could be expected that the English would be the gainers from it.

The Führer replied that Germany's fundamental attitude on these questions, as the Mufti himself had already stated, was clear. Germany stood for uncompromising war against the Jews. That naturally included active opposition to the Jewish national home in Palestine, which was nothing other than a centre, in the form of a state, for the exercise of destructive influence by Jewish interests. Germany was also aware that the assertion that the Jews were carrying out the function of economic pioneers in Palestine was a lie. The work there was done only by the Arabs, not by the Jews. Germany was resolved, step by step, to ask one European nation after the other to solve its Jewish problem, and at the proper time direct a similar appeal to non-European nations as well.

Germany was at the present time engaged in a life and death struggle with two citadels of Jewish power: Great Britain and Soviet Russia. Theoretically there was a difference between

England's capitalism and Soviet Russia's communism; actually, however, the Jews in both countries were pursuing a common goal. This was the decisive struggle; on the political plane, it presented itself in the main as a conflict between Germany and England, but ideologically it was a battle between National Socialism and the Jews. It went without saying that Germany would furnish positive and practical aid to the Arabs involved in the same struggle, because platonic promises were useless in a war for survival or destruction in which the Jews were able to mobilize all of England's power for their ends.

The aid to the Arabs would have to be material aid. Of how little help sympathies alone were in such a battle had been demonstrated plainly by the operation in Iraq, where circumstances had not permitted the rendering of really effective, practical aid. In spite of all the sympathies, German aid had not been sufficient and Iraq was overcome by the power of Britain, that is, the guardian of the Jews.

The Mufti could not but be aware, however, that the outcome of the struggle going on at present would also decide the fate of the Arab world. The Führer therefore had to think and speak coolly and deliberately, as a rational man and primarily as a soldier, as the leader of the German and allied armies. Everything of a nature to help in this titanic battle for the common cause, and thus also for the Arabs, would have to be done. Anything, however, that might contribute to weakening the military situation must be put aside, no matter how unpopular this move might be.

Germany was now engaged in very severe battles to force the gateway to the northern Caucasus region. The difficulties were mainly with regard to maintaining the supply, which was most difficult as a result of the destruction of railroads and highways as well as of the oncoming winter. If at such a moment, the Führer were to raise the problem of Syria in a declaration, those elements in France which were under de Gaulle's influence would receive new strength. They would interpret the Führer's declaration as an intention to break up France's colonial empire and appeal to their fellow countrymen that they should rather make common cause with the English to try to

save what still could be saved. A German declaration regarding
Syria would in France be understood to refer to the French colonies in general, and that would at the present time create new
troubles in western Europe, which means that a portion of the
German armed forces would be immobilized in the west and
no longer be available for the campaign in the east.

The Führer then made the following statement to the Mufti,
enjoining him to lock it in the uttermost depths of his heart:

1. He (the Führer) would carry on the battle to the total destruction of the Judeo–Communist empire in Europe.

2. At some moment which was impossible to set exactly today but which in any event was not distant, the German armies
would in the course of this struggle reach the southern exit
from Caucasia.

3. As soon as this had happened, the Führer would on his own
give the Arab world the assurance that its hour of liberation
had arrived. Germany's objective would then be solely the destruction of the Jewish element residing in the Arab sphere
under the protection of British power. In that hour the Mufti
would be the most authoritative spokesman for the Arab world.
It would then be his task to set off the Arab operations which
he had secretly prepared. When that time had come, Germany
could also be indifferent to French reaction to such a declaration.

Once Germany had forced open the road to Iran and Iraq
through Rostov, it would be also the beginning of the end of the
British world empire. He (the Führer) hoped that the coming
year would make it possible for Germany to thrust open the
Caucasian gate to the Middle East. For the good of their common
cause, it would be better if the Arab proclamation were put off
for a few more months than if Germany were to create difficulties for herself without being able thereby to help the Arabs.

He (the Führer) fully appreciated the eagerness of the Arabs
for a public declaration of the sort requested by the Grand
Mufti. But he would beg him to consider that he (the Führer)
himself was the Chief of State of the German Reich for five long
years during which he was unable to make to his own home-

land the announcement of its liberation. He had to wait with that until the announcement could be made on the basis of a situation brought about by the force of arms that the *Anschluss* had been carried out.

The moment that Germany's tank divisions and air squadrons had made their appearance south of the Caucasus, the public appeal requested by the Grand Mufti could go out to the Arab world.

The Grand Mufti replied that it was his view that everything would come to pass just as the Führer had indicated. He was fully reassured and satisfied by the words which he had heard from the Chief of the German State. He asked, however, whether it would not be possible, secretly at least, to enter into an agreement with Germany of the kind he had just outlined for the Führer.

The Führer replied that he had just now given the Grand Mufti precisely that confidential declaration.

The Grand Mufti thanked him for it and stated in conclusion that he was taking his leave from the Führer in full confidence and with reiterated thanks for the interest shown in the Arab cause.

Schmidt

Documents 21–23

The Anglo-American Committee of Inquiry, 1946

An Anglo-American Inquiry Committee was appointed in November 1945 to examine the status of the Jews in former Axis-occupied countries and to find out how many were impelled by their conditions to migrate. Britain, weakened by the war, found itself under growing pressure from Jews and Arabs alike and the Labour Government decided, therefore, to invite the United States to participate in finding a solution. The Report of the Committee was published on 1 May 1945 (Document 21). President Truman welcomed its recommendation that the immigration and land laws of the 1939 White Paper were to be rescinded. Prime Minister Attlee, on the other hand, declared that the report would have to be 'considered as a

whole in all its implications'. Arab reaction was hostile (Document
22); the Arab League announced that Arabs would not stand by with
their arms folded. The Ihud (Association) group led by Dr J. L.
Magnes and Professor M. Buber (who submitted Document 23 to the
Committee), favoured a bi-national solution, equal political rights
for Arabs and Jews, and a Federative Union of Palestine and the
neighbouring countries. Ihud found little support among the Jewish
Community. It had, in the beginning, a few Arab sympathizers, but
some of them were assassinated by supporters of the Mufti and the
others dropped out.

Document 21

Recommendations and Comments

The European Problem

Recommendation No. 1. We have to report that such information as we received about countries other than Palestine gave
no hope of substantial assistance in finding homes for Jews wishing or impelled to leave Europe.

But Palestine alone cannot meet the emigration needs of the
Jewish victims of Nazi and Fascist persecution; the whole world
shares responsibility for them and indeed for the resettlement
of all 'displaced persons'.

We therefore recommend that our Governments together,
and in association with other countries, should endeavour immediately to find new homes for all such 'displaced persons',
irrespective of creed or nationality, whose ties with their former communities have been irreparably broken.

Though emigration will solve the problems of some victims
of persecution, the overwhelming majority, including a considerable number of Jews, will continue to live in Europe. We
recommend therefore that our Governments endeavour to
secure that immediate effect is given to the provision of the
United Nations Charter calling for 'universal respect for, and
observation of, human rights and fundamental freedoms for
all without distinction as to race, sex, language or religion'.

Comment. In recommending that our Governments, in association with other countries, should endeavour to find new
homes for 'displaced persons', we do not suggest that any
country should be asked to make a permanent change in its
immigration policy. The conditions which we have seen in
Europe are unprecedented and so unlikely to arise again that
we are convinced that special provision could and should be
made in existing immigration laws to meet this unique and
peculiarly distressing situation. Furthermore, we believe that
much could be accomplished – particularly in regard to those
'displaced persons', including Jews, who have relatives in countries outside Europe – by a relaxation of administrative regulations.

Our investigations have led us to believe that a considerable
number of Jews will continue to live in most European countries. In our view the mass emigration of all European Jews
would be of service neither to the Jews themselves nor to
Europe. Every effort should be made to enable the Jews to rebuild their shattered communities, while permitting those Jews
who wish to do so to emigrate. In order to achieve this, restitution of Jewish property should be effected as soon as possible.
Our investigations showed us that the Governments chiefly concerned had for the most part already passed legislation to this
end. A real obstacle, however, to individual restitution is that
the attempt to give effect to this legislation is frequently a cause
of active anti-Semitism. We suggest that, for the reconstruction
of the Jewish communities, restitution of their corporate property, either through reparations payments or through other
means, is of the first importance.

Nazi occupation has left behind it a legacy of anti-Semitism.
This cannot be combated by legislation alone. The only really
effective antidotes are the enforcement by each Government
of guaranteed civil liberties and equal rights, a programme of
education in the positive principles of democracy, the sanction
of a strong world public opinion – combined with economic
recovery and stability.

Refugee Immigration into Palestine

Recommendation No. 2. We recommend (a) that 100,000 certificates be authorized immediately for the admission into
Palestine of Jews who have been the victims of Nazi and Fascist
persecution; (b) that these certificates be awarded as far as
possible in 1946 and that actual immigration be pushed forward
as rapidly as conditions will permit.

Comment. The number of Jewish survivors of Nazi and Fascist
persecution with whom we have to deal far exceeds 100,000:
indeed there are more than that number in Germany, Austria
and Italy alone. Although nearly a year has passed since their
liberation, the majority of those in Germany and Austria are
still living in assembly centres, the so-called 'camps', island
communities in the midst of those at whose hands they suffered
so much.

In their interests and in the interests of Europe, the centres
should be closed and their camp life ended. Most of them have
cogent reasons for wishing to leave Europe. Many are the sole
survivors of their families and few have any ties binding them
to the countries in which they used to live.

Since the end of hostilities, little has been done to provide
for their resettlement elsewhere. Immigration laws and restrictions bar their entry to most countries and much time must pass
before such laws and restrictions can be altered and effect
given to the alterations.

Some can go to countries where they have relatives; others
may secure inclusion in certain quotas. Their number is com-
paratively small.

We know of no country to which the great majority can go
in the immediate future other than Palestine. Furthermore, that
is where almost all of them want to go. There they are sure
that they will receive a welcome denied them elsewhere. There
they hope to enjoy peace and rebuild their lives.

We believe it is essential that they should be given an opportunity to do so at the earliest possible time. Furthermore, we
have the assurances of the leaders of the Jewish Agency that
they will be supported and cared for.

We recommend the authorization and issue of 100,000 certificates for these reasons and because we feel that their immediate issue will have a most salutary effect upon the whole
situation.

In the awarding of these certificates priority should, as far as
possible, be given to those in the centres and to those liberated
in Germany and Austria who are no longer in the centres but
remain in those countries. We do not desire that other Jewish
victims who wish or will be impelled by their circumstances to
leave the countries where they now are or that those who fled
from persecution before the outbreak of war should be excluded. We appreciate that there will be difficulty in deciding
questions of priority, but none the less we urge that so far as
possible such a system should be adhered to, and that, in applying it, primary consideration should be given to the aged and
infirm, to the very young and also to skilled workmen whose
services will be needed for many months on work rendered
necessary by the large influx.

It should be made clear that no advantage in the obtaining of
a certificate is to be gained by migrating from one country to
another or by entering Palestine illegally.

Receiving so large a number will be a heavy burden on Palestine. We feel sure that the authorities will shoulder it and that
they will have the full cooperation of the Jewish Agency.

Difficult problems will confront those responsible for organizing and carrying out the movement. The many organizations
– public and private – working in Europe will certainly render
all the aid they can ; we mention UNRRA especially. Cooperation by all throughout is necessary.

We are sure that the Government of the United States, which
has shown such keen interest in this matter, will participate
vigorously and generously with the Government of Great Britain in its fulfilment. There are many ways in which help can be
given.

Those who have opposed the admission of these unfortunate
people into Palestine should know that we have fully considered all that they have put before us. We hope that they will
look upon the situation again, that they will appreciate the

considerations which have led us to our conclusion, and that above all, if they cannot see their way to help, at least they will not make the position of these sufferers more difficult.

Principles of Government: No Arab, No Jewish State

Recommendation No. 3. In order to dispose, once and for all, of the exclusive claims of Jews and Arabs to Palestine, we regard it as essential that a clear statement of the following principles should be made:

(1) That Jew shall not dominate Arab and Arab shall not dominate Jew in Palestine. (2) That Palestine shall be neither a Jewish state nor an Arab state. (3) That the form of government ultimately to be established, shall, under international guarantees, fully protect and preserve the interests in the Holy Land of Christendom and of the Muslim and Jewish faiths.

Thus Palestine must ultimately become a state which guards the rights and interests of Muslims, Jews and Christians alike and accords to the inhabitants, as a whole, the fullest measure of self-government consistent with the three paramount principles set forth above.

Comment. Throughout the long and bloody struggle of Jew and Arab in Palestine, each crying fiercely: 'This land is mine' – except for the brief reference in the Report of the Royal Commission (hereinafter referred to as the Peel Report) and the little evidence, written and oral, that we received on this point – the great interest of the Christian world in Palestine has been completely overlooked, glossed over or brushed aside.

We therefore emphatically declare that Palestine is a Holy Land, sacred to Christian, to Jew and to Muslim alike; and because it is a Holy Land, Palestine is not, and can never become, a land which any race or religion can justly claim as its very own.

We further, in the same emphatic way, affirm that the fact that it is the Holy Land sets Palestine completely apart from other lands and dedicates it to the precepts and practices of the brotherhood of man, not those of narrow nationalism.

For another reason, in the light of its long history, and particularly its history of the last thirty years, Palestine cannot be regarded as either a purely Arab or a purely Jewish land.

The Jews have a historic connexion with the country. The Jewish National Home, though embodying a minority of the population, is today a really established under international guarantee. It has a right to continued existence, protection and development.

Yet Palestine is not, and never can be, a purely Jewish land. It lies at the crossroads of the Arab world. Its Arab population, descended from long-time inhabitants of the area, rightly look upon Palestine as their homeland.

It is, therefore, neither just nor practicable that Palestine should become either an Arab state, in which an Arab majority would control the destiny of a Jewish minority, or a Jewish state, in which a Jewish majority would control that of an Arab minority. In neither case would minority guarantees afford adequate protection for the subordinated group.

A Palestinian put the matter thus: 'In the hearts of us Jews there has always been a fear that some day this country would be turned into an Arab state and the Arabs would rule over us. This fear has at times reached the proportions of terror. . . . Now this same feeling of fear has started up in the hearts of Arabs . . . fear lest the Jews acquire the ascendancy and rule over them.'

Palestine, then, must be established as a country in which the legitimate national aspirations of both Jews and Arabs can be reconciled without either side fearing the ascendancy of the other. In our view this cannot be done under any form of constitution in which a mere numerical majority is decisive, since it is precisely the struggle for a numerical majority which bedevils Arab-Jewish relations. To ensure genuine self-government for both the Arab and the Jewish communities, this struggle must be made purposeless by the constitution itself.

Mandate and United Nations Trusteeship

Recommendation No. 4. We have reached the conclusion that the hostility between Jews and Arabs and, in particular, the determination of each to achieve domination, if necessary by violence, make it almost certain that, now and for some time to come, any attempt to establish either an independent Palestinian state or independent Palestinian states would result in civil strife such as might threaten the peace of the world. We therefore recommend that until this hostility disappears the Government of Palestine be continued as at present under mandate pending the execution of a trusteeship agreement under the United Nations.

Comment. We recognize that, in view of the powerful forces, both Arab and Jewish, operating from outside Palestine, the task of Great Britain, as Mandatory, has not been easy. The Peel Commission declared in 1937 that the Mandate was unworkable and the Permanent Mandates Commission of the League of Nations thereupon pointed out that it became almost unworkable once it was publicly declared to be so by such a body. Two years later the British Government, having come to the conclusion that the alternative of partition proposed by the Peel Commission was also unworkable, announced their intention of taking steps to terminate the Mandate by establishment of an independent Palestine state.

Our recommendations are based on what we believe at this stage to be as fair a measure of justice to all as we can find in view of what has gone before and of all that has been done. We recognize that they are not in accord with the claims of either party, and furthermore that they involve a departure from the recent policy of the Mandatory.

We recognize that, if they are adopted, they will involve a long period of trusteeship, which will mean a very heavy burden for any single Government to undertake, a burden which would be lightened if the difficulties were appreciated and the trustees had the support of other members of the United Nations.

Equality of standards

Recommendation No. 5. Looking toward a form of ultimate self-government consistent with the three principles laid down

in Recommendation No. 3, we recommend that the Mandatory
or trustee should proclaim the principle that Arab economic,
educational and political advancement in Palestine is of equal
importance with that of the Jews; and should at once prepare
measures designed to bridge the gap which now exists and raise
the Arab standard of living to that of the Jews; and to bring the
two peoples to a full appreciation of their common interest and
common destiny in the land where both belong.

Comment. Our examination of conditions in Palestine led us
to the conclusion that one of the chief causes of friction is the
great disparity between the Jewish and Arab standards of living. Even under conditions of war, which brought considerable
financial benefits to the Arabs, this disparity has not been ap-
preciably reduced. Only by a deliberate and carefully planned
policy on the part of the Mandatory can the Arab standard of
living be raised to that of the Jews. In stressing the need for
such a policy we would particularly call attention to the dis-
crepancies between the social services, including hospitals,
available in Palestine for Jews and Arabs.

Social Aid

We fully recognize that the Jewish social services are financed
to a very great extent by the Jewish community in Palestine,
with the assistance of outside Jewish organizations; and we
would stress that nothing should be done which would bring
these social services down to the level of those provided for the
Arabs, or halt the constant improvements now being made in
them.

We suggest that consideration be given to the advisability of
encouraging the formation by the Arabs of an Arab community
on the lines of the Jewish community which now largely controls and finances Jewish social services. The Arabs will have
to rely, to a far greater extent than the Jews, on financial aid
from the Government. But the Jews of Palestine should accept
the necessity that taxation, raised from both Jews and Arabs,
will have to be spent very largely on the Arabs in order to
bridge the gap which now exists between the standard of living
of the two peoples.

Further Immigration Policy

Recommendation No. 6. We recommend that pending the early
reference to the United Nations and the execution of a trusteeship agreement, the Mandatory should administer Palestine
according to the Mandate, which declares, with regard to immigration, that 'the administration of Palestine, while ensuring
that the rights and position of other sections of the population
are not prejudiced, shall facilitate Jewish immigration under
suitable conditions'.

Comment. We have recommended the admission of 100,000
immigrants, victims of Nazi persecution, as soon as possible.
We now deal with the position after the admission of that
number. We cannot look far into the future. We cannot construct a yardstick for annual immigration. Until a trusteeship
agreement is executed it is our clear opinion that Palestine
should be administered in accordance with the terms of the
Mandate quoted above.

Further than that we cannot go in the form of a recommendation. In this disordered world, speculation as to the economic
position of any country a few years ahead would be a hazardous proceeding. It is particularly difficult to predict what, after
a few years have passed, will be the economic and political
condition of Palestine. We hope that the present friction and
turbulence will soon die away and be replaced by an era of
peace, absent so long from the Holy Land; that the Jew and
Arab will soon realize that collaboration is to their mutual advantage, but no one can say how long this will take.

The possibility of the country sustaining a largely increased
population at a decent standard of living depends largely on
whether or not plans referred to in Recommendation No. 8
can be brought to fruition.

The Peel Commission stated that political as well as economic considerations have to be taken into account in regard to
immigration, and recommend a 'political high level' of 12,000
a year. We cannot recommend the fixing of a minimum or of a
maximum for annual immigration in the future. There are too
many uncertain factors.

We desire, however, to state certain considerations which we agree should be taken into account in determining what number of immigrants there should be in any period. It is the right of every independent nation to determine in the interests of its people the number of immigrants to be admitted to its lands. Similarly, it must, we think, be conceded that it should be the right of the Government of Palestine to decide, having regard to the well-being of all the people of Palestine, the number of immigrants to be admitted within any given period.

In Palestine there is the Jewish National Home, created in consequence of the Balfour Declaration. Some may think that that declaration was wrong and should not have been made; some that it was a conception on a grand scale and that effect can be given to one of the most daring and significant colonization plans in history. Controversy as to which view is right is fruitless. The national home is there. Its roots are deep in the soil of Palestine. It cannot be argued out of existence; neither can the achievements of the Jewish pioneers.

The Government of Palestine in having regard to the well-being of all the people of Palestine cannot ignore the interests of so large a section of the population. It cannot ignore the achievements of the last quarter of a century. No Government of Palestine doing its duty to the people of that land can fail to do its best not only to maintain the national home but also to foster its proper development and such development must, in our view, involve immigration.

The well-being of all the people of Palestine, be they Jews, Arabs or neither, must be the governing consideration. We reject the view that there shall be no further Jewish immigration into Palestine without Arab acquiescence, a view which would result in the Arab dominating the Jew. We also reject the insistent Jewish demand that forced Jewish immigration must proceed apace in order to produce as quickly as possible a Jewish majority and a Jewish state. The well-being of the Jews must not be subordinated to that of the Arabs; nor that of the Arabs to the Jews. The well-being of both, the economic situation of Palestine as a whole, the degree of execution of plans for further development, all have to be carefully considered in deciding the number of immigrants for any particular period.

Palestine is a land sacred to three faiths and must not become the land of any one of them to the exclusion of the others, and Jewish immigration for the development of the national home must not become a policy of discrimination against other immigrants. Any person, therefore, who desired and is qualified under applicable laws to enter Palestine must not be refused admission or subjected to discrimination on the ground that he is not a Jew. All provisions respecting immigration must be drawn, executed and applied with that principle always firmly in mind.

Further, while we recognize that any Jew who enters Palestine in accordance with its laws is there of right, we expressly disapprove of the position taken in some Jewish quarters that Palestine has in some way been ceded or granted as their state to the Jews of the world, that every Jew everywhere is, merely because he is a Jew, a citizen of Palestine and therefore can enter Palestine as of right without regard to conditions imposed by the Government upon entry and that therefore there can be no illegal immigration of Jews into Palestine. We declare and affirm that any immigrant Jew who enters Palestine contrary to its laws is an illegal immigrant.

[Recommendations 7-9 deal with land policy, economic development, and education. Ed.]

Document 22

The Arab Case for Palestine : Evidence Submitted by the Arab Office, Jerusalem, to the Anglo-American Committee of Inquiry, March 1946

The Problem of Palestine

1. The whole Arab people is unalterably opposed to the attempt to impose Jewish immigration and settlement upon it, and ultimately to establish a Jewish state in Palestine. Its opposition is based primarily upon right. The Arabs of Palestine are descen-

dants of the indigenous inhabitants of the country, who have
been in occupation of it since the beginning of history; they
cannot agree that it is right to subject an indigenous population
against its will to alien immigrants, whose claim is based upon
a historical connexion which ceased effectively many centuries
ago. Moreover they form the majority of the population; as
such they cannot submit to a policy of immigration which if
pursued for long will turn them from a majority into a minority
in an alien state; and they claim the democratic right of a
majority to make its own decisions in matters of urgent national concern . . .

2. In addition to the question of right, the Arabs oppose the
claims of political Zionism because of the effects which Zionist
settlement has already had upon their situation and is likely to
have to an even greater extent in the future. Negatively, it has
diverted the whole course of their national development. Geographically Palestine is part of Syria; its indigenous inhabitants
belong to the Syrian branch of the Arab family of nations; all
their culture and tradition link them to the other Arab peoples;
and until 1917 Palestine formed part of the Ottoman Empire
which included also several of the other Arab countries. The
presence and claims of the Zionists, and the support given them
by certain Western powers have resulted in Palestine being cut
off from the other Arab countries and subjected to a regime,
administrative, legal, fiscal and educational, different from that
of the sister-countries. Quite apart from the inconvenience to
individuals and the dislocation of trade which this separation
has caused, it has prevented Palestine participating fully in the
general development of the Arab world.

First, while the other Arab countries have attained or are
near to the attainment of self-government and full membership
of the UNO, Palestine is still under Mandate and has taken no
step towards self-government; not only are there no representative institutions, but no Palestinian can rise to the higher
ranks of the administration. This is inacceptable on grounds of
principle, and also because of its evil consequence. It is a
hardship to individual Palestinians whose opportunities of responsibility are thus curtailed; and it is demoralizing to the

population to live under a government which has no basis in their consent and to which they can feel no attachment or loyalty.

Secondly, while the other Arab countries are working through the Arab League to strengthen their ties and coordinate their policies, Palestine (although her Arab inhabitants are formally represented in the League's Council) cannot participate fully in this movement so long as she has no indigenous government; thus the chasm between the administrative system and the institutions of Palestine and those of the neighbouring countries is growing, and her traditional Arab character is being weakened.

Thirdly, while the other Arab countries have succeeded in or are on the way to achieving a satisfactory definition of their relations with the Western powers and with the world-community, expressed in their treaties with Great Britain and other Powers and their membership of the United Nations Organization, Palestine has not yet been able to establish any definite status for herself in the world, and her international destiny is still obscure.

3. All these evils are due entirely to the presence of the Zionists and the support given to them by certain of the powers; there is no doubt that, had it not been for that, Arab Palestine would by now be a self-governing member of the UNO and the Arab League. Moreover, in addition to the obstacles which Zionism has thus placed in the way of Palestine's development, the presence of the Zionists gives rise to various positive evils which will increase if Zionist immigration continues.

The entry of incessant waves of immigrants prevents normal economic and social development and causes constant dislocation of the country's life; in so far as it reacts upon prices and values and makes the whole economy dependent upon the constant inflow of capital from abroad it may even in certain circumstances lead to economic disaster. It is bound moreover to arouse continuous political unrest and prevent the establishment of that political stability on which the prosperity and health of the country depend. This unrest is likely to increase in frequency and violence as the Jews come nearer to being the majority and the Arabs a minority.

Even if economic and social equilibrium is re-established, it will be to the detriment of the Arabs. The superior capital resources at the disposal of the Jews, their greater experience of modern economic technique and the existence of a deliberate policy of expansion and domination have already gone far toward giving them the economic mastery of Palestine. The biggest concessionary companies are in their hands; they possess a large proportion of the total cultivable land, and an even larger one of the land in the highest category of fertility; and the land they possess is mostly inalienable to non-Jews. The continuance of land-purchase and immigration, taken together with the refusal of Jews to employ Arabs on their lands or in their enterprises and the great increase in the Arab population, will create a situation in which the Arab population is pushed to the margin of cultivation and a landless proletariat, rural and urban, comes into existence. This evil can be palliated but not cured by attempts at increasing the absorptive capacity or the industrial production of Palestine; the possibility of such improvements is limited, they would take a long time to carry out, and would scarcely do more than keep pace with the rapid growth of the Arab population; moreover in present circumstances they would be used primarily for the benefit of the Jews and thus might increase the disparity between the two communities.

Nor is the evil economic only. Zionism is essentially a political movement, aiming at the creation of a state: immigration, land-purchase and economic expansion are only aspects of a general political strategy. If Zionism succeeds in its aim, the Arabs will become a minority in their own country; a minority which can hope for no more than a minor share in the government, for the state is to be a Jewish state, and which will find itself not only deprived of that international status which the other Arab countries possess but cut off from living contact with the Arab world of which it is an integral part.

It should not be forgotten too that Palestine contains places holy to Muslims and Christians, and neither Arab Muslims nor Arab Christians would willingly see such places subjected to the ultimate control of a Jewish Government.

4. These dangers would be serious enough at any time, but are

particularly so in this age, when the first task of the awakening Arab nation is to come to terms with the West; to define its relationship with the Western Powers and with the westernized world community on a basis of equality and mutual respect, and to adapt what is best in Western civilization to the needs of its own genius. Zionist policy is one of the greatest obstacles to the achievement of this task : both because Zionism represents to the Arabs one side of the Western spirit and because of the support given to it by some of the Western powers. In fact Zionism has become in Arab eyes a test of Western intentions towards them. So long as the attempt of the Zionists to impose a Jewish state upon the inhabitants of Palestine is supported by some or all of the Western Governments, so long will it be difficult if not impossible for the Arabs to establish a satisfactory relationship with the Western world and its civilization, and they will tend to turn away from the West in political hostility and spiritual isolation; this will be disastrous both for the Arabs themselves and for those Western nations which have dealings with them.

5. There are no benefits obtained or to be expected from Zionism commensurate with its evils and its dangers. The alleged social and economic benefits are much less than is claimed. The increase in the Arab population is not primarily due to Zionist immigration, and in any case would not necessarily be a sign of prosperity. The rise in money wages and earnings is largely illusory, being offset by the rise in the cost of living. In so far as real wages and the standard of living have risen, this is primarily an expression of a general trend common to all Middle Eastern countries. The inflow of capital has gone largely to raising money prices and real estate values. The whole economy is dangerously dependent upon the citrus industry. The benefits derived from the establishment of industries and the exploitation of the country's few natural resources have been largely neutralized by the failure of Jewish enterprises to employ Arabs.

The Zionist contention that their social organizations provide health and social services for the Arab population is exaggerated; only a minute proportion of the Arabs, for example,

are looked after by Jewish health organizations. Even if true it
would prove nothing except that the Government was neglect-
ing its responsibilities in regard to the welfare of the population. Arab voluntary social organizations have grown up
independently of Jewish bodies and without help from them.
Even in so far as social and economic benefits have come to the
Arabs from Zionist settlement, it remains true on the one hand
that they are more than counterbalanced by the dangers of
that settlement, and on the other that they are only incidental
and are in no way necessary for the progress of the Arab people.
The main stimulus to Arab economic and social progress does
not come from the example or assistance of the Zionists but
from the natural tendency of the whole Middle Eastern areas,
from the work of the Government and above all from the newly
awakened will to progress of the Arabs themselves. The Arabs
may have started later than the Jews on the road of modern
social and economic organization, but they are now fully
awake and are progressing fast. This is shown in the economic
sphere for example by the continued development of the Arab
citrus industry and financial organizations, in the social sphere
by the growth of the labour movement and the new Land
Development Scheme.

If any proof were needed of this, it could be found in the progress made during the last three decades by the neighbouring
countries. None of the Arab countries is stagnant today: even
without the example and capital of the Zionists, they are building up industries, improving methods and extending the scope
of agriculture, establishing systems of public education and increasing the amenities of life. In some countries and spheres
the progress has been greater than among the Arabs of Palestine,
and in all of them it is healthier and more normal.

The Zionists claim further that they are acting as mediators
of Western civilization to the Middle East. Even if their claim
were true, the services they were rendering would be incidental
only: the Arab world has been in direct touch with the West
for a hundred years, and has its own reawakened cultural movement, and thus it has no need of a mediator. Moreover the claim
is untrue: so long as Jewish cultural life in Palestine expresses

itself through the medium of the Hebrew language, its influence on the surrounding world is bound to be negligible; in fact, Arab culture today is almost wholly uninfluenced by the Jews, and practically no Arabs take part in the work of Jewish cultural or educational institutions. In a deeper sense the presence of the Zionists is even an obstacle to the understanding of Western civilization, in so far as it more than any other factor is tending to induce in the Arabs an unsympathetic attitude towards the West and all its works.

6. Opposition to the policy of the Zionists is shared by all sections of the Palestinian Arab people. It is not confined to the townspeople but is universal among the rural population, who stand to suffer most from the gradual alienation of the most fertile land to the Jewish National Fund. It is felt not only by the landowners and middle class but by the working population, both for national reasons and for reasons of their own. It is not an invention of the educated class; if that class have seen the danger more clearly and sooner than others, and if they have assumed the leadership of the opposition, that is no more than their duty and function.

Moreover not only the Arab Muslim majority are opposed to Zionism but also and equally the Arab Christian minority who reject Zionism both because they share to the full in the national sentiments of other Arabs and because as Christians they cannot accept that their Holy Places should be subject to Jewish control, and cannot understand how any Christian nation could accept it.

7. The sentiments of the Palestinian Arabs are fully shared by the other Arab countries, both by their Government and their peoples. Their support has shown itself in many ways: in pan-Arab Conferences, in the moral and material support given by the whole Arab world to the revolt in 1936–9, in the diplomatic activities of Arab Governments, and most recently in the formation of the Arab League, which has taken the defence of Palestine as one of its main objectives. The members of the Arab League are now taking active measures to prevent the alienation of Arab lands to the Zionists and Jewish domination of the economic life of the Middle East . . .

8. In the Arab view, any solution of the problem created by Zionist aspirations must satisfy certain conditions :

(i) It must recognize the right of the indigenous inhabitants of Palestine to continue in occupation of the country and to preserve its traditional character.

(ii) It must recognize that questions like immigration, which affect the whole nature and destiny of the country, should be decided in accordance with democratic principles by the will of the population.

(iii) It must accept the principle that the only way by which the will of the population can be expressed is through the establishment of responsible representative government. (The Arabs find something inconsistent in the attitude of Zionists who demand the establishment of a free democratic commonwealth in Palestine and then hasten to add that this should not take place until the Jews are in a majority.)

(iv) This representative Government should be based upon the principle of absolute equality of all citizens irrespective of race and religion.

(v) The form of Government should be such as to make possible the development of a spirit of loyalty and cohesion among all elements of the community, which will override all sectional attachments. In other words it should be a Government which the whole community could regard as their own, which should be rooted in their consent and have a moral claim upon their obedience.

(vi) The settlement should recognize the fact that by geography and history Palestine is inescapably part of the Arab world; that the only alternative to its being part of the Arab world and accepting the implications of its position is complete isolation, which would be disastrous from every point of view; and that whether they like it or not the Jews in Palestine are dependent upon the goodwill of the Arabs.

(vii) The settlement should be such as to make possible a satisfactory definition within the framework of UNO of the relations between Palestine and the Western Powers who possess interests in the country.

(viii) The settlement should take into account that Zionism

is essentially a political movement aiming at the creation of a Jewish state and should therefore avoid making any concession which might encourage Zionists in the hope that this aim can be achieved in any circumstances.

9. In accordance with these principles, the Arabs urge the establishment in Palestine of a democratic government representative of all sections of the population on a level of absolute equality; the termination of the Mandate once the Government has been established; and the entry of Palestine into the United Nations Organization as a full member of the working community.

Pending the establishment of a representative Government, all further Jewish immigration should be stopped, in pursuance of the principle that a decision on so important a matter should only be taken with the consent of the inhabitants of the country and that until representative institutions are established there is no way of determining consent. Strict measures should also continue to be taken to check illegal immigration. Once a Palestinian state has come into existence, if any section of the population favours a policy of further immigration it will be able to press its case in accordance with normal democratic procedure; but in this as in other matters the minority must abide by the decision of the majority.

Similarly, all further transfer of land from Arabs to Jews should be prohibited prior to the creation of self-governing institutions. The Land Transfer Regulations should be made more stringent and extended to the whole area of the country, and severe measures be taken to prevent infringement of them. Here again once self-government exists matters concerning land will be decided in the normal democratic manner.

10. The Arabs are irrevocably opposed to political Zionism, but in no way hostile to the Jews as such nor to their Jewish fellow-citizens of Palestine. Those Jews who have already entered Palestine, and who have obtained or shall obtain Palestinian citizenship by due legal process will be full citizens of the Palestinian state, enjoying full civil and political rights and a fair share in government and administration. There is no question of their being thrust into the position of a 'minority' in the bad sense of

a closed community, which dwells apart from the main stream of the state's life and which exists by sufferance of the majority. They will be given the opportunity of belonging to and helping to mould the full community of the Palestinian state, joined to the Arabs by links of interest and goodwill, not the goodwill of the strong to the powerless, but of one citizen to another.

It is to be hoped that in course of time the exclusiveness of the Jews will be neutralized by the development of loyalty to the state and the emergence of new groupings which cut across communal divisions. This however will take time; and during the transitional period the Arabs recognize the need for giving special consideration to the peculiar position and the needs of the Jews. No attempt would be made to interfere with their communal organization, their personal status or their religious observances. Their schools and cultural institutions would be left to operate unchecked except for that general control which all governments exercise over education. In the districts in which they are most closely settled they would possess municipal autonomy and Hebrew would be an official language of administration, justice and education.

11. The Palestinian state would be an Arab state not (as should be clear from the preceding paragraph) in any narrow racial sense, nor in the sense that non-Arabs should be placed in a position of inferiority, but because the form and policy of its government would be based on a recognition of two facts: first that the majority of the citizens are Arabs, and secondly that Palestine is part of the Arab world and has no future except through close cooperation with the other Arab states. Thus among the main objects of the Government would be to preserve and enrich the country's Arab heritage, and to draw closer the relations between Palestine and the other Arab countries. The Cairo Pact of March 1945 provided for the representation of Palestine on the Council of the Arab League even before its independence should be a reality; once it was really self-governing, it would participate fully in all the work of the League, in the cultural and economic no less than the political sphere. This would be of benefit to the Jewish no less than the

Arab citizens of Palestine, since it would ensure those good relations with the Arab world without which their economic development would be impossible.

12. The state would apply as soon as possible for admission into UNO, and would of course be prepared to bear its full share of the burdens of establishing a world security-system. It would willingly place at the disposal of the Security Council whatever bases or other facilities were required, provided those bases were really used for the purpose for which they were intended and not in order to interfere in the internal affairs of the country, and provided also Palestine and the other Arab states were adequately represented on the controlling body.

The state would recognize also the world's interest in the maintenance of a satisfactory regime for the Muslim, Christian and Jewish Holy Places. In the Arab view however the need for such a regime does not involve foreign interference in or control of Palestine; no opportunity should be given to great powers to use the Holy Places as instruments of policy. The Holy Places can be most satisfactorily and appropriately guarded by a Government representative of the inhabitants, who include adherents of all three faiths and have every interest in preserving the holy character of their country.

Nor in the Arab view would any sort of foreign interference or control be justified by the need to protect the Christian minorities. The Christians are Arabs, who belong fully to the national community and share fully in its struggle. They would have all the rights and duties of citizens of a Palestinian state, and would continue to have their own communal organizations and institutions. They themselves would ask for no more, having learnt from the example of other Middle Eastern countries the dangers of an illusory foreign 'protection' of minorities.

13. In economic and social matters the Government of Palestine would follow a progressive policy with the aim of raising the standard of living and increasing the welfare of all sections of the population, and using the country's natural resources in the way most beneficial to all. Its first task naturally would be to improve the condition of the Arab peasants and thus to bridge the economic and social gulf which at present divides the two

communities. Industry would be encouraged, but only in so far as its economic basis was sound and as part of a general policy of economic development for the whole Arab world; commercial and financial ties with the other Arab countries would so far as possible be strengthened, and tariffs decreased or abolished.

14. The Arabs believe that no other proposals would satisfy the conditions of a just and lasting settlement. In their view there are insuperable objections of principle or of practice to all other suggested solutions of the problem.

(1) The idea of partition and the establishment of a Jewish state in a part of Palestine is inadmissible for the same reasons of principle as the idea of establishing a Jewish state in the whole country. If it is unjust to the Arabs to impose a Jewish state on the whole of Palestine, it is equally unjust to impose it in any part of the country. Moreover, as the Woodhead Commission showed, there are grave practical difficulties in the way of partition; commerce would be strangled, communications dislocated and the public finances upset. It would also be impossible to devise frontiers which did not leave a large Arab minority in the Jewish state. This minority would not willingly accept its subjection to the Zionists, and it would not allow itself to be transferred to the Arab state. Moreover, partition would not satisfy the Zionists. It cannot be too often repeated that Zionism is a political movement aiming at the domination at least of the whole of Palestine; to give it a foothold in part of Palestine would be to encourage it to press for more and to provide it with a base for its activities. Because of this, because of the pressure of population and in order to escape from its isolation it would inevitably be thrown into enmity with the surrounding Arab states and this enmity would disturb the stability of the whole Middle East.

(2) Another proposal is for the establishment of a bi-national state, based upon political parity, in Palestine and its incorporation into a Syrian or Arab Federation. The Arabs would reject this as denying the majority its normal position and rights. There are also serious practical objections to the idea of a bi-national state, which cannot exist unless there is a strong

sense of unity and common interest overriding the differences
between the two parties. Moreover, the point made in regard
to the previous suggestion may be repeated here : this scheme
would in no way satisfy the Zionists, it would simply encourage
them to hope for more and improve their chances of obtaining
it ...

Document 23

The Case for a Bi-national State *

The Arab Contention

The Arabs say that 'the existence of the Jewish National Home,
whatever its size, bars the way to the attainment by the Arabs
of Palestine of the same national status as that attained, or
soon to be attained, by all the other Arabs of Asia' (Royal Commission, p. 307). That is so. And they ask if they are not as fit
for self-government as the Arabs of other countries. They are.

Arab Concessions

But the whole history of Palestine shows that it just has not
been made for uni-national sovereign independence. This is an
inescapable fact which no one can disregard. Although the
Arabs cannot have a uni-national independent Arab Palestine,
they can enjoy independence in a bi-national Palestine together
with their Jewish fellow-citizens. This will afford them a maximum of national freedom. What the bi-national state will take
away from them is sovereign independence in Palestine. There
are other Arab states with sovereign independence. But we
contend that the sovereign independence of tiny Palestine,
whether it be Jewish sovereignty or Arab sovereignty, is a ques-
tionable good in this post-war period, when even great states
must relinquish something of their sovereignty and seek union,
if the world is not to perish. We contend that for this Holy Land

---

*Reprinted from M. Buber and J. L. Magnes, *Arab-Jewish Unity*.
London : Victor Gollancz Ltd., 1947.

the idea of a bi-national Palestine is at least as inspiring as that
of an Arab sovereign Palestine or a Jewish sovereign Palestine.

Jewish Concessions

On the other hand, the bi-national Palestine would deprive the
Jews of their one chance of a Jewish state. But this bi-national
Palestine would be the one state in the world where they would
be a constituent nation, i.e. an equal nationality within the
body politic, and not a minority as everywhere else. The absence
of a Jewish state would make more difficult direct access by the
Jewish people to UNO. To compensate for this, some form
should be devised for giving the Jewish people a recognized
place within the structure of the United Nations Organization.

Nevertheless, the concessions the Jews would have to make
on these matters are, we think, more far-reaching than the
concessions the Arabs of Palestine would have to make. But
the hard facts of the situation are that this is not a Jewish land
and it is not an Arab land – it is the Holy Land, a bi-national
country – and it is in the light of such hard facts that the problem must be approached.

The Advantages of a Bi-national Palestine

Before proceeding to outline our suggestions as to the political
structure of the bi-national Palestine, we should like finally to
point out some of the advantages of bi-nationalism based on
parity in a country which has two nationalities.

FAILURE OF MINORITY GUARANTEES

1. The breakdown of the minority guarantees provided for
in the Versailles Peace treaties is proof that in a bi-national
country the only safeguard for a minority is equality with the
majority. There is no prospect of peace in a country where
there is a dominant people and a subordinate people. The
single nation-state is a proper form for a country where there
is but one legally recognized nationality, as, for example, the
United States. But in countries with more than one recognized

nationality – and they are numerous in Europe and in Asia – bitterness is engendered among the minority because the civil service, the military, the economic key positions, foreign affairs, are in the hands of the ruling class of the majority nation. Parity in a multi-national country is the only just relationship between the peoples.

SWITZERLAND

2. The multi-national state is an effective method of affording full protection for the national languages, cultures and institutions of each nationality. That there can be full cultural autonomy combined with full allegiance to the multi-national political state is proven in Switzerland's history for more than 100 years. The Swiss are divided by language, religion and culture; nor do the linguistic and religious groupings coincide in the various cantons. Yet all of these divergencies have not been obstacles to political unity. This is a newer form of democracy which is as important for multi-national states as the more familiar form of democracy is for uni-national states. The Swiss example is most relevant to Palestine, although there are, of course, many points of difference.

OTHER MULTI-NATIONAL COUNTRIES

The Soviet Union is a newer example of a multi-national state. The new Yugoslav state is an attempt at multi-national federalism. Professor Seton Watson outlines a bi-national solution of the age-long problem of Transylvania. Roumanian domination, Hungarian domination, partition, had all been tried without success.

BI-NATIONALISM A HIGH IDEAL

3. In many senses the multi-national state represents a higher, more modern and more hopeful ideal than the uni-national sovereign independent state. The old way of having a major people and a minor people in a state of various nationalities is reactionary. The progressive conception is parity among the peoples of the multi-national state. The way of peace in the world today and tomorrow is through federation, union. Divid-

ing up the world into tiny nationalistic sovereign states has not
been the success the advocates of self-determination had hoped
for at the end of the First World War. (Cobban, *National Self-
Determination*.) The peoples who have been placed by fate or
by history in the same country have warred with one another
for domination throughout the centuries. The majority have
tried to make the state homogeneous through keeping down the
minority nationalities. The federal multi-national state, based on
the parity of the nationalities, is a most hopeful way of enabling
them to retain their national identity, and yet of coalescing in
a larger political framework. It results in separate nationalities,
yet a single citizenship. This is a noble goal to which the youth
of multi-national countries can be taught to give their enthusiasm and their energies. It is a modern challenge to the intelligence and the moral qualities of the peoples constituting
multi-national lands.

Documents 24–25

The United Nations Takes Over

British Foreign Secretary Ernest Bevin announced on 14 February
1947 that His Majesty's Government had decided to refer the
Palestine problem to the United Nations. Tension inside Palestine had
risen, illegal Jewish immigration continued, there was growing
restiveness in the Arab countries: Palestine, Bevin said, could not
be so divided as to create two viable states, since the Arabs would
never agree to it, the Mandate could not be administered in its
present form, and Britain was going to ask the United Nations how
it could be amended.

The United Nations set up a UN Special Committee on Palestine
(UNSCOP) composed of representatives of eleven member states.
Its report and recommendations were published on 31 August 1947
(Document 24). The Jewish Agency accepted the partition plan as
the 'indispensable minimum', the Arab governments and the Arab
Higher Executive rejected it. On 29 November 1947 the UN General
Assembly endorsed the partition plan by a vote of thirty-three to
thirteen (Document 25). The two-thirds majority included the United
States and the Soviet Union but not Britain.

Document 24

Summary of the Report of UNSCOP
(UN Special Committee on Palestine)

31 August 1947

(a) *General Recommendations of the Committee*

The eleven unanimously adopted resolutions of the Committee
were:

That the Mandate should be terminated and Palestine granted
independence at the earliest practicable date (recommendations
I and II);

That there should be a short transitional period preceding
the granting of independence to Palestine during which the
authority responsible for administering Palestine should be
responsible to the United Nations (recommendations III and
IV);

That the sacred character of the Holy Places and the rights
of religious communities in Palestine should be preserved and
stipulations concerning them inserted in the constitution of any
state or states to be created and that a system should be found
for settling impartially any disputes involving religious rights
(recommendation V);

That the General Assembly should take steps to see that the
problem of distressed European Jews should be dealt with as a
matter of urgency so as to alleviate their plight and the Palestine problem (recommendation VI);

That the constitution of the new state or states should be
fundamentally democratic and should contain guarantees for
the respect of human rights and fundamental freedoms and for
the protection of minorities (recommendation VII);

That the undertakings contained in the Charter whereby
states are to settle their disputes by peaceful means and to
refrain from the threat or use of force in international relations in any way inconsistent with the purposes of the United

Nations should be incorporated in the constitutional provisions applying to Palestine (recommendation VIII);

That the economic unity of Palestine should be preserved (recommendation IX);

That states whose nationals had enjoyed in Palestine privileges and immunities of foreigners, including those formerly enjoyed by capitulation or usage in the Ottoman Empire, should be invited to renounce any rights pertaining to them (recommendation X);

That the General Assembly should appeal to the peoples of Palestine to cooperate with the United Nations in its efforts to settle the situation there and exert every effort to put an end to acts of violence (recommendations XI);

In addition to these eleven unanimously approved recommendations, the Special Committee, with two members (Uruguay and Guatamala) dissenting, and one member recording no opinion, also approved the following twelfth recommendation:

Recommendation XII. The Jewish Problem in General

It is recommended that

In the appraisal of the Palestine question, it be accepted as incontrovertible that any solution for Palestine cannot be considered as a solution of the Jewish problem in general.

(b) Majority Proposal: Plan of Partition with Economic Union

According to the plan of the majority (the representatives of Canada, Czechoslovakia, Guatemala, Netherlands, Peru, Sweden and Uruguay), Palestine was to be constituted into an Arab State, a Jewish State and the City of Jerusalem. The Arab and the Jewish States would become independent after a transitional period of two years beginning on 1 September 1947. Before their independence could be recognized, however, they must adopt a constitution in line with the pertinent recommendations of the Committee and make to the United Nations a declaration containing certain guarantees, and sign a treaty by which a system of economic collaboration would be established and the economic union of Palestine created.

The plan provided, *inter alia*, that during the transitional period, the United Kingdom would carry on the administration of Palestine under the auspices of the United Nations and on such conditions and under such supervision as the United Kingdom and the United Nations might agree upon. During this period a stated number of Jewish immigrants was to be admitted. Constituent Assemblies were to be elected by the populations of the areas which were to comprise the Arab and Jewish States, respectively, and were to draw up the constitution of the States.

These constitutions were to provide for the establishment in each State of a legislative body elected by universal suffrage and by secret ballot on the basis of proportional representation and an executive body responsible to the legislature. They would also contain various guarantees, e.g. for the protection of the Holy Places and religious buildings and sites, and of religious and minority rights.

The Constituent Assembly in each State would appoint a provisional government empowered to make the declaration and sign the Treaty of Economic Union, after which the independence of the State would be recognized. The Declaration would contain provisions for the protection of the Holy Places and religious buildings and sites and for religious and minority rights. It would also contain provisions regarding citizenship.

A treaty would be entered into between the two States, which would contain provisions to establish the economic union of Palestine and to provide for other matters of common interest. A Joint Economic Board would be established consisting of representatives of the two States and members appointed by the Economic and Social Council of the United Nations to organize and administer the objectives of the Economic Union.

The City of Jerusalem would be placed, after the transitional period, under the International Trusteeship System by means of a Trusteeship Agreement, which would designate the United Nations as the Administering Authority. The plan contained recommended boundaries for the city and provisions concerning the governor and the police force.

The plan also proposed boundaries for both the Arab and Jewish States.

(c) Minority Proposal. Plan of a Federal State

Three UNSCOP members (the representatives of India, Iran and Yugoslavia) proposed an independent federal state. This plan provided, *inter alia*, that an independent federal state of Palestine would be created following a transitional period not exceeding three years, during which responsibility for administering Palestine and preparing it for independence would be entrusted to an authority to be decided by the General Assembly.

The independent federal state would comprise an Arab State and a Jewish State. Jerusalem would be its capital.

During the transitional period a Constituent Assembly would be elected by popular vote and convened by the administering authority on the basis of electoral provisions which would ensure the fullest representation of the population.

The Constituent Assembly would draw up the constitution of the federal state, which was to contain, *inter alia*, the following provisions:

The federal state would comprise a federal government and governments of the Arab and Jewish States, respectively.

Full authority would be vested in the federal government with regard to national defence, foreign relations, immigration, currency, taxation for federal purposes, foreign and inter-state waterways, transport and communications, copyrights and patents.

The Arab and Jewish States would enjoy full powers of local self-government and would have authority over education, taxation for local purposes, the right of residence, commercial licences, land permits, grazing rights, inter-state migration, settlement, police, punishment of crime, social institutions and services, public housing, public health, local roads, agriculture and local industries.

The organs of government would include a head of state, an executive body, a representative federal legislative body composed of two chambers, and a federal court. The executive would be responsible to the legislative body.

Election to one chamber of the federal legislative body would be on the basis of proportional representation of the population as a whole, and to the other on the basis of equal representation of the Arab and Jewish citizens of Palestine. Legislation would be enacted when approved by majority votes in both chambers ; in the event of disagreement between the two chambers, the issue would be submitted to an arbitral body of five members including not less than two Arabs and two Jews.

The federal court would be the final court of appeal regarding constitutional matters. Its members, who would include not less than four Arabs and three Jews, would be elected by both chambers of the federal legislative body.

The constitution was to guarantee equal rights for all minorities and fundamental human rights and freedoms. It would guarantee, *inter alia*, free access to the Holy Places and protect religious interests.

The constitution would provide for an undertaking to settle international disputes by peaceful means.

There would be a single Palestinian nationality and citizenship.

The constitution would provide for equitable participation of representatives of both communities in delegations to international conferences.

A permanent international body was to be set up for the supervision and protection of the Holy Places, to be composed of three representatives designated by the United Nations and one representative of each of the recognized faiths having an interest in the matter, as might be determined by the United Nations.

For a period of three years from the beginning of the transitional period Jewish immigrants would be permitted into the Jewish State in such numbers as not to exceed its absorptive capacity, and having due regard for the rights of the existing population within that State and their anticipated natural rate of increase. An international commission, composed of three Arab, three Jewish and three United Nations representatives, would be appointed to estimate the absorptive capacity of the Jewish State. The commission would cease to exist at the end of the three-year period mentioned above.

The minority plan also laid down the boundaries of the proposed Arab and Jewish areas of the federal state.

Document 25

UN General Assembly Resolution on the Future Government of Palestine (Partition Resolution)

29 November 1947

The General Assembly,

Having met in special session at the request of the mandatory Power to constitute and instruct a special committee to prepare for the consideration of the question of the future government of Palestine at the second regular session;

Having constituted a Special Committee and instructed it to investigate all questions and issues relevant to the problem of Palestine, and to prepare proposals for the solution of the problem, and

Having received and examined the report of the Special Committee (document A/364) including a number of unanimous recommendations and a plan of partition with economic union approved by the majority of the Special Committee,

Considers that the present situation in Palestine is one which is likely to impair the general welfare and friendly relations among nations;

Takes note of the declaration by the mandatory Power that it plans to complete its evacuation of Palestine by 1 August 1948;

Recommends to the United Kingdom, as the mandatory Power for Palestine, and to all other Members of the United Nations the adoption and implementation, with regard to the future government of Palestine, of the Plan of Partition with Economic Union set out below;

Requests that

(a) The Security Council take the necessary measures as provided for in the plan for its implementation ;

(b) The Security Council consider, if circumstances during the transitional period require such consideration, whether the situation in Palestine constitutes a threat to the peace. If it decides that such a threat exists, and in order to maintain international peace and security, the Security Council should supplement the authorization of the General Assembly by taking measures, under Articles 39 and 41 of the Charter, to empower the United Nations Commission, as provided in this resolution, to exercise in Palestine the functions which are assigned to it by this resolution ;

(c) The Security Council determine as a threat to the peace, breach of the peace or act of aggression, in accordance with Article 39 of the Charter, any attempt to alter by force the settlement envisaged by this resolution ;

(d) The Trusteeship Council be informed of the responsibilities envisaged for it in this plan;

Calls upon the inhabitants of Palestine to take such steps as may be necessary on their part to put this plan into effect;

Appeals to all Governments and all peoples to refrain from taking any action which might hamper or delay the carrying out of these recommendations, and

Authorizes the Secretary-General to reimburse travel and subsistence expenses of the members of the commission referred to in Part I, Section B, paragraph 1 below, on such basis and in such form as he may determine most appropriate in the circumstances, and to provide the Commission with the necessary staff to assist in carrying out the functions assigned to the Commission by the General Assembly.

Plan of Partition with Economic Union

Part I – Future Constitution and Government of Palestine

A. TERMINATION OF MANDATE
PARTITION AND INDEPENDENCE

1. The Mandate for Palestine shall terminate as soon as possible but in any case not later than 1 August 1948.

2. The armed forces of the mandatory Power shall be progressively withdrawn from Palestine, the withdrawal to be completed as soon as possible but in any case not later than 1 August 1948.

The mandatory Power shall advise the Commission, as far in advance as possible, of its intention to terminate the Mandate and to evacuate each area.

The mandatory Power shall use its best endeavours to ensure that an area situated in the territory of the Jewish State, including a seaport and hinterland adequate to provide facilities for a substantial immigration, shall be evacuated at the earliest possible date and in any event not later than 1 February 1948.

3. Independent Arab and Jewish States and the Special International Regime for the City of Jerusalem, set forth in part III of this plan, shall come into existence in Palestine two months after the evacuation of the armed forces of the mandatory Power has been completed but in any case not later than 1 October 1948. The boundaries of the Arab State, the Jewish State, and the City of Jerusalem shall be described in parts II and III below.

4. The period between the adoption by the General Assembly of its recommendation on the question of Palestine and the establishment of the independence of the Arab and Jewish States shall be a transitional period.

B. STEPS PREPARATORY TO INDEPENDENCE

1. A Commission shall be set up consisting of one representative of each of five Member States. The Members represented on the Commission shall be elected by the General Assembly

on as broad a basis, geographically and otherwise, as possible.

2. The administration of Palestine shall, as the mandatory Power withdraws its armed forces, be progressively turned over to the Commission, which shall act in conformity with the recommendations of the General Assembly, under the guidance of the Security Council. The mandatory Power shall to the fullest possible extent coordinate its plans for withdrawal with the plans of the Commission to take over and administer areas which have been evacuated.

In the discharge of this administrative responsibility the Commission shall have authority to issue necessary regulations and take other measures as required.

The mandatory Power shall not take any action to prevent, obstruct or delay the implementation by the Commission of the measures recommended by the General Assembly.

3. On its arrival in Palestine the Commission shall proceed to carry out measures for the establishment of the frontiers of the Arab and Jewish States and the City of Jerusalem in accordance with the general lines of the recommendations of the General Assembly on the partition of Palestine. Nevertheless, the boundaries as described in part II of this plan are to be modified in such a way that village areas as a rule will not be divided by state boundaries unless pressing reasons make that necessary.

4. The Commission, after consultation with the democratic parties and other public organizations of the Arab and Jewish States, shall select and establish in each State as rapidly as possible a Provisional Council of Government. The activities of both the Arab and Jewish Provisional Councils of Government shall be carried out under the general direction of the Commission.

If by 1 April 1948 a Provisional Council of Government cannot be selected for either of the States, or, if selected, cannot carry out its functions, the Commission shall communicate that fact to the Security Council for such action with respect to that State as the Security Council may deem proper, and to the Secretary-General for communication to the Members of the United Nations.

5. Subject to the provisions of these recommendations during the transitional period the Provisional Councils of Government, acting under the Commission, shall have full authority in the areas under their control, including authority over matters of immigration and land regulation

6. The Provisional Council of Government of each State, acting under the Commission, shall progressively receive from the Commission full responsibility for the administration of that State in the period between the termination of the Mandate and the establishment of the State's independence.

7. The Commission shall instruct the Provisional Councils of Government of both the Arab and Jewish States, after their formation, to proceed to the establishment of administrative organs of government, central and local.

8. The Provisional Council of Government of each State shall, within the shortest time possible, recruit an armed militia from the residents of that State, sufficient in number to maintain internal order and to prevent frontier clashes.

This armed militia in each State shall, for operational purposes, be under the command of Jewish or Arab officers resident in that State, but general political and military control, including the choice of the militia's High Command, shall be exercised by the Commission.

9. The Provisional Council of Government of each State shall, not later than two months after the withdrawal of the armed forces of the mandatory Power, hold elections to the Constituent Assembly which shall be conducted on democratic lines.

The election regulations in each State shall be drawn up by the Provisional Council of Government and approved by the Commission.

Qualified voters for each State for this election shall be persons over eighteen years of age who are: (a) Palestinian citizens residing in that State and (b) Arabs and Jews residing in the State, although not Palestinian citizens, who, before voting, have signed a notice of intention to become citizens of such State.

Arabs and Jews residing in the City of Jerusalem who have signed a notice of intention to become citizens, the Arabs of the Arab State and the Jews of the Jewish State, shall be entitled to vote in the Arab and Jewish States respectively.

Women may vote and be elected to the Constituent Assemblies.

During the transitional period no Jew shall be permitted to establish residence in the area of the proposed Arab State, and no Arab shall be permitted to establish residence in the area of the proposed Jewish State, except by special leave of the Commission.

10. The Constituent Assembly of each State shall draft a democratic constitution for its State and choose a provisional government to succeed the Provisional Council of Government appointed by the Commission. The constitutions of the States shall embody chapters 1 and 2 of the Declaration provided for in section C below and include *inter alia* provisions for:

(*a*) Establishing in each State a legislative body elected by universal suffrage and by secret ballot on the basis of proportional representation, and an executive body responsible to the legislature;

(*b*) Settling all international disputes in which the State may be involved by peaceful means in such a manner that international peace and security, and justice, are not endangered;

(c) Accepting the obligation of the State to refrain in its international relations from the threat or use of force against the territorial integrity or political independence of any State, or in any other manner inconsistent with the purposes of the United Nations;

(*d*) Guaranteeing to all persons equal and non-discriminatory rights in civil, political, economic and religious matters and the enjoyment of human rights and fundamental freedoms, including freedom of religion, language, speech and publication, education assembly and association;

(*e*) Preserving freedom of transit and visit for all residents and citizens of the other State in Palestine and the City of Jerusalem, subject to considerations of national security, provided that each State shall control residence within its borders.

11. The Commission shall appoint a preparatory economic commission of three members to make whatever arrangements

are possible for economic cooperation, with a view to establishing, as soon as practicable, the Economic Union and the Joint Economic Board, as provided in section D below.

12. During the period between the adoption of the recommendations on the question of Palestine by the General Assembly and the termination of the Mandate, the mandatory Power in Palestine shall maintain full responsibility for administration in areas from which it has not withdrawn its armed forces. The Commission shall assist the Mandatory Power in the carrying out of these functions Similarly the mandatory Power shall cooperate with the Commission in the execution of its functions.

13. With a view to ensuring that there shall be continuity in the functioning of administrative services and that, on the withdrawal of the armed forces of the mandatory Power, the whole administration shall be in charge of the Provisional Councils and the Joint Economic Board, respectively, acting under the Commission, there shall be a progressive transfer, from the mandatory Power to the Commission, of responsibility for all the functions of government, including that of maintaining law and order in the areas from which the forces of the mandatory Power have been withdrawn.

14. The Commission shall be guided in its activities by the recommendations of the General Assembly and by such instructions as the Security Council may consider necessary to issue.

The measures taken by the Commission, within the recommendations of the General Assembly, shall become immediately effective unless the Commission has previously received contrary instructions from the Security Council.

The Commission shall render periodic monthly progress reports, or more frequently if desirable, to the Security Council.

15. The Commission shall make its final report to the next regular session of the General Assembly and to the Security Council simultaneously.

C. DECLARATION

A declaration shall be made to the United Nations by the provisional government of each proposed State before independence. It shall contain *inter alia* the following clauses:

GENERAL PROVISION

The stipulations contained in the declaration are recognized as fundamental laws of the State and no law, regulation or official action shall conflict or interfere with these stipulations, nor shall any law, regulation or official action prevail over them.

CHAPTER I. HOLY PLACES, RELIGIOUS BUILDINGS
AND SITES

1. Existing rights in respect of Holy Places and religious buildings or sites shall not be denied or impaired.

2. In so far as Holy Places are concerned, the liberty of access, visit and transit shall be guaranteed, in conformity with existing rights, to all residents and citizens of the other State and of the City of Jerusalem, as well as to aliens, without distinction as to nationality, subject to requirements of national security, public order and decorum.

Similarly, freedom of worship shall be guaranteed in conformity with existing rights, subject to the maintenance of public order and decorum.

3. Holy Places and religious buildings or sites shall be preserved. No act shall be permitted which may in any way impair their sacred character. If at any time it appears to the Government that any particular Holy Place, religious building or site is in need of urgent repair, the Government may call upon the community or communities concerned to carry out such repair. The Government may carry it out itself at the expense of the community or communities concerned if no action is taken within a reasonable time.

4. No taxation shall be levied in respect of any Holy Place, religious building or site which was exempt from taxation on the date of the creation of the State.

No change in the incidence of such taxation shall be made which would either discriminate between the owners or occupiers of Holy Places, religious buildings or sites, or would place such owners or occupiers in a position less favourable in relation to the general incidence of taxation than existed at the time of the adoption of the Assembly's recommendation.

5. The Governor of the City of Jerusalem shall have the right

to determine whether the provisions of the Constitution of the State in relation to Holy Places, religious buildings and sites within the borders of the State and the religious rights appertaining thereto, are being properly applied and respected, and to make decisions on the basis of existing rights in cases of disputes which may arise between the different religious communities or the rites of a religious community with respect to such places, buildings and sites. He shall receive full cooperation and such privilages and immunities as are necessary for the exercise of his functions in the State.

CHAPTER II. RELIGIOUS AND MINORITY RIGHTS

1. Freedom of conscience and the free exercise of all forms of worship, subject only to the maintenance of public order and morals, shall be ensured to all.

2. No discrimination of any kind shall be made between the inhabitants on the ground of race, religion, language or sex.

3. All persons within the jurisdiction of the State shall be entitled to equal protection of the laws.

4. The family law and personal status of the various minorities and their religious interests, including endowments, shall be respected.

5. Except as may be required for the maintenance of public order and good government, no measure shall be taken to obstruct or interfere with the enterprise of religious or charitable bodies of all faiths or to discriminate against any representative or member of these bodies on the ground of his religion or nationality.

6. The State shall ensure adequate primary and secondary education for the Arab and Jewish minority, respectively, in its own language and its cultural traditions.

The right of each community to maintain its own schools for the education of its own members in its own language, while conforming to such educational requirements of a general nature as the State may impose, shall not be denied or impaired. Foreign educational establishments shall continue their activity on the basis of their existing rights.

7. No restriction shall be imposed on the free use by any

citizen of the State of any language in private intercourse, in commerce, in religion, in the Press or in publications of any kind, or at public meetings.[1]

8. No expropriation of land owned by an Arab in the Jewish State (by a Jew in the Arab State)[2] shall be allowed except for public purposes. In all cases of expropriation full compensation as fixed by the Supreme Court shall be paid previous to dispossession.

CHAPTER III. CITIZENSHIP, INTERNATIONAL CONVENTIONS
  FINANCIAL OBLIGATIONS

  1. *Citizenship.* Palestinian citizens residing in Palestine outside the City of Jerusalem, as well as Arabs and Jews who, not holding Palestinian citizenship, reside in Palestine outside the City of Jerusalem shall, upon the recognition of independence, become citizens of the State in which they are resident and enjoy full civil and political rights. Persons over the age of eighteen years may opt, within one year from the date of recognition of independence of the State in which they reside, for citizenship of the other State, providing that no Arab residing in the area of proposed Jewish State shall have the right to opt for citizenship in the proposed Jewish State and no Jews residing in the proposed Jewish State shall have the right to opt for citizenship in the proposed Arab State. The exercise of this right of option will be taken to include the wives and children under eighteen years of age of persons so opting.

  Arabs residing in the area of the proposed Jewish State and Jews residing in the area of the proposed Arab State who have signed a notice of intention to opt for citizenship of the other State shall be eligible to vote in the elections to the Constituent

---

1. The following stipulation shall be added to the declaration concerning the Jewish State: 'In the Jewish State adequate facilities shall be given to Arabic-speaking citizens for the use of their language, either orally or in writing, in the legislature, before the Courts and in the administration.'

2. In the declaration concerning the Arab State, the words 'by an Arab in the Jewish State' should be replaced by the words 'by a Jew in the Arab State'.

Assembly of that State, but not in the elections to the Constituent Assembly of the State in which they reside.

2. *International conventions*. (*a*) The State shall be bound by all the international agreements and conventions, both general and special, to which Palestine has become a party. Subject to any right of denunciation provided for therein, such agreements and conventions shall be respected by the State throughout the period for which they were concluded.

(*b*) Any dispute about the applicability and continued validity of international conventions or treaties signed or adhered to by the mandatory Power on behalf of Palestine shall be referred to the International Court of Justice in accordance with the provisions of the Statute of the Court.

3. *Financial obligations*. (*a*) The State shall respect and fulfil all financial obligations of whatever nature assumed on behalf of Palestine by the mandatory Power during the exercise of the Mandate and recognized by the State. This provision includes the right of public servants to pensions, compensation or gratuities.

(*b*) These obligations shall be fulfilled through participation in the Joint Economic Board in respect of those obligations applicable to Palestine as a whole, and individually in respect of those applicable to, and fairly apportionable between, the States.

(*c*) A Court of Claims, affiliated with the Joint Economic Board, and composed of one member appointed by the United Nations, one representative of the United Kingdom and one representative of the State concerned, should be established. Any dispute between the United Kingdom and the States respecting claims not recognized by the latter should be referred to that Court.

(*d*) Commercial concessions granted in respect of any part of Palestine prior to the adoption of the resolution by the General Assembly shall continue to be valid according to their terms, unless modified by agreement between the concession-holder and the State.

[Section D has been deleted: 'Economic Union and Transit'. Part II of the Resolution deals with the borders of the new State; Part III with 'Capitulations'. Ed.]

Part 3

Israel and the Arab World 1948-67

Part 3 of the Reader extends from the establishment of the state of Israel in May 1948 to the aftermath of the third Arab–Israeli war in 1967. The United Nations resolution about the partition of Palestine was bitterly resented by the Palestinian Arabs and their supporters in the neighbouring countries who tried to prevent with the force of arms the establishment of a Zionist state by the 'Jewish usurpers'. This attempt failed and Israel, as a result, seized areas beyond those defined in the U N resolution. The armistice of 1949 did not restore peace; an Arab refugee problem came into being, guerrilla attacks, Israel retaliation and Arab blockage of the Suez Canal and the Gulf of Aqaba led to the second and third Arab–Israeli Wars.

Document 26

State of Israel Proclamation of Independence

The Proclamation of Independence was published by the Provisional State Council in Tel Aviv on 14 May 1948. The Provisional State Council was the forerunner of the Knesset, the Israeli parliament. The British Mandate was terminated the following day and regular armed forces of Transjordan, Egypt, Syria and other Arab countries entered Palestine.

*

The Land of Israel was the birthplace of the Jewish people. Here their spiritual, religious and national identity was formed. Here they achieved independence and created a culture of national and universal significance. Here they wrote and gave the Bible to the world.

Exiled from the Land of Israel the Jewish people remained faithful to it in all the countries of their dispersion, never ceasing to pray and hope for their return and the restoration of their national freedom.

Impelled by this historic association, Jews strove throughout the centuries to go back to the land of their fathers and regain their statehood. In recent decades they returned in their masses. They reclaimed the wilderness, revived their language, built cities and villages, and established a vigorous and ever-growing community, with its own economic and cultural life. They sought peace, yet were prepared to defend themselves. They brought the blessings of progress to all inhabitants of the country and looked forward to sovereign independence.

In the year 1897 the First Zionist Congress, inspired by Theodor Herzl's vision of the Jewish State, proclaimed the right of the Jewish people to national revival in their own country.

This right was acknowledged by the Balfour Declaration of 2 November 1917, and re-affirmed by the Mandate of the

League of Nations, which gave explicit international recognition to the historic connexion of the Jewish people with Palestine and their right to reconstitute their National Home.

The recent holocaust, which engulfed millions of Jews in Europe, proved anew the need to solve the problem of the homelessness and lack of independence of the Jewish people by means of the re-establishment of the Jewish State, which would open the gates to all Jews and endow the Jewish people with equality of status among the family of nations.

The survivors of the disastrous slaughter in Europe, and also Jews from other lands, have not desisted from their efforts to reach Eretz-Yisrael, in face of difficulties, obstacles and perils; and have not ceased to urge their right to a life of dignity, freedom and honest toil in their ancestral land.

In the Second World War the Jewish people in Palestine made their full contribution to the struggle of the freedom-loving nations against the Nazi evil. The sacrifices of their soldiers and their war effort gained them the right to rank with the nations which founded the United Nations.

On 29 November 1947 the General Assembly of the United Nations adopted a Resolution requiring the establishment of a Jewish State in Palestine. The General Assembly called upon the inhabitants of the country to take all the necessary steps on their part to put the plan into effect. This recognition by the United Nations of the right of the Jewish people to establish their independent State is unassailable.

It is the natural right of the Jewish people to lead, as do all other nations, an independent existence in its sovereign State.

ACCORDINGLY WE, the members of the National Council, representing the Jewish people in Palestine and the World Zionist Movement, are met together in solemn assembly today, the day of termination of the British Mandate for Palestine; and by virtue of the natural and historic right of the Jewish people and of the Resolution of the General Assembly of the United Nations.

WE HEREBY PROCLAIM the establishment of the Jewish State in Palestine, to be called *Medinath Yisrael* [The State of Israel].

WE HEREBY DECLARE that, as from the termination of the Mandate at midnight 14–15 May 1948, and pending the setting up of the duly elected bodies of the State in accordance with a Constitution, to be drawn up by the Constituent Assembly not later than 1 October 1948, the National Council shall act as the Provisional State Council, and that the National Administration shall constitute the Provisional Government of the Jewish State, which shall be known as Israel.

THE STATE OF ISRAEL will be open to the immigration of Jews from all countries of their dispersion; will promote the development of the country for the benefit of all its inhabitants; will be based on the principles of liberty, justice and peace as conceived by the Prophets of Israel; will uphold the full social and political equality of all its citizens, without distinction of religion, race, or sex; will guarantee freedom of religion, conscience, education and culture; will safeguard the Holy Places of all religions; and will loyally uphold the principles of the United Nations Charter.

THE STATE OF ISRAEL will be ready to cooperate with the organs and representatives of the United Nations in the implementation of the Resolution of the Assembly of 29 November 1947, and will take steps to bring about the Economic Union over the whole of Palestine.

We appeal to the United Nations to assist the Jewish people in the building of its State and to admit Israel into the family of nations.

In the midst of wanton aggression, we yet call upon the Arab inhabitants of the State of Israel to preserve the ways of peace and play their part in the development of the State, on the basis of full and equal citizenship and due representation in all its bodies and institutions – provisional and permanent.

We extend our hand in peace and neighbourliness to all the neighbouring states and their peoples, and invite them to cooperate with the independent Jewish nation for the common good of all. The State of Israel is prepared to make its contribution to the progress of the Middle East as a whole.

Our call goes out to the Jewish people all over the world to rally to our side in the task of immigration and development, and to stand by us in the great struggle for the fulfilment of the dream of generations for the redemption of Israel.

With trust in the Rock of Israel, we set our hand to this Declaration, at this Session of the Provisional State Council, on the soil of the Homeland in the city of Tel Aviv, on this Sabbath eve, the fifth of Iyar, 5708, the fourteenth of May, 1948.

Document 27

The Law of Return

The 'Law of Return' was passed unanimously by the Knesset on 5 July 1950 and written into the state legislation.

*

The Law of Return states:
1. Every Jew has the right to immigrate to the country.
2. (a) Immigration shall be on the basis of immigration visas.
   (b) Immigrant visas shall be issued to any Jew expressing a desire to settle in Israel except if the Minister of Immigration is satisfied that the applicant:
      (i) acts against the Jewish nation; or
      (ii) may threaten the public health or State security.
3. (a) A Jew who comes to Israel and after his arrival expresses a desire to settle there may, while in Israel, obtain an immigrant certificate.
   (b) The exceptions listed in Article 2 (b) shall apply also with respect to the issue of an immigrant certificate, but a person shall not be regarded as a threat to public health as a result of an illness that he contracts after his arrival in Israel.
4. Every Jew who migrated to the country before this law goes into effect, and every Jew who was born in the country either before or after the law is effective enjoys the same status as any person who migrated on the basis of this law.
5. The Minister of Immigration is delegated to enforce this

law and he may enact regulations in connexion with its implementation and for the issue of immigrant visas and immigrant certificates.

Document 28

The Manifesto of the United Arab Republic (Preamble)

The manifesto concerning the principles to govern the new Federal State of the United Arab Republic was published in April 1963. It was prepared in connexion with an abortive attempt to establish federal union in the Arab world. Signed by Gamal Abdel Nasser and the presidents of Iraq and Syria, it is of interest mainly in view of the reference to Palestine.

*

In the name of the Merciful Compassionate God,

In the name of the Almighty God,

The three delegations representing the United Arab Republic, Syria and Iraq met in Cairo and in response to the will of the Arab people in the three regions and the great Arab fatherland, brotherly talks began between the three delegations on Saturday, 6 April, and ended on Wednesday, 17 April, 1963.

The delegations in all their discussions were inspired by faith that Arab unity was an inevitable aim deriving its principles from the oneness of language bearing culture and thought, common history-making sentiment and conscience, common national struggle deciding and defining destiny, common spiritual values stemming from Divine messages and common social and economic understanding based on liberty and socialism.

The delegations were guided by the will of the masses of the Arab peoples, demanding unity, struggling to attain it and sacrificing in its defence, and realizing that the hard core of the union is to be formed by the unification of the parts of the homeland which have acquired their freedom and independence and in which nationalist, progressive governments have emerged with the determination to destroy the alliance of feudalism, capital, reaction and imperialism, and to liberate the working forces of the people in order to join them in alliance and to express their genuine will.

The revolution of 23 July was a historical turning point at which the Arab people in Egypt, discovering their identity and regaining their free will, set out on their quest for freedom, Arabism and union. The revolution of the 14th of Ramadan [8 February] illuminated the true Arab face of Iraq, and the path leading it to the horizons of unity, envisaged by the zealous elements of the 14 July revolution. The revolution of 8 March put Syria back into the line of the union destroyed by the setback of reactionary secession, having destroyed all the obstacles which the reactionaries and imperialism had determinedly put up in the path of union.

The three Revolutions thus met which affirmed again that unity is a revolutionary action deriving its conceptions from the people's faith, its power from their will, and its objectives from their aspirations for freedom and socialism.

Unity is a revolution – a revolution because it is popular, a revolution because it is progressive, and a revolution because it is a powerful tide in the current of civilization.

Unity is especially a revolution because it is profoundly connected with the Palestine cause and with the national duty to liberate that country. It was the disaster of Palestine that revealed the conspiracy of the reactionary classes and exposed the treacheries of the hired regional parties and their denial of the people's objectives and aspirations. It was the disaster of Palestine that showed the weakness and backwardness of the economic and social systems that prevailed in the country, released the revolutionary energies of our people and awakened the spirit of revolt against imperialism, injustice, poverty and underdevelopment. It was the disaster of Palestine that clearly indicated the path of salvation, the path of unity, freedom and socialism. This was kept in mind by the delegations during their talks. If unity is a sacred objective, it is also the instrument of the popular struggle and its means to achieve its major objectives of freedom and security in liberating all the parts of the Arab homeland and in establishing a society of sufficiency and justice, a society of socialism, in continuing the revolutionary tide without deviation or relapse and its extension to embrace the greater Arab homeland, and in contributing to the progress of human civilization and consolidation of world peace.

It was unanimously agreed that unity between the three regions would be based, as required by the Arab people, on the principles of democracy and socialism, would be a real and strong unity which would consider the regional circumstances to consolidate the ties of unity on a basis of practical understanding, not ignore the reasons for partitioning and separation, and make the power of each region a power for the Federal State of the Arab Nation, and make the Federal State a power for each of its regions as well as for the whole Arab Nation.

Document 29
The Draft Constitution of the Palestine Liberation Organization

The charter of the Palestine Liberation Organization (PLO) was prepared under Egyptian auspices following an agreement at the Arab Summit Conference in 1963 by Ahmed Shukairy, a lawyer born in Palestine who represented Saudi Arabia and later Syria in the UN and ultimately became President of the PLO. The role of the PLO on the eve of the Arab–Israeli war was later criticized in the Arab capitals and Shukairy forced to resign in December 1967.

*

1. In accordance with this constitution, an organization known as 'The Palestine Liberation Organization' shall be formed, and shall launch its responsibilities in accordance with the principles of the National Charter and clauses of this constitution.

2. All the Palestinians are natural members in the Liberation Organization exercising their duty in the liberation of their homeland in accordance with their abilities and efficiency.

3. The Palestinian people shall form the larger base for this

Organization; and the Organization, after its creation, shall work closely and constantly with the Palestine people for the sake of their organization and mobilization so they may be able to assume their responsibility in the liberation of their country.

4. Until suitable conditions are available for holding free general elections among all the Palestinians and in all the countries in which they reside, the Liberation Organization shall be set up in accordance with the rules set in this constitution.

5. Measures listed in this constitution shall be taken for the convocation of a Palestinian General Assembly in which shall be represented all Palestinian factions, emigrants and residents, including organizations, societies, unions, trade unions and representatives of [Palestinian] public opinions of various ideological trends; this assembly shall be called 'The National Assembly of the Palestine Liberation Organization'.

6. In preparation and facilitation of work of the assembly, the Palestinian representative at the Arab League [i.e., Ahmed Shukairy] shall, after holding consultations with various Palestinian factions, form:

a) A Preparatory Committee in every Arab country hosting a minimum of 10,000 Palestinians; the mission of each one of these committees is to prepare lists according to which Palestinian candidates in the respective Arab country will be chosen as members of the assembly; these committees shall also prepare studies and proposals which may help the assembly carry out its work; these studies and proposals shall be presented to the Coordination Committee listed below.

b) A Coordination Committee, with headquarters in Jerusalem; the mission of this committee shall be to issue invitations to the assembly, adopt all necessary measures for the holding of the assembly, and coordinate all proposals and studies as well as lists of candidates to the assembly, as specified in the clause above; also the committee shall prepare a provisional agenda – or as a whole, undertake all that is required for the holding and success of the assembly in the execution of its mission.

7. The National Assembly shall be held once every two years; its venue rotates between Jerusalem and Gaza; the National Assembly shall meet for the first time on 14 May 1964, in the city of Jerusalem.

8. To facilitate its work, the Assembly shall form the following committees:

a) The Political Committee: shall be in charge of studying the political sides of the Palestine question in the Arab and international fields.

b) The Charter By-laws and Lists Committee: shall consider the National Charter as well as the various by-laws and lists required by the Organization in the execution of its duties.

c) The Financial Committee: shall formulate a complete plan for the National Palestinian Fund required for financing the Organization.

d) Information Committee: shall work out a complete scheme for information and offices to be established in various parts of the world.

e) The Juridical Committee: shall study the various legal aspects of the Palestine question, be it in relation to principles of International Law, UN Charter, or international documents pertaining to the Palestine question.

f) Proposals and Nomination Committee: shall coordinate proposals and nominations submitted to the Assembly.

g) Awakening Committee: shall study ways and means for the upbringing of the new generations both ideologically and spiritually so they may serve their country and work for the liberation of their homeland.

h) The National Organization Committee: shall lay down general plans pertaining to trade unions, federations, sports organizations and scouts groups; this is in accordance with rules and laws in effect in Arab countries.

9. The National Assembly shall have a Presidency Office composed of the President, two Vice-Presidents, a Secretary, and a Secretary General; these officers shall be elected by the National Assembly when it meets.

10. These (above-listed eight committees) shall submit their reports and recommendations to the National Assembly which,

in turn, shall discuss them and issue the necessary resolutions.

11. The National Assembly shall have an executive apparatus to be called 'The Executive Committee of the Liberation Organization' which shall practise all responsibilities of the Liberation Organization in accordance with the general plans and resolutions issued by the National Assembly.

12. The Executive Committee shall be formed of fifteen members elected by the National Assembly; the Committee shall in its turn elect a President, two Vice-Presidents and a Secretary General.

13. The Executive Committee can be called to a meeting in the time and place decided by the President, or by a proposal submitted by five members of the Committee.

14. The President of the Executive Committee shall represent the Palestinians at the Arab League; therefore, his office shall be in Cairo since the Arab League Headquarters is there.

15. The Executive Committee shall establish the following departments:

a) Department of Political and Information Affairs.

b) Department of the National Fund.

c) Department of General Affairs.

Each one of these departments shall have a Director General and the needed number of employees. Duties of each one of these departments shall be defined by special by-laws prepared by the Executive Committee.

16. The Executive Committee has the right of calling the National Assembly to meet in a place and time it specifies; it has the right also to call to a meeting any committee of the National Assembly to study certain subjects.

17. The Executive Committee shall have a consultative council to be known as 'The Shura [Consultative] Council'; the Executive Committee shall select the president and members of this council from people of opinion and prestige among the Palestinians; prerogatives of the Consultative Council are in matters proposed to it by the Executive Committee.

18. The Arab states shall avail the sons of Palestine the op-

portunity of enlisting in their regular armies on the widest scale possible.

19. Private Palestinian contingents shall be formed in accordance with the military needs and plans decided by the Unified Arab Military Command in agreement and cooperation with the concerned Arab states.

20. A Fund, to be known as 'The National Palestinian Fund', shall be established to finance operations of the Executive Committee: the Fund shall have a board of Directors whose members shall be elected by the National Assembly.

21. Sources of the Fund are to be from:

a) Fixed taxes levied on Palestinians and collected in accordance with special laws.

b) Financial assistance offered by the Arab governments and people.

c) A 'Liberation Stamp' to be issued by the Arab states and be used in postal and other transactions.

d) Donations on national occasions.

e) Loans and assistance given by the Arabs or by friendly nations.

22. Committees, to be known as 'Support Palestine Committees', shall be established in Arab and friendly countries to collect donations and to support the Liberation Organization.

23. The Executive Committee shall have the right to issue by-laws for fulfilment of provisions of this constitution.

24. This draft constitution shall be submitted to the National Assembly for consideration; what is ratified of it cannot be changed except by a two thirds majority of the National Assembly.

Document 30

*United Nations General Assembly
Resolution on the Internationalization
of Jerusalem*

This UN Resolution (No. 303 [IV]) and the following one (Document
31 – Resolution 619 [VII]) are among those most frequently quoted
in the discussions about the Arab–Israeli conflict.

*

9 *December* 1949

The General Assembly,

Having regard to its resolution 181 (II) of 29 November 1947
and 194 (III) of 11 December 1948,

Having studied the reports of the United Nations Conciliation Commission for Palestine set up under the latter resolution,

I. Decides

In relation to Jerusalem,

Believing that the principles underlying its previous resolutions concerning this matter, and in particular its resolution of
29 November 1947, represent a just and equitable settlement
of the question,

1. To restate, therefore, its intention that Jerusalem should be
placed under a permanent international regime which should
envisage appropriate guarantees for the protection of the Holy
Places, both within and outside Jerusalem and to confirm specifically the following provisions of General Assembly resolution
181 (II):

(1) The City of Jerusalem shall be established as a *corpus
separatum* under a special international regime and shall be
administered by the United Nations; (2) The Trusteeship Council shall be designated to discharge the responsibilities of the
Administering Authority . . .; and (3) The City of Jerusalem shall
include the present municipality of Jerusalem plus the surrounding villages and towns, the most eastern of which shall
be Abu Dis; the most southern, Bethlehem; the most western,

Ein Karim (including also the built-up area of Motsa); and the most northern, Shu'fat, as indicated on the attached sketch-map; [*map not reproduced: Ed.*]

2. To request for this purpose that the Trusteeship Council at its next session, whether special or regular, complete the preparation of the Statute of Jerusalem, omitting the now in-applicable provisions, such as Articles 32 and 39, and, without prejudice to the fundamental principles of the international regime for Jerusalem set forth in General Assembly resolution 181 (II) introducing therein amendments in the direction of its greater democratization, approve the Statute, and proceed im-mediately with its implementation. The Trusteeship Council shall not allow any actions taken by any interested Government or Governments to divert it from adopting and implementing the Statute of Jerusalem;

II. *Calls upon* the States concerned, to make formal under-takings, at an early date and in the light of their obligations as Members of the United Nations, that they will approach these matters with good will, and be guided by the terms of the present resolution.

Document 31

UN Security Council Resolution Concerning Restrictions on the Passage of Ships through the Suez Canal

1 September 1951

The Security Council

1. *Recalling* that in its resolution of 11 August 1949 (S/1376) relating to the conclusion of Armistice Agreements between Israel and the neighbouring Arab States, it drew attention to the pledges, in these Agreements 'against any further acts of hostility between the Parties';

2. *Recalling* further that in its resolution of 17 November 1950 (S/1907) it reminded the States concerned that the Armis-tice Agreements to which they were parties contemplated 'the

return of permanent peace in Palestine', and therefore urged them and the other States in the area to take all such steps as would lead to the settlement of the issues between them;

3. *Noting* the report of the Chief of Staff of the Truce Supervision Organization to the Security Council of 12 June 1951 (S/2194);

4. *Further noting* that the Chief of Staff of the Truce Supervision Organization recalled the statement of the senior Egyptian delegate in Rhodes on 13 January 1949, to the effect that his delegation was 'inspired with every spirit of cooperation, conciliation and a sincere desire to restore peace in Palestine', and that the Egyptian Government has not complied with the earnest plea of the Chief of Staff made to the Egyptian delegate on 12 June 1951, that it desist from the present practice of interfering with the passage through the Suez Canal of goods destined for Israel;

5. *Considering* that since the Armistice regime, which has been in existence for nearly two and a half years, is of a permanent character, neither party can reasonably assert that it is actively a belligerent or requires to exercise the right of visit, search, and seizure for any legitimate purpose of self-defence;

6. *Finds* that the maintenance of the practice mentioned in paragraph 4 above is inconsistent with the objectives of a peaceful settlement between the parties and the establishment of a permanent peace in Palestine set forth in the Armistice Agreement;

7. *Finds further* that such practice is an abuse of the exercise of the right of visit, search and seizure;

8. *Further finds* that that practice cannot in the prevailing circumstances be justified on the ground that it is necessary for self-defence;

9. *And further noting* that the restrictions on the passage of goods through the Suez Canal to Israel ports are denying to nations at no time connected with the conflict in Palestine valuable supplies required for their economic reconstruction, and that these restrictions together with sanctions applied by Egypt to certain ships which have visited Israel ports represent un-

justified interference with the rights of nations to navigate the seas and to trade freely with one another, including the Arab States and Israel;

10. *Calls upon* Egypt to terminate the restrictions on the passage of international commercial shipping and goods through the Suez Canal wherever bound and to cease all interference with such shipping beyond that essential to the safety of shipping in the Canal itself and to the observance of international conventions in force.

Document 32
President Nasser on Zionism and Israel

The following excerpts are from Nasser's *The Philosophy of the Revolution*, and speeches on various occasions between 1960 and 1963. Nasser served as an army officer in the Palestine War of 1948. The liberation of Palestine has been one of the chief planks of his political programme, but there have been conflicting statements as to whether there was a definitive plan for the liberation. On several occasions, he announced that his army would soon be ready to enter Palestine on 'a carpet of blood', on others that the time was not ripe yet.

*

From *The Philosophy of the Revolution*

As far as I am concerned I remember that the first elements of Arab consciousness began to filter into my mind as a student in secondary schools, wherefrom I went out with my fellow schoolboys on strike on 2 November of every year as a protest against the Balfour Declaration whereby England gave the Jews a national home usurped unjustly from its legal owners.

When I asked myself at that time why I left my school enthusiastically and why I was angry for this land which I never saw I could not find an answer except the echoes of sentiment. Later a form of comprehension of this subject began when I was a cadet in the Military College studying the Palestine campaigns in particular and the history and conditions of this region in general which rendered it, throughout the last century, an easy prey ravaged by the claws of a pack of hungry beasts.

My comprehension began to be clearer as the foundation of its facts stood out when I began to study, as a student in the Staff College, the Palestine campaign and the problems of the Mediterranean in greater detail.

And when the Palestine crisis loomed on the horizon I was firmly convinced that the fighting in Palestine was not fighting on foreign territory. Nor was it inspired by sentiment. It was a duty imposed by self-defence.

Address by the President Gamal Abdel Nasser in Aleppo (17 February 1960)

Yesterday, the elderly Foreign Minister of Israel threatened the UAR and said that Israel would not tolerate the ban on Israeli ships transiting the Suez Canal.

I would like to tell her and her master, Ben Gurion, as well as the Israeli people, that Israeli ships and cargoes will not, under any circumstances, transit the Canal.

Once these cargoes arrive in Port Said or in any other port in the UAR they become the property of the people of Palestine against whom Zionism and imperialism have conspired.

Eleven years after this tragedy, the people of Palestine have not changed. They, and we, are working for the restoration of their rights in their homeland. The rights of the people of Palestine are Arab rights above all. We feel it is our sacred duty to regain those rights for the people of Palestine.

By this unity which is binding you and the power of Arab unity and Arab nationalism, we can march along the road of freedom and liberation in order to get back the usurped rights of the Palestine Arabs.

Speech by the President Gamal Abdel Nasser at a
Mass Rally of the Youth Organizations in
Damascus (18 October 1960)

Now for the Palestinian issue. Wherever I have been in this or
the Southern Region I hear the strong call for the liberation of
this Arab territory of Palestine, and I would like to tell you,
Brethren, that all that we are now doing is just a part of the
battle for Palestine. Once we are fully emancipated from the
shackles of colonialism and the intrigues of colonialist agents,
we shall take a further step forward towards the liberation of
Palestine.

When we have brought our armed forces to full strength and
made our own armaments we will take another step forward
towards the liberation of Palestine, and when we have manu-
factured jet aircraft and tanks we will embark upon the final
stage of this liberation.

Address by the President Gamal Abdel Nasser on the
Eleventh Anniversary of the Revolution at the
Republican Square, Cairo (22 July 1963)

Work and readiness are the only means to protect the Arab's
right in Palestine.

Arab unity is our hope of liberating Palestine and restoring
the rights of the people of Palestine.

Arab unity is a sort of preparation, a human and national
preparation as well as a preparation with weapons and plans
in all fields. It is not enough to deliver speeches declaring that
we would liberate Palestine and liberate it just on paper for
political consumption. As I said before, we do not have any
defined plan for the liberation of Palestine. I mention this because I find it my duty to say it. But we have a plan to be implemented in case of any Israeli aggression against us or against
any Arab country.

In this case, we know well what to do. We have to be

prepared. We have a plan for this preparation and for the unification of the Arab world which is the only means to protect
the Arab land and safeguard Arab Nationalism.

God be with you and may his peace and mercy be upon you.

Speech Delivered by President Gamal Abdel Nasser
at Alexandria on the Return on Another
Contingent of U A R Troops in Yemen
(11 August 1963)

The Armed Forces are getting ready for the restoration of the
rights of the Palestine people because the Palestine battle was
a smear on the entire Arab nation. No one can forget the
shame brought by the battle of 1948. The rights of the Palestine people must be restored. Therefore, we must get ready to
face Israel and Zionism as well as imperialism which stands
behind them.

Document 33

Ahmed Shukairy: The Palestine Refugees

Excerpts from a speech at the United Nations by Shukairy in 1958
when serving as a member of the Saudi Arabian mission.

*

The Five Principles

Having portrayed the refugees' problem against its lengthy
background of United Nations' action, of the Conciliation
Commission and the relief Agency, we come to the crucial question. What is next? What is the solution?

In my submission, this is the question which must engage
our attention and call for our action; and I shall endeavour to
answer the question in a manner devoid of any decoration. For

when the destiny of a whole people is involved, when the fundamental human rights are in question, and lastly when the peace of the world is at stake, there should be no fineness in our approach. The need calls for plain talking characterized with frankness, and sharp frankness indeed.

It is for these reasons that it becomes our duty to answer the question in all the candour under our command. In this spirit, Mr Chairman, I propose now to deal with three matters: The solution of the problem, the fundamental principles of the solution, and the measures and sanctions to implement the solution.

Beginning with the fundamental principle of the solution, I must reiterate, even to the point of redundance, that these fundamental principles constitute the only basis for the solution to the refugee question. No matter how we view the problem, no solution can offer a chance for a peaceful settlement unless it takes full cognizance of the following five principles:

FIRST: The *de facto* situation created by Israel is entirely unacceptable as a basis for the solution of the Palestine problem in general, or the refugee question in particular. This *de facto* situation is the *fait accompli* of military action that does not vest rights non-existing, or divest rights already existing.

SECOND: The rights of the refugees to their homes and homeland are not related to, or in any way dependent upon, the consent or refusal of Israel. These rights are natural, inherent and self-existing. They are not bestowed even by the United Nations, let alone Israel. They cannot be denied even by the United Nations, let alone Israel. They are vested in the refugees; they reside with the refugees. Thus, consent or no consent, these rights are theirs imprescriptible, irresistible and indivisible.

THIRD: Resettlement, reintegration, rehabilitation or any similar projects, no matter what their connotation may be, are not a solution by themselves. They should be planned or implemented not as aims, but merely as a means to meet the legitimate aspirations of the refugees and to the extent of giving effect to their inherent right to their homeland.

FOURTH: The relief programme of the refugees is no solution to the problem, neither is it a substitute, no matter for how long it is continued. It is a humanitarian measure having no political implications.

FIFTH: Works projects, and self-support programmes are not a solution ; nor a solution to avoid the solution. Self-supporting or dependent, a refugee remains a refugee and his status remains an international problem until it is finally and satisfactorily solved.

To recast such a background has become the more necessary after we heard yesterday the statement on behalf of the United States. The Distinguished Representative of the United States, in his outline of the background of the refugee question, has omitted certain truths entirely, related half-truths on certain aspects and finally arrived at wrongful conclusions on the substance of the problem.

As to the termination of the mandate of the Agency in favour of a better system as implied in the statement of the United States, we have serious misgivings of paramount nature. I must assure the Distinguished Representative of the United States that no Arab state, and no refugee, to use the words of the Distinguished Representative of the United States, feels it 'best to let matters ride as in the past'. To the refugees, continuation of relief is a source of great humiliation. To the Arab governments it is a source of distress. If 'some' feel differently, I assure the Distinguished Representative of the United States, it is not the Arabs anyhow. These refugees who are costing you 7 cents a day per head, have properties, revenues, fortunes in their homeland. The minute they lay hand on their properties they will be the first to thank you and plead the discontinuation of relief. It is only then that the UN responsibility ends, but not before.

I must, therefore, make it quite clear to the Committee in general and to the Distinguished Representative of the United States in particular, that we shall resist any attempt which directly or indirectly reduces in any degree the right of the refugees to repatriation. At a later stage of the debate, I will show the flaw in the reasoning underlying the position of the United States on the question. I simply wish to say here and now that any measure that might be in the direction of even scratching the right to repatriation or absolving the United Nations from its responsibility will be resisted in the Committee and in the Arab world.

With these five principles in mind, I can turn now to the solution of the problem. Here I would say that we need not look for a solution. The solution is there. It is repatriation and nothing but repatriation. It is the only solution that does not dishonour, but certainly does honour the Charter. It is the only solution that does not defeat, but rather does endorse the resolution of the United Nations. It is the only solution that does not defame the bill of human rights, but surely gives it a worthy fame. Lastly, it is the only solution that constitutes an investment of peace, and an asset of confidence in this organization.

After all, repatriation is one of those principles that cannot be questioned by the United Nations. It does not stand by our acceptance, nor does it lapse by our non-acceptance. To borrow a legal term, repatriation is a right *In Rem*, that can be exercised against the whole world, if need be. It springs from the right to a homeland, which is not subject to waiver, surrender, or compensation. Compensation is one remedy open for individual property rights, but a homeland does not submit to compensation even for the most precious possessions of this planet, and indeed the whole universe with all its fabulous riches. This is no exaggeration, unless I exaggerate your feelings towards your respective homelands.

Document 34

*Erskine Childers: The Other Exodus**

Erskine Childers, an Irish journalist, has published articles bitterly critical of Israeli policies. The present article was originally published in the London weekly the *Spectator* (12 May 1961) and provoked a great deal of controversy. Childers, the grandson of a well-known Irish patriot and writer, also worked for the British Broadcasting

*Reprinted by permission of The Spectator Limited.

Corporation and subsequently became a leading official in Irish
television.

                                        *

The Palestine Arab refugees wait, and multiply, and are de-
bated at the United Nations. In thirteen years, their numbers
have increased from 650,000 to 1,145,000. Most of them survive only on rations from the UN agency, UNRWA. Their subsistence has already cost £110,000,000. Each year, UNRWA has
to plead at New York for the funds to carry on, against widespread and especially Western lack of sympathy. There is one
reason for this impatience: the attitude created towards these
refugees by Israeli argument. For over ten years, Israeli spokesmen have claimed that

> Unless we understand how this problem was caused we cannot
> rightly judge how it should be solved. . . . The responsibility of the
> Arab governments is threefold. Theirs is the initiative for its crea-
> tion. Theirs is the onus for its endurance. Above all – theirs is the
> capacity for its solution.
>
>   (Abba Eban to the UN, 1957)

In this inquiry, I propose only briefly to examine the last
two of these three claims. The last, about a 'solution', is that
if the Arab host governments were willing, they could resettle
the refugees quite easily outside Palestine – where, as Israel
claims and as President Kennedy's 1960 election platform also
had it, 'there is room and opportunity for them'. This is not
even remotely true. UNRWA's new chief, Dr John Davis, has
now bluntly and bravely warned against 'facile assumptions
that it rests with the host governments to solve the problem . . .
the simple truth is that the jobs . . . do not exist today within
the host countries'. Nor can the jobs be created, Dr Davis
reports, because most of the refugees are unskilled peasants –
precisely the host countries' worst problem among their own
rapidly expanding populations.

These Arabs, in short, are displaced persons in the fullest,
most tragic meaning of the term – an economic truth cruelly
different from the myth. But there is also the political myth,
and it too has been soothing our highly pragmatic Western
conscience for thirteen years. This is the Israeli charge, solemnly made every year and then reproduced around the world, that

these refugees are – to quote a character in Leon Uris's *Exodus*
– 'kept caged like animals in suffering as a deliberate political
weapon'.

This again, Dr Davis has now bravely called a 'misconcep-
tion'. The reality here is that the refugees themselves fanatic-
ally oppose any resettlement outside Palestine. UNRWA even
had to persuade them that concrete huts, even in the UN camps,
replacing their squalid tents and hovels, would not be the thin
end of a resettlement wedge. Unlike other refugees, these refuse
to move; they insist on going home.

Why? The answer, I believe, lies in the third of the three
issues Israel argues – in the cause itself of the mass exodus. The
very fact that cause is argued by both sides is significant. Israel
claims that the Arabs left because they were ordered to, and
deliberately incited into panic, by their own leaders who wanted
the field cleared for the 1948 war. It is also argued that there
would today be no Arab refugees if the Arab states had not
attacked the new Jewish state on 15 May 1948 (though 800,000
had already fled before that date). The Arabs charge that their
people were evicted at bayonet-point and by panic deliberately
incited by the Zionists.

Examining every official Israeli statement about the Arab
exodus, I was struck by the fact that no primary evidence of
evacuation orders was ever produced. The charge, Israel
claimed, was 'documented'; but where were the documents?
There had allegedly been Arab radio broadcasts ordering the
evacuation; but no dates, names of stations, or texts of messages were ever cited. In Israel in 1958, as a guest of the Foreign
Office and therefore doubly hopeful of serious assistance, I
asked to be shown the proofs, I was assured they existed, and
was promised them. None had been offered when I left, but I
was again assured. I asked to have the material sent on to me.
I am still waiting.

While in Israel, however, I met Dr Leo Kohn, professor of
political science at the Hebrew University and an ambassador
rank adviser to the Israeli Foreign Office. He had written one
of the first official pamphlets on the Arab refugees. I asked him
for concrete evidence of the Arab evacuation orders.

Agitatedly, Dr Kohn replied: 'Evidence? Evidence? What more could you want than this?' and he took up his own pamphlet. 'Look at this *Economist* report', and he pointed to a quotation. 'You will surely not suggest that the *Economist* is a Zionist journal?'

The quotation is one of about five that appear in every Israeli speech and pamphlet, and are in turn used by every sympathetic analysis. It seemed very impressive: it referred to the exodus from Haifa, and to an Arab broadcast order as one major reason for that exodus.

I decided to turn up the relevant (2 October 1948) issue of the *Economist*. The passage that has literally gone around the world was certainly there, but I had already noticed one curious word in it. This was a description of the massacre at Deir Yassin as an 'incident'. No impartial observer of Palestine in 1948 calls what happened at this avowedly non-belligerent, unarmed Arab village in April 1948 an 'incident' – any more than Lidice is called an 'incident'. Over 250 old men, women and children were deliberately butchered, stripped and mutilated or thrown into a well, by men of the Zionist Irgun Zvai Leumi.

Seen in its place in the full *Economist* article, it was at once clear that Dr Kohn's quotation was a second-hand account, inserted as that of an eye-witness at Haifa, by the journal's own correspondent who had not been in that city at the time. And in the rest of the same article, written by the *Economist* correspondent himself, but never quoted by Israel, the second great wave of refugees were described as 'all destitute, as the Jewish troops gave them an hour in which to quit, but simultaneously requisitioned all transport'.

It was now essential to check all other, even secondary, Israeli 'evidence'. Another stock quotation down the years has been that, supposedly, of the Greek-Catholic Archbishop of Galilee. For example, Israel's Abba Eban told the UN Special Political Committee in 1957 that the Archbishop had 'fully confirmed' that the Arabs were urged to flee by their own leaders.

I wrote to His Grace, asking for his evidence of such orders.

I hold signed letters from him, with permission to publish, in which he has categorically denied ever alleging Arab evacuation orders; he states that no such orders were ever given. He says that his name has been abused for years; and that the Arabs fled through panic and forcible eviction by Jewish troops.

As none of the other stock quotations in Israeli propaganda were worth comment, I next decided to test the undocumented charge that the Arab evacuation orders were broadcast by Arab radio – which could be done thoroughly because the BBC monitored all Middle Eastern broadcasts throughout 1948. The records, and companion ones by a US monitoring unit, can be seen at the British Museum.

There was not a single order, or appeal, or suggestion about evacuation from Palestine from any Arab radio station, inside or outside Palestine, in 1948. There is repeated monitored record of Arab appeals, even flat orders, to the civilians of Palestine to stay put. To select only two examples: on 4 April, as the first great wave of flight began, Damascus Radio broadcast an appeal to everyone to stay at their homes and jobs. On 24 April, with the exodus now a flood, Palestine Arab leaders warned that

Certain elements and Jewish agents are spreading defeatist news to create chaos and panic among the peaceful population. Some cowards are deserting their houses, villages or cities. . . . Zionist agents and corrupt cowards will be severely punished.

(*Al-Inqaz*, the Arab Liberation Radio, at 12.00 hours)

Even Jewish broadcasts (in Hebrew) mentioned such Arab appeals to stay put. Zionist newspapers in Palestine reported the same: none so much as hinted at any Arab evacuation orders.

The fact is that Israel's official charges, which have vitally influenced the last ten years of Western thought about the refugees, are demonstrably and totally hollow. And from this alone, suspicion is justified. Why make such charges at all? On the face of it, this mass exodus might have been entirely the result of 'normal' panic and wartime dislocation.

We need not even touch upon Arab evidence that panic was quite deliberately incited. The evidence is there, on the Zionist record. For example, on 27 March, four days before the big offensive against Arab centres by the official Zionist (Haganah) forces, the Irgun's radio unit broadcast in Arabic. Irgun, a terrorist organization like the Stern Gang, was officially disowned by Ben Gurion and the Haganah. Yet just four days before the Haganah offensive Irgun warned 'Arabs in urban agglomerations' that typhus, cholera and similar diseases would break out 'heavily' among them 'in April and May'.

The effect may be imagined. Two weeks later, it was this same Irgun, apparently so solicitous of Arab welfare, that butchered the people of Deir Yassin. Irgun then called a press conference to announce the deed; paraded other captured Arabs through Jewish quarters of Jerusalem to be spat upon; then released them to tell their kin of the experience. Arthur Koestler called the 'bloodbath' of Deir Yassin 'the psychologically decisive factor in this spectacular exodus'. But this was only Irgun, it may be said. Is there evidence that official Zionist forces – the Haganah under Ben Gurion and the Jewish Agency – were inciting panic? An Israeli government pamphlet of 1958 states that 'the Jews tried, by every means open to them, to stop the Arab evacuation' (this same 1958 pamphlet has diluted Deir Yassin to 'the one and only instance of Jewish highhanded [sic] action in this war').

There is one recorded instance of such an appeal. It is beyond dispute even by Arabs, that in Haifa the late gentle Mayor, Shabetai Levi, with the tears streaming down his face, implored the city's Arabs to stay. But elsewhere in Haifa, Arthur Koestler wrote in his book that Haganah loudspeaker vans and the Haganah radio promised that city's Arabs escort to 'Arab territory', and 'hinted at terrible consequences if their warning were disregarded'. There are many witnesses of this loudspeaker method elsewhere. In Jerusalem the Arabic warning from the vans was, 'The road to Jericho is open! Fly from Jerusalem before you are all killed!' (Meyer Levin in *Jerusalem Embattled*). Bertha Vester, a Christian missionary, reported that another theme was, 'Unless you leave your homes, the fate of

Deir Yassin will be your fate.' The Haganah radio station also broadcast, in Arabic, repeated news of Arabs fleeing 'in terror and fear' from named places.

Still, however, we have plumbed this exodus only so far as panic is concerned. There are UN and *Economist* reports of forcible expulsion, which is something else. How much evidence is there for this? And were only the 'unofficial' Irgun and Stern forces responsible? This is what Nathan Chofshi, one of the original Jewish pioneers in Palestine, wrote in an ashamed rebuttal of an American Zionist rabbi's charges of evacuation orders :

If Rabbi Kaplan really wanted to know what happened, we old Jewish settlers in Palestine who witnessed the fight could tell him how and in what manner we, Jews, forced the Arabs to leave cities and villages . . . some of them were driven out by force of arms; others were made to leave by deceit, lyin and false gpromises. It is enough to cite the cities of Jaffa, Lydda, Ramleh, Beersheba, Acre from among numberless others. (*Jewish Newsletter*, New York, 9 February 1959.)

Were official Zionist troops involved at any of these places? I propose to select, for the sake of brevity, only the Lydda-Ramleh area. It was about the exodus from this area, among others, that the *Economist* reported, 'Jewish troops gave them an hour to quit.'

In their latest book, which has been publicly endorsed by Ben Gurion, Jon Kimche and his brother devoted considerable detail to the Zionist offensive against Lydda and Ramleh. It was undertaken by official Israeli forces under Yigael Allon. And the immediately responsible officer was Moshe Dayan, commander of the 1956 Sinai attack, now a Cabinet Minister. Kimche has described how, on 11 July 1948, Dayan, with his columns,

drove at full speed into Lydda, shooting up the town and creating confusion and a degree of terror among the population . . . its Arab population of 30,000 either fled or were herded on the road to Ramallah. The next day Ramleh also surrendered and its Arab population suffered the same fate. Both towns were sacked by the victorious Israelis.

Ramallah, on the road to which these particular Arabs – numbering over 60,000 from this one area alone – were herded, was up in the Judean hills, outside Zionist-held territory. The 'road to Jericho', which Arabs in Jerusalem were warned to take, brought them into the Jordan Valley. Some 85,000 are still there in one UN camp alone, under the Mount of Temptation. The Arab population of Acre, mentioned by Chofshi, exceeded 45,000 : Acre was attacked by official Zionist troops.

From this analysis of only some of the sources of the Arab exodus, then, it is clear beyond all doubt that official Zionist forces were responsible for expulsion of thousands upon thousands of Arabs, and for deliberate incitement to panic. Seen from the viewpoint of the Arab refugees themselves, little more would need to be said. And needless to say, even those Arabs expelled or who fled through 'unofficially' incited panic can hardly be asked to look differently on the Israeli Government today. It pays former Irgunists and Sternists the same war pensions as former Haganah troops; its denial of expulsion is total.

But is it conceivable that Ben Gurion and his colleagues could have deliberately contemplated an 'emptying' of Palestine? That a motive existed is beyond doubt The UN partition scheme had in no way solved the 'Arab problem' that a Jewish state would face. It would have given Zionism what its leaders publicly called the 'irreducible minimum' of territory in a Palestine they claimed should entirely belong to them. And we know that the official Zionist movement had in fact no intention of accepting the UN territorial award. Six weeks before the British Mandate ended, before the Israeli state was proclaimed, and before the Arab states sent in their armies, an all-out Zionist military offensive was launched. Later, Ben Gurion publicly said of this offensive :

As fighting spread, the [Arab] exodus was joined by Bedouin and fellahin [peasants], but not the remotest Jewish homestead was abandoned and nothing a tottering [British] administration could unkindly do stopped us from reaching our goal on 14 May 1948, in a state made larger and Jewish by the Haganah. (cf. *Rebirth and Destiny of Israel.*)

The Jewish state envisaged by the UN would have contained a 45 per cent Arab population: the extra territory attacked by the Zionists before 14 May would have increased that ratio – for example, by more than 80,000 Arabs in Jaffa alone. But it was not just a question of numbers. The Arabs owned and occupied far too much of the territory's productive and social facilities to enable anything like the mass Jewish immigration of which Zionists dreamed.

What this meant in terms of motive can be seen in the statistics that followed the Arab exodus. More than 80 per cent of the entire land area of Israel is land abandoned by the Arab refugees. Nearly a quarter of all the standing buildings in Israel had been occupied by those Arabs. Ten thousand shops, stores and other firms inside new Israel had been Arab. Half of all the citrus fruit holdings in the new state had belonged to the Arabs now made refugees. By 1954, more than one third of the entire Jewish population of Israel was living on 'absentee property' – most of it now 'absorbed' into the Israeli economy, and unilaterally sequestered by Israeli legislation against a 'global' compensation offer.

It is, then, little wonder that old Chaim Weizmann, Israel's first President, described the Arab exodus as a 'miraculous simplification of Israel's tasks'. But was it 'miraculous'? Unexpected? In no way part of combined military and economic planning of nascent Israel's leaders?

We come to perhaps the most grave evidence of all. The mass exodus began in April 1948. By June, the UN Mediator was fully seised of it. He formally demanded a statement of policy from the new Israeli government about the refugees. At first, he could get no satisfaction. Then, in an official letter dated 1 August 1948, Israel's Foreign Minister replied.

It was only four months since the first waves of flight; only eleven weeks since Israel had been proclaimed, ostensibly calling on the Arabs to 'play their part in the development of the state'. And it was at this time that a government since claiming that this whole exodus was unexpected and despite its implorings, formally denied the refugees the right of return. Israel did not merely plead 'security', but told the United Nations:

On the economic side, the reintegration of the returning Arabs into normal life, and even their mere sustenance, would present an insuperable problem. The difficulties of accommodation, employment, and ordinary livelihood would be insuperable.

The case rests. This is not the place to discuss a 'solution', and no summary conclusion is needed, save perhaps to recall the words of an official Israeli spokesman, though in rather different import:

Unless we understand how this problem was caused, we cannot rightly judge how it should be solved.

The Arabs of Palestine now enter their fourteenth year of exile. If you go among them in the hills of Judea, they will take you by the arm to a crest of land and point downwards, across the rusty skeins of barbed wire. 'Can you see it – over there beside those trees? That is my home.'

It his shaming beyond all brief descriptions to move among these million people, as a Westerner. It is shaming for many Jews, and some speak out as Nathan Chofshi has bravely done:

We came and turned the native Arabs into tragic refugees. And still we dare to slander and malign them, to besmirch their name. Instead of being deeply ashamed of what we did and trying to undo some of the evil we committed . . . we justify our terrible acts and even attempt to glorify them.

Document 35
Abba Eban: The Refugee Problem

Excerpts from a speech (17 November 1958) by the chief Israeli representative to the United Nations who subsequently became Foreign Minister of Israel.

*

The Arab refugee problem was caused by a war of aggression, launched by the Arab states against Israel in 1947 and 1948. Let there be no mistake. If there had been no war against Israel, with its consequent harvest of bloodshed, misery, panic and flight, there would be no problem of Arab refugees today. Once you determine the responsibility for that war, you have determined the responsibility for the refugee problem. Nothing in the history of our generation is clearer or less controversial than the initiative of Arab governments for the conflict out of which the refugee tragedy emerged. The historic origins of that conflict are clearly defined by the confessions of Arab governments themselves: 'This will be a war of extermination,' declared the Secretary General of the Arab League speaking for the governments of six Arab states; 'It will be a momentous massacre to be spoken of like the Mongolian massacre and the Crusades.'

The assault began on the last day of November 1947. From then until the expiration of the British Mandate in May 1948 the Arab States, in concert with Palestine Arab leaders, plunged the land into turmoil and chaos. On the day of Israel's Declaration of Independence, on 14 May 1948, the armed forces of Egypt, Jordan, Syria, Lebanon and Iraq, supported by contingents from Saudi Arabia and the Yemen, crossed their frontiers and marched against Israel. The perils which then confronted our community; the danger which darkened every life and home; the successful repulse of the assault and the emergence of Israel into the life of the world community are all chapters of past history, gone but not forgotten. But the traces of that conflict still remain deeply inscribed upon our region's life. Caught up in the havoc and tension of war; demoralized by the flight of their leaders; urged on by irresponsible promises that they would return to inherit the spoils of Israel's destruction – hundreds of thousands of Arabs sought the shelter of Arab lands. A survey by an international body in 1957 described these violent events in the following terms:

As early as the first months of 1948 the Arab League issued orders exhorting the people to seek a temporary refuge in neighbouring countries, later to return to their abodes in the wake of the victorious Arab armies and obtain their share of abandoned Jewish property. (*Research Group for European Migration Problems Bulletin*, Vol. V No. 1, 1957, p. 10.)

Contemporary statements by Arab leaders fully confirm this version. On 16 August 1948 Msgr. George Hakim, the Greek Catholic Archbishop of Galilee, recalled:

The refugees had been confident that their absence from Palestine would not last long; that they would return within a few days – within a week or two; their leaders had promised them that the Arab armies would crush the 'Zionist gangs' very quickly and that there would be no need for panic or fear of a long exile.

A month later, on 15 September 1948, Mr Emile Ghoury who had been the Secretary of the Arab Higher Committee at the time of the Arab invasion of Israel declared:

I do not want to impugn anyone but only to help the refugees. The fact that there are these refugees is the direct consequence of the action of the Arab States in opposing partition and the Jewish State. The Arab States agreed upon this policy unanimously and they must share in the solution of the problem.

No less compelling than these avowals by Arab leaders are the judgements of United Nations organs. In April 1948, when the flight of the refugees was in full swing, the United Nations Palestine Commission inscribed its verdict on the tablets of history:

Arab opposition to the plan of the Assembly of 29 November 1947 has taken the form of organized efforts by strong Arab elements, both inside and outside Palestine, to prevent its implementation and to thwart its objectives by threats and acts of violence, including repeated armed incursions into Palestine territory. The Commission has had to report to the Security Council that powerful Arab interests, both inside and outside Palestine, are defying the resolution of the General Assembly and are engaged in a deliberate effort to alter by force the settlement envisaged therein.

This is a description of the events between November 1947 and May 1948 when the Arab exodus began. Months later, when the tide of battle rolled away, its consequences of bereavement, devastation and panic were left behind. At the General Assembly meetings in 1948 the United Nations Acting Mediator recorded a grave international judgement:

The Arab states had forcibly opposed the existence of the Jewish State in Palestine in direct opposition to the wishes of two thirds of the members of the Assembly. Nevertheless their armed intervention proved useless. The [Mediator's] report was based solely on the fact that the Arab states had no right to resort to force and that the United Nations should exert its authority to prevent such a use of force.

The significance of the Arab assault upon Israel by five neighbouring states had been reflected in a letter addressed by the Secretary General of the United Nations to representatives of the permanent members of the Security Council on 16 May 1948 : 'The Egyptian Government,' wrote the Secretary General,

has declared in a cablegram to the President of the Security Council on 15 May that Egyptian armed forces have entered Palestine and it has engaged in 'armed intervention' in that country. On 16 May I received a cablegram from the Arab League making similar statements on behalf of the Arab states. I consider it my duty to emphasize to you that *this is the first time since the adoption of the Charter that member states have openly declared that they have engaged in armed intervention outside their own territory*.

These are only a few of the documents which set out the responsibility of the Arab governments for the warfare of which the refugees are the main surviving victims. Even after a full decade it is difficult to sit here with equanimity and listen to Arab representatives disengaging themselves from any responsibility for the travail and anguish which they caused. I recall this history not for the purpose of recrimination, but because of its direct bearing on the Committee's discussion. Should not the representatives of Arab states, as the authors of this tragedy, come here in a mood of humility and repentance rather than in shrill and negative indignation? Since these governments have, by acts of policy, created this tragic problem, *does it not follow that the world community has an unimpeachable right to claim their full assistance in its solution?* How can governments create a vast humanitarian problem by their action – then wash their hands of all responsibility for its alleviation? The claim of the world community on the co-operation of Arab governments is all the more compelling when we reflect that these states, in their vast lands, command all the resources and conditions which would enable them to liberate the refugees from their plight, in full dignity and freedom.

With this history in mind the Committee should not find it difficult to reject the assertion that the guilt for the refugee problem lies with the United Nations itself. The refugee problem was not created by the General Assembly's recommendation for the establishment of Israel. It was created by the attempts of Arab governments to destroy that recommendation by force. The crisis arose not as Arab spokesmen have said because the United Nations adopted a resolution eleven years ago; it arose because Arab governments attacked that resolution by force. If the United Nations proposal had been peacefully accepted, there would be no refugee problem today hanging as a cloud upon the tense horizons of the Middle East.

The next question is – why has the problem endured?

In his statement to the Committee on 10 November 1958, the representative of the United States said:

> In our view it is not good enough consciously to perpetuate for over a decade the dependent status of nearly a million refugees.

Other speakers in this debate have echoed a similar sense of frustration.

Apart from the question of its origin, the perpetuation of this refugee problem is an unnatural event, running against the whole course of experience and precedent. Since the end of the Second World War, problems affecting forty million refugees have confronted governments in various parts of the world. In no case, except that of the Arab refugees, amounting to less than two per cent of the whole, has the international community shown constant responsibility and provided lavish aid. In every other case a solution has been found by the integration of refugees into their host countries. Nine million Koreans; 900,000 refugees from the conflict in Vietnam; 8½ million Hindus and Sikhs leaving Pakistan for India ; 6½ million Muslims fleeing India to Pakistan ; 700,000 Chinese refugees in Hong

Kong; 13 million Germans from the Sudetenland, Poland and other East European states reaching West and East Germany; thousands of Turkish refugees from Bulgaria; 440,000 Finns separated from their homeland by a change of frontier; 450,000 refugees from Arab lands arrived destitute in Israel, and an equal number converging on Israel from the remnants of the Jewish holocaust in Europe – these form the tragic procession of the world's refugee population in the past two decades. *In every case but that of the Arab refugees now in Arab lands the countries in which the refugees sought shelter have facilitated their integration.* In this case alone has integration been obstructed.

The paradox is the more astonishing when we reflect that the kinship of language, religion, social background and national sentiment existing between the Arab refugees and their Arab host countries has been at least as intimate as those existing between any other host countries and any other refugee groups. It is impossible to escape the conclusion that the integration of Arab refugees into the life of the Arab world is an objectively feasible process which has been resisted for political reasons.

In a learned study on refugee problems published by the Carnegie Endowment for International Peace in November 1957 under the title *Century of the Homeless Man* Dr Elfan Rees, Advisor on Refugees to the World Council of Churches, sums up the international experience in the following terms:

No large-scale refugee problem has ever been solved by repatriation, and there are certainly no grounds for believing that this particular problem can be so solved. Nothing can bring it about except wars which in our time would leave nothing to go back to. War has never solved a refugee problem and it is not in the books that a modern war would.

Those words should be compared with Mr Shukairy's peroration, in which he seems to look forward to a settlement of the refugee problem by a war launched for the extinction of Israel's independence. Such a war, whose result would not be that envisaged by Mr Shukairy, would be more likely to create new refugee problems than to solve the existing ones.

Dr Rees's Report continues :

This then is not a case of a refugee rejecting a particular solution but of the international community having to reject it as dangerous and impossible. It is time this was done with more frankness and force than has been used hitherto. Until it is – real danger remains, and these refugee problems will be unnecessarily perpetuated by the rejection of other and viable solutions.

The Carnegie Endowment publication concludes :

The facts we must face force us to the conclusion that for most of the world refugees the only solution is integration where they are.

Another important study on refugee problems carried out last year has been published by the Research Group for European Migration. This study reaches the following grave conclusion :

The official attitude of the [Arab] host countries is well known. It is one of seeking to prevent any sort of adaptation and integration because the refugees are seen as a political means of pressure to get Israel wiped off the map or to get the greatest possible number of concessions.

It is painfully evident that this refugee problem has been artificially maintained for political motives against all the economic, social and cultural forces which, had they been allowed free play, would have brought about a solution.

Recent years have witnessed a great expansion of economic potentialities in the Middle East. The revenues of the oil-bearing countries have opened up great opportunities of work and development, into which the refugees by virtue of their linguistic and national background could fit without any sense of dislocation. The expansion in the areas of Arab sovereignty has also created opportunities of employment which did not exist in the days of colonial tutelage. There cannot be any doubt that if free movement had been granted to the refugees there would have been a spontaneous absorption of thousands of them into these expanded Arab economies. It is precisely this that Arab governments have obstructed. In his report to the

Eighth session of the General Assembly the Director of
UNRWA describes Arab policies on free movement in a highly
significant passage :

The full benefit of the spread of this large capital investment [in
Arab countries] will be felt only if restrictions on the movement
of refugees are withdrawn. This is a measure which was proposed
in the original three-year plan but little has been done so far to give
effect to it. Such freedom of movement would enable refugees to
take full advantage of the opportunities for work arising in countries such as Iraq, Saudi Arabia and the Persian Gulf Sheikhdoms
where economic development has already taken place.

There has, of course, been some movement of refugees into
the new labour opportunities of the region. The force of economic attraction has sometimes prevailed. But these potentialities can only be fully realized if political resistance to integration is overcome. There are broad opportunities in the Arab
world for refugees to build new lives; but the governments
concerned have so far sought to debar refugees from using
them. In the survey published by the Carnegie Endowment the
obstructive record of Arab governments is set out in graphic
words :

The history of UNRWA has been a clinical study in frustration.
No Agency has been better led or more devoutly served but the
organized intransigence of the refugees and the calculated indifference of the Arab states concerned have brought all its plans to
nought. By chicanery it is feeding the dead, by political pressure it is
feeding non-refugees, its relief supplies have been subjected in some
instances to import duty, its personnel policies are grossly interfered
with and its 'constructive measures', necessarily requiring the concurrence of governments, have been pigeon-holed. The net result is
that relief is being provided in 1957 to refugees who could have
been rehabilitated in 1951 with 'home and jobs', without prejudice
to their just claims.

In a survey on *Social Forces in the Middle East 1956*, Dr
Channing B. Richardson of Hamilton University writes :

Towards UNRWA the attitudes of the Arab governments vary
between suspicion and obstruction. It cannot be denied that the

outside observer gains the impression that the Arab governments have no great desire to solve the refugee problem.

In June 1957 the Chairman of the Near Eastern Sub-Committee of the United States Senate Foreign Relations Committee reported at the end of an illuminating survey:

The fact is that the Arab states have for ten years used the Palestine refugees as political hostages in their struggle with Israel. While Arab delegates in the United Nations have condemned the plight of their brothers in the refugee camps nothing has been done to assist them in a practical way lest political leverage against Israel be lost.

The failure or refusal of Arab governments to achieve a permanent economic integration of refugees in their huge lands appears all the more remarkable when we contrast it with the achievements of other countries when confronted by the challenge and opportunity of absorbing their kinsmen into their midst. Israel with her small territory, her meagre water resources and her hard-pressed finances, has found homes, work and citizenship in the past ten years for nearly a million newcomers arriving in destitution no less acute than those of Arab refugees. These refugees from Arab lands left their homes, property and jobs behind. Their standards of physique and nutrition were in many cases pathetically low. They have had to undergo processes of adaptation to a social, linguistic and national ethos far removed from any that they had known before. Thus, integration in this case has been far more arduous than it would be for Arab refugees in Arab lands, where no such differences exist between the society and culture of the host country and those with which the refugees are already familiar. If Israel in these conditions could assimilate nearly one million refugees – 450,000 of them from Arab lands – how much more easily could the vast Arab world find a home for a similar number of Arab refugees if only the same impulse of kinship asserted itself.

This is concisely described in the report published by the Carnegie Endowment:

There is another aspect of the Middle East refugee problem that is also frequently ignored. It is necessary to remember that concurrently with the perpetuation of the Arab refugee problem more that 400,000 Jews have been forced to leave their homes in Iraq, the Yemen, and North Africa. They have not been counted as refugees because they were readily and immediately received as new immigrants into Israel. Nevertheless they were forced to leave their traditional homes against their will and to abandon, in the process, all that they possessed. The latest addition to their number are the 20,000 Jews for whom life has become impossible in Egypt. Fifteen thousand of them have sought asylum in Israel while the remainder are in Europe seeking other solutions to their problem.

Nor is this an isolated example of what can be achieved by governments in circumstances much less favourable than those which the Arab states command. Less than two weeks ago the representative of Finland, in the Third Committee of this Assembly, gave the following moving account of what a small country can achieve in refugee integration :

In 1944 the 3,300,000 people who lived within the present boundaries of Finland had to receive in a couple of weeks' time around 440,000 displaced persons, all Finnish citizens who had left their homesteads after the new frontier line had cut off some 13 per cent of our territory from the rest of Finland. ... As in 1944 practically no emigration of the displaced persons was possible and none of them could be sent back to their earlier home region, complete integration was the only solution. It was an extremely heavy economic burden taking into consideration that there was no international aid, that the reparation of war destruction and the payment of war indemnities all came simultaneously and that the displaced persons came practically empty handed.

I will not ask the Committee to consider the other numerous precedents. Enough has been said to prove the crucial point that there is no objective difficulty in solving such problems provided the will for a solution exists.

Indeed, compared with other problems, the Arab refugee problem is one of the easiest to solve.

The Research Group for European Migration points out in its report (pp. 25–26) that

The Palestine refugees have the closest possible affinities of national sentiment, language, religion and social organization with the Arab host countries and the standard of living of the majority of the refugee population is little different from those of the inhabitants of the countries that have given them refuge or will do so in the future.

The same point is made in the report of a Special Study Commission to the Near East and Africa dispatched by the Committee on Foreign Affairs of the United States House of Representatives, the source of a great proportion of UN relief funds:

Unlike refugees in other parts of the world the Palestine refugees are no different in language and social organization from the other Arabs. Resettlement therefore would be in familiar environment. If the local governments are unwilling to tackle the problem except on their own terms there is little incentive for outside governments to continue financial support. Original humanitarian impulse which led to the creation and perpetuation of UNRWA is gradually being perverted into a political weapon. (19 May 1958)

Most of the recent literature describes Arab resistance to integration by two methods – political opposition to integration; and careful scrutiny of UNRWA's activities to ensure that they do not develop into permanent solutions. The policy of obstruction however also has a third heading. I refer to the rejection of economic development proposals which seemed to hold the promise of a refugee solution. The thinking behind these plans was simple but imaginative. The international community was willing to create special opportunities of livelihood by irrigating new areas of land, establishing new farms or, in some cases, new village communities with industrial as well as agricultural activity. Refugees were to be placed into these newly created labour opportunities. The result would be a reduction of the number of refugees receiving relief and progress towards lightening the international burden.

None of these schemes has won Arab acceptance. Many of them have been rejected precisely because their implementation would help solve the refugee problem. A typical and spec-

tacular instance is to be found in the long negotiations
conducted between 1953 and 1956 on a project for the coordi-
nated use of the Jordan and Yarmuk Rivers. Israel was prepared,
despite certain disavowal – indeed is still prepared – to cooperate in this plan. Ambassador Eric Johnston has summed
up his experience in the following words:

Between 1953 and 1956, at the request of President Eisenhower, I
undertook to negotiate with these states a comprehensive Jordan
Valley development plan that would have provided for the irrigation
of some 225,000 acres. . . . After two years of discussion, technical
experts of Israel, Jordan, Lebanon and Syria agreed upon every
important detail of a unified Jordan plan. But in October 1956 it was
rejected for political reasons at a meeting of the Arab League. . . .
Three years have passed and no agreement has yet been reached on
developing the Jordan. Every year a billion cubic metres of precious
water still roll down the ancient stream, wasted, to the Dead
Sea.

In the light of these experiences it cannot be doubted that
Arab governments have been determined that the refugees
shall remain refugees; and that the aim of wrecking any alternative to 'repatriation' has been pursued by these governments
with an ingenuity worthy of a better cause. With an international agency working for integration; with millions of dollars expended every year to move refugees away from a life
of dependence, the Arab governments have brought us to a
point where there are more refugees on United Nations rolls
than ever before.

Any discussion of this problem revolves around the two
themes of resettlement, and what is called 'repatriation'. There
is a growing scepticism about the feasibility of repatriation.
These hundreds of thousands of Arab refugees are now in Arab
lands on the soil of their kinsmen. They have been nourished
for ten years on one single theme – hatred of Israel; refusal to
recognize Israel's sovereignty; resentment against Israel's existence; the dream of securing Israel's extinction. All these implacable sentiments found expression in the address by the
representative of Saudi Arabia.

Repatriation would mean that hundreds of thousands of people would be introduced into a state whose existence they oppose, whose flag they despise and whose destruction they are resolved to seek. The refugees are all Arabs; and the countries in which they find themselves are Arab countries. Yet the advocates of repatriation contend that these Arab refugees should be settled in a non-Arab country, in the only social and cultural environment which is alien to their background and tradition. The Arab refugees are to be uprooted from the soil of nations to which they are akin and loyal – and placed in a state to which they are alien and hostile. Israel, whose sovereignty and safety are already assailed by the states surrounding her, is invited to add to its perils by the influx from hostile territories of masses of people steeped in the hatred of her existence. All this is to happen in a region where the Arab nations possess unlimited opportunities for resettling their kinsmen, and in which Israel has already contributed to a solution of the refugee problems of Asia and Africa by receiving 450,000 refugees from Arab lands among its immigrants.

Surely the Committee will not find it difficult to understand why this solution finds such little favour. In discussing the rights and duties of individuals let us not forget the rights and duties of states. Israel is a small sovereign state whose primary preoccupation is that of its safety. It cannot in conscience entertain a solution which would involve its own disruption, and bring misery and disillusionment to refugees who have surely suffered enough from false hopes and vain illusions. While every state is entitled to respect for its security needs, Israel is surely unique in the acuteness of the threats which surround her. No other state on the face of the globe is surrounded, as we are, by hostile neighbours who openly avow its destruction. To suggest that in addition to facing external perils from the north, south and east, we should import a massive quantity of hatred and rancour into our midst is to demand something beyond prudence or reason.

There are three other considerations which must be placed on the scale against repatriation. First the word itself is not accurately used in this context. Transplanting an Arab refugee

from an Arab land to a non-Arab land is not really 'repatriation'. 'Patria' is not a mere geographical concept. Resettlement of a refugee in Israel would be not repatriation, but
alienation from Arab society; a true repatriation of an Arab
refugee would be a process which brought him into union with
people who share his conditions of language and heritage, his
impulses of national loyalty and cultural identity.

Second, the validity of the 'repatriation' concept is further
undermined when we examine the structure of the refugee
population. More than 50 per cent of the Arab refugees are
under fifteen years of age. This means that at the time of Israel's
establishment many of those, if born at all at that time, were
under five years of age. We thus reach the striking fact that a
majority of the refugee population can have no conscious memory of Israel at all.

Thirdly those who speak of repatriation to Israel might not
always be aware of the measure of existing integration of
refugees into countries of their present residence. In the kingdom of Jordan, refugees have full citizenship and participate
fully in the government of the country. They are entitled to
vote and be elected to the Jordanian parliament. Indeed many
of them hold high rank in the government of the kingdom.
Thousands of refugees are enrolled in the Jordanian army and
its National Guard. It is, to say the least, eccentric to suggest
that people who are citizens of another land and are actually
or potentially enrolled in the armed forces of a country at war
with Israel are simultaneously endowed with an optional right
of Israel citizenship.

In the Syrian region of Egypt refugees have not been granted
citizenship; but, by virtue of a law of July 1956, their status is,
to a large degree, assimilated to that of citizens. This is especially so in respect of the right to work and to establish commercial enterprises. According to the law of July 1956, refugees
are subject to compulsory military service in the Syrian army.
Here again, to adduce an unconditional right 'repatriation'
would signify that those who are citizens of a state foreign and
hostile to Israel have a simultaneous right to be regarded as
Israel citizens! Is there any state represented here which

would acknowledge a right of entry to those who having left its shores have become the citizens of a foreign and hostile state, and have taken military service under governments which proclaim a state of war against it?

This is merely a striking example of the sharp paradox which we enter if we try to reconcile the slogan of 'repatriation' with the actual context, the hard facts of Arab–Israel relations.

I do not believe it necessary to speak at any length on the point that resettlement in Arab countries is free from all the disadvantages which adhere to 'repatriation'. Every condition which has ever contributed to a solution of refugee problems by integration is present in this case. With its expanse of territory, its great rivers, its resources of mineral wealth, its accessibility to international aid, the Arab world is easily capable of absorbing an additional population, not only without danger to itself, but with actual reinforcement of its security and welfare ...

Document 36

Golda Meir: A Call for Disarmament

From an address by the then Israeli Foreign Minister before the UN General Assembly on 9 October 1962.

*

The small and new countries, emerging into a world of armed camps, suffer twofold. Our immediate aim is rapid development, but since the danger of war still looms over every dispute, we are constantly burdened with defence expenditures to the detriment of our development needs. We too quickly learn the bitter lesson that those who threaten others must be deterred by some equilibrium, and let not those whose declared policy is to attack their neighbour cry out in mock indignation when the latter seeks some means of defence.

My government rejects war as a means of settling disputes. From the day that the state of Israel was established, my government has called for settling all outstanding differences by direct negotiations.

We do not rest content with calling upon the great powers to find a way to disarmament, and to settle outstanding problems by negotiation and conciliation between them. We are prepared to put this into practice in the dispute in which we are involved with our neighbours. As we have done in the past, we call again upon the Arab states to agree to complete disarmament with mutual inspection, covering all types of weapons, and to accept that method of direct negotiations as the only means for solving all differences between them and Israel . . .

There are many that are misled by two fallacies regarding the Middle East. The first is that it is an Arab region. In fact there are in it more non-Arabs than Arabs – Muslims, Christians and Jews. This composite pattern of peoples of various faiths and cultures has always been the pattern of the Middle East, each people with its historic continuity, past, present and future.

The second fallacy is that all would be well in that region if it were not for the tension between the Arab states and Israel. I would be the last to underrate the difficulties and dangers which arise from that conflict. But this is only one source of tension in a part of the world which is, unhappily, the scene of so much political instability, economic and social backwardness, rivalry and friction between different countries and regions and the pressures of the cold war. Anyone who follows the affairs of the Middle East knows that during this last year the focus of trouble in the area has been the bitter struggles within the Arab world which have made of the Arab League no longer even a façade of unity.

Israel longs for the day when the political independence and territorial integrity of every single state in the area – Arab and non-Arab – will be assured and when we can all concentrate

on the welfare of our people. When I refer to the turmoil in the
Arab world, it is because we are a Middle Eastern country and
therefore affected by all that affects the peace of our area.

As far as the Israel–Arab dispute itself is concerned, it is well
to see clearly what is the basic problem. It is the denial by the
Arab states of Israel's right to exist. If this attitude were to
change, and if the Arab states and Israel were to discuss their
differences at the conference table in a frank and open manner,
I am positive that solutions could be found on all the specific
issues.

Year after year Israel has come on this rostrum with one
demand – peace between it and its Arab neighbours. May I
say here that we were grateful to the distinguished Deputy
Foreign Minister of Ghana when he drew our attention again
to the important statement of President Nkrumah during the
15th General Assembly, in which he called for recognition of
the political realities in the Middle East and for insurance
against non-aggression. We are entirely in agreement with that
view.

The Arab denial of Israel's right of existence has a direct
bearing on the distressing refugee problem. We are willing, and
always have been willing, to discuss with the Arab governments
what can best be done to secure the future of the refugees in
the light of the political and economic realities in the region.
But a natural solution to the problem is frustrated by the Arab
dream of destroying Israel and openly proclaimed Arab intention of using the refugees for this purpose.

This design has been openly propagated even from the rostrum of this Assembly. This small spot of land, in which the
Jewish people have revived their ancient home and nationhood, must again be wrested from them and they again be
scattered to the four corners of the earth. Our neighbours have
tried to achieve this by various means, open or guerilla warfare,
economic boycott, propaganda and threats.

Negotiations and conciliation are proclaimed from the rostrum as the method to solve all other problems in the world
except this one, which must, according to these spokesmen,
be resolved by force. For every other nation, they claim co-

existence, practised in peace. For Israel, non-existence, to be achieved by war. This doctrine not only runs counter to the basic principles of the United Nations Charter; its acceptance strikes at the very roots of our organization.

The world of today is overwhelmed by ideological disputes, international conflicts and economic controversies. In face of this situation, the basic concepts of the Charter, on the eschewing of force, on the unremitting search for peace, on international cooperation, on negotiation as the means to solve problems, have gained a new depth and significance. As long as negotiation is sought, there is hope. Those who rule out negotiation in the Middle East, those who year after year engage in sterile and stereotyped speeches of hostility, should know that their attitude is irrelevant to the basic theme of the international community and can have no echo in an organization which has proclaimed peace to be synonymous with human survival: that they are assaulting the foundations of human progress.

The policy of the Israel government has been and continues to be peace. It is peace, not only for the world, but also between us and our neighbours. We believe in coexistence and cooperation everywhere and we shall do everything in our power towards that end ...

Despite all the speeches which we have heard from Arab representatives, we are convinced that for us and for our neighbours the day must come when we shall live in amity and cooperation. Then will the entire Middle East become a region where the tens of millions of people will dwell in peace and then will its economic potentialities and rich cultural heritage achieve fulfilment. This Israel believes and towards this end we shall devote all our efforts.

Document 37

*Fayez A. Sayegh: Zionist Colonialism
in Palestine*

This statement is from a booklet published in Beirut in 1965 by a
leading spokesman of the Palestinian refugees maintaining that the
Liberation of Palestine from the Zionist usurpers was the only
possible solution of the problem.

*

In 1948 the Palestinian Arab people was forcibly dispossessed.
Most Palestinians were evicted from their country. Their un-
yielding resistance and their costly sacrifices over three decades
had failed to avert the national catastrophe.

But those sacrifices were not in vain. For they safeguarded
the Palestinian national rights and underscored the legitimacy
of the Arabs' claim to their national heritage. Rights unde-
fended are rights surrendered. Unopposed and acquiesced in,
usurpation is legitimized by default. For forfeiture of its patri-
mony, the Palestinian generation of the inter-war era will be
indicted by the Palestinian generations to come. It lost indeed –
but not without fighting. It was dislodged indeed – but not for
want of the will to defend its heritage.

Nor has the people of Palestine retroactively bestowed un-
deserved legitimacy upon the Zionist colonization of Palestine
by recognizing the *fait accompli* after the fact. Many have been
the self-appointed counsellors of 'realism', urging upon Palestinians acknowledgement of the new *status quo* in Palestine
and acceptance of their exile 'in good grace'; and many have
been the lucrative offers of economic aid for 'resettlement' and
'rehabilitation' outside Palestine. But the people which had
remained for thirty years undaunted by the combined power
of British Imperialism and Zionist Colonialism, and which subsequently refused to allow the seizure of its land and the
dispersal of its body to conquer its soul, also knew very well
how to resist those siren-calls.

The Zionist settler-state, therefore, has remained a usurper, lacking even the semblance of legitimacy – because the people of Palestine has remained loyal to its heritage and faithful to its rights . . .

The people of Palestine, notwithstanding all its travails and misfortunes, still has undiminished faith in its future.

And the people of Palestine knows that the pathway to that future is the liberation of its homeland.

It was in this belief that the Palestinian people – after sixteen years of dispersion and exile, during which it had reposed its faith in its return to its country in world conscience and international public opinion, in the United Nations, and/or in the Arab states – chose at last to seize the initiative. In 1964, it reasserted its corporate personality by creating the Palestine Liberation Organization.

Only in the liberation of Palestine, spearheaded by Palestinians prepared to pay the price, can the supreme sacrifices of past generations of Palestinians be vindicated, and the visions and hopes of living Palestinians be transformed into reality.

Documents 38–42

Towards the Third Round

The Arab–Israeli conflict again escalated with the Egyptian decision in mid May 1967 to concentrate troops in Sinai and the announcement that the Straits of Tiran would be closed to Israeli shipping. In his speech on 25 May Nasser said that 'under no circumstances' would he allow the Israeli flag to pass the Straits. On the day after: 'Recently we felt we are strong enough, that if we were to enter a battle with Israel, with God's help, we could triumph' (Document 39). On the 29th: 'The issue now at hand is not the Gulf of Aqaba but the rights of the Palestinian people' (Document 41). Meanwhile Hassanain Haykal, Egypt's leading spokesman, had explained (on 26 May – Document 40) why a war with Israel was inevitable. On 9 June, after the Egyptian defeat, Nasser announced his resignation (Document 42), but several hours after, following demonstrations in Cairo, withdrew it. The summing up of the war and its pre-history as Nasser saw it appears in Part 4 of this Reader (page 237).

Document 38

Nasser's Speech at UAR Advanced Air Headquarters,
25 May 1967

The entire country looks up to you today. The entire Arab
nation supports you. It is clear that in these circumstances the
entire people support you completely and consider the armed
forces as their hope today. It is also a fact that the entire Arab
nation supports our armed forces in the current situation
through which the entire Arab nation is passing.

What I wish to say is that we are now in 1967 and not in
1956 after the tripartite aggression. A great deal was said then
and all the secrets revealed had a double interpretation. Israel,
its commanders and rulers, boasted a great deal after 1956. I
have read every word written about the 1956 events and I also
know exactly what happened in 1956.

On the night of 29 October 1956 the Israeli aggression against
us began. Fighting began on 30 October. We received the Anglo-
French ultimatum which asked us to withdraw several miles
west of the Suez Canal. On 31 October the Anglo-French attack
on us began. The air raids began at sunset on 31 October. At
the same time all our forces in Sinai were withdrawn completely to inside Egypt.

Thus in 1956 we did not have an opportunity to fight Israel.
We decided to withdraw before the actual fighting with Israel
began. Despite our decision to withdraw Israel was unable to
occupy any of our positions except after we left them. Yet
Israel created a major uproar, boasted and said a great deal
about the Sinai campaign and the Sinai battle. Everyone of
you knows all the rubbish that was said. They probably believed what they said themselves.

Today, more than ten years after Suez, all the secrets have
been exposed. The most important secret concerns when they
brought Ben Gurion to France to employ him as a dog for
imperialism, to begin the operation. Ben Gurion refused to
undertake anything unless he was given a written guarantee

that they would protect him from the Egyptian bombers and the Egyptian Air Force. All this is now no longer secret. The entire world knows. It was on this basis that France sent fighter aircraft to Ben Gurion, and it was also on this basis that Britain pledged to Ben Gurion to bomb Egyptian airfields within twenty-four hours after the aggression began.

This goes to show how much they took into account the Egyptian forces. Ben Gurion himself said he had to think about the Haifa–Jerusalem–Tel Aviv triangle, which holds one third of Israel's population. He could not attack Egypt out of fear of the Egyptian Air Force and bombers. At that time we had a few Ilyushin bombers. We had just acquired them to arm ourselves. Today we have many Ilyushins and other aircraft. There is a great difference between yesterday and today, between 1956 and 1967. Why do I say all this? I say it because we are in a confrontation with Israel. Israel today is not backed by Britain and France as was the case in 1956. It has the United States supporting it and supplying it with arms. But the world cannot again accept the plotting which took place in 1956.

Israel has been clamouring since 1956. They spoke of Israel's competence and high standard of training. It was backed in this by the West and the Western press. They capitalized on the Sinai campaign where no fighting actually took place because we withdrew to confront Britain and France.

Today we have a chance to prove the fact. We have, indeed, a chance to make the world see matters in their true perspective. We are now face to face with Israel. In recent days Israel has been making aggressive threats and boasting. On 12 May a very impertinent statement was made. Anyone reading this statement must believe that these people are so boastful and deceitful that one simply cannot remain silent. The statement said that the Israeli commanders announced they would carry out military operations against Syria in order to occupy Damascus and overthrow the Syrian government. On the same day the Israeli Premier, Eshkol, made a very threatening statement against Syria. At the same time the commentaries said that Israel believed that Egypt could not make a move because it was bogged down in Yemen.

Of course they say that we are bogged down in Yemen and have problems there. We are in Yemen but they seem to have believed the lies they have been saying all these years about our being in Yemen. It is very possible that the Israelis themselves believed such lies. We are capable of carrying out our duties in Yemen and at the same time doing our national duty here in Egypt, both in defending our borders and in attacking if Israel attacks any Arab country.

On 13 May we received accurate information that Israel was concentrating on the Syrian border huge armed forces of about 11 to 13 brigades. These forces were divided into two fronts, one south of Lake Tiberias and the other north of the Lake. The decision made by Israel at this time was to carry out an attack against Syria starting on 17 May. On 14 May we took action, discussed the matter and contacted our Syrian brothers. The Syrians also had this information. Based on the information Lt-Gen. Mahmud Fawzi left for Syria to coordinate matters. We told them that we had decided that if Syria was attacked Egypt would enter the battle right from the start. This was the situation on 14 May; forces began to move in the direction of Sinai to take up their normal positions.

News agencies reported yesterday that these military movements must have been the result of a previously well laid plan. I say that the sequence of events determined the plan. We had no plan prior to 13 May because we believed that Israel would not have dared to make such an impertinent statement.

On 16 May we requested the withdrawal of the United Nations Emergency Force [UNEF] in a letter from Lt-Gen. Mahmud Fawzi. We requested the complete withdrawal of the UNEF. A major worldwide campaign, led by the United States, Britain and Canada, began opposing the withdrawal of the UNEF from Egypt. Thus we felt that attempts were being made to turn the UNEF into a force serving neo-imperialism. It is obvious that the UNEF entered Egypt with our approval and therefore cannot continue to stay in Egypt except with our approval. Until yesterday a great deal was said about the UNEF. A campaign is also being mounted against the UN Secretary-General because he made a faithful and honest decision and could not surrender to the pressure brought to bear upon him by the United States, Britain and Canada to make the UNEF an instrument for implementing imperialism's plans.

It is quite natural, and I say this quite frankly, that had the UNEF ignored its basic task and turned to working for the aims of imperialism we would have regarded it as a hostile force and forcibly disarmed it. We are definitely capable of doing such a job. I say this now not to discredit the UNEF but to those who have neo-imperialist ideas and who want the UN to achieve their neo-imperialist aims – that there is not a single nation which respects itself and enjoys full sovereignty which could accept these methods in any shape or form. At the same time I say that the UNEF has honourably and faithfully carried out its duties. The UN Secretary-General refused to succumb to pressure. He issued immediate orders to the UNEF to withdraw. Consequently we praise the UNEF which has stayed ten years in our country serving peace. And when they left – at a time when we found that the neo-imperialist force wanted to divert them from their basic task – we gave them a cheerful send-off and saluted them.

Our forces are now in Sinai and we are fully mobilized both in Gaza and Sinai. We notice that there is a great deal of talk about peace these days. Peace, peace, international peace, international security, UN intervention, and so on and so forth, all appears daily in the press. Why is it that no one spoke about peace, the UN and security when on 12 May the Israeli premier and the Israeli commanders made their statements that they would occupy Damascus, overthrow the Syrian regime, strike vigorously at Syria, and occupy a part of Syria? It was obvious that the press approved of the statements made by the Israeli premier and commanders.

There is talk about peace now. What peace? If there is a true desire for peace we say that we also work for peace. But does peace mean ignoring the rights of the Palestinian people because of the passage of time? Does peace mean that we should concede our rights because of the passage of time? Nowadays they speak about a UN presence in the region for the sake of peace. Does a UN presence in the region for peace mean that we should close our eyes to everything? The UN has adopted a number of resolutions in favour of the Palestinian people. Israel has implemented none of these resolutions. This brought no reaction from the UN.

Today US Senators, members of the House of Representatives, the press and the entire world speak in favour of Israel, of the Jews. But nothing is said in the Arabs' favour. The UN resolutions which favour the Arabs have not been implemented. What does this mean? No one is speaking in the Arabs' favour. How does the UN stand with regard to the Palestinian people? How does it stand with regard to the rights of the Palestinian people? How does it stand with regard to the tragedy which has continued since 1948? Talk of peace is heard only when Israel is in danger. But when Arab rights and the rights of the Palestinian people are lost, no one speaks about peace, rights, or anything like this.

It is clear, therefore, that an alliance exists between the Western powers, chiefly represented by the United States and Britain, with Israel. There is a political alliance. This political alliance prompts the Western powers to give military equipment to Israel. Yesterday and the day before yesterday the entire world was speaking about Sharm al-Shaikh, navigation in the Gulf of Aqaba, and Eilat Port. This morning I heard the BBC say that in 1956 Abdel Nasser promised to open the Gulf of Aqaba.

Of course, this is not true. It was copied from a British paper called the *Daily Mail*. No such thing happened. Abdel Nasser would never forfeit any UAR right. As I said, we would never give away a grain of sand from our soil or our country.

The armed forces' responsibility is now yours. The armed forces yesterday occupied Sharm al-Shaikh. What does this mean? It is affirmation of our rights and our sovereignty over the Gulf of Aqaba, which constitutes Egyptian territorial waters. Under no circumstances will we allow the Israeli flag to pass through the Gulf of Aqaba.

The Jews threaten war. We tell them you are welcome, we

are ready for war. Our armed forces and all our people are
ready for war, but under no circumstances will we abandon
any of our rights. This water is ours. War might be an opportunity for the Jews, for Israel and Rabin, to test their forces
against ours and to see that what they wrote about the 1956
battle and the occupation of Sinai was all a lot of nonsense.

With all this there is imperialism, Israel and reaction. Reaction casts doubt on everything and so does the Islamic
alliance. We all know that the Islamic alliance is now represented by three states: the kingdom of Saudi Arabia, the
kingdom of Jordan and Iran. They are saying that the purpose
of the Islamic alliance is to reunite the Muslim against Israel.
I would like the Islamic alliance to serve the Palestine question
in only one way – by preventing the supply of oil to Israel. The
oil which now reaches Israel, which reaches Eilat, comes from
some of the Islamic alliance states. It goes to Eilat from Iran.
Who then is supplying Israel with oil? The Islamic alliance –
Iran, an Islamic alliance state. Such is the Islamic alliance. It
is an imperialist alliance and this means it sides with Zionism
because Zionism is the main ally of imperialism.

The Arab world, which is now mobilized to the highest
degree, knows all this. It knows how to deal with the imperialist agents, the allies of Zionism and the fifth column.

They say they want to coordinate their plans with us. We
cannot coordinate our plans in any way with Islamic alliance
members because it would mean giving our plans to the Jews
and to Israel. This is a vital battle. When we said that we were
ready for the battle we meant that we would surely fight if
Syria or any other Arab state was subjected to aggression.

The armed forces are now everywhere. The army and all the
forces are now mobilized and so are the people. They are all
behind you, praying for you day and night and believing that
you are the pride of their nation, of the Arab nation. This is
the feeling of the Arab people in Egypt and outside Egypt. We
are confident that you will honour the trust. Everyone of us is
ready to die and not give away a grain of his country's sand.
This for us is the greatest honour. It is the greatest honour for
us to defend our country. We are not scared by the imperialist,

Zionist or reactionary campaigns. We are independent and we know the taste of freedom. We have built a strong national army and achieved our aims. We are building our country. There is currently a propaganda campaign, a psychological campaign, and a campaign of doubt against us. We leave all this behind us and follow the course of duty and victory. May God be with you.

Document 39

Nasser's Speech to Arab Trade Unionists, 26 May 1967

Thank you for this initiative. You have provided me with an opportunity to see you. I have actually heard your speeches and resolutions, there is nothing to add during this meeting to what you have already said. You, the Arab workers' federations, represent the biggest force in the Arab world.

We can achieve much by Arab action, which is a main part of our battle. We must develop and build our countries to face the challenge of our enemies. The Arab world now is very different from what it was ten days ago. Israel is also different from what it was ten days ago. Despair has never found its way into Arab hearts and never will. The Arabs insist on their rights and are determined to regain the rights of the Palestinian people. The Arabs must accomplish this set intention and this aim. The first elements of this aim appeared in the test of Syria and Egypt in facing the Israeli threat. I believe that this test was a major starting point and basis from which to achieve complete cohesion in the Arab world. What we see today in the masses of the Arab people everywhere is their desire to fight. The Arab people want to regain the rights of the people of Palestine.

For several years, many people have raised doubts about our intentions towards Palestine. But talk is easy and action is difficult, very difficult. We emerged wounded from the 1956 battle. Britain, Israel and France attacked us then. We sustained heavy losses in 1956. Later, union was achieved. The 1961 secession occurred when we had only just got completely together and had barely begun to stand firmly on our feet.

Later the Yemeni revolution broke out. We considered it our duty to rescue our brothers, simply because of the principles and ideals which we advocated and still advocate.

We were waiting for the day when we would be fully prepared and confident of being able to adopt strong measures if we were to enter the battle with Israel. I say nothing aimlessly. One day two years ago, I stood up to say that we have no plan to liberate Palestine and that revolutionary action is our only course to liberate Palestine. I spoke at the summit conferences. The summit conferences were meant to prepare the Arab states to defend themselves.

Recently we felt we are strong enough, that if we were to enter a battle with Israel, with God's help, we could triumph. On this basis, we decided to take actual steps.

A great deal has been said in the past about the UN Emergency Force [UNEF]. Many people blamed us for UNEF's presence. We were not strong enough. Should we have listened to them, or rather built and trained our Army while UNEF still existed? I said once that we could tell UNEF to leave within half an hour. Once we were fully prepared we could ask UNEF to leave. And this is what actually happened.

The same thing happened with regard to Sharm al-Shaikh. We were also attacked on this score by some Arabs. Taking Sharm al-Shaikh meant confrontation with Israel. Taking such action also meant that we were ready to enter a general war with Israel. It was not a separate operation. Therefore we had to take this fact into consideration when moving to Sharm al-Shaikh. The present operation was mounted on this basis.

Actually I was authorized by the [Arab Socialist Union's] Supreme Executive Committee to implement this plan at the right time. The right time came when Syria was threatened with aggression. We sent reconnaissance aircraft over Israel. Not a single brigade was stationed opposite us on the Israeli side of the border. All Israeli brigades were confronting Syria. All but four brigades have now moved south to confront Egypt.

Those four are still on the border with Syria. We are confident
that once we have entered the battle we will triumph, God
willing.

With regard to military plans, there is complete coordination of military action between us and Syria. We will operate
as one army fighting a single battle for the sake of a common
objective – the objective of the Arab nation.

The problem today is not just Israel, but also those behind it.
If Israel embarks on an aggression against Syria or Egypt the
battle against Israel will be a general one and not confined to
one spot on the Syrian or Egyptian borders. The battle will be
a general one and our basic objective will be to destroy Israel.
I probably could not have said such things five or even three
years ago. If I had said such things and had been unable to
carry them out my words would have been empty and worthless.

Today, some eleven years after 1956, I say such things because I am confident. I know what we have here in Egypt and
what Syria has. I also know that other states – Iraq, for instance,
has sent its troops to Syria; Algeria will send troops; Kuwait
also will send troops. They will send armoured and infantry
units. This is Arab power. This is the true resurrection of the
Arab nation, which at one time was probably in despair.

Today people must know the reality of the Arab world. What
is Israel? Israel today is the United States. The United States is
the chief defender of Israel. As for Britain, I consider it America's lackey. Britain does not have an independent policy. Wilson
always follows Johnson's steps and says what he wants him to
say. All Western countries take Israel's view.

The Gulf of Aqaba was a closed waterway prior to 1956.
We used to search British, US, French and all other ships. After
the tripartite aggression – and we all know the tripartite plot
– we left the area to UNEF which came here under a UN resolution to make possible the withdrawal of Britain, France and
Israel. The Israelis say they opened the maritime route. I say
they told lies and believed their own lies. We withdrew because
the British and the French attacked us. This battle was never
between us and Israel alone.

I have recently been with the armed forces. All the armed forces are ready for a battle face to face between the Arabs and Israel. Those behind Israel are also welcome.

We must know and learn a big lesson today. We must actually see that in its hypocrisy and in its talks with the Arabs, the United States sides with Israel 100 per cent and is partial in favour of Israel. Why is Britain biased towards Israel? The West is on Israel's side. General de Gaulle's personality caused him to remain impartial on this question and not to toe the US or the British line; France therefore did not take sides with Israel.

The Soviet Union's attitude was great and splendid. It supported the Arabs and the Arab nation. It went to the extent of stating that, together with the Arabs and the Arab nation, it would resist any interference or aggression.

Today every Arab knows foes and friends. If we do not learn who our enemies and our friends are, Israel will always be able to benefit from this behaviour. It is clear that the United States is an enemy of the Arab because it is completely biased in favour of Israel. It is also clear that Britain is an enemy of the Arabs because she, too, is completely biased in favour of Israel. On this basis we must treat our enemies and those who side with our enemies as our actual enemies. We can accord them such treatment. In fact we are not states without status. We are states of status, occupying an important place in the world. Our states have thousands of years of civilization behind them – 7,000 years of civilization. Indeed, we can do much; we can expose the hypocrisy – the hypocrisy of our enemies if they try to persuade us that they wish to serve our interests. The United States seeks to serve only Israel's interests. Britain also seeks to serve only Israel's interests.

The question is not one of international law. Why all this uproar because of the closure of the Gulf of Aqaba? When Eshkol and Rabin threatened Syria, nobody spoke about peace or threats to peace. They actually hate the progressive regime in Syria. The United States, Britain and reaction – which is the friend of the United States and Britain – do not favour the national progressive regime in Syria. Israel, of course, shares their feelings. Israel is an ally of the United States and Britain. When Israel threatened Syria, they kept quiet and accepted what it said. But when we exercise one of our legitimate rights, as we always do, they turn the world upside down and speak about threats to peace and about a crisis in the Middle East. They fabricate these matters and threaten us with war.

We shall not relinquish our rights. We shall not concede our right in the Gulf of Aqaba. Today, the people of Egypt, the Syrian Army, and the Egyptian Army comprise one front. We want the entire front surrounding Israel to become one front. We want this. Naturally there are obstacles at present. Of course, Wasfi al-Tall is a spy for the Americans and the British. We cannot cooperate with these spies in any form, because the battle is one of destiny and the spies have no place in this battle. We want the front to become one united front around Israel. We will not relinquish the rights of the people of Palestine, as I have said before. I was told at the time that I might have to wait seventy years. During the crusaders' occupation, the Arabs waited seventy years before a suitable opportunity arose and they drove away the crusaders. Some people commented that Abdel Nasser said we should shelve the Palestinian question for seventy years. I do not mean exactly seventy years, but I say that as a people with an ancient civilization, as an Arab people, we are determined that the Palestine question will not be liquidated or forgotten. The whole question, then, is the proper time to achieve our aims. We are preparing ourselves constantly.

You are the hope of the Arab nation and its vanguard. As workers, you are actually building the Arab nation. The quicker we build, the quicker we will be able to achieve our aim. I thank you for your visit and wish you every success. Please convey my greetings and best wishes to the Arab workers in every Arab country.

Document 40

Hassanain Haykal : An Armed Clash with Israel
Is Inevitable – Why?

(From *Al Ahram*, 26 May 1967)

It is extremely difficult to write about current events, particularly when such events are as swift and violent as a hurricane.
But it is easy to write about what has already happened, to
give an account and analysis of facts. It is also safe to write
about what could take place in the future, because the future
is boundless. Tomorrow never comes because every day has a
tomorrow. The real problem is to speak about what is taking
place while it happens. Then every interpretation may endure
only a few minutes or even seconds.

There are two considerations which make the problem even
more difficult: the topic is one of destiny and life, and there is
the need for rational, intelligent writing without indulging in a
long composition or platitudes.

What I am going to say after this introduction will in fact
be no more than a collection of observations which I think are
important at present. The first observation is that I believe an
armed clash between the UAR and Israel is inevitable. This
armed clash could occur at any moment, at any place along
the line of confrontation between the Egyptian forces and the
enemy Israeli forces – on land, air or sea along the area extending from Gaza in the North to the Gulf of Aqaba at Sharm
al-Shaikh in the South. But why do I emphasize this in such
a manner? There are many reasons, particularly the psychological factor and its effect on the balance of power in the
Middle East.

Passage through the Gulf of Aqaba is economically important to Israel at a time when it is suffering the symptoms a man
has on waking up after a long, boisterous and drunken party.
The fountains of German reparations are drying up. Israel has
also drained the sources of contributions and gifts. Although
emergency sources will emerge as a result of the present crisis,

particularly with the help of Western propaganda trumpets, people in the West, at least many of them, are getting tired of an entity which has been unable to lead a normal life, like a child who does not want to grow up, who cannot depend on himself and does not want to take on any responsibility. Israel is suffering from an economic crisis. There are over 100,000 unemployed, nearly one quarter of Israel's manpower. The new blow had added to the economic plight. Israel attached great importance to its trade with East Africa and Asia. This trade depended on one route : the Red Sea via the Gulf of Aqaba, to Eilat. There were many projects for enlarging the port of Eilat, which at present can handle 400,000 tons a year. In addition, there were the oil lines. Israel has built two pipelines to carry Iranian oil from Eilat to the Haifa oil refinery. Israel has also dreamed of digging a canal from Eilat to Ashdod to compete with or replace the Suez Canal.

In my personal opinion all these important economic matters and questions are not the decisive factor which will influence or dictate the Israeli reaction to the closure of the Gulf of Aqaba. The decisive factor in my opinion is the psychological factor. The economic aspect swings back and forth between yes and no. From this aspect the challenge of war can be either accepted or put off. But the psychological factor cannot swing back and forth. From this aspect there is one answer : Yes. It is in the light of the compelling psychological factor that the needs of security, of survival itself, make acceptance of the challenge of war inevitable.

One thing is clear : The closure of the Gulf of Aqaba to Israeli navigation and the ban on the import of strategic goods, even when carried by non-Israeli ships, means first and last that the Arab nation represented by the UAR has succeeded for the first time, *vis-à-vis* Israel, in changing by force a *fait accompli* imposed on it by force. This is the essence of the problem, regardless of the complications surrounding it and future contingencies.

As for the complications, we can find in the past ample justification for Arab resistance. We could say that the British Mandate in Palestine had sold Palestine to Zionism in accordance with a resolution adopted by the League of Nations. This is true. We could say that the UN betrayed Palestine, and this is true. We could say Arab reaction from the Jordanian King Abdullah to the Saudi King Faisal connived at the plot against Palestine, and this is true. We could say about the Gulf of Aqaba that in 1956 imperialism, represented by the British and French forces, imposed a *fait accompli* during this period from autumn 1956 to spring 1967. It was imperialist not Israeli arms which imposed this *fait accompli*. We could say all this is seeking to justify Arab resistance. But the naked and rocky truth which remains after all this is that the accomplished fact was aggressively imposed by force. The Arabs did not have the force to resist the accomplished fact, let alone to change it by force and to impose a substitute consistent with their rights and interests.

As for the contingencies which may be precipitated by this new development, I do not think I need go into detail.

Israel has built its existence, security and future on force. The prevalent philosophy of its rulers has been that the Arab quakes before the forbidding glance, and that nothing deters him but fear. Thus Israeli intimidation reached its peak. Provocation went beyond tolerable bounds. But all of this, from the Israeli point of view, had the psychological aim of convincing the Arabs that Israel could do anything and that the Arabs could do nothing; that Israel was omnipotent and could impose any accomplished fact, while the Arabs were weak and had to accept any accomplished fact. Despite the error and danger in this Israeli philosophy – because two or even three million Israelis cannot by military force or by myth dominate a sea of eighty million Arabs – this philosophy remained a conviction deeply embedded in Israeli thinking, planning and action for many disturbing years, without any Arab challenge capable of restoring matters to their proper perspective.

Now this is the first time the Arabs have challenged Israel in an attempt to change an accomplished fact by force and to replace it by force with an alternative accomplished fact consistent with their rights and interests. The opening of the Gulf of Aqaba to Israel was an accomplished fact imposed by the force of imperialist arms. This week the closure of the Gulf of Aqaba to Israel was an alternative accomplished fact imposed and now being protected by the force of Arab arms. To Israel this is the most dangerous aspect of the current situation.... Therefore it is not a matter of the Gulf of Aqaba but of something bigger. It is the whole philosophy of Israeli security. It is the philosophy on which Israeli existence has pivoted since its birth and on which it will pivot in the future.

Hence I say that Israel must resort to arms. Therefore I say that an armed clash between UAR and the Israeli enemy is inevitable.

As from now, we must expect the enemy to deal us the first blow in the battle. But as we wait for that first blow, we should try to minimize its effect as much as possible. The second blow will then follow. But this will be the blow we will deliver against the enemy in retaliation and deterrence. It will be the most effective blow we can possibly deal. Why do I say this now? My point of view is as follows:

When one studies the strategy of the Egyptian action of the ten great days from 14 to 23 May in which the positions and balance in the Middle East changed, one will immediately perceive two factors which at first sight may appear contradictory. The first factor: Egypt was ready and prepared. The second factor: the Egyptian action was a complete surprise, even to Egypt in so far as it was a reaction to a specific situation, namely, Israel's threat to and readiness to invade Syria.

By analysing the first factor in the strategy of the Egyptian action during the ten great days which changed the positions and balance in the Middle East we find that there are roots extending from the spring of 1967 back to the time when the UAR called for the Arab summit conferences. The first summit conference was convened in January 1964. The first item submitted by the UAR to that conference was the Jordan headwaters. At that time the anti-Egyptian Western propaganda which was backed by the reactionary elements sought, discreetly at times but most of the time shamelessly, to hamper Egyptian policy at that time by two propaganda themes: (1) that Egypt's whole aim in the summit conferences policy was to settle the Yemeni issue with Saudi Arabia; (2) that when Egypt called for the summit conferences it wanted to abandon the responsibility of action for Palestine, in accordance with the traditional method which says that when you face a problem for which you cannot find a solution the only way to bury and get rid of it is to form a commission to discuss and study it. All this, of course, was untrue, since Egypt at the time imagined that the Arab summit conferences could draw up the policy of the liberation battle and could prepare for it. Egypt wanted unified action to be the front of a broad movement which might have worldwide political influence serving the strategy of battle. Besides, unified Arab action might be beneficial in providing possibilities for defending Arab countries which at that time did not have reassuring defences. At the same time Egypt believed that when the time came for earnest action, loyalty and fidelity to the trust dictated that it should primarily depend on itself.

Accordingly the summit conferences were a broad front suitable for worldwide political influence. It was also possible for them to help strengthen the defence of Arab countries surrounding Israel. Behind this broad front and the consolidation of the other Arab countries surrounding Israel Egypt could prepare and mobilize its own effective forces.

The remainder of the story of the summit conferences is known and I do not propose to repeat it. It ended in utter failure because of Arab reactionary rancour, and because reaction had greater hatred for Arab social progress than for the Israeli enemy, which wants to humiliate all the Arabs whatever their social views. The broad front for unified Arab action therefore collapsed with the failure of the summit conferences. The possibilities of strengthening the defence of the other Arab countries surrounding Israel did not sufficiently materialize as they should have done. Egypt was unable to control all those circumstances but it was able to control the third objective, namely, to prepare and mobilize its effective forces.

Anti-Egyptian Western propaganda, backed by the Arab reactionary elements, continued to attack Egypt fiercely. The attack went to the length of spreading the belief that the entire

Egyptian Army had perished in Yemen, had been scattered into aimless groups, and that the remainder had been killed, wounded or captured. Similarly it was said that the Egyptian economy was collapsing and could not stand on its feet, let alone bear the weight of any bold venture and carry on with it. But Egypt knew the truth and was confident that the truth would appear to the entire Arab nation one day when the time was ripe for serious action.

Egypt, then, was prepared and ready. This is the first fact about the strategy of Egyptian action during the ten great days.

I will now come to the second factor in the crisis. This factor is that the Egyptian action was a complete surprise. It appears, and it is now almost certain, that the forces hostile to Egypt, that is imperialism, Arab reaction and Israel, had come in the end to believe their own propaganda. People sometimes fall prey to the lies they themselves fabricate. Something of that sort must certainly have happened, otherwise Israel would not have persisted in its threats against Syria and gone to the length of the cry of 'March on Damascus'. It must have felt certain that there would be no decisive Egyptian reaction, because there were insufficient forces for any initiative or retaliatory action.

It was this Israeli threat to Syria and information confirming it concerning intentions and plans that precipitated the emergency situation to which Egypt had to react immediately, even though it came as a surprise to it. There was preparation and mobilization of the effective Egyptian forces. There was national consciousness and abidance by its principles. There was creative leadership. What I meant to say is that Egypt was not prepared for this specific contingency but was prepared for all contingencies, including such a one.

Now, to turn to the march of events during the ten great days which changed the situation and the balance of the Middle East. Events began to move. One calculated and effective step followed another: the decision was taken to implement the joint defence agreement with Syria – this is the decision which Lt-Gen Mahmud Fawzi, the Chief of Staff of the Egyptian Armed Forces, carried on the five-hour visit to Damascus. Then

followed the message addressed by Lt-Gen. Mahmud Fawzi
to the Commander of the UN Emergency Force to withdraw his
forces from the Egyptian borders with Israel. The Egyptian
Armed Forces then, without waiting, actually began occupying all the border positions. The Foreign Minister Mahmud
Riyad then sent his message to the UN Secretary-General U
Thant on the withdrawal and evacuation of the Emergency
Forces in the UAR and Gaza. Then followed the advance on
Sharm al-Shaikh, the entrance to the Gulf of Aqaba; the order
was issued to close the Gulf of Aqaba to Israeli shipping and to
strategic goods for Israel even if transported aboard non-Israeli
ships ; and all the US initiatives were rejected. All these actions
were backed by a massive, ready force enjoying a morale brim-
ming over with a fighting spirit the like of which the Middle
East has never seen.

Two results were thus achieved, that is to say : (1) The plan
against Syria collapsed; the invasion of Syria became impossible because all of the enemy forces streamed into the South
to confront the Egyptian concentration. (2) The accomplished
fact, which the British-French invasion, and not the Israeli
Army, had imposed in 1956 to the benefit of Israel, was changed.

In other words the strategy of this stage achieved its first objective by frustrating the plot to invade Syria, and, moveover,
it achieved another longed-for and precious objective: the return of the armed forces to direct confrontation wich Israel
and the closing once again of the door to the Gulf of Aqaba in
Israel's face.

Is this, then, the end of the matter? I would answer that I
have explained – or rather tried to explain – with the first
observation in this inquiry that the problem has not ended but
rather has hardly begun. This is because I am confident that
for many reasons, chiefly the psychological, Israel cannot
accept or remain indifferent to what has taken place. In my
opinion it simply cannot do so. This means, and that is what I
intend to say in the second observation of this inquiry, that the
next move is up to Israel. Israel has to reply now. It has to deal
a blow. We have to be ready for it, as I said, to minimize its
effect as much as possible. Then it will be our turn to deal the

second blow, which we will deliver with the utmost possible effectiveness.

In short, Egypt has exercised its power and achieved the objectives of this stage without resorting to arms so far. But Israel has no alternative but to use arms if it wants to exercise power. This means that the logic of the fearful confrontation now taking place between Egypt, which is fortified by the might of the masses of the Arab nation, and Israel, which is fortified by the illusion of American might, dictates that Egypt after all it has now succeeded in achieving must wait, even though it has to wait for a blow. This is necessitated also by the sound conduct of the battle, particularly from the international point of view. Let Israel begin. Let our second blow then be ready. Let it be a knockout.

Document 41

Gamal Abdel Nasser:
Speech to National Assembly Members
on 29 May 1967

Brothers, when Brother Anwar as-Sadat informed me of your decision to meet me I told him that I myself was prepared to call on you at the National Assembly, but he said you were determined to come. I therefore responded to this and I thank you heartily for your consideration.

I was naturally not surprised by the law which Brother Anwar as-Sadat read because I was notified of it before I came here. However, I wish to thank you very much for your feelings and for the powers given me. I did not ask for such powers because I felt that you and I were as one, that we could cooperate and work for the sublime interest of this country, giving a great example of unselfishness and of work for the welfare of all. Thanks be to God, for four years now the National Assembly has been working and has given great examples. We have given great examples in cooperation and unselfishness and in placing before us the sublime and highest objective – the interest of this nation.

I am proud of this resolution and law. I promise you that I
will use it only when necessary. I will, however, send all the
laws to you. Thank you once again. The great gesture of moral
support represented by this law is very valuable to my spirit
and heart. I heartily thank you for this feeling and this initia
tive.

The circumstances through which we are now passing are
in fact difficult ones because we are not only confronting Israel
but also those who created Israel and who are behind Israel.
We are confronting Israel and the West as well – the West,
which created Israel and which despised us Arabs and which
ignored us before and since 1948. They had no regard whatsoever for our feelings, our hopes in life, or our rights. The West
completely ignored us, and the Arab nation was unable to
check the West's course.

Then came the events of 1956 – the Suez battle. We all know
what happened in 1956. When we rose to demand our rights.
Britain, France and Israel opposed us, and we were faced with
the tripartite aggression. We resisted, however, and proclaimed
that we would fight to the last drop of our blood. God gave us
success and God's victory was great.

Subsequently we were able to rise and to build. Now, eleven
years after 1956, we are restoring things to what they were in
1956. This is from the material aspect. In my opinion this material aspect is only a small part, whereas the spiritual aspect
is the great side of the issue. The spiritual aspect involves the
renaissance of the Arab nation, the revival of the Palestine
question, and the restoration of confidence to every Arab and
to every Palestinian. This is on the basis that if we are able to
restore conditions to what the were before 1956 God will surely
help and urge us to restore the situation to what it was in 1948.
[*prolonged applause.*]

Brothers, the revolt, upheaval and commotion which we
now see taking place in every Arab country are not only because we have returned to the Gulf of Aqaba or rid ourselves
of the UNEF, but because we have restored Arab honour and
renewed Arab hopes.

Israel used to boast a great deal, and the Western powers,

headed by the United States and Britain, used to ignore and even despise us and consider us of no value. But now that the time has come – and I have already said in the past that we will decide the time and place and not allow them to decide – we must be ready for triumph and not for a recurrence of the 1948 comedies. We shall triumph, God willing.

Preparations have already been made. We are now ready to confront Israel. They have claimed many things about the 1956 Suez war, but no one believed them after the secrets of the 1956 collusion were uncovered – that mean collusion in which Israel took part. Now we are ready for the confrontation. We are now ready to deal with the entire Palestine question.

The issue now at hand is not the Gulf of Aqaba, the Straits of Tiran, or the withdrawal of the UNEF, but the rights of the Palestine people. It is the aggression which took place in Palestine in 1948 with the collaboration of Britain and the United States. It is the expulsion of the Arabs from Palestine, the usurpation of their rights, and the plunder of their property. It is the disavowal of all the UN resolutions in favour of the Palestinian people.

The issue today is far more serious than they say. They want to confine the issue to the Straits of Tiran, the UNEF and the right of passage. We demand the full rights of the Palestinian people. We say this out of our belief that Arab rights cannot be squandered because the Arabs throughout the Arab world are demanding these Arab rights.

We are not afraid of the United States and its threats, of Britain and her threats, or of the entire Western world and its partiality to Israel. The United States and Britain are partial to Israel and give no consideration to the Arabs, to the entire Arab nation. Why? Because we have made them believe that we cannot distinguish between friend and foe. We must make them know that we know who our foes are and who our friends are and treat them accordingly.

If the United States and Britain are partial to Israel, we must say that our enemy is not only Israel but also the United States and Britain and treat them as such. If the Western Powers disavow our rights and ridicule and despise us, we Arabs must teach them to respect us and take us seriously. Otherwise all our talk about Palestine, the Palestine people, and Palestinian rights will be null and void and of no consequence. We must treat enemies as enemies and friends as friends.

I said yesterday that the States that champion freedom and peace have supported us. I spoke of the support given us by India, Pakistan, Afghanistan, Yugoslavia, Malaysia, the Chinese People's Republic and the Asian and African States.

After my statements yesterday I met the War Minister Shams Badran and learned from him what took place in Moscow. I wish to tell you today that the Soviet Union is a friendly Power and stands by us as a friend. In all our dealings with the Soviet Union – and I have been dealing with the USSR since 1955 – it has not made a single request of us. The USSR has never interfered in our policy or internal affairs. This is the USSR as we have always known it. In fact, it is we who have made urgent requests of the USSR. Last year we asked for wheat and they sent it to us. When I also asked for all kinds of arms they gave them to us. When I met Shams Badran yesterday he handed me a message from the Soviet Premier Kosygin saying that the USSR supported us in this battle and would not allow any Power to intervene until matters were restored to what they were in 1956.

Brothers, we must distinguish between friend and foe, friend and hypocrite. We must be able to tell who is making requests, who has ulterior motives and who is applying economic pressure. We must also know those who offer their friendship to us for no other reason than a desire for freedom and peace.

In the name of the UAR people, I thank the people of the USSR for their great attitude which is the attitude of a real friend. This is the kind of attitude we expect. I said yesterday that we had not requested the USSR or any other state to intervene, because we really want to avoid any confrontation which might lead to a world war and also because we really work for peace and advocate world peace. When we voiced the policy of non-alignment, our chief aim was world peace.

Brothers, we will work for world peace with all the power at our disposal, but we will also hold tenaciously to our rights with all the power at our disposal. This is our course. On this occasion, I address myself to our brothers in Aden and say: Although occupied with this battle, we have not forgotten you. We are with you. We have not forgotten the struggle of Aden and the occupied South for liberation. Aden and the occupied South must be liberated and colonialism must end. We are with them; present matters have not taken our minds from Aden.

I thank you for taking the trouble to pay this visit. Moreover, your presence is an honour to the Qubbah Palace, and I am pleased to have met you. Peace be with you.

Document 42

Gamal Abdel Nasser: Resignation Broadcast,
9 June 1967

Brothers, at times of triumph and tribulation, in the sweet hours and bitter hours, we have become accustomed to sit together to discuss things, to speak frankly of facts, believing that only in this way can we always find the right path however difficult circumstances may be.

We cannot hide from ourselves the fact that we have met with a grave setback in the last few days, but I am confident that we all can and, in a short time, will overcome our difficult situation, although this calls for much patience and wisdom as well as moral courage and ability to work on our part. Before that, brothers, we need to cast a glance back over past events so that we shall be able to follow developments and the line of our march leading to the present conditions.

All of us know how the crisis started in the Middle East. At the beginning of last May there was an enemy plan for the invasion of Syria and the statements by his politicians and all his military leaders openly said so. There was plenty of evidence concerning the plan. Sources of our Syrian brothers were categorical on this and our own reliable information confirmed it. Add to this the fact that our friends in the Soviet Union warned the parliamentary delegation, which was on a visit to

Moscow, at the beginning of last month, that there was a pre-meditated plan against Syria. We considered it our duty not to accept this silently. This was the duty of Arab brotherhood, it was also the duty of national security. Whoever starts with Syria will finish with Egypt.

Our armed forces moved to our frontiers with a competence which the enemy acknowledged even before our friends. Several steps followed. There was the withdrawal of the United Nations Emergency Force and the return of our forces to the Sharm al-Shaikh post, the controlling point in the Straits of Tiran, which had been used by the Israeli enemy as one of the after-effects of the tripartite aggression against us in 1956. The enemy's flag passing in front of our forces was intolerable, apart from other reasons connected with the dearest aspirations of the Arab nation.

Accurate calculations were made of the enemy's strength and showed us that our armed forces, at the level of equipment and training which they had reached, were capable of repelling the enemy and deterring him. We realized that the possibility of an armed clash existed and accepted the risk.

Before us were several factors – national, Arab and international. A message from the US President Lyndon Johnson was handed to our Ambassador in Washington on 26 May asking us to show self-restraint and not to be the first to fire, or else we should have to face grave consequences. On the very same night, the Soviet Ambassador asked to have an urgent meeting with me at 05.30 [*as broadcast*] after midnight. He informed me of an urgent request from the Soviet government not to be the first to open fire.

In the morning of last Monday, 5 June, the enemy struck. If we say now it was a stronger blow than we had expected, we must say at the same time, and with complete certainty, that it was bigger than the potential at his disposal. It became very clear from the first moment that there were other powers behind the enemy – they came to settle their accounts with the Arab national movement. Indeed, there were surprises worthy of note:

(1) The enemy, whom we were expecting from the east and north, came from the west – a fact which clearly showed that facilities exceeding his own capacity and his calculated strength had been made available to him.

(2) The enemy covered at one go all military and civilian air-fields in the UAR. This means that he was relying on some force other than his own normal strength to protect his skies against any retaliatory action from our side. The enemy was also leaving other Arab fronts to be tackled with outside assistance which he had been able to obtain.

(3) There is clear evidence of imperialist collusion with the enemy – an imperialist collusion, trying to benefit from the lesson of the open collusion of 1956, by resorting this time to abject and wicked concealment. Nevertheless, what is now established is that American and British aircraft carriers were off the shores of the enemy helping his war effort. Also, British aircraft raided, in broad daylight, positions on the Syrian and Egyptian fronts, in addition to operations by a number of American aircraft reconnoitring some of our positions. The in-evitable result of this was that our land forces, fighting most violent and brave battles in the open desert, found themselves at the difficult time without adequate air cover in face of the decisive superiority of the enemy air forces. Indeed it can be said without emotion or exaggeration, that the enemy was operating with an air force three times stronger than his nor-mal force.

The same conditions were faced by the forces of the Jordan-ian Army, fighting a brave battle under the leadership of King Hussain who – let me say for the sake of truth and honesty – adopted an excellent stand; and I admit that my heart was bleeding while I was following the battles of his heroic Arab Army in Jerusalem and other parts of the West Bank on the night when the enemy and his plotting forces massed no less than 400 aircraft over the Jordanian front.

There were other honourable and marvellous efforts. The Algerian people, under their great leader Hawwari Boumedi-enne, gave without reservation and without stinting for the battle. The people of Iraq and their faithful leader Abdel Rahman Arif gave without reservation or stinting for the battle. The Syrian Army fought heroically, consolidated by the forces of the great Syrian people and under the leadership of their national government. The peoples and governments of Sudan, Kuwait, Yemen, Lebanon, Tunisia and Morocco adopted honourable stands. All the peoples of the Arab nation, without exception, adopted a stand of manhood and dignity all along the Arab homeland; a stand of resolution and determination that Arab right shall not be lost, shall not be humiliated, and that the war in its defence is advancing, regardless of sacrifice and setbacks, on the road of the sure and inevitable victory. There were also great nations outside the Arab homeland who gave us invaluable moral support.

But the plot, and we must say this with the courage of men, was bigger and fiercer. The enemy's main concentration was on the Egyptian front which he attacked with all his main force of armoured vehicles and infantry, supported by air supremacy the dimensions of which I have outlined for you. The nature of the desert did not permit a full defence, especially in face of the enemy's air supremacy. I realized that the armed battle might not go in our favour. I, with others, tried to use all sources of Arab strength. Arab oil came in to play its part. The Suez Canal came in to play its part. A great role is still reserved for general Arab action. I am fully confident that it will measure up to its task. Our Armed Forces in Sinai were obliged to evacuate the first line of defence. They fought fearful tank and air battles on the second line of defence.

We then responded to the cease-fire resolution, in view of assurances contained in the latest Soviet draft resolution, to the Security Council, as well as French statements to the effect that no one must reap any territorial expansion from the recent aggression, and in view of world public opinion, especially in Asia and Africa, which appreciates our position and feels the ugliness of the forces of international domination which pounced on us.

We now have several urgent tasks before us. The first is to remove the traces of this aggression against us and to stand by the Arab nation resolutely and firmly; despite the setback, the Arab nation, with all its potential and resources, is in a position to insist on the removal of the traces of the aggression.

The second task is to learn the lesson of the setback. In this connexion there are three vital facts : (1) The elimination of imperialism in the Arab world will leave Israel with its own intrinsic power; yet, whatever the circumstances, however long it may take, the Arab intrinsic power is greater and more effective. (2) Redirecting Arab interests in the service of Arab rights is an essential safeguard : the American Sixth Fleet moved with Arab oil, and there are Arab bases, placed forcibly and against the will of the peoples, in the service of aggression. (3) The situation now demands a united word from the entire Arab nation; this, in the present circumstances, is irreplaceable guarantee.

Now we arrive at an important point in this heart-searching by asking ourselves: does this mean that we do not bear responsibility for the consequences of the setback ? I tell you truthfully and despite any factors on which I might have based my attitude during the crisis, that I am ready to bear the whole responsibility. I have taken a decision in which I want you all to help me. I have decided to give up completely and finally every official post and every political role and return to the ranks of the masses and do my duty with them like every other citizen.

The forces of imperialism imagine that Gamal Abdel Nasser is their enemy. I want it to be clear to them that their enemy is the entire Arab nation, not just Gamal Abdel Nasser. The forces hostile to the Arab national movement try to portray this movement as an empire of Abdel Nasser. This is not true, because the aspiration for Arab unity began before Abdel Nasser and will remain after Abdel Nasser. I always used to tell you that the nation remains, and that the individual – whatever his role and however great his contribution to the causes of his homeland – is only a tool of the popular will, and not its creator.

In accordance with Article 110 of the Provisional Constitution promulgated in March 1964 I have entrusted my colleague, friend and brother Zakariya Muhiedin with taking over the post of President and carrying out the constitutional provisions on this point. After this decision, I place all I have at his disposal in dealing with the grave situation through which our people are passing.

In doing this I am not liquidating the revolution – indeed the revolution is not the monopoly of any one generation of revolutionaries. I take pride in the brothers of this generation of revolutionaries. It has brought to pass the evacuation of British imperialism, has won the independence of Egypt and defined its Arab personality, and has combated the policy of spheres of influence in the Arab world ; it has led the social revolution and created a deep transformation in the Egyptian reality by establishing the people's control over the sources of their wealth and the result of Arab action; it recovered the Suez Canal and laid down the foundation of industrial upsurge in Egypt; it built the High Dam to bring fertile greenness to the barren desert; it laid down a power network over the whole of the north of the Nile Valley; it made oil resources gush out after a long wait. More important still, it gave the leadership of political action to the alliance of the people's working forces, the constant source of renewed leaderships carrying the banners of Egyptian and Arab struggle through its successive stages, building socialism, succeeding and triumphing.

I have unlimited faith in this alliance as the leader of national action : the peasants, the workers, the soldiers, the intellectuals and national capital. Its unity and cohesion and creative response within the framework of this unity are capable of creating – through work, serious work, difficult work, as I have said more than once – colossal miracles for this country in order to be a strength for itself, for its Arab nation, for the movement of national revolution and for world peace based on justice.

The sacrifices made by our people and their burning spirit during the crisis and the glorious pages of heroism written by the officers and soldiers of our armed forces with their blood will remain an unquenchable torch in our history and a great inspiration for the future and its great hopes. The people were splendid as usual, noble as their nature, believing, sincere and loyal. The members of our armed forces were an honourable example of Arab man in every age and every place. They defended the grains of sand in the desert to the last drop of their blood. In the air, they were, despite enemy supremacy, legends of dedication and sacrifice, of courage and willingness to perform the duty in the best way.

This is an hour for action; not an hour for sorrow. It is a situation calling for ideals and not for selfishness or personal feelings. All my heart is with you, and I want all your hearts to be with me. May God be with us all, a hope in our hearts, a light and guidance. Peace and the blessing of God be with you.

Part 4

Views and Comments: The Arab–Israeli
Conflict Today and Tomorrow

This section of the Reader presents a selection of
Israeli and Arab views about the prospects of war
and peace in the Middle East as expressed
since the war of 1967, as well as the analysis and/or
the opinions of outside observers. Three wars in
twenty years have not brought a solution of the
conflict any nearer; a renewal of fighting at
some future date is again thought likely as no
substantial progress has been made in the attempts to
mediate between the two sides. There is, moreover,
the distinct danger of big power involvement, and,
as a result, the transformation of a local conflict
into a world crisis.

'The Most Severe Crisis': Nasser's Revolution Anniversary Speech at Cairo University, 23 July 1967*

Brother compatriots, the fifteenth anniversary of the revolution of 23 July 1952 comes while we are living through a crisis. We will not be exaggerating if we say that this is the most severe crisis we have faced in the history of our revolutionary work.

At no time has our work been easy. We have always had to face all kinds of political, economic and military dangers. Every victory we have achieved came after difficulties and hardships which we bore patiently.

To carry out the revolution of 23 July was not an easy job for our people after seventy years of British occupation. For seventy years the British, in collaboration with the feudalists and the capitalists, ruled this country with the backing of 80,000 British soldiers in the Suez Canal zone. Nor was our people's resistance to the policy of pacts and zones of influence which others tried to impose on us an easy job at a time when the national liberation movement had not attained the present level of independence and non-subservience.

Moreover, our people's acceptance of the challenge to build the High Dam was not an easy job in the face of the arrogance of the United States, which thought that by withdrawing a Western offer to finance the High Dam it could harm the Egyptian economy and reveal our people as incapable of assuming the responsibility of executing such a project, which is unequalled anywhere in the world. In fact by its arrogance the

---

* This speech was delivered on the fifteenth anniversary of the Egyptian revolution, on 23 July 1967 at Cairo University. It is the most detailed survey from the Arab point of view of the events leading to the Arab–Israeli war.

United States wanted our people to lose confidence in themselves and to overthrow our revolutionary regime.

Nor was our people's endurance of the horrors of the Suez war an easy job. In 1956 our people were attacked by three states, two of which were big powers. The aggression has utilized the base that imperialism had established in the heart of the Arab homeland to threaten and terrorize this homeland, once overtly and the second time covertly.

Our people's progress in the field of socialist reconstruction, self-reliance and justice and their attempt to increase national wealth through the enormous process of industrialization; reclamation of vast lands; electrification of the entire country; restoration of all foreign interests; elimination of monopolism, capitalism and feudalism; redistribution of land; provision for education, health and social security services; and the participation of the workers in the profits and administration of firms – all this, brothers, was not an easy job in this country where foreign and feudalist interests once dominated the national resources. It was not an easy job in the heart of this Arab world which was dominated by foreign and feudalist interests. Whatever happens in our country has its repercussions in our entire Arab world whether we like it or not.

Our people's acceptance of the responsibilities of Arab solidarity, the common struggle and of destiny was not an easy job. In exercising these responsibilities we resisted the attempt to invade Syria in 1957, accepted the consequences of unity and secession, supported the revolution in Iraq in 1958, supported the Algerian revolution from 1954 to 1962, and backed the Yemeni revolution and the revolution in South Arabia. The latest problem we have confronted and are still confronting is the attempt to invade Syria.

Brothers, our work has never been easy. The road of the struggle is strewn with dangers, the way to glory with sacrifices, and the way to great hopes with great sacrifices. Should the peoples fail to take this course they would face rigidity and backwardness. They would take no chances and would not face life – the sweet and bitter. Those who do not shoulder responsibilities have no right to entertain hopes. Those who do not take chances become the prisoner of fear itself because of their fear. This is not the quality of vigorous peoples; it is not their nature or their course.

I have said that the crisis we now face is one of the severest we have faced in the history of our revolutionary action for more than one reason. For one thing, this crisis which we are confronting, although it is not the gravest and most difficult we have faced, certainly marks the highest degree of hypocrisy and meanness we have encountered. Imperialism – we must admit this – has benefited from all its encounters with us and with the other peoples who have frequently been exposed to its assaults. This time imperialism did not face us overtly as it did in 1956. But imperialism made an effort – and we must admit that it was skilful – to conceal its role and hide its collusion. In the end perhaps imperialism left nothing to incriminate it but its fingerprints. But this is one thing and catching imperialism redhanded as we did in 1956 is something else.

For another thing, this is perhaps the first revolution anniversary that has found our homeland in the midst of a savage conspiracy. Despite their courage and insistence on confronting it, our people undoubtedly at the same time are experiencing deep sorrow and severe pain.

Brothers, perhaps Almighty God wanted to test us to judge whether we deserve what we have achieved, whether we are able to protect our achievements, and whether we have the courage to be patient and stand firm against affliction. Brothers, perhaps Almighty God also wanted to give us a lesson to teach us what we had not learned, to remind us of some things we might have forgotten, and to cleanse our souls of the blemishes that have affected us and the shortcomings that we must avoid [applause] as we build our new society. Whatever the Almighty's will may be, we accept His test as our destiny. We are fully confident that He is with us : He will protect our struggle should we set out to struggle; grant us victory if we be determined to triumph and open the road to justice to us; endow us with victory if we be determined to be the victor; and open the road of justice to us if we be able to place ourselves on His right path.

Brother compatriots, I do not want to take you back to the circumstances which paved the way to this crisis. I explained some of these circumstances to you in my address to the nation on 9 June right after the setback. Also I realize, and we must all realize, that what happened has happened and there is no use wailing over the debris. Now it is more important to learn the lesson, overcome the setback, rise above it, and proceed triumphantly on our road towards the achievement of our aspirations.

But I do believe that we must ponder certain important matters so that we may all be able to achieve the highest degree of clarity. The first thing which should be clear to us all is that it was we who started the crisis in the Middle East. We all know that this crisis began with Israel's attempt to invade Syria. It is quite clear to us all that in that attempt Israel was not working for itself alone but also for the forces which had got impatient with the Arab revolutionary movement.

The information we received about the invasion of Syria came from many sources. Our Syrian brothers had information that Israel had mobilized eighteen brigades on their front. We confirmed this information. It became evident to us that Israel had mobilized no less than thirteen brigades on the Syrian front. Our parliamentary delegation headed by Anwar as-Sadat was on a visit to Moscow, and our Soviet friends informed Anwar as-Sadat at that time that the invasion of Syria was imminent.

What were we to do? We could have remained silent, we could have waited, or we could have just issued statements and cables of support. But if this homeland had accepted such behaviour it would have meant that it was deserting its mission, its role and even its personality. There was a joint defence agreement between us and Syria. We do not consider our agreements with the peoples of our Arab nation or others merely ink on paper. To us these agreements are sacred, an honour and an obligation. Between us and Syria, between us and all Arab peoples there was and always will be something far greater and more lasting than agreements and treaties: faith in the common struggle and the common fate. Therefore it was imperative that we take concrete steps to face the danger threatening Syria, especially since the statements of Israeli political and military leaders at the time and their open threats to Syria – as reported in the press and frankly noted at the UN – left no room for anyone to doubt any information or to wait or hesitate.

The second question : when we decided to move, our actions led to certain practical results. First we asked for the withdrawal of the UN Emergency Force. Then we restored Egyptian sovereignty rights in the Gulf of Aqaba. This was one of the things our Arab brothers had always insisted on. It was natural that such steps had a great impact on the area and the world.

The third question : by moving and taking the initiative to repel the danger to Syria, we realized – particularly from an international point of view – that the question was whether we should strike first in an armed battle. Had we done this we would have exposed ourselves to very serious consequences, greater than we would have been able to tolerate. First we would have faced direct US military action against us on the pretext that we had fired the first bullet in the battle.

Here I should like to draw your attention to certain important points. The first is the US warnings. Perhaps you have read about these US warnings. President Johnson's adviser summoned our Ambassador in Washington at a late hour at night and told him that Israel had information that we were going to attack. The adviser said this would put us in a serious situation and urged us to exercise self-restraint. They also said they were telling Israel the same thing so that it would also exercise self-restraint. We also received messages from President Johnson referring to the UN and urging us to exercise self-restraint.

The second point – which perhaps I have discussed before – is that on the following day the Russian Ambassador asked to see me and conveyed to me a message from the Soviet Premier urging self-restraint. He informed me about a message he had sent to the Israeli Premier and said that any action on our part would expose the world to great danger.

The third point is that the entire international community
was against the outbreak of war. President de Gaulle was clear
when he said France would define its attitude on the basis of
who fired the first shot.

The fourth point is that we were the victims of a diplomatic
trick, a political deception in which we had not imagined a
major Power would involve itself. This political trick was
played by the United States. It was represented in the US President's speech, his appeals, his request that we cooperate with
the UN Secretary-General, and his offer to send the Vice-
President to discuss with us ways to save the entire world from
this crisis. The UN Secretary-General came here and we cooperated with him to the maximum. The Secretary-General
asked for a breathing-space with regard to the Gulf of Aqaba
and we agreed to this. He said he wanted this breathing-space
so that all concerned would have time to pause and deal with
matters. The first thing we pointed out to him was that no
Israeli ships would be allowed to pass through the Canal [*sic*],
that no strategic shipments would be allowed to pass, and, in
the meantime, we would not search any ships. We accepted
this and considered it a proposal by the Secretary-General of
the UN, providing a breathing-space for all to discuss the matter.

After that an envoy of the US President arrived here. The
emissary suggested that a Vice-President go to the United
States. I approved the idea on the understanding that the Vice-
President would meet President Johnson and explain our atti-
tude to him. Then I sent a letter to the US President telling him:
We welcome the visit of the US Vice-President but at the same
time I am prepared to send Vice-President Zakariya Muhiedin
to Washington to meet you and explain the Arab view to you.
Naturally, the next day I received the reply that they welcomed
Zakariya Muhiedin's trip to Washington to meet the American
President and they requested that we set a date. We set it for
Tuesday 6 June, and we all know that the aggression began on
5 June.

What does this mean? It means that large-scale political
and diplomatic activities were going on and it was right in the

light of these activities to think that the explosion would not occur soon.

The fifth point: in spite of all this, we were not reassured about all these things. We knew that something was in the making and that it would not be long in coming. It was obvious that something was being planned against us. In fact, I had felt for two years that something would be prepared against us, since the cessation of US aid and America's warnings to us not to arm or enlarge our army, nor to follow a course of technical development, nor to seek military development.

When we concentrated our forces I estimated that the likelihood of war breaking out was 20 per cent. Before we closed the Gulf of Aqaba, we convened a meeting of the Higher Executive Committee at my home. We discussed the closure of the Gulf of Aqaba. That meeting took place on 22 May. At that meeting I told them that the possibility of war was 50 per cent. At another meeting I said that the likelihood of war was 80 per cent. At our meeting of the Higher Executive Committee it was obvious that our action would be defensive, that we would attack only if aggression was launched against Syria, and that we would be on the alert. At that meeting no one spoke at all of attacking Israel. There was no intention at all that we would launch an offensive against Israel. As I explained earlier it was clear from all our analyses that any attack on Israel would expose us to great dangers. The foremost of these dangers would be an American attack on us in view of the statements America made saying that it guaranteed the borders of the states in this area. It was obvious to us that when America said it guaranteed the borders of the states in this area and would not tolerate any changes in this area, America did not at all mean the Arab states, but by this it meant Israel. It meant that if an aggression was carried out against Israel, America would implement the statement made by President Kennedy that America guaranteed all the borders in this area.

On these grounds there was no discussion at all of launching an attack on Israel. But our entire operation at the Joint Command was defensive. As we estimated at that time, our concentrations were a deterrent action so that Israel would not commit aggression against Syria.

On 23 May we announced the closure of the Gulf of Aqaba to Israeli ships. Then came the political changes in Israel at the beginning of June. As we followed what was going on there, the probability of war became 100 per cent.

What does this mean? It means that we did not trust in the least all the political and diplomatic activities of the United States. We realized that something was being planned and that it would not take long.

On Friday 2 June I personally went to the Armed Forces Supreme Command HQ. I participated at a meeting which was attended by all senior officers of the armed forces. At that meeting I gave my view before listening to theirs. I said at that meeting on Friday 2 June that we must expect the enemy to strike a blow within 48 to 72 hours and no later on the basis of the indications of events and developments. I also said at that meeting that I expected the aggression to take place on Monday 5 June and the first blow to be struck at our Air Force. The Air Force commander was present at the meeting.

What does this mean? It means that we did not under-estimate the situation as a result of all the diplomatic con-tacts, the dispatch of the UN Secretary-General, and Johnson's approval of a visit by Zakariya Muhiedin. It was quite clear on any political calculation that Israel was bound to take military action, especially after Iraqi forces had moved and Jordan had joined the joint defence agreements.

Question No. 6: After what has happened, we must faithfully and honourably admit that the military battle did not go as we had expected and hoped. It confirmed the proverb that pre-caution does not deter fate.

I do not wish now to talk about the causes, nor will I permit myself or this people, while the battle continues, to apportion blame. This is a matter for history and the struggle of our people. But I can say with satisfaction, good will and a con-science ready to give an account at any time that first and last the responsibility was mine. I said this in my address to the nation on 9 June, and I say it now and will continue to say it, bearing all the consequences and accepting any judgement of it. Actually this was why I decided to resign on 9 June. I wanted to take the responsibility and step down, and I wanted the enemies of the Egyptian people and the Arab nation to know that the issue is not Abdel Nasser or Abdel Nasser's ambitions, as they said. The Egyptian people's struggle began before Abdel Nasser and will go on after Abdel Nasser. The Arab nation sought its unity before Abdel Nasser. I have said and will always say that I am not the leader of this people. The greatest honour I desire is to be their representative at a particular stage in their continuous struggle, a struggle not dependent on any individual.

Question No. 7 concerns the US role. A large part of the part played by the United States is still vague. We know only a little about this part. The secrets of the 1956 Suez war became known only last year – exactly ten years after the war. Therefore, we shall not know the secrets of the 1967 war now. It will be some years before we know everything.

A large part of the US role in the recent aggression is still vague. But we already know a few things. We have already found the answers to several questions. What was behind the political and diplomatic part which the United States played before the battle? This role included the call for self-restraint, the threat that any action taken by us would expose the entire region to dangers, the proposal to send the US Vice-President to confer with us on the subject, the approval of Zakariya Muhiedin's trip to Washington to meet Johnson to confer on the subject and to try to reach a solution. All this took place before the aggression, before the battle.

It was a deception. We must ask : in whose interest was this deception? Certainly, it was in the interest of the imperialist-Israeli aggression. The deception was part of a US plan drawn up two years ago. The aim of this plan was to overthrow the free revolutionary regimes, which do not heed the words of the big Powers and refuse to be under anyone's influence.

What was behind the part played by the Sixth Fleet near our shores a few days before the war? How many arms were transported to Israel in the period from the outset of the crisis to the day of the aggression? How many aircraft reached Israel? How many volunteer pilots? How do we explain the huge air power which the enemy used on all Arab fronts? They attacked the Egyptian, Jordanian and Syrian fronts simultaneously. They also sent aircraft to attack Iraqi airports. On the evening on 7 June just before dawn, King Hussain contacted me by telephone saying that 400 aircraft were attacking the Jordanian front and were seen on his radar equipment. Where did these aircraft come from?

How do we explain the role of the US espionage ship *Liberty*? You have all read in the papers that an American ship named *Liberty* was near our territorial waters – probably in these waters – and that the Israelis thought it was an Egyptian warship and attacked it with torpedo boats. Some 34 officers and crew of this US ship were killed in this incident. For whom was the US ship with all its scientific equipment working? It was said that the ship was there to decode operational messages. It was also said that those messages were sent to the United States. Later it was said that the messages were sent to Israel. Messages can be radioed very rapidly. It was also said that those messages were sent to US embassies in the area. What did the Americans do? When the Israelis hit them they pulled themselves together, hushed up the story, and went to Malta to repair the ship. Had we attacked the US ship, the Americans would have given us an ultimatum because we are neither an American colony nor an imperialist bridgehead. Nor are we in the US sphere of influence.

There is another question: why were the US aircraft over our front lines? On Wednesday 7 June two aircraft bearing US markings were seen over our lines. At first I did not believe it, but the information was certain. We then issued a statement saying that American aircraft had flown over our lines and over the front. We also said that we, therefore, believed the Americans were participating in the operation. We also spoke of the aircraft that were attacking Jordan and said that there had been a non-Israeli air attack on Jordan. We broadcast a statement including details about the two aircraft we had observed in flight.

In the evening I received a letter from President Johnson. He contacted the Soviet Head of State and requested him to send us a letter because at that time we did not have relations with him. He said it was true that there were two US aircraft over our lines, but they were going to the aid of the USS Liberty the spy ship.

The question arises: were there other US aircraft? A second question is: would they have made their admission had we not broadcast the statement? In fact, one asks oneself such questions about the things one knows.

What is the explanation of the US attitude at the UN and after the end of the operations? The US attitude at the UN after the operations was fully to endorse Israel's point of view. The US position at the UN was for unconditional surrender by the Arabs. This was the US position at the UN after the operations had ended. What does this mean?

There is an appalling difference between the two US attitudes – the attitude in 1956 when America was surprised by the tripartite aggression against us and the attitude in 1967 when America was not taken by surprise. In 1956 America was surprised by the tripartite aggression against us. In 1967, despite the letters and the agreement to send Zakariya Muhiedin, America was not surprised by the Israeli aggression against us. When America was surprised it stood steadfast against the aggression and demanded that it be halted and that the aggressive forces withdraw. But when America was not taken by surprise, it supported the aggression and brought pressure to bear on any state which America could influence in any way. The result was the failure of the UN as we have seen.

It is certain that America was not taken by surprise. Stories began to be told. These days American papers abound in news reports saying that the issue has provoked discussions at the highest levels in America. US papers and the American Life magazine said that Israel submitted to the US President the view that it should launch an attack, saying that it felt superior. US newspapers also say that the US President sought the views of the US Chief of Staff and the US Intelligence Director and that they agreed. Accordingly, Israel was allowed to launch the offensive and to perpetrate aggression. At the same time Israel obtained guarantees from the United States that, should the Arabs enter Israel, the Sixth Fleet would intercept them and if Israel entered the Arab countries, America would support Israel. These stories were published in newspapers. The Israeli Premier Eshkol has thanked the US President for telling him: The Sixth Fleet is there for you and to help you. Eshkol replied in a soothing manner to the US President and told him: I am afraid that when we become exposed to danger, you will be busy with Vietnam or you may be spending the weekend at your Texas ranch. But the US President emphatically assured him that the Sixth Fleet would protect him should the Arabs cross the borders into Israel. These articles, statements and all these stories were published in the papers. Therefore, the USA was not surprised by the aggression . . .

[The second part of the speech, which has been deleted here, was devoted to domestic problems. Ed.]

The Six Day War: Abba Eban's Speech at the Special Assembly of the United Nations, 19 June 1967*

The subject of our discussion is the Middle East, its past agony and its future hope. We speak of a region whose destiny has profoundly affected the entire human experience. In the heart of that region, at the very centre of its geography and history, lives a very small nation called Israel. This nation gave birth to the currents of thought which have fashioned the life of the Mediterranean world and of vast regions beyond. It has now been re-established as the home and sanctuary of a people which has seen six million of its sons exterminated in the greatest catastrophe ever endured by a family of the human race.

In recent weeks the Middle East has passed through a crisis whose shadows darken the world. This crisis has many consequences but only one cause. Israel's rights to peace, security,

* Reprinted from the *Jerusalem Post*.

sovereignty, economic development and maritime freedom –
indeed its very right to exist – has been forcibly denied and aggressively attacked. This is the true origin of the tension which
torments the Middle East. All the other elements of the conflict
are the consequences of this single cause. There has been danger, there is still peril in the Middle East because Israel's existence, sovereignty and vital interests have been and are
violently assailed.

The threat to Israel's existence, its peace, security, sovereignty and development has been directed against her in the
first instance by the neighbouring Arab states. But all the conditions of tension, all the impulses of aggression in the Middle
East have been aggravated by the policy of one of the great
powers which under our Charter bear primary responsibilities
for the maintenance of international peace and security. I
shall show how the Soviet Union has been unfaithful to that
trust. The burden of responsibility lies heavy upon her.

I come to this rostrum to speak for a united people which,
having faced danger to the national survival, is unshakably
resolved to resist any course which would renew the perils
from which it has emerged.

The General Assembly is chiefly preoccupied by the situation against which Israel defended itself on the morning of
5 June. I shall invite every peace-loving state represented here
to ask itself how it would have acted on that day if it faced
similar dangers. But if our discussion is to have any weight or
depth, we must understand that great events are not born in a
single instant of time. It is beyond all honest doubt that, between 14 May and 5 June, Arab governments, led and directed
by President Nasser, methodically prepared and mounted an
aggressive assault designed to bring about Israel's immediate
and total destruction. My authority for that conviction rests on
the statements and actions of Arab governments themselves.
There is every reason to believe what they say and to observe
what they do.

During Israel's first decade, the intention to work for her destruction by physical violence has always been part of the offi-

cial doctrine and policy of Arab states. But many members of the United Nations hoped and believed that relative stability would ensure from the arrangements discussed in the General Assembly in March 1957. An attempt has been made to inaugurate a period of non-belligerency and coexistence in the relations between the UAR and Israel. A United Nations emergency force was to separate the armies in Sinai and Gaza. The Maritime Powers were to exercise free and innocent passage in the Gulf of Aqaba and the Straits of Tiran. Terrorist attacks against Israel were to cease. The Suez Canal was to be opened to Israel shipping, as the Security Council had decided six years before.

In March 1957 these hopes and expectations were endorsed in the General Assembly by the United States, France, the United Kingdom, Canada and other states in Europe, the Americas, Africa, Asia and Australia. These assurances, expressed with special solemnity by the four governments which I have mentioned, induced Israel to give up positions which she then held at Gaza and at the entrance to the Straits of Tiran and in Sinai. Non-belligerency, maritime freedom and immunity from terrorist attack were henceforth to be secured, not by Israel's own pressure but by the concerted will of the international community. Egypt expressed no opposition to these arrangements. Bright hopes for the future illuminated this hall ten years ago.

There were times during the past decade when it really seemed that a certain stability had been achieved. As we look back it becomes plain that the Arab governments regarded the 1957 arrangements merely as a breathing space enabling them to gather strength for a later assault. At the end of 1962 President Nasser began to prepare Arab opinion for an armed attack that was to take place within a few brief years. As his armaments grew his aggressive designs came more into light. On 23 December 1962 Nasser said :

> We feel that the soil of Palestine is the soil of Egypt, and of the whole Arab world. Why do we all mobilize? Because we feel that the land of Palestine is part of our land, and are ready to sacrifice ourselves for it.

The present Foreign Minister of Egypt, Mahmoud Riad, echoed his master's voice:

The sacred Arab struggle will not come to an end until Palestine is restored to its owners.

In March 1963 the official Cairo radio continued the campaign of menace:

Arab unity is taking shape towards the great goal – i.e. the triumphant return to Palestine with the banner of unity flying high in front of the holy Arab march.

The newspaper *Al Gumhuriya* published an official announcement on the same day:

The noose around Israel's neck is tightening gradually. . . . Israel is mightier than the empires which were vanquished in the Arab East and West. . . . The Arab people will take possession of their full rights in their united homeland.

Egypt is not a country in which the press utters views and opinions independently of the official will. There is thus significance in the statement of *Al Akhbar* on 4 April 1963:

The liquidation of Israel will not be realized through a declaration of war against Israel by Arab states, but *Arab unity and inter-Arab understanding will serve as a hangman's rope for Israel.*

The Assembly will note that the imagery of a hangman's rope or of a tightening noose occurs frequently in the macabre vocabulary of Nasserism. He sees himself perpetually presiding over a scaffold. In June 1967 the metaphor of encirclement and strangulation was to come vividly to life, in Israel's hour of solitude and danger.

In February 1964 Nasser enunciated in simple terms what was to become his country's policy during the period of preparation:

The possibilities of the future will be war with Israel. It is we who will dictate the time. It is we who will dictate the place.

A similar chorus of threats arose during this period from other Arab capitals. President Arif of Iraq and President

Ben Bella of Algeria were especially emphatic and repetitive in their threat to liquidate Israel. The Syrian attitude was more ominous because it affected a neighbouring frontier. Syrian war propaganda has been particularly intense in the past few years. In 1964 the Syrian Defence Minister, General Abdulla Ziada, announced:

> The Syrian army stands as a mountain to crush Israel and demolish her. This army knows how to crush its enemies.

Early last year Syria began to proclaim and carry out what it called a 'popular war' against Israel. The Syrian concept of 'popular war' expressed itself in the dispatch of trained terrorist groups into Israel territory to blow up installations and communication centres, to kill, maim, cripple and terrorize civilians in peaceful homes and farms. Sometimes the terrorists, trained in Syria, were dispatched through Jordan or Lebanon. The terrorist war was formally declared by President Al-Atassi on 22 May 1966, when he addressed soldiers on the Israel–Syrian front:

> We raise the slogan of the people's liberation war. We want total war with no limits, a war that will destroy the Zionist base.

The Syrian Defence Minister, Hafiz Asad, said two days later:

> We say: We shall never call for, nor accept, peace. We shall only accept war and the restoration of the usurped land. We have resolved to drench this land with our blood, to oust you, aggressors, and throw you into the sea for good. We must meet as soon as possible and fight a single liberation war on the level of the whole area against Israel, Imperialism and all the enemies of the people.

Mr President, from that day to this, not a week passed without Syrian officials adding to this turgid stream of invective and hate. From that day to this, there has not been a single month without terrorist acts, offensive to every impulse of human compassion and international civility, being directed from Syria against Israel citizens and territory. I would have no difficulty in filling the General Assembly's records with a thousand official statements by Arab leaders in the past two years announcing their intention to destroy Israel by diverse forms of organized physical violence. The Arab populations have been conditioned by their leaders to the anticipation of a total war, preceded by the constant harassment of the prospective victim.

From 1948 to this very day there has not been one statement by any Arab representative of a neighbouring Arab state indicating readiness to respect existing agreements or the permanent renunciation of force to recognize Israel's sovereign right of existence or to apply to Israel any of the central provisions of the United Nations Charter.

For some time Israel showed a stoic patience in her reaction to these words of menace. This was because the threats were not accompanied by a capacity to carry them into effect. But the inevitable result of this campaign of menace was the burden of a heavy race of arms. We strove to maintain an adequate deterrent strength and the decade beginning in March 1957 was not monopolized by security considerations alone. Behind the wall of a strong defence, with eyes vigilantly fixed on dangerous borders, we embarked on a constructive era in the national enterprise. These were years of swift expansion in our agriculture and industry, of intensive progress in the sciences and arts, of a widening international vocation, symbolized in the growth of strong links with the developing world. At the end of this first decade, Israel had established relations of commerce and culture with all the Americas, and with most of the countries of Western, Central and Eastern Europe. In her second decade she built constructive links with the emerging countries of the developing world with whom we are tied by a common aspiration to translate national freedom into creative economic growth and progress.

Fortified by friendships in all five continents, inspired by its role in the great drama of developments, intensely preoccupied by tasks of spiritual cooperation with kindred communities in various parts of the world, and in the efforts to assure the Jewish survival after the disastrous blows of Nazi oppressions, tenaciously involved in the development of original social ideas,

Israel went on with its work. We could not concern ourselves exclusively with the torrent of hatred pouring in upon us from Arab governments. In the era of modern communication a nation is not entirely dependent on its regional context. The wide world is open to the voice of friendship. Arab hostility towards Israel became increasingly isolated, while our position in the international family became more deeply entrenched. Many in the world drew confidence from the fact that a very small nation could, by its exertion and example, rise to respected levels in social progress, scientific progress and the human arts, and so our policy was to deter the aggression of our neighbours so long as it was endurable, to resist it only when failure to resist would have invited its intensified renewal, to withstand Arab violence without being obsessed by it, and even to search patiently here and there for any glimmer of moderation and realism in the Arab mind. We also pursued the hope of bringing all the great powers to a harmonious policy in support of the security and sovereignty of Middle Eastern states. It was not easy to take this course. The sacrifice imposed upon our population by Arab violence was cumulative in its effects, but as it piled up month by month the toll of death and bereavement was heavy and in the last few years it was evident that this organized murder was directed by a central hand.

We were able to limit our response to this aggression so long as its own scope appeared to be limited. President Nasser seemed for some years to be accumulating inflammable material without an immediate desire to set it alight. He was heavily engaged in domination and conquest elsewhere. His speeches were strong against Israel, but his bullets, guns and poison gases were for the time being used to intimidate other Arab states and to maintain a colonial war against the villagers of the Yemen and the peoples of the Arabian Peninsula.

But Israel's danger was great. The military build-up in Egypt proceeded at an intensive rate. It was designed to enable Egypt to press its war plans against Israel while maintaining its violent adventures elsewhere. In the face of these developments, Israel was forced to devote an increasing part of its resources to self-defence. With the declaration by Syria of the doctrine of a 'day by day military confrontation', the situation in the Middle East grew darker. The Palestine Liberation Organization, the Palestine Liberation Army, the Unified Arab Command, the intensified expansion of military forces and equipment in Egypt, Syria, Lebanon, Jordan and more remote parts of the Arab continent – these were the signals of a growing danger to which we sought to alert the mind and conscience of the world.

In three tense weeks between 14 May and 5 June, Egypt, Syria and Jordan, assisted and incited by more distant Arab states, embarked on a policy of immediate and total aggression.

June 1967 was to be the month of decision. The 'final solution' was at hand.

There was no convincing motive for the aggressive design which was now unfolded. Egyptian and Soviet sources had claimed that a concentrated Israeli invasion of Syria was expected during the second or third week in May. No claim could be more frivolous or far-fetched. It is true that Syria was sending terrorists into Israel to lay mines on public roads and, on one occasion, to bombard the Israeli settlement at Manara from the Lebanese border. The accumulation of such actions had sometimes evoked Israeli responses always limited in scope and time. All that Syria had to do to ensure perfect tranquility on her frontier with Israel was to discourage the terrorist war. Not only did she not discourage these actions – she encouraged them, she gave them every moral and practical support. But the picture of Israeli troop concentrations in strength for an invasion of Syria was a monstrous fiction. Twice Syria refused to cooperate with suggestions by the UN authorities, and accepted by Israel, for a simultaneous and reciprocal inspection of the Israel–Syrian frontier. On one occasion the Soviet Ambassador complained to my Prime Minister of heavy troop concentrations in the north of Israel. When invited to join the Prime Minister that very moment in a visit to any part of Israel which he would like to see, the distinguished envoy brusquely refused. The prospect of finding out the truth at first hand seemed to fill him with a profound disquiet. But by 9 May, the Secretary-General of the United Nations from his own sources on the ground had ascertained that no Israeli troop concentration existed. This fact had been directly communicated to the Syrian and Egyptian governments. The excuse had been shattered, but the allegations still remained. The steps which I now describe could not possibly have any motive or justification if an Israeli troop concentration, as both Egypt and Syria knew, did not exist. Indeed the Egyptian build-up ceased to be described by its authors as the result of any threat to Syria.

On 14 May Egyptian forces began to move into Sinai.

On 16 May the Egyptian Command ordered the United Nations Emergency Force to leave the border. The following morning the reason became clear. For on 17 May 1967, at 6 in the morning, Radio Cairo broadcast that Field-Marshal Amer had issued alert orders to the Egyptian armed forces. Nor did he mention Syria as the excuse. This announcement reads:

1. The state of preparedness of the Egyptian armed forces will increase to the full level of preparedness for war, beginning 14.30 hours last Sunday.

2. Formations and units allocated in accordance with the operational plans will advance from their present locations to the designated positions.

3. The armed forces are to be in full preparedness to carry out any combat tasks on the Israel front in accordance with developments.

On 18 May Egypt called for the total removal of the United Nations Emergency Force. The Secretary-General of the United Nations acceded to this request and moved to carry out, without reference to the Security Council or the General Assembly, without carrying out the procedures indicated by Secretary-General Hammarskjöld in the event of a request for a withdrawal being made, without heeding the protesting voices of some of the permanent members of the Security Council and of the government at whose initiative the force had been established, without consulting Israel on the consequent prejudice to her military security and her vital maritime freedom, and without seeking such delay as would enable alternative measures to be concerted for preventing belligerency by sea and a dangerous confrontation of forces by land.

It is often said that United Nations procedures are painfully slow. This decision was disastrously swift. Its effect was to make Sinai safe for belligerency from north to south, to create a sudden disruption of the local security balance, and to leave an international maritime interest exposed to almost certain threat. I have already said that Israel's attitude to the peace-keeping functions of the United Nations has been trauma-tically affected by its experience. What is the use of a fire brigade which vanishes from the scene as soon as the first smoke and flames appear? Is it surprising that we are firmly resolved never again to allow a vital Israel interest and our very se-curity to rest on such a fragile foundation?

The clouds now gathered thick and fast. Between 14 May and 23 May Egyptian concentrations in Sinai increased day by day. Israel took corresponding measures. In the absence of an agreement to the contrary it is, of course, legal for any state to place its armies wherever it chooses in its territory. It is equally true that nothing could be more uncongenial to the prospect of peace than to have large armies facing each other across a narrow space, with one of them clearly bent on an early assault. For the purpose of the concentration was not in doubt. On 18 May, at 24.00 hours, the Cairo radio, *Saut el-Arab*, published the following order of the day by Abdul Mushin Murtagi, the General then commanding Sinai:

The Egyptian forces have taken up positions in accordance with a definite plan.

Our forces are definitely ready to carry the battle beyond the borders of Egypt.

Morale is very high among the members of our armed forces because this is the day for which they have been waiting – to make a holy war in order to return the plundered land to its owners.

In many meetings with army personnel they asked when the holy war would begin – the time has come to give them their wish.

On 21 May General Amer gave the order to mobilize re-serves. Now came the decisive step. All doubt that Egypt had decided upon immediate or early war was now dispelled. Appearing at an Air Force Base at 6 o'clock in the morning, President Nasser announced that he would blockade the Gulf of Aqaba to Israeli ships, adding : 'The Jews threaten war and we say : by all means, we are ready for war.'

But the Jews were not threatening war. Prime Minister Eshkol was calling for a de-escalation of forces. Nasser treated this as a sign of weakness.

On 25 May Cairo Radio announced :

The Arab people is firmly resolved to wipe Israel off the map and to restore the honour of the Arabs of Palestine.

On the following day, 26 May, Nasser spoke again :

The Arab people wants to fight. We have been waiting for the right time when we will be completely ready. Recently we have felt that our strength has been sufficient and that if we make battle with Israel we shall be able, with the help of God, to conquer. Sharm al-Shaikh implies a confrontation with Israel. Taking this step makes it imperative that we be ready to undertake a total war with Israel.

Writing in *Al Ahram*, on 26 May, Nasser's mouthpiece, Hassanain Haykal, wrote, with engaging realism :

I consider that there is no alternative to armed conflict between the United Arab Republic and the Israeli enemy. This is the first time that the Arab challenge to Israel attempts to change an existing fact in order to impose a different fact in its place.

On 28 May, Nasser had a press conference. He was having them every day. He said :

We will not accept any possibility of coexistence with Israel.

And on the following day :

If we have succeeded to restore the situation to what it was before 1956, there is no doubt that God will help us and will inspire us to restore the situation to what it was prior to 1948.

There are various ways of threatening Israel's liquidation. Few ways could be clearer than this.

The troop concentrations and blockade were now to be accompanied by encirclement. The noose was to be fitted around the victim's neck. Other Arab states were closing the ring. On 30 May Nasser signed the Defence Agreement with Jordan, and described its purpose in these terms :

The armies of Egypt, Jordan, Syria and Lebanon are stationed on the borders of Israel in order to face the challenge. Behind them stand the armies of Iraq, Algeria, Kuwait, Sudan and the whole of the Arab nation.

This deed will astound the world. Today they will know that the Arabs are ready for the fray. The hour of decision has arrived.

On 4 June Nasser made a statement on Cairo Radio after signing the protocol associating Iraq with the Egyptian-Jordanian Defence Pact. Here are his words :

... We are facing you in the battle and are burning with desire for it to start, in order to obtain revenge. This will make the world realize what the Arabs are and what Israel is ...

Mr President, nothing has been more startling in recent weeks than to read discussions about who planned, who organized, who initiated, who wanted and who launched this war. Here we have a series of statements, mounting in crescendo from vague warning through open threat, to precise intention.

Here we have the vast mass of the Egyptian armies in Sinai with seven infantry and two armoured divisions, the greatest force ever assembled in that Peninsula in all its history. Here we have 40,000 regular Syrian troops poised to strike at the Jordan Valley from advantageous positions in the hills. Here we have the mobilized forces of Jordan, with their artillery and mortars trained on Israel's population centres in Jerusalem and along the vulnerable narrow coastal plain. Troops from Iraq, Kuwait and Algeria converge towards the battle-front at Egypt's behest. 900 tanks face Israel on the Sinai border, while 200 more are poised to strike the isolated town of Eilat at Israel's southern tip. The military dispositions tell their own story. The Northern Negev was to be invaded by armour and bombarded from the Gaza Strip. From 27 May onward,

Egyptian air squadrons in Sinai were equipped with operation orders instructing them in detail on the manner in which Israeli airfields, pathetically few in number, were to be bombarded, thus exposing Israel's crowded cities to easy and merciless assault. Egyptian air sorties came in and out of Israel's southern desert to reconnoitre, inspect and prepare for the assault. An illicit blockade had cut Israel off from all her commerce with the eastern half of the world.

Those who write this story in years to come will give a special place in their narrative to Nasser's blatant decision to close the Straits of Tiran in Israel's face. It is not difficult to understand why this outrage had a drastic impact. In 1957 the maritime nations, within the framework of the United Nations General Assembly, correctly enunciated the doctrine of free and innocent passage to the Straits. When that doctrine was proclaimed – and incidentally, not challenged by the Egyptian representative at that time – it was little more than an abstract principle for the maritime world. For Israel it was a great but still unfulfilled prospect, it was not yet a reality. But during the ten years in which we and the other states of the maritime community have relied upon that doctrine and upon established usage, the principle had become a reality consecrated by hundreds of sailings under dozens of flags and the establishment of a whole complex of commerce and industry and communication. A new dimension has been added to the map of the world's communication. And on that dimension we have constructed Israel's bridge towards the friendly states of Asia and Africa, a network of relationships which is the chief pride of Israel in the second decade of its independence and on which its economic future depends.

All this, then, had grown up as an effective usage under the United Nations' flag. Does Mr Nasser really think that he can come upon the scene in ten minutes and cancel the established legal usage and interests of ten years?

There was in his wanton act a quality of malice. For surely the closing of the Straits of Tiran gave no benefit whatever to Egypt except the perverse joy of inflicting injury on others.

It was an anarchic act, because it showed a total disregard for the law of nations, the application of which in this specific case had not been challenged for ten years. And it was, in the literal sense, an act of arrogance, because there are other nations in Asia and East Africa that trade with the port of Eilat, as they have every right to do, through the Straits of Tiran and across the Gulf of Aqaba. Other sovereign states from Japan to Ethiopia, from Thailand to Uganda, from Cambodia to Madagascar, have a sovereign right to decide for themselves whether they wish or do not wish to trade with Israel. These countries are not colonies of Cairo. They can trade with Israel or not trade with Israel as they wish, and President Nasser is not the policeman of other African and Asian states.

Here then was a wanton intervention in the sovereign rights of other states in the eastern half of the world to decide for themselves whether or not they wish to establish trade relations with either or both of the two ports at the head of the Gulf of Aqaba.

When we examine, then, the implications of this act, we have no cause to wonder that the international shock was great. There was another reason, too, for that shock. Blockades have traditionally been regarded, in the pre-Charter parlance, as acts of war. To blockade, after all, is to attempt strangulation — and sovereign states are entitled not to have their State strangled.

The blockade is by definition an act of war, imposed and enforced through violence.

Never in history have blockade and peace existed side by side. From 24 May onward the question of who started the war or who fired the first shot became momentously irrelevant. There is no difference in civil law between murdering a man by slow strangulation or killing him by a shot in the head. From the moment at which the blockade was imposed, active hostilities had commenced and Israel owed Egypt nothing of her Charter rights. If a foreign power sought to close Odessa, or Copenhagen or Marseilles or New York Harbour by the use of force, what would happen? Would there be any discussion about who had fired the first shot? Would anyone ask whether aggression had begun? Less than a decade ago the Soviet Union proposed a draft resolution in the General Assembly on the question of defining aggression. The resolution reads:

> In an international conflict, that State shall be declared an attacker which first commits one of the following acts:
> a. Naval blockade of the coastal ports of another State.

This act constituted in the Soviet view aggression as distinguished from other specific acts designated in the Soviet draft as indirect aggression. In this particular case the consequences of Nasser's action had been fully announced in advance. On 1 March 1967 my predecessor announced that:

> Interference, by armed force, with ships of the Israel flag exercising free and innocent passage in the Gulf of Aqaba and through the Straits of Tiran will be regarded by Israel as an attack entitling it to exercise its inherent right of self-defence under Article 51 of the United Nations Charter and to take all such measures as are necessary to ensure the free and innocent passage of its ships in the Gulf and in the Straits.

The representative of France declared that any obstruction of free passage in the Straits or Gulf was contrary to international law 'entailing a possible resort to the measures authorized by Article 51 of the Charter'.

The United States, inside and outside of the United Nations, gave specific endorsement to Israel's right to invoke her inherent right of self-defence against any attempt to blockade the Gulf. Nasser was speaking with acute precision when he stated that Israel now faced the choice either between being choked to death in her southern maritime approaches or to await the death blow from Northern Sinai.

Nobody who lived through those days in Israel, between 23 May and 5 June, will ever forget the air of doom that hovered over our country. Hemmed in by hostile armies ready to strike, affronted and beset by a flagrant act of war, bombarded day and night by predictions of her approaching extinction, forced into a total mobilization of all her manpower, her economy and commerce beating with feeble pulse, her main supplies of vital fuel choked by a belligerent act, Israel faced the greatest peril of her existence that she had known since her resistance against aggression nineteen years before, at the hour of her birth. There was peril wherever she looked and she faced it in deepening solitude. On 24 May and on succeeding days, the Security Council conducted a desultory debate which sometimes reached a point of levity. The Soviet Representative asserted that he saw no reason for discussing the Middle Eastern situation at all. The Bulgarian delegate uttered these unbelievable words:

At the present moment there is really no need for an urgent meeting of the Security Council.

A crushing siege bore down upon us. Multitudes throughout the world trembled for Israel's fate. The single consolation lay in the surge of public opinion which rose up in Israel's defence. From Paris to Montevideo, from New York to Amsterdam, tens of thousands of persons of all ages, peoples and affiliations marched in horrified protest at the approaching stage of genocide. Writers and scientists, religious leaders, trade union movements and even the Communist parties in France, Holland, Switzerland, Norway, Austria and Finland asserted their view that Israel was a peace-loving state whose peace was being wantonly denied. In the history of our generation it is difficult to think of any other hour in which progressive world opinion rallied in such tension and agony of spirit.

To understand the full depth of pain and shock, it is necessary to grasp the full significance of what Israel's danger meant. A small sovereign state had its existence threatened by lawless violence. The threat to Israel was a menace to the very foundations of the international order. The state thus threatened bore a name which stirred the deepest memories of civilized mankind and the people of the remnant of millions, who, in living memory, had been wiped out by a dictatorship more powerful, though scarcely more malicious, than Nasser's Egypt. What Nasser had predicted, what he had worked for with undeflecting purpose, had come to pass – the noose was tightly drawn.

On the fateful morning of 5 June, when Egyptian forces moved by air and land against Israel's western coast and southern territory, our country's choice was plain. The choice was to live or perish, to defend the national existence or to forfeit it for all time.

From these dire moments Israel emerged in five heroic days from awful peril to successful and glorious resistance. Alone, unaided, neither seeking nor receiving help, our nation rose in self-defence. So long as men cherish freedom, so long as small states strive for the dignity of existence, the exploits of Israel's armies will be told from one generation to another with the deepest pride. The Soviet Union has described our resistance as aggression and sought to have it condemned. We reject this accusation with all our might. Here was armed force employed in a just and righteous cause, as righteous as the defenders at Valley Forge, as just as the expulsion of Hitler's bombers from the British skies, as noble as the protection of Stalingrad against the Nazi hordes, so was the defence of Israel's security and existence against those who sought our nation's destruction.

What should be condemned is not Israel's action, but the attempt to condemn it. Never have freedom, honour, justice, national interest and international morality been so righteously protected. While fighting raged on the Egyptian–Israel frontier and on the Syrian front, we still hoped to contain the conflict. Jordan was given every chance to remain outside the struggle. Even after Jordan had bombarded and bombed Israel territory at several points we still proposed to the Jordanian monarch that he abstain from general hostilities. A message to this effect reached him several hours after the outbreak of hostilities on the southern front on 5 June.

Jordan answered not with words but with shells. Artillery opened fire fiercely along the whole front with special emphasis on the Jerusalem area. Thus Jordan's responsibility for the second phase of the concerted aggression is established beyond doubt. This responsibility cannot fail to have its consquences in the peace settlement. As death and injury rained on the city, Jordan had become the source and origin of Jerusalem's fierce ordeal. The inhabitants of the city can never forget this fact, or fail to draw its conclusions.

Mr President, I have spoken of Israel's defence against the assaults of neighbouring states. This is not the entire story. Whatever happens in the Middle East for good or ill, for peace or conflict, is powerfully affected by what great great powers do or omit to do. When the Soviet Union initiates a discussion here, our gaze is inexorably drawn to the story of its role in recent Middle Eastern history. It is a sad and shocking story, it must be frankly told.

Since 1955 the Soviet Union has supplied the Arab states with 2,000 tanks, of which more than 1,000 have gone to Egypt. The Soviet Union has supplied the Arab states with 700 modern fighter aircraft and bombers, more recently with ground missiles, and Egypt alone has received from the USSR 540 field guns, 130 medium guns, 200 120-mm. mortars, anti-aircraft guns, 175 rocket launchers, 650 anti-tank guns, seven destroyers, a number of Luna M and SPKA 2 ground-to-ground missiles, 14 submarines and 46 torpedo boats of various types including missile-carrying boats. The Egyptian Army has been trained by Soviet experts. This has been attested to by Egyptian officers captured by Israel. Most of this equipment was supplied to the Arab states after the Cairo Summit Conference of Arab leaders in January 1964 had agreed on a specific programme for the destruction of Israel, after they had announced and hastened to fulfil this plan by accelerating their arms purchases from the Soviet Union. The proportions of Soviet assistance are attested to by the startling fact that in Sinai alone the Egyptians abandoned equipment and offensive weapons of Soviet manufacture whose value is estimated at two billion dollars.

Together with the supply of offensive weapons, the Soviet Union has encouraged the military preparations of the Arab States.

Since 1961 the Soviet Union has assisted Egypt in its desire to conquer Israel. The great amount of offensive equipment supplied to the Arab states strengthens this assessment.

A great power which professes its devotion to peaceful

settlement and the rights of states has for fourteen years afflicted the Middle East with a headlong armaments race, with the paralysis of the United Nations as an instrument of security and against those who defend it.

The constant increase and escalation of Soviet armaments in Arab countries has driven Israel to a corresponding, though far smaller, procurement programme. Israel's arms purchases were precisely geared on the successive phases of Arab, and especially Egyptian, rearmament. On many occasions in recent months we and others have vainly sought to secure Soviet agreement for a reciprocal reduction of arms supplies in our region. These efforts have borne no fruit. The expenditure on social and economic progress of one half of what has been put into the purchase of Soviet arms would have been sufficient to redeem Egypt from its social and economic ills. A corresponding diversion of resources from military to social expenditure would have taken place in Israel. A viable balance of forces could have been achieved at a lower level of armaments, while our region could have moved forward to higher standards of human and social welfare. For Israel's attitude is clear. We should like to see the arms race slowed down. But if the race is joined, we are determined not to lose it. A fearful waste of economic energy in the Middle East is the direct result of the Soviet role in the constant stimulation of the race in arms.

It is clear from Arab sources that the Soviet Union has played a provocative role in spreading alarmist and incendiary reports of Israel intentions amongst Arab governments.

On 9 June President Nasser said:

Our friends in the USSR warned the visiting parliamentary delegation in Moscow, at the beginning of last month, that there exists a plan of attack against Syria.

Similarly an announcement by Tass of 23 May states:

The Foreign Affairs and Security Committee of the Knesset have accorded the Cabinet special powers to carry out war operations against Syria. Israeli forces concentrating on the Syrian border have been put in a state of alert for war. General mobilization has also been proclaimed in the country ...

'There was not one word of truth in this story. But its diffusion in the Arab countries could only have an incendiary result.

Cairo Radio broadcast on 28 May (0500 hours) an address by Marsh Grechko at a farewell party in honour of the former Egyptian Minister of Defence, Shams ed-Din Badran :

The USSR, her armed forces, her people and government will stand by the Arabs and will continue to encourage and support them. We are your faithful friends and we shall continue aiding you because this is the policy of the Soviet nation, its Party and government. On behalf of the Ministry of Defence and in the name of the Soviet nation we wish you success and victory.

This promise of military support came less than a week after the illicit closing of the Tiran Straits, an act which the USSR has done nothing to condemn.

The USSR has exercised her veto right in the Security Council five times. Each time a just and constructive judgement has been frustrated. On 22 January 1964 France, the United Kingdom and the United States presented a draft resolution to facilitate work on the west bank of the River Jordan in the B'not Ya'akov Canal Project. The Soviet veto held up regional water development for several years. On 29 March 1964 a New Zealand resolution simply reiterating UN policy on blockade along the Suez Canal was frustrated by Soviet dissent. On 19 August 1963 a United Kingdom and United States resolution on the murder of two Israelis at Almagor was denied adoption by Soviet opposition. On 21 December 1964 the USSR vetoed a United Kingdom and United States resolution on incidents at Tel Dan, including the shelling of Dan, Dafna and Sha'ar Yashuv. On 2 November 1966 Argentina, Japan, the Netherlands, New Zealand and Nigeria joined to express regret at 'infiltration from Syria and loss of human life caused by the incidents in October and November 1966'. This was one of the few resolutions sponsored by member-states from five continents.

The Soviet use of veto has had a dual effect. First, it prevented any resolution which an Arab state has opposed from being adopted by the Council. Secondly, it has inhibited the Security Council from taking constructive action in disputes between an Arab state and Israel because of the certain knowledge that the veto would be applied in what was deemed to be the Arab interest. The consequences of the Soviet veto policy have been to deny Israel any possibility of just and equitable treatment in the Security Council, and to nullify the Council as a constructive factor in the affairs of the Middle East.

Does all this really add up to a constructive intervention by the USSR in the Arab–Israel tension? The position becomes graver when we recall the unbridled invective against the Permanent Representative of Israel in the Security Council. In its words and in the letter to the Israel government, the USSR has formulated an obscene comparison between the Israel Defence Forces and the Hitlerite hordes which overran Europe in the Second World War. There is a flagrant breach of international morality and human decency in this comparison. Our nation never compromised with Hitler Germany. It never signed a pact with it as did the USSR in 1939.

To associate the name of Israel with the accursed tyrant who engulfed the Jewish people in a tidal wave of slaughter is to violate every canon of elementary taste and fundamental truth.

In the light of this history, the General Assembly will easily understand Israel's reaction to the Soviet initiative in convening this Special Session for the purpose of condemning our country and recommending a withdrawal to the position that existed before 5 June.

Your [the Soviet] government's record in the stimulation of the arms race, in the paralysis of the Security Council, in the encouragement throughout the Arab world of unfounded suspicion concerning Israel's intentions, your constant refusal to say a single word of criticism at any time of declarations threatening the violent overthrow of Israel's sovereignty and existence – all this gravely undermines your claims to objectivity. You come here in our eyes not as a judge or as a prosecutor, but rather as a legitimate object of international criticism for the part that you have played in the sombre events which have brought our region to a point of explosive tension.

If the Soviet Union had made an equal distribution of the friendship amongst the peoples of the Middle East, if it had refrained from exploiting regional rancours and tensions for the purpose of its own global policy, if it had stood in even-handed devotion to the legitimate interests of all states, the crisis which now commands our attention and anxiety would never have occurred. To the charge of aggression I answer that Israel's resistance at the lowest ebb of its fortunes will resound across history, together with the uprising of our battered remnants in the Warsaw Ghetto, as a triumphant assertion of human freedom. From the dawn of its history the people now rebuilding a state in Israel has struggled often in desperate conditions against tyranny and aggression. Our action on 5 June falls nobly within that tradition. We have tried to show that even a small state and a small people have the right to live. I believe that we shall not be found alone in the assertion of that right, which is the very essence of the Charter of the United Nations. Similarly, the suggestion that everything goes back to where it was before 5 June is totally unacceptable. The General Assembly cannot ignore the fact that the Security Council, where the primary responsibility lay, has emphatically rejected such a course. It was not Israel, but Syria, Egypt and Jordan, who violently shattered the previous situation to smithereens. It cannot be recaptured. It is a fact of technology that it is easier to fly to the moon than to reconstruct a broken egg. The Security Council acted wisely in rejecting a backward step, advocated by the Soviet Union. To go back to the situation out of which the conflict arose would mean that all the conditions for renewed hostilities would be brought together again. I repeat what I said to the Security Council. Our watchword is not 'backward to belligerency' but 'forward to peace'.

What the Assembly should prescribe is not a formula for renewed hostilities, but a series of principles for the construction of a new future in the Middle East. With the cease-fire established, our progress must be not backward to an armistice regime which has collapsed under the weight of years and the brunt of hostility. History summons us forward to permanent

peace and the peace that we envisage can only be elaborated
in frank and lucid dialogue between Israel and each of the
states which have participated in the attempt to overthrow her
sovereignty and undermine her existence. We dare not be satisfied with intermediate arrangements which are neither war
nor peace. Such patchwork ideas carry within themselves the
seeds of future tragedy. Free from external pressures and
interventions, imbued with a common love for a region which
they are destined to share, the Arab and Jewish nations must
now transcend their conflicts in dedication to a new Mediterranean future in concert with a renascent Europe and an Africa
and Asia which have emerged at last to their independent role
on the stage of history.

In free negotiation with each of our neighbours we shall offer
durable and just solutions redounding to our mutual advantage
and honour. The Arab states can no longer be permitted to
recognize Israel's existence only for the purpose of plotting its
elimination. They have come face to face with us in conflict.
Let them now come face to face with us in peace.

In peaceful conditions we could imagine communications
running from Haifa to Beirut and Damascus in the north, to
Amman and beyond in the east, and to Cairo in the south. The
opening of these blocked arteries would stimulate the life,
thought and commerce in the region beyond any level otherwise conceivable. Across the southern Negev, communication
between the Nile Valley and the fertile crescent could be resumed without any change in political jurisdiction. What is
now often described as a wedge between Arab lands would
become a bridge. The kingdom of Jordan, now cut off from
its maritime outlet, could freely import and export its goods
on the Israeli coast. On the Red Sea, cooperative action could
expedite the port developments at Eilat and Aqaba, which give
Israel and Jordan their contact with a resurgent East Africa
and a developing Asia.

The Middle East, lying athwart three continents, could become a busy centre of air communications, which are now
impeded by boycotts and the necessity to take circuitous routes.
Radio, telephone and postal communications, which now end

abruptly in mid-air, would unite a divided region. The Middle East, with its historic monuments and scenic beauty, could attract a vast movement of travellers and pilgrims if existing impediments were removed. Resources which lie across national frontiers – the minerals of the Dead Sea and the phosphates of the Negev and the Arava – could be developed in mutual interchange of technical knowledge. Economic cooperation in agricultural and industrial development could lead to supranational arrangements like those which mark the European community. The United Nations could establish an economic commission for the Middle East, similar to the commissions now at work in Europe, Latin America and the Far East. The specialized agencies could intensify their support of health and educational development with greater efficiency if a regional harmony were attained. The development of arid zones, the desalination of water and the conquest of tropical disease are common interests of the entire region, congenial to a sharing of knowledge and experience.

In the institutions of scientific research and higher education of both sides of the frontiers, young Israelis and Arabs could join in a mutual discourse of learning. The old prejudices could be replaced by a new comprehension and respect, born of a reciprocal dialogue in the intellectual domain. In such a Middle East, military budgets would spontaneously find a less exacting point of equilibrium. Excessive sums devoted to security could be diverted to development projects.

Thus, in full respect of the region's diversity, an entirely new story, never known or told before, would unfold across the Eastern Mediterranean. For the first time in history, no Mediterranean nation is in subjection. All are endowed with sovereign freedom. The challenge now is to use this freedom for creative growth. There is only one road to that end. It is the road of recognition, of direct contact, of true cooperation. It is the road of peaceful coexistence. This road, as the ancient prophets of Israel foretold, leads to Jerusalem.

Jerusalem, now united after her tragic division, is no longer an arena for gun emplacements and barbed wire. In our nation's long history there have been few hours more intensely

moving than the hour of our reunion with the Western Wall.
A people had come back to the cradle of its birth. It has renewed its links with the memories which that reunion evokes.
For twenty years there has not been free access by men of all
faiths to the shrines which they hold in unique reverence. This
access now exists. Israel is resolved to give effective expression,
in cooperation with the world's great religions, to the immunity
and sanctity of all the Holy Places. The prospect of a negotiated peace is less remote than it may seem. Israel waged her
defensive struggle in pursuit of two objectives – security and
peace. Peace and security, with their territorial, economic and
demographic implications, can only be built by the free negotiation which is the true essence of sovereign responsibility. A
call to the recent combatants to negotiate the conditions of
their future coexistence is the only constructive course which
this Assembly could take.

We ask the great powers to remove our tormented region
from the scope of global rivalries, to summon its governments
to build their common future themselves, to assist it, if they
will, to develop social and cultural levels worthy of its
past.

We ask the developing countries to support a dynamic and
forward-looking policy and not to drag the new future back
into the outworn past.

To the small nations, which form the bulk of the international family, we offer the experience which teaches us that
small communities can best secure their interests by maximal
self-reliance. Nobody will help those who will not help themselves; we ask the small nations in the solidarity of our smallness, to help us stand firm against intimidation and threat such
as those by which we are now assailed. We ask world opinion,
which rallied to us in our plight, to accompany us faithfully
in our new opportunity. We ask the United Nations, which was
prevented from offering us security in our recent peril, to respect our independent quest for the peace and security which
are the Charter's higher ends. We shall do what the Security
Council decided should be done – and reject the course which
the Security Council emphatically and wisely rejected. It may

seem that Israel stands alone against numerous and powerful adversaries. But we have faith in the undying forces in our nation's history which have so often given the final victory to spirit over matter, to inner truth over mere quantity. We believe in the vigilance of history which has guarded our steps. The Guardian of Israel neither slumbers nor sleeps.

The Middle East, tired of wars, is ripe for a new emergence of human vitality. Let the opportunity not fall again from our hands.

The Right of Israel

By Yizhak Rabin*

Your Excellency, President of the State, Mr Prime Minister, President of the Hebrew University, Rector of the University; Governors, Teachers, Ladies and Gentlemen:

I stand in awe before you, leaders of the generation, here in this venerable and impressive place overlooking Israel's eternal capital and the birthplace of our Nation's earliest history.

Together with other distinguished personalities who are no doubt worthy of this honour, you have chosen to do me great honour in conferring upon me the title of Doctor of Philosophy. Permit me to express to you here my feelings on this occasion. I regard myself, at this time, as a representative of the entire Israel Forces, of its thousands of officers and tens of thousands of soldiers who brought the State of Israel its victory in the Six Day War. It may be asked why the University saw fit to grant the title of Honorary Doctor of Philosophy to a soldier in recognition of his martial activities. What is there in common to military activity and the academic world which represents civilization and culture? What is there in common

---

*The text of an address by Rabin, formerly Israeli chief of staff and at present Israeli ambassador in the United States, on the occasion of receiving an honorary doctorate from the Hebrew University, 28 June 1967.

between those whose profession is violence and spiritual values? I, however, am honoured that through me you are expressing such deep appreciation to my comrades in arms and to the uniqueness of the Israel Defence Forces, which is no more than an extension of the unique spirit of the entire Jewish People.

The world has recognized the fact that the Israel Defence Forces are different from other enemies. Although its first task is the military task of ensuring security, the Israel Defence Forces undertake numerous tasks of peace, tasks not of destruction but of construction and of the strengthening of the Nation's cultural and moral resources.

Our educational work has been praised widely and was given national recognition, when in 1966 it was granted the Israel Prize for Education, The Nahal, which combines military training and agricultural settlement, teachers in border villages contributing to social and cultural enrichment, these are but a few small examples of the Israel Defence Forces' uniqueness in this sphere.

However, today, the University has conferred this honorary title on us in recognition of our Army's superiority of spirit and morals as it was revealed in the heat of war, for we are standing in this place by virtue of battle which though forced upon us was forged into a victory astounding the world.

War is intrinsically harsh and cruel, bloody and tear-stained, but particularly this war, which we have just undergone, brought forth rare and magnificent instances of heroism and courage, together with humane expressions of brotherhood, comradeship, and spiritual greatness.

Whoever has not seen a tank crew continue its attack with its commander killed and its vehicle badly damaged, whoever has not seen sappers endangering their lives to extricate wounded comrades from a minefield, whoever has not seen the anxiety and the effort of the entire Air Force devoted to rescuing a pilot who has fallen in enemy territory, cannot know the meaning of devotion between comrades in arms.

The entire Nation was exalted and many wept upon hearing the news of the capture of the Old City. Our Sabra Youth and most certainly our soldiers do not tend to sentimentality and shy away from revealing it in public. However, the strain of battle, the anxiety which preceded it, and the sense of salvation and of direct participation of every soldier in the forging of the heart of Jewish history cracked the shell of hardness and shyness and released well-springs of excitement and spiritual emotion. The paratroopers, who conquered the Wailing Wall, leaned on its stones and wept, and as a symbol this was a rare occasion, almost unparalleled in human history. Such phrases and clichés are not generally used in our Army but this scene on the Temple Mount beyond the power of verbal description revealed as though by a lightning flash deep truths. And more than this, the joy of triumph seized the whole nation. Nevertheless we find more and more and more a strange phenomenon among our fighters. Their joy is incomplete, and more than a small portion of sorrow and shock prevails in their festivities. And there are those who abstain from all celebration. The warriors in the front lines saw with their own eyes not only the glory of victory but the price of victory. Their comrades who fell beside them bleeding. And I know that even the terrible price which our enemies paid touched the hearts of many of our men. It may be that the Jewish People never learned and never accustomed itself to feel the triumph of conquest and victory and therefore we receive it with mixed feelings.

The Six Day War revealed many instances of heroism far beyond the single attack which dashes unthinkingly forward. In many places desperate and lengthy battles raged. In Rafiah, in El Arish, in Um Kataf, in Jerusalem, and in Ramat Hagollan, there, and in many other places the soldiers of Israel were revealed as heroic in spirit, in courage, and in persistence which cannot leave anyone indifferent once he has seen this great and exalting human revelation. We speak a great deal of the few against the many. In this war perhaps for the first time since the Arab invasions of the spring of 1948 and the battles of Negba and Degania, units of the Israel Forces stood in all sectors, few against many. This means that relatively small units of our soldiers often entered seemingly endless networks of fortification, surrounded by hundreds and thousands of enemy troops and faced with the task of forcing their way, hour after hour, in this jungle of dangers, even after the momentum of the first attack has passed and all that remains is the necessity of belief in our strength, the lack of alternative and the goal for which we are fighting, to summon up every spiritual resource in order to continue the fight to its very end.

Thus our armoured Forces broke through on all fronts, our paratroopers fought their way into Rafiah and Jerusalem, our sappers cleared minefields under enemy fire. The units which broke the enemy lines and came to their objectives after hours upon hours of struggle continuing on and on, while their comrades fell right and left and they continued forward, only forward. These soldiers were carried forward by spiritual values, by deep spiritual resources, far more than by their weapons or the technique of warfare.

We have always demanded the cream of our youth for the Israel Defence Forces when we coined the slogan *Hatovim l'Tayis* – The Best to Flying, and this was a phrase which became a value. We meant not only technical and manual skills. We meant that if our airmen were to be capable of defeating the forces of four enemy countries within a few short hours, they must have moral values and human values.

Our airmen, who struck the enemies' planes so accurately that no one in the world understands how it was done and people seek technological explanations of secret weapons; our armoured troops who stood and beat the enemy even when their equipment was inferior to his; our soldiers in all various branches of the Israel Defence Forces who overcame our enemies everywhere, despite their superior numbers and fortifications; all these revealed not only coolness and courage in battle but a burning faith in their righteousness, an understanding that only their personal stand against the greatest of dangers could bring to their country and to their families victory, and that if the victory was not theirs the alternative was destruction.

Furthermore, in every sector our Forces' commanders, of all ranks, far outshone the enemies' commanders. Their under-

standing, their will, their ability to improvise, their care for
soldiers and, above all, their leading troops into battle, these are
not matters of material or of technique. They have no rational
explanation except in terms of a deep consciousness of the
moral justice of their fight.

All of this springs from the soul and leads back to the spirit.
Our warriors prevailed not by their weapons but by the consciousness of a mission, by a consciousness of righteousness, by
a deep love for their homeland and an understanding of the
difficult task laid upon them; to ensure the existence of our
people in its homeland, to protect, even at the price of their
lives, the right of the Nation of Israel to live in its own State,
free, independent and peaceful.

This Army, which I had the privilege of commanding
through these battles, came from the people and returns to
the people, to the people which rises in its hour of crisis and
overcomes all enemies by virtue of its moral values, its spiritual readiness in the hour of need.

As the representative of the Israel Defence Forces, and in the
name of everyone of its soldiers, I accept with pride your recognition.

*'We Shall Triumph': President Nasser's speech at the
National Congress of the Arab Socialist Union at
Cairo University, 23 July 1968*

[The first part of the speech, which is omitted, was devoted to
questions of domestic policy. Ed.]

The Middle East crisis : I do not want to go back to the circumstances which led to the Middle East crisis. All the details are
known, starting with the premeditated aggression against Arab
territory, to the imperialist collusion with the Israeli enemy, to
the 5 June setback and its serious and sad results for our Arab
nation. As you know, we lost the major part of our military
power. We accepted the political solution experiment for
several reasons. At that time we had no alternative to talking

about a political solution; we had no armed forces to depend on. At the same time we are not advocates of war for the sake of war – not at all. If we can obtain our rights through political action, as happened in 1957, fine; if not, we have no alternative but to struggle for our rights and to liberate our land.

Furthermore, we want world public opinion to be on our side and really to know our position. At the same time, we must consider our present friends and our possible friends before we consider our enemies. A major part of the battle is taking place on an international level and under the eyes of public opinion throughout the entire world, which wants to live in peace.

We realized from the beginning, as we were trying a political solution, that it was a difficult and thorny road because the enemy was drunk with victory. We know that the principle that what has been taken by force cannot be regained by anything but force is a sound and correct principle in all circumstances. But we tried sincerely and are still trying sincerely on a basis from which we do not deviate. This basis is clear and definite in UAR policy: no negotiations with Israel, no peace with Israel, no recognition of Israel, and no deals at the expense of Palestinian soil or the Palestinian people.

These are the foundations on which we proceeded in regard to solving the Middle East crisis peacefully. However, since 23 November and until now, give and take has been going on with the UN representative. Have we achieved anything? We have achieved nothing. We cooperated to the maximum with the UN Secretary-General's representative. We accepted the Security Council resolution, but Israel did not.

No projects exist now for a peaceful solution, and it does not seem to me that there will be any in the future. We hear what the representatives of the UN Secretary-General says, and we express our opinion on what we hear. So far our opinion has been clear.

With regard to a political solution, we will not in any way agree to give away one inch of Arab territory in any Arab country.

It is clear that Israel, which rejected the Security Council resolution, has many aims. The first is to achieve a political objective, because it won a military victory but did not achieve a political gain. Israel wants direct negotiations and wants a peace treaty signed. We reject this. Israel thus won a military victory but has so far been unable to achieve the political objective – signing a peace treaty with any of the Arab states surrounding it.

Therefore Israel will not withdraw. Why should it withdraw from the territory it occupied after achieving a crushing military victory? Israel, as they say, will remain in this territory hoping that conditions or regimes will be changed and replaced by regimes which will agree to the conclusion of a peace treaty with Israel [shouts of 'God forbid' from audience].

How would the conditions change? Israel knows that the occupation burdens the hearts of all the sons of the Arab nation. Occupation represents fragmentation. Occupation is something out of the ordinary and is like a nightmare to all of us. Israel and the imperialist forces working behind it would be able to influence the domestic fronts and might be able to change the regimes and replace them with others which would agree to the conclusion of peace with Israel. As long as Israel knows that we have not yet attained a crushing offensive military strength, it will remain where it is, hoping to achieve political victory through a changing of regimes.

Israel continues to refuse the Security Council resolution. Israel refuses to discuss the Security Council resolution. Israel says: We will remain in our places along the cease-fire lines until you agree to negotiate with us and conclude a peace treaty. Naturally we counter this by rebuilding our armed forces. A year ago after the defeat, we had no armed forces. We now have armed forces which may be greater than those existing before the battle. We are working for the development of the armed forces in order to attain supremacy because our enemy is a cunning enemy backed by a force which gives him everything – money and arms.

After this, we shall discuss the possibilities of the military and political solutions. Because of its nature, the crisis cannot last long. We have been waiting for one year. Our area is a sensitive one. The status quo cannot be accepted. This status

quo is against nature and creates a situation conducive to quick
ignition and explosion at any time.

There exists a basic and principal commitment which is a
question of life or death : the liberation of the land inch by inch
is necessary even if one martyr must fall on every inch of land.
That is clear. A war to regain a right is a legal war. However,
we shall allow no one to provoke us. We shall decide, prepare
and arrange things. This is a lengthy matter which demands
our patience and endurance. We must be patient and stand
fast in order to triumph and attain supremacy. Having attained
supremacy, we shall triumph.

Life will be meaningless and worthless to us, however, until
every inch of Arab soil is liberated. To us the liberation of Arab
soil represents an indivisible whole. In no circumstances is there
an alternative to the departure of the occupation forces from
all occupied territory. Prior to this departure, there can be no
peace in the Middle East in any circumstances. If there is no
peace in the Middle East, it is very doubtful that the repercussions will be restricted to borders of the Middle East.

We do not address ourselves to Israel alone but to the whole
world. We have nothing to say as far as Israel is concerned.
Israel's role has been exposed. Its role as a stooge of world
imperialism and colonialism has been fully exposed. However,
our talk today is addressed to the world, which is anxious for
peace and adheres to peace. We add that peace in this part of
the world will not be achieved by the mere elimination of
the consequences of the 5 June aggression. Real peace should
take into consideration the legal rights of the Palestinian
people.

The third subject is the armed forces. When we study the
causes of the defeat – I have studied the causes of the defeat
and attended command meetings which discussed everything
that took place – when we study the causes of the defeat, it
becomes clear to us that there was no deficiency among the
officers and soldiers. We must know this well. A mistake was
made and it is painful to go back over its details.

Four fifths of our forces did not encounter the enemy and
had no opportunity to fight. They were placed in extremely

bad conditions. It is not advantageous to talk now about the past except within the limits necessary to reassess matters and to benefit from the lessons of the battle. Our soldiers and officers who entered the battles proved that they could stand firm and die. The Egyptian soldier is a fighting soldier who does not fear death. I fought with the Egyptian peasant soldier in 1948 and saw how he welcomes death.

We should therefore be doing our soldiers and officers an injustice if we looked at them on the basis of what has taken place. The fact is that a very large part of the army did not enter battle. Each of us knows that during the withdrawal operation the hostile forces were finally able to inflict the heaviest losses on us. We have now learned and benefited from the lessons of the battle. We have compensated for much of the loss our armed forces suffered last year. As I said before, we have attained defence capability. We shall now strive to transform our army into a strong offensive army supplied with the most up-to-date weapons.

I witnessed an exercise before leaving for the Soviet Union. I saw our armed forces that participated in it. I can say that in the past year they achieved as much as five years of work. One can say that we now have capable armed forces. However it is all-essential that we understand that the officers and soldiers are doing a very difficult job. They are now working day and night. Every officer and NCO feels that the whole country is watching him and assigning him a duty which will determine our fate and future. Each of them feels that the nation is giving him the responsibility. They are therefore carrying out this duty. However, our armed forces must bide their time and be ready to take the opportunity to achieve what they are duty bound to achieve.

We, as a people, fully support our armed forces and have full faith in them because when the people lose confidence in their armed forces, they also lose confidence in themselves and in their destiny. The people must give to their armed forces because there is no alternative. It is my duty to say that the people have given. What have they given? They have given their sons. The best of their sons are now members of the armed forces.

The soldiers and officers of the armed forces are our sons. The people feel and live with them constantly. The people feel that the armed forces are living under difficult psychological and physical conditions as a result of their hard work, great efforts, training and exhausting conditions. To live under such conditions day after day is painful to the soul and to our armed forces, who see the enemy on the other bank of the Canal.

The fourth question is my recent visit to the Soviet Union and to Yugoslavia. Brothers, I mainly went to thank the leaders and people of the Soviet Union for everything they have given us and to discuss the situation. However, there is a fact which we must realize and know: Had it not been for the Soviet Union, we would now find ourselves facing the enemy without any weapons and compelled to accept his conditions. The United States would not have given us a single round of ammunition. It has given us and will give us nothing, but it gives Israel everything from guns to aircraft and missiles.

In reality, we have so far paid not one millieme for the arms we obtained from the Soviet Union to equip our armed forces. Actually, were it a question of payment, we have no money to buy arms. We all know the situation. We took part of the Soviet weapons as a gift and concluded a contract for the remainder for which we shall pay in the future in long-term instalments. Had it not been for the Soviet Union and its agreement to supply us with arms, we should now be in a position similar to our position a year ago. We should have no weapons and should be compelled to accept Israel's condition under its threat.

At the same time, there exists a question which we must fully realize and understand: Why does the Soviet Union give us all these things? Why? We have one common aim with the Soviet Union – to resist imperialism. We do not want foreign influence in our part of the world. For its part, the Soviet Union is most anxious to oppose imperialism and to liquidate the imperialist concentrations to the south of its borders. Our ideological and national interest is against imperialism; the Soviet Union's ideological interest and strategy are against imperialism. I wish to tell you frankly and clearly that the Soviet Union has never tried, not even in our most crucial times, to dictate conditions to us or to ask anything of us. On the contrary, it has always been we who have asked.

Naturally, I did not pay my recent visit to the Soviet Union to express gratitude only, but to ask for things as well. After expressing my gratitude. I asked for things and, after asking, I told them that I was ashamed. Do you not want anything from us? We ask you for things. But they answered: We have nothing to ask of you. I am actually telling this to you and to history so we may know who our friends and enemies are.

We went on asking for hours but they did not make one request of us. Even when I told them I felt ashamed that we were making many demands while they had asked nothing of us – I wish they had a request which we could fulfil – I asked if they had nothing to ask of us. They told us: We take this stand on the basis of our ideology – the ideology of national liberation and the peoples' struggle. We have nothing to ask.

The Soviet Union did not try to dictate any conditions to us. In our constant dealings with it, the Soviet Union has not tried to dictate any conditions – not even when we differed, and we differed with the Soviet Union in 1959. At that time there was agreement on the first stage of the High Dam, the first industrialization agreement and the arms deal agreement. Despite this, despite the difference which reached such extent that it was published in the newspapers, no attempt was made to apply pressure and no word of threat was uttered by the Soviet Union. Sincerity prompts me to say this.

There is another point. This is the element of the Soviet Navy and its appearance in the Mediterranean. I say that the states of the region, all the liberated states in the region, welcome the appearance of the Soviet Navy in the Mediterranean Sea as an element to balance the US Sixth Fleet, which sought to turn the Mediterranean into an American sea. The Soviet Navy did not threaten us. The Sixth Fleet is a strategic reserve for Israel, according to the Israel Premier himself. When the US Navy leaves the Mediterranean, then those who wonder about the danger of the presence of the Soviet Navy will be able to speak and be heard.

On this occasion, I may make a quick reference to our

attitude towards the United States. US policy has failed rapidly in this region. No one other than an obvious agent can openly declare friendship for the United States. The entire Arab world is aware of what the United States has done. We expected something different from the United States, or at least we did not expect all that has happened. However, that is the United States' business.

Giving arms to Israel while it is occupying Arab territory means that the United States supports Israel in the occupation of the Arab territory. Giving aircraft to Israel while it is occupying Arab territory means that the United States supports Israel in the occupation of the Arab territory. The complete US support for Israel at the United Nations and the adoption and defence of the Israeli point of view means that the United States supports Israel's occupation of the Arab territory. The US refusal to make a statement stipulating the need for the withdrawal of the Israeli forces to the positions they occupied before 5 June is proof that the United States supports Israel and, indeed, colludes with Israel in what it has done and is doing. Every member of the Arab nation is aware of this.

This matter is not confined to the Arab nation but also includes other states. Last year, it appeared that some CENTO member-states wanted to absolve themselves of CENTO, which was formerly called the Baghdad Pact. Yesterday we read that the Turkish students were throwing Sixth Fleet crews into the sea. Why? No sensible man in the United States asks himself why this has happened in the Arab world and in other states.

The United States, which possesses means of power that no other state has had the chance to possess throughout history or in our era, should really ask itself what the people want of it. The people want the United States to adopt an attitude based on justice, an attitude based on equality, for as a great Power the United States should also have great principles which reject aggression and occupation and in no circumstances agree to support the aggressor and give him arms.

I shall now refer to my visit to Yugoslavia. I visited Yugoslavia for a short time. Maybe we stayed two nights there. The purpose of the visit was to prove our appreciation for President Tito's visit to us last August. He decided to come in August, the warmest time, last year. Such a gesture on his part deserves great appreciation. President Tito is our friend. After the set-back, he actually played a very great role everywhere and in all states against aggression, occupation and Israel's methods. At the same time we discussed the new conference of non-aligned states.

We shall now speak about the economic situation. Despite all the conditions of war, the Egyptian economic situation is sound in its entirety. Industry has obtained investments, new factories are being opened daily, and agricultural products are setting records. This does not mean that we have no economic problems. No. We have economic problems. We have problems in respect of hard currency, the balance of payments and investments required for development. We want to employ the largest number of people and therefore we need a large amount of money. However, despite these problems, the economy is proceeding on its course. There were hopes that economic pressure would make us hungry and would place us in a situation so that we could not import wheat or food. Now, one year later, we are able to stand fast. There is wheat, flour and corn. There are no crises involving supplies, all this despite the fact that we have made an unprecedented allocation for the defence budget this year – over £E300 million.

The next point I wish to discuss concerns youth and its role. Concern about youth is one of the most important phenomena in our homeland. We must develop this concern. The worst thing that can happen to any country is to have its youth feel indifferent. We want our youth to be interested in everything. The conditions of youth must be one of our most important subjects, because youth is the hope of the homeland. Young people participating in public affairs is a healthy sign and a guarantee of hope for the future. This is the reason for the concern about the representation of youth at this Congress.

We also believe that the university's positive participation in forming concepts is necessary. I have spoken, perhaps in this very hall, of this many times in past years. The university must be the stronghold protecting national social development and opening the way before it. I never cease to say that the guarantees for the future are the universities, concern about the universities, and democracy.

The next point is Arab action. The battle against the enemy must have priority over everything else. The battle demands a single Arab nation. Up to now we have been trying by all means to attain this aim.

A meeting was held at Khartoum. I have spoken previously about the Khartoum meeting and its importance. We called for another summit conference but did not insist on it and substituted bilateral coordination instead. We are not about to be side-tracked. Some have tried to drag us along, but we are not prepared to be dragged.

There is one battle which is absorbing all our efforts in preparing for it; we have no time for anything else. It is the battle against the enemy. Our attitude towards any Arab state depends on the state's attitude towards the battle. Naturally, some states have sent us forces, Sudan and Algeria for instance. Their forces are with us. Other Arab countries such as Iraq and Kuwait have forces with us too. Some states have helped us to resist economically and have adhered to the Arab support agreement such as Saudi Arabia, Libya and Kuwait. I believe that Arab action can progress day after day in spite of the slow rate of progress.

The next point concerns Palestinian *feday* activity. We are fully committed to offering all help to the Palestinian *feday* action. We consider that the Palestinian struggle last year was a big sign of change in the whole Arab situation. Not only we but the entire world senses this indication that the Palestinian people have risen to champion their own cause by themselves and to defend their rights by themselves.

The ninth point concerns psychological warfare. Psychological warfare means an attempt to arouse doubt about everything. Its aim is to strike at the domestic front. But attempts to cast suspicion are not new to us. As we have said, in 1957 there were eleven clandestine radios broadcasting against us. Attempts to arouse suspicions are useless so far as the masses of the Arab nation are concerned.

Suspicion campaigns act in various directions. Firstly, they try to distort the essential wide-scale diplomatic activity of the UAR and to depict it as accepting suspect plans. Of course, it is our duty to launch a diplomatic offensive and expose Israel throughout the world. Of course, psychological warfare is being used in an effort to depict this diplomatic offensive as acceptance of suspicious plans.

Psychological warfare also seeks to speak of the Soviet Union and holds that our relations with the USSR have expanded and become closer and that this will drive us into communism and embroil us in subservience. All of us know these points and I do not have to repeat them.

There is a big difference between cooperation and subservience. When we concluded the 1955 arms deal with the Soviet Union they said there was danger in the arms deal because it would drag us into subservience. They cited examples. When we began to conclude the High Dam agreement with the Soviet Union, they said Soviet experts would come to work at the High Dam and that this would lead to some sort of subservience. More than 5,000 Soviet experts came to the High Dam, but none of them interfered in our domestic affairs and none of them tried to convert any of the people of Aswan to communism. Nothing of the sort happened.

Today they are saying the same thing. For example, they say the Soviet experts in the Army mean domination of the army and subservience. I have said before that we asked the Soviet Union for these experts and that the Soviet Union was not receptive to giving us experts, saying it would expose us to attack. But in fact, after the 5 June events, anyone with insight who could evaluate things felt that we needed training and that we had a great deal to learn about war. Thus we asked for and got the military experts. They are helping us. We have, in fact, benefited from them; we have benefited from them in all fields.

What the psychological warfare suggested when we received arms in 1955 and when we concluded the High Dam agreement in 1960 may again be suggested this time.

Brothers, we feel that the entire Arab nation must feel grateful to the Soviet Union. Had it not been for the Soviet Union,
as I have already said, we should now find ourselves with no
arms in the face of the Israeli militarism, which has been
blinded by its victory of June 1967. Egypt's independence – and
I say this to all people – is not for sale, is not for anyone to
buy and is not for mortgage. This will continue to be the case.
It is this attitude that has placed us in the difficult situations we
are experiencing. Had we agreed to subservience, such as that
represented by the Baghdad Pact which we were asked under
threats to join, we should have accepted subservience some
years ago, long ago and there would have been no need for us
to wage all these battles. We have not accepted subservience,
we will never accept it and for this reason we have been struggling and fighting for freedom, independence and the building
of a free homeland and free citizens.

There has also been the psychological war – poisoned news.
It was reported in recent dispatches that demonstrations had
been started in Alexandria and that travellers were the source
of this information. Our country is an open, not a closed, country. Our country is not a closed country – people can come and
go. Thousands of people enter and leave our country every
hour. These reports reflect a form of psychological war involving false reports to influence us and to prove that the domestic
front is not strong and is not steadfast and, at the same time, to
influence the domestic front and shake it so that imperialism,
Israel and those who stand behind Israel can achieve their
purpose.

Our enemies have succeeded in winning a military victory,
but our country has not fallen, has not accepted defeat, but
has decided to stand fast. They have applied economic pressure to us and, despite this pressure, we have not surrendered
but have marched on. We have imposed restrictions on ourselves and have accepted these restrictions. Our enemies have
failed to destroy us economically. Hence, there remains one
thing for them to do – to strike at the domestic front and to
break up the alliance of the people's working forces because
if the domestic front collapses the hostile imperialist forces and

Israel will achieve the aims they have so far been unable to achieve

The tenth and last point is the inevitability of victory and the conditions for victory. Brothers, there is no alternative to victory for our nation. The nation is capable of achieving victory provided it mobilizes its forces and benefits properly from its energy and conditions, and also if we can build up and safeguard our domestic front according to the needs of the battle. The domestic front is the pillar of the fighting front. We must expose, defeat and crush all enemy attempts to influence the domestic front.

Now comes your role, brothers, comrades in the struggle, and members of the ASU National Congress. You are the command of the alliance of the people's working forces. You are the more capable of cohesion with these forces. You are the more capable of guiding them through work, struggle, clarity and truth. The battle is all the people's battle. It is the battle for the people's lives, and all the people must participate in it. It must be a victory for life and for the people. May God grant you success. Peace be with you.

The Moment of Truth

Towards a Middle East Dialogue
by Cecil Hourani *

This essay is addressed to the educated classes in the Arab countries: to those who still participate actively in the political, social, and intellectual life of their countries, and to those who have been excluded forcibly or by their own free will. To all I trust it will have a message of hope. Destructive as much of my argument is, my aim is positive and constructive. On the understanding of our errors in the past may be built the new society of the future. I have

---

*Cecil Hourani, who was for ten years an adviser to President Bourguiba of Tunisia, lives now in Beirut. His essay was originally published in *El Nahar*, Beirut, and appeared in English in *Encounter*, November 1967.

294 The Israel–Arab Reader

*no recrimination against states or individuals. Time and history will
provide their own judgement. The moment is one for solidarity and
mutual tolerance, and above all for a free discussion among ourselves. In a climate of honest self-criticism and free expression those
truths may emerge which can lead us from our present disarray to
a new vision of ourselves and the world we would like to build.*

At this moment when the destiny of the Arab nation is being
decided, it is the duty of every Arab thinker to witness to the
truth as he sees it, without fear and without dissimulation. For
too long has the field of publicity and expression been left in
the hands of professional demagogues, blackmailers, and semi-
educated fanatics. Our silence on the one hand, their vocifera-
tion on the other, have led the Arab nation not merely to
disaster, but to the brink of disintegration.

The primary condition of a redressment of this situation is to
see things as they are, in all their brutal clarity : then to take
action to change them in the light of the ideals and objectives
we set ourselves. A victory over ourselves is more important
than a physical defeat on the battlefield. Governments, states,
regimes, frontiers, are all transient things, subject to fluctuations and fortune. What is important is that a people should
survive, not as a mere agglomeration of individuals, but as a
living, creative force in history. We can only survive by acting
positively ourselves, not by reacting negatively to what others
may do, or seek to do, to us.

History has given to the Arab nation in the twentieth century
a unique chance to return to the community of living creative
forces in the world : a conjunction of international affairs which
made possible the independence of all our territories ; and the
discovery of enormous wealth which with almost no effort on
our part gives us the means to accomplish all we need to re-
fashion our society and to raise it to prosperity and progress.

This unique chance we are now in danger of losing. Our
sovereign and political liberty gives us the means to bring about
our own destruction more easily than we can construct our
future. Our very freedom implies dangers greater than existed
when we were dependent. No one will now save us from the
consequences of our own mistakes and follies, except ourselves.

The fact that we inhabit certain territories in this world of strategic importance or material wealth is not a sufficient guarantee of our safety or survival. We can be driven from these territories, or lose control of these riches. We can commit suicide as a nation. And history will then judge us as a people who did not know how to use the chances which had been offered them, and condemn us to the fate we shall have deserved.

The most dramatic, but not the only, example of our weakness, and of our failure to recognize both our weakness and our strength, lies in our relationship with the Zionist movement and with the state of Israel.

We have been able neither to come to terms with them: nor to destroy them: nor even to contain them.

As a result of our failure to decide what position to adopt, or to take the necessary measures of self-defence, we have allowed Israel to usurp the whole of Palestine, and to occupy the most important strategic positions in the Near East.

While it is true that the Zionist movement did not develop wholly in relationship to the Arab world, but also in an international climate outside our control, nevertheless since the establishment of Israel in 1948, against our will, our struggle against that state has taken place within the framework of the international community, and largely within the United Nations Organization. The frontiers established in 1948 as a result of the cease-fire were not wholly advantageous to Israel, because they set a territorial limit to Zionism.

The Arab objective, therefore, if we had thought clearly and calmly, should have been the *containment of Israel* within its boundaries as limited by *de facto* arrangements arrived at after two wars we had lost, rather than its conquest and destruction.

That we were unable to distinguish clearly between containment and conquest was due primarily to a psychological weakness in us: *that which we do not like we pretend does not exist.* Because we refused to recognize a situation which was distasteful to us, we were unable to define our own relationship to that situation, or to distinguish between what we would have liked ideally, and what we were capable of achieving in practice.

As a policy of containment, the moves of the UAR until 5 June 1967 could have been successful. But it had implicit dangers, the greatest of which was that in the minds of those who were practising it, it could be at any moment transformed successfully into a policy of conquest. By this confusion in their own minds about their aims, and by their misjudgement of their own strength, the Arab governments brought about the disaster of 5 June. They also lost the battle of public opinion. By foolish and irresponsible statements they allowed themselves to appear as the aggressor instead of the victims. While they talked of war and conquest, Israel prepared it.

For years Israel had cultivated the image of herself as a small defenceless state surrounded by heavily armed neighbours bent on destroying her. While in fact we were trying to contain her, some of our spokesmen, for home consumption, were exaggerating our military capacities and promising our people conquests. This gave Israel a pretext for arming to the teeth. The balance of power which Israel was trying to maintain was not one between Israel and Egypt, but between Israel and all her neighbours combined. The higher technical skills of the Israelis, and the integration of her armed forces into her civilian population, combined with supplies of arms qualitatively at least equal to those of the Arabs, in fact gave her an advantage which we should have foreseen.

The greatest defeat, however, was not that on the battlefield or in propaganda and public opinion, but that which our governments inflicted on their own people: countless lives lost uselessly; a great new exodus of refugees from their homes; economic losses and misery not yet calculable; a new despair and a new humiliation.

What greater proof of our capacities for self-deception and moral cowardice than that Ahmed Shukairy still sits with our responsible leaders, or the claims of one Arab Head of State that we were not defeated because we did not use our full strength? Does not all this make one suspect that the 'final victory' of which some talk would be nothing less than a *coup de grâce* delivered to the Arabs?

This is indeed our moment of truth: but some of our leaders

cannot make up their minds whether they want to be Torero or Bull!

Another consequence of our unwillingness to accept as real what we do not like is that *when reality catches up with us, it is always too late.* At every *débâcle* we regret that we did not accept a situation which no longer exists. In 1948 we regretted that we had not accepted the 1947 UN plea for partition. In May 1967 we were trying to go back to pre-Suez. Today we would be happy – and are actually demanding the UN – to go back to things as they were before 5 June. From every defeat we reap a new regret and a new nostalgia, but never seem to learn a new lesson.

Yet every human situation – except annihilation – contains within it the seeds of its final reversal. Take for example the creation of Israel in 1948. It is true that in relation to our right to the total possession of Palestine this represented an Arab loss : but there were also gains to us in what happened in 1948. We won independence for part of Palestine in place of total dependence on the Mandatory Power before. Under the Mandatory Regime, Jewish immigration and the expansion of Zionism could have continued in the whole of Palestine: after 1948 Zionism was confined to a tiny territory which was strategically weak and scarcely viable economically. Had we consolidated the independence we had gained, we could have contained Israel, and with it World Zionism, for fifty years, after which Israel itself would have ceased to be a threat to us, and become just another Levantine state, part Jewish, part Arab, but overwhelmingly Oriental.

Instead of which, twenty years later, we have not only lost what remained of Arab Palestine: we have also helped Zionism to leap forward yet another stage in its dynamic progress towards full Jewish nationalism. The enormous material and moral support which the state of Israel received from Jewish citizens of other countries in the recent crisis shows that what extreme Zionists have always hoped, and moderate Jews always feared, is happening : namely the polarization of Jewish nationalism around the state of Israel, and the progressive alienation of Jews from the societies in which they have been assimilated or at least accepted. The potential population of Israel is thus not the unborn generations in that country alone, but Jews from everywhere in the world.

Shall we in one, or ten, or twenty years, seek another 'victory' like the one we have just gained, and lose the other side of the Jordan, the fertile plains of Jaulan and Hauran in Syria, and the Litani and Hasbani rivers in Lebanon? And shall we still have Ahmed Shukairy with us to consecrate the final victory of stupidity over intelligence, of fanaticism over common sense, of dishonesty over truth?

The answer lies with us. What we do in reaction to the events of the last few weeks will determine the future of our people not for ten or twenty years, but for centuries. This time there can be no second chance. Either we continue on the same road that has led us to our present state, defeats, retreats, *débâcles*, and the rapid transformation of our settled urban and peasant populations in the Near East into a new nomadism: or we take positive measures to stop the process of disintegration, to limit the collapse, and to transform our military defeat into a political and a psychological victory.

What are these positive measures, and what are the psychological victories we may hope to gain?

We must first of all ask ourselves the question: What does victory mean in terms of our actual situation and our real strength? Does it mean victory over others – Israel, or the Anglo-Americans, or Western imperialism or international indifference, or all together? Does it mean we can impose our terms on others, draw frontiers as we want, dictate the conditions on which we agree to live with the rest of the world, and make others see us as we would like to see ourselves?

Our first effort must surely be to win a victory over ourselves: over defeatism on the one hand, extremism on the other. These two dangers are in fact intimately linked together. The real defeatists are not those who look facts in the face, accept them, and try to remedy the situation which brought them about, but those who refuse to do this, who deny facts, and who are thus preparing for new defeats.

The extremists are those who argue that our concepts were

correct, but that we did not implement them seriously: and that therefore we should continue along the same path, but use more violent methods.

If, however, our concepts were wrong, the use of the same methods even in a more violent form can only lead us to another defeat. It is therefore essential to re-think our basic ideas in terms of *reality*, rather than of wishes. What could we realistically hope to achieve?

I have pointed out the disastrous effects of not having formulated clearly in our minds the distinction between the containment and the conquest of Israel. The principal reason why we did not make this distinction, and imagined that we could at any moment switch from one to the other, was our failure to appreciate our own strength and weakness relatively to Israel and the rest of the world. We must therefore examine this question honestly and fearlessly.

1. The first basic truth we must face is that the Arabs as a whole do not yet have the scientific and technological skills, nor the general level of education among the masses, which make possible the waging of large-scale modern warfare. This is not merely a deduction from recent events: it is a statistically demonstrable fact. We do not have the educational facilities or standards at home, nor enough students abroad, to provide the General Staff, the officers, and the men capable of using modern weapons and modern methods. Nor do we have civilian populations sufficiently disciplined and educated to collaborate with the armed forces and the civil authorities to the degree which modern warfare demands.

By not recognizing this fact, our military leaders tried to fight the wrong kind of war. It is a classical accusation made against General Staffs that they use methods appropriate to the previous war. Our military thinkers and planners were trying to fight the next one. As a result our soldiers were not only unable to use the modern weapons that were placed in their hands: they were actually handicapped by them. Trapped in the tanks they could not manoeuvre, relying on the air support that never came, they fell easy victims to their enemies. And the material they had to abandon will be incorporated into the army of Israel, so that in fact we have helped to arm our opponents.

2. The second truth is that the rate of technological and scientific advance is so rapid in the modern world that even if in twenty years we can catch up with the military standards of today, we shall still be out-distanced by the Israelis, whose technological and scientific skills are the product not only of their own schools and research institutes, but of Jewish – and non-Jewish – talent throughout the world.

3. The third truth is that even if we had been able to defeat Israel militarily, we would have been deprived of the fruit of that victory by some of the great powers, who would have intervened to save Israel's political existence.

4. The fourth truth is that in twenty years, or even less, even if we succeed in bringing our scientific and technological skills to a point where we could wage a modern war, warfare itself will have taken on quite another aspect. The possession of nuclear weapons by smaller powers – including the Arab states and Israel – will offer a choice either of mutual annihilation or of international control: and in neither case shall we be able to get our own way on our own terms.

It is evident, therefore, that if we think primarily in terms of military power we shall be making a fundamental error. This does not mean that we should disarm. It does mean that we must re-appraise our own strength, and find a new relationship between military power on the one hand, and our political, economic, and geo-political assets on the other.

What are the conclusions we should draw from these facts about our relationship to Israel? We must first of all realize that the immediate consequence of the present war has been to modify the strategic situation in favour of Israel, which has now reached more natural frontiers than she had before both of defence and attack. If therefore we try to rectify this situation by military force, we shall be in an even weaker position than we were in 1948, in 1956, or before 5 June 1967. And not only are we in a weaker position to attack: we are also less able to defend ourselves.

The conclusions to be drawn are two: in the first place, the resort to military force as a basic element in Arab policy towards Israel is an error. In the second place, our best chance of containing Israel lies in international pressures either within or outside the United Nations. These international pressures, of whatever nature, have, however, a price. What is the price we are prepared to pay, is a question I leave to later on.

If the balance of military power has now been seriously upset in favour of Israel, there are other aspects of the balance of power which remain in our favour. Some of these have always existed, though we have not used them properly: others spring from the defeat of 5 June itself, for in all situations lie the seeds of their reversal. In the first place, Israel's military victory was a limited one – limited by those territorial, geo-political factors which make the physical conquest of the Arab world impossible. Military occupation is one thing, permanent conquest and domination quite another. In the second place, Israel's military victory was not a political one: it has not led her any nearer to that peace on her terms which she would like, or any nearer to the negotiating table with the Arabs. It has on the contrary brought against her a coalition of international pressures which never existed before, and liquidated the fruit of twenty years' work to win friends in Africa and Asia.

If military force is not the Arabs' best card, neither is it Israel's. By a military action far out of proportion to the immediate situation it had to face, Israel has brought into play other factors which in the long run may modify the situation within Israel in ways which their present leaders had never envisaged.

Firstly, let us suppose that international pressures do not succeed in forcing Israel to withdraw to her pre-5 June frontiers. By incorporating the Gaza Strip and the West Bank into her territory, the proportion of Arabs to Jews in Israel will be radically changed. The higher birth-rate of the Arabs will give them equality in numbers, then a majority, in a few years. And as the proportion of 'Arab' Jews to European Jews is also changing, the total population of Palestine will eventually, and before long, take on an oriental character. As we acquire some of their virtues, and they acquire some of our defects, the gap between Arab and Jew will narrow, and in fifty years could almost disappear.

Secondly, it is clear that the Zionist movement as a whole, and the Israeli leaders in particular, must now face a dramatic dilemma as a result of their *blitzkrieg* of 5 June. This dilemma is the following: If the Israeli government accepts the Arabs within the territories she controls as full Israeli citizens, with equal civil and political rights, the concept of Israel which has hitherto been incorporated into her laws will have to be changed. Israel will no longer be a Jewish state, in which, as it does now, full citizenship requires not only membership of the Jewish religion, but Jewish ancestry. It will become a Jewish-Arab state in which nationality will be a function of residence or citizenship. Israel, in other words, as she has been since 1948, will no longer exist, and Palestine, with Arabs and Jews living together, will have been restored.

If, on the other hand, the Israeli authorities refuse to accept the Arabs as full citizens with equal civil and political rights, she will have on her hands a large population which she will be unable to liquidate or to govern.

It is the perception of this dilemma which is now leading some of the Israeli leaders to force the hands of the others and to try to have it both ways: to keep the territories they have conquered, and try to reduce the Arab population in numbers by encouraging their exodus across the Jordan. It is not difficult to foresee that the next step will be to encourage a new wave of Jewish immigration into Israel, to replace as many Arabs as possible in as short a period as possible.

If the extremists within Israel succeed in forcing the hand of the more reasonable, and getting the world Zionist movement to follow, then they will in fact make forever impossible their dream of an Arab–Jewish *rapprochement*. For the way in which the Arabs are ultimately going to judge the advantages of peace or war in their relations with Israel will depend on the way Israel treats the Arabs within its borders. If there is a genuine attempt to live together with the Arabs on terms of complete equality and within the same juro-political framework, the way to an eventual conciliation between Israel, or Palestine, and the rest of the Arab world will have been opened. But if the Arabs are excluded from full citizenship, and reduced to the status of a colonized, dependent population, no peace will ever be possible, either inside or outside Palestine.

It is not difficult to draw logical conclusions about what Arab policy should be in the light of this situation, and of this dilemma which faces Israel. If the goals of Arab policy should be, as I have suggested, (1) the containment of Israel within whatever boundaries we can get international pressure to agree to and to stabilize, (2) the gradual transformation of Israel from a European-dominated 'exclusive' Jewish state into a predominantly oriental Arab–Jewish state, then the problem of whether or not to make a formal 'peace' becomes a secondary one. It will no longer be a question of principle on which no Arab leader can compromise: it becomes a question of expediency and efficacy. But there is no reason why we should accept the Israeli argument that peace can only be obtained by direct negotiations with them. Since the United Nations, or some other international group, will have to be a party to any attempt to stabilize frontiers, all our efforts to obtain a settlement can be canalized through that organization. What we cannot afford is to have no policy at all: to be unable to support the conditions of war, and incapable of profiting from the advantages of peace.

The formulation of a consistent Arab policy towards Israel within the framework of the international community is thus perfectly possible and not difficult if we define both our aims and our methods. I have stated what these aims could be. As for the methods, a few are obvious, although others may also be found, and the way these methods are used will be up to the Arab negotiators to determine.

1. We should do all we can to secure the return to the frontiers as they were before 5 June 1967, not indeed as a final settlement but as a first step towards an arrangement in which the questions of frontiers, the rights of the refugees to return, and compensation will find a solution. The means we adopt to bring pressure on other powers to accept our point of view

should be realistic, however: that is to say they should be capable of success, and they should not do us more harm than they can bring us benefits.

It is unlikely that we shall be able to achieve our objective without making some concessions. What these concessions might be, it is up to those governments who would have to make them to decide. But we should hope and insist that these governments would not act unilaterally, and thereby prejudice the outcome of any compromise they may accept.

2. In the event of our being unable to accept the terms on which a withdrawal from occupied territories is offered us, our second line of policy should be based on the principle that the forcible occupation of a territory involves a responsibility towards the inhabitants of that territory. We should not only bring the maximum international pressure to prevent Israel from expelling Arabs and expropriating their possessions in favour of new Jewish immigrants: we should bring the same international pressure on Israel to accord full political and civil rights to her Arab population, as well as the right of the Arab refugees to return. If all Palestine is re-united, there is no reason why any Palestinian should be prevented from returning to his country : not only the refugee masses now living in camps (old and new) should return: in addition all those Palestinians who have been able to find work and prosperity in the Arab countries should go back and help to rebuild the Palestine Arab community, and play their proper role in re-establishing the rights of the Arabs in their own country. The returning Arabs will not be a fifth column : one cannot be a fifth column in one's own country. The relations which the Palestinian Arabs within Palestine are then able or willing to establish with the Jews will be their own responsibility. The other Arab countries must help them by all means in their struggle to restore their rights and their human dignity : but the primary responsibility for their future will lie with the Palestinians themselves.

There remains one more question perhaps more important than any I have yet discussed, because in the long run it will determine our relations with the Jews and their relations with us. *The fate and the peace of the Near East should not be left to the initiative of Israel alone.* Even if Israel opts for the closed, exclusive type of society, and rejects the Arabs as fellow-citizens, *we should not do the same.* If there is no room in Israeli society for the Arabs, we should show that there is room in Arab society for the Jews. This has always been the pattern of our society, and the greatest victory of militant Zionism would be to get us to abandon it and to adopt their concept of the state. For in their hearts they know that a closed, exclusive, fanatic Israel can never coexist with an open, liberal, and tolerant Arab society. There are Jews, however, in Israel and throughout the world who also reject the narrow vision and fanatical aims of some of their leaders, and who can be our allies in combating the introduction of racial nationalism into the Near East. Our greatest victory will be the day when the Jews in Palestine will prefer to live in an Arab society rather than in an Israeli one. It is up to us to make that possible.

I have suggested that we formulate and try to implement a consistent Arab policy towards Israel within the framework of the international community, which means in effect the United Nations. But it is not only in the problem of Israel that the international community can be of service to us. In many of our foreign relations our numbers and our potential strength make the UN a suitable instrument of action. This implies, however, a correct appraisal of our strength and our weakness in the world.

Our greatest mistake in the past has been to overestimate our actual and to underestimate our potential strength. From this combination of misjudgements spring almost all the errors of our international behaviour. We have formulated and pursued policies we could not implement: we have neglected to practise policies which might have succeeded.

Nothing illustrates this truth better than the international policies we had adopted towards Israel. All our attempts to find military solutions have ended in failure, and led to subsequent political and diplomatic failures. On the other hand, our diplomatic, political and economic efforts have often met with success until we lost our advantages by pushing them too far, or not realizing what these advantages were.

For example, the St James's Conference in London in 1939 between the British government and some of the Arab governments led to the White Paper, which was in our favour, but which we rejected. In 1948 we secured the evacuation of British civil and military authorities from Palestine, but we did not take the necessary steps to take their place. In 1948 again, after our first unsuccessful war, we could have turned our military defeat into a limited political victory and confined Israel to an insignificant territory. Instead, we preferred our theoretical rights and principles to our real advantages. By 1967 – and this was the basic cause of Israel's aggression on 5 June – we had succeeded in building up an economic situation in Jordan and most of the other Arab countries to a point where foreign investors were beginning to have serious doubts about putting money in Israel if that meant exclusion from Arab markets. We had also isolated Israel diplomatically in wide areas of international life. We lost all these advantages by failing to analyse the situation correctly. We did not perceive that the disparity between Israel's growing economic and diplomatic difficulties and her military strength would inevitably tempt her to restore the balance by a generalized rather than a localized military action. Instead of removing all possible pretexts for such an action we provided the pretexts they had difficulty in inventing themselves ...

The greatest sources of weakness in the last twenty years has been the introduction into Arab political life of methods of government and of ideological slogans which are unsuitable and irrelevant to the actual conditions of the Arab countries. These methods and slogans have not only poisoned the relations between different Arab countries, they have also blinded some of their regimes to their real problems and their real interests.

The military regimes, for example, which have installed themselves in certain Arab countries since 1949 had their only justification in terms of the necessity of meeting external dangers. They have now given a public demonstration of their incompetence in war. What reason do we have to suppose that they are likely to be more successful in economic planning and development, in education, foreign affairs, finance, or culture?

Among the most harmful consequences of military regimes to the political, economic and social structure of the countries they have tried to govern is the exclusion from public life which they have deliberately or indirectly effected of vast numbers of educated and skilled citizens, who now languish idle either in their own countries, or in exile in others. This fact represents an enormous loss in terms of an investment in human resources going back at least forty years. The resulting poverty of technicians is felt not only in civilian affairs, but even in the armies themselves, so that it can reasonably be argued that the military regimes instead of strengthening their armed forces have in reality weakened them.

The introduction of ideological slogans and political and economic doctrines which derive from contexts radically different from those of the Arab countries has done even more harm to these countries both in their relations with each other and in their internal affairs. They have divided the Arab world into camps on issues which are not really relevant or along lines which do not make sense.

First of all, that between the so-called 'progressive' or 'revolutionary' and the 'reactionary' or 'conservative' regimes. It is interesting and significant that all those regimes which call themselves 'progressive' are, in fact, military. What has led some of our leaders to adopt the language and imitate the style of movements and regimes with which they really have nothing in common? There are two basic reasons: the desire to find foreign allies and friends, and the need to seek popular support. Since most of the Arab countries have only recently emerged from Western domination or colonization, it was natural for leaders seeking an easy popularity among the masses to align themselves with the enemies of the West in foreign policy, and to promise them economic and social welfare through 'land reforms', 'nationalization', and other elements of the programme of certain socialist countries.

Except in Egypt, however, the 'progressive' military regimes have not only failed to implement socialist programmes: they have actually lowered gross national products and seriously damaged the economic welfare of some sections of the population without improving that of others. Nor have they been able, or willing, to take those social and juridical measures which would have given a progressive character to their regimes, at least on paper. Not one of the 'progressive' regimes, for example, has abolished polygamy. On the contrary, some of them have been trying to reintroduce a conservative interpretation of Islam into public life. And certain of the regimes which have been classified as 'conservative' or 'reactionary' have done much for their populations in terms of economic progress and social legislation.

Secondly, the attempt to identify Arab nationalism with the 'progressive' as opposed to the 'reactionary' regimes has led to a senseless and dangerous conflict between some of the Arab governments, just as it has inflamed and divided public opinion all over the Arab world. We must reject and resist the claim that any one regime or party or leader has a monopoly on Arab nationalism, and refuse to accept that differences of opinion or of interests provide an adequate basis for classifying regimes or individuals as genuine nationalists or traitors. The poisonous campaigns waged by the radio stations and the press in certain countries should be condemned, ignored, or ridiculed, and every pressure should be brought on those governments which utilize or permit them to put an end to this scandal of the Arab world.

The introduction into Arab life of political and social doctrines which are not relevant to it at its present stage not only weakens the Arab countries by dividing them on irrelevant issues; it also diverts their attention from their real problems. The only valid distinction at this time between the Arab countries lies in the degree of their economic and social development, and in the resources they possess to promote their progress. The real difference is between the less and the more underdeveloped, and between the rich and the poor. There is no reason why we should anticipate the problems of more highly developed societies before we have reached the stage where these problems become real and demand solutions. There is no reason why we should adopt the language and the political forms of social and economic conflicts which are not relevant to our societies.

The most immediate and urgent problems which face nearly all the Arab countries are those involved in establishing the minimum conditions on which a modern society may eventually be built. While the nature of that society, and the social and economic content of the measures to be taken to bring it into existence, must certainly be studied and discussed, and will certainly provide eventually the grounds for divergent opinions and political movements, we have not yet reached that stage. There is a wide area for action where interests are common and basic enough for us to ignore or at least to postpone questions which may divide us at a moment when we need to be united.

For some of the underdeveloped countries of the world the necessity of finding an outside source for the capital investments and the technical skills they lack forces them to an involvement in the ideological conflict and divisions of the more developed world. No such necessity exists for the Arab world, which has all the material, and many of the human resources, which it needs. There is sufficient capital and liquidity to make us independent of outside financial help, and to promote our own economic and social progress provided we use our resources intelligently, and take a broad view of both the existing and the future needs of the Arab world as a whole. We have vast territories, enormous natural resources, and vital strategic positions. What we need is to exploit them in terms of today's and tomorrow's needs. Countries which are rich today may not be always: others which are poor today possess potentialities which may one day make them rich. The total human and natural resources of the Arab world must be studied and then exploited in the light of a general plan, a moving idea.

It is this great responsibility which now faces the educated

classes in the Arab countries. They have a unique chance which
is not given to many of the educated classes of more developed
countries and societies, weighed down as they often are by
traditions and already established patterns of life which do not
give much scope to originality or to individual initiative. It is
our good fortune to be born at a time when not only great
tasks await us, but when the possibility of action is also present.

Instead of the sterile and irrelevant discussions, the bitter
divisions and mutual suspicions which dominate our political
and intellectual life, we should try to establish among ourselves
an understanding, an agreement on principles, a mutual confidence which will make possible the action which must now
be undertaken if the Arab world is to be saved from a rapid
decline.

The Argument between Arabs and Jews

An Exchange between Arnold Toynbee
and J. L. Talmon*

London, 3 July 1967

Dear Professor Talmon,

I have just been staying with my son Philip and I have read
your paper 'For Total Peace in the Middle East' which Isaiah
Berlin passed on to him. I believe, like you, that this is the moment for everyone of good will and good sense to make an
all-out effort to get total, genuine, and lasting peace there. I
believe there is a real opportunity for this, if we seize it now.
I am just back from the United States, and, three weeks ago,
I stuck my neck out by writing, for the United Press International, an article saying this, and making some concrete

* This exchange of letters between Professors Toynbee and Talmon, dated July 1967, appeared in *Encounter*, October 1967.
PROFESSOR ARNOLD TOYNBEE, who refers to himself as 'a
Western spokesman for the Arab cause', is the author of many
studies of Islamic history, politics and culture. J. L. TALMON is
Professor of Modern History at the Hebrew University of Jerusalem.

proposals for bringing it about. The United Press tell me that my article has been reproduced pretty widely in the US press, so a copy of it may come into your hands some time, but, as there is no time to lose, I am writing to you now direct.

I feel a responsibility for doing anything I can to help towards getting a permanent peace now. I have a number of reasons. (1) I am British, so I have a share of responsibility for my country's past actions. (2) As a young man during the First World War, I was working as a 'temporary Foreign Office clerk' on Middle Eastern affairs, particularly on British wartime commitments in the Middle East, so I know the history of these from the inside. (3) I am known as a Western spokesman for the Arab cause, and it is therefore just possible that what I say in public now might have some influence in the Arab world, though it is perhaps more likely that the Arabs might write me off with the verdict that I am no friend of theirs after all. Anyway, I believe that the truest act of friendship that any friend of either the Arabs or the Israelis can do for them at this moment is to try to help them to see that the facts make genuine peace a prime interest for both parties. (4) Being now an old man, with grandchildren, I feel what Johnson and Kosygin seem to have felt when they met. One's grandchildren symbolize for me, in a concrete way, all the future generations of the human race – 70 million unborn generations who might be deprived, by our generation, of their right to life if we, in our time, were to stumble into an atomic third world war. (5) Thinking also in terms of the present, I want to see something done now which, besides saving the world from an enormous catastrophe, will reduce present human suffering in the Middle East to a minimum. I should have been as much horrified at genocide of Jews in the Middle East as I was horrified at it in Europe. I also think it very wrong to treat any people, living or unborn, as political pawns, instead of treating them as suffering human beings whose alleviation ought to have priority over any political considerations. In discussing the Arab states' policy with my Arab friends, I have always pointed out to them that West Germany's post-war policy towards refugees from Eastern Germany and from east of the Oder-Neisse line has not only been humane, but has paid dividends to Western Germany, economically and therefore also politically. Israelis should look ahead for their grandchildren.

Now about the facts that each side has to face and about practical possibilities for a settlement.

In your paper, you yourself have put your finger on the fact that Israel has to face. A series of more and more sensational victories in successive wars does not, in itself, give Israel the vital thing that she wants and needs: that is, real peace with her Arab neighbours. So long as Israel has not mutually agreed permanent frontiers, but only a military front, always smouldering and periodically flaring up into full-blown hostilities, Israel has to stay constantly on the alert and cannot concentrate her energies on her own internal development, which is and always has been her real objective. She has demonstrated now conclusively that, in war, she can always conquer more Arab territory without any foreign military aid; but, the more of this that she occupies, the more she will become militarily over-extended, and the larger the proportion of her limited and precious man-power she will have to keep unprofitably mobilized. The Arab world has the same passive military advantage as Russia and China have: there is virtually no end to it. So Israel's overriding interest is genuine peace; even the greatest military victories will be fruitless unless they can be converted into that.

The Arabs have to face the fact that Israel has come to stay; that a three-times repeated experience has shown that they cannot defeat her; that the Soviet Union is not going to war with the United States for the Arabs' sake; and that, in the unlikely event of the Arabs becoming, one day, able to destroy Israel, the United States would not let this happen.

I need not dwell on your psychological analysis of the present-day Arab state of mind. It is masterly; you have shown a power of sympathetic understanding by which you have entered into it imaginatively. This is very important and very encouraging, because Israel, as the present victor, holds the initiative. The party that has suffered injustice and has been humiliated is the one that is the more sensitive and that therefore needs the more delicate handling. The Palestinian Arabs have suffered injustice. To put it simply, they have been made to pay for the genocide of Jews in Europe which was committed by Germans, not by Arabs. The Arabs as a whole have been humiliated, because, in the establishment, first of the Jewish National Home and then of the state of Israel, the Arabs have, as you point out, never been consulted. It has all been done over their heads. They have been treated as 'natives' with no more than sub-human rights. For a people with a great, but no longer actual, historic past, this is infuriating. The present Arab and present Chinese states of mind have the same explanation.

So I would plead with Israel to make the first move towards achieving the total genuine and lasting peace which is the supreme common interest of Israel, the Palestinian Arab refugees, and the Arab states. For Israel publicly to make the first move would be magnanimous as well as far-sighted. I suggest that Israel should now propose that the two sides should make the following simultaneous declaration:

The Arab states and the Palestinian Arab people pledge themselves to recognize, *bona fide*, the existence of Israel with the intention of making a permanent peace with her, and they also guarantee to negotiate permanent frontiers with Israel on approximately the 1948 armistice lines. Israel pledges herself to accept these agreed frontiers *bona fide*, with the intention, on her side, of making permanent peace, and she also undertakes to take the initiative in bringing about a satisfactory permanent settlement of the problem of the 1948 refugees.[1]

If both sides would give these reciprocal pledges in a formal agreement of the kind that used to be called 'preliminaries of peace', this would open the way for a negotiated treaty about details, and then things that have so far been impossible would become possible, e.g.:

1. The repatriation of the 1967 refugees was taken for granted in this letter. Ed.

1. In the conversion of the 1948 armistice lines into permanent frontiers, there could be minor rectifications, so long as these offset each other fairly on balance.

2. There could be a mutual opening-up of communications that are vital to both parties. Israel could be assured of a right of way not only through the Straits of Tiran but through the Suez Canal too. Egypt could be assured of a right of way, across Israel, to Lebanon, Syria, Jordan and Saudi Arabia, thus removing the 'Polish corridor' irritant of Israel's having split the Arab world in two by extending from the Mediterranean coast to the Gulf of Aqaba. Syria and Jordan could be given a free port at Haifa, with a right of way to it, and Jordan could be given a second one at Jaffa.

3. The 1948 Palestinian Arab refugees could (a) be given monetary compensation for the loss of their property situated in Israel; (b) be given an extra indemnity for having been forced, as innocent victims of the conflict between Israel and the Arab states, to spend twenty years as refugees; (c) be given the option of either returning to their former homes on condition of becoming loyal citizens of Israel (as the Galilean Arabs have been during the present crisis) or else being settled on good land outside Israel; (d) a fund could be raised for the refugees' resettlement, whether inside Israel or outside it. I am sure the majority will opt for resettlement *outside* Israel; but for Israel to offer the choice of returning home (on condition of their becoming *bona fide* loyal Israeli citizens) is psychologically very important for producing a change of heart among the refugees. If Israel appealed to the world to help her raise a fund for these four purposes, money would pour in.

4. Water for irrigation: in the London *Times* a few days ago, there was an important letter from Edmund de Rothschild about this, followed up next day by a long and constructive article by a desalination expert. They make the point that, even though desalination has not yet been made possible at an economic price, it would pay the world to subsidize it for the use of Israel and Jordan. This would (a) make it no longer necessary to pay a pittance to the refugees; (b) in combination with the Jordan water, it would supply abundant water for *both* Israel *and* Jordan, and would therefore make it unnecessary for them to contend with each other over their respective shares of Jordan water.

The future of the Old City of Jerusalem is a question of special urgency and danger. It is of crucial importance that Israel should not take unilateral action for annexing it. This would not be valid in international law; it could not be accepted by the United Nations; it would make genuine peace between Israel and the Arabs impossible; and it would arouse the whole Muslim world, and probably a large part of the Christian world too, not only against Israel, but against the Jews in general. It might seriously prejudice the diaspora's position in many countries.

Moreover, possession of the Temple area (the Muslims' Haram al-Sherif) would be an embarrassment for Israel. She would have either to refrain from rebuilding the Temple or else she would have to demolish the Dome of the Rock and the Al Aqsa Mosque, which would really be unthinkable. Of course, Israelis and all other Jews must have free access to the Wailing Wall. I like the Pope's proposal for an international trusteeship for the holy places of *all* religions in Palestine. But any change of sovereignty here would be most provocative unless it were freely negotiated in exchange for some equivalent *quid pro quo*. For instance, Jordan might conceivably say to Israel: 'Cede to us the fields, now in Israel, that belong to villages on the Jordan side of the frontier, and then we will cede to you the south-west corner of the Old City of Jerusalem, up to the western face of the Wailing Wall.' A bargain on these lines would be all right, but unilateral action by Israel would be disastrous.

Well, I am writing this to you, and am sending copies to Isaiah Berlin and to a friend of mine in Baltimore, Maryland, Rabbi Agus.

I am now an old man, and most of my treasure is therefore in future generations. This is why I care so much, and why I am writing this letter to you.

Please make any use of my letter that you think useful. I am not marking it 'confidential'.

Yours sincerely,

Arnold Toynbee

Jerusalem, 18 July, 1967

Dear Professor Toynbee,

I expressed to you by wire my first deeply felt reaction to your letter as soon as I finished reading it. I wish to apologize to you now for the ten days delay in sending you the detailed reply which I promised in my telegram. This was the last week of term at our University, teaching having been resumed at the end of June, after the interruption caused by mobilization and war. I had also wished to show your letter to friends at the University and to a few persons in government circles for their comments. Finally, I needed time to ponder over what you say and sort out my own thoughts in the light of the feelings and ideas which animate the people of Israel at this moment.

May I say at the outset that I have reason to claim that I voice the sentiments of most Israelis in the appreciation of the moral fervour and sense of urgency which motivate your letter. I speak however only for myself when I deal with your concrete proposals and offer my own suggestions. All the same, I know for certain that a very strong volume of Israeli opinion shares my views on the practical prospects of an Arab-Israeli settlement; and I do not think I exaggerate if I add that, given the proper response from the other side, the suggestions voiced in the second part of this letter may easily become acceptable to the vast majority of the people of Israel, and – Israel being a genuine democracy – to its government.

You list a number of reasons for your feeling of 'responsibility for doing anything [you] can to help towards getting a permanent peace now'. I would add one reason which you do not mention, but which to me outweighs perhaps all those enumerated by you, for in a sense it contains them all. I seemed to hear in your letter the voice of Arnold Toynbee who in the *Study of History* had been speaking to me not just as the architect of a colossal edifice, but, if I may say so, as a prophet who stands in awe before the mystery of Time and is engaged in a passionate quest for overriding purpose and redeeming significance in History. Some of us who are living in 'permanent and anguished intimacy with the mystery of Jewish martyrdom and survival' could not help responding to these 'Judaic' ingredients in your work, and therefore felt especially pained by what to us, Jews and Zionists, appeared as a failure to accord to Judaism and its contemporary mutation, Israel, their due place in your scheme of civilizations merging and falling, vast spiritual forces shaping and dissolving them, all that supposedly leading to some salvationist denouement in the end, but now suddenly faced by the mortal danger of total and meaningless destruction.

I welcome, therefore, most heartily your letter as some kind of opening to a friendly and fruitful dialogue. And it is not in any spirit of polemic or out of a wish to put into your mouth things which you did not say in your letter, but out of deep respect and genuine inner need, that I feel compelled to make these few, general comments before I come to your suggestions.

Zionism did not start with Hitler, and to us, therefore, the emergence of Israel could not be summed up in the statement that the Arabs 'have been made to pay for the genocide of Jews in Europe which was committed by Germans, not by Arabs'.

Just as we would not base our right to exist as an independent state in the Middle East solely on our right of conquest and demand of the Arabs simply to bow to that fact of nature (or history), so we could not possibly subordinate the immemorial aspiration of the Jewish people, admittedly much quickened by the rise of nationalism in the world at large, and made unbearably urgent by murderous persecution, to the exclusive resolve of the Arabs. Whatever the degree of our imaginative understanding of Arab resentment at not having been consulted on the Balfour Declaration and the Palestine Mandate and for having had their objections overridden by the UN and their armed resistance to partition (the solution contrived to meet a clash of rights) overpowered by the Jews in 1948; and whatever the measure of our embarrassed sympathy for the terrible plight of the Palestine refugees, we could not put into question the very basis of our existence.

It is probably too much to ask – in this fallen state of mankind – of a nationalist movement to see the point of the other side and to make concessions to it readily and altruistically. Many as may have been the Zionist sins of commission or omission in this respect, every one of their attempts at a compromise had all along been met by Arabs with the absolute and implacable refusal to recognize any Jewish claim. This was bound to lead to the half-despairing, half-defiant reaction that since nothing could be done with them, it had to be done in spite of and even against them. Arab intransigence has proved a disastrous policy to the Arab interests. Every crisis culminating in armed clash cost the Arabs more and more, and weakened their position still further, which again deepened Arab neurosis on the point of Israel.

Wounded pride of a race with glorious memories is not an ignoble feeling. But an obsessive sense of injury and self-pity are conducive to sterile self-centredness and stultifying misanthropy. Where would we Jews have been today, had we never ceased to remember all the scores and been reliving all the humiliations we had suffered at the hand of every possible nation with which we had come into contact throughout our long history? What would have happened to the persecuted and maltreated of our race, had we behaved like the Arab States towards the Arab refugees: 'May they suffer and rot, for it is all the doing of the Jews, and we must not make it easier for the enemy, but should on the contrary keep that sore running.' Is there any hope of breaking this vicious circle – the source of so much misery to the peoples of the Middle East, and now threatening to engulf the whole world in an unspeakable catastrophe?

A man greatly revered by both of us, my late teacher R. H. Tawney, wrote:

It is the tragedy of a world where man must walk by sight that the discovery of the reconciling formula is always left to future generations, in which passion has cooled into curiosity, and the agonies of peoples have become the exercise in the schools. The devil who builds bridges does not span such chasms till much that is precious to mankind has vanished down them for ever.

Surely enough blood has flowed down the chasms for the reconciling formula to be evolved and accepted at last. It is infinitely sad that *homo sapiens* should be so slow-witted, and that his reason should be so dominated and twisted by irra-

tional drives and intractable aversions that only an overwhelming shock and inexorable *faits accomplis* are able to make the
sweet voice of reason heard.

I entirely agree with you that on the morrow of the third
Arab–Israel war in twenty years, the most self-absorbed nationalists on both sides should be ripe for the acceptance of
the fact that galling as it is not to be able to attain one's supreme goal in its undiminished totality, that is the way the jealous gods will it. It may be hard upon the Arabs impelled by a
vision of a pan-Arab Empire from Iran to the Atlantic to find
the Jews planted on the Eastern shore of the Mediterranean.
But the war to the bitter end advocated by the extremists,
while most unlikely to wipe out Israel, is sure to bring, at once,
the Arab states under Soviet domination, with Russian 'advisers' and 'technicians' in every office and regiment: a strange
consummation of the dream of an Islamic renaissance. Even
those no longer very numerous Jews who are still capable of
becoming intoxicated with verses on the vastness of the Kingdom promised by the Almighty to His children have to wake up
to the fact that God has played them an unfair trick in putting
so many Arabs on the banks of the Jordan and scattering so
many more in the countries around. The Israelis may defeat
them again and again, but only to find the promised 'rest and
inheritance' removed further and further, and themselves condemned to live by the sword instead of walking by the spirit, to
be a Sparta and not the combination of Jerusalem and Athens –
the fondest dream of the noblest among the prospects of Zionism.

There is in fact no need to persuade Israel of the desirability
and necessity of peace. All the effort is required on the other
side. As to the actual terms envisaged by Israel, these would
be a function of Arab readiness to recognize Israel and make a
genuine peace with her. The graver our fears, the stiffer the
guarantees we think necessary for our survival and security;
the greater the confidence the Arabs are able to inspire, the
more lenient are our terms likely to be.

You single out two items as all-important and indeed all-embracing: refugees and frontiers.

Only yesterday I was deeply impressed by a person whom I was always inclined to consider something of an extremist exclaiming with heat, 'But we should pawn all we have to the tenth generation to solve this terrible problem of Arab refugees!'

I feel sure that, on this, all but one of your suggestions would be met: monetary compensation, extra-indemnity, participation in an international fund for resettlement. The difficulty would frankly be the suggestion of an Israeli offer to the Arab refugees of 1948 of the choice of returning home. You consider this as more important for its symbolic significance by expressing the certainty that the 'majority will opt for resettlement outside Israel'. As you know, we have made such an offer to the 1967 refugees who, seized by panic (out of implacable hostility to Israel or out of a desire to be with their own next of kin) crossed to the East Bank of the Jordan during and since the recent hostilities. We do not know yet how many will avail themselves of the offer to return to the West Bank. While I can see the human and symbolic significance, indeed the duty, of allowing such an option to the recent refugees, I doubt whether there is a case for doing the same in regard to the refugees of twenty years ago. It would not only create very grave problems for Israel. It would also impose upon the refugees, transplanted into realities quite different from those they knew a generation ago, strains and stresses which they would be spared if resettled in an Arab land or overseas. This does not mean that we shall not be prepared, as we have been in the past, to allow reunion of families or make special consideration where warranted.

This world should become one and a fit place for men and women of different races and religions to live together. Yet I cannot help remembering to what extent precisely regimes which claim to be inspired by a universal creed, which subordinates racial peculiarity and national self-assertion to proletarian solidarity and universal brotherhood, have found no other solution to their nationalities problem but in the expulsion of millions of women and children, and in the annexation of vast territories to which their historic claim bears no comparison at all to the strength of the Jewish claim to Palestine. Even in such advanced and rich countries like Belgium and Canada racial conflict is assuming a virulence which baffles all observers. Incidentally, in absorbing some hundreds of thousands of Jewish immigrants or refugees from the Arab countries, Israel has carried out something of an exchange of populations.

As to the territorial terms, again, I and many like me hold the realistic opinion that territory densely populated by Arabs is not only not an asset to Israel, but a liability which even from the strategic point of view outweighs the supposed strategic advantages of what is called 'more defensible frontiers'. But there are reservations. Israel is entitled to security, and while I do not wish to be an annexationist, I could not consider the 1949 (you say by mistake 1948) armistice frontiers as sacrosanct, and would think rectifications for which you make an allowance in your letter to be justified and indeed indispensable on those trouble spots like the Syrian ridge, the Sinai border, the Straits of Tiran. But I hasten to add that if other effective guarantees for our security could be devised – by way of demilitarization, international force (not one always exposed to be sent unilaterally packing), international government – I dare say there would not be any insistent pressure for far-reaching territorial changes. The Gaza Strip cannot remain an Egyptian enclave.

Israel has repeatedly offered Jordan free access to Israeli ports on the Mediterranean, and although I cannot see the necessity for Syria, which has good ports of her own, of free access to Haifa, surely in an atmosphere of good-neighbourly relations this request, like the question of a right of way for Egypt through Israeli Arab territory to the other Arab states, would not present an insurmountable obstacle. But for this, free passage for Israeli shipping through the Suez Canal is a precondition.

The question of Jerusalem is a point *sui generis*, and on this our opinions are likely to differ. Of one thing I can assure you: there is no person or group of persons, of any standing in

322   *The Israel–Arab Reader*

Israel, even among the ultra-orthodox, who would dream of rebuilding the Temple and destroying Muslim or other sanctuaries. The whole matter is not worth a moment of your anxiety. At the same time, public opinion in Israel is so unanimous and determined on the retention of Jerusalem that no government would survive a week if it showed signs of giving in on that. I invite the historian Arnold Toynbee to weigh the pros and cons of this issue in historical perspective and with the historian's detachment, difficult as it is to treat this loaded problem in that way.

If Israel is prepared, and indeed is most anxious, to submit all holy places to international administration and supervision exercised by the accredited representatives of the various religions, Christian and Muslim, with extra-territoriality guaranteed, why should there be all that fuss about sovereignty over the areas which do not contain any holy places? In what way was the Hashemite dynasty of Jordan, whose rule over Jordan resulted from the pure post-World War I accident and indeed a British embarrassment, a more trustworthy guardian than an Israeli government, which (as you hint) has hostages in all the Christian nations? The Jordanians have not left a single synagogue standing in Old Jerusalem and paved the road with tombstones from the ancient cemetery on the Mount of Olives. Are we not faced here with a residue of that unhappy, age-long special attitude to the nation of deicides, whose inferiority to Christendom (and Islam) must be made especially manifest, and the members of which must never be allowed to rule or command the members of the true and triumphant faith? Internationalization? I seem to detect signs that the Vatican has by no means made up its mind on the desirability of a Jerusalem run by the UN, in which pagan, communist-atheist and Muslim, not to speak of Protestant powers, constitute the vast majority. Finally, may I recall the tremendous agitation against the incorporation of Rome, the capital of Christendom, the seat of the Holy See, into the kingdom of Italy in the nineteenth century. It requires an effort of imagination today to visualize a situation in which Rome is not the capital of Italy, but the free state of the Pope or an international city.

This brings me to my last and most immediately practical point: how to go about getting peace.

Like very many Israelis I fervently desire an early arrangement with King Hussain of Jordan. In order not to lose myself in too sanguine illustrations I would say no more than that this solution appears to me to be the least impossible of all solutions talked of. The Israelis have genuine respect and a sneaking affection for the brave little King, and one can hear expressions of almost sympathetic regret that he should have made the terrible blunder he did. Incidentally, the total absence in Israel of any hatred or contempt for the Arabs as such is best illustrated by the fact that the spate of songs and poems of war and victory has not produced a single hate hymn; and never has any note of abuse crept into radio or press. There have been only minor cases of plunder which received prompt punishment, although in the heat of firing and sniping there seems to have been some unnecessary destruction of houses. The people left homeless were soon provided with shelter. I believe it is our interest to come to terms with Jordan and that Hussain stands to gain no less than we from such a settlement which would return to him most of the West Bank, except Jerusalem, its immediate vicinity and a few strategic points elsewhere, while ensuring to Jordanians some form of free access to Jerusalem and the holy places of Islam. I believe, like you, that the international community, especially the West, would be enthusiastically ready to offer very large sums and sponsor a joint international venture, with Israel and Jordan as partners, designed to resettle the refugees, execute those public works of irrigation and desalination you mention, solving thereby not only the refugee problem, but restoring Hussain to his former position. A common stake in joint prosperity would thus be created. Would Hussain dare to take such a step alone? Objectively speaking, Egypt and Syria can afford not to conclude any arrangement with Israel and play the part of the intransigent patriots; Jordan just cannot exist without it. Hussain had been for so long cruelly vilified and ill-used by the more powerful Arab states. In the war he and his army have acquitted themselves very honourably and the sacrifices made by them have been infinitely greater than those by other Arab states. So he has done more than his share to fight for Arab honour.

It is quite possible that once the shouting against Hussain for having come to terms with Israel had died down, the other Arab states would tire of their excitement and get down to their internal affairs and gradually slide into some *modus vivendi*, or even follow Hussain's example fairly soon.

Now I am going to stick out my neck with a good many Jews just as you in your words stuck out your neck with your Arabs. I dislike the idea of a separate little autonomous Arab state on the west bank of Jordan which would be a camouflaged Israeli protectorate. Not only because I doubt its economic viability, am apprehensive of the crushing financial and administrative burden it is sure to impose upon Israel, fear its irredentism, and the grave security problems arising out of it. I recoil from the idea of Jews lording it over others. It is at variance with the image of Judaism I cherish, and the example of other nations makes me fear the dangers to the moral fibre, the psychological balance, and spiritual values lying in wait for a master race.

I pray that we shall not be compelled to assume that role, which may happen if an arrangement with Jordan proves impossible and the other Arab states refuse to establish peace with Israel.

You speak movingly of your grandchildren. I understand you well. I am a younger man and I have two small children. When I look into their eyes, I think of the million Jewish children whom the Nazis separated from their parents, starved to death and killed in the gas chambers. At such moments my heart goes out to all the children of the world, Arab, Vietnamese, and all others, and I feel like crying aloud: 'Never, never again.'

                                                    Yours sincerely,
                                                    J. L. Talmon

Palestine and Israel

By Albert Hourani*

At the heart of the Middle Eastern problem lies the problem of Palestine: the struggle of Palestinian Arabs and Jewish settlers for possession and mastery of the land. Now that the Powers have been drawn in and a local crisis has become a worldwide one, it is easy to forget the local causes of it; but it is dangerous, for unless they are treated the crisis may return.

The struggle of Arabs and Jews for Palestine cannot be explained by ancient religious hostility. Jews (and Christians) had always lived among the mainly Arab Muslim population of Palestine, and relations between them had usually been correct. But in the 1880s a new type of Jewish immigration began, mainly from Eastern Europe, inspired by the Zionist idea of a Jewish national home: this soon aroused the hostility of Ottoman officials and part of the population.

During its thirty years of rule, 1917–47, Britain bound itself by the Balfour Declaration and the Mandate to encourage the Jewish national home, subject to the rights of the existing population; immigration increased, particularly after the rise of Hitler, and Arab opposition became almost universal and drew in the surrounding Arab states.

This hostility sprang from the attempt to implant a new society in a land already occupied by an old one. When the settlers came they found a complete society already there: farmers, craftsmen and merchants, ancient towns and villages, religious institutions, a culture expressed in Arabic, a leadership which formed part of the Arab Ottoman élite. The aim of the newcomers was not to be absorbed into it but to create their own society with its farms and cities, institutions, Hebrew culture and political leaders.

*Albert Hourani is Director of the Middle Eastern Centre and Fellow of St Antony's College, Oxford. His article was first published in the *Observer* (London) 3 September 1967. (Reprinted by permission of the Observer Foreign News Service.)

In the age of European expansion, other such attempts were made to plant new societies amidst old ones. They always caused strain, but Zionist settlement in Palestine had special features. The new Jewish society, by the nature of the Zionist idea, was to be a complete and exclusive one. Its aim was to create a wholly Jewish economy: land bought by the Jewish National Fund became the inalienable property of the Jewish people and no non-Jew could ever be employed on it.

It is true the Zionists bought their land. But in the Middle East political power and ownership of land have always gone together, and the Arabs were convinced that if the Jews had power they would seize the greater part of the land. That the Jews *would* take power became first a danger, then a certainty, as the Jewish population grew. Because of the nature of the Zionist idea, the new Jewish society was an expanding society, open to all who wished to come in. In 1922 Jews formed 13 per cent of the population of Palestine; in 1935, 28 per cent; in 1947, 33 per cent.

As numbers grew, the idea of a Jewish national home turned into that of a Jewish state, and this was unacceptable to the Arabs, not only because by the 1930s most of them were moved by the idea of an Arab state of which Palestine would be part, but because in a Jewish state they would have no choice (whatever guarantee the Mandate might contain) except between being a powerless minority and leaving their country.

Some Zionist leaders did indeed talk of a 'bi-national state', but attempts at political agreement broke on the question of immigration. The Arabs wanted to preserve the Arab character of Palestine, and so wanted little or no Jewish immigration. The Zionists wanted to keep the doors of Palestine open, no matter what the form of government.

Here lay the dilemma of their policy: they wanted agreement with the Arabs and they wanted unlimited immigration, but they could not have both, and if forced to choose most of them would choose immigration.

The British, who were politically responsible, had no clear or stable policy on this matter. They had obligations to the

Arabs and so opposed the idea of a Jewish state: they had obligations to the Zionists and so permitted immigration, not as much as the Jews wanted but enough to make a Jewish state possible. In 1948, unable to reach agreement with the two parties, they withdrew in circumstances which made fighting inevitable, and there happened what the Arabs had feared for so long.

The dynamic, exclusive, alien society which had grown up among them seized power in the greater part of Palestine, with encouragement and help from some Western states, secured control of the land and brought in immigrants on a large scale; and two thirds of the Arab inhabitants lost their lands and homes.

All wars create refugees, and after the armies have departed the peasants and merchants return to take up their lives again. Civilized governments accept that they have a responsibility for those who live in the land they rule. But after the armistice agreements of 1949 Israel refused – with limited exceptions – to allow the Arab refugees to return. In a situation like this everything becomes political, and the Israelis made political use of the refugees.

By refusing to consider the refugee problem except in the framework of a peace settlement with the surrounding Arab states, they linked together two matters which had no moral connexion; for the return of the refugees was an obligation which they owed not to the surrounding Arab states but to the Palestinian Arabs themselves, as inhabitants of the land they had conquered. To make such a connexion was the more tempting because Israel did not really wish the refugees to return. Even at a peace settlement it would only have offered to take back a small number; for what it wanted was to have the land without its inhabitants, so as to settle its own immigrants.

(This policy was made morally acceptable to Israelis and the outside world by the 'myth' that the Arabs left willingly under orders from their leaders. No more than the most tenuous evidence was produced for this, and, in fact, the flight of the Arabs presents no mystery. Some left for reasons of prudence, some from panic during the fighting, some were forced to go by the Israeli Army. What has happened this year throws some light on this. It is clear that no Arab government ordered the Palestinians to leave this year, but a quarter of the inhabitants of the West Bank left in two months – and for the same reasons.)

Nothing could show more clearly that the basic dilemma of Zionist policy was still there. If it wanted land for immigrants, it was sensible to stop the return of the refugees. But if it wanted peace with the Arabs, then it was fatal.

After 1948, the first step to peace was that Israel should recognize its responsibility to the Arabs who lived in its territory but had been displaced by the fighting. Only this could have set in motion a train of events leading towards peace; and only Israel, as victor and beneficiary of the war, could have taken the step. Israel never did so, and its attitude was accepted by the Western powers. Every year the United Nations passed a resolution calling for the return or compensation of the refugees, but no one tried seriously to carry it out.

The assumption which underlay the attitude of Israel and the Western powers was that sooner or later the refugees would melt away, absorbed into the surrounding Arab peoples, and then the problem of Palestine would cease to exist. But this was a false assumption. It was not a mass of individuals who fled in 1948, it was the greater part of a society. A common land and language, a common political fate, and the shock of exile created a Palestine Arab nation. After 1948 it lived scattered.

Allowing for natural increase, by the beginning of this year there must have been rather more than two million Palestinian Arabs: almost 400,000 in the Gaza Strip, 300,000 in Israel, 1,300,000 in Jordan, 150,000 each in Lebanon and Syria. About two thirds of them were still registered refugees. Many of these had become wholly or partly self-supporting; if more had not, it was not (as was often said) because the host-countries did not wish them to be settled, but because the absorption of refugees depended on the pace of economic development, and this was bound to be slow in the early stages. In no country was their position satisfactory.

In Jordan they had full citizenship, but Palestinians and Transjordanians had not yet been welded into a complete unity, and positions of real power remained in Transjordanian hands; an intelligent policy of development created an economy into which some of them were absorbed, but the refugees formed a third of the whole population, and a country with such limited resources could not absorb so large a number in twenty years.

In Israel, their position was tolerable: they had civil and political rights, but fewer opportunities of higher education and skilled employment than Jews, they lived under a strict military control (until a relaxation in recent months), and were virtually shut out of the political community.

Thus the Palestinian Arabs remained in being as a nation which had lost almost everything but was determined to continue to exist: that is to say, to live with one another, and to live in Palestine. After 1948 this was the heart of the 'Palestine problem'; the *de facto* existence of Israel was not in serious danger, but what remained to be assured was the existence of the Palestinian nation. Its attitude to Israel was shared by the other Arab nations, for many reasons. The individual losses of the refugees were felt throughout Jordan, Syria and Lebanon, which belonged to the same geographical and historical unit as Palestine, and where almost every family had Palestinian connexions.

More widespread still was a sense of human indignity, a feeling that in the eyes of Israel and the West the Arabs were surplus human beings, to be removed and dumped elsewhere to redress a wrong not they but Europe had done to the Jews. It seemed to most Arabs that Western governments talked in one way about the rights of the Jews and in another about those of the Arabs. They often said that Israel was here to stay; they never said that the Palestinian Arab nation was here to stay. They talked in language of high principles and threats about Israel's right to free navigation; they used a milder language about the right of the refugees to return or compensation.

Unwise statements by Arab spokesmen about throwing Israel into the sea were widely quoted and condemned; no one seemed to care that Israel had, in fact, thrown a large number of Arabs into the desert.

Together with this went an almost universal fear. So long as Israel remained open to all Jews who wished to immigrate, so long as it could maintain Western standards of technology and hope for wide support in Europe and America, there would be a danger of its expanding into the territory of the surrounding states. Sooner or later, most Arabs believed, Israel would absorb the rest of Palestine, and perhaps parts of southern Syria and Lebanon as well; for a second time the Palestinians would have to move out, and would find themselves walking down the road to Jericho or scrambling across the Jordan bridges.

Whatever their differences on other matters, the Arab states were united in their attitude to Israel, and attracted the support – within limits – of most Afro-Asian and communist states. But coalitions are fragile, in particular if they include states of unequal strength. The common object which brings them together becomes entangled with the separate interests and claims of each, and it was this which led the Arabs into statements and acts which were self-defeating. The essential point of their propaganda was justice for the Palestinian Arabs.

Before 1948 it had been possible to argue that a Jewish state should not be set up because this would be unjust to the Arabs; but once Israel had become a member of the UN, to talk in terms of its disappearance as a state was to embarrass allies and touch a sensitive spot in the European conscience. The official policy to the Arab states was not to destroy Israel but to return to the settlement of 1947–8 and a fulfilment of all the UN resolutions; but at the same time they insisted they were still in a state of active belligerence.

This was a dangerous policy for a weaker party to adopt towards a stronger: it gave Israel a licence to attack whenever it could claim that its interests were in danger. Israel indeed always remained balanced between two policies: it wanted peace with the Arabs if it could obtain it on its own terms; but war with the Arabs might give it better frontiers.

An Arab policy based on inferior power but expressed in extreme terms played into Israel's hands. This was shown clearly in the events of May and June. For ten years Egypt and Jordan had kept their frontiers with Israel quiet, and there is no reason to think they wanted a change. But the Syrian frontier was disturbed because of the difficult problem of the demilitarized zone.

Syria began supporting Palestinian activist groups; Israel replied, first by an unprovoked attack on Jordan, not Syria, then by threats which constituted a challenge to Egypt. Egypt replied by sending its Army to the frontier. In so doing Egypt acted as prisoner of the hopes it had aroused, but clearly it did not expect to fight. Egypt's acts were directed towards a political settlement, and its mistake was to think not that the Russians would support it more than they did, but that the Americans would restrain Israel more than they did – that the United States could or would force Israel to give Egypt a victory which might lead to further demands.

Israel called the Egyptian bluff in circumstances which brought it the greatest possible support in the Western world, not only because of Egypt's bad relations with the US and Britain but because of foolish statements by Arab leaders skilfully used by Zionist propaganda.

The frightening wave of anti-Arab feeling which swept Europe and America in June is not the subject of this article. Ordinary people, Jews and non-Jews, certainly felt that Israel was threatened with destruction. It is more difficult to believe that the Israel Government thought so, knowing its own military strength and that it had a guarantee (implicit or formal) from the strongest Power in the world. However that may be, the defensive war soon became a 'defensive-offensive' one, and once more what the Palestinians had feared came true.

The Israeli victory has changed many things in the Middle East, but it has not changed the problem of Palestine. The Palestinian Arab people are still there, still in ruin and exile, still determined to exist. Perhaps two thirds of them are now under Israeli rule; many more refugees have been created, and it is not certain that Israel will allow most of them to return; many who are not refugees have been ruined by the occupation of half Jordan; every individual Palestinian has now suffered or lost something because of Israel.

The attitude of the Palestinians towards Jordan may well have changed, and if the West Bank is returned Jordan may become a more solid and united state. But in spite of Israeli hopes and efforts, there is no reason to believe that the attitude of Palestinian Arabs towards Israel has changed, except to be hardened by new losses. The Arab states have more and not less reason to think of Israel as an expansionist state which, with the help or acquiescence of the US, may dominate politically and economically the region lying between Nile and Euphrates.

It seems not impossible that the Arab states will be persuaded to make a declaration of non-belligerence and the Israelis to withdraw from the conquered lands. Even so, the basic dilemma of Israeli policy remains. The Palestinian Arabs are the estranged neighbours with whom Israel must be reconciled if it is to become 'like all nations'; and it remains true, as it has been since 1948, that the first step towards a stable *modus vivendi* is one which only Israel can take – to accept its responsibility towards the indigenous people of the land it controls, and to grant the refugees the right of return or compensation.

In the long run it may be in Israel's interest to do this: only as a mixed state has it a chance of being accepted by its neighbours. But in the short run, the desire for security and for further immigration works against it. It seems more likely than not that Israel will do nothing. If so, it may stay in Gaza and the West Bank; part of the Arab population may be squeezed out; the rump of Jordan may be absorbed into some other state; and in a few more years the Palestinian Arab nation may rise once more to haunt Israel, this time inside as well as outside its frontiers.

Israel and the Arabs

By J. L. Talmon*

The Arab–Israeli dispute has become a world issue. This time
the world has had a lucky escape, possibly thanks to the swift-
ness and completeness of the Israeli victory. No one can be
sure of such good luck in the case of another round.

Who are the parties to the Israel–Arab conflict? Clearly not
only the Jews of Israel on the one side, and the Palestine Arabs
on the other. They are Israel – representing in some way world
Jewry – and the Arab world acting on behalf of the Palestine
Arabs.

To me, after reading Dr Hourani's article 'Palestine and
Israel' in the *Observer* last week, the conflict illustrates that
the view one takes on the particular rights and wrongs is determined by one's disposition towards the general case – recognition or non-recognition of an overriding right, a will to
war or a will to peace.

But no one who believes and claims for his own people the
right of national liberation and self-determination may decry
Zionists settlement as 'imperialist invasion'. Nor must its significance be reduced to the dimensions of an asylum for a mob
of refugees driven out by Hitler and then thrown upon the
Arabs, who had no share in the persecution. It was only natural, once the urge for corporate self-expression in conditions
of sovereign mastery over their own fate – the most potent
and universal impulse in modern times – had seized the heirs
of one of the most ancient peoples on earth, that the aspiration
should rivet itself to their ancient home, where their identity
was first evolved and where their distinct and so significant
contribution to mankind's heritage was shaped.

---

*J. L. Talmon is Professor of Modern History at the Hebrew
University, Jerusalem. His answer to Albert Hourani was published
in the *Observer* (London), 10 September 1967. (Reprinted by permission of the Observer Foreign News Service.)

Millions of Europe's Jews were then overtaken by a wave of murderous persecutions without precedent. Literally hunted for their lives, they had no government to appeal to for protection, no tribunal to turn to for redress – delivered into the hands of assassins on the sole condition that they would be put to death. This traumatic experience fired the Israelis with the desperate resolve to gain, in one place in the world, political sovereignty, without having to rely on the protection or help of others, and to fight for it to death.

On the plane of lesser urgency, the annihilation of that compact and vital Jewish civilization in central and eastern Europe, coupled with the loss of cohesion in Jewish life in the remaining Diaspora, has left Israel as sole guarantor of the survival of the corporate identity of the Jews as a people. This explains the recent upsurge of first anguished and then proud solidarity with Israel in all parts of Jewry.

But what about the Arab rights and claims? I would classify myself as one of those Zionists who, though passionately convinced of the rightness of the Jewish case, are nevertheless made acutely uneasy by the thought of the Arabs. They can find no sustenance in ascribing to the Arabs some special dose of original sin and selfish greed, let alone inferiority. Dr Weizmann aptly described our position when he spoke of the Jewish–Arab conflict as a clash of rights, for which a solution could be found only on the lines of least injustice, and where no perfect justice was possible.

Dr Hourani seems to make the distinction between the Palestine Arabs as a mass of human beings and Palestinian Arab nationhood. On the sufferings of the former, I must confess I have no answer, no more than to the bafflingly cruel mystery why innocent people suffer and die when states engage in wars, nor to the chilling fact that there has not been a nation in history, including the mightiest Powers and richest civilizations on earth, which has not established itself through invading, subjugating, expelling, or indeed annihilating vast native populations. Dr Hourani himself admits that the situation of the Arabs under Israeli jurisdiction has been tolerable.

Just as there is no justification for the claim that Israel is in any way an obstacle to the flowering of an Arab renaissance in the vast territories around Palestine, there is no ground for maintaining that Palestinian Arab national identity and culture have suffered mortal injury from the encroachment of the Jews. The Arabs themselves had until recently been vehemently denying the existence of such an entity as Palestine, insisting that the Holy Land was nothing but southern Syria, as administratively it was under the Turks. There has never been a distinct Arab–Palestinian culture, literature, dialect or national consciousness. Although it is one of the holy Muslim cities, Jerusalem has never played any role comparable to Cairo, Damascus or Baghdad in Arab history. And so, while the obliteration of Jewish Israel would make the survival of the Jewish entity very problematic, even a complete de-Arabization of Palestine – which is hardly at stake – would have no vital effect on the Arab totality nor, in the last analysis, on even the aspiration towards permanent Arab unity.

Admittedly, not much thought was given to the Palestine Arabs before or at the end of the First World War. Britain, which issued the Balfour Declaration of 1917, and the countries which endorsed the Mandate on Palestine in 1921, had all been nurtured on biblical reminiscences of the eternal bond between the children of Israel and their promised land. They knew next to nothing of the Arabs, nor were they particularly worried about the rights of the native populations of the partitioned Ottoman Empire – especially since the Arabs had emerged after the First World War from centuries of Turkish bondage with large self-governing territories, in comparison with which what was promised to the Jews seemed so little.

For a fleeting moment it seemed also as if the Weizmann–Faisal agreement might ensure a *modus vivendi* between the diverse aspirations of the two races. Addicted to their idealistic endeavour, so pathetically eager to turn the desert into garden, the Jews would at first meet any argument about the Arabs with vague expressions of benevolence, quite sincerely disclaiming any wish to hurt them. They were passionately anxious to build up a normal integrated Jewish society and to disprove the slander of their detractors that they were made only for usury and commerce and not for labour and toil. They were also afraid of being put in the position of European planters in Asia and Africa, and so they insisted on employing only Jewish labour on the Jewish national land.

Then, in 1937, when the clash between Arabs and Jews became too acute, the Jews accepted the Royal (or Peel) Commission plan for partition, although by then the need for a refuge from anti-Semitic persecution was already desperately urgent. It was rejected uncompromisingly by the Arabs. The same happened in 1947 – when the United Nations, with the United States and Russia acting as sponsors, resolved upon partition. The Arabs have never since tired of proclaiming a state of war against Israel. In violent and bloodcurdling language they continued to voice their intention to wipe out Israel, and indeed its inhabitants. Survivors of Auschwitz could not be expected to treat such threats as mere rhetoric or figures of speech. Nor could they be blamed if they resolved to acts of war, when day in and day out it was not only dinned into their ears that a state of siege was on, but demonstrated to them in the form of infiltration, sabotage, murder and arson.

It was as if God had hardened the heart of Pharaoh: the more intransigent the form of Arab enmity towards Israel, the worse were the consequences for the Arabs themselves. The armed resistance of the Arab states to the UN plan created the refugee problem; the resumption of fighting after the first cease-fire resulted in the loss of more Arab territory; Arab sabotage on the one hand and alliance with Russia on the other only led to a strengthening of Israel's might; finally, this year, the attempt to strangle Israel brought the Arabs a most humiliating *débâcle*.

The armistice agreements concluded in 1949 between the new State of Israel and the Arab countries contained *prima facie* all the guarantees for peace, if not in form, at least in substance. They forbade hostile propaganda, acts of sabotage, operations by military or paramilitary formations, above all armed intrusions or incursions by Army detachments.

In a state of war no points of contact are possible. Hence the irrelevance of the empirical approach, so dear to Anglo-Saxon statesmanship, which sets its hopes on gradual, imperceptible sliding from a state of half-war, half-peace into a state of full peace, from contact and cooperation in small things – such as sharing the waters of the Jordan – to sustained neighbourly give-and-take in all spheres.

This is the context of the question of refugees. Acute as the problem is in terms of human suffering, and few Jews, sons of a nation of exiles and refugees, can be callously indifferent to this aspect of the problem, the state of war makes its solution quite impossible. The world is understandably deeply exercised by the plight of hundreds of thousands of refugees wasting away their lives in camps in pitiable conditions.

One often hears the well-intentioned opinion that this is the most serious obstacle to peace, and that if this tragedy were to be put out of the way, peace could easily be established. The Arabs themselves have never said that the return of the Arab refugees to Palestine was their condition for peace; quite the reverse. In October 1949 the Egyptian Foreign Minister said: 'It should be known and well understood that in demanding the return of the refugees to Palestine the Arabs mean their return as masters of their country and not as slaves. More clearly, they envisage the liquidation of Israel.' In a speech in 1964 President Nasser stated: 'There have been attempts to separate the issues and present them in an imaginary way, as if the question of Israel is just the problem of refugees, and that once this problem is solved the Palestine question would be solved and no trace would be left of it. The Israeli danger lies in the very existence of Israel and in what this state represents.'

If war was the objective, no one could blame the Israelis for believing that the demand for the readmission of refugees, or compensation for them, was motivated not just by the wish to see them restored to their homes, but by the desire to use them as an instrument, a Trojan horse, to disrupt Israel. Besides, the way to solve the refugee problem is surely not by revanchism. What Pandora's boxes would be opened if all nations whose members had been driven from their homes by armed hostilities were to resort to war to right the wrong or merely to wreak vengeance.

Israel has already absorbed in the last twenty years about 600,000 Jewish immigrants from the Arab countries. The Arab refugee problem is intractable, not because no solution can be found through their resettlement and absorption elsewhere in the Arab countries, but because of the implacable Arab refusal even to consider such a possibility lest this blunt the edge of the refugee issue as a political weapon. In fact, the refugee problem is not the sole or even the main obstacle to peace: it is the state of war that is the chief obstacle to the solution of the refugee problem. But Arabs would not, and perhaps could not, see that, because Israel has become to them an obsession, indeed a neurosis.

The Arabs are a proud race enamoured of the memories of their past glories. When they woke up so late from their long lethargy, they were, like all late-comers, in a great haste to recover their place in the sun. They were then faced by the inexorable facts of actual weakness, underdevelopment and vast misery. The combination of resentment towards the West and the envious desire to appropriate and utilize its achievements and levers of power, plus the frustrations encountered in the attempt to skip centuries of social and economic development, led Arabs to put all the blame on imperialism – although in comparative terms the brunt of imperialism was felt much more heavily by other races.

World support for Zionist settlement, for which Arab consent was neither sought nor obtained, and then the establishment of Israel, assumed in the eyes of Arab nationalism the dimensions of a mortal injury, especially as it came from the hands of the Jews, whom they had been accustomed to despise as second-class citizens and a non-martial race of infidels.

The Palestine issue has become the symbol and focus of all Arab frustrations. Their sense of grievance blinds them to the historic rights, the background of tragedy behind the Jewish aspirations, the ardour and high idealism motivating them and the genuine interest of the civilized world in the restoration of Jewish statehood.

The student of Arab opinion and Arab thought is often horrified to watch the growth of the anti-Israel obsession to the point of it having become the cornerstone of a kind of systematic Manichean metaphysic, with the Jew as devil incarnate.

The paramount task at present is to put an end to the general atmosphere of 'kill him before he kills you'. The Arabs threaten to kill the Jews; the Jews then feel they must forestall the Arabs; the Arabs are convinced the Jews are out to kill them off, and so when an armed clash occurs they start running; the Arabs swear bloody vengeance; the Jews insist on maximum guarantees. Any historian knows what a corroding effect this sense of a state of mortal emergency has on peace, morality and freedom. The Arabs are now, understandably, in a state of shock. But one believes one perceives wiser and more prudent counsels stirring among some of them, although for the time being these are too inhibited to come out into the open.

Israel is still more deeply divided. There are those who anxiously 'await a telephone call from King Hussain', hoping for an arrangement with him whereby Jordan would receive back most of the West Bank, except some strategic points and, of course, excepting Jerusalem, plus access to and possibly control over the Muslim holy places. These hopes also assume that worldwide financial support, combined with a substantial Israeli contribution – by way of compensation – would not only make the resettlement of refugees possible, but also put Hussain back on his feet, and create a network of joint, international-sponsored ventures in the form of vast works for desalination, irrigation, and so on, for the benefit of all concerned.

There are the others who, pointing to Arab intransigence, claim to see in the triumph of Israel arms the hand of God. Such a chance occurs only once in history, they say. The present generation of Israelis has no right to barter away the promised inheritance, which belongs to all generations. There can be no retreat from the strategic frontiers, particularly on the Jordan, the Heights of Golan, and the Suez Canal. (Others would be content with the demilitarization of Sinai.) They insist on the sacrosanct character of the geo-political entity that is Palestine.

While the mystics and romantics are obsessed with the danger from outside, the moderate realists fear the enormous difficulties inside, arising out of the presence of a large compact territorial Arab minority. They are also beset by grave moral scruples and are apprehensive of world public opinion. To this the former, among them a surprising number of declared leftists, retort by condemning their adversaries as men of small Zionist faith, who also lack confidence in the ability of Israel to treat an Arab minority humanely and well and to solve all the social and economic problems involved.

In the hopeless view they take of the Arab readiness to recognize the existence of Israel, the hawks of Israel are most likely to add fuel to the hawks in the Arab world. This paradoxical 'alliance' can be countered, and the vicious circle broken, only by an 'alliance' of the moderate realists on both sides. And I can only hope that my friend Hourani and men like him will heed this appeal to their moral obligation towards their own people and mankind in general.

The Origins of the Middle East Crisis[1]

By Hal Draper*

We have just seen War No. 3 in the tragedy known as the Israel–Arab conflict; and we find ourselves in the position of

---

1. This article is a somewhat condensed and edited version of a talk given in Berkeley shortly after the outbreak of the Third Arab–Israeli War, dealing with the historical background of the conflict but not with the current situation, which was discussed separately. Fully detailed documentation for the material contained here may be found in a book which has just been published, Zionism, Israel and the Arabs: The Historical Background of the Middle East Tragedy (Berkeley, 1967), edited by myself, comprising articles from the Independent Socialist press. H.D.

*Hal Draper is an editor of New Politics and author of 'Berkeley:

being unable to cheer for either side in this clash of chauvinisms. At this time I am going to devote myself mainly to the myths and illusions about the Israeli side of the story, for the simple reason that it is these myths and illusions that you mainly read and hear about.

It is not possible to understand what has happened merely by looking at what happened in the last couple of weeks. Behind War No. 3 is a closely connected chain of events and issues going far back. The main link in this chain is the story of a *nation that has been destroyed*.

That sounds like an echo of what we hear all around, viz. the threat of the Arab states to destroy the state of Israel – the threat which is the hallmark of Arab chauvinism. But while this is a threat, there *was* a nation that was destroyed in Palestine – already. It is this destroyed nation whose fate has been the crux of the Middle East tragedy, for its fate has been used and is being used as a football by each side.

When I was born, there was an Arab nation in Palestine, in whose midst Jews had lived for 2000 years in relative peace. Where is this nation now, and what has been done to it? The answer is at the heart of the programme which we face now.

Today the leaders of the Arab states are saying, 'We aim to destroy the nation which inhabits Palestine', and they are rightly denounced for this. But towards the end of the nineteenth century, a movement arose which did in fact set itself the aim of destroying the nation which inhabited Palestine then; and moreover it did so. That movement was the Zionist movement.

Everyone talks nowadays about 'the Jews' and 'the Arabs', with doubtful justice. There are Jews and Jews, as there are Arabs and Arabs: and right now I am talking not about 'the

The New Student Revolt'. His article appeared in *New Politics*, Winter 1967, and is reprinted by permission of the author. An article in a similar vein by the late Isaac Deutscher ('On the Israel–Arab War') was published in the *New Left Review*, London, July–August 1967. It was answered in detail by Simha Flapan in *Les Temps Modernes*, Paris, November 1967. Ed.

342   *The Israel–Arab Reader*

Jews', but about the Zionist movement. Israel today is run by the old men of the world Zionist movement, and it is still the Zionist ideology which rules Israeli policy. The European survivors of Hitler's death camps are not the Jews who run Israel; their terrible fate has been a tool used by the men who run Israel, so that the crimes of the Nazis have been used to deflect the attention of world public opinion from the crimes committed in Palestine.

For present purposes, there are three things to understand about this Zionist ideology, which still rules the rulers of Israel. To present the first, I quote a typical example of anti-Semitic literature:

> The converted Jew remains a Jew, no matter how much he objects to it ... Jews and Jewesses endeavour in vain to obliterate their descent through conversion or intermarriage with the Indo-Germanic and Mongolian races, for the Jewish type is indestructible ... Jewish noses cannot be reformed, and the black wavy hair of the Jews will not change through conversion into blond, nor can its curves be straightened out by constant combing.

There is more of the same where this comes from. Obviously from the Nazi commentary on the Nuremberg Laws, or from Streicher's *Stürmer*, or perhaps from Gerald L. K. Smith? Not at all: it is from a classic of Zionism, Moses Hess's *Rom und Jerusalem*. It is easily possible to quote pages and pages more of this same mystical blood-tribalism from the best Zionist sources, all sounding as if it came from the arsenal of the anti-Semites.

For Zionism is, first of all, a doctrine about a tribal blood-mystique which makes all Jews a single nation no matter where they live or how. It asserts that Jews are inevitably *aliens* everywhere, just as the anti-Semites say they are; and that anti-Semitism is correct in feeling this. This is the first element in Zionism.

Secondly: it follows that the Jews must reconstitute their 'nation' in a state territory; but not just *any* state territory. In fact there is a point of view called 'territorialism', as distinct from Zionism, which looked for the establishment of a Jewish

nation in a land other than Palestine. But Zionism demands that
the Jewish 'nation' take over Palestine – only Palestine; and
by Palestine it means the ancient Jewish state and its boundaries, *Eretz Israel*, no less. This is what the tribal mystique
demands.

Thirdly: the Zionist ideology dictates that this Jewish state
must be set up not only by Jews who want to live in such a
state. One of the tasks of the Zionist movement is to move *all*
Jews, from all countries of the world, into Palestine, now Israel.
In Zionist slang, this is called the 'Ingathering of the Exiles';
for it is an article of basic faith that all Jews living outside this
territory are living literally in exile, and always will merely be
exiles, nothing else. It was not very many years ago that a
writer in *Davar*, the organ of the Israeli ruling party, made
the suggestion that a good way of uprooting all those American Jews who declined to go to Israel was to send a gang of
anti-Semitic agitators there to make the ground hot under their
feet so that they would move. This, of course, is not usually the
course recommended on paper, as against persuasion. But how
persuasion graduates into denunciation and arm-twisting was
seen in the early fifties when David Ben Gurion, on a visit to
the US, denounced the Zionist Organization of America as
traitors to Zionism because its leaders were not working actively to get the entire Jewish population of the US to move to
Israel. It must be understood (though American Zionists sys-
tematically obfuscate it to the best of their ability) that the
Israeli leaders and world Zionist leaders sincerely believe in
their mission to 'ingather' *all* the Jews of the world to the state
of Israel, and that they have devoted their lives to this mission.

The Zionists have always been fond of saying that they are
tired of the Jews being a 'peculiar people', that they have
been 'peculiar' long enough. They want (they say) the Jews
to be a people like any other, and to have a state just like any
other state. In Israel, I would tell you, they have succeeded
notably in *this* aim: Israel more and more has become a state
like any other state. In this stridently militarist Zionist state, the
current of Jewish humanism which was one of the glories of
the Jewish people from Maimonides to Spinoza and after, is

today represented only by a minority – a minority whose voices are rarely heard abroad, and hardly at all in the US; but it is this minority which represents the only Israel with whom one can identify.

Soon after the creation of Israel the press was full of enthusiastic reports by American Jewish tourists who went to Israel and came back to relate the wonders that they saw there (and there are many to see). One that I remember most vividly was a tourist who was quoted as follows in the course of his burbling: 'Why, you walk around Tel Aviv, and you know what? Even the *policemen* are Jewish!' That's true, naturally. The cops are Jewish in Israel – and they are still cops. The militarists in Israel are Jewish – and they are militarists. And the people who destroyed the Arab Palestinian nation which I mentioned were, alas, also Jewish – though I do not believe that they will go down in the annals of history alongside Maimonides and Spinoza.

The destruction of that Palestinian nation went through four periods. The first period goes from the beginning of the Zionist movement up to World War I. This was a period of slow immigration of Jews into Palestine and of gradual land-buying. By the time it ended Jews constituted something under ten per cent of the population. Despite Zionism's profession that this was the thin edge of the wedge in its long-term aim to establish a Jewish state in the land inhabited by Arabs, it was not taken seriously enough to occasion much resistance until the second period, inaugurated by the 1917 Balfour Declaration.

It was in this period that British imperialism, taking over the area, started its decades-long policy of playing Zionists against Arabs in order to maintain its imperialist control. The Zionist leadership willingly and knowingly collaborated with the British. They knew that, at this stage, it was not they who could control the Arab people living in the land; only British imperialism could do it for them. To be sure, they were not *puppets* of the British: they were junior partners, in an enterprise in which each partner considered that it was using the other for its own ends.

This was also the period of the beginning of Arab nationalism, of an Arab national liberation movement. This movement had every right to fight for liberation from Britain (or
in other parts of the Middle East, from France). To supporters
of Arab freedom, the Zionist movement could have appeared
only as what it actually was: a partner of the European imperialists. It makes no difference whatsoever that the Zionists
played this baneful role not out of love for Britain but in pursuit of their own expansion. The fact is that Britain used the
Zionist tool to increase the number of Jewish settlers so as to
play them off against the indigenous Arab population. Thus it
was inevitable that Jewish immigration should appear to the
Arabs as a tool of imperialist domination, for it was so.

It was therefore during the 1920s that, for pretty much the
first time in Palestine, there began sporadic Arab attacks
against Jewish settlers. On the one side, these were the first stirrings of an Arab national liberation movement, directed not
only against the British but also against the allies of the British
who were at hand, viz. Zionist infiltrators into the country.
On the other hand – and here you get the typically tragic
element in this story which goes through it from beginning to
end – these stirrings took on strong overtones of the backward
social and religious aims of the Arab movement; for progressive social elements were weak, working-class formations
were incipient. But this hardly can change the fact that there
was a legitimate nationalist movement under way.

The third period – which was to prove decisive to the outcome – came with the onset of the Nazis' anti-Jewish drive,
first in Germany itself, and then in the course of World War II
in the rest of Nazi-occupied Europe, up to the mass extermination campaign and its death camps. It should be added that, in
the period immediately following the war, there was also the
onset of Soviet anti-Semitism on a big scale, thereby boosting
the impact of what had happened during the war.

This is the period that everyone knows about; some think it
is all one has to know. But there is more to this than meets the
myopic eye.

To be sure, for the Jewish remnant Europe represented

burning ground: they had to get out – somehow, somewhere, anywhere. This plight of the Jewish refugees – one of the most terrible in the history of man's bestiality to man – was what dramatically captured the sympathy of everyone decent in the world; it is this that is tied up in the public mind with the exodus to Palestine. This is entirely true as far as it goes; but one has to know something else too. *This terrible plight and this great world sympathy were not enough to open the gates of a single Western country to those Jewish refugees!*

During those years we Independent Socialists called for opening the doors of the United States to the Jewish victims of Hitlerism, those who were left. I can tell you that in this great 'liberal' country, crawling with liberals, there was hardly an echo of such a notion, of opening the doors of *this* country to the poor Jews for whom everyone's heart bled – in print.

One reason for this is clear and can be easily documented. Morris Ernst, the famous civil liberties lawyer who was involved at the time, has told the story, among others: about how the leaders of the Zionist movement exerted all the influence they could muster to make sure that the US did *not* open up immigration to these Jews – for the simple reason that they wanted to herd these same Jews to Palestine. This is what their Zionist ideology demanded. White Christian America was only too glad to go along with this 'solution'! Who wanted a few hundred thousand miserable Jewish refugees coming into the country? Not our liberal Americans, who were so heart-stricken by Nazi brutality. Not the British, who took in an inconsequential token number. Nor anyone else. These Jewish victims were people on the planet without a visa. Liberals in this country, as elsewhere, had a convenient way of salving their tender consciences; all they had to do was parrot the line which the Zionists industriously provided them: 'They want to go only to Palestine ...'

Now there is no point in anyone's arguing to what extent this was really true or not, or of how many it was true, because no one ever gave them the chance to decide whether they wanted to go to Palestine or to some other country that was open to them. The doors were shut against them, with the help of the whole Zionist apparatus and of other 'influential' Jews who were no more enthusiastic about 'flooding' the country with poor Jews than their WASP neighbours. First it was made damned sure that Palestine was the only possible haven, and then they might possibly be asked where they wanted to go, as if they had a free choice! In my eyes, this is one of the basest crimes committed by the Zionist leadership.

In this way the Jewish survivors of the Hitlerite death camps were herded towards Palestine, to keep the US and other countries from being contaminated by their presence (for some) or to make sure that they were properly 'ingathered' (for others). Of course, Palestine was not really open either, being still under the control of the British, but here at least the Zionist movement was willing to go all-out to crash the gates, with heavy financing from many an American Jew who himself had no sympathy for Zionism but could be convinced that Palestine was certainly a more suitable haven than New York.

This turn brought the Zionist movement into conflict with the same British imperialism whose junior partner it had been. The partners' paths now diverged. The Jewish refugees – fleeing from a horror behind them, and rejected on all sides – became the human material the Zionists needed to carry out the goal they had set a half century before: to dispossess the Arab nation of Palestine and install a Jewish state in its stead – and to do this with the sympathy of a good deal of the world.

The Palestinian Arabs, as well as their Arab neighbours, had a very simple comment to make on this situation: 'Hitler's extermination programme was a great crime, but why does that mean that *we* have to give up our land to the Jews? It is the world's problem, not just ours.' I should like to see someone refute this.

We must note that by this time the Zionist movement had finally come out openly with its proclaimed intention of taking Palestine away as a Jewish state. This had been done in 1942, in the so-called 'Biltmore Programme'. (Up to then, the Zionists had used doubletalk about a 'Jewish homeland' to confuse the picture.) Now that the cards were on the table, there were even some Zionists – or at least people who considered themselves to be Zionists – who were outraged. It was around this time that the Ihud was founded in Palestine by Rabbi Judah Magnes. The idea of a bi-national state in Palestine was counterposed to the official Zionist programme: instead of a 'Jewish state' it meant a state in which both Jews and Arabs could live peacefully and tranquilly together; but it was rejected. Instead, the Zionists said, 'We are going to take the whole country'; and they did.

Here I need only sketch how this happened. After a series of doubledealing manoeuvres by the great powers (particularly the US, Britain and Russia) which it would take too long to go into, by 1947 the United Nations decided on a partition plan. There were to be two separate states in Palestine, a Jewish state and an Arab Palestinian state. By this time, there was indeed a Jewish majority in the territory assigned to the Jewish state – something like a 60 per cent majority – and therefore one could feel that this majority had the right to invoke the right to self-determination. I might as well mention that, at that time (1948), I did myself believe and write that the Palestinian Jews had the *right* to make this mistaken choice (for, of course, a right exists only if it includes the right to make a mistake). I mention this only to make clear that I believed and wrote at that time that the attack on the new state of Israel by the Arab states was an aggression and a violation of the right to self-determination.

But at that moment Israel was still new-born, and there were different ways in which it could defend itself – in a progressive and democratic way, and in a racist and expansionist way. The answer to *that* historical question was not long in coming: it was given right away by the same Zionist leaders who were also the rulers of the new state power. From its first hour the Zionist power took the road of a reactionary and racist purge of the Arabs as such. At this point I am not talking about the foreign Arab states, but of the Arabs of Israel themselves, the great mass of whom never took up arms against Israel or aided the aggressors.

A new act in the Middle East tragedy begins here; although

it is a crime smaller in magnitude than Hitler's against the Jews, it is still one of the most shameful in recent history. The Zionist rulers utilized the attack by the *foreign* Arab states to run the *Palestinian* Arabs off their land, by means of a series of laws and measures which were taken not only in 1948-9 but which went right on into the 1950s. The 40 per cent of the population which was Arab in the partitioned territory was reduced to about 10 per cent in the new state of Israel. Immense proportions of Arab-owned land were simply robbed from them, by 'legal' means. By 1954 over one third of the Jewish population then in Israel was settled on land that had been stolen from the Palestinian Arabs. And the Arab state of Palestine which had been created by the partition never came into existence; by the end of the war, five sections of it had been grabbed by Israel and were never given up, and the West Jordan area was incorporated into the state of Jordan.

Thus the Arab nation of Palestine was destroyed, except as a discriminated-against remnant in Israel, and even the truncated Arab state of Palestine set up by partition was destroyed. I am entirely willing to denounce anyone who wants to destroy any existing state, including Israel; but some thought should be given to this recent history by those who are willing to denounce *only* the threat to destroy Israel.

The great land robbery of the Israeli Arabs was the despoiling of a whole people. It was carried out in various ways, but generally speaking the pattern was this: any Arab who had left his village during the war for any reason whatsoever was declared an 'absentee' and his land was taken away by Zionist agencies. The Zionist myth has it that all these Palestinian Arabs left at the behest of the foreign Arab invaders and in cahoots with them. This is a big lie. There was a war on, and even if they *fled from* the Arab invaders and in fear of them, and even if they fled only to a neighbouring village, they became 'absentees'. They also fled from the British; they not only fled from the invading Arabs but also fled from the Zionist troops – the Haganah and the Irgun. This was especially true after the massacre at Deir Yassin.

Deir Yassin was the name of an Arab village in Palestine,

whose people were outstandingly *hostile* to the Arab invaders. In 1948 a battalion of the Irgun (the right-wing Zionist force) attacked the village. There were no armed men in the village, and no arms. Purely for terroristic purposes, the Irgun sacked the village and massacred 250 men, women and children. One hundred and fifty bodies were thrown down a well; ninety were left scattered around. This massacre was deliberately directed by the Irgun against a village known to be *friendly* to the Jews, as an example. Although the dirty job was done by the Irgun, the official-Zionist Haganah knew of the planned attack; immediately afterwards the Irgun, instead of being pilloried in horror by the Zionist movement, was welcomed by the Haganah into a new pact of collaboration. (The Irgun's leader, Begin, by the way, was taken into the Israeli cabinet along with General Dayan just before the outbreak of the recent Third War.)

Of course, the Irgun was able to show the way to the Haganah because it was semi-fascist; but the Haganah leaders learned fast. Before the First War had ended the Haganah too was attacking and ousting unarmed and non-belligerent Arab villagers, although naturally not as brutally as the Irgun (since they were democrats and 'socialists'). Especially after the Deir Yassin massacre, it was only necessary that any troops show up, and the Arab peasants got out of the way, as anyone else would do. They thus became 'absentees', and their land was taken away by a series of laws over the next several years. *All* of the Zionist parties, from 'left' to right, sanctioned this robbery. There was even a legal category known as 'present absentees', who were very much present as Arab citizens of Israel but who were legally accounted to be 'absentees' because they had been absent from their village on a certain date – and therefore could be legally robbed of their land. The largest portion of this stolen land went to the kibbutzim – not only the kibbutzim run by the Mapai (right-wing social democrats) but even more went to the kibbutzim of the Mapam (who claimed to be left social-ists), whose leaders regularly made clear that their hearts bled for the plight of the Israeli Arabs. However, their hearts also bled for their land, even more.

Along the border areas, Palestinian Arabs were pushed over the line into the Gaza Strip, or into Jordan and then they were shot on sight as 'infiltrators' if they tried to come back. It was in ways like this – which I sketch here only briefly – that Israel's rulers created the massive Arab refugee problem. Literally they surrounded the country with a circle of hatred – *hatred which they themselves had caused* – the hatred of the despoiled Palestinian Arabs looking over from the other side of the border and seeing their own lands being tilled by strangers whom the Zionists had brought from thousands of miles away to take their place.

This robbery is not transmuted into justice just because some of these strangers were Jewish refugees from Europe against whom another crime had been committed by someone else. The Zionist agencies welcomed these despairing refugees to their new life by putting them on the marches of the hate-encircled state so that they would have to defend themselves, their lives, and their stolen gifts from the previous Arab owners. (Thus the 'exiles' were not only 'ingathered' but also very useful.)

Meanwhile in Israel, the 10 per cent of the Palestinian Arabs left – who had not only not taken up arms but had not fled – were placed under military control like an occupied enemy people, and discriminated against in many ways. It is not without reason that they have been called the 'niggers of Israel'; but as a matter of fact the American Negroes would not have taken lying down what the Israeli Arabs had to endure for two decades.

On the borders – for example, in the Gaza Strip – the dispossessed and robbed Arabs lived a wretched existence under the control of Egypt, but the Egyptians only used them for their own purposes as pawns, while keeping their help to a minimum. They were not admitted into Egypt proper. They were forced to fester there so that their misery and hatred might make them a bone in the throat of the Israelis; at the same time Israel was as little interested as Nasser in arriving at a deal for the settlement of the Arab refugee problem.

Every now and then some of the refugees would 'infiltrate'

– that is, slip across into Israel to visit his own land or till his own soil or try to take back his own belongings – and would be shot to death by those same Jewish policemen and guards who so delighted the heart of the Jewish tourist mentioned earlier. As a result the Israelis complained bitterly about the 'infiltrators' who were so evil as to do this. The terrible situation escalated. Infiltrators began to commit acts of sabotage on the property that had been stolen from them, or struck out more blindly at the robbers. The Israelis began to resort to organized military reprisals to terrorize them into acquiescence. In 1953 there was a massacre organized by Israeli armed forces in the Arab village of Kibya. In 1955 – a year that more or less marked a turning-point for the worse – there was a big attack by an organized Israeli military force on Gaza; more and more Israeli leaders oriented towards 'preventive' war, since military force was their only answer to the problem created by their own crimes. This was the traditional and classic answer of the militarist and expansionist mentality; it is the same answer as was recommended by General MacArthur on how to treat Koreans and Chinese and other such 'gooks' – you show them who's master – that's what they can understand, etc. The answer of the Israeli militarists was, similarly: kill and terrorize the 'gooks' and 'teach them a lesson' so that they won't do it again.

There were negotiations over the plight of the Arab refugees but neither side was interested in a real settlement – not the Israeli side and not the Egyptian and Arab side. For Nasser, the Arab refugees leading their wretched existence were useful tools to harass the Israelis. As for Israel, at the same time that they argued that they could not restore the land to the Arabs they had robbed, they were industriously bringing in whole Jewish populations, from Yemen and Morocco, for example (not to speak of the whole Jewish population of the US which Ben Gurion was so vainly anxious to move to Israel). There was plenty of room in Israel for such hundreds of thousands of Jews, but in the negotiations over the Arab refugee problem there was not a *dunam* of land that could be spared. The decisive thing to remember is that, from the Zionist viewpoint, for every single despoiled Arab who would be readmitted to Israel there was a Jew who could therefore not be 'ingathered'.

The problem was not *how* Israel and the Arab states could have made peace; the problem was that neither side wanted to make peace, except of course on capitulatory terms. They did not then, and they do not now.

For Nasser, the Israel issue was a pawn in the inter-Arab struggle for power. It was also a useful distraction from the internal failures of his bureaucratic-military regime, which lacked any progressive domestic programme. In both Egypt and Jordan, the pressure of the refugees within the country was relieved only by pointing them outward, against Israel. As for Israel, it must be remembered that Zionism still did not rule the 'Land of Israel' as the Zionist programme demanded; the 'Land of Israel' still included territories outside of the state of Israel. Israeli expansionism was implicit in this, and also in the fact that, if room was going to be made for the millions of 'exiles' who were to be ingathered, more land was needed. In 1955 Israeli leaders (some eagerly convinced of the necessity of 'preventive' war, some dragging their feet) were looking for some pretext to launch a war against Egypt and the Arab alliance. As it happened, British and French imperialism brought them to launch that aggression themselves. In 1956, openly and in the sight of the whole world, side by side with the two leading European imperialisms (of which it was once again a junior partner), Israel invaded Egypt as its partners struck at the Suez Canal.

The point is not that Nasser is or was a dove of peace, himself, as has been made clear. One of the reasons why Nasser was not in a position to give warlike substance to his blowhard threats was that he was too preoccupied with internal difficulties and too weak. But if Nasser was no dove, it is still true that Israel exposed itself to the whole world as an open aggressor in alliance with European imperialism. Every dirty expansionist plan it had been accused of turned out to be true. Even after the British and French enterprise failed, Israel fought to retain the land it had grabbed in Egypt and gave it up only after immense international pressure.

This pattern must be remembered in the light also of the way in which the recent Third War was initiated: i.e. with Nasser taking the situation to the brink, talking loudly about destroying Israel, while the Israelis went straight to the business at hand by precipitating the shooting war.

There is one other story to be told for this period – the story of a pogrom. This pogrom was directed against an Arab village in Israel named Kfar Kassem. On the day that Israel attacked Egypt in 1956, the Israeli government declared a new curfew for its Arab citizens (who, remember, were under military control anway, even without a war). The new decree advanced the curfew from 11 p.m. to 5 p.m. Israeli officers showed up in Kfar Kassem, as well as other places, to make known the change on that day. They were told that the men had already gone out to the fields; the officers' reply was, roughly speaking, 'Don't bother us with details'. In the evening, when the men of the village returned from working in the fields after the new curfew hour, they were shot down in cold blood by the Israeli soldiers – for violating a curfew that had never been told them. The government admitted that forty-six men were thus killed; the number wounded was not made public. The government admission applied only to Kfar Kassem but it was reliably reported that the same thing happened that day at other Arab villages. Even this much was admitted by the government only after a week had passed and the reports could no longer be hushed up. All of Israel was appalled. Some underlings were made the scapegoats.

It was clear, then, that the Zionist programme of making Israel a 'state like any other state' had come true: it had its own Jewish policemen, it had its own soldiers, it had its own militarists, and now it had its own pogroms.

In 1967 the road that started in Deir Yassin and goes through Kfar Kassem has now reached the bank of the Jordan, where Arab refugees are once again being pushed out and around by the Israelis, as they have been for the last twenty years. It would be useful to go through the whole chapter subsequent to

1956, leading up to the Third War, but, aside from time considerations, we would only find that it is more of the same thing: the tragedy of one reactionary chauvinism versus another reactionary chauvinism.

There is an image that haunts me, about this whole tragic embroilment in the Middle East. Buck deer in the mating season will fight each other, and now and again it has happened that they will entangle their antlers and be unable to disengage. Unable to break loose, unable to win, locked in a static hopeless combat until they die and rot and their bleached bones are found by some hunter in the forest, their skeletons are grisly evidence of a tragedy which destroyed them both, ensnarled.

It may be that, in the Middle East entanglement, the Arabs, or some of the Arabs, can survive this conflict. But it is doubtful whether, in the long run, the Jews of Israel can. What the Zionists have made out of Israel is a new ghetto – a state ghetto with state boundaries. That's not a new life for the Jews; that is more of the old life of which the Jews have had more than their share. This generation of Zionist hawks ruling Israel is a curse. No matter how many more great military victories they win the sea of Arab peoples ringing them cannot be eliminated from the picture, and hatred grows. It may be another decade or two before the Arab states become modernized enough to wage war effectively; and then it will take more than euphoria over military heroes to point a way for Israel.

There are some in Israel who know and say what has been said here – more who know and fewer who say – and it is to be hoped that the next generation will be more willing to listen to their kind, to the kind of Jews who represent what is best in the history of Jewish humanism and social idealism rather than those who worship the Moloch of a 'state like any other state'.

Perfidy and Aggression

By N. T. Fedorenko*

The attention of the whole world has been focused in these past days on the Middle East, where Israel has committed open and perfidious aggression against the Arab states.

The United Nations Organization, whose mission it is to maintain international peace and security, naturally could not pass by the Israeli aggression. First the Security Council was urgently called into session, to discuss, in particular, the Soviet demand for cessation of hostilities by Israel and withdrawal of Israeli troops from UAR, Jordanian and Syrian territory occupied as a result of the aggression. Then, on the initiative of the Soviet Union, a special emergency session of the General Assembly was convened on 17 June.

The Security Council debates showed up the broad imperialist conspiracy against the Arab states and peoples of the Middle East. It was proved that the Israeli aggression was not an accidental thing, not the result of any mistake or misunderstanding. No, it was a carefully plotted imperialist provocation, the timing of which was planned on all sides. This aggression was to secure political changes in the Middle East in the interest of imperialism, notably American imperialism, to alter the 'balance of strength' in the area. Its purpose was to undermine the Arab national liberation movement, to weaken the progressive regimes in the UAR, Syria and other Arab countries. Israel acted as the instrument of more powerful imperialist states, and above all the US.

The Israeli army was built up and trained with the help of the imperialist Western powers. Tel Aviv was given every protection and encouragement, particularly in Washington, to prepare it for aggression against the Arab states.

---

*N. T. Fedorenko, Soviet Permanent Delegate to the UN, played a leading part in the United Nations' discussions before, during and after the crisis of June 1967. His article appeared in the Soviet weekly *New Times*, 28 June 1967.

The peoples of the UAR and other Arab countries have scored historic victories in these past years in their struggle to attain national independence and freedom. Important social restructuring and reform in the interests of the working masses has been carried out in these countries. The imperialists could not stomach the fact that in this struggle the Arab peoples lean on the friendship and support of the Soviet Union and other socialist states.

Writing in *US News and World Report*, General Max Johnson, formerly planning officer for the US Joint Chiefs of Staff, openly voiced the sentiment of the American military chiefs. 'The growing hostility of Middle Eastern nations towards the United States and friendliness towards the Soviet Union,' he wrote, 'has been a strategic loss of great proportions.' And he linked the events in Vietnam with the position in the Middle East, pointing out that this area was a 'strategic crossroads' between Europe, Asia and Africa.

And indeed, remote though South-east Asia and the Gulf of Tonkin are geographically from the Middle East and the Eastern Mediterranean, few will question that the American aggression in Vietnam was bound to have the most pernicious effect on the general political situation in the world; and it was by no means the last factor in Israel's aggression against the Arab states.

The colonialists also refused to accept that Arab riches should belong to the Arabs themselves and that it is the Arab countries' lawful right to determine their own path of development. The imperialist forces got busy and the Israeli aggression was unleashed just when more and more of the Arab countries had begun taking measures to consolidate national independence.

The Israeli aggression is pointed against the national freedom and state independence of the millions of Arabs – from Kuwait, Damascus and Baghdad to Cairo, Algiers and Casablanca. There is not a shadow of doubt that behind Tel Aviv stand the imperialist forces which want to hamstring the free national development of the Arab states. It is these forces that lavishly supplied Tel Aviv with the needful means and gave it economic, moral and political assistance and support.

It should be added that behind the Israeli extremists it is easy to discover not only the Pentagon generals but the incorrigible militarists in West Germany. That Bonn has directly abetted the Israeli extremists is not to to be concealed by any smoke-screens of 'neutrality'. Bonn not only engaged in incitement, it not only sacrificed diplomatic relations with a number of Arab states for the sake of close partnership with Israel; it also supplied arms and equipment for the Israeli army. At the height of the Middle East crisis, West Germany demonstratively dispatched a large consignment of gas-masks to Israel. Thus there grew up on the soil of fevered militarism, on the common basis of adventurism, of hatred for all things progressive, of hostility to the Arab peoples' struggle to consolidate indepen-dence and achieve social progress, an alliance of Tel Aviv extremist circles not only with Washington but with Bonn.

On the eve of the Israeli attack an atmosphere of hysteria was artificially created in the country and tension whipped up to prepare the ground for aggression. The Arab states were showered with accusations. The events that followed showed that the U A R, Syria and the other Arab states had no aggres-sive intentions, that they had not been preparing to strike, and that it was Israel that had been girding feverishly for its brigand attack on the Arab countries. It was not the peoples, not the Arab countries that had an interest in kindling military conflict, but the forces of imperialism, the oil monopolies, of whom Israel is the confederate.

It is not surprising that when the question of Israel's aggres-sion against the Arab states came before the Security Council, the aggressor had open defenders and abettors there, who sought to obstruct the work of the Council and enable Israel to ignore the Council's decisions, gain time for more conquests, and carry out its criminal plans.

That is why the Security Council had to hold a practically continuous series of emergency meetings and pass three sepa-rate resolutions on what was in effect one and the same question, reiterating its demand that Israel cease hostilities forthwith.

Thanks to the support given them by the United States – a permanent member of the Security Council – and by certain other members of the Council, who prevented the passage of a decision condemning the aggressor and demanding the immediate withdrawal of his troops to the positions held before the hostilities, the Tel Aviv rulers were able insolently to ignore the Security Council decisions and continue and extend their aggression, overrunning more and more Arab territory.

Even after the Security Council had ordered an immediate cease-fire and termination of hostilities, Israel treacherously – contrary to two Security Council resolutions (of 6 and 7 June) – invaded the Syrian Arab Republic, occupied part of its territory, and bombed Cairo and the Damascus area.

The Tel Aviv rulers deliberately deceived the Security Council, assuring it that Israel was complying with its decisions while in reality they continued the aggression. It came to light during the debates that the bombing attacks on Cairo and Damascus and the invasion of Syria had taken place at the very time when Israel's representative in the Security Council had been making his hypocritical speeches and misleading Council members so as to distract attention from the criminal acts of the Israeli military. The Israeli authorities also did everything they could to prevent the UN observers on the spot from discharging their functions and keeping the Security Council informed of what was happening.

This perfidy of Tel Aviv was indignantly condemned by the socialist and Afro-Asian members of the Security Council. The Soviet delegation called the Council's attention to the dangerous war psychosis that has come to reign in the Israeli capital. Threats and ultimatums of a rare insolence and cynicism have been issuing from there. Plans of expansion, plans of seizing new territories, plans of recarving the map of the Middle East have been intensively prepared.

The overweening aggressors have taken over the notorious Nazi theories of geopolitics, of *Lebensraum*, of establishing a 'new order' and 'vital frontiers' in the Middle East. The peoples are familiar with these ultimatums, these insensate theories, this talk of a 'new order' and of recarving the political map. It was the Nazi conquistadors that set out to recarve the map of Europe and the world, and attempted by armed force to impose what they called a 'new order', until the fascist beast's spine was broken by the combined efforts of the Soviet Union and other peoples. How monstrous that these devices of the Nazi brigands, condemned by the International Military Tribunal in 1946, have now been revived by a government claiming to represent a people which suffered so bitterly at the Nazi butchers' hands!

Incoming reports show that the Arab population of Gaza, Jerusalem and other areas is being forcibly driven out. In the territories seized by Israeli troops occupation authorities are being set up, military governors of towns and regions are being appointed. Judging by all the indications, the system is being employed which the Nazi invaders used in the countries they occupied in World War II.

Israel's Prime Minister Eshkol declared on 12 June: 'Have no illusions, Israel will not agree to revert to the situation which existed until a week ago. . . . We are entitled to determine what are the true and vital interests of our country and how they shall be secured. The position that existed until now shall never again return.' General Moshe Dayan has proclaimed the same ambitions, declaring the other day that 'if they [the Arab countries] don't want to talk to us, to sit down with us, then we shall stay where we are.' 'I don't think,' he went on, 'that we should in any way give back the Gaza Strip to Egypt or the western part of Jordan to King Hussain.'

Do these statements not show up the aggressor's true face and his expansionist plans, carefully laid long beforehand and executed when he thought the moment opportune?

Nor are the Israeli aggressors original in their methods of carrying out their expansionist policies. Like the Nazis, they try to deceive the peoples by shifting the blame to the victim of aggression. They also emulate their American masters, who are waging barbarous war on the Vietnamese people and trying to dictate terms from positions of strength.

The facts go to show that, in the Middle East and in South-east Asia and in Latin America alike, the same criminal hand is at work and the same imperialist methods are being employed. Like the soil of Vietnam, Arab soil has been drenched with napalm, and on it, too, infamous crimes against civilian populations have been and are still being perpetrated. It is all part of a single imperialist plot against freedom-loving peoples defending their sovereignty and freedom against colonial oppressors, upholding the great cause of national liberation.

In the Security Council the representative of Jordan, in a wrathful indictment of Tel Aviv, pointed to the similarity of Israel's policy and methods to the policy and methods of the Nazis. 'Both,' he said, 'have the concept of expansion, both have the concept of race, both have the concept of force, of acquiring lands by invasion and the use of force, and both have fifth columns.'

Already in the first hours of Israel's aggression against the Arab states the Soviet Union branded the Israeli invaders and firmly demanded condemnation of their perfidious and criminal acts, immediate cessation of hostilities and the withdrawal of Israeli troops behind the armistice lines.

In a resolution tabled on 8 June, the Soviet Union called on the Security Council to emphatically condemn Israel's aggressive acts and its violation of the Security Council resolutions, the UN Charter and the principles of the United Nations, and to demand that Israel immediately cease hostilities against neighbouring Arab states and withdraw all its troops from their territory to behind the armistice lines.

However, the United States, Britain and some other Western Powers, set their face against condemnation of the aggressor and the demand for the immediate withdrawal of his troops from the occupied territories. The Security Council proved unable to pass the decision that the emergency dictated. Yet under the UN Charter, as the organ primarily responsible for the maintenance of international peace and security, it should have done so.

Some Western representatives even tried to make out that

the question of the withdrawal of Israel's troops from the occupied territories should be linked with some sort of other conditions, with a general settlement in the Middle East, and so on and so forth. The Soviet delegation firmly rejected all such attempts.

The Washington diplomats hastened to introduce their own resolution, which, so far from condemning Israel's aggression and demanding the withdrawal of its troops, actually attempted to put the Arab states at a disadvantage *vis-à-vis* the aggressor and hedge about the withdrawal of Israeli troops with various demands which in the final count would limit the Arab states' sovereign rights. Essentially, the American resolution only encouraged the Israeli extremists' expansionist ambitions. Accordingly, the Arab countries and the Soviet Union decidedly rejected it.

The Soviet delegation asked the US and other Western delegations outright: Did they agree to the immediate and unconditional withdrawal of Israel's troops from the territories it had seized to behind the armistice lines? Were they willing to recognize that continued occupation of Arab territory by the Israeli armed forces was unlawful, criminal and contrary to the UN Charter and the elementary principles of modern international law? But the Security Council never did get a clear answer to these questions.

The representatives of India and Mali emphasized in their Security Council speeches the need to order withdrawal of both sides' armed forces behind the armistice lines and only then discuss other problems, relating to so-called deeper causes of the tension in the Middle East. The stand taken in the Council by India, in particular, was based on the well-known principle of international law that an aggressor must not be allowed to profit by his aggression.

Because of the Western powers' attitude, however, the Security Council at the initial stage was only able to order the cessation of hostilities. But that was only a preliminary measure, essential to protect the victims of aggression from Israel's brigand forces. It was altogether insufficient. For it was the Security Council's duty under the UN Charter to put an end to the aggression and restore the lawful rights of the attacked Arab states – the UAR, Syria and Jordan.

The Soviet Union accordingly continued to insist that the Security Council should vote on the Soviet resolution. Yet even in the concluding phase of the Council's work the attitude of the Western members, notably the US and Britain, who openly support Israel's aggressive policy, made it impossible for the Council to pass the necessary decision.

The Soviet resolution's demand for the immediate withdrawal of Israeli troops from the occupied Arab territories received the votes of the socialist (USSR and Bulgaria) and Afro-Asian (India, Mali, Ethiopia and Nigeria) member countries of the Council. The Western states, while not venturing to vote openly against this lawful and just demand, resorted to the 'hidden veto' by abstaining. Thus, the Soviet resolution did not go through.

Heavy responsibility for this rests on the states which failed in their duty as members of the Security Council. The result was to produce a situation that called for emergency action by the United Nations and all freedom-loving countries to stop the continuing aggression in the Middle East.

It was clear that further discussion of the matter in the Security Council could not at present yield the proper results. It thus became necessary to seek other ways of exerting a sobering influence on the aggressor.

In the circumstances the Soviet government felt that the UN General Assembly should discuss the situation, in accordance with Article 11 of the UN Charter, and take decisions designed to liquidate the consequences of the aggression and effect the immediate withdrawal of Israeli troops behind the armistice lines.

The Soviet government asked for a special emergency session of the UN General Assembly to be convened immediately for this purpose. A majority of UN member states responded at once with support for the Soviet government's proposal. It is significant, however, that the United States and Israel opposed this Soviet initiative.

The special emergency session of the General Assembly opened in New York on 17 June. In view of the great importance of the question before it, the Soviet delegation is led by Premier Kosygin. Many other leading statesmen of UN member nations are also attending. The session has only begun. But one can already say that except for a narrow group of accomplices of the aggressor, the members of the UN uphold the rights of the Arab peoples.

Even now the Israeli aggressors remain on the soil they have seized from neighbouring Arab peoples. What are they counting on? Is Tel Aviv perhaps waiting for a special invitation? Does it think that the peoples of the world, the United Nations Organization, will accept its seizure and occupation of foreign territory? Does it imagine that the Arab countries, the Soviet Union, the socialist states and other freedom-loving peoples will allow it to profit by its insolent and perfidious aggression, to dictate terms from positions of strength, the positions of an invader seeking to wrest away by force lands that belong to Arab countries?

Anyone who imagines any such thing is profoundly mistaken. The Tel Aviv government should have no illusions: Israel will have to pay in full for its brigand actions. And the United Nations Organization must pass its authoritative judgement, must do its duty under the Charter.

New York
17 June

Holy War

By I. F. Stone*

Stripped of propaganda and sentiment, the Palestine problem is, simply, the struggle of two different peoples for the same strip of land. For the Jews, the establishment of Israel was a

* I. F. Stone, a Washington correspondent for twenty-five years, is publisher and editor of *I. F. Stone's Weekly*. This essay first appeared in the *New York Review of Books*, 3 August 1967, and is reprinted by permission of the author.

Return, with all the mystical significance the capital R implies. For the Arabs it was another invasion. This has led to three wars between them in twenty years. Each has been a victory for the Jews. With each victory the size of Israel has grown. So has the number of Arab homeless.

Now to find a solution which will satisfy both peoples is like trying to square a circle. In the language of mathematics, the aspirations of the Jews and the Arabs are incommensurable. Their conflicting ambitions cannot be fitted into the confines of any ethical system which transcends the tribalistic. This is what frustrates the benevolent outsider, anxious to satisfy both peoples. For two years Jean-Paul Sartre has been trying to draw Israelis and Arabs into a confrontation in a special number of his review, *Les Temps Modernes*. The third war between them broke out while it was on the press.

This long-awaited special issue on *Le Conflit israélo-arabe* is the first confrontation in print of Arab and Israeli intellectuals. But it turns out to be 991 pages not so much of dialogue as of dual monologue. The two sets of contributors sit not just in separate rooms, like employers and strikers in a bitter labour dispute, but in separate universes where the simplest fact often turns out to have diametrically opposite meanings. Physics has begun to uncover a new conundrum in the worlds of matter and anti-matter, occupying the same space and time but locked off from each other by their obverse natures, forever twin yet forever sundered. The Israeli–Arab quarrel is the closest analogue in the realm of international politics.

The conditions exacted for the joint appearance of Israelis and Arabs in the same issue of *Les Temps Modernes* excluded not only collaboration but normal editorial mediation or midwifery. Claude Lanzmann, who edited this special issue, explains in his Introduction that the choice of authors and of subjects had to be left 'in full sovereignity' (*en toute souveraineté*) to each of the two parties. The Arabs threatened to withdraw if an article was included by A. Razak Abdel-Kader, an Algerian who is an advocate of Israeli–Arab reconciliation. When the Israelis objected that *Les Temps Modernes* at least allow Abdel-Kader to express himself as an individual, the

Arabs insisted on an absolute veto: there would be no issue if
Abdel-Kader were in it.

In his Preface Jean-Paul Sartre lays bare the conflicting emotions which led him to embark on so difficult a task as to
attempt the role – in some degree – of peacemaker between
Arab and Israeli. They awaken the memories of his finest hours.
One was that of the Resistance. 'For all those who went
through this experience,' M. Sartre writes, 'it is unbearable to
imagine that another Jewish community, wherever it may be,
whatever it may be, should endure this Calvary anew and
furnish martyrs to a new massacre.' The other was Sartre's aid
to the Arabs in their struggle for Algerian independence. These
memories bind him to both peoples, and give him the respect of
both, as the welcome he received in both Egypt and Israel last
year attests. His aim in presenting their views is, he says wist-
fully, merely to *inform*. His hope is that information in itself
will prove pacifying 'because it tends more or less slowly to
replace passion by knowledge'. But the roots of this struggle
lie deeper than reason. It is not at all certain that information
will replace passion with knowledge.

The experiences from which M. Sartre draws his emotional
ties are irrelevant to this new struggle. Both sides draw from
them conclusions which must horrify the man of rationalist
tradition and universalist ideals. The bulk of the Jews and the
Israelis draw from the Hitler period the conviction that, in this
world, when threatened one must be prepared to kill or be
killed. The Arabs draw from the Algerian conflict the conviction that, even in dealing with so rational and civilized a
people as the French, liberation was made possible only by
resorting to the gun and the knife. Both Israeli and Arabs in
other words feel that only force can assure justice. In this they
agree, and this sets them on a collision course. For the Jews
believe justice requires the recognition of Israel as a fact; for
the Arabs, to recognize the fact is to acquiesce in the wrong
done them by the conquest of Palestine. If God as some now say
is dead, He no doubt died of trying to find an equitable solution
to the Arab-Jewish problem.

The argument between them begins with the Bible. 'I give this country to your posterity,' God said to Abraham (Genesis XV, 18) 'from the river of Egypt up to the great river, Euphrates.' Among the Jews, whether religious or secular mystics, this is the origin of their right to the Promised Land. The opening article in the Arab section of *Les Temps Modernes* retorts that the 'posterity' referred to in Genesis includes the descendants of Ishmael since he was the son of Abraham by his concubine Ketirah, and the ancestor of all the Arabs, Christian or Muslim.

All this may seem anachronistic nonsense, but this is an anachronistic quarrel. The Bible is still the best guide to it. Nowhere else can one find a parallel for its ethnocentric fury. Nowhere that I know of is there a word of pity in the Bible for the Canaanites whom the Hebrews slaughtered in taking possession. Of all the nonsense which marks the Jewish–Arab quarrel none is more nonsensical than the talk from both sides about the Holy Land as a symbol of peace. No bit of territory on earth has been soaked in the blood of more battles. Nowhere has religion been so zestful an excuse for fratricidal strife. The Hebrew *shalom* and the Arabic *salaam* are equally shams, relics of a common past as Bedouins. To this day inter-tribal war is the favourite sport of the Bedouins; to announce 'peace' in the very first word is a necessity if any chance encounter is not to precipitate bloodshed.

In biblical perspective the Jews have been going in and out of Palestine for 3,000 years. They came down from the Euphrates under Abraham; returned from Egypt under Moses and Joshua; came back again from the Babylonian captivity and were dispersed again after Jerusalem fell to the Romans in A.D. 70 This is the third return. The Arabs feel they have a superior claim because they stayed put. This appearance side by side in *Les Temps Modernes* provides less than the full and undiluted flavour of an ancient sibling rivalry. Both sides have put their better foot forward. The Arab section includes no sample of the bloodcurdling broadcasts in which the Arab radios indulge; the Israeli, no contribution from the right-wing

368   *The Israel–Arab Reader*

Zionists who dream of a greater Israel from the Nile to the Euphrates (as promised in Genesis) with complete indifference to the fate of the Arab inhabitants. On neither side is there a frank exposition of the *Realpolitik* which led Arab nationalists like Nasser to see war on Israel as the one way to achieve Arab unity, and leads Jewish nationalists like Ben Gurion and Dayan to see Arab disunity and backwardness as essential elements for Israeli security and growth. No voice on the Arab side preaches a Holy War in which all Israel would be massacred, while no voice on the Israeli side expresses the cheerfully cynical view one may hear in private that Israel has no realistic alternative but to hand the Arabs a bloody nose every five or ten years until they accept the loss of Palestine as irreversible.

The picture, however, is not wholly symmetrical. There is first of all the asymmetry of the victorious and the defeated. The victor is ready to talk with the defeated if the latter will acquiesce in defeat. The defeated, naturally, is less inclined to this kind of objectivity. The editor, Claude Lanzmann, speaks of an 'asymmetry between the two collections of articles which derives at one and the same time from a radical difference in their way of looking at the conflict and from the difference in the nature of the political regimes in the countries involved'. Even if not expressly authorized by their governments or organizations to participate, M. Lanzmann explains, all the Arabs except the North Africans wrote only after consultation and defend a common position while the Israelis 'as is normal in a Western-style democracy' speak either for themselves or for one of their numerous parties. But this diversity may be exaggerated. On the fundamental issue which divides the two sides, no Arab contributor is prepared to advocate recognition of the state of Israel, while only one Israeli contributor is prepared to advocate its transformation into something other than a basically Jewish state.

The depth of this nationalistic difference may be measured by what happened to Israel's Communist Party. Elsewhere national centrifugal tendencies have made their appearance in the once monolithic world of communism. In Israel the same

nationalist tendencies split the Communist Party into two, one
Jewish the other Arab. The days when Arab Communists faithfully followed Moscow's line straight into the jails of Egypt,
Iraq, Syria and Jordan by supporting the 1947 partition plan
have long passed away. Today Arab and Jewish Communists
no longer find common ground.[1] It would be hard to find an
Arab who would agree with Moshe Sneh, head of the Jewish
Communist Party (Maki) in Israel, when he told *L'Express*
(19–25 June), 'our war is just and legitimate. What united the
thirteen Arab states against us, irrespective of their regime,
was not anti-imperialism but pan-Arabism and anti-Jewish
chauvinism.' He added boldly that Moscow in supporting the
Arabs had 'turned its back on the politics of the international
left and on the spirit of Tashkent'. But even Sneh's bitter rival,
Meir Vilner, the Jewish leader of, and one of the few Jews left
in, the Arab Communist Party (Rakah), expresses himself in
Les Temps Modernes in terms with which no Arab contributor
to it agrees. M. Vilner is for the return of all the refugees who
wish to, for full equality to Arabs in Israel and for a neutralist
policy, but he defends the existence of Israel as a legitimate
fact and denies that 'one can in any way compare the people
[of Israel] to Algerian *colons* or the Crusaders'. The comparisons
rejected by the leader of the Arab Communist Party in Israel
are the favourite comparisons of the Arabs outside Israel. The
diversity of viewpoint on the Israeli side thus ends with the
basic agreement on its right to exist, and to exist as a Jewish
state. This is precisely where the Arab disagreement begins.

   The gulf between Arab and Jewish views becomes even
clearer when one reads two supplementary pieces contributed
by two French Jews, Maxime Rodinson, a distinguished sociologist and Orientalist, and Robert Misrahi, a well-known writer
of the Left. The former takes the Arab and the latter the Zionist
side. But while M. Misrahi's article appears with the Israelis, M.
Rodinson's contribution – by far the most brilliant in the whole

---

   1. The relative strength of the two since the split may be seen
from the fact that the Jewish branch was able to elect only one
deputy while the Arab branch, which draws the largest vote among
the Arab minority, elected three, two Arabs and one Jew.

volume – appears alone. He refused, for reasons of principle, to appear in the Arab ensemble. It is not hard to see why. For while M. Rodinson gives strong support to every basic Arab historical contention, he is too much the humanist (and in the last analysis no doubt the Jew) to welcome an apocalyptic solution at the expense of Israel's existence. There is still a gulf between M. Rodinson's pro-Arab position and the most moderate view any Arab statesman has yet dared express, that of Tunisia's President Bourguiba. Bourguiba's famous speech in Jericho, 3 March 1965, is reprinted in an appendix by *Les Temps Modernes*, along with an interview he gave *Le Nouvel Observateur* (15 April) a month later. But Bourguiba's speech, though it created a sensation by its relative moderation, merely suggested that the Arabs proceed to regain Palestine as they did Tunisia by a series of more or less peaceful compromises. When *Le Nouvel Observateur* asked him whether this did not imply the progressive disappearance of the state of Israel, he would not go beyond the cryptic reply, 'That is not certain.'

The Arab section of the symposium is nevertheless far from being uniform. A Moroccan, Abdallah Laroui, a professor of literature in Rabat, not only ends by saying that the possibilities of peaceful settlement must be kept open because a war would settle nothing, but even goes so far as to express the hope that the time may come when a settlement is possible without making a new exile, i.e. of the Israelis, pay for the end of another exile, i.e. of the Arabs from Palestine. He even suggests that, under certain conditions, a Jewish community 'with or without political authority' – a most daring remark – may prove compatible with Arab progress and development.

When we examine these conditions, we come to the heart of the fears expressed by the Arabs in this symposium. The Palestinian Arabs, from the first beginnings of Zionism, foresaw the danger of being swamped and dislodged by Jewish immigration. Neighbouring Arab states feared that this immigration would stimulate a continuous territorial expansion at their expense and create a Jewish state powerful enough to dominate the area. The relative size and population of Israel when compared to its Arab neighbours are deceptive and may make these fears seem foolish, but historically the Middle East has often been conquered and dominated by relatively small bands of determined intruders. Even now, as the recent fighting showed, tiny Israel could without difficulty have occupied Damascus, Amman and Cairo, and – were it not for the big powers and the UN – dictated terms to its Arab neighbours.

It was the attempt of the British to allay Arab apprehension by setting limits on Jewish immigration that precipitated the struggle between the British and the Jews. The 1917 Balfour Declaration, when it promised a 'Jewish National Home' in Palestine, also said – in a passage Zionists have always preferred to forget – 'that nothing shall be done which may prejudice the civil and religious rights of the existing non-Jewish communities in Palestine'. British White Papers in 1922, in 1930, and again in 1939 tried to fulfil this companion pledge by steps which would have kept the Jews a permanent minority. It is this persistent and – as events have shown – justifiable Arab fear which is reflected in M. Laroui's article. In calling the Palestine problem 'A Problem of the Occident' his basic point is that if the Occident wipes out anti-Semitism, or keeps it within harmless proportions, making refuge in Israel unnecessary for the bulk of Jewry, and Israel divorces its politics from the Zionist dream of gathering in all the Jews from Exile, this will end the danger of an inexorable expansion in search of *lebensraum* at the expense of the Palestinian Arabs, and finally make peace possible between the two peoples. Since immigration into Israel has dwindled in recent years, this Arab fear seems at the moment less a matter of reality than of Zionist theory and of a past experience which leads them to take it seriously.

The suggestion that Israel abandon its supra-nationalist dream finds its only echo on the other side of this collection of essays in Israel's No. 1 maverick and champion of Arab rights, Uri Avnery. Avnery was born in Germany in 1923 and went to Palestine at the age of ten, the year Hitler took power. He began his political career on the far nationalist right, as a member of the Irgun terrorist group in the struggle against the

British, but has since swung over to the far left of Israeli opinion, to the point where he is considered anti-nationalist. In the wake of the first Suez war, he supported the Egyptian demand for evacuation of the Canal Zone and in 1959 he formed an Israeli committee to aid the Algerian rebels. At one time he organized a movement which asserted that the Israelis were no longer Jews but 'Canaanites' and therefore one with the Arabs, forcibly converted remnants of the same indigenous stock. When this far-out conception attracted few Jews and even fewer Canaanites, he formed a 'Semitic Action' movement which has now become 'The Movement of New Forces'. This polled 1.2 per cent of the vote in the 1965 elections and by virtue of proportional representation put Avnery into Parliament. Avnery has been more successful as a publisher. He has made his weekly *Haolam Hazeh* ('This World') the largest in Israel by combining non-conformist politics with what the rather puritanical Israelis call pornography, though that weekly's girlie pictures would seem as old-fashioned as the *Police Gazette* in America.

Avnery writes in *Les Temps Modernes* that he would turn Israel into a secular, pluralist, and multi-national state. He would abolish the Law of Return which gives every Jew the right to enter Israel and automatically become a citizen. Avnery says this pan-Judaism of Zionism feeds the anti-Zionism of pan-Arabism by keeping alive 'the myth of an Israel submerged by millions of immigrants who, finding no place to settle, would oblige the government to expand the country by force of arms'.

Yet Avnery, who asks Israel to give up its Zionist essence, turns out to be a Jewish nationalist, too. After sketching out a plan for an Arab Palestinian state west of the Jordan, Avnery writes, 'The Arabic reader will justly ask at this point, "And the return of Israel to the limits of the UN Plan of 1947?"' Since Israel in the 1947–8 fighting seized about 23 per cent more territory than was allotted to it in the 1947 partition plan, this implies a modification of frontiers in favour of the Arab state which was supposed to be linked with it in an economically united Palestine. But to this natural Arab question Avnery replies,[2] 'Frankly we see no possibility of this kind. The Arab armies are already fifteen kilometres from Israel's most populous city (Tel Aviv) and at Nathanya are even closer to the sea.' The Arabs may feel that Avnery is as unwilling to give up the fruits of conquest as any non-'Canaanite'. Avnery is as reluctant as any conventional Zionist to see his fellow Canaanite too close to Tel Aviv.

It is easy to understand why neither side trusts the other. In any case M. Sartre's symposium is a confrontation largely of moderates and Leftists, and on neither side do these elements command majority support. Another complexity is that while in settled societies the Left tends to be less nationalistic than the Right, in colonial societies the revolutionary left is often more nationalistic than the native conservative and propertied classes.

The overwhelming majority opinion on both sides, even as expressed in a symposium as skewed leftward as this one, shows little tendency to compromise. The Arabs argue that Israel is a colonialist implantation in the Middle East, supported from the beginning by imperialist powers; that it is an enemy of Arab union and progress; that the sufferings of the Jews in the West were the consequence of an anti-Semitism the Arabs have never shared; and that there is no reason why the Arabs of Palestine should be displaced from their homes in recompense for wrongs committed by Hitler Germany. M. Laroui alone is sympathetic enough to say that if the Jewish National Home had been established in Uganda, the Arabs who felt compassion for the sufferings of the Jews of Europe would have shown themselves as uncomprehending of the rights of the natives as the West has been in Palestine. At the other end of the Arab spectrum a fellow Moroccan, a journalist, Tahar Benziane, ends up in classic anti-Semitism, blaming the Jews themselves, their separatism and their sense of superiority, for the prejudice against them. Benziane sees the only solution not just in the liquidation of Israel but in the disappearance of world

---

2. Avnery was writing, of course, before the new outbreak of warfare had again changed these borders to Israel's advantage.

Jewry through assimilation. His would indeed be a Final Solution. This bitter and hateful opinion, widespread in the Arab world, explains why Nazism found so ready an echo before the war in the Middle East and Nazi criminals so welcome a refuge in Egypt. It also disposes of the semantic nonsense that Arabs being Semite cannot be anti-Semitic!

The Zionist argument is that the Jewish immigration was a return to the Jewish homeland. Robert Misrahi even goes so far as to argue that the Jews had an older claim to Palestine than the Arabs since the Jews had lived there in the ancient kingdom of the Hebrews long before the *Hijra* of Muhammad. Misrahi argues the familiar Zionist thesis that their struggle against Britain proves them to be anti-imperialist, that their colonies are socialist, that their enemies are the feudal elements in the Arab world, and that the Arab refugees are the moral responsibility of the Arab leaders since it was on their urging that the Arabs ran away.

There is a good deal of simplistic sophistry in the Zionist case. The whole earth would have to be reshuffled if claims 2,000 years old to *irredenta* were suddenly to be allowed. Zionism from its beginning tried to gain its aims by offering to serve as outpost in the Arab world for one of the great empires. Herzl sought to win first the Sultan and then the Kaiser by such arguments. Considerations of imperial strategy finally won the Balfour Declaration from Britain. The fact that the Jewish community in Palestine afterward fought the British is no more evidence of its not being a colonial implantation than similar wars of British colonists against the mother country, from the American Revolution to Rhodesia. In the case of Palestine, as of other such struggles, the Mother Country was assailed because it showed more concern for the native majority than was palatable to the colonist minority. The argument that the refugees ran away 'voluntarily' or because their leaders urged them to do so until after the fighting was over not only rests on a myth but is irrelevant. Have refugees no right to return? Have German Jews no right to recover their properties because they too fled?

The myth that the Arab refugees fled because the Arab radios urged them to do so was analysed by Erskine Childers in the London *Spectator* of 12 May 1961. An examination of British and US radio monitoring records turned up no such appeals; on the contrary there were appeals and 'even orders to the civilians of Palestine, *to stay put*'. The most balanced and humane discussion of the question may be found in Christopher Sykes's book *Crossroads to Israel: 1917–48* (pages 350–57). 'It can be said with a high degree of certainty', Mr Sykes wrote,

that most of the time in the first half of 1948 the mass exodus was the natural, thoughtless, pitiful movement of ignorant people who had been badly led and who in the day of trial found themselves forsaken by their leaders.... But if the exodus was by and large an accident of war in the first stage, in the later stages it was consciously and mercilessly helped on by Jewish threats and aggression toward Arab populations ... It is to be noted, however, that where the Arabs had leaders who refused to be stampeded into panic flight, the people came to no harm.

Jewish terrorism, not only by the Irgun, in such savage massacres as Deir Yassin, but in milder form by the Haganah, itself 'encouraged' Arabs to leave areas the Jews wished to take over for strategic or demographic reasons. They tried to make as much of Israel as free of Arabs as possible.

The effort to equate the expulsion of the Arabs from Palestine with the new Jewish immigration out of the Arab countries is not so simple nor so equitable as it is made to appear in Zionist propaganda. The Palestinian Arabs feel about this 'swap' as German Jews would if denied restitution on the grounds that they had been 'swapped' for German refugees from the Sudetenland. In a sanely conceived settlement, some allowance should equitably be made for Jewish properties left behind in Arab countries. What is objectionable in the simplified version of this question is the idea that Palestinian Arabs whom Israel didn't want should have no objection to being 'exchanged' for Arabic Jews it did want. One uprooting cannot morally be equated with the other.

A certain moral imbecility marks all ethnocentric movements. The Others are always either less than human, and thus
their interests may be ignored, or more than human, and therefore so dangerous that it is right to destroy them. The latter is
the underlying pan-Arab attitude towards the Jews; the former
is Zionism's basic attitude towards the Arabs. M. Avnery notes
that Herzl in his book *The Jewish State*, which launched the
modern Zionist movement, dealt with working hours, housing
for workers, and even the national flag but had not one word
to say about the Arabs! For the Zionists the Arab was the In-
visible Man. Psychologically he was not there. Achad Ha-Am,
the Russian Jew who became a great Hebrew philosopher, tried
to draw attention as early as 1891 to the fact that Palestine
was not an empty territory and that this posed problems. But
as little attention was paid to him as was later accorded his
successors in 'spiritual Zionism', men like Buber and Judah
Magnes who tried to preach *Ihud*, 'unity', i.e. with the Arabs.
Of all the formulas with which Zionism comforted itself none
was more false and more enduring than Israel Zangwill's phrase
about 'a land without people for a people without a land'. Buber related that Max Nordau, hearing for the first time that
there was an Arab population in Palestine, ran to Herzl crying,
'I didn't know that – but then we are committing an injustice.'
R. J. Zwi Werblowsky, Dean of the Faculty of Letters at the
Hebrew University, in the first article of this anthology's Israeli
section, writes, with admirable objectivity, 'There can be no
doubt that if Nordau's reaction had been more general, it would
seriously have paralysed the *élan* of the Zionist movement.' It
took refuge, he writes, in 'a moral myopia'.

This moral myopia makes it possible for Zionists to dwell on
the 1900 years of Exile in which the Jews have longed for Palestine but dismiss as nugatory the nineteen years in which Arab
refugees have also longed for it. 'Homelessness' is the major
theme of Zionism, but this pathetic passion is denied to Arab
refugees. Even Meir Yaari, the head of Mapam, the leader
of the 'Marxist' Zionists of Hashomer Hatzair, who long
preached bi-nationalism, says Israel can only accept a minority
of the Arab refugees because the essential reason for the crea-

tion of Israel was to 'welcome the mass of immigrant Jews returning to their historic fatherland'! If there is not room enough for both, the Jews must have precedence. This is what leads Gabran Majdalany, a Ba'ath Socialist, to write that Israel is 'a racist state founded from its start on discrimination between Jew and non-Jew'. He compares the Zionists to the Muslim Brotherhood who 'dream of a Muslim Israel in which the non-Muslims will be the gentiles, second-class citizens sometimes tolerated but more often repressed'. It is painful to hear his bitter reproach:

Some people admit the inevitably racist character of Israel but justify it by the continual persecutions to which the Jews have been subjected during the history of Europe and by the massacres of the Second World War. We consider that, far from serving as justification, these facts constitute an aggravating circumstance; for those who have known the effects of racism and of discrimination in their own flesh and human dignity, are less excusably racist than those who can only imagine the negative effects of prejudice.

When Israel's Defence Minister, Moshe Dayan, was on *Face the Nation* on 11 June, after Israel's latest victories, the colloquy occurred.

SYDNEY GRUSON (*New York Times*): Is there any possible way that Israel could absorb the huge number of Arabs whose territory it has gained control of now?

GEN. DAYAN: Economically we can; but I think that is not in accord with our aims in the future. It would turn Israel into either a bi-national or poly-Arab-Jewish state instead of the Jewish state, and we want to have a Jewish state. We can absorb them, but then it won't be the same country.

MR GRUSON: And it is necessary in your opinion to maintain this as a Jewish state and purely a Jewish state?

GEN. DAYAN: Absolutely – absolutely. We want a Jewish state like the French have a French state.

This must deeply disturb the thoughtful Jewish reader. Ferdinand and Isabella in expelling the Jews and Moors from Spain were in the same way saying they wanted a Spain as 'Spanish', (i.e. Christian) as France was French. It is not hard to recall more recent parallels.

It is a pity the editors of *Les Temps Modernes* didn't widen their symposium to include a Jewish as distinct from an Israeli point of view. For Israel is creating a kind of moral schizophrenia in world Jewry. In the outside world the welfare of Jewry depends on the maintenance of secular, non-racial, pluralistic societies. In Israel, Jewry finds itself defending a society in which mixed marriages cannot be legalized, in which non-Jews have a lesser status than Jews, and in which the ideal is racial and exclusionist. Jews must fight elsewhere for their very security and existence – against principles and practices they find themselves defending in Israel. Those from the outside world, even in their moments of greatest enthusiasm amid Israel's accomplishments, feel twinges of claustrophobia, not just geographical but spiritual. Those caught up in prophetic fervour soon begin to feel that the light they hoped to see out of Zion is only that of another narrow nationalism.

Such moments lead to a re-examination of Zionist ideology. That longing for Zion on which it is predicated may be exaggerated. Its reality is indisputable but its strength can easily be overestimated. Not until after World War II was it ever strong enough to attract more than a trickle of Jews to the Holy Land. By the tragic dialectic of history, Israel would not have been born without Hitler. It took the murder of six million in his human ovens to awaken sufficient nationalist zeal in Jewry and sufficient humanitarian compassion in the West to bring a Jewish state to birth in Palestine. Even then humanitarian compassion was not strong enough to open the gates of the West to Jewish immigration in contrition. The capitalist West and the communist East preferred to displace Arabs than to welcome the Jewish 'displaced persons' in Europe's postwar refugee camps.

It must also be recognized, despite Zionist ideology, that the periods of greatest Jewish creative accomplishment have been associated with pluralistic civilizations in their time of expansion and tolerance : in the Hellenistic period, in the Arab civilization of North Africa and Spain, and in Western Europe and America. Universal values can only be the fruit of a universal vision ; the greatness of the Prophets lay in their overcoming of ethnocentricity. A Lilliputian nationalism cannot distil truths for all mankind. Here lies the roots of a growing divergence between Jew and Israeli; the former with a sense of mission as a Witness in the human wilderness, the latter concerned only with his own tribe's welfare.

But Jewry can no more turn its back on Israel than Israel on Jewry. The ideal solution would allow the Jews to make their contributions as citizens in the diverse societies and nations which are their homes while Israel finds acceptance as a Jewish state in a renascent Arab civilization. This would end Arab fears of a huge inflow to Israel. The Jews have as much reason to be apprehensive about that prospect as the Arabs.

It can only come as the result of a sharp recrudescence in persecution elsewhere in the world. Zionism grows on Jewish catastrophe. Even now it casts longing eyes on Russian Jewry. But would it not be better, more humanizing, and more just, were the Soviet Union to wipe out anti-Semitism and to accord its Jews the same rights of cultural autonomy and expression it gives all its other nationalities? The Russian Jews have fought for Russia, bled for the Revolution, made no small contribution to Russian literature and thought; why should they be cast out? This would be a spiritual catastrophe for Russia as well as Jewry even though it would supply another flow of desperate refugees to an Israel already short of Jews if it is to expand as the Zionist militants hope to expand it.

Israel has deprived anti-Semitism of its mystique. For the visitor to Israel, anti-Semitism no longer seems a mysterious anomaly but only another variant of minority-majority friction. *Es is schwer zu sein a Yid* ('It's hard to be a Jew') was the title of Sholom Aleichem's most famous story. Now we see that it's hard to be a goy in Tel Aviv, especially an Arab goy. Mohammad Watad, a Muslim Israeli, one of the five Arabic contributors to the Israeli side of this symposium, begins his essay with words which startlingly resemble the hostile dialogue Jews encounter elsewhere. 'I am often asked,' he writes, 'about my "double" life which is at one and the same time

that of an Arab and that of an Israeli citizen.' Another Arab
contributor from Israel, Ibrahim Shabath, a Christian who
teaches Hebrew in Arabic schools and is editor-in-chief of *Al
Mirsad*, the Mapam paper in Arabic, deplores the fact that
nineteen years after the creation of Israel 'the Arabs are still
considered strangers by the Jews'. He relates a recent conversation with Ben Gurion. 'You must know,' Ben Gurion told
him, 'that Israel is the country of the Jews and only of the
Jews. Every Arab who lives here has the same rights as any
minority citizen in any country of the world, but he must admit
the fact that he lives in a Jewish country.' The implications
must chill Jews in the outside world.

The Arab citizen of Israel, Shabath complains, 'is the victim
today of the same prejudices and the same generalizations as
the Jewish people elsewhere'. The bitterest account of what
they undergo may be found in an anonymous report sent to
the United Nations in 1964 by a group of Arabs who tried un-
successfully to found an independent socialist Arab movement
and publication. Military authorities, despite a Supreme Court
order, refused to permit this, and the courts declined to over-
rule the military. Their petition is reprinted in the Israeli section of this symposium. Though the military rule complained
of was abolished last year, and police regulations substituted,
it is too soon – especially because of the new outbreak of warfare – to determine what the effect will be on Arab civil liberties. Israelis admit with pleasure that neither in the Christian
villages of Central Galilee nor in the Muslim villages of the
so-called 'Triangle' was there the slightest evidence of any Fifth
Column activity. Those Israelis who have fought for an end of
all discrimination against the Arabs argue that they have demonstrated their loyalty and deserve fully to be trusted.

It is to Israel's credit that the Arab minority is given place
in its section to voice these complaints while no similar place is
opened for ethnic minority opinion in the Arabic section. Indeed except for Lebanon and to some degree Tunisia there is
no place in the Arab world where the dissident of any kind
enjoys freedom of the press. There is no frank discussion of

this in the Arab section. One of the most vigorous and acute
expositions of the Arab point of view, for example, is an article
by an Egyptian writer, Lotfallah Soliman, who has played a
distinguished role in bringing modern ideas to the young intellectuals of his country since World War II. His autobiographi-
cal sketch says cryptically if discreetly, 'He lives presently in
Paris.' I stumbled on a more candid explanation. In preparing
for this review, I read an earlier article in *Les Temps Modernes*
(Aug.–Sept. 1960) by Adel Montasser on *La répression anti-
démocratique en Egypte*. Appended to it was a list of intellectuals imprisoned by Nasser. Among them was Lotfallah
Soliman. Obviously it's hard to be a free Egyptian intellectual
in Nasser's Egypt. Many of those then imprisoned have since
been freed, but it is significant that a writer as trenchant and
devoted as Soliman has to work in exile.

It is true that the full roster of Arab minority complaints in
Israel had to be presented anonymously for fear of the authorities. But in the Arab section of this book no place was
allowed even anonymously for the Jewish and the various
Christian minorities to voice their complaints. As a result the
Arab contributors were able to write as if their countries, unlike Europe, were models of tolerance. They hark back to the
great days of Arabic Spain where (except for certain interludes
not mentioned) Christian and Jew enjoyed full equality, religious, cultural and political, with the Muslim: Spain did not
become synonymous with intolerance, Inquisition and obscur-
antism until the Christian Reconquest. But today no Arab
country except, precariously, Lebanon, dimly resembles Moor-
ish Spain. As a result the Jews from the Arabic countries tend
to hate the Arab far more than Jews from Europe who have
never lived under his rule, which often recalls medieval Christendom. A glimpse of these realities may be found in the most
moving article in this whole symposium. This is by Atallah
Mansour, a young Christian Arabic Israeli novelist of peasant
origin who has published two novels, one in Arabic and the
other in Hebrew, and worked as a journalist on Avnery's paper
Haolam Hazeh and on the staff of *Haaretz*, Israel's best and
most objective daily paper. M. Mansour knows doubly what it

is to be a 'Jew'. He is as an Arab a 'Jew' to the Israelis and as a Christian a 'Jew' to the Muslims. He tells a touching story of an accidental encounter in (of all places) the Paris Metro with a young man who turned out like him to be Greek-rite Christian though from Egypt. They exchanged stories of their troubles, like two Jews in the Diaspora. 'We in Egypt,' the younger stranger told him, 'have the same feelings as you. There is no law discriminating between us and the Muslims. But the governmental administration, at least on the everyday level, prefers Mahmoud to Boulos and Ahmed to Simaan' – i.e. the man with the Muslim name to the man with the Christian. 'Omar Sharif, the well-known movie actor,' the Egyptian Christian added, 'is Christian in origin. But he had to change his Christian name for a Muslim to please the public.' In Israel, similarly, Ibrahim often becomes Abraham to pass as a Jew and to avoid widespread housing discrimination.

If in this account I have given more space to the Arab than the Israeli side it is because as a Jew, closely bound emotionally with the birth of Israel,[3] I feel honour bound to report the Arab side, especially since the US press is so overwhelmingly pro-Zionist. For me, the Arab–Jewish struggle is a tragedy. The essence of tragedy is a struggle of right against right. Its catharsis is the cleansing pity of seeing how good men do evil despite themselves out of unavoidable circumstance and irresistible compulsion. When evil men do evil, their deeds belong to the realm of pathology. But when good men do evil, we confront the essence of human tragedy. In a tragic struggle, the victors become the guilty and must make amends to the defeated. For me the Arab problem is also the No. 1 Jewish problem. How

3. I first arrived in Palestine on Balfour Day, 2 November 1945, the day the Haganah blew up bridges and watch towers to begin its struggle against the British and immigration restrictions. The following spring I was the first newspaperman to travel with illegal Jewish immigrants from the Polish–Czech border through the British blockade. In 1947 I celebrated Passover in the British detention camps in Cyprus and in 1948 I covered the Arab–Jewish war. See my *Underground to Palestine* (1946) and *This Is Israel* (1948). I was back in 1949, 1950, 1951, 1956 and 1964.

we act towards the Arabs will determine what kind of people we become: either oppressors and racists in our turn like those from whom we have suffered, or a nobler race able to transcend the tribal xenophobias that afflict mankind.[4]

Israel's swift and extraordinary victories have suddenly transmuted this ideal from the realm of impractical sentiment to urgent necessity. The new frontiers of military conquest have gathered in most of the Arab refugees. Zionism's dream, the 'ingathering of the exiles', has been achieved, though in an ironic form; it is the Arab exiles who are back. They cannot be gotten rid of as easily as in 1948. Something in the order of 100,000 have again been 'encouraged' to leave, but the impact on public opinion abroad and in Israel has forced the State to declare that it will allow them to return. While the UN proves impotent to settle the conflict and the Arab powers are unwilling to negotiate from a situation of weakness, Israel can to some degree determine its future by the way in which it treats its new Arab subjects or citizens. The wrangles of the powers will go on for months but these people must be fed, clothed, and housed. How they are treated will change the world's picture of Israel and of Jewry, soften or intensify Arab anger, build a bridge to peace or make new war certain. To establish an Arab state on the West Bank and to link it with Israel, perhaps also with Jordan, in a Confederation, would turn these Arab neighbours, if fraternally treated, from enemies

---

4. In September, Black Star will publish a vigorous little book *The Aryanization of the Jewish State* by Michael Selzer, a young Pakistani Jew who lived in Israel. It may help Jewry and Israel to understand that the way to a fraternal life with the Arabs inside and outside Israel must begin with the eradication of the prejudices that greet the Oriental and Arabic-speaking Jews in Israel who now make up over half the population of the country. The bias against the Arab extends to a bias against the Jews from the Arab countries. In this, as in so many other respects, Israel presents in miniature all the problems of the outside world. Were the rest of the planet to disappear, Israel could regenerate from itself – as from a new Ark – all the bigotries, follies, and feuds of a vanished mankind (as well as some of its most splendid accomplishments).

into a buffer, and give Israel the protection of strategic frontiers. But it would be better to give the West Bank back to
Jordan than to try to create a puppet state – a kind of Arab
Bantustan – consigning the Arabs to second-class status under
Israel's control. This would only foster Arab resentment. To
avoid giving the Arabs first-class citizenship by putting them
in the reservation of a second-class state is too transparently
clever.

What is required in the treatment of the Arab refugees Israel
has gathered in is the conquest both of Jewish exclusivism and
the resentful hostility of the Arabs. Even the malarial marshes
of the Emek and the sandy wastes of the Negev could not have
looked more bleakly forbidding to earlier generations of Zionist pioneers than these steep and arid mountains of prejudice.
But I for one have a glimmer of hope. Every year I have gone
to Palestine and later Israel I have found situations which
seemed impossible. Yet Zionist zeal and intelligence overcame
them. Perhaps this extraordinarily dynamic, progressive and
devoted community can even if need be transcend its essential
self.

I was encouraged to find in this volume that the most objective view of the Arab question on the Israeli side was written by
Yehudah Harbaki, a Haifa-born professional soldier, a briga-
dier general, but a general who holds a diploma in philosophy
and Arabic studies from the Hebrew University and from Har-
vard. He has written a book on *Nuclear War and Nuclear
Peace*. His article 'Hawks or Doves' is extraordinary in its
ability to rise above prejudice and sentiment. He does not shut
his eyes at all to the Arab case. He feels peace can come only
if we have the strength to confront its full human reality.
'Marx affirms,' he concludes, 'that knowledge of the truth frees
man from the determinism of history.' It is only, General Harkabi says, when Israel is prepared 'to accept the truth in its
entirety that it will find the new strength necessary to maintain
and consolidate its existence'. The path to safety and the path
to greatness lies in reconciliation. The other route, now that
the West Bank and Gaza are under Israeli jurisdiction, leads

to two new perils. The Arab populations now in the conquered territories make guerrilla war possible within Israel's own boundaries. And externally, if enmity deepens and tension rises between Israel and the Arab states, both sides will by one means or another obtain nuclear weapons for the next round.

This will change the whole situation. No longer will Israeli and Arab be able to play the game of war in anachronistic fashion as an extension of politics by other means. Neither will they be able to depend on a mutual balance of terror like the great powers with their 'second strike' capacity. In this pygmy struggle the first strike will determine the outcome and leave nothing behind. Nor will the great powers be able to stand aside and let their satellites play out their little war, as in 1948, 1956, and 1967. I have not dwelt here on the responsibility of the great powers, because if they did not exist the essential differences in the Arab–Israeli quarrel would still remain, and because both sides use the great-power question as an excuse to ignore their own responsibilities. The problem for the new generation of Arabs is the social reconstruction of their decayed societies; the problem will not go away if Israel disappears. Indeed their task is made more difficult by the failure to recognize Israel since that means a continued emphasis on militarization, diversion of resources, and domination by military men. For Israel, the problem is reconciliation with the Arabs; the problem will not go away even if Moscow and Washington lie down together like the lion and the lamb or blow each other to bits. But the great powers for their part cannot continue the cynical game of arming both sides in a struggle for influence when the nuclear stage is reached. It is significant that the one place where the Israeli and Arab contributors to this symposium tend to common conclusions is in the essay discussing the common nuclear danger. To denuclearize the Middle East, to defuse it, will require some kind of neutralization. Otherwise the Arab–Israeli conflict may some day set off a wider Final Solution. That irascible Old Testament God of Vengeance is fully capable, if provoked, of turning the whole planet into a crematorium.

I. F. Stone Reconsiders Zionism

By Marie Syrkin*

In a lengthy review of *Le Conflit israelo–arabe*, the special issue
of Jean-Paul Sartre's *Les Temps Modernes* devoted to the Arab–
Israel conflict, I. F. Stone re-examines the Zionist case, (the
New York Review of Books, 3 August 1967). Mr Stone explains
that 'as a Jew, closely bound emotionally with the birth of
Israel' he felt 'honour bound to report the Arab side, especially
since the US press is so overwhelmingly pro-Zionist'. Whatever
the reasons for his posture, his conclusions and arguments must
stand on their own. It is unfortunate that his declared stance
as the man of 'rationalist and universalist ideals' offers a protective shade to the weighted scale in which he judges Arab
and Jewish claims. Familiar mis-statements dismissed as the
usual anti-Israel line when coming from Arab propagandists,
the American Council for Judaism or Mr Fedorenko, are admittedly more distressing when repeated by a respected writer
of intellectual independence. Mr Stone concludes: 'If God as
some now say is dead, He no doubt died of trying to find an
equitable solution to the Arab-Jewish problem.' I am more
inclined to attribute the demise to despair at the wilful casuis-
try of some of the high-minded disputants.

In reviewing the Arab and Israeli contributions to *Les Temps
Modernes*, Mr Stone complains that both sides 'have put their
better foot forward'. The Arabs fail to include their 'bloodcurdling broadcasts' demanding the extermination of Israel;
the Israeli section offers no contribution from 'right-wing Zionists' with expansionist dreams, also 'no voice on the Arab side
preaches a Holy War in which all Israel would be massacred,
while no voice on the Israeli side expresses the cheerful cynical

*Marie Syrkin, formerly a Professor of English Literature, is now a
member of the Jewish Agency Executive in New York. Her answer
to I. F. Stone was published in *Midstream*, October 1967. © The
Theodor Herzl Foundation, Inc.

view one may hear in private that Israel has no realistic alternative but to hand the Arabs a bloody nose every five or ten years until they accept the loss of Palestine as irreversible'.

This plea for honesty disguises a dishonest equation. The cries for the extermination of Israel, as every reader of the daily press knows, emanate, beginning with Nasser, from the Presidents, Prime Ministers and Foreign Ministers of the Arab states; the expansionist visions of 'the right-wing Zionists' are limited to a small group of extremists who at no time since the creation of Israel have controlled its government or have made its policy. On what basis does Mr Stone equate the openly declared official policy of all the Arab states with the views of minority groups in Israel whose programmes have been consistently repudiated by the Israeli people and government? And by what yardstick are the Arab will for a 'Holy War in which all Israel would be massacred' and the Israeli will to oppose this ambition given a common measure? Mr Stone describes the Israeli determination as 'cheerfully cynical'. Neither the adverb nor the adjective seems appropriate. I, too, have heard in many not so private conversations in Israel the view that as long as Arabs were bent on the destruction of the country, Israelis would be obliged to demonstrate, at whatever sacrifice, that it cannot be done; but to detect cheer or cynicism in this resolution is, to say the least, far-fetched.

The burden of Mr Stone's analysis is the dispossessed Arab, and no matter where his argument strays he returns to this central question. Of the Arab refugees, Mr Stone writes: 'The argument that the refugees ran away "voluntarily" or because their leaders urged them to do so until after the fighting was over not only rests on a myth but is irrelevant. Have refugees no right to return? Have German Jews no right to recover their properties because they too fled?' And he continues: 'Jewish terrorism, not only by the Irgun, in such savage massacres as Deir Yassin, but in milder form by the Haganah itself, "encouraged" Arabs to leave areas the Jews wished to take over.'

First as to the 'myth'. It is hard to understand why Mr Stone finds it necessary to quote a notoriously pro-Arab advocate like Erskine Childers or any other commentator to make his point. Mr Stone was in Israel in 1948 and gave an enthusiastic account of the Israel struggle. In *This Is Israel*, published in 1948, Mr Stone wrote: 'Ill-armed, out-numbered, however desperate their circumstances, the Jews stood fast. The Arabs very early began to run away. First the wealthiest families went; it was estimated that 20,000 of them left the country in the first two months of internal hostilities. By the end of January, the exodus was already so alarming that the Palestine Arab Higher Committee in alarm asked neighbouring Arab countries to refuse visas to these refugees and to seal the borders against them. *While the Arab guerrillas were moving in, the Arab civilian population was moving out.*' (Emphasis added – M.S.)

Mr Stone goes on to describe the 'phenomenon' of the 'sudden flight' of Arabs from Tiberias and Haifa. Not one word in Mr Stone's first-hand, on-the-spot report suggests the 'milder' terrorism of the Haganah which he now discovered in retrospect. On the contrary, his own account fully supports the 'myth'. Admittedly, Mr Stone is entitled to change his mind about the rights of the Zionist case in the course of twenty years – there have been changes of heart in regard to Israel from Soviet Russia to De Gaulle – but he should not revise history. Either what he himself saw in 1948 or what he reads now about 1948 is accurate. Which is the myth and who is being mythopoeic?

I can bear witness to the correctness of Mr Stone's 1948 reporting. In June 1948, when I arrived in Israel, the overwhelming sentiment of the Israelis was still bewilderment at the 'phenomenon' of the mass flight of the Arabs. As I pieced together the diverse explanations, a fairly consistent picture emerged. The first waves of departure – in January by the well-to-do Arabs, in March by thousands of Arab villagers from the Sharon coastal plain after the picking of the citrus crop – were clearly in response to the directives of their leaders in anticipation of Arab bombardment. The Jewish farmers were so troubled by what the departure boded that they begged the

Arabs to stay. This phase of the exodus was obviously disciplined and well-organized.

The process gathered momentum as the fighting increased and the Jews, instead of being driven into the sea, were proving victorious. When the Arabs of Tiberias suddenly fled in long convoys (the British provided transport) the astonished Jewish Community Council of Tiberias issued the following statement: 'We did not dispossess them; they themselves chose this course. But the day will come when the Arabs will return to their homes and property in this town. In the meantime let no citizen touch their property.' Such was the initial reaction in April 1948.

The circumstances surrounding the flight of 70,000 Arabs from Haifa after the Haganah victory on 22 April has fortunately been fully reported by the British authorities who are surely free of the suspicion of pro-Jewish bias. On 26 April the Haifa British Chief of Police, A. J. Bridmead, reported: 'The situation in Haifa remains unchanged. Every effort is being made by the Jews to persuade the Arab populace to stay and carry on with their normal lives, to get their shops and businesses open and to be assured that their lives and interests will be safe.' In a supplementary report issued the same day, Bridmead repeated: 'An appeal has been made to the Arabs by the Jews to reopen their shops and businesses in order to relieve the difficulties of feeding the Arab population. Evacuation was still going on yesterday and several trips were made by Z craft to Acre. Roads too were crowded. *Arab leaders* [my emphasis] reiterated their determination to evacuate the entire Arab population, and they have been given the loan of ten three-ton military trucks as from this morning to assist the evacuation.' On 28 April Bridmead was again reporting: 'The Jews are still making every effort to persuade the Arab population to remain and settle back into their normal lives in the town.'

A British eye-witness account published in the London *Economist* (2 October 1948) offers an explanation for the stampede: 'So far as I know, most of the British civilian residents whose advice was asked by Arab friends told the latter that they would be wise to stay. Various factors influenced their decision to seek safety in flight. There is but little doubt that by far the most potent of these factors was the announcement made over the air by the Arab Higher Executive urging all Arabs in Haifa to quit. The reason given was that upon the final withdrawal of the British the combined armies of the Arab states would invade Palestine and drive the Jews into the sea.'

All this is familiar, readily available information and I am bringing Mr Stone no news. I am concerned with his readers. It is obvious from the dates that the Arab exodus began months before 'such savage massacres as Deir Yassin', which took place on 9 April. (Note Mr Stone's plural though the outrage perpetrated by the Irgun was a unique occurrence deplored and repudiated by the Jewish community of Palestine.) It is also obvious from Bridmead's report that 'Arab leaders' with whom he was negotiating insisted on the evacuation of Haifa. None of this precludes the irrational panic and mass psychosis to which the Arabs fell prey; the exodus assumed proportions not anticipated by its instigators. However, the Jews can hardly be held responsible for the too complete success of the Arab scheme to clear the decks for an Arab invasion. The Arabs of Nazareth, who did not join the exodus, and other villages in Galilee that followed the example of Nazareth, were well able to withstand the Haganah 'encouragement' that Mr Stone suspects. The most straightforward explanation of Arab flight is still that provided by the Jordanian daily, *Al Difaa*, which voiced the sentiments of the refugees themselves: 'The Arab governments told us, "Get out so that we can get in." So we got out, but they did not get in.' (6 September 1954.)

The Arabs fled; they were not driven out. Equally true is that the Jews of Palestine, at first baffled and alarmed by something they could not understand, subsequently shed no tears for defectors who had cast their lot with the Arab invaders. The Arab onslaught transformed the situation physically and psychologically.

So much for the 'myth'. How about Mr Stone's argument that it is in any case 'irrelevant'? When Mr Stone asks, 'Have

German Jews no right to recover their properties because they too fled?' his implied comparison of the Palestinian Arabs with the Nazi victims and consequently of the Israelis and the Nazis is disquietingly reminiscent of the crudest Arab propaganda and of the diatribes of the representatives of the Soviet Union at the General Assembly. It is shocking to hear this line from Mr Stone. What choice except the gas chamber remained for German Jews who did not manage to escape? Mr Stone can hardly pretend that the Arabs ran from systematic extermination. This 'too' thrown in so casually to associate the fate of German Jewry with that of the Palestinian Arabs in the reader's mind is a sample of Mr Stone's fair play. If Mr Stone is convinced of the unqualified right of all refugees to return, why does he not raise his voice for the return of millions of German refugees to East Prussia, Pomerania and Silesia? In the context of war and its aftermaths, such a demand would be as absurd as in the case of the Arab refugees. However, reparation for abandoned Arab property is another matter and subject to negotiation as the Israeli government has repeatedly stated.

The Arab states have made no secret of the objective of an Arab 'return' – the liquidation of Israel. Nasser put it simply and candidly: 'If the Arabs return to Israel, Israel will cease to exist.' (*Zürcher Woche*, 1 September 1961.) The numerous official Arab pronouncements on 'the refugees' right to annihilate Israel' are not the statements of extremist groups but official Arab policy enunciated by Arab statesmen. Consequently when Mr Stone asks, 'Have refugees no right to return?' and conjures up the image of despoiled and persecuted German Jews, he should consider Shukairy's Palestine Liberation Organization, an army of 300,000 refugees concentrated in the Gaza Strip. That a would-be invading army fails of its purpose does not make it innocent or innocuous.

A good example of the complexities of the situation is provided by the new refugee problems resulting from the Israeli victory of June 1967. Some 150,000 Arabs fled from the West Bank of Jordan to the East Bank. They fled for a variety of reasons chief among them the conviction that Israeli soldiers

would massacre them; they had been promised that the victorious Arabs would slaughter every Israeli 'man, woman and
child'. Hussain's broadcast to his people gave full instructions
as to how to treat a conquered enemy : 'Kill the Jews wherever
you find them. Kill them with your hands, with your nails and
teeth.' It is hardly surprising that Arabs so commanded expected no better from the soldiers of Israel. As in 1948, Arab atro-
city propaganda back-fired. But unlike 1948 the Israelis were
neither bewildered nor alarmed. If Arabs preferred the East
Bank of the Jordan to life on the West Bank under Israeli
occupation, Israelis could readily make peace with this pre-
dilection. They remembered how savagely Jordan had shelled
Jerusalem despite all urging by Israel that Hussain not join the
Arab attack. They knew that had Israel been defeated there
would have been no Jewish equivalent of the East Bank and no
Jewish refugees. Nevertheless, after the cessation of hostilities,
Israel agreed to repatriate all *bona fide* residents of the West
Bank who had fled. Yet after this decision, in the course of the
negotiations, the Jordanian Finance Minister, Abdul Wahab
Majali, publicly urged the refugees to return 'to help your
brothers continue their political action and remain a thorn in
the flesh of the aggressor until the crisis had been solved'. It is
hardly surprising that after this pronouncement some members
of the Israeli Cabinet, meeting on 13 August, several days after
the Jordanian Finance Minister's counsel, raised the question of
the advisability of the return of these 'thorns'. Though the
Cabinet re-affirmed its previous decision despite this blatant
provocation, no government can be expected to welcome a
returning Fifth Column, even the Israeli.

No doubt just as Mr Stone, despite his own testimony of
1948, now finds it possible to write of 'the expulsion of the
Arabs from Palestine' so the contemporary reports of corres-
pondents who watched the trek of Arabs across the Allenby
Bridge from the West Bank to the East Bank will weigh little
with the scribes of the future or, for that matter, of the present.
Already the whole anti-Semitic, anti-Israel cabal from Fascist
to Communist, from Black Power to White Power, is in full
swing, as Soviet cartoons *à la* Streicher and accounts of Israeli

'massacres' of Arabs in the publications of SNCC and of the white supremacist National States Rights party indicate. The notion that TV, radio and instant reporting have made the distortion of events taking place under our eyes more troublesome than in the past appears to be increasingly naive. The Arab who on the Israeli side of the Allenby Bridge testifies in the presence of the Red Cross and neutral observers that he is leaving voluntarily, and signs a document to that effect, may tell an opposite tale to the Jordanians on the other side of the bridge. That the Jordanian government urges refugees to return and even ventures to recommend insurrection merely confirms the statement of the UNRWA chief representative in West Jordan who stated on 4 July that not one of the twenty refugee camps in West Jordan was affected by the hostilities during the war, nor one resident killed. (Reported by Martha Gellhorn in the *Guardian*.)

In a sense Mr Stone is right when he declares that the discussion as to whether Arab refugees fled voluntarily or were driven out is 'irrelevant'. It is irrelevant because his objection to the resettlement of Arab refugees or to any reasonable accommodation with reality is based on his rejection of the right of Israel to exist as a Jewish state. He believes that General Dayan's statement, 'We want a Jewish state like the French have a French state' must 'deeply disturb the thoughtful Jewish reader'. He is equally shocked by a reported conversation with Ben Gurion in which the latter said: 'You must know that Israel is the country of the Jews and only of the Jews. Every Arab who lives here has the same rights as any minority citizen in any country of the world, but he must admit the fact that he lives in a Jewish country.' Mr Stone observes, 'The implications must chill Jews in the outside world.'

Presumably he accepts the existence of France, or Soviet Russia, or China, or the United States without frost-bite. While we judge the democratic character of these states by the rights enjoyed by their ethnic or religious minorities, each of these states has a dominant majority culture. Why is a Jewish state, while giving full political rights to all its citizens and prepared to respect their cultural and religious differences, more disturbing than any other democratic national state? Israeli Arabs speak Arabic and are Muslims or Christians; the Jewish majority speaks Hebrew and is Jewish, and the Arabs would be the first to protest linguistic or religious 'integration'. Their minority rights are precious just as are the rights of minorities in the United States or, hopefully, in Soviet Russia. But Mr Stone, thoroughly congealed, is only able to compare a Jewish state with Spain of the Inquisition and, in an indecent innuendo, with 'more recent parallels'.

If Mr Stone were advocating the abolition of all national states and raising the vision of the Federation of the World and the Parliament of Man his ideological horror of a 'Jewish country' would be comprehensible. But he is not unfurling a belated internationalist banner under whose folds the tribes will merge. On the contrary, he is sympathetic to national claims, and particularly sensitive to the claims of Arab nationalism. It is only Jewish nationalism that by definition becomes 'narrow', 'tribal', 'exclusive', or 'racist'. For Israel to call itself a Jewish state is 'supra-nationalist', unlike the other countries of the earth whose national character leaves thoughtful Jews and non-Jews unchilled. In the vocabulary of Jewish Leftists as of Jewish bourgeois assimilationists (*vide* the Council of Judaism's espousal of Mr Stone), Jewish nationalism is always 'chauvinism'; it is never 'emergent', 'renascent', 'progressive', 'revolutionary'. No matter how many national 'liberation movements' may burgeon with radical and liberal approval in Asia or Africa, Jewish nationalism is a suspect growth to be eradicated as energetically by the hammer and sickle as by the Fascist axe. A totalitarian Egypt, where former Nazi henchmen not only receive refuge but are influential in the government, is acclaimed in preference to socially advanced Israel. The Left has long abandoned its old-fashioned Utopian enchantment with internationalism and has developed a sturdy regard for the national identity of all the tribes of the globe – yellow, black, red – with the one exception already noted. I am certain that the same Russian Communists who proscribe the study of Hebrew in the Soviet Union as reaction-

ary will, without batting an eyelid, endorse SNCC's suggestion that Swahili be taught in American public schools.

Mr Stone finds nothing reprehensible in love of country if
Arabs do the loving. Writing in *Ramparts* (July 1967), he writes :
'The refugees lost their farms, their villages, their offices, their
cities, their country.' In the mounting crescendo of this listing,
the climactic 'their country' is worth noting. And in the *New
York Review of Books* he comments on the longing of the Arab
refugees for Palestine. '"Homelessness" is the major theme of
Zionism but this pathetic passion is denied to Arab refugees.'
The homelessness in question here is, of course, national homelessness.

Mr Stone stresses not only the Arab refugee who – whatever
the explanation – left his home and his home town but the
Palestinian who lost his country. And he charges the Zionists
with a 'moral imbecility' which enabled them to ignore the
existence of a native Palestinian population when they began
the return to the ancient homeland. Through the Jewish return
to Palestine a Palestinian people was ruthlessly dispossessed.
Here Mr Stone echoes the theme song of Arab belligerence.

Though it seems late in the day to re-argue the ABCs of the
Zionist case, the current barrage from both the extreme Right
and Left makes a few reminders mandatory, particularly as
many well-intentioned people are troubled by such charges.
Did Jewish aggressors set up their homeland in total disregard
of a native people with prior claims?

Now for the ABCs: To make his point Mr Stone comes up
with all kinds of nuggets from his mining of *Les Temps
Modernes*. Herzl never mentioned the Arabs in *The Jewish State*
(1896); Nordau wept when he learned of the existence of Arabs.
Mr Stone fails to mention the fact that by the time Herzl wrote
Old-New Land, he was well aware of the Arabs and dreamed
of happy coexistence. But whatever were the deficiencies of
early Zionist fantasies, the Balfour Declaration issued in 1917
took full cognizance of the 600,000 local Arabs. The underlying
assumption of the Declaration was that while over 97 per cent
of the huge territories liberated by the Allies from the Turks

would be devoted to the setting up of independent Arab states, the 'small notch' of Palestine would be reserved for the creation of a Jewish state. This 'small notch' (Lord Balfour's term) was in 1922 further reduced by two thirds through the amputation of the East Bank of Palestine for the establishment of Trans-jordan, later Jordan.

By the time the Mandate was in effect, five independent Arab states were established on the territory freed from Turkish rule. Saudi Arabia, Iraq, Syria, Lebanon and Transjordan were allotted an area covering 1,200,000 square miles. The ten thousand square miles left to Western Palestine constituted less than 1 per cent of the total area and was less than a third of the area originally promised by the Balfour Declaration. The Partition Resolution of 1947, accepted by the Jews and fought by the Arabs, further lopped away at the continually diminishing 'notch'. A glance at the map of the region shows the ratio between the huge Arab lands and the tiny state of Israel.

But the Arabs and their supporters reject this comparison as irrelevant. That the Arabs received much and the Jews little has nothing to do with the case. Arab nationalism cannot be sated by less than 100 per cent gratification; 90 per cent plus won't do. What about the Palestinian Arabs? Why should they surrender their Palestinian identity to become Syrians or Jordanians as the Jews irrationally suggest? True, all Arabs are brothers when the pan-Arab dream beckons but it is criminal imperialist aggression to suggest that the Arabs, particularly the Palestinians, relinquish one jot of their national claim because of Jewish need, Hitler's victims and the rest. Such is the Arab argument.

If a genuine Palestinian nationalism had been violated then it would be Quixotic folly to ask the Arabs of Palestine to abandon their rights in favour of the unfortunate Jews. But did such a violation take place? At the end of World War I the inhabitants of the land treasured for centuries by Jews as Zion did not view themselves as a distinct Palestinian nation. *Palestine did not exist as a political or national entity as far as the Arabs were concerned.* For them it was merely a geographical locality, the south of Syria. Whereas no one doubts the fierce

authenticity of Arab nationalism, *Palestinian* Arab nationalism is an artificial creation with no roots before the British
Mandate. As recently as 31 May 1956, Ahmed Shukairy, the
extremist chief of the Palestine Liberation Organization, declared before the Security Council: 'It is common knowledge
that Palestine is nothing but southern Syria.'

Nor were the Zionist pioneers who came to an abandoned
wasteland forty or fifty years ago afflicted by 'moral imbecility'. They may have been simple-minded in believing that the
swamps they drained, the stony soil they irrigated – incidentally, swamps and deserts *purchased* at fancy prices by the
Jewish National Fund – would make them welcome neighbours, but there was nothing wrong with their ethics. They were
socialist idealists who believed that to reclaim a marsh through
their own toil and devotion and to establish agricultural settlements on soil on which no one had been able to live for generations was a gain for all and a loss to none. They took literally
the business about to each according to his need from each
according to his capacity. The result of their personal sacrifices was the green countryside which now enables Arabs to
point to the flourishing land of which they were 'despoiled'.

Simple-minded though the pioneers may have been in believing that their physical reclamation of desolate wastes would
win them affection or gratitude, they were right in their estimate of the economic and demographic results of their labour.
Far from dispossessing Arabs, Zionist colonization resulted in
their numerical increase.

According to the 1922 census taken by the British government only 186,000 Arabs lived in the area which later became
Israel. The increase in the Arab population of Palestine took
place not only because of a very high rate of natural increase
due to improved health conditions and standards of living but
also because Palestine became a country of Arab *immigration*
from adjacent Arab countries. Arabs were attracted, mainly
from Syria and Egypt, to the Jewish areas of Mandated Palestine by the swift industrial and agricultural growth which the
Jews had started and were constantly enlarging and

diversifying. This is confirmed by the testimony in an UNRWA
bulletin of 1962 :

A considerable movement of people is known to have occurred,
particularly during the Second World War years when new opportunities of employment opened up in the towns and on military
works in Palestine. These wartime prospects and, generally, the
higher rate of industrialization in Palestine than in neighbouring
countries attracted many immigrants from those countries, and
many of them entered Palestine without their presence being
officially recorded.
(UNRWA Reviews, Information Paper No. 6, Beirut, September
1962.)

In the whole of Palestine the Arab population doubled between 1920 and 1940, growing from 600,000 to well over a
million. In Jordan, closed to Jewish immigration, the population remained static. Paradoxically, in the period between the
issuance of the Balfour Declaration and the establishment of
Israel, Palestine changed from a country of Arab emigration to
one of Arab immigration – a phenomenon observable in none
of the adjacent Arab countries.

Perhaps the most telling demonstration of what had actually taken place has ironically been provided by Israel's June
victory. When publicity focused on the Arab refugees, the overwhelming bulk were discovered dwelling on the West Bank, the
part of Palestine annexed in 1948 by Jordan, and in Gaza, the
Palestinian city, occupied by Egypt. The refugees, maintained
by UNRWA in camps whose standard of living was higher
than that of many an Arab village, had never left Palestine.

Will Mr Stone, who deplores 'Lilliputian nationalism', make
a holy cause of a fixation on a particular village or street? No
matter how dear a home or a home town to the residents,
people are shifted despite their wishes for so trivial a cause
as the construction of a new dam or highway. Israel, a country
of immigrants gathered from remote corners of the world, understandably perceives no gross injustice in the resettlement of
Arabs on territory formerly Palestine – or on adjacent territory
– a resettlement requiring no adjustment in landscape, language, climate, religion or social mores. The opposition of the

Arab states to any of the numerous proposals for the productive resettlement of the Palestinian Arabs is predicated on the
simple proposition that Israel must be destroyed. Economically,
territorially, above all, humanly, the deliberately created Arab
refugee problem lends itself to just solution once the Arab premise of the liquidation of Israel swiftly through a hostile influx or slowly through an uncontrolled demographic change is
abandoned. The pseudo-humanitarian premise that Arab nationalism in full panoply down to its most tenuous ramifications merits tender regard, whatever the cost to the one small
Jewish state, only bolsters Arab appetite and intransigence.

In addition to dwelling on the 'expulsion' of the Arabs, Mr
Stone finds much wrong with Israel. He complains that Israel
is creating a kind of 'moral schizophrenia in world Jewry'.
Outside Israel, Jewish welfare depends on the existence of 'secular, non-racial, pluralistic societies'; yet Jews defend a society
in Israel in which 'the ideal is racial and exclusionist'. Israel
is a theocratic state, with second-class Arab citizens and with
ingrained prejudice against oriental Jews. Mr Stone makes
these charges categorically without offering a shred of evidence of their truth. Blanket denunciations, if false, can only
be answered with a blanket denial. The one specific point Mr
Stone makes ('In Israel Jewry finds itself defending a society in
which mixed marriages cannot be legalized') is patently untrue.
Both in Israel and outside of Israel the requirements of rigid
orthodoxy instead of being defended, are constantly under attack. If Mr Stone read the Hebrew press he would appreciate
the vigour of its self-criticism in this and other respects. Israel
has many imperfections but to pretend that any of its inadequacies are its 'ideal' rather than the result of human failure
or of the economic and political pressures to which the small
beleaguered land has been subject since its establishment is
again to judge Israel by an invidious criterion applied to no
other people. No country in the world has so bold a social vision
or has tried so bravely to integrate the excluded of the earth
who came to it – were they survivors of the gas chambers or
despoiled Oriental Jews. Born in great travail to find an answer

for Jewish need and to achieve Jewish national independence, it is not called upon to answer non-existent needs or desires which have ample scope for their satisfaction elsewhere.

Mr Stone perceives a growing divergence between Jew and Israeli : 'the former with a sense of mission as a Witness in the human wilderness, the latter concerned only with his own tribe's welfare.' The reverse, of course, is true. It is the Israelis whose concerns are global, whose emissaries penetrated Hitler's Europe, who brought Eichmann to justice, whose instructors teach new and advanced social techniques to emergent countries in Africa, whose kibbutzim serve as laboratories to Africans and Indians and Burmese and Europeans, whose social dynamism and accomplishments inspire all poor and undeveloped countries. The world sympathy for Israel last June was not a tribute to tribal egoism but to courage and vision on an unprecedented scale.

Mr Stone makes another nasty charge. Since Zionism 'grows on Jewish catastrophe', it now 'casts longing eyes on Russian Jewry'. Mr Stone wants to know if it would not be better if the Soviet Union wiped out anti-Semitism and gave equal rights to its Jewish citizens. Better than what? Better than another large-scale Jewish catastrophe which Israel apparently desires? This is a disgraceful accusation. Israel is in the foreground of Jewish agitation for unrestricted cultural rights for Russian Jews. Among the rights sought is the right of emigration for those Russian Jews who have families in Israel or elsewhere. Were there to be free emigration from Russia, Israel would be delighted if Russian Jews came. But that is a very different matter from desiring another 'catastrophe' which would supply 'another flow of desperate refugees to an Israel already short of Jews if it is to expand as the Zionist militants hope to expand it'. Here we get a double dig; not only is Israel lusting for Jewish tragedy but it is expansionist. Let me tell Mr Stone a secret: not only Zionist 'militants' want Jewish immigration; all Israel does. The call for *Aliyah* (Immigration) has gone out not to 'expand' but further to develop the country. Ben Gurion's great dream is to 'expand' into the Negev, the desert that constitutes two thirds of Israel. This creative vision

– to regenerate sand and stone as the Emek was reclaimed – is Israel's 'hope'. Mr Stone who so eloquently expounds universal values and universal visions should be warier of lending his authority to vicious anti-Israel smears.

Finally Mr Stone suggests : 'The ideal solution would allow the Jews to make their contributions as citizens in the diverse societies and nations which are their homes while Israel finds acceptance as a Jewish state in a renascent Arab civilization. This would end Arab fears of a huge inflow to Israel.' At first reading, most Zionists would enthusiastically embrace such a solution; that's what they have been wanting all along – a renascent Jewish state to be accepted by a renascent Arab civilization. Stone might be quoting Herzl. But a second reading is less reassuring. To calm Arab fears of a 'huge inflow', Jewish immigration to Israel would presumably be restricted (though Mr Stone appreciates that the prospect of an inundation is slight). If, despite his cautious phrasing, I read Mr Stone correctly, the one group that the 'exclusionist' Jewish state could rightly exclude would be Jews. Such is the *reductio ad absurdum* of Mr Stone's universalism.

Given a will to peace on the part of the Arabs all the problems of the Arab–Israeli conflict can be settled reasonably and to the advantage of Jew and Arab. This includes the definition of boundaries and the integration of refugees into a productive life, but the elementary recognition of Israel's right to exist is the precondition of any settlement. And the emergence of Israel as a Jewish country with the same rights for self-defence and normal development as other democratic countries should scar no psyche able to envision 'renascent' civilizations all over the globe.

A word of warning should be added. The Zionist visionaries who came with the Bible and socialist tracts to build a 'just society' in the desert have lost many illusions. They have learned the stern lessons of recent history. I have watched this transformation. In 1936, on my first visit to Palestine, I attended a *seder* in Ein Harod, a kibbutz in the Emek. In addition to the traditional questions – why is this night different? – the children asked *Kashes* of their own. One of the questions was, 'Why do the Arabs live on the hills and we in the valley?' The answer, understandable only to those aware of the exposed position of the kibbutzim, was, 'Because we want peace and friendship.'

The children who heard this answer grew up to fight for hills in three wars since 1948. Last July, three weeks after the end of the 1967 battles, I was in Galilee in a kibbutz shelled for months from the Syrian ridges. I saw the destroyed cottages and the underground shelters where the children routinely slept. The next morning I visited the Golan Heights, the fortified Syrian hills bristling with Russian armour from which Syrian soldiers equally routinely attacked the kibbutz. The ridge was scaled by Israeli soldiers on the last day of the fighting and the bunkers dismantled in one of the toughest fights of the war. Perhaps the most illuminating circumstance of this battle was that the kibbutzim, not the Israeli military, insisted on the capture of the ridge: 'Our children must sleep in beds not in shelters.' Anyone standing among the masses of Russian armour on the ridge and seeing the guns pointed at the settlements would probably find it difficult to continue prating about Israeli expansionism. Until the Arabs make peace, Israel needs viable borders; as long as Israel is under attack by Arabs who out-number her twenty to one, it will perforce be militant. If instead of indulging in strictly one-sided pieties, the self-declared humanists and universalists would unequivocally grant the rights of the farmer in valley rather than of the gunner on the hill, peace might come sooner. Otherwise the enemies of Israel may be caught in the vice of a self-fulfilling prophecy to the detriment of all.

The Arab–Israeli War: The Consequences of Defeat

By Bernard Lewis*

I

Since the end of the third Arab–Israeli war the vocabulary of Middle Eastern politics has been enriched with a new formula – 'the removal of the consequences of aggression'. The phrase presents some obvious difficulties of definition concerning the origin of the aggression, the nature of its consequences and the manner of their removal. All these are subject to a wide diversity of interpretations. However, the meaning of the Arab states in putting forward this formula as a demand is quite clear; it is that Israel is the aggressor, that the occupation of Arab lands and the departure of their Arab inhabitants are the consequences of aggression, and that these consequences should be reversed.

It is possible that in certain circumstances the conquerors might be willing to give up their conquests; it is even conceivable that the refugees might return – though this would make them unique among the countless millions in Europe, Asia and Africa who have fled or been driven from their homes in our brutal century. But far more has happened than the occupation of lands and the movement of peoples, important as these may be. In the world of reality, events cannot be unmade, and their effects persist, even when their results vanish. Sometimes these events are of such dimensions as to involve radical reassessments: governments reassess policies at the periphery of their interests and people at the centre of crisis reassess their governments. It seems likely that the war and crisis in the Middle East in the summer of 1967 formed such a turning point. The four chief parties concerned – the Arabs, Israel, the Soviet Union

* Bernard Lewis is Professor of the History of the Near and Middle East at the University of London. Reprinted by special permission from *Foreign Affairs*, January 1968. Copyright by the Council on Foreign Relations, Inc., New York.

and the West – must have been pondering the significance of these events and the lessons to be learnt from them.

The Russians were involved in the crisis from the start – indeed, without descending to the conspiratorial conception of history or returning to the polemics of the Cold War, we can say with reasonable assurance that they had no small part in creating it. One contribution, which they shared with other powers, was the dispatch of large quantities of modern, sophisticated weapons to the area; another, more distinctively their own, was their unswerving support for the Arab states in any and every encounter, irrespective of circumstances. A good example of this is the recurrent problem of clashes on the Syrian–Israeli border. Most observers – and governments – were content to treat each incident on its merits and to blame one side or the other as seemed appropriate. But the Soviet government invariably supported the Syrians, even when they were palpably in the wrong, and on several occasions even used its veto in the Security Council to save the Syrians from a mildly critical resolution. On 3 November 1966, the veto was applied against an inoffensive resolution sponsored, among others, by two African states – a remarkable indication of how far the Soviet government was prepared to go in support of its Arab protégés.

This kind of action would in itself have led Arab governments to form a high – and, as it turned out, exaggerated – assessment of Soviet willingness to stand by them in a crisis. There is, in addition, some evidence of Soviet help at a more intimate level than the politics of the United Nations. Syrian gunnery on the border, it is said, showed a degree of professional efficiency out of accord with the previous and subsequent performances of the Syrian army; Syrian diplomacy, on both border issues and questions of oil transit payments, was conducted with a professional finesse that suggested greater reserves of skill and experience than are normally available to short-lived governments in Damascus.

In his television address on Friday, 9 June, President Nasser explained how the crisis had begun. On 15 May, he said, it had become clear from Israeli statements that they intended to attack Syria. This was confirmed by information from Syrian sources and also by reports from the Egyptian intelligence services. Moreover, 'our friends in the Soviet Union informed the parliamentary delegation which visited Moscow early last month that there was a premeditated intention to attack Syria. It was our duty not to stay with our arms crossed. It was a duty of Arab solidarity, and also a guarantee for our national security.' It was for this reason, said the President, that he had sent his forces to the frontier. This had led successively to the withdrawal of UNEF, the Egyptian occupation of Sharm al-Shaikh, and the declaration of a blockade of the Gulf of Aqaba, since 'the passage of the enemy flag in front of our troops was intolerable, and inflicted the deepest wound on the feelings of the Arab nation'.

President Nasser of course acted, as always, by his own choice, but we may believe him when he says that the original impetus came from Syrian and Russian warnings. Both Syrian and, what is more important, Russian spokesmen have throughout taken the same line. But were these warnings based on a genuine danger – or even on a genuine belief that such a danger existed? The evidence adduced, apart from vague references to information received, consisted of two points : an alleged concentration of large Israeli forces on the Syrian frontier, and menacing speeches by Mr Eshkol. Neither piece of evidence amounts to much. The speeches were no more than routine warnings of reprisals in what had become a standardized pattern, intended to discourage Syrian and soothe Israeli hotheads – an exercise which should have been familiar to Arab leaders. The troop concentration, as is clear from the reports of the UN truce observers, never took place. The Syrians may have misread the situation and panicked; the Russians will not have done so, and the conclusion is inescapable that the Soviet Government, for reasons of its own, either planned or connived at the launching of what became a new and dangerous crisis in Israel–Arab relations.

The suggestion has been made that the Soviet purpose was to provide a distraction in the Middle East and thus relieve the pressure on Vietnam. This would assume, first, that they intended, from the start, to create a major international crisis, involving the powers and especially the United States, and, second, that they counted on the willingness of the United States to become involved. Both assumptions seem unlikely. A more probable explanation is that they aimed at something much more limited and local, a scare rather than a crisis, and that its purpose was to save the tottering Syrian regime from collapse. The Soviets had invested a good deal of time, effort and money in the left-wing Ba'athist government and had achieved a closer relationship with it than with any other government not under Communist control. In May 1967 that government, and with it the Soviet position in Syria, was in grave danger. It was already more than a year old – a dangerous age in Damascus. Based on an uneasy alliance between members of Muslim religious minority groups, it was unpopular with the Sunnis,[1] and further weakened by the split between Alawis and Druzes. Worst of all, some of its supporters had gratuitously antagonized the powerful Islamic establishment. Like other 'revolutionary' and 'progressive' regimes in the Arab world, the Ba'athists had confined their radicalism to politics and economics and had usually refrained from attacking Islamic beliefs, traditions or institutions. They had therefore encountered nothing more than the grumbles of a population accustomed to acquiesce in the vagaries of authoritarian government. There are, however, limits to acquiescence, and at the beginning of May the publication in an army-sponsored magazine of an article denouncing religion and belief in God evoked a menacing wave of popular resentment against a regime which now seemed to be threatening the most cherished values of a Muslim people. The government beat a hasty retreat, attributing the article to the CIA, but the damage was already done. The Ba'athists and their Russian backers may well have decided that a little diversion, based on the unfailing theme of Palestine, might be useful. As the crisis developed, and seemed to be tending towards a diplomatic victory for the revolutionary Arab states, and therefore for Russia, wider and more tempting prospects appeared

1. At one time the Ba'athist government was known as the *'Adas* (lentil) regime – an acronym of 'Alawis, Druzes and Isma'ilis.

– the collapse of Western influence, the consolidation of Russian influence in the revolutionary Arab states, and its extension to the remaining Arab states in the Middle East and North Africa.

In backing them so far, the Russians were clearly assuming that the Arabs would win – if necessary in a war, but probably without one. The West would be hypnotized into accepting Arab demands; Israel, abandoned by her Western friends, perhaps even under their pressure, would be forced to give way. The dispatch of a Russian fleet to the eastern Mediterranean, of a strength obviously insufficient to confront the US Sixth Fleet, can only have been intended to overawe Israel, with American acquiescence. The world would learn that the friends of the Soviets prosper, while the friends of the West do not.

For a while the world seemed to be learning just that. The West faltered and fumbled; Israel, unsure of Western attitudes, hesitated; President Nasser, triumphant, threw caution to the winds. After nationalizing the Suez Canal in 1956, he had astutely sat back, declared himself satisfied and left the next move to his opponents. After closing the Straits of Tiran, he declared explicitly that this was a preliminary to the final confrontation with Israel, for which he was now ready. The other revolutionary Arab states were with him; even his Arab enemies felt obliged to make the necessary accommodations. That the Russian encouraged him to go so far is unlikely; they certainly did not prevent him.

The Six Day War and its sequel showed that the Russians had failed badly in their military and political intelligence and assessments – not perhaps of the West, but of Israel and the Arabs. No doubt they were misled about the one by their own anti-Semitic stereotypes, about the other by the wishful thinking of their Arab informants. The correction of error is difficult in a dictatorship. By Monday evening, 6 June, informed opinion – by Tuesday almost everyone in the free world – knew how the battle was going. It was not until Tuesday night (Wednesday morning in the Middle East) that the Soviet delegate to the UN agreed to an unconditional ceasefire. The extra time he

had striven to gain for the Arabs served only to consolidate
their defeat.

From Wednesday morning the signs multiplied that the Russians were engaged in a reappraisal – probably agonizing. They
were surprised, disconcerted and very angry. Their public fury
was directed against Israel; in addition, they were probably not
unmoved by the swift collapse of Arab arms and by President
Nasser's attempt, through the false charge of American and
British participation, to drag them into war.

The Russians had reason to be angry. Soviet prestige – the
reputation of Soviet arms and guidance, the value of Soviet
friendship, the credibility of Soviet warnings – had received a
damaging blow, with far-reaching repercussions. The Russians
had suffered this blow because, through the extent of their
commitment to the Arabs, they had in effect entrusted the
safety of Soviet prestige to the keeping of Arab governments
over which they had no real control. They had taken great
chances, which turned out badly ; they had done so for very
dubious gains. The Arab leaders were very unwise to assume
that the Soviets would accept, for their sake, risks which they
had not accepted for Berlin or Vietnam. This miscalculation
was disastrous for the Arabs; it was also most unfortunate for
the Soviet Union.

The root of the trouble was that the Arab governments, even
that of Syria, were not satellites, and were therefore ultimately
uncontrollable. The Soviet government, in dealing with the
Middle East, found themselves in a position of responsibility
without power – a reversal of their normal experience. It is not
surprising that they were disturbed.

In this predicament, the Soviet leadership had, basically, a
choice between two policies: either to consolidate its hold on
the revolutionary Arab governments and transform them into
satellites, or to attempt some measure of disengagement. This
in turn is linked with the larger, global choice before them,
between détente and coexistence, on the one hand, and active
hostility toward the United States on the other. Both choices
are affected by changing and conflicting pressures within the
collective leadership which succeeded Khrushchev.

One of these pressures is that of the so-called Stalinists – more precisely, the exponents of repression and chauvinism. These circles are strongly affected by old-fashioned anti-Semitism, which can become a powerful factor in determining attitudes both towards a Jewish state and towards its enemies. The point is sometimes made that Jewish or pro-Jewish sentiments can lead to unbalanced and unrealistic policies. This is of course true. It is equally true, though less obvious, that anti-Jewish sentiments can have the same effect. The hysterical violence and traditional anti-Semitic symbolism of Soviet attacks on Israel show that the offence of the Israelis, in Soviet eyes, were greatly aggravated by the fact that they were Jews. These Soviet reactions also suggest that one of the motives of a pro-Arab policy may have been a desire to hurt the Jews, and that this emotional impulsion may have warped the judgement of policy-makers and led them to a degree of indulgence to Arab wishes which was ultimately harmful to Soviet and even Arab interests. This phenomenon is not unknown in other countries ; in the Soviet Union it was not countered or corrected by any pressure, emotional or otherwise, in the opposite direction.

11

Anti-Jewish prejudice may have pushed the policy of supporting Arab nationalism to ill-judged extremes; it was not of course the sole or even the main motive for this policy, which rested on a fairly realistic assessment of the condition of the Arab world and the importance of the Middle Eastern bridgehead for Soviet activities in Asia and Africa.

This importance was enhanced, rather than reduced, by the Arab defeat, and for the moment there was much to tempt the Russians into a closer involvement. The regimes they had supported were in danger of overthrow, with further damaging effects to Soviet prestige. China seemed ready to usurp Russia's place as the patron of Arab nationalism, and was gaining the support of Arab Communists. The blow to Western influence, on the other hand, was far heavier than to Russian influence, and affected even those countries that were under conservative regimes. For a while the Russians seem to have toyed with the

The Israel–Arab Reader

idea of establishing Communist regimes in the Arab lands – and then to have abandoned it as too dangerous.

It is not difficult to see why. To transform the Arab countries into satellites would be an expensive, difficult and hazardous operation, and would never be safe unless the regimes were sustained, as in Eastern Europe, by the threat or presence of Soviet force. Even in Eastern Europe, this policy has become precarious; it would be still more so in countries that have no land frontier with the Soviet Union. Moreover, such an intervention in the Arab lands would endanger the new, hard-won and greatly valued understanding with Turkey and Iran – both of them, despite their recent rethinking, still members of Western-oriented alliances. In addition, it soon became clear that the Chinese menace was not yet a serious factor, and that collapse of Western influence was by no means as complete as had at first appeared. The Syrian episode had shown that Islam was still the strongest loyalty of the people, and that outraged Islamic feelings could still shake or destroy a government which really tried to enforce its 'progressive' and 'revolutionary' principles. An attempt to create 'popular democracies' could arouse very powerful forces indeed.

Finally, and most important of all, the danger of a direct confrontation with the United States remained. It was this danger that had induced the Soviet government, at the height of the crisis, to draw back from armed intervention to save the Arabs. An adventurous policy in the Middle East could easily lead to a new danger of confrontation – and to another withdrawal, with even more damaging effects on Soviet prestige. In avoiding an entanglement with the Arabs and a collision with the United States, the Soviet leadership would be faithful to tradition. During the centuries of expansion, by which the Principality of Muscovy grew into the great Russian Empire, the greater Soviet Union and the still greater Soviet bloc, two principles were almost always respected: to advance by land into adjoining regions to which troops and settlers could easily be moved, and to avoid a clash with a superior or even an equal power.

The dilemma of the Soviet government was acute. A closer

involvement in the Middle East was too dangerous – yet disengagement seemed politically impossible. The collective
leadership could not make the sudden changes of policy that
were possible for Stalin or Khrushchev; the internal pressures
were too strong, and the status of the Soviet Union as a superpower was heavily committed. The Russian demand to Egypt,
at the time of President Podgorny's visit, for a purge of bourgeois elements in the Egyptian government and army, could
be interpreted either way – as a prelude to bolshevization or to
abandonment. As an emergency measure, an airlift of arms
was organized, to save the Nasserist and Ba'athist regimes from
collapse. But while Soviet prestige clearly required that these
regimes survive the war and its immediate aftermath, it did
not necessarily require their indefinite continuance, and at one
point there were some indications that the Soviets might regard
them as expendable. Later they seem to have decided to hold
on to President Nasser, and to support him against his possible
successors on the left or the right. To do this, they needed to
undertake some further re-equipment of the Egyptian armed
forces, and to extend – and more especially to publicize – their
own military and political activities in Egypt. Whether these
represent a holding operation or a new adventure is an open
question. It is still too early to assess the future development of
Soviet policy in the Middle East, nor indeed is it certain that
this policy has yet been decided. Much will obviously depend
on the attitudes of the Western powers and, above all, of the
United States.

There are, however, some signs of its probable direction.
The Soviets will certainly continue to give vociferous support
to the Arab case against Israel, especially at the United Nations. They will try to salvage their battered prestige and hope
that, as on previous occasions, they will find someone in the
West to help them in this task. But in all probability they will
take care not to get into a position again where their prestige
can be endangered by governments and armies which they do
not control. The most likely development is a policy based on
relations with individual Arab states rather than on Arabism,
and aimed at the kind of relationship that they have sought to

establish with Turkey, Iran and Pakistan. The question is how far they will be allowed to extricate themselves if they desire to do so.

Like the Soviet Union, the Western powers have been able to draw certain inferences from what has happened. For a while it seemed that the West, and particularly the United States, had been outmanoeuvred. The ring was closing around Israel; even pro-Western Arab rulers, whatever their real feelings, were lining up behind President Nasser. Communist Russia could support Arab nationalist demands to the full; the United States and Britain, captives of their own freedom and their own standards, could not, and were thus forced to appear as enemies of the Arabs. Their only choice was of what kind : as enemies to be respected and conciliated, or to be despised and ignored. For the United States, a far more terrible choice was being prepared – whether to abandon Israel to destruction, or to be trapped in a land war in South-west as well as South-east Asia.

Fortunately for the United States, no such choice was needed. Through no particular wisdom or merit of their own, the Western powers emerged from a dangerous situation with what turned out to be only minor injuries. Like the Russians, they had learned that their control over their friends was very limited. They were fortunate in that the state which was generally regarded as their protégé did not need to be rescued. The danger remained.

For a while, it seemed that despite their failure against Israel, the Russians had won a considerable political success against the United States and Britain, which found themselves being ignominiously evicted from most Arab countries. But even this was deceptive. The two most powerful Arab weapons against the West – the oil boycott and, for Britain, the sterling balances – both proved ineffective. The stoppage of oil exports did greater and swifter damage to the sellers than to the buyers. Arabian money transferred from London to Switzerland, at low or no interest rates, found its way back to London, to earn high interest for its new custodians. Even the closing of the Suez Canal did less harm than was feared, and for the United

States even brought some marginal advantage – some additional exports and the slowing down of Russian supplies to North Vietnam. The inconvenience to Britain was more serious, but much of this was of a transitional nature, until new arrangements could become fully effective. The heaviest sufferers were India, some other Asian and East African states, and above all the Egyptians themselves.

As the flames and the dust subsided, there were signs that the damage to Anglo-American diplomacy was less severe than had at first appeared. Some Arab leaders were beginning to wonder whether they were wise to identify themselves entirely with one camp in the global conflict, and whether indeed they had chosen the right one. Before very long, several Arab states began to make overtures to the West, and even President Nasser flew a kite, no doubt expecting, on the basis of past experience, that Western governments would respond with eager gratitude to the opportunity once again to feed his people and sustain his regime. This time, however, he had overestimated the American capacity to absorb calumny, abuse and injury, and the response from Washington was disappointing. In London he fared somewhat better, though the extent of British complaisance, and its value to Egypt, are still not clear.

That President Nasser should have found it necessary to seek London's good offices – for pressure in Jerusalem or intercession in Washington – is a measure of the failure of another kind of Western policy, that of General de Gaulle. Previous French policy towards Israel had been based on the assumptions that nothing could be achieved with the Arab states, and that one small ally in the Middle East was better than none at all. In a calculation unconnected with the Middle East, both assumptions were now abandoned. By supporting the Russian and Arab line against Israel, the General incurred some immediate losses – in the political and commercial good will of Israel, and in the confidence of Europe, at a time when the credibility of his friendship was rather important to him. In compensation, he gained warm words from Moscow and the Arab capitals. Whether he will gain any more from them is dubious. They for their part have already learnt that his support made no real difference to them; they are unlikely to pay for more than they receive.

III

In the West as in Russia the question that arises is a basic and simple one – how much trouble is the Middle East worth? On both sides there seems to be a growing appreciation of the advantages of disengagement – as far as is feasible – from an area of high risks, great costs, dubious returns and, above all, of diminishing importance, as it is being by-passed by strategic, economic and technological developments and overshadowed by the urgent problems of East Asia. These must, increasingly, dominate political and strategic thinking in Washington and Moscow.

For the powers of the Communist and Western blocs the possibility exists, however remotely, of extricating themselves from the Middle Eastern quicksands. No such possibility is open to the countries of the Middle East, which must make the best they can of conditions in their area – including, for as long as may be necessary, the policies of the great and not-so-great powers. The lessons of the war will thus appear to these countries in a somewhat different form.

What Israel learnt is what victors always learn from victory – that is, that they were right all along. On two points in particular the crisis and war confirmed Israeli beliefs: that their survival depended, ultimately, on their willingness and ability to fight for it, and that they could not trust the United Nations, where their enemies had a built-in position of advantage. The Soviet veto in the Security Council is always available to the Arabs, even on the most trivial matters; the combination of the Communist bloc and the quaintly named 'nonaligned' states in the General Assembly is sufficient to prevent any solution acceptable to Israel, if not to enforce one acceptable to the Arabs. 'If the Arabs table a resolution tomorrow that the earth is flat,' said an Israeli minister, 'they can count on at least forty votes.'

Reliance on their own military and political strength in the

Middle East and mistrust of 'United Nations auspices' are two basic Israeli conclusions from recent events. A third is that, of all the powers of the outside world, the only one that really matters to Israel is the United States. Even in the euphoria of victory, Israelis know that American goodwill is fundamental to them. Basically, there are three things that Israel wants from Washington: first, to deter the Russians, as in June 1967, from direct military intervention against them; second, to refrain from imposing, alone or with others, a solution which Israel judges contrary to her interests; third to ensure that Israel's armaments do not fall dangerously below the level of the Arab states. In other words, they wish to be sure that the Americans will neither undermine their position nor allow Russia to do so. Given this assurance, they feel confident that they can cope with their Arab neighbours. The ultimately more serious problem of their Arab subjects, with its implications for the whole future of their state, society and ethos, remains unresolved, and there is little sign of agreement, inside Israel, on how to tackle it.

A victory, said the Duke of Wellington, is the greatest tragedy in the world, except a defeat. The Arabs suffered this greater tragedy, and the problems confronting them – problems of understanding and of action – have a terrible urgency quite different from the milder dilemmas of the Americans, the Russians, even of the Israelis.

The first and obvious question was – what went wrong? Why had they suffered a double defeat – a military defeat in the field, at the hands of a nation inferior in numbers, weapons, territory and resources, and a political defeat at the United Nations, despite every appearance of overwhelming political superiority? At the moment of crisis and war, it was the Arab states which found themselves isolated from world opinion, and even some of those governments which supported them were clearly acting against their own public opinion at home.[2]

---

2. The line-up of Communist, Fascist, personal, revolutionary and traditional dictatorships on the Arab side raises difficult problems for those who believe that economics and ideology, not politics, are the determining factors in international as in other affairs.

Even the full mobilization of the Soviet regular and auxiliary forces in the General Assembly failed to secure the necessary majority for the resolutions that the Arabs wanted. It was a political defeat hardly less striking than the military defeat which had preceded it.

War and defeat are the classical motors of social and political change. Sometimes they lead to major transformations, as in Germany and Russia after the First World War; sometimes to a mood of sullen resentment and withdrawal, as in the South after the American Civil War, and in Spain after 1898. Defeat is especially cogent when inflicted by the carriers of another civilization with a different and challenging religion or ideology. The defeat in Palestine in 1948 was the first such shock suffered directly by the Eastern Arabs. The earlier defeats of Islam at the hands of West and East European imperialism had been sustained by the Turks and Persians, who, as the dominant peoples of Islam, had shielded the Arabs from the realities of politics and war. The vague encounters of the Anglo-French period added little of value to their experience; on the contrary, by providing easy victories over embarrassed and half-hearted opponents they fostered a dangerous illusion of strength.

The shock of defeat in 1948, in place of the expected victory parade, was all the greater in that it was inflicted, not by the mighty imperial powers, but by the despised and familiar Jews. The *nakba* (disaster), as the Arabs called it, gave rise to an extensive literature, much of it concerned with the political and military blunders of Arab leaders, but some of it, as for example the well-known works by Mr Musa Alami and Professor Constantine Zurayk, attempting to penetrate to the deeper social and cultural causes of the Arab failure.

Politically, the defeat was seen as a failure of the regimes – the parliamentary and constitutional monarchies and republics – which had conducted the war. The lesson learnt was the need for a more radical and more violent approach. The traditional and authoritarian regimes, as in Jordan and Saudi Arabia, managed to survive, but the liberal-style regimes in Syria Egypt and Iraq were swept away. They were succeeded by military governments, with programmes of revolutionary change, later designated socialism, and of Arab nationalism. In international relations, their anti-Western attitudes gradually became pro-Soviet, when the Soviet Union finally emerged as the most serious and dangerous antagonist of the West and of Western civilization.

The second defeat, in 1956, brought no comparable soul-searching or upheaval. This was because the military defeat was compensated by a great political victory, and because the significance of the struggle was blurred by myths. Three beliefs, in particular, shaped Arab thinking on these events; first, that Egypt was defeated by France and Britain, not just by Israel; second, that a cause of defeat was Arab disunity, which left Egypt alone to face the tripartite attack; third, that Egypt was saved from the consequences of defeat by the intervention of Russia, her new friend since the previous year.

The third of these is an obvious myth – a successful combined effort of delusion and self-delusion. The record of October and November 1956 makes it quite clear that the Soviet government did not speak out until the American President and other spokesmen had explained, not once but several times, that the United States did not support Britain, France or Israel, and disapproved of their action. Then and only then did the Soviets take up the Egyptian cause and utter dire threats against the aggressors. And even after that, they were powerless to secure the Israeli withdrawal from Sinai, which was brought about by the American government alone. Yet the myth of the Soviet rescue became an article of faith, and was reaffirmed by King Hussain in Moscow as late as 3 October 1967.

The military myths were more excusable, and were, in part at least, solidly based on fact. Egypt had indeed fought alone; Israel had not. The Egyptian interpretation of events was further encouraged by a flow of revelations and confessions.[3] The

3. Notably by General Dayan's *Diary of the Sinai Campaign* (Hebrew, 1965; English translation 1966) and by the publication in *The Times* of London, 29 April–6 May 1967, of Mr Anthony Nutting's account of the Suez crisis, later brought out in book form, *No End of a Lesson: the Story of Suez.*

study of these revelations may well have contributed to President Nasser's – perhaps also to Moscow's – misjudgement of the relative military and political strengths of Israel and Egypt.

The myth of 1956 – Egypt, alone, embattled and ultimately victorious against three enemies – stood for more than ten years. The events of 1967 should finally have dispelled it. This time the defeat was political as well as military. Three Arab states on Israel's borders, with help from others, were overwhelmed by Israel alone. There have been attempts to refurbish the old myths and create new ones; they have had only limited success.

There is still little willingness to face the facts – far less than in 1948–9, when discussion was still free and often realistic. The relatively minor defeat of that time was called *nakba*, disaster. The far greater defeat of 1967 is firmly labelled *naksa*, setback. This word is used even in press translations or summaries of foreign comments, and serves to render such terms as defeat and disaster, which are tabu. The universal adoption of this word is a striking example of the nationalization of language and its use to control thought and conceal reality.

Discussion so far has been mainly on the tactical level, and has concentrated on such things as military and political errors and unwise propaganda. In some Arab countries, as for example, in North Africa and South Arabia, rulers and leaders have been quick to draw inferences from the new balance of power within the Arab world, and to realign their policies accordingly. There are as yet few outward signs of any desire to examine the deeper causes of the Arab predicament: the basic weaknesses of Arab society in an age of disruption and transition; the inadequacy of Arab political structures and ideas;[4] the widening sociological and therefore technological gap.

What are the prospects of peace in the Middle East? In the

---

4. It is striking that, of the three Arab armies engaged, the Jordanian, with every disadvantage of numbers, terrain and armament, acquitted itself best. Simple, old-fashioned tribal and monarchical loyalties were more effective in maintaining morale than the revolutionary nationalism of Egypt and Syria.

outside world, the realists, like other people, are divided into two groups: the pro-Arab realists, who say that it is unrealistic to expect the Arabs to recognize Israel, and the pro-Israel realists, who say that it is unrealistic to expect Israel to relinquish her gains without substantial guarantees. Stated in this form, the two views are mutually exclusive – and both could well be right. There is, however, a faint hope that the Arabs may in the last resort prove less implacable than the pro-Arabs in their hostility to Israel. One Arab leader, President Bourguiba, was prepared, however reluctantly, to accept the fact of Israel's existence even before the war. Other leaders in the East may be coming to the conclusion that some form of recognition is the least disagreeable of the alternatives that face them. The problem remains whether, in a context of unstable regimes, contested succession and external incitement, they will have the courage and ability to act on such beliefs.

In the past, it has sometimes been argued that the Arab–Israeli conflict prevents great-power agreement, sometimes that the great-power conflict prevents the Arabs and Israelis from coming to terms. Certainly outside intervention has more than once increased tensions, provoked crises and prevented solutions. The effect of the United Nations on problems in the Middle East and elsewhere has often been like that of modern medicine on major diseases – enough to prevent the patient from dying of natural causes, but not enough to make him well. Chronic invalidism is not a happy state.

It may well be that the best hope for the Middle East lies in its diminishing importance, which may in time lead to the great powers losing interest in the area. This would not be the first time. The decline of European interest in the Middle East in the fifteenth and sixteenth centuries, and its effects, are well known. An earlier example may be found in the fourth century A.D., when the last of a long series of wars between Rome and Persia came to an end. While the struggle between the two great powers of the ancient world continued, both were active in Arabia – politically, militarily, commercially. During the long peace from A.D. 384 to 520, both lost interest. During the centuries of neglect, the trade routes were diverted, the caravan cities abandoned and much of Arabia reverted to nomadism.

It would not be easy for the great powers to lose interest and might well be painful for the Middle East, where the final fulfilment of the long-standing demand for the end of imperialism could have disconcerting political and economic effects. Without foreign stimulation, there would be grave danger of deterioration and regression; without foreign irritants, there might also be some hope of peace.

Is Peace in the Middle East Possible?

By Walter Laqueur*

Beyond the artillery duels at Suez, beyond the Security Council meetings and the Arab summits, the search is going on for solutions to the Middle East conflict. A scheme for an autonomous Arab state on the west bank of the Jordan has been proposed; there are blue-prints for an Israeli–Jordan confederation, even for a bi-national state. A corridor giving Jordan access to the Mediterranean has been suggested, as has the internationalization of the Sinai Desert. There are even pretenders to the throne of the kingdom of Jerusalem – one in Nathania, one in London and, for all one knows, others elsewhere. The settlement of the Gaza Strip refugees on the West Bank is envisaged by some, a new canal from Eilat to Ashdod by others, to make Suez unnecessary.

Such suggestions are only natural; war is usually followed by a peace settlement of sorts, a compromise between extreme demands and positions. Unfortunately, there is at this moment little hope that the Arab–Israeli war will end in such a fashion. Most of the schemes that have been advanced, however well-

* Walter Laqueur is Director of the Institute of Contemporary History and the Wiener Library in London, Professor at the University of Reading and Professor in the History of Ideas and Politics at Brandeis University. His article appeared first in the *New York Times Sunday Magazine*, 27 August 1967. © 1967 by The New York Times Company. Reprinted by permission.

meaning and ingenious, are irrelevant. The more ambitious they are, the more quickly they collapse at the first collision with harsh facts. Had the recent war been over the possession of certain territories, over the refugee question, over the Jordan waters – or over all these bones of contention together – solutions could be found. It would take a few months, at most a few years, for passions to cool down, and then, after much haggling, a sensible compromise could be worked out. The extremists on both sides would shout, 'No, never!' But in the course of time most people would be reconciled to the new state of affairs. After a generation, with a little luck, the *modus vivendi* reached would no longer be questioned.

If there were such a chance Israel would be well advised to seize it with both hands : 'Agree with thine adversary quickly, while thou art in the way with him.' No sacrifice – not even Jerusalem – would be too heavy to ensure a lasting peace between Israel and its Arab neighbours. (Jerusalem is the crown of the state it is now claimed, Israel cannot exist without it. But Israel did exist without the Wailing Wall for nineteen years ; the state would not collapse without it.) However the struggle is not about Jerusalem, about the borders of Israel, the refugees of the Jordan waters. To reduce it to a simple formula, it is a conflict between Arab pride and dignity and Jewish survival. Such a conflict cannot be solved by territorial concessions or Jordan water projects of which, there are by now a half-dozen. Technically, the refugee problem *could* be solved – an international loan of several billion dollars would make their absorption possible, some on the West Bank, others in underpopulated regions of Iraq and Syria. But all these schemes presuppose Arab willingness to negotiate with Israel, to accept the existence of the Jewish state. And for this they are not yet ready.

Their case is well known; Palestine was an Arab country up to the end of the First World War, when Britain imposed the Jewish community on the Arabs, who were thus asked to atone for the sins of the Christian peoples of Europe. Following Zionist invasion and aggression, the Jewish refugee problem was solved by creating an Arab refugee problem. The establishment of a Jewish state was thus a crying injustice; moved by collective guilt feelings about the Jews, the European peoples ignored the fact that morally, and in every other respect, right was on the side of the Arabs.

The case is familiar, and so are the counter-arguments: that Palestine was a Turkish province inhabited by a few hundred thousand Arabs at the time of the Balfour Declaration; that Jerusalem had a Jewish majority well before 1917; the Zionism has built up a flourishing country from what was largely desert; that a Jewish state came into being because the Arabs rejected a bi-national state; that Israel expanded beyond the borders of the United Nations resolution of 1947 as a result of invasion by Arab armies; that the loss of a war is a misfortune, but not a moral argument; that nations have never come into being in accordance with the moral law, but as the result of migration, settlement, invasion and other forms of peaceful, or not so peaceful, conquest. All this is familiar; no useful purpose will be served by pursuing this discussion.

It was the historical misfortune of the Jewish state that it appeared as a latecomer among the nations, and that it came into conflict with a people who had grave, if different, problems of their own. The Arabs are a proud people, with a long and distinguished history. They kept the flame of civilization burning while most of Europe was shrouded in darkness. But this golden age was followed by centuries of sad decline until, in the nineteenth century, it was suddenly realized that the West, which they had despised and ignored, had forged ahead in every respect, while the Arab world had stagnated. Attempts were made to copy the institutions of the West; their failure generated resentment and hatred.

This kind of response was not peculiar to the Arabs: there have been similar reactions in other parts of the world. There are interesting parallels between the Cultural Revolution in China and the present irrational eruptions in the Arab world; the Middle Kingdom, like the Arab world, had for centuries ignored the 'Western barbarians' until it woke up to the painful realization of its own backwardness. Wounded national pride made it imperative to catch up with the technological achievements of the West – which, it soon turned out, was not so easy as had at first been thought. There was also a profound urge to seek revenge for all the humiliations suffered during the colonial age. In the case of the Arabs, the creation of Israel, and the Arab failure to destroy the Jewish state, was a further blow to national pride.

Nasser saw it as his main task to restore Arab self-respect and dignity. He did his best to modernize his country; given Egypt's desperate poverty, this was an uphill struggle in which no quick results could be expected. Meanwhile, national pride was to be restored by defiance of the West and by intense propaganda which conjured up a dream world of Arab power and glory.

At first there was much goodwill towards Nasserism. In their willingness to come to terms with this movement, the Western powers, especially America, leaned over backward, ignoring attacks and insults. Like progressive parents, they showed infinite patience towards the misdeeds of their young. The results were calamitous.

In the meantime, a new generation had grown up in the Arab world, spoon-fed on the new slogans: Arab might was invincible, the confrontation with Israel inevitable. Why wait? Why not remove at once that Western outpost, the 'imperialist poisoned dagger', as they called it? This was the attitude of the new generation of revolutionary and progressive Arab nationalists. But the progressive veneer was not very deep; there was as much hatred for the Jewish worker as for the Jewish capitalist. In Lebanon, traditionally the least fanatical Arab country, a popular singer aroused applause on the eve of the last war with a new song about Israel: 'Kill them, crush them, suck their blood.' The Syrian government was (and is) almost Maoist in its inspiration: it constantly emphasizes the class struggle, the proletarian nations, the vanguard of the working class. But when it really got excited, its broadcasts assumed a different tone: 'By God, if it is decreed that we have to wade through seven seas of blood and that the whole nation has to sink in blood to get revenge for its honour and dignity,

then we will wade through the seas of blood and we will risk
everything. . . .' No more atheism, class struggle or dialectical
materialism ; instead, God, blood, nation, revenge, honour,
dignity.

Then came the five-day war and the totally unexpected defeat. Placards in the streets of Cairo and Damascus still displayed quaking little Jews cowering under the bayonets of
steady-eyed confident Arab soldiers. It was totally inexplicable,
and utterly unacceptable. The self-image of the Arabs was that
of a proud people distinguished above all by courage and the
military virtues; the Jews were cowards who would not dare to
fight. The war had been seen as a walkover. Surely Israel could
not have defeated the Arab armies single-handed. Surely it was
the element of surprise, the treacherous sudden attack for
which the Arabs had been unprepared.

A generation educated in the belief that Arab armies are invincible could not possibly accept defeat, nor would it consider
for a single moment that both its self-appraisal, and its image
of Israel, may have been mistaken. Instead there was a call to
renew the fighting immediately. If Nasser was a spent force,
salvation would come from Boumedienne and the Syrian
leaders. Boumedienne is a political featherweight, whose army
was worsted even by the Moroccans – numerically inferior
and not one of the world's greatest fighting forces. Nasser, even
in defeat, is a giant in comparison with the men who rule in
Damascus.

But these are the imperatives of a desperate situation: new
heroes are needed to wreak revenge. There are some sensible
voices, calling for self-criticism and a more realistic policy,
but they are half-muted; they come from faraway countries
like Tunisia and Morocco. Those nearer Israel do not dare to
speak up : the director of Cairo Radio was no doubt right when
he said that the Arabs would kill any leader contemplating
peace with Israel. The Arab governments had armed thousands of Palestinian volunteers (not to mention their own
peoples); they had promised the liberation of Palestine; for
more than a decade they had proclaimed that Israel was a

cancer in the body politic of the Arab world and that it would be eradicated. They cannot now retreat. They fear that in their rage and frustration the masses would turn against them. The masses cannot be told that it is, for the time being, hopeless to continue the war.

It is not a reassuring picture – the Arabs, 'lost in stormy visions, keep with phantoms an unprofitable strife'. Nor does it leave much room for optimism. But any scheme to settle the Middle East crisis which ignores these psychological currents is doomed from the outset.

There are, in theory at any rate, three possibilities for a peaceful settlement. According to one school of thought, a solution could be imposed if only someone powerful enough would take the initiative. There would be resistance from both sides, especially from the Arabs. But provided there was courageous leadership, the fires of passion would die down after the inevitable period of shouting ('We shall never surrender').

Israel could be made to give up much, though not all, of its territorial conquests, if presented with a real, foolproof, big-power guarantee of its frontiers, and an Arab recognition of its existence. Israel would undertake to accept back all those refugees who wanted to return, the assumption being that not many would. Jordan would receive a corridor to the Mediterranean, or some other arrangement could be made. Israel would be given the right of free passage through the Suez Canal – in the very near future if not immediately. United Nations forces would be stationed permanently along the borders, and some of the most critical spots could be demilitarized (Sharm al-Shaikh, Sinai, the Syrian hills overlooking Galilee). A special status would be worked out for Jerusalem, safeguarding Israel sovereignty, Arab rights, free access to everyone – perhaps as an Israeli–United Nations condominium. The transfer of a permanent UN commission to Jerusalem might be envisaged. There would be substantial international loans for the Jordan waters project, and for other Arab–Israeli development schemes to make cooperation attractive.

Not all Arab countries would be willing to collaborate

immediately, but once negotiations started between Israel and one Arab government, the conviction would grow in all Arab capitals that recognition of Israel could not be indefinitely postponed. It might take years, success might be only partial, but in the end a new *modus vivendi* would emerge; in due time it would be tolerated, if not enthusiastically accepted, by both Arabs and Jews.

I wish I could feel more optimistic about these visions; there are a great many variants, but they are all based on too many assumptions that are, at present, unreal. They all imply American–Soviet cooperation, but the Soviet Union does not see the slightest reason to impose any solution on the Arabs that would be unacceptable to them. Nor should the extent to which Moscow and Washington can impose solutions be overrated. For the Arab capitals there is always China in the event of a Soviet 'betrayal'.

It is unlikely that any Israeli government (except perhaps one headed by Dayan, an unlikely contingency at present) would be able to convince the public that some of its recent gains should be given up. Israelis would no doubt argue that a new greatpower guarantee would be no more reliable and effective than any previous one. What if agreement were reached about the freedom of passage through the Suez Canal, and the Straits of Tiran, and then Nasser, after a few years, again imposed a blockade? Since there are no foolproof guarantees, would it not be more prudent from the Israeli point of view to hold on to what they have? If one or several Arab leaders decided to enter into negotiations with Israel, would there be any certainty that they would not be doing so merely to gain time, until they were ready for the next round of fighting? Should Israel pay for a recognition which might well be meaningless? Assuming even a sincere wish on the part of some Arab leaders to reach agreement with Israel, what guarantee is there that it would be honoured by their successors? In the present state of turbulence in the Arab world, no ruler is secure. Those most likely to talk with Israel are the ones most exposed, their countries most vulnerable to a Syrian-style coup. In the present mood, demagogues preaching war are infinitely more in line with the general sentiment in the Arab world than responsible leaders aiming at constructive solutions. Why talk to Israel, if the defeat of the 'Zionist gangster state' is just a matter of one more attempt? (It used to be the 'gangster dwarf state', but the dwarf has grown.) Surely the far greater resources of the Arab states will prevail; next time the Arab armies will not wait for the enemy to attack – the element of surprise will give them victory.

Israeli diplomats have argued for a long time that there is only one obstacle to lasting peace in the Middle East – the absence of courageous Arab leadership. It is, I fear, an over-simplification. Arabs have been accustomed for two decades to an 'I-am-more-anti-Israel-than-thou' competition among the Arab leaders. It is quite unrealistic to expect that any one of them now will tell his people that it was a mistake and that it is all over.

The second school of thought maintains that it is up to Israel to make not only the first step but also most of the concessions. For, even if the Israelis have won one campaign, they have not won the war. Israel is still a small enclave surrounded by 80 million enemies. Time works for the Arabs; in the long run, Israel cannot defeat them. It will survive only if it ceases to be a Western outpost and integrates itself into the Afro–Asian world to which it really belongs; it must join the third world if it is to survive.

Within a big Arab federation, Israel would play an important role. True, the Arabs may demand the cessation of immigration – but then, not many immigrants will come anyway. Half of Israel is now Middle Eastern in origin, and there have been Israeli voices advocating integration in recent years. The only realistic policy in the long run is therefore to recognize that revolutionary Arab nationalism is the wave of the future, the present victory merely a brief episode interrupting an irreversible historic movement – the rise to political conscious-ness of the Arab masses, as personified by Nasser and the Syrian leaders. Consequently, Israel should extend the hand of friend-ship to the Arab leaders, give up all its gains and perhaps go even further and try to win Arab friendship by accepting Nasser's leadership.

There may be a grain of truth in this series of arguments. Nasser-style or Syrian-style radical Arab nationalism may well prevail in more Arab countries in the coming years; the long-term survival of Israel is not yet assured. Gestures play an inordinate role in the Middle Eastern politics (a few declarations by de Gaulle made the Arabs forget that he, not America, equipped the Israeli Army). It is possible that some Israeli gestures of goodwill towards the Arabs, some unilateral acts or concessions, would have a beneficial effect, and it is a matter of regret that they have not been made.

Yet basically this school of thought is mistaken in most of its assumptions. Whether a big population is a blessing or a curse in the modern world is by no means certain; what matters, militarily as well as technologically, is quality, not quantity. If the Arab–Israeli conflict were to go nuclear, the Arab countries, above all Egypt, would be as much exposed as Israel. Whether time works for the Arabs is not certain either; for the last twenty years it has not. As a result of their refusal to live in peace with Israel the Arab countries have had to spend a good share of their gross national product on armaments and various kinds of anti-Israel warfare. As a result, the real growth of their economies has been very small – in the region of 2.5 per cent per annum. (Israel's rate of growth has been almost three times as high.)

The present outlook for the Arab world – especially Egypt, Syria and Jordan – is grave: it faces economic ruin. And yet today the Arabs feel obliged to devote an even higher percentage of their income to rearming. Talk about the wave of the future is meaningless unless supported by Soviet or Chinese (or Japanese or Western) rates of growth. But even if the future of the Arabs were much brighter, even if time were working for them, how could Israel become a member of the Arab world?

Geographically and historically, Israel is, of course, far closer to the Mediterranean world – Italy, Greece, Turkey – than to the Afro–Asian bloc. The Third World is passing through a profound crisis – politically, socially, economically – a crisis nowhere more palpably felt than in the Arab countries. There has been little if any advance towards political stability and economic progress. In recent years the Arab countries have fallen further back in comparison with both the Western and the Eastern bloc, and this has produced a profound malaise bordering occasionally on collective hysteria. Israel has by no means solved its own problems, but it has tackled modernization fairly successfully; it is a far from perfect country, but it is reasonably democratic, reasonably effective. It could try to cut its ties with the Jews in the West; it could attempt to copy Egypt or Syria, with demonstrations in the streets of Jerusalem and Tel Aviv crying, 'Down with American imperialism! Long live Frantz Fanon and the Third World!' Such behaviour might warm the hearts of some observers in the West, but it would carry little conviction in the Arab world.

A reasonable man may try to gain the confidence and friendship of the unreasonable by behaving like them, but it is not the surest way to success. The political psychology of backwardness is an organic growth; hate and resentment are the products of certain mechanisms that do not exist in Israel. Israel was never a colony and does not suffer from a colonial hangover; it has been successful where most Arab countries have failed. Israel could pretend to be part of the 'wretched of the earth', but I fear no one would believe it. Countries like Egypt and Syria are at present in (to put it cautiously) a disturbed frame of mind. One must sympathize with them in their plight and hope for a change in the not-too-distant future. But agreement cannot be reached by voluntary adaptation to political psychosis. The present delusions in the Arab world may not last; there is hope of change in the long term, hope of a sobering-up process and more rational response to the challenges facing the Arab world. Then, and only then, will there be a chance for a real meeting of minds.

There is a third, less spectacular way to work for peace in the Middle East – by trying to defuse some of the most explosive issues. The administration of conquered territories presents Israel with enormous economic problems (unemployment on

the West Bank is now 20 per cent). In the long haul, there will
be grave security problems, too, and the full implications of
absorbing a million Arabs into Israel have not yet been entirely
grasped in Israel. When they are, there may be greater readiness to negotiate. But, on the whole, what is negotiable as far
as Israel is concerned will probably shrink as time passes. *Rien
ne dure que le provisoire.* If the Arabs are unwilling to enter
into direct negotiations, if they make preparations for a new
war, the conviction will grow in Israel that it may as well hold
on to its new territories, which give it undoubted military advantages.

The Arab states, above all Egypt and Jordan, and to a lesser
degree Syria, are at present under far greater pressure. Jordan
has lost half its agricultural output, Egypt half its foreign currency earnings. This means economic disaster, for Russia cannot indefinitely support Egypt's economy. And who is going
to save poor Jordan? Yet Nasser, or whoever may succeed him,
can in no circumstances enter into direct negotiations with
Israel; so long as Nasser refuses, King Hussain has to refuse,
too.

After the present round of inconclusive talks among Arab
leaders, they will probably agree that while recognition of
Israel and a peace settlement are out of the question, there
should be talks through some intermediary in an attempt to
solve certain particular issues : Egypt wants to reopen the Suez
Canal to regain some of its foreign currency earnings; Jordan
wants to negotiate about the refugees and the West Bank. Yet
even the choice of a mediator presents difficulties. America and
Russia cannot mediate for obvious reasons, and Israel has
reservations about France. Will it be Mr Fanfani then, or Mr
Maurer? Israel may agree to the reopening of the canal if there
is free passage for Israeli ships. It is more than doubtful whether
Nasser could accede to this demand, even if there should be a
face-saving formula. Prospects for a partial agreement with
Jordan are better, but even this is not likely to come soon.

Public opinion in the Arab world (outside Jordan) is not
aware of the extent of the military defeat and does not see the
necessity for any compromise with Israel. The leaders are

aware of the defeat, but they cannot undo now the effects of many years of anti-Israel propaganda. Nor can they switch their policy suddenly. Israel contends that the reward of victory should be peace ; the Arabs, that there cannot be peace and that there should be unconditional withdrawal. Between these two positions there is no meeting ground.

A total Israeli victory would have compelled the Arab countries to change their position, but in Arab eyes what has happened is only a temporary setback. The Soviet Union is said to have replaced about half of the Arab aircraft and a quarter of the tanks; in a year, all the losses may be made good. But much more than that – and years of retraining – will be needed for a successful offensive against Israel. The Crusaders, it is said, were defeated by the Arabs after many decades; but are such historical parallels really of much help in recent times? Algeria and Syria press for the immediate renewal of a Chinese-style people's war. But the equation is not convincing : Dayan is not Marshal Ky, the Palestine Liberation Army is not the Vietcong, and Syria is not China. Israel would not be defeated; at most it would again be provoked into full-scale military action.

My own feeling is that the present confusion in the Arab world will persist for a long time, that attempts may be made in both directions – halfhearted negotiations and perhaps a little guerrilla war. At present, and for years to come, the Arab leaders can make neither war nor peace. No decisive action should be expected; and as the economic and political difficulties of the various regimes grow more severe, there will be more internal crises, greater instability. This long-drawn-out crisis may in the end have a sobering effect: the Arabs may realize that 'dull and endless strife' is unprofitable, that the unsuccessful attempt to defeat Israel, which is sapping their strength and energy, is gradually making the Middle East a backwater of history, and preventing the general development of the Arab world. The Israeli victory will still be painful, but it would no longer receive priority in Arab eyes, and gradually energies would be directed into different channels to prevent even greater disasters to the Arab cause than the loss of Palestine. This is a possibility; unfortunately, it is no certainty; in any case, it will be a long haul back.

There is a sharp conflict of interest between America and Russia in the Middle East: the Soviet Union has now gained access to Middle East bases and warm-water ports, admittedly at an enormous price, and its political influence in Egypt and Syria seems unassailable. The United States aim, on the other hand, is not to allow the eastern Mediterranean to become a Soviet *mare nostrum*. But there is also a sphere of common interest: neither power wants another war which could have more dangerous consequences than even the one in Vietnam. The one way to prevent a war is to limit the arms race, to isolate the conflict as much as possible.

Montesquieu once said: 'Happy the nations whose annals of history are boring to read.' The boring years in the Middle East were always the happy ones. It cannot be too often stressed that the intrinsic importance of the Middle East is usually overrated in both East and West. If the West showed that it could get along indefinitely without Arab oil and even without the Suez Canal, that Egypt and Syria are simply not that important, it would be the greatest possible contribution not only to Middle Eastern mental hygiene but also to improved relations between the West and the Arab world. So long as the Nassers, Boumediennes and Atassis feel that the whole world's attention is focused on them, they will fret and strut on the Middle Eastern stage, adopting dramatic poses, uttering dire threats.

There is no cure for the Middle East sickness, but there is one sure way to alleviate it: to reduce the problems to their real size, not to take so terribly seriously the pocket Napoleons and Mao Tse-tungs, their trips, speeches, declarations, threats and promises. They flourish with publicity and wither when ignored. Half the battle for the future of the Middle East will be won on the day when news about this part of the world will be relegated from page 1 to page 16 in the *New York Times* and other leading newspapers.

Part 5

From War to War?

The documents and articles contained in the present section refer to developments since the Six Day War in 1967, with the exception of the National Covenant of the Palestine Liberation Organization. This manifesto, drawn up in May 1964, superseded the earlier Draft Constitution. The Palestine Liberation Organization is the biggest of the Palestinian refugee organizations; its manifesto has been modified since in various points. The Al Fatah 'Seven Points' and the interview with the leader of the organization, Yassir Arafat, both published in 1969, offer more recent interpretations of the aims of this movement. The Arab National Movement (the predecessor of the Popular Front) was founded in the Lebanon in 1948. It did not join Al Fatah which in its view was not radical enough and it has since split into two factions led by Dr George Habbash and Naif Hawatme respectively. The 'Platform of the Popular Front for the Liberation of Palestine' was formulated by the latter, the extreme left-wing faction of the movement. General Harkabi, the author of several studies on Arab–Israeli problems, now teaches at the Hebrew University, Jerusalem. The essay on Fatah Doctrine is taken from a more detailed study: 'Fedayeen Action and Arab Strategy' published by the Institute of Strategic Studies in London in December 1968. Nasser's speech at the Arab Socialist Union Congress in March 1969 and the Syrian Ba'ath Party Resolution of April 1969 reflect the stand taken by the Egyptian and Syrian governments in the dispute since the armistice of June 1967.The

excerpts from articles by Hassanain Haykal, the
leading Egyptian journalist, define in more detail the
objectives of the war of attrition against Israel as seen
from Cairo. Ahmad Baha ed-Dine is another
prominent Egyptian journalist, editor of the weekly
Mussawar; the ideas expressed in his article were later
discussed at greater length in a book by the same author
which attracted much attention in Arab circles.
'Two Years Later' written by Foreign Minister Abba
Eban and General Dayan's speech present Israeli points
of view on both the short-term issues involved in the
Arab–Israeli dispute and the long-term perspectives.
Yehoshua Arieli is professor of history at the Hebrew
University, Jerusalem; his speech reflecting the
opinions of the anti-annexationist movement in Israel
was made at an international symposium in Tel Aviv
in March 1969 sponsored by the monthly New Outlook.
'Sartre looks at the Middle East again' is based on an
interview with Arturo Schwartz, editor of the
Quaderni del Medio Oriente. Sartre had visited the
Middle East shortly before the Six Day War. Professor
Bernard Lewis argues in his essay originally written for
Foreign Affairs, that the two main problems of the
area – the East–West rivalry and the Arab–Israeli
conflict – while likely to persist are not necessarily
connected. Professor Uri Ra'anan of the Fletcher School of
Law and Diplomacy discusses in his contribution first
published in Midstream in May 1969 Soviet interest in
the M`ddle East and the possibilities of US Soviet
agreement.

Security Council Resolution on the
Middle East, 22 November 1967

THE SECURITY COUNCIL,

Expressing its continuing concern with the grave situation in the Middle East,

Emphasizing the inadmissibility of the acquisition of territory by war and the need to work for a just and lasting peace in which every state in the area can live in security,

Emphasizing further that all member states in their acceptance of the Charter of the United Nations have undertaken a commitment to act in accordance with Article 2 of the Charter.

1. *Affirms* that the fulfilment of Charter principles requires the establishment of a just and lasting peace in the Middle East which should include the application of both the following principles:

(i) Withdrawal of Israeli armed forces from territories of recent conflict;

(ii) Termination of all claims or states of belligerency and respect for and acknowledgement of the sovereignty, territorial integrity and political independence of every state in the area and their right to live in peace within secure and recognized boundaries free from threats or acts of force;

2. *Affirms further* the necessity

(a) For guaranteeing freedom of navigation through international waterways in the area;

(b) For achieving a just settlement of the refugee problem;

(c) For guaranteeing the territorial inviolability and political independence of every state in the area, through measures including the establishment of demilitarized zones;

3. *Requests* the Secretary General to designate a special representative to proceed to the Middle East to establish and maintain contacts with the states concerned in order to

promote agreement and assist efforts to achieve a peaceful and
accepted settlement in accordance with the provisions and
principles in this resolution.

4. *Requests* the Secretary General to report to the Security
Council on the progress of the efforts of the special representative as soon as possible.

National Covenant of the Palestine Liberation Organization

Statement of Proclamation of the Organization
In the name of God, the Magnificent, the Compassionate,

Believing in the right of the Palestine Arab people to its sacred
homeland Palestine and affirming the inevitability of the battle
to liberate the usurped part from it, and its determination to
bring out its effective revolutionary entity and the mobilization
of the capabilities and potentialities and its material, and spiritual forces;

And in realization of the will and determination of our
people to wage the battle of liberating its homeland forcefully
and vigorously in harmony with its role as the effective and
fighting vanguard of the sacred march;

And in realization of a genuine and dear national aspiration
embodied in the resolutions of the League of Arab States, and
the First Arab Summit Conference;

And depending upon God the Almighty and in the name of
the First Arab Palestine Congress held in the city of Jerusalem
this day on the 16th of Muharram of the year 1384, corresponding to 28 May 1964, I do hereby proclaim the establishment of the Palestine Liberation Organization as a mobilizing
leadership of the forces of the Palestine Arab people to wage
the battle of liberation, as a shield for the rights and aspirations
of the people of Palestine and as a road to victory.

Ahmed Shukairy
Chairman of The First Palestine Congress

The Palestinian National Covenant : Introduction

In the name of Almighty, the Magnificent, the most Merciful,

We, the Palestinian Arab people, who waged fierce and continuous battles to safeguard its homeland, to defend its dignity and honour, and who offered all through the years continuous caravans of immortal martyrs, and who wrote the noblest pages of sacrifice, offering and giving.

We, the Palestinian Arab people, who faced the forces of evil, injustice and aggression, against whom the forces of international Zionism and colonialism conspired and worked to displace it, dispossess it from its homeland and property, abused what is holy in it and who in spite of all this refused to weaken or submit.

We, The Palestinian Arab people, who believe in its Arabism and in its right to regain its homeland, to realize its freedom and dignity, and who have determined to amass its forces and mobilize its efforts and capabilities in order to continue its struggle and to move forward on the path of holy war until complete and final victory has been attained.

We, The Palestinian Arab people, depending upon our right of self-defence and the complete restoration of our lost homeland – a right that has been recognized by international covenants and common practices including the Charter of the United Nations – and in implementation of the principles of human rights and comprehending the international political relations, with its various ramifications and limits, and considering the past experiences in all that pertains to the causes of the catastrophe, and the means to face it.

And embarking from the Palestine Arab reality, and for the sake of the honour of the Palestinian individual and his right to free and dignified life,

And realizing the national grave responsibility placed upon our shoulders, for the sake of all this,

We, the Palestinian Arab people, dictate and declare this Palestinian National Covenant and vow to realize it.

Article 1. Palestine is an Arab homeland bound by strong

Arab national ties to the rest of the Arab Countries and which together form the large Arab Homeland.

Article 2. Palestine with its boundaries at the time of the British Mandate is a regional indivisible unit.

Article 3. The Palestinian Arab people has the legitimate right to its homeland and is an inseparable part of the Arab Nation. It shares the sufferings and aspirations of The Arab Nation and its struggle for freedom, sovereignty, progress and unity.

Article 4. The people of Palestine determine its destiny when it completes the liberation of its homeland in accordance with its own wishes and free will and choice.

Article 5. The Palestinian personality is a permanent and genuine characteristic that does not disappear. It is transferred from fathers to sons.

Article 6. The Palestinians are those Arab citizens who were living normally in Palestine up to 1947, whether they remained or were expelled. Every child who was born to a Palestinian parent after this date whether in Palestine or outside is a Palestinian.

Article 7. Jews of Palestinian origin are considered Palestinians if they are willing to live peacefully and loyally in Palestine.

Article 8. Bringing up Palestinian youth in Arab and nationalist manner is a fundamental national duty. All means of guidance, education and enlightenment should be utilized to introduce the youth to its homeland in a deep spiritual way that will constantly and firmly bind them together.

Article 9. Doctrines whether political, social or economic, shall not distract the people of Palestine from the primary duty of liberating their homeland. All Palestinians constitute one national front and work with all their feelings and spiritual and material potentialities to free their homeland.

Article 10. Palestinians have three mottoes: National Unity, National Mobilization, and Liberation. Once liberation is completed, the people of Palestine shall choose for its public life whatever political, economic or social system they want.

Article 11. The Palestinian people firmly believe in Arab unity, and in order to play its role in realizing this goal, it must, at this stage of its struggle, preserve its Palestinian personality and all its constituents. It must strengthen the consciousness of its existence and stand against any attempt or plan that may weaken or disintegrate its personality.

Article 12. Arab unity and the liberation of Palestine are two complementary goals; each prepares for the attainment of the other. Arab unity leads to the liberation of Palestine, and the liberation of Palestine leads to Arab unity. Working for both must go side by side.

Article 13. The destiny of the Arab Nation and even the essence of Arab existence are firmly tied to the destiny of the Palestine question. From this firm bond stems the effort and struggle of the Arab Nation to liberate Palestine. The people of Palestine assume a vanguard role in achieving this sacred national goal.

Article 14. The liberation of Palestine, from an Arab viewpoint, is a national duty. Its responsibilities fall upon the entire Arab Nation, governments and peoples, the Palestinian people being in the foreground. For this purpose, the Arab Nation must mobilize its military, spiritual and material potentialities; specifically, it must give to the Palestinian Arab people all possible support and backing and place at its disposal all opportunities and means to enable them to perform their role in liberating their homeland.

Article 15. The liberation of Palestine, from a spiritual viewpoint, prepares for the Holy Land an atmosphere of tranquillity and peace, in which all the Holy Places will be safeguarded, and the free worship and visit to all will be guaranteed, without any discrimination of race, colour, tongue, or religion. For all this the Palestinian people look forward to the support of all the spiritual forces in the world.

Article 16. The liberation of Palestine, from an international viewpoint, is a defensive act necessitated by the demands of self-defence as stated in the Charter of the United Nations. That is why the people of Palestine, desiring to befriend all nations which love freedom, justice, and peace, look forward to their support in restoring the legitimate situation to Palestine, establishing peace and security in its territory, and enabling its people to exercise national sovereignty and freedom.

Article 17. The partitioning of Palestine in 1947 and the establishment of Israel are illegal and false regardless of the loss of time, because they were contrary to the wish of the Palestine people and its natural right to its homeland, and in violation of the basic principles embodied in the Charter of the United Nations, foremost among which is the right to self-determination.

Article 18. The Balfour Declaration, the Mandate system and all that has been based upon them are considered fraud. The claims of historic and spiritual ties between Jews and Palestine are not in agreement with the facts of history or with the true basis of sound statehood. Judaism because it is a divine religion is not a nationality with independent existence. Furthermore the Jews are not one people with an independent personality because they are citizens of the countries to which they belong.

Article 19. Zionism is a colonialist movement in its inception, aggressive and expansionist in its goal, racist and segregationist in its configurations and fascist in its means and aims. Israel in its capacity as the spearhead of this destructive movement and the pillar of colonialism is a permanent source of tension and turmoil in the Middle East in particular and to the international community in general. Because of this the people of Palestine is worthy of the support and sustenance of the community of nations.

Article 20. The causes of peace and security and the needs of right and justice demand from all nations, in order to safeguard true relationships among peoples and to maintain the loyalty of citizens to their homeland, that they consider Zionism an illegal movement and outlaw its presence and activities.

Article 21. The Palestine people believes in the principle of justice, freedom, sovereignty, self-determination, human dignity, and the right of peoples to practise these principles. It also supports all international efforts to bring about peace on the basis of justice and free international cooperation.

Article 22. The people of Palestine believe in peaceful coexistence on the basis of legal existence, for there can be no coexistence with aggression, nor can there be peace with occupation and colonialism.

Article 23. In realizing the goals and principles of this Covenant the Palestine Liberation Organization carries out its complete role to liberate Palestine in accordance with the fundamental law of this Organization.

Article 24. This Organization does not exercise any regional sovereignty over the Western Bank in the Hashemite Kingdom of Jordan, on the Gaza Strip or the Himmah Area. Its activities will be on the national popular level in the liberational, organizational, political and financial fields.

Article 25. This Organization is encharged with the movement of the Palestine people in its struggle to liberate its homeland in all liberational, organizational, political, and financial matters, and in all other needs of the Palestine Question in the Arab and international spheres.

Article 26. The Liberation Organization cooperates with all Arab governments, each according to its ability, and does not interfere in the internal affairs of any Arab State.

Article 27. This Organization shall have its flag, oath and a national anthem. All this shall be resolved in accordance with a special system.

Article 28. The Fundamental Law for the Palestine Liberation Organization is attached to this Covenant. This law defines the manner of establishing the Organization, its organs, institutions, the specialties of each one of them, and all the needed duties thrust upon it in accordance with this Covenant.

Article 29. This Covenant cannot be amended except by two-thirds majority of the National Council of the Palestine Liberation Organization in a special session called for this purpose.

Al Fatah

The Seven Points, passed by the Central Committee of
Al Fatah, January 1969

1. *Al Fatah*, the Palestine National Liberation Movement,
is the expression of the Palestinian people and of its will to
free its land from Zionist colonization in order to recover its
national identity.

2. *Al Fatah*, the Palestine National Liberation Movement, is
not struggling against the Jews as an ethnic and religious community. It is struggling against Israel as the expression of
colonization based on a theocratic, racist and expansionist system and of Zionism and colonialism.

3. *Al Fatah*, the Palestine National Liberation Movement,
rejects any solution that does not take account of the existence
of the Palestinian people and its right to dispose of itself.

4. *Al Fatah*, the Palestine National Liberation Movement, categorically rejects the Security Council Resolution of
22 November 1967 and the Jarring mission to which it
gave rise.

This resolution ignores the national rights of the Palestinian
people – failing to mention its existence. Any solution claiming
to be peaceful which ignores this basic factor, will thereby be
doomed to failure.

In any event, the acceptance of the resolution of 22 November 1967, or any pseudo-political solution, by whatsoever party,
is in no way binding upon the Palestinian people, which is determined to pursue mercilessly its struggle against foreign
occupation and Zionist colonization.

5. *Al Fatah*, the Palestine National Liberation Movement,
solemnly proclaims that the final objective of its struggle is the
restoration of the independent, democratic State of Palestine,
all of whose citizens will enjoy equal rights irrespective of their
religion.

6. Since Palestine forms part of the Arab fatherland, *Al
Fatah*, the Palestine National Liberation Movement, will work

for the State of Palestine to contribute actively towards the establishment of a progressive and united Arab society.

7. The struggle of the Palestinian People, like that of the Vietnamese people and other peoples of Asia, Africa and Latin America, is part of the historic process of the liberation of the oppressed peoples from colonialism and imperialism.

An Interview with 'Abu Ammar' (Yassir Arafat)*

Q: Al Fatah has offered an alternative to the Jews in Palestine – that is the creation of a progressive, democratic state for all. How do you reconcile this with the slogan 'Long live Palestine Arab and Free'?

Abu Ammar: A democratic, progressive state in Palestine is not in contradiction to that state being Arab. The social, geographical and historical factors play a major role in determining the nature and identity of any state. Anyone who has tried to look at the Palestine problem in its historic perspective would realize that the Zionist state has failed to make itself acceptable because it is an artificially created alien state in the midst of an Arab world.

Palestine has acquired its identity through the historical development of the area. It is impossible for any Palestinian State to isolate itself from its geographical surroundings. It has been proved historically that any state, created on the land of Palestine which had been aliens to the area, was unable to survive.

It is claimed that the main reason for the establishment of the state of Israel was to find a solution to the Jewish problem, but the experience of the past twenty years has proved that the absorbing capacity of the state has been insufficient to solve the problem of the 16 million Jews in the world.

The Zionist Movement has, as a result, to face one of two alternatives: either to carry on an expansionist policy which

---

*Text of an interview with the leader of Al Fatah, published in *Free Palestine*, August 1969.

will enable it to absorb all the Jews of the world or to admit
the failure of its experience and try and find a solution for those
Jews who have been uprooted from their countries of origin to
be settled on the land of Palestine.

We have offered our solution: that is the creation of a democratic Palestinian state for all those who wish to live in peace
on the land of peace. Such a state can only acquire stability
and viability by forming a part of the surrounding area, which
is the Arab area. Otherwise this state with its Jewish, Christian
and Muslim citizens would be another alien and temporary
phenomena in the area, which will arouse the antagonism of its
neighbours, exactly as did the first Jewish state and the Crusaders' state. Neither of these states lasted for more than seventy years.

The word 'Arab' implies a common culture, a common
language and a common background. The majority of the
inhabitants of any future state of Palestine will be Arab, if
we consider that there are at present 2,500,000 Palestinian Arabs
of the Muslim and Christian faiths and another 1,250,000 Arabs
of the Jewish faith who live in what is now the state of Israel.

Q: The immediate objective of your Movement is the liberation of your occupied homeland. What are your long-term objectives after achieving liberation? How do you envisage the
future state of Palestine?

Abu Ammar: As you have rightly mentioned, the immediate
objective of Al Fatah is the total liberation of Palestine from
Zionism and the destruction of any racial or sectarian notion
which might exist among the Arabs.

Accordingly, we believe the only way to realize our objective is by overcoming our differences and achieving national
unity. Our struggle in its present stage is a struggle for survival
and for recovering our national identity. We aim ultimately at
the establishment of an independent, progressive, democratic
state in Palestine, which will guarantee equal rights to all its
citizens, regardless of race or religion.

We wish to liberate the Jews from Zionism, and to make them
realize that the purpose behind the creation of the state of

Israel, namely to provide a haven for the persecuted Jews, has instead thrown them into a ghetto of their own making.

We wish to help build a progressive society based on liberty and equality for all. We also aim at participating actively in any struggle led by any Arab nation to achieve freedom and independence and to help build the united progressive Arab society of the future.

We support the struggle of all oppressed peoples in the world and we believe in the right for self-determination to all nations. We do not know for how long our struggle will go on until the liberation of our homeland is achieved. It might be a few years, or perhaps tens of years. It will be up to the generation that will finally liberate Palestine to decide upon the structure of their state.

Q: The Palestine National Liberation Movement has certainly been able to achieve a break-through in what used to be a Zionist domain: the Western Leftist movements. Al Fatah has become to many synonymous with freedom fighting and an expression of struggle against oppression everywhere. Yet the new Zionist propaganda tactic is to smear it, by accusing it of accepting help from what is termed by them as 'reactionary sources'. What have you to say to this?

Abu Ammar: Our Revolution accepts help, whether technological, material or military, from all sources. We seek the support of all those who wish to see Palestine liberated from Zionism, provided it is unconditional. We address ourselves equally to those who wish to offer help because they wish to see the holy places liberated or to those revolutionaries in Africa, Asia and Latin America who consider our struggle as part of the struggle against oppression everywhere.

We have formed very strong ties with the liberation movements all over the world – in Cuba, in China, in Algeria and in Vietnam. We must not forget that in a war of liberation we should make use of every available source and means that will help us reach our ultimate goal – that is the liberation of our homeland.

I would also like to point out that other nations who have entered a war of liberation have adopted the same methods:

for example in Vietnam the National Liberation Front includes twenty-three different organizations ranging from the Catholics and Buddhists, to the Communists.

Can anyone accuse the Vietnamese Revolution of being a reactionary force? Add to this that the Palestinian Revolution in undertaking to lead the struggle against the Zionists, and to prevent any further aggression against the rest of the Arab world is entitled to use all the resources available in the Arab area.

Q: Plans for a 'peaceful settlement' of what is termed as an 'Arab–Israeli' conflict seem to be speeding up, with the Four-Power talks going ahead. Both the United States and the Soviet Union are eager to impose such a solution. How will Al Fatah react or rather act?

Abu Ammar: The United Nations Security Council and the big powers have chosen to call their solutions 'peaceful', whereas, in fact they are political solutions which are in no way related to peace as they all aim at safeguarding the state of Israel and ignoring the Palestinian Revolution. As such we declare that we will not under any circumstances accept any so-called peaceful solution which is being concocted by either the 'big states or the 'small' states. We regard any such settlement as a document of self-humiliation which our people are forcibly asked to accept.

I believe that if our generation is unable to liberate its homeland, it should not commit the crime of accepting a *fait accompli*, which will prevent the future generations from carrying on the struggle for liberation.

What seems strange is that the call for a peaceful settlement started to be heard only when the Zionist enemy began to feel the blows dealt him by our Revolution.

I would like to mention here that immediately following the June War 1967, when President Johnson was asked about the problem in the Middle East, he replied, 'Is there a problem?' This goes to prove that a problem exists only when Israel considers it as existing. We, the Palestinian people, refuse to capitulate or to give legality to usurpation. As long as Israel is an invading, racialist, fascist state, it will be rejected. Let no one think that any resolution taken outside the will of the Palestinians will ever acquire viability or legality.

We have waited twenty years for world conscience to awaken but it was at the cost of more dispersion. And here I would like to state that in this we do not only have the support of the Palestinian masses, but also of the whole Arab masses. We must also not forget that our Movement started before 5 June 1967, with the purpose of liberating Palestine and we will not throw away our arms until victory, no matter who stands in our way.

Q: Your Movement has on more than one occasion declared that it will not interfere in the affairs of other Arab countries. Don't you think that owing to recent developments in certain neighbouring Arab countries, this policy should be revised, especially as these developments aim at threatening the Palestinian Revolution?

Abu Ammar: We will not interfere in the internal affairs of any Arab country that will not in its turn put obstacles in the way of our Revolution or threaten its continuation.

Q: During her last visit to Britain, Golda Meir denied the existence of a Palestinian people or a Palestinian resistance movement. What is your answer?

Abu Ammar: Her predecessor, Levi Eshkol, also denied our existence for a very long time. Yet before his death, in an interview with the American magazine *Newsweek*, he had to admit that we do exist. In 1967 Moshe Dayan claimed that the Palestinian resistance was like an egg in his hand, which he could crush any time. Yet in 1969 he was quoted as advising the Israelis to 'deepen their graves'. Our answer therefore to Golda Meir and to anyone who doubts our existence can be found in our actions inside the occupied territories, whether in Haifa or Jerusalem or Tel Aviv or Eilat or elsewhere. Besides, you are now living amongst us and you can judge whether a Palestinian Resistance Movement exists or not.

Q: Besides the military field, what are Al Fatah's achievements, for example, in other fields such as the emancipation of women, the education of children, social services and so on?

Abu Ammar: As a progressive revolution we consider that all members of our society, whether men or women, should enjoy equal rights. We therefore encourage the total emancipation of all our women and we endeavour to give them every opportunity to participate actively in our struggle. The Palestinian woman has since the days of the Mandate fought side by side with our men. In the occupied territories at present, it is our valiant sisters who are leading the civilian resistance against the occupying forces.

We do not place any obstacles or restrictions in the face of any woman who wishes to join in our Movement. In fact, we are encouraging them to join both our military and political ranks.

As for the education of children, we have established schools for both girls and boys; we have the 'Cubs' training centres, we have organizations for caring for the families of our martyrs. We have founded our own hospitals and clinics which provide free medical treatment to the displaced persons in their camps. In fact, we know that our struggle is a long-term one and we are preparing ourselves accordingly.

Q: How many times did you personally cross the Jordan since 1967?

Abu Ammar: I do not answer personal questions, but I have entered the occupied territories every time that my military command has asked me to do so.

Q: Do you consider your struggle as part of the struggle against imperialism and colonialism everywhere and why?

Abu Ammar: Our struggle is part and parcel of every struggle against imperialism, injustice and oppression in the world. It is part of the world revolution which aims at establishing social justice and liberating mankind. Outside the Palestinian and Arab masses our greatest support comes from all freedom-loving people who have realized the true nature of Zionism and its association with imperialism and neo-colonialism. Israel's natural allies are sufficient proof of this. We only have to look at the support it receives from the United States, at its close links with the racist republics of South Africa and Rhodesia.

As for its ties with the puppet regime of South Vietnam, let us only remember that its defence minister Moshe Dayan found it necessary and useful to spend a few months there learning their methods. The 1956 aggression against Egypt is another very clear example of the reasons for the creation of a Zionist state in the area. To sum up, we consider Israel as playing the new role of the East India Company in the Middle East.

Q: Do you accept non-Palestinians in your fighting forces?

Abu Ammar: We have at present both Arab and non-Arab freedom fighters in our ranks.

Q: Why do you think Al Fatah has had such an appeal on both the national and international levels?

Abu Ammar: Al Fatah has revolutionized the approach to the Palestinian problem. It has been the active force behind the resurgence of the Palestinian entity, which has established itself as the major element in the conflict. It is a true expression of the new Arab determination to resist invasion and oppression. Above all, it is part of the world movements for liberation and as such must attract freedom-loving people everywhere. Al Fatah was the first movement which translated the Palestinian aspirations into actions and which by its nature represents the true Palestinian determination.

Platform of the Populur Front for the Liberation of Palestine

I

The Arab bourgeoisie has developed armies which are not prepared to sacrifice their own interests or to risk their privileges. Arab militarism has become an apparatus for oppressing revolutionary socialist movements within the Arab states, while at the same time it claims to be staunchly anti-imperialist. Under the guise of the national question, the bourgeoisie has used its armies to strengthen its bureaucratic power over the masses, and to prevent the workers and peasants from acquiring political power. So far it has demanded the help of the workers and peasants without organizing them or without developing a proletarian ideology. The national bourgeoisie usually comes to power through military coups and without any activity on the part of the masses, as soon as it has captured power it reinforces its bureaucratic position. Through widespread application of terror it is able to talk about revolution while at the same time it suppresses all the revolutionary movements and arrests everyone who tries to advocate revolutionary action.

The Arab bourgeoisie has used the question of Palestine to divert the Arab masses from realizing their own interests and their own domestic problems. The bourgeoisie always concentrated hopes on a victory outside the state's boundaries, in Palestine, and in this way they were able to preserve their class interests and their bureaucratic positions.

The war of June 1967 disproved the bourgeois theory of conventional war. The best strategy for Israel is to strike rapidly. The enemy is not able to mobilize its armies for a long period of time because this would intensify its economic crisis. It gets complete support from US imperialism and for these reasons it needs quick wars. Therefore for our poor people the best strategy in the long run is a people's war. Our people must overcome their weaknesses and exploit the weaknesses of the enemy by mobilizing the Palestinian and Arab peoples. The weakening of imperialism and Zionism in the Arab world demands revolutionary war as the means to confront them.

II

The Palestinian struggle is a part of the whole Arab liberation movement and of the world liberation movement. The Arab bourgeoisie and world imperialism are trying to impose a peaceful solution on this Palestinian problem but this suggestion merely promotes the interests of imperialism and of Zionism, doubt in the efficacy of people's war as a means of liberation and the preservation of the relations of the Arab bourgeoisie with the imperialist world market.

The Arab bourgeoisie is afraid of being isolated from this market and of losing its role as a mediator of world capitalism

That is why the Arab oil-producing countries broke off the boycott against the West (instituted during the June War) and for this reason MacNamara, as head of the World Bank, was ready to offer credits to them.

When the Arab bourgeoisie strive for a peaceful solution, they are in fact striving for the profit which they can get from their role as mediator between the imperialist market and the internal market. The Arab bourgeoisie are not yet opposed to the activity of the guerrillas, and sometimes they even help them; but this is because the presence of the guerrillas is a means of pressure for a peaceful solution. As long as the guerrillas don't have a clear class affiliation and a clear political stand they are unable to resist the implication of such a peaceful solution; but the conflict between the guerrillas and those who strive for a peaceful solution is unavoidable. Therefore the guerrillas must take steps to transform their actions into a people's war with clear goals.

III

The basic weakness of the guerrilla movement is the absence of a revolutionary ideology, which could illuminate the horizons of the Palestinian fighters and would incarnate the stages of a militant political programme. Without a revolutionary ideology the national struggle will remain imprisoned within its immediate practical and material needs. The Arab bourgeoisie is quite prepared for a limited satisfaction of the needs of the national struggle, as long as it respects the limits that the bourgeoisie sets. A clear illustration of this is the material help that Saudi Arabia offers Al Fatah while Al Fatah declares that she will not interfere in the internal affairs of any Arab countries.

Since most of the guerrilla movements have no ideological weapons, the Arab bourgeoisie can decide their fate. Therefore, the struggle of the Palestinian people must be supported by the workers and peasants, who will fight against any form of domination by imperialism, Zionism or the Arab bourgeoisie.

IV

We must not be satisfied with ignoring the problems of our struggle, saying that our struggle is a national one and not a class struggle. The national struggle reflects the class struggle. The national struggle is a struggle for land and those who struggle for it are the peasants who were driven away from their land. The bourgeoisie is always ready to lead such a movement, hoping to gain control of the internal market. If the bourgeoisie succeeds in bringing the national movement under its control, which strengthens its position, it can lead the movement under the guise of a peaceful solution into compromises with imperialism and Zionism.

Therefore, the fact that the liberation struggle is mainly a class struggle emphasizes the necessity for the workers and peasants to play a leading role in the national liberation movement. If the petty bourgeoisie take the leading role, the national revolution will fall as a victim of the class interests of this leadership. It is a great mistake to start by saying that the Zionist challenge demands national unity, for this shows that one does not understand the real class structure of Zionism.

The struggle against Israel is first of all a class struggle. Therefore the oppressed class is the only class which is able to face a confrontation with Zionism.

V

The decisive battle must be in Palestine. The armed people's struggle in Palestine can help itself with the simplest weapons in order to ruin the economies and the war machinery of their Zionist enemy. The moving of the people's struggle into Palestine depends upon agitating and organizing the masses, more than depending upon border actions in the Jordan Valley, although these actions are of importance for the struggle in Palestine.

When guerrilla organizations began their actions in the occupied areas, they were faced with a brutal military repression by the armed forces of Zionism. Because these organizations had no revolutionary ideology and so no programme, they gave in to demands of self-preservation and retreated into eastern Jordan. All their activity turned into border actions. This presence of the guerrilla organizations in Jordan enables the Jordanian bourgeoisie and their secret agents to crush these organizations when they are no longer useful as pressure for a peaceful solution.

VI

We must not neglect the struggle in east Jordan for this land is connected with Palestine more than with the other Arab countries. The problem of the revolution in Palestine is dialectically connected with the problem of the revolution in Jordan. A chain of plots between the Jordanian monarchy, imperialism and Zionism have proved this connexion.

The struggle in east Jordan must take the correct path, that of class struggle. The Palestinian struggle must not be used as a means of propping up the Jordanian monarchy, under the mask of national unity, and the main problem in Jordan is the creation of a Marxist-Leninist party with a clear action programme according to which it can organize the masses and enable them to carry out the national and class struggle. The harmony of the struggle in the two regions must be realized through coordinating organs whose tasks will be to guarantee reserves inside Palestine and to mobilize the peasants and soldiers in the border-territories.

This is the only way in which Amman can become an Arab Hanoi: a base for the revolutionaries fighting inside Palestine.

Al Fatah's Doctrine*

by Y. Harkabi

Fatah's prescription for facing the challenge inherent in [its] dilemma was Revolutionary War waged on guerrilla warfare

*Reprinted by special permission from *Adelphi Papers* No. 53

lines. Its merit is that it does not require such long and tedious preparations as a conventional war, for it can be launched with small forces. Revolutions, Fatah reasons, once set in motion, generate their own forces and acquire momentum.

The armed struggle is the basic factor for expanding the revolution and its continuation; in short, causing a revolution in the life of this society. Such historic changes are usually achieved by wars, calamities and uncontrollable economic fluctuations. The nearest means of producing such a convulsion and a great historic change in the course of the national development of the Arab nation is by creating an appropriate environment for a decisive fateful battle between the Arabs and the Zionist enemy.

Arab politicians usually subordinated the Palestinian issue to their interests and policy, and manipulated it accordingly. Fatah signifies an attempt to reverse this trend and subordinate all other Arab problems to the goal of liberating Palestine. Before, the Palestinians orbited round the Arab state; now, Fatah tries to stage a Copernican revolution, and reverse the relationship.

Fatah sets out the objective of the war against Israel in bold type:

The liberation action is not only the wiping out of an imperialist base but, what is more important, the extinction of a society [*inqirad mujtama*]. Therefore armed violence will necessarily assume diverse forms in addition to the liquidation of the armed forces of the Zionist occupying state, namely, it should turn to the destruction of the factors sustaining the Zionist society in all their forms: industrial, agricultural and financial. The armed violence necessarily should also aim at the destruction of the various military, political, economic, financial and intellectual institutions of the Zionist occupation state, to prevent any possibility of a re-emergence of a new Zionist society. Military defeat is not the sole goal in the Palestinian Liberation War, but it is the blotting out of the Zionist character of the occupied land, be it human or social.

(December 1968), 'Fedayeen Action and Arab Strategy'. Institute of Strategic Studies, London.

Or:

The Jewish state is an aberrant mistaken phenomenon in our nation's history and therefore there is no alternative but to wipe out the existential trace [*alathar alwujudi*] of this artificial phenomenon.

Lt-Col. Sha'ir, an officer in the command of the PLO Army, also expresses the objective in unmistakable terms:

The chief objective and the fundamental effort for the Popular War concerning the liberation of Palestine is the reoccupation of the usurped land regardless of the method, be it smashing or annihilation [*ibada*], because the enemy when he usurped Palestine did not think of the fate of our people, of things holy to it and its lawful rights, in the lands of his forefathers.

Arab declarations of objectives frequently used extreme expressions like 'throwing the Jews into the sea' which implied genocide. Fatah endeavours in its publications to avoid such notorious expressions, stressing that the purpose is limited to the destruction of the state, not of its people. The formula most frequently used in its writings is 'liquidation, or the uprooting of the Zionist existence or entity'. However, when the implications of this objective come to be spelled out, it is realized that Zionism is not only a political regime or a superstructure of sorts, but is embodied in a *society*. Therefore, this *society* has to be liquidated, which underlines that achieving it will require a great deal of killing. The Arabs' objective of destroying the state of Israel (what may be called a 'politicide') drives them to genocide. Since the existence of Israel is founded on the existence of a concentration of Jews so their dispersion should precede the demise of the state. Thus, despite Fatah's efforts, it comes back to the Arab objective in its extremist version.

Fatah stresses that Jews will be allowed to live in a democratic Arab Palestine after Israel's extinction. In order for the country to become Arab again, the sheer numerical predominance of Jews over Palestinian Arabs requires part of the Jewish population to disappear. How?

Fatah's recognition of the right of a Jewish minority to exist
is nothing new. It recalls the fundamental Islamic position,
which grants the Jews security on the condition of their subordination as a tolerated minority.

The Arab position is enmeshed in this complexity arising
from the impossibility of destroying Israel as a state without
destroying a considerable part of her inhabitants. To escape
from this dilemma the Arab objective is sometimes expressed
in another formula showing perhaps improved articulation
without changing the issue: 'the de-zionization of Israel'. Since
the basic meaning of Zionism was the achievement of Jewish
statehood, de-zionizing Israel has only one implication, that
Israel will cease being a Jewish state; not Israel but Palestine.
Israel and Zionism are organically connected. De-zionizing Israel is only a contradiction in terms.

Fatah senses the difficulties in the Arab position:

> Examining the Palestinian issue from all its aspects, we realize
> the necessity to satisfy many parties by our solution. For instance,
> if we consider world public opinion has some weight and influence,
> we must put out a solution which will satisfy public opinion or be
> acceptable to it, even be it with difficulty. Of course, when we
> speak about the need for satisfying world opinion, we do not
> mean in the kind of solution to the Palestine issue, but in its
> method. Public opinion has no right to dispute the imperative
> necessity of its solution [i.e. by destruction of the state], but its
> right to know the method, so that public opinion will not castigate
> us with Fascism, anti-Semitism or other inhuman epithets.

What is more important for the present discussions is the
influence of the objective on the nature of the war by which
Fatah hopes to achieve its aim. Such a war is different from
one directed towards a change of the political regime, or towards harassment of the representatives of a remote country
until the government prefers to relinquish its rule in that area.
In order to achieve the purpose of liquidating a society or wip-
ping out its 'existential trace', war must be of great extent
and intensity and become really total.

The question that is crucial to any evaluation of Fatah's
position is the degree to which guerrilla warfare can suit such

an objective. This will be taken up at the conclusion of this paper.

Fatah exhorted the Palestinians to become the driving force in the conflict, not by agitation in the Arab countries as they had previously, not by pushing the Arab states to action, but by starting actual fighting themselves. *Fedayeen* action should be developed into a fully fledged War of National Liberation. Only by what Fatah terms an 'armed struggle' can the Palestinians solve their problems and regain Palestine.

Fatah stressed its disbelief in the possibility of a political solution. Arab politics are treated, especially before the Six Day War, with marked disapproval. Politics are sickening when juxtaposed with the sublimity of the 'armed struggle'. The Palestinians will be able to concentrate on their conflict only if they extricate themselves from inter-Arab rivalries and exercise neutrality. If they take sides in any Arab issue, they will antagonize the opponents of the side they support, who will then try to make things difficult for them. The Palestinian problem should be put above Arab politics. Only by freeing themselves from Arab rivalries will the Palestinians be able to acquire liberty of action in their affairs.

There are inconsistencies in the writings and pronouncements of Fatah on how far the Palestinians are capable of accomplishing by themselves the liberation of Palestine. On the one hand, there are announcements that the forces of the Palestinian masses are irresistible and can achieve this goal. On the other hand, there is recognition that the last stroke will have to be dealt by the concerted forces of the Arab armies.

The war Fatah aspires to wage is called, in its parlance, the 'Palestinian Revolution', to signify as well the transformation it will cause in the Palestinians themselves who from passive onlookers will become dynamic fighters.

This trend towards Palestinian activism and the palestinization of the conflict has to be seen against its historical background. Its psychological aspects should also be tackled, otherwise the human dimension of such developments will evade us. However, in offering psychological explanations, it should always be borne in mind how tentative they are so long as they are based on intuition, and how corrupting they may be by inspiring in the writer, and even the reader, a false sense of clairvoyance.

The mid 1960s saw the re-emergence of the Palestinians as contestants in the Arab–Israel conflict, after about seventeen years in which the confrontation was mainly at states level. The entry of the Arab armies into the war in 1948 transformed the conflict from a civil one between Jews and Arabs in Palestine, or an intra-state war, to an inter-state war. The activities surrounding the setting up of the Palestine Liberation Organization and the *fedayeen* organizations signify in some respects an attempt to revert to the previous state of affairs. This development of the Palestinians' reassertion embodied elements of both protest and reproach towards the Arab states for their failure to fulfil their obligation towards the Palestinians. Fatah, by emphasizing that the 'Palestinian people is the only true available stock [*rasid*] for the war of return', insinuates that the others are not so trustworthy.

On the other hand, the Arab states handing over to the Palestinians the leading role in the conflict implied an abdication of sorts by the Arab states and an avowal of their failure. It is not mere coincidence that the Summit Meetings which established the PLO were convened as a result of, presumably, the most dismal of Arab failures between 1948 and the Six Day War. All the Arab leaders had committed themselves to preventing Israel from completing her project of pumping water from Lake Tiberias (what Arabs called 'the diversion of the Jordan'). When the time came, they realized their helplessness.

The relationship between the Palestinians and the Arabs has always been ambivalent, each accused the other of being responsible for their inadequacies in the conflict. The Arab states blamed the Palestinians for selling land to the Jews, for their feeble resistance during the Mandate, and for their acting as agents for Israel Intelligence. Their existence epitomized the calamities that befell the Arab world as a result of the Arab–Israel conflict, and the Palestinians were blamed for them.

The Palestinians blamed the Arab states for their halfhearted activities in the conflict, their irresolution, internal bickerings, the restrictions they imposed on the Palestinians, and their manipulation of the conflict to their narrow interests.

Despite that element of protest against the Arab states embodied in the Palestinians' organizations, they could be created only with the help of some Arab official quarters. The PLO did not come into being only by Palestinian spontaneity. It was established from above by the Summit Meetings and derived its authority and part of its finances from them. The Fatah acted under the aegis of the Syrian radical Ba'ath. Thus protest and dependence intermingled.

Palestinian activism came in the early 1960s to be cherished widely in Palestinian circles. Palestinian initiative seemed vital after the Arab states' failure. Mr Nashashibi ends his book as follows: 'O Palestinians, if you do not restore the land, you will not return to it, and it will not return to you.'

An important factor in the Palestinian move for the 'repalestinization' of the conflict was the influence of the Algerian War. It was a source of both pride and inspiration. If the Algerians prevailed over a great power such as France, so it was argued, there was hope in defeating small Israel.

Hence the effort to draw analogies between Algeria and Palestine and the effort to describe Israel as only another colonialist case, whose fate is doomed as part of the general historical trend of the liquidation of colonies.

Palestinian ideologists argued that previous presentation of the conflict as an inter-state one was erroneous. It was an imperialist ruse aimed at excluding the Palestinians from their natural role, thus 'liquidating' the conflict. This argument was, too, an apologia for the Arabs themselves as they too described the conflict as international. They were only deluded and their failing was only naïveté. Both Israel and the imperialists conspired to blur the 'liberation' aspect of the conflict.

Naming the conflict a 'War of National Liberation' after it had already reached a mature age, and the identification of 'War of National Liberation' with guerrilla warfare, produced among Palestinians an inclination to project it backwards and describe the conflict as if the Palestinians had waged continuous popular guerrilla warfare against the Jews. The history of the events in Palestine from World War 1 is being rewritten to appear as a continuous popular resistance and heroic uprisings. The blame for failure is focused on the leadership. Naji Alush in his book *Arab Resistance in Palestine 1917–1948* gives a Marxist explanation for this failing. Because of its class interests the Palestinian leadership tied its destiny to colonialism, and betrayed the national cause.

Palestinian radio programmes abound with plays and descriptions of brave resistance against the Jews in Palestine. Small ambushes or attacks on Jewish settlers are elevated into heroic acts of guerrilla warfare. Thus, heroism anticipated in the future is reinforced by inspiration drawn from the past, and if the real past cannot be a source of such inspiration, some retouching is done. Such an account may have another merit: it implies that the Palestinians are not only imitators of Mao and Che, but preceded them.

The allure of activism is presumably very powerful for the Palestinians. The Palestinians suffered not only from the agony of defeat, deprivation, refugee status, living in camps, but from contempt by the other Arabs. Losing their land and property was a blow to their dignity, as traditionally the criterion for position and prestige in Arab society is ownership of real estate. Activism and 'revolutionarism' are means of gaining self-respect especially for the younger generation. This generation is ambivalent towards their parents – they reproach them for their weaknesses and failings, calling them 'the generation of defeat', or 'the defeated generation' (*jil al-hazima, al-jil al-munhar*). Whereas the young generation dubbed itself (already before the Six Day War) the 'generation of resistance' or 'the generation of revenge' (*jil al-muqawama, jil al-naqma*). On the other hand, in order to bolster themselves up as Palestinians, they have to praise the Palestinian record and stress the continuity of the struggle.

Activism has the psychological function of atoning for past failings and inadequacies. It symbolizes the Palestinians' regeneration, and a reaction against fatalism, proverbial in Arab society, about which the young generation feels uneasy. Activism is a manly quality, hailed in a masculine society, and a reaction against emotionalism treated derogatorily in Arab political literature, including Fatah's 'Revolutionarism' (*thauria*) exerts a strong influence in most of the Arab world signifying a radical change, spectacular and forceful, a protest against the past, and a guarantee of success for the future. The adjective 'revolutionary' is attached to all kinds of nouns in Arab political literature as a word of approbation and optimism.

Fatah described what this Palestinian revolution will accomplish :

> The staging of the revolutionary movement is a conscious transcendence of the circumstances of the Arab Palestinian people, of the traditional leadership, of the stagnated situations, of the opportunism and the self-seeking political arrangements, or those directed from beyond the Palestinian pale, it is a rejection of this fragmented reality. The Palestinian revolutionary movement on this level is a social revolution and a mutation in the social relationship of the Palestinian Arab people.

It is not by sheer accident that the third Fatah pamphlet entitled *The Revolution and Violence, The Road to Victory* is a selective précis of Frantz Fanon's book *The Wretched of the Earth*. Fanon's influence is manifested in other Fatah writings, especially on the psychological impact of Israel on the Arabs and on the transformations that their armed struggle will produce in the Palestinians. 'Violence', 'Violent Struggle', and 'Vengeance' are expressions of great frequency in Fatah literature. The reader of these texts is introduced to a world of simmering frustrated hatred and a drive for unquenchable vengeance.

Violence is described as imperative in wiping out colonialism, for between the colonialist and the colonized there is such a contradiction that no coexistence is possible. One of the two has to be liquidated. (Descriptions of the Arab–Israel conflict as both a zero-sum game and a deadly quarrel are frequent in Arab publications.) Such a conflict is 'a war of annihilation of one of the rivals, either wiping out the national entity, or wiping out colonialism. . . . The colonized will be liberated from violence by violence.' The 'Palestinian Revolution' is such a cataclysmic event that it can only be achieved by violence.

Violence liberates people from their shortcomings and anxieties. It inculcates in them both courage and fearlessness concerning death. Violence has a therapuetic effect, purifying society of its diseases. 'Violence will purify the individuals from venom, it will redeem the colonized from inferiority complex, it will return courage to the countryman.' In a memorandum to Arab journalists, Fatah stated: 'Blazing our armed revolution inside the occupied territory [i.e. Israel – it was written before the Six Day War] is a healing medicine for all our people's diseases.'

The praising of violence as purgative may imply also an element of self-indictment for flaws which will now be rectified, and a desire to exorcize the record of failings. The praising of violence may have as well the function of giving cathartic satisfaction as a substitute for operational action.

Violence, Fatah asserts, will have a unifying influence on people, forging one nation from them. It will draw the individuals from the pettiness of their ego, and imbue them with the effusiveness of collective endeavour, as bloodshed will produce a common experience binding them together. Thus, 'the territoriality, [i.e. the fragmentation into different Arab states] which was imposed by imperialism and Arab leaderships and which was sustained by traditional circumstances in the societies, will end.'

The struggle, besides its political goals, will have as a by-product an important impact on those who participate in it. It is 'a creative struggling' (*nidalia khallaqa*). Violence, Revolutionarism, Activism, 'the battle of vengeance', 'armed struggle', all coalesce in an apocalyptic vision of heroic and just aggression meting out revenge on Israel.

Fatah ideologists have been inclined to deal with general ideas of guerrilla warfare, rather than specifying in detail how their objectives will be accomplished through it. Like the other exponents of guerrilla warfare Fatah deals with the more practical problems, by means of tracing the phases by which the war or the revolution will evolve. It is called 'revolution' in which warfare proper is only a part of a larger complex of activities, mobilizing the support and the participation in the struggle of the masses, and their own transformation through it.

The pamphlet entitled *How Will The Armed Popular Revolution Explode?* dwells on the mechanism and process of this 'revolution'. It explains that a revolution originates when the oppressed people become aware of the evils of the present reality, and as a result of the growth of an urge to avenge themselves upon it. Needless to say, the reality here is Israel. Though the feelings of revolt against the oppressive reality are spontaneous, they have to be assisted and to be organized. The revolution has to be orchestrated by stages, by its leaders, the 'Revolutionary Vanguard'.

In Fatah's descriptions of the stages and their names there are some inconsistencies. They may originate either from different authorship, reflecting diverse influences, or be caused by simple imprecision and vagueness. This vagueness is even more accentuated by the lack of differentiation between the organizational and the operational aspects of the stages, and the relationship between the two.

The parts of Fatah's writings which deal with the phases of war make uneasy reading. Fatah's terminology and formulation may seem both esoteric and highfalutin. However, what may be more wearisome for the reader who is not versed in such parlance is the generality and abstraction of the discussion. It contains a mixture of a terminology influenced by Marxist literature, attempting to interpret developments in a rational way, with mythical overtones expressed in figures of speech like the 'ignition' or 'detonation' or a revolution, and leaves the reader wondering how it is to be done.

The organizational stages symbolize the expansion of the circles of those involved in the revolution or war. Stage one is the *Formation of the Revolutionary Vanguard*. This is achieved by 'the movement of revolutionary gathering of the revengeful conscious wills'. 'The individual of the Revolutionary Vanguard is distinguished by his revolutionary intuition.' His task is 'to discover the vital tide in his society, for its own sake and for its usefulness for action and movement, and then to realize what obstacles hamper his movement in accordance with history's logic'. Thus,

the Revolutionary Vanguard signifies the type of human who inter-acts positively with the reality [of his predicament], and so ele-vates himself by his consciousness until he releases himself from reality's grip, in order to pursue the superseding of this reality by another, which differs basically in its values and traits. To take a concrete example, the reality of Arab Palestinian people is frag-mented, disfigured and corrupted, and shows signs of stagnation. However, despite this stagnation and immobility, the historical direction imposes the existence of a current of vitality among the Palestinian people, so long as the Palestinian man treasures ven-geance on this reality. As this wish for vengeance grows, the current of vitality congeals in the form of a Revolutionary Vanguard.

The second stage is the *Formation of the Revolutionary Organization*. In it the Revolutionary Vanguard achieves a psychological mobilization of the Palestinian masses by stimu-lating their urge for revenge, until 'the constructive revolu-tionary anxiety embraces all the Palestinian Arabs'. It is thus called the stage of *Revolutionary Embracing (al-shumul al-thauri)*. Indoctrination of the masses will not precede the stag-ing of the armed struggle but will be achieved by it. 'Mistaken are those who advocate the need for rousing a national con-sciousness before the armed struggle assumes a concrete form. ... Ineluctably the armed struggle and mass consciousness will go side by side, because the armed struggle will make the masses feel their active personality and restore their self-confidence.' The Vanguard will galvanize the masses by means of its example and sacrifice in guerrilla activities.

Fatah's publications state that irresistible might is stored in the Arab masses. They are 'latent volcanoes', they are the main 'instrument' of the struggle. This explosive capacity has to be activated and this task is allotted to the Vanguard.

The revolution's success is dependent on cooperation between the Vanguard and the masses. 'The Revolution in its com-position has a leadership and a basis, necessitates the accomplishment of a conscious interaction between the basis, which is the masses, and the leadership, in order to ensure the revolution's success and continuation.'

The third stage is the *Formation of the Supporting Arab Front*. Popular support for the 'Palestinian Revolution' is to be secured in all Arab countries in order to safeguard rear bases in Arab countries for the war, and as a means of putting pressure on the Arab governments not to slacken or deviate from aiding the Palestinian Revolution by pursuit of their local interests. The Supporting Arab Front is thus expressed on two levels, the popular and the governmental. The popular support is used as an instrument of pressure against the Arab governments.

In the same publications the overall development of the revolution is divided into two major stages: one, *Organization and Mobilization*, called elsewhere the *Phases of Revolutionary Maturing*, comprises the organizational stages already enumerated. The second stage is called that of the *Revolutionary Explosion (marhal atal-tafjir al-thauri)*. The stage of the Revolutionary Explosion is described in colourful language: 'The hating revengeful masses plunge into the road of revolution in a pressing and vehement fashion as pouring forces that burn everything that stands in their way.' In this stage 'tempests of revenge' will be let loose. However, the Vanguard should ensure mass discipline to prevent violence going berserk. 'The Revolution's Will should obey its regulating brain.'

While the first stage is preparatory, the second is the main interesting stage. Unfortunately, Fatah's description of it is rather rudimentary. Even the question of the timing of its beginning is not clear. Fatah specified: 'Our operations in the occupied territory can never reach the stage of the aspired revolution unless all Palestinian groups are polarized around the revolution.' Fatah does have an ambition to become the central leader of all the Palestinians, proving that the other movements, which have not matured round what has been described as a Revolutionary Vanguard like itself, are artificial and 'counterfeited'. Thus the stage of revolution will arrive only when Fatah has mobilized *all* the Palestinians.

Nevertheless, Fatah's small action at the beginning of January 1965 is frequently hailed as the 'detonation of the revolution', implying that the revolution started then. By the same token, at the beginning of 1968, Fatah's official journal celebrated the fourth anniversary 'of our Palestinian people's revolution in the occupied territory'. Perhaps this ambiguity as to the timing of the revolutionary stage stems from Fatah's emphasis of the need to precipitate action. Once action is launched the development proceeds spontaneously.

The theories of guerrilla warfare have been developed in the twentieth century several times over. They have been popularized and romanticized to the extent of becoming almost part of this generation's culture. No wonder that Fatah repeats ideas expounded elsewhere. It would be excessive to expect its approach to be completely original, nor does it pretend to be all original. Actually, the temptation to pose as original is less than the confidence Fatah can draw from the success of these theories in China, Algeria, Cuba or Vietnam. These successes are presented as precedents guaranteeing Fatah's success as well. The feeling of kinship of sorts in a family of successful revolutionaries and guerrilla fighters inspires optimism and pride. Thus, Fatah makes no bones about its indebtedness to the exponents of guerrilla warfare. Its spokesmen are fond of explaining that, although they have learnt from others, they rely only on their own specific experience. No doubt the singularity of the Palestinian case limits the possibility of benefiting from lessons from elsewhere.

The main guerrilla treatises of Mao Tse-tung, Giap, Che Guevara and Régis Debray, have been translated into Arabic in several editions, and serialized in the press. In its main series of 'Revolutionary Lessons and Trials', Fatah published pamphlets bearing the titles *The Chinese Experience*, *The Vietnamese Experience* and *The Cuban Experience*.

In their books on guerrilla warfare, General Talas and Colonel Sha'ir too give long and detailed accounts of the doctrines of guerrilla warfare as developed by its major exponents.

Though Algeria, as an Arab case, should have served as the main source of inspiration, it seems that the greatest influence was exerted by Cuba. (Algeria has not codified her guerrilla experience in the same way as the other guerrilla practitioners. At least such a publication, if it does exist, has not come to the general notice. Perhaps the reason is that Boumedienne was more of a commander of the regular forces outside Algeria in Tunisia than a guerrilla leader.)

The reasons for Fatah's seeing Cuba as the main source of inspiration seem obvious: Mao has stressed that guerrilla warfare can succeed only in a large country like China where the guerrillas can establish a base out of the reach of enemy forces. Mao has specified that guerrilla warfare cannot succeed in a country the size of Belgium. Mao's words thus disprove Fatah, whereas Cuba is a success story of guerrilla warfare in a small country.

Che Guevara radiates optimism. He lightheartedly urged taking the plunge before conditions matured, while Mao is both more cautious and sombre. The first sentence of the Fatah pamphlet on Cuba reads: 'The Cuban experience has proved the error of those who see a need for waiting until the maturing of the objective and the subjective circumstances for the revolution, instead of the continuous effort to accelerate the formation of these circumstances.'

In China and Vietnam the bearers of the revolution were the Communist Party. Fatah disapproves of the need to set out as a party. In Cuba it all started from the wanderings of the first twelve people in the Sierra Maestra. Thus the Cuban model suits Fatah better, precisely because it was not a popular movement.

General Talas, who dedicated his book to Guevara, and praises him to the skies as the 'guide of War of National Liberation', explains in the introduction that his main contribution was the idea of the 'revolutionary focus', the nucleus of the revolt which, though numerically small, can start the movement off and win.

Representatives of Fatah and the other organizations established relations with China, Vietnam and Cuba, and were given help and advice. Some of Fatah's leaders were sent to Algeria and China for training.

During the years 1963 to 1967 there was a spate of articles in the Arab press on the different aspects of Arab strategy against Israel. A wide range of problems was discussed, such as the kind of war the Arabs should wage, how it should be initiated, analyses of strategic strengths and weaknesses of the two sides, the impact of nuclear weapons – should Israel acquire them, problems arising from Western intervention, the influence of Egyptian missiles, the timing of war, the possibilities of a preventive war by Israel, and the whole field of guerrilla warfare.

To the strategic analyst part of this material may seem amateur – an exercise in imitation of the style of strategic discussions in the West. However these publications are interesting as they throw light on the mood and thinking of some important Arab circles. It would be tedious to try fully to report on the views expressed. My purpose is to isolate some of the strands of thought on guerrilla warfare and Arab strategy in general not in a micro-historic way – tracing chronologically the details of the debate in Arab countries, identifying the people who took part in it, and the circles they represented – but rather in a conceptual way, reconstructing the possible different positions on the problem of the Arab programme of action against Israel.

The basic suitability of guerrilla warfare as advocated by Fatah was questioned. Naji Alush writing his book in 1963–4 directed his criticism against articles published in 1962 in *Our Palestine*: the journal in which Fatah made its ideological debut Alush asked:

Why should we suppose that the Israeli Army will stand with its hands tied in the face of *fedayeen*'s attacks? The Israeli Army will destroy Arab villages and cities, and even may take a decisive step, and, for example, occupy the whole West Bank . . .
The Journal considered that in the present circumstances the Arab armies are incapable of wiping out Israel, wheras it sees that the Palestinian entity is capable of accomplishing this miracle. How

will it be? With the help of the Arab states and the non-Arab states?

Naturally we see the Revolutionary Road, which *Our Palestine* has chosen, as an unwarranted one, because it is built on improvisation, excitement and spontaneity. It will restore the issue to 1947 [i.e. to another defeat]. . . .

Smashing Israel cannot be done by *fedayeen*'s attacks because of the completeness of her preparations and arms.

The relevance of the Algerian case to the Palestinian condition came under criticism from several quarters. Naji Alush admonished, 'The legend of the liberation of Algeria may push the liberation of Palestine into an abyss. The heroic triumph of the Algerian revolt made some Palestinians and some progressive Arabs fancy that following the same road will bring the same result.'

Alush spelled out the differences between Algeria and Palestine, invoking the authority of an analysis by Professor Walid al-Khalidi:

1. *The Combat Area.* Algeria was a colony with a small French minority and ten million Algerians. Palestine is divided into three: a small Arab minority in Israel concentrated in a few zones, and limited in its possibilities of action; the West Bank has become a Jordanian colony occupied by the 'Forces of the Desert and mercenaries', where the Palestinians are prohibited from organizing themselves; the Gaza Strip is administered as occupied territory by an Arab government withholding from its inhabitants self-government which might have transformed them into a nucleus from which serious action for the liberation of Palestine could have been developed. The Palestinians in Gaza and the West Bank have first to overcome Arab government domination, before they can organize themselves for war.

2. *The Nature of the Battle.* In Algeria it was a battle for independence . . . which is not the case in Palestine. There is a battle for the uprooting of a state recognized by the United Nations, supported by world public opinion and the principal capitalist states. . . . Britain and the United States were ready to accept the independence of Algeria, but they are not ready to accept the liquidation of the Zionists' state. The Algerian struggle for independence could be compared to the Palestinians' struggle before

1948 ... after 1948 the nature of the situation changed in Palestine.

3. Algerians could have bases in Tunisia and Morocco. However, no Arab government will tolerate the organization of the Palestinians on its territory, unless they constitute a part of its forces and are subservient to its policy.

4. *The Problem of Power.* The Algerian people could paralyse, by employing guerrilla warfare, a large French army, owing to the vastness of Algeria which is 852,600 square miles, in which there are many mountains, thick bushes and roadless regions, which rendered movement of the army difficult and made way for successful guerrilla warfare. As regards Palestine, most of the occupied territory is a plain, settled with fortified settlements, connected by an extensive network of roads, which facilitates army movements and renders the task of *fedayeen* difficult.

5. When the revolution erupted in Algeria, its active organizations were in Algeria. As regards the Palestinians, the organization of a revolution must grow outside of the occupied territory.... Since the revolutionary organizations are outside the boundaries of the Zionists' state, any action by them necessitates an armed invasion against which the usurping state will launch a military operation directed against the Arab neighbouring countries.

6. In Algeria, the fighters were men attached to their people who left the towns and their sham for the bosom of the masses. The propagandists of revolution in Palestine are chatterboxes of the bourgeoisie who prefer coffee houses in Beirut, Damascus, or Gaza to the sands of the occupied territory and the mountains of what was left in Palestine west of the Jordan. They organize themselves in Gaza, Lebanon, and Kuwait issuing thousands of proclamations without remembering once where the battlefield is, or discovering its boundaries and purpose.

7. Arab states' aid to Algeria was very small, yet, despite its smallness, Algeria achieved victory because her conditions made that meagre aid sufficient. However, in the battle for Palestine, the aid will not be adequate even if it is large. This is because the aim is to uproot the usurping state and not to spread fear and ruin inside its borders. The Palestinian people, divided and oppressed, cannot mobilize the necessary power to squash the Zionists' state which is defended by 300,000 well-trained and well-armed soldiers.

8. The Algerian campaign took a territorial shape [i.e. pertaining to one Arab people or state] ... the struggle stopped at the traditional borders of Algeria, and it recognized the borders drawn by

colonialism. This nature of territoriality made the Palestinians demand a territorial struggle [i.e. by the 'Palestinian entity' as distinct
from the rest of the Arabs], but that is impossible in Palestine.
Algeria could be liberated without a clash with Tunisia or Morocco
and their reactionary governments, while the revolutionary operation for the liberation of Palestine must collide with the government of Jordan.

No doubt this is sound criticism. It spares the need for a military evaluation of guerrilla prospects in the area, which, coming from an Israeli, might be suspected as partisan.

'The Struggle Continues': President Nasser's Speech at the opening of the second session of the Arab Socialist Union National Congress at Cairo University, 27 March 1969

In the name of God the All-Merciful, we open the Arab Socialist Union National Congress.

Brothers, before beginning with the proceedings of the session
I ask you to observe one minute's silence in memory of General
Abdel Mun'im Riyad – the brave soldier who offered his life
on the battlefield and who gave a high example of Egyptian
military honour, and in memory of all our heroic martyrs on
the Egyptian front, and the martyrs of the Palestine resistance
and the martyrs of the Palestine masses confidently and faithfully struggling on their soil.

Compatriots, members of the ASU National Congress, your
Congress is now holding its second session in accordance with
the 30th March statement – that the elected ASU National Congress should exist until the effects of the aggression were overcome and should hold a plenary session every three months
to follow up and guide the stages of the struggle and adopt
whatever it deemed appropriate in this respect.

Although the agenda of this session includes many questions,
the foremost question under the 30th March statement – and
the primary question of concern to the masses – is one before

any other: this is the question of the comprehensive struggle of our people and nation to restore and establish their rights and to liberate and honour the land. There is no other issue before this question, under the 30th March statement and by virtue of our masses' concern. There is no other issue above this question by virtue of the current phase of the foremost issue of comprehensive Arab struggle, which is the centre of attention and the sphere of every sacrifice and hope we offer or expect.

This session of the National Congress begins when our struggle is in a very important and at the same time very dangerous phase. This phase is reflected in particular in both the military and political sides of the Middle East crisis.

On the military side, the phase is apparent in the continued escalation of military operations along the Egyptian front, the escalation of the Palestine resistance organizations, and the escalation of the Palestine people's steadfastness, which is openly and fully challenging the Israeli occupation. At the same time, the enemy's wrath has escalated. We see the effects of this in the repeated raids on Jordanian towns and cities on the pretext of deterring the Palestine resistance.

Brothers, this means that with this escalation we are entering a stage which is inevitable, with the continuation of Israeli aggression on one side, and on the other with our increased capacity for steadfastness and daily support for our comprehensive force in defending our sacred rights. We are now entering a stage in which we should expect strikes by the enemy and in which we should return the enemy's strikes more heavily. We will discuss this in detail later.

On the political side, the phase is apparent in the collaboration of international political activity surrounding the Middle East crisis, which is crystallizing in the forthcoming meeting of the four big-power permanent member states of the Security Council, which issued the 22 November 1967 resolution on the Middle East crisis. The meeting, coming about eighteen months after adoption of the resolution, is to discuss that resolution and what has been done to implement it, in the midst of pressures affirming to every fair observer and every individual sincerely concerned about peace that the Middle East crisis cannot possibly wait any longer.

It is a miracle that the crisis has lasted so long without exploding – an explosion which would have far-reaching and unlimited effects. This means that politically and militarily we are entering a very critical and sensitive stage. Representatives of the four big powers will meet in New York. These powers will study and debate various possibilities. The importance of the subject is that the attitude of these four powers will be a new measurement that will help us clearly and beyond doubt to determine the attitudes of enemies and friends. Perhaps I should sincerely say that the attitudes of the various States in this connexion will determine for each the extent of their relations with our Arab nation for years to come, whatever the consequences.

In this connexion, and without awaiting other details on the political side, which I will deal with later, I wish to explain to you that the destiny of the Middle East will be determined in the Middle East itself and that nobody can dictate to the Arab nation what this nation regards as against justice or its lawful, historical rights. Peace cannot be imposed, but peace can come by itself if justice forms the basis. We should alway' remember that the balance of power may change but the fov dations of justice are always firmly rooted and perpetual.

Brother compatriots, members of the Congress, the current session of your Congress begins with a new military and political phase – a phase in which events are moving faster and taking a serious turn. Therefore we must be extremely alert cautious and fully prepared ...

Brothers, we will now take a look at some of our fronts near the enemy lines.

First, the Egyptian front. When we refer to the Egyptian front, we begin with the issue of the reconstruction of the armed forces. We all know the situation of our armed forces after the aggression and the cease-fire decision. The reconstruction of our armed forces was a difficult operation. It was not at all an easy operation. First of all we were in need of arms, then we needed reorganization, then we needed hard training. All this requires the exertion of great efforts and means that our officers and soldiers must accustom themselves to leading a hard – a very hard – life. Naturally, the formation, organization and training of our armed forces is not enough. We must also train the brains that command these forces and units. This too has not been an easy task. The formation, training and command of all levels of our leadership has not been easy. When we speak about the reconstruction of the armed forces, we mean that we are reconstructing an army in whose arming, organization, training and command we have confidence. The armed forces command is the brain that directs the battle and fighting. We also refer to the standard and efficiency of the men in our armed forces.

All these operations were delicate operations that require planning. What was wanted was fighting spirit, a spirit of sacrifice, and the restoration of confidence in our armed forces after the defamatory campaign to which our armed forces had been exposed in the world.

In reality we lost the battle in 1967 without coming face-to-face with the enemy. We lost the war without entering into it. We lost the battle without fighting. Despite this, our armed forces were exposed to many defamatory campaigns. The only confrontation in 1967 took place on 5 June. On that day, our armed forces fought well. However, in view of what happened to our air force on 5 June, instructions to withdraw were issued on 6 June. So, since we did not have the opportunity to enter the war we cannot say that we lost. We did not have the opportunity to confront the enemy. What happened was that an attempt was made to defame our armed forces so that the people would lose their confidence in the armed forces and so that the armed forces would lose confidence in themselves.

Therefore, after the organization and arming of our armed forces and after the creation of a command, we had to examine the standard of our men and the spirit of confidence which was restored. We had to see that the fighting spirit was spread among all members of our armed forces. We had to feel the spirit of sacrifice return among the members of our armed forces and to see that cohesion was present between officers and men. We had to see that everyone was sacrificing his time and that we worked day and night.

Brothers, I saw all this during my visits to the armed forces. The people gave a good example of their feelings when they attended the funeral of the martyr Abdel Mun'im Riyad. Abdel Mun'im Riyad worked till midnight every day. All members of the armed forces knew this. He used to pay constant visits to army units. He had constant discussions with everyone. The members of our armed forces were used to sudden visits by Abdel Mun'im Riyad at any post.

During my recent visits to the armed forces at the time of the feast [Id al-Adha], a soldier spoke to me about a certain issue. When the soldier approached me I thought that he was going to complain to me or that he was going to refer to a private issue. However, he did not speak to me about a private issue. He spoke about an issue concerning the use of the arms in his unit. In fact, when he said what he wanted, I asked him: Do you not want anything? He said: No, I do not want anything. I asked him: Have you no complaints? He said: No, I have no complaints. I asked him: From what college did you graduate? He said: I graduated from the Faculty of Arts of Cairo University. We discussed the subject he brought up. Abdel Mun'im Riyad also spoke to him on the same subject. At the end of our visit that night we went to rest. After dinner I noticed that Abdel Mun'im Riyad had asked for the soldier who spoke to us earlier. Riyad sat down with him and asked him about the details of the subject for which he had had no time during the visit. He sat with him and talked about all issues.

This is the spirit of our men in the armed forces. This is the spirit of the Chief of Staff of our armed forces and the spirit of a soldier of the Egyptian armed forces which are now in position on the battlefield.

Brothers, the efforts to train our armed forces are great. We know that the enemy had been preparing for this battle since 1956. This fact appeared in books written by the enemy. They said they were mobilizing themselves until they saw that we were about to become stronger than they. They launched their aggression against us at that time so that they could prevent us from becoming their superiors.

We have learned many lessons from what happened in 1967. We are now working hard day and night to make good our losses. With regard to training, training means one is deprived of leave for a long period, for there is training day and night. We feel that the officers and men of the armed forces are doing difficult work and are assuming heavy responsibilities. They work for long periods without leave, but every one of them knows that we want to make good our losses in the shortest period possible. We also want to use the weapons we have received with full competence. This is as far as training is concerned.

So far as science and technology are concerned, we are endeavouring to catch up with what we have missed in all types. We are developing and expanding our war industry. When I speak in this way some people may think that I am divulging secrets. Well, I am not divulging secrets. How can we enter the war if we are not trained and if we do not have a command, arms and armed forces in which we have complete confidence?

With regard to arms, the subject of the supply of arms demands our careful consideration. By such consideration we learn a few lessons, and also we can be more sure of the correctness of the course we have maintained. Several points have to be considered in this matter.

(i) The Soviet Union is supplying us with the weapons we need. Immediately after the setback and the aggression the Soviet Union began supplying us with arms, with aircraft. We were able in a short period to obtain enough arms to help us meet any Israeli aggression. Had it not been for these arms we could not have succeeded in attaining a position from which we could answer or repel the enemy.

(ii) The United States and its allies are supplying arms to our enemy. There is a distinction between the US supply of arms to Israel and the Soviet supply of arms to us. After the

June 1967 aggression Israel had more arms than it needed, while we hardly had enough. Moreover, we needed the arms to defend our homelands and to liberate our occupied territories. The supply of arms to Israel – which was the aggressor – could only mean that Israel was being encouraged to continue the aggression and to insist on achieving gains from this aggression.

(iii) The Soviet Union is supplying us with the arms we need without exerting pressure on our current financial resources, which are bearing the heavy burden of the war. It is enough to tell you that we have not yet paid a single penny for all the arms we have received so far from the Soviet Union. The first consignment of arms we received from the Soviet Union was free. After that, all other arms consignments were paid for with long-term loans.

I want you to know that the United States gives arms to Israel practically free of charge. The US Export-import Bank offers Israel long-term loans with which it purchases arms for nominal sums, while generous American donations to Israel take care of these loans when the time for payment comes.

(iv) When arms are obtained from states and not by smuggling, the matter is no longer a commercial deal but is firmly linked with the countries exporting the arms. A country cannot possibly give arms to a country contrary to its own policy. This means quite frankly that the imperialist powers cannot give arms to countries which openly oppose and challenge imperialism, even if these countries are ready to pay for the arms in hard currency. They cannot get the arms until they succumb to imperialism, or if there is hope of making them succumb to imperialism. We tried this with Britain in 1953 and with the United States in 1954. I want to say quite clearly that, supposing we did have the foreign hard currency to purchase the arms, if we could manage that – and I say that we could manage – if we had the currency and went to Washington or London to purchase the arms, we would not get anything. Proof of this is clearly before our eyes.

(v) From the point of view of our national independence, in particular from the point of view of our main and basic existence, our supply of arms from the Soviet Union is a firm guarantee and the only door open to us. This makes us always feel most grateful for the Soviet Union's attitude to us, to our questions of destiny and to our legitimate struggle for our cause.

We have obtained arms from the Soviet Union since 1955. From 1955 to this date, the Soviet Union has neither dictated any political restriction nor made a single condition. It has not made any request which could affect our national prestige. Relations are based mainly on the belief in the popular liberation movement, hostility to imperialism, and resistance to imperialist influence and plans.

After obtaining arms, we must grasp arms. The armed forces are now day and night doing so, grasping and training so that the arms may have full weight on the battlefield. After obtaining the arms, we asked the Soviet Union to provide us with Soviet military technicians – who are at present with our armed forces in their various units and corps. We asked the Soviet Union for technicians and have insisted on our request. Why? To compensate for shortcomings. These shortcomings appeared in various fields in June 1967 – in the use of arms, in the command and in various aspects. We also asked the Russians to assist us in training, in grasping arms, and in modernizing the various commands – from the supreme to the subordinate commands. I insisted on requestioning Soviet experts for deployment with the armed forces because of my conviction that to confront the Israeli enemy we needed the full assistance of Soviet arms and also of those who could instruct us on the use of the arms and who could help us in command training.

In fact, we have benefited a great deal in the recent months from the Soviet experts and advisers who are with our units. They have left their families behind and are earnestly working with us day and night so that we may benefit from their experience and so that our armed forces may attain full proficiency to enable them to stage the battle to liberate the land. . .

Brother citizens, members of the National Congress. Before leaving the subject of the Egyptian front to view the remaining

Arab fronts surrounding the enemy, we must stop carefully to consider the excellent activities that the Arab Sinai Organization had begun to carry out. The activities of this organization, which was founded by the young people of Sinai and by other groups of young people from the whole of the homeland who have voluntarily joined its ranks – who defied danger and found their way to this dear part of our nation – began to be felt a few months ago.

During the past few weeks the organization began to expand its activities in extremely dangerous circumstances, and to fight the enemy in unsuitable natural conditions. Despite all this, the young people of this organization carried out their great and extremely dangerous tasks in solemn silence. Their attacks were direct. They came face-to-face with the enemy's military forces concentrated in the desert. Our young people formed fighting patrols and clashed with the enemy. They raided enemy headquarters and laid mines. Not a single day passed without the sound of the explosion of these mines reaching the enemy's ears. These explosions inflicted personal and material losses on the enemy.

Regardless of the enemy's repeated threats of revenge against the activities of this organization no one is now able to prevent these national young people from carrying out their role in the battle. The Arab *fedayeen* action is linked with the Israeli occupation of Arab soil. Therefore, as long as this occupation continues, the people's resistance against it cannot be stopped. This resistance is manifested in all possible ways, both in a negative way and in a popular or military way. This resistance will continue until the end of the occupation.

Brothers, we shall now move on to consider the other fronts of Arab military action. The matters I shall discuss are not secret, because some of Israel's leaders have discussed them and the facts may have also been published by newspapers in Israel or in some Arab newspapers.

The second point I want to discuss is the eastern command. Actually, ever since June 1967 we have been thinking of coordinating the joint Arab fronts. Meetings and other long secret conferences actually took place, until it was eventually possible ot establish the eastern front and form a command for this eastern front. This command is actually of great importance. Therefore it is necessary that there should be an eastern front and a western front. It is also necessary that there should be complete coordination between the eastern and western fronts. The enemy is aware of this importance and of what can possibly result from the formation of strong eastern and western fronts.

The importance of the eastern front was stressed in one of the books of the Strategic Studies Institute. The book points out that Israel's principal target these days is to break up his eastern front. I can say that the establishment of the eastern front has succeeded to a great extent. What has been achieved?

The eastern front has been formed composed of Syria, Iraq and Jordan. A command for this eastern command has been formed and complete coordination has been achieved between the forces of Syria, Iraq and Jordan. What I am now saying is not a secret, because the Israeli Defence Minister discussed it in the Israeli newspapers. Contacts are now taking place between the eastern front and Kuwait and Saudi Arabia.

After this short discussion of the eastern front I will now speak about the resistance forces. We have spoken about the resistance forces before and revealed our view on them. We have also spoken of our policy. Our policy towards the resistance forces is summed up in consolidation of the resistance forces by every material and military means. We have also said that it is the right of the Palestine people to resist occupation, to fight and to demand their full rights.

We will now speak about the Palestine popular resistance. As we speak about the Palestine popular resistance, which has broken out everywhere in the territory the enemy occupied after June 1967, we must mention the resistance being carried out in valiant Gaza – the Palestine Arab people in valiant Gaza, these people who refuse to surrender. We are aware of the difficult circumstances the people of Gaza are facing in economic and other ways. Despite these circumstances, however,

Gaza refuses in every way – through its young men, its sons, its daughters, its men and its old people – refuses to surrender or to keep silent.

We must also mention the Palestine popular resistance in the West Bank. We must mention the Palestine popular resistance in Jerusalem and the reaction by Israel, seeking to turn Jerusalem into a Jewish city. I tell our brothers, the people of Jerusalem, that we, the people of the UAR, give our pledge that we shall in no circumstances accept the *fait accompli* Israel seeks to impose in Jerusalem. Arab Jerusalem is a part of the Arab nation and no one can abandon Arab Jerusalem ...

Brother citizens, I am aware that there is a big question in your mind and in the mind of our people and nation. The question is: When will the battle be? I should like to tell you – out of a sense of responsibility – that I cannot answer this question. I can only say that everything physically possible is being mobilized for the day of the battle. In fact, superhuman efforts are being made for the battle. This is being done with the work, knowledge, faith and resolve of our men in all fields of national struggle, both at the front and on the home front immediately behind it.

Therefore I hope that you will see eye to eye with me that we should not accelerate the battle to make it take place before its due time, not even by one day. However, I promise you in the meantime that we shall not delay the battle, not even by one day, from the date it is due.

Brother citizens, members of the National Congress, before leaving military matters to discuss political matters, I must remind you that the War Minister will be here with you tomorrow at a closed session to give you further details which you would like to know and on which you may ask for explanations. The same thing will apply to the Foreign Minister, who will also attend the closed session with you tomorrow. He will talk to you about things that you would like to know within his field.

For this reason, I shall make my talk about political matters as brief as possible so as not to place obstacles before the

contacts among the four big powers which will begin in the
next few days. However, it might be appropriate to review certain general topics so that we may not expect more than the
circumstances allow.

1. No one can ask us to do more than we committed ourselves to do when we accepted the 22 November 1967 Security
Council resolution. Despite our absolute belief in a principle
which we have declared and which we shall untiringly repeat
– that what has been taken by force can be regained only by
force – we have presented everything possible, within the principles in which we believe, to the UN Middle East envoy Gun-
nar Jarring, who is to supervise the implementation of the
Security Council resolution.

2. We have realized from the beginning that any hope in
Ambassador Jarring's mission is difficult to realize because Israel rejects the Security Council resolution. It rejects the resolution because it provides for two things of great importance.
These are: (i) the need for withdrawal from Arab territories
occupied after 5 June, and (ii) that no territory can be annexed
by aggression. Israel wants to expand and is seeking land. We
have brought to the attention of the world statements by Israeli
leaders and officials sufficient to condemn them and to expose
their intentions and plans.

3. Towards the end of last year the problem was again taken
to the Security Council in an indirect manner. It was evident
then that Ambassador Jarring was unable to proceed with his
mission and that the authority issuing the resolution should
express another view on it before it was too late.

4. Since that time three new attempts have emerged. The
first was a timetable presented by the Soviet Union for the implementation of the resolution. The second was a set of ideas
contributing to the implementation of the resolution. These
ideas have been presented by France for discussion at a four-
power meeting, proposed by her, to include the four big powers
which are permanent Security Council members, in their capacity as the effective force in the Council. Finally, a few days
ago, there was the US working document.

5. I do not want to express an opinion after which it might

be said that we are making difficulties before the meeting of the four big powers. However, I cannot conceal from you that the USA bears a great responsibility for the dangerous road on which the Middle East crisis is proceeding. From the beginning of the crisis, the US attitude has been identical to that of Israel all along the line and without reservations, despite its alleged friendships with the Arab world – which are a subject of great doubt, and despite its enormous interests in the Arab world – about which there is no doubt. Following the recent US Presidential elections, which brought in a new government, we tried – and I add further that we are still trying – but I am bound in honesty to say immediately that so far I do not see any indications of a change in the US attitude, which supports Israel all the way.

Brothers, after perusing the recent US working document, I can assert that the US attitude is one of complete support for the Israeli point of view. I have only one answer to this US support for Israel – the constant support before and after June 1967 – I have only one answer. It is that we Arabs will in no circumstances surrender or accept any pressure.

Brothers, the Israeli newspapers reported that the USA had accepted Israel's point of view, during Eban's visit, on the subject of negotiations between the Arabs and Israel and on the subject of refugees. The Israeli newspapers said that the USA had adopted Israel's point of view on these subjects.

Brothers, the serious situation that may arise if the big four countries, in their capacity as the principal powers in the Security Council, are unable to find a means of implementing the Council's resolution – this situation we and everybody are aware of.

Brother compatriots, members of the National Congress, whatever the case may be, before and after all this, one fact above all remains. Our Arab nation will always have the last word concerning the most important issues of its struggle. Our nation will not give up any of its principles, rights or territory. It will work, struggle, resist and fight so that its destiny will always be guarded by its will. God is its supporter. Peace be with you.

Syrian Ba'ath Party Congress Resolutions:
Text of Statement by Ba'ath Regional Command on
the Party's Extraordinary Fourth Regional
Congress, April 1969

Brother citizens, the Extraordinary Fourth Regional Congress
was convened at a time when the Arab nation stands, with all
its present and future aspirations and hopes, at a cross roads.
It will either assert itself, its freedom and its rights in life and
determine its future, or slip again into a lost road to live deprived and powerless. This national situation imposed itself on
the conference throughout. In a responsible spirit the past
stage, including both its achievements and its gaps, was reviewed. In the light of this, the congress was able to arrive at
a unified view of the future, avoiding the gaps and enabling
the achievements to take effect. It was also able to surmount
the crisis and begin a new stage which it is hoped will be filled
with action and achievement.

The recent crisis tackled by the congress is not the first of its
type in the history of the party. Throughout its march, the
party, like any other revolutionary party, has faced bitter
strife from within and acute domestic struggles, but has always
emerged strong and more capable of confronting future events
however hard these may be. Nevertheless, in view of the present circumstances of the Arab homeland, the recent crisis
was the most dangerous and sensitive crisis for the future of
the current stage of our people. The Syrian Region, in the light
of its doctrinal line which it raised through the party's leadership, has become one of the main guarantees for continuing
the line opposing colonialism, imperialism and Zoinism in a
constructive way. Prompted by our national and domestic responsibility, it behoves us to defend the party leading the revolution in this Region.

There were various past and recent causes for the difficult,
hard conditions which the Arab homeland has experienced
since the setback, and the party's own conditions have played

a major role in these causes. In the light of the situation imposed by the setback, liberation has become the noblest and principal aim of this stage, and the armed struggle has become the axis of the party's policy in all fields. It was natural that views should differ on the means and methods to guarantee the best possible situation for confronting the occupation and aggression in our land. This has led to attitudes which differ in certain aspects from the attitudes of the political Command.

Those resolutions adopted by congresses convened after 23 February [1966] on building up the party and developing sound party relations have not been fully implemented. Furthermore, there has been a coordination between the implementation of the congresses' resolutions on domestic policy and the realization of the slogan 'Every citizen has his role in the battle' on the one hand, and major advances in building the material base of the revolution on the other. There has also been no coordination between the will of the revolution to build the ideological army and the provision of the means and the adoption of the practical steps necessary to achieve this.

In addition to a number of other factors, these circumstances have led to the appearance of the signs of a crisis which continued to develop to the point when some measures were adopted that led to a collision course. The crisis thus extended beyond the party framework to become a domestic and national crisis which affected both the Arab masses and leaders. Action to end this crisis in a manner ensuring party unity and the preservation of the revolution became a general domestic and national demand.

The party's bases, represented by the regional congress members, called for an extraordinary congress in accordance with the party's statutes. The Command agreed to call the congress for an extraordinary session which was attended by the representatives of the various popular organizations and some party organizations abroad. The meetings continued from 20 March to 31 March 1969. The reports submitted to the congress regarding the crisis and its causes, as well as ways of tackling it, were discussed. The congress discussions were comprehensive, objective, and within the framework of the domestic and national responsibility demanded by the present fateful stage.

Brother citizens, on the basis of the fateful circumstances facing the Arab nation, which dictate that the main aim of the Arab people in this stage should be the liberation of the land from the colonialist Zionist occupation and working for the unification of all the human, military, political and economic efforts and resources and placing them in the service of the armed struggle battle to achieve the aim of liberation; and out of the party's obligation to face its historic responsibilities towards the Arab revolution; the congress has adopted the following resolutions and recommendations: ...

In connexion with the battle. Everything we say, build and plan is in accordance with the logic of the current fateful battle in all its dimensions and requirements. This Region has had a clear policy towards the battle based on principle. The policy was drawn up by the former party congresses on the basis of the slogan 'Everything for the battle'. In addition to affirming the resolutions of the former congresses in this connexion, the congress has decided: (a) To complete popular mobilization in keeping with the new stage. (b) To stress the achievement of effective coordination between the Arab fronts.

In the field of Arab policy. The party has always believed that Arab unity and the battle in which the Arab nation is now engaged are two faces of the same fact, namely the Arab nation's awareness of its nationhood. Both are a living and practical expression of this awareness. Any step on the path to comprehensive unity gives support to the battle and is a step towards victory. Any victory we win in the battle will undoubtedly strengthen the Arab people's self-confidence and self-knowledge, and their ability to apply this knowledge in establishing unity.

In view of the fateful circumstances of the Arab homeland and the hostile plot against the Arab land and national existence, and on the strength of its absolute faith in the sound character of the Arab nation, the congress has recommended the following: (a) That all initiatives be taken to achieve any possible step towards unity with the progressive Arab states, to work in all circumstances to create an atmosphere for unity, and to produce with these states a unified policy for the present stage. (b) To continue the work to bring all Arab resources into the battle and to achieve a unified Arab military stand and provide the necessary atmosphere for this stand.

In the field of foreign policy. The congress views with satisfaction the fact that this Region has done everything necessary to strengthen relations with our friends, especially the Soviet Union and the states of the socialist camp, and to develop these relations to serve the battle of freedom and existence in which the Arab nation is engaged. Also, the congress expresses satisfaction that this Region has responded to France's ban on arms for Israel, and that the Region is willing to develop friendly relations with France and do everything necessary to encourage the just French policy concerning the aggression. The congress is gratified at this Region's firm stand towards all those states whose attitudes have proved them to be enemies of the Arab people and this people's legitimate aspirations to a free dignified life. These states include particularly the USA, Britain and Western Germany.

The congress has also viewed with satisfaction the great efforts by this Region in political struggle on the international level, including influencing world opinion – a political struggle which supports the armed struggle. The congress has decided to continue to work for implementation of the party congresses' resolutions on foreign affairs, stressing especially the party's strategy of faith in armed struggle, rejection of so-called peaceful solutions, and the determination of our attitude towards other states in the light of their policies on the Palestine issue.

In the party field. (a) All measures adopted because of the crisis shall be abolished and the Command shall restore the situation to normality immediately. (b) The regional congress denounces the exchanges of uncorroborated accusations which accompanied the crisis and enhanced it, and asks the Command to pay special attention to dealing with such a phenomenon, which threatens proper moral practices within the party. (c) The party bases called for a regional congress and the Command's response to this call has strengthened the party's organization principles and confirmed that the solution to any crisis within the party can only be achieved through its institutions.

Brother citizens, the concern for the forward march of the party and the revolution shown by friends throughout the world, many Arab brothers and honourable progressive and mass organizations in this country, and the responsible, mature attitude shown by all citizens throughout the crisis, have greatly impressed the party's bases and congress members. The party Command praises these friendly and fraternal attitudes and renews its pledge to perform all its commitments of struggle in domestic, Arab and international policies. The Command underlines the importance of complete expression, in both policies and actions, of the Arab people's historic determination to retrieve the usurped land and restore the disgraced dignity.

Long live the struggle of the Arab people against imperialism and Zionism! Long live the struggle of the Palestinian Arab people for the liberation of their usurped land! Glory and immortality to the martyrs of the resistance and *fedayeen* movements throughout the battlefields!

The Regional Command of the Ba'ath Party.

The Strategy of the War of Attrition

By Hassanain Haykal*

The coming stage of the struggle will be full of great and precious sacrifices. No matter how saddening or painful this may be, it is a destiny from which there can be no escape in view of several considerations arising from the battle fronts in the Arab–Israeli conflict:

1. ... In the Israeli view, supported so far by Britain and the USA, the present cease-fire lines provide an opportunity for

---

*Excerpts from articles published in *Al Ahram*, 27 March, 11 April, 25 April, 1969.

forcing the Arab nation to submit completely to a plan for domination of which Israel is only the spearhead. This view assumes that, placed as they are along the cease-fire lines, the Arabs are in no position to reject anything.

In the Arab view, supported by the USSR and understood by France, the present cease-fire lines are new burdens in an old crisis, a new more serious complication in an already dangerous situation, and such a complication twice compounded would be the last foundation on which any long or short-term solution can be based.

2. Israel believes that the present cease-fire lines will enable it to exert a dual-purpose pressure on Egypt, Syria and Jordan to secure the following:

(a) Recognition of the 1948 armistice lines as the international boundaries of Israel; (b) annexation of new areas, on the West Bank, the Golan Heights, and perhaps in the Egyptian Sinai desert as well where claims might exist but have not been made public yet.

In the face of this dual-purpose pressure, however, none of the three Arab states directly concerned can either : (a) make any bargains over its national territory under any pressure; ... once a state concedes part of its territory, it collapses and loses any justification for its continued existence; or (b) decide on anything inside the Palestinian territory, because the Palestinian people now speak for themselves and nobody has the right to speak on their behalf, particularly in matters affecting their land ...

3. There is a time bomb in the shape of the cease-fire lines. This is a dangerous situation for which the influence of the USA and of pro-Israeli world opinion are to blame more than anybody else . . . . It was inevitable that the cease-fire lines turned into a time-bomb, for the Arab states which accepted the cease-fire did so because they had no alternative and because they wanted to wait for the results of the efforts that might be made by the forces concerned with the peace of the area and the world. But the state of no alternative is liable to change and waiting has a limit.

The enemy has poured fuel on the fire. When the enemy felt

the Arab impatience growing at the cease-fire lines, he tried to prolong the situation by the only means he has : violence . . .

It is only natural for us to become impatient at the cease-fire lines. Likewise, the enemy's violence will increase, for this is his nature. Accordingly, we must expect that the enemy will increase his violence, extending it to the entire cease-fire lines and beyond them to any spot he can.

All this means that a different stage of confrontation will develop and will be full of great and precious sacrifices, as I have already said. We shall lose heroes. . . . We shall lose installations built with much sweat . . .

I was one of those who after the battles of 1967 wrote frankly that one of the advantages achieved by the enemy was his occupation of Sinai which had brought the Canal area within range of his guns. No matter how hard or painful this may be, the area installations must be considered exposed to danger. Undoubtedly, it is one of our prime duties to defend every wall against the enemy guns as long as this is possible. But the vulnerability of the areas to the enemy guns must not for one single moment prevent us from acting. Otherwise, the enemy would be successful in using the hostage as he had calculated from the start. In fact, this area has been in danger since the day it came within range of the enemy guns in June 1967. Whatever solution is achieved for the Middle East crisis – even if it is a peaceful or diplomatic solution – the enemy will most likely vent his wrath by pouring fire into this area before withdrawing from it.

The phase which prevailed for almost a year after the June battles could be described as the phase of calm along the cease-fire lines. It was a phase in which calm was the rule and impatience was the exception, expressing signs of the Arab rejection that has been suppressed by the state of waiting without alternative.

But for some months, the features of a new phase have been developing and have not taken clear shape. It is the phase of impatience along the cease-fire lines. It is a phase in which impatience is the rule and calm is the exception. This phase will grow every day because the enemy has only violence, and human experience has shown that violence does not extinguish fires but fans them, turning impatience into indignation, indignation into wrath, and wrath into an explosion. The enemy's losses during the growing phase of impatience will be great no matter how hard he tries to conceal or deny them. We shall benefit from this phase no matter how many heroes we lose in the battlefield, no matter how valuable the installations exposed to enemy fire on and away from the battlefield. I will only speak of some of the benefits and completely ignore the rest.

1. The enemy has exploited the shock the Arabs suffered following their defeat in the battles of June 1967 and the period of calm that followed, to unburden himself of the commitments of general mobilization which he could not endure for long because of his limited manpower resources ...

2. When the Arab resistance operations rose in intensity inside the occupied territory, the enemy employed a brigade of paratroopers to help the Nahal, police and intelligence forces. He also employed a squadron of helicopters, learning from the US experiences in Vietnam. Thus the enemy's burden was increased.

3. When the civil disobedience waves began against the enemy authority and later turned into bloody clashes in Gaza, Nablus, Hebron and Jerusalem, the enemy rushed to set up an electronic defence line to prevent the resistance men from entering the occupied territory. Thus, he was able to divert some of his forces to deal with the Palestinian cities which rose with pride and dignity against the enemy's authority and presence. The line, however, failed to achieve the desired aim and the enemy had to deploy part of his force in the occupied area surrounding Jerusalem.

4. When the artillery exchanges along the Suez Canal increased and Egyptian armed resistance patrols entered Sinai, as the Israeli delegate to the Security Council said, and fought battles near the Mitlah pass, the enemy immediately thought of setting up a defence line of steel installations along the east bank of the Canal. This led to more clashes and the Egyptian

artillery fire was so strong that it destroyed a large part of these installations and prevented the setting up of others. Israel then rushed to declare partial mobilization to reinforce its troops in Sinai. Thus, the size of the Israeli forces almost doubled, from one and a half divisions to almost three divisions.

5. With the continuation of the artillery operations along the Egyptian front and the pouring of troops into Sinai, Israel resorted to another method for dealing with the resistance organizations. It is called 'active pursuit' by aircraft . . .

6. The use of Israeli aircraft in such battles is likely to have several effects: (a) the aircraft will be in constant need of maintenance due to extensive use. (b) The aircraft will be continuously exposed to being shot down . . . (c) The Arab fighters will become accustomed to living under the threat of air strikes and to fighting this threat. This in itself will help to dispel the state of unjustified panic that had developed after the six-day battles. Furthermore, aircraft may be effective in strategic operations but in tactical operations, without the conditions of a comprehensive war, the effect will be limited, particularly on fighters who are helped by the nature of the ground on which they are fighting and by their training to protect themselves against air attacks.

7. When Israel increased its troop concentrations in Sinai, the Arab Sinai Organization began to play its most serious part, for this increase has provided it with more targets for more effective blows . . .

The new phase along the battle fronts has meant the following to us: (1) Loss of more heroes; (2) further exposure of our installations to danger; (3) the cease-fire line is proving to the world every day that it is a time bomb; (4) the growing belief of our masses in their right to self-defence and their power to practise it, despite the shackles imposed by the stage of waiting without alternative; and (5) preparation of our fighters for the battle so that they will not be taken by surprise as in June 1967.

To the enemy, the new phase has meant: (1) Increase in the

occupation costs; (2) loss of more blood; (3) exhaustion of more equipment; and (4) increase of economic burdens because of the confrontation.

The difference between us and the enemy is that whatever losses we suffer will not be high compared with our losses in June 1967, while anything the enemy loses will be great after its cheaply won victory in 1967 . . .

The Israeli enemy does not appear to be at his best these days. Usually our enemy is orderly and organized, but these days he appears confused and contradictory. There is a great deal of evidence of this. . . . Perhaps the most striking evidence of apparent confusion and contradiction can be summed up as follows:

1. So far the enemy has not taken an appropriate decision on the defence of his positions in Sinai. Will he adopt a static or mobile defence? Both methods have advantages and contain dangers. Static defence from reinforced positions would save him men and would not require him to increase his concentrations in the open desert. It would at the same time rob him of his best advantage: the capability of rapid movement . . .

2. When the recent fierce artillery battles began, the Israeli Defence Minister Gen. Moshe Dayan described them 'as a kind of fireworks – neither harmful nor beneficial'. Nevertheless, a few days later the Israeli Army began constructing what they later called the Bar Lev Line, after the Israeli Army Chief of Staff. It seems Bar Lev was once one of the leading proponents of the static defence method. The Bar Lev Line is composed of more than 100 reinforced concrete positions. . . . When the Egyptian artillery destroyed more than half of these fortified positions, the enemy rapidly increased his concentrations in the desert.

3. When the Egyptian forces advanced one step in their strategy of positive defence and launched combat patrol operations across the Canal to attack the Israeli positions and engage in face-to-face combat with the men and officers in those positions, the enemy's behaviour was a vivid example of his state of confusion and contradiction. The first operation was

carried out last Sunday night. The enemy kept it secret despite his losses. He did not expect Egypt to say anything about it because any such statement would be tantamount to an admission of violating the cease-fire line by crossing the Suez Canal. When the Egyptian military spokesman mentioned the operation in his daily statement about incidents on the fighting front, the enemy appeared surprised. The enemy restrained himself, and eighteen hours after the operation and three hours after the statement by the Egyptian military spokesman, he hastened to issue an admission of the operation. He tried however to minimize its significance.

When Monday night's operation followed, Israel was the first to issue a statement on it. Again Israel's statement was an attempt to minimize the significance of the operation. This attempt was reinforced by the statement of the UN Israeli delegate that instructions had been issued to him to lodge a complaint against Jordan to the President of the Security Council on operations of the 'saboteurs' – meaning the Palestine resistance organizations – but that Israel did not intend to lodge any complaint about operations by the Egyptian combat patrols, because those operations were so insignificant as to deserve no attention.

Nevertheless, at dawn on Tuesday the Israeli Air Force retaliated against an Egyptian radar unit which is on Jordanian territory in accordance with the requirements of the direct military coordination between the two countries and within the framework of the activities of the Eastern Command.... Even the Israeli retaliatory operation was not as well planned as usual. The Israeli raid on the Egyptian radar position near the town of Mazar in the Karak district did not take the Egyptian anti-aircraft artillery responsible for protecting the position by surprise, even though the attack took place at dawn. Radar equipment worth not more than $10,000 was destroyed, but Israel lost a Vautour and a Mirage worth not less than $10,000,000 ...

My purpose in this article is not merely to cite the evidence of the enemy's current state of confusion and contradiction.

This is only an introduction to my purpose. But there is one question that must be answered in connexion with this introduction before arriving at my main purpose. The question is: What is the explanation of this current state of the enemy?

The only explanation is that on most of the Arab fronts the enemy is facing something for which he is not prepared ...

On the Egyptian front, to be specific, the Israeli enemy imagined that any bullet fired on the Egyptian front would be 'a political bullet' intended either to bring pressure to bear on the great powers to convince them that the Middle East situation was about to explode, or to influence the Arab masses and convince them of the earnest intention to fight. Conceived in this frame of mind, Israel's assessments overlook the most important factor in the Arab stand on all the fighting fronts: the incentive of liberation. The enemy forgets that the picture changed fundamentally after 1967. Before then, the enemy claimed the Arabs were working to bring about his defeat. ... Since 1967, the enemy no longer accuses the Arabs of working to defeat him, although in fact their sole aim in life is now to bring about his defeat by any means. The enemy acquits the Arabs now not because he feels reassured about their intentions, but because he feels reassured about their present capabilities. Yet, the enemy forgets the incentive of liberation, which was not as strong before 1967. ... In view of this powerful incentive, the enemy should not make his calculations according to the traditional criteria, but on the basis of different factors that will definitely prove their effectiveness. ... After the introduction and the related question, the purpose of this article is to draw attention to a number of vital points at the present stage of the Arab–Israeli struggle.

1. The Israeli enemy will soon wake up from the confusion and contradiction that now afflict him. This is because he has many means, above all his military strength, which will enable him to recover his balance quickly. Military force will be the first means the enemy will use intensively to rid himself of the state of confusion and contradiction now afflicting him. This means that the enemy will strike violent blows so as at least

to regain the initiative and, if he can, to reduce the pent-up power of the Arab incentive of liberation which has gathered force since the setback ...

The Israelis planned their war with us in a modern, logical way which involved no miracles or near-miracles. But when they arrived to fight us, we were not really there. This was due to many factors – previously discussed by me – which imposed defeat without a fight on the Arab force. Acute anxiety prevailed in Israel before the decision was taken to enter the war on 5 June 1967. Israel's Grand Old Man Ben Gurion was against the risk. The former Premier Levi Eshkol was hesitant. Israel entered a war which the Arabs entered not with their strength but with their shortcomings. In fairness, and according to all sources of reference, it must be said that the units that had the opportunity to fight acquitted themselves well. The reasons for the Arab shortcomings were at a higher level than the sacrifices of those who fought. It will suffice to say that four fifths of the Egyptian force in Sinai did not have an opportunity to engage the enemy ...

The first thing, then, the enemy will use to recover his balance and rid himself of the state of confusion and contradiction that now afflicts him is his military strength. He will strike with it because it is the only weapon he has, and because the legend of its victory is the most precious thing he possesses. All this means that the enemy will strike and strike violently. He cannot recover his balance and regain the initiative unless he drives the Arabs back, at least psychologically, to their position at the end of the battles of June 1967.

2. No one should exaggerate in presenting the evidence of Israel's confusion and contradiction. This is not yet the end, nor even the beginning of the end. What is now taking place on the Arab fronts is closer to being the beginning of the beginning. The next part of the road will be rough beyond imagination. I can even say that the famous saying that we will wrest our territory from the enemy's occupation inch by inch is not a mere slogan but it is most probably what will actually happen, because we will fight on every inch of this land.

We must face the rough road with steady hearts and not

be swayed by joy one day because the enemy lost two or three aircraft, or because dozens of his soldiers fell to our guns, or because our fighting patrols hit his positions. We must, in return, expect unlimited losses in men and equipment on our side. If one day we give ourselves to tumultuous rejoicing, we may find ourselves in the grip of gloomy grief the next day. We must not let the days pass in this way – one very cold and another very hot ...

What I said about the need to put the brakes on feelings now may appear to be a call for people to become computers, devoid of sentiment. This is impossible, because it is inhuman. This is not exactly what I am asking. I am trying to avoid further human misfortune. ... It is usual for many to resort to hope to bridge the wide gap between reality and their desires. The danger is that such hopes may become daydreams. Daydreams may exceed capability and disable it. This will double the strength of any enemy strikes ...

Someone might contradict by asking: Why do I say this when we are moving along a road which we must follow to the end? The answer is: This is what should really be said at this time and in these circumstances. It is the nature of war to strike, to be prepared to be struck by the enemy without letting this be a surprise, and to be prepared at all times to give death to the enemy, and to take death from him. Such is the nature of war ...

To my mind there is one chief method which cannot be ignored or avoided in tipping the balance of fear and assurance in the Arab–Israeli conflict in favour of the Arabs. This course, which meets all the requirements and necessities and is in harmony with logic and nature – this main course to tip the balance in our favour, or merely precisely to adjust it, is: to inflict a clear defeat on the Israeli Army in battle, in one military battle.

I should like to be more specific because there is no room under present conditions for irresponsible talk. I would make the following points: (1) I am not speaking about the enemy's defeat in the war, but his defeat in a battle. There is still a long way to go before the enemy can be defeated in the war. The possibilities for this are still not within sight. But the enemy's defeat in one battle presupposes capabilities which could be available at an early stage in the long period before the end of the war. (2) I am not speaking of a battle on the scale of that of 5 June 1967 – a 5 June in reverse, with the Arabs taking the initiative and Israel taken by surprise. Most likely 5 June will not be repeated either in form or in effect. In the coming battle neither we nor the enemy will be taken by surprise. . . . I am speaking about a limited battle which would result in a clear victory for the Arabs and a clear defeat for Israel – naturally within the limits of that battle. (3) The requirements and necessities I am speaking about, and which will impose the military battle, do not include any marked consideration for the so-called revenge for injured Arab dignity . . .

To these three reservations regarding the battle, which I consider necessary and vital, I should like to add more, in the hope that they will give a clearer picture of what I am saying. (1) The current artillery exchanges along the Egyptian front are not the battle I am thinking of – the battle that I feel the requirements and necessities are imposing. What I am envisaging is far greater and broader. The artillery exchanges are important, indeed very important, but they are not the battle which can achieve the aim of inflicting a clear defeat on the Israeli Army. (2) Neither are the activities of the resistance organizations at their present level the battle I am thinking of or the battle imposed by the requirements and possibilities. . . . (3) In simple and general terms the battle I am speaking about . . . is one in which the Arab forces might, for example, destroy two or three Israeli Army divisions, annihilate between 10,000 and 20,000 Israeli soldiers, and force the Israeli Army to retreat from the positions it occupies to other positions, even if only a few kilometres back.

I am speaking, then, about a battle and not the war; about a battle that is limited as battles naturally are; about a real battle, however, resulting in a clear defeat for the Israeli Army. Such a limited battle would have unlimited effects on the war . . .

    1. It would destroy a myth which Israel is trying to implant

in the minds – the myth that the Israeli Army is invincible. Myths have great psychological effect ...

2. The Israeli Army is the backbone of Israeli society. We can say that the greatest achievement placed on record by the Arab resistance against Zionism – an achievement resulting from the simple act of refusal – has been to dispel the Zionist dreams. Because of the Arab refusal, Israel has become the society of a besieged stronghold – a military garrison society ...

3. Such a battle would reveal to the Israeli citizens a truth which would destroy the effects of the battles of June 1967. In the aftermath of these battles, Israeli society began to believe in the Israeli Army's ability to protect it. Once this belief is destroyed or shaken, once Israeli society begins to doubt its Army's ability to protect it, a series of reactions may set in with unpredictable consequences.

4. Furthermore, such a battle would shake the influence of the ruling military establishment. The establishment has the whip hand in directing and implementing Israeli policy on the excuse of acting as Israeli's sole protector and guardian of Zionist plans.

5. Such a battle would destroy the philosophy of Israeli strategy, which affirms the possibility of 'imposing peace' on the Arabs. Imposing peace is, in fact, a false expression which actually means 'waging war'.

6. Such a battle and its consequences would cause the USA to change its policy towards the Middle East crisis in particular, and towards the Middle East after the crisis in general.

There are two clear features of US policy. One which concerns the Middle East crisis is that the USA is not in a hurry to help in finding a solution to the crisis. No matter how serious or complicated the situation may become, the USA will continue to move slowly as long as Israel is militarily in a stronger position. The situation would surely change once the Israel position of strength was shaken.

The other phenomenon concerns the Middle East after its present crisis. It is that the USA sees in Israel an instrument for attaining its aims in the area. No matter how far the Arabs go in their revolt against the US influence and how much they defy this influence, the US aims are guaranteed as long as Israel remains capable of intimidating the Arabs. If Israel's ability to intimidate becomes doubtful, US policy will have to seek another course. Israel has proved to the USA that for the time being it is more useful to it than the Arabs. Although all the US interests in the Middle East lie with the Arabs, the USA continues to support Israel. The strange contradiction in the Middle East at present is that the USA is protecting its interests in the Arab world by supporting Israel. Israel is thus the gun pointed at the Arabs, the gun which the USA is brandishing to attain its aims and protect its interests ...

After all this, the question remains : is such a battle possible? The answer is : I do not claim military experience, yet I say that there is no doubt or suspicion as to the possibilities of such a battle which could inflict defeat on the Israeli Army. My belief is based on the following considerations:

1. The only myths in the Israeli system are those fabricated by bold and daring propaganda or by great imagination. Israeli society is not a straw as some believe, nor a rock as others imagine. ... Israeli society cannot live independently. It is a society which cannot produce any genuine economic or political force. What matters most is the intrinsic force and not the apparent force, which is deceptive in most cases. Myths that are based on apparent force are bound to be dispelled by experience, especially if met by a capable force.

2. Israel has lost its once-in-a-lifetime opportunity. After 5 June 1967 its myth acquired all the elements it needed. Yet Israel could not attain its goal of turning the end of the battle into the end of the war. Arab steadfastness proved that the battle has ended but the war will continue. Thus Israel has lost its opportunity.

3. In any future battle, the Israeli Army would fight under conditions different from those in all previous battles. The Israeli Army would not be able to advance easily from its present positions along the Jordan river, the Suez Canal and the Golan Heights without finding itself passing through densely populated Arab areas, with the danger that these would absorb

all its striking forces, exhaust it and make it easy to pounce on the Israeli Army's scattered remains one by one. With the exception of the Air Force effort, the Israeli Army would have to fight a sustained battle or a defensive battle, whereas it is accustomed to fighting offensive battles with its characteristic tactics of indirect approach and fast outflanking movements. The Israeli lines of communication between the bases and the fronts have become long and arduous, especially in times of operations. As a result of the long lines of communication it would be impossible for the Israeli Army to move quickly on the Arab fronts as it did in the past when it was able to strike on one front and then switch its forces by its short lines of communication to strike at another Arab front . . .

4. In any future battle the Israeli Army would face Arab armies with different standards of firepower and its use, different command structures benefiting from past experience, and a higher morale, as the Arab forces would be aware of fighting for the heart of their homeland and not only for its borders.

At the beginning of my article I said that a battle ending in a clear defeat for the Israeli Army should be the chief method of tipping the balance of fear and assurance. . . . I did not say it is the only method because there are other secondary methods. . . . I will give the following examples in this respect.

1. Our acceptance of the Security Council resolution on the Middle East – the resolution which international society has endorsed – is a valuable step, particularly since Israel has rejected the resolution and thereby defied the whole of international society. Despite Israel's daily proclaimed disrespect for the international organization, the question is not so simple. I mean that the Israeli citizens' awareness of being at odds with the entire world will undoubtedly influence their mood, and so affect the balance of fear and assurance in the Arab–Israeli conflict.

2. The Soviet Union's support for the Arabs and its continued help to them in rebuilding their military forces after the tragedy of June 1967 will undoubtedly affect the feelings of the Israeli people in the balance of fear and assurance.

3. France's stand cannot fail to affect the balance of fear and assurance for the Israeli inhabitants who realize that the greater part of their military power in 1967 came from France and that – from 1954 to 1964 at least – France was an ally of Israel joined by special ties.

4. The current four-power talks in New York arouse Israel's suspicions, to say the least, because they indicate clearly that the Middle East crisis cannot for long remain confined to the Middle East and that it might lead to a nuclear confrontation between the great powers. The talks may produce a solution to the problem which – to put it at its lowest – will fail to give Israel everything it feels to be within its reach. Irrespective of their results and what the Arabs think of these results, the talks will play their part in affecting the balance of fear and assurance in the Israeli people's feelings.

I expect Israel will take this article and submit a copy of it to the Security Council, as it has done in the past, saying : Look, they admit that the battle is the only course and that the political attempts are only secondary courses paving the way for the chief method. Taking all the Israeli attempts into consideration, and we must admit its tireless activities, I should like to say : Our aim is to eliminate the aggression. How we wish that all the secondary methods might lead to the attaining of that aim! Facts and evidence keep reminding us that what has to be done must be done.

Returning to Palestine

By Ahmed Baha ed-Dine

The withdrawal of the forces of aggression behind the frontiers of 5 June 1967 is undoubtedly the logical slogan, conforming with the phase through which we are passing at this time. It denotes the scope of the 'first indispensable step' which has to be taken before we can even contemplate going on to the next stages. *Nevertheless, it would be an error to imagine that 'the elimination of the consequences of aggression' implies the restoration of the exact same situation in the Arab world as existed prior to the aggression.*

Many situations will change and many ideas and methods will be modified.

We should also now be thinking of what ought to change – in particular with regard to the Palestinian problem itself.

The most elementary lesson we can draw from the defeat is to ask ourselves the following question: Have the ways we have been following up to now in order to try to solve the Palestinian problem been adequate or should we be thinking of other means and new methods ... with a view to fully restoring the rights of the Arabs?

The conditions which existed in the Arab world from 1948 to 1967 fossilized the Arab position towards the Palestinian problem. For close to twenty years, the Arabs have obtained no other result than a verbal 'rejection' of the state of affairs created in 1948. Now that this 'frozen' situation has been thawed by Israeli aggression, we find ourselves facing a new situation that can be moulded anew.

At this time, news is reaching us concerning the heroic Palestinian resistance put up in the occupied territory – a resistance which is the only serious step imaginable prior to realizing and consolidating our aims. Consequently we must draw the most important lesson of our defeat from that reality.

Before we envisage the possibility of different circumstances, of leaving our defence trenches in order to tackle the Palestine problem anew, we must admit that the simplest and most important line of 'defence' against Israel would be, in the first place, for *Palestine to become a reality.*

The Zionist invasion of 1948 succeeded in tearing away one part of Palestine, while we Arabs, instead of preserving what was left to us of that country, and seeing to it that it was made monolithic, firm and able to demand its rights, set about dismembering that part of the territory of Palestine which we controlled.

The Zionist invasion of 1948 set out to gather together Jewish

immigrants and refugees from all over the world and to transform them into active citizens – farmers, artisans and fighters;
while the Arabs reconciled themselves to the Palestinian citizens being transformed into emigrants and refugees.

In the course of the years, the idea of creating a Palestinian
entity and a Palestinian organization took form and began to
develop. It is thus that the Palestinian (Liberation) Organization
came into being, although it lacked one of the most important
conditions enabling it to speak on behalf of the people and the
homeland; namely, the territory. Yet, this territory, though reduced, did exist. The Palestinian 'struggle' was consequently
directed from Cairo, Beirut and every other Arab country –
but not Palestine.

This state of affairs gave the world the feeling that Palestine
no longer existed; that there was no real Palestinian people lay-
ing claim to its own territory; that it was merely a case of the
neighbouring Arab states putting up a resistance to another state
named Israel.

Somewhat similar situations – but with innumerable variants
and nuances – have been imposed on some other countries by
international and colonialist circumstances. In this way Korea
was divided into two sides, each side claiming to represent the
country's only authentic state; but neither did away with itself
because the colonialists were occupying the other state. In Vietnam, foreign forces imposed divisions upon the country, recognizing the victory of the national revolution in North Vietnam
and preserving a colonialist base in the South. But the ampu-
tated nation which did not succeed in having its own right
triumph fully – instead of knuckling under, mustered its strength
and turned itself into a base for the liberation of its usurped,
colonized nation.

What should we do, as a result?

It is clear that the indispensable point of departure, which
must be examined and organized immediately, is the re-establishment of a state called Palestine. This state would include
Jordan – consisting of the west and the east bank of the Jordan
– and the Gaza sector. In other words, it would comprise the

remaining parts of Palestine, to which would be added the area which was Transjordan and which has become integrated with Palestine in the course of the years. It might be argued that this proposal would change nothing and simply suggest a change of name. Our reply to this is that any political initiative may confine itself to titles and be void of substance, but may equally, by persevering action, bring about a radical change and assume a new substance.

Only the restoration of the name, 'Palestine', could have a major psychological – and subsequently political – influence on the world, and affect the future of this problem. The authentic name of the country would be reborn; the Palestinian state, of which one part was usurped, would rise up solidly along the front line against the usurper and claim its legitimate rights.

The re-establishment of the name of Palestine on Palestinian soil should be accompanied by the return of the Palestinian people to the soil of Palestine.

What actually has happened during the past nineteen years to the Palestinian people, with the exception of those who stayed in their own homes on the west bank of the Jordan?

The Palestinian faced the following dilemma: either to become a powerless refugee living in tents, or to become an ex-Palestinian emigrant in some other part of the world – Canada, Latin America or one of the Arab countries from Algeria to the West to Kuwait in the East.

Who emigrated? The most capable, competent and gifted of Palestine's sons. Those who had succeeded in their careers as businessmen, engineers, doctors, economists and journalists. The élite among these competent and intelligent people had no other path open before them than emigration, than working outside Palestine and choosing some other nationality than the Palestinian. Only those who had left families in their country of origin kept up any ties with Palestine, while the others detached themselves from it completely. Thus, at the very same time that Israel was knocking at every door to attract Jews from Yemen, from Europe and the Maghreb in order to transform them into citizens and thereby enhance the density of her own population and her demographic and social solidity, the Arabs, for their part, were allowing the Palestinian entity, as a demographic reality and as a civilization, to disintegrate, to disperse and gradually to lose its most precious asset: its human resources.

The restoration of the name of the Palestinian state would of course be of no value as long as it was not accompanied by real action aimed at turning the tide of emigration and dispersion into to one of return and regrouping. Before talking of 'returning' to occupied Palestinian territory, we must achieve the return to the territory where Palestinians are still living. The Arab bulwark deployed to face Israel cannot be composed of a desert zone of refugee camps and of a society becoming more depleted from day to day. On the contrary, it should be supported by a society that is economically, socially, politically and therefore militarily, powerful.

A different kind of life must be launched in Palestine – a life that could absorb the capacities of its people, that would not encourage them to emigrate but instead would attract former emigrants to return to their country. Though it is true that such a new life is an expression of the duty of patriotism and the wish to solve the Palestine problem, it is no less true that Palestine must make it possible for all to work there, to live, to advance and to develop in that country.

Our call for a return to Palestine is not a marginal or secondary problem. Despite the current international and political interest surrounding the Palestinian problem it is indispensable that a Palestine exist. Palestine, which is the principal party to this problem, must affirm its presence, demonstrate that it exists, and prove that its existence is real and meaningful. It must express its claims and exert continuing pressure. It was precisely the feeling of the importance of this factor that undoubtedly prompted the Summit Conferences to create a Palestinian entity represented by the Palestine Liberation Organization. What was it, however, that caused that organization to fail and what was its weak point? The factor which proved fatal to the organization was the lack of a territory, and of a people attached to that territory. Its existence was more fragile than that of the Jewish Agency before the creation of the state of Israel. In fact, the Jewish Agency and even the Zionist Movement itself only owe their effectiveness to the fact that they were attached to a territory, to their concentration on Palestinian territory, through the agricultural settlements, the towns and the population centres which they controlled.

The call for a return is not a subsidiary problem. The human factor is the decisive one in this national struggle, the bitter struggle which sets noble national destinies against those of an invading people that is seeking to create a new nationalism. In the final instance, it is the human factor which will prove decisive, and above all it will be the Palestinian human factor, aided and supported by the Arab human factor as its strategic extension. The Palestinian human factor does not depend only on quantity but also on quality; as much in the sphere of education as of skills, productivity and the country's economic, political, social and military institutions.

It is of little importance, after all, what the regime of the country will be: whether it will be a monarchy or something else. The homeland is greater than the regime in power. People may disagree regarding the regime, with all that this implies, but there can be no disagreement concerning the national homeland itself. No one makes it a pre-condition that the regime of his country be according to his own tastes before thinking of living, working and fighting there. The Palestinian's feelings concerning the return to the country and the Palestinian cause, his struggle and activities, should be no less strong than that of the Jew who emigrates from the other end of the earth to a country he has never seen, which he does not know and whose language he does not even speak. Undoubtedly, the Palestinian attachment is no less powerful than that attraction.

Let the Palestinian of today – of Lebanese, Kuwaiti or Argentinian nationality – be able to benefit solely from his Palestinian nationality. The Palestinians must be in Palestine if Palestine is to belong to the Palestinians.

Those who are ready to sacrifice their lives today fighting in the occupied territories under extremely difficult conditions

show that they are tackling the problem in a sound manner and
that their way is perfectly feasible.

The proposal, however, raises a delicate and sensitive point –
of the Palestinian refugees. And here I refer to those living in
the camps situated around Israel's frontiers in Gaza, Syria,
Lebanon and Jordan. Since 1948, that is, for the past twenty
years, approximately one million Palestinians have been living
in tents in the refugee camps supported by international welfare
organizations. Their circumstances are such that they cannot
lead any sort of civilized lives; they are not cultivating the land,
they are not working and they are not learning properly.

They are living in tents because they constitute the main contingent of those who were literally driven off their land and
out of their dwellings. Their kind of life symbolizes to them the
determination of the Palestinian people to reoccupy their
homes, or at least to apply the resolutions successively adopted
by the United Nations in their favour. No one wants to eliminate the refugee problem either by abandoning their right to
return or by diverting them from claiming that right. The
following question arises, however: should this large mass of
Palestinian people, after twenty years of living in tents, continue
to live in these same tents for a further period, whose duration
no one knows?

I believe that to be impossible, unjust to the refugees and
without any purpose.

In this comprehensive proposal I have put forward for the
renaissance of 'the Palestinian state', I don't have any precise
answers to this question. But, nevertheless, I can define the objective and refer it to the writers, the experts, the thinkers and
the politicians to discuss the ways it could be fulfilled.

The aim is a double one:

1. To reform the life of that dispersed mass of human beings
on the land of Palestine which we control. These people should,
upon Palestinian soil, transform themselves into a powerful,
enlightened, advanced and productive society, that will promote its agriculture and arm itself. A kind of 'powerful clim
ate' along the front line with Israel could be created. Finally

this human mass will no longer find itself behind barriers of infirmity, illiteracy, incapacity and stunted development ;

2. To prevent any action liable to put an end to their right to return or in any way to undermine their cause.

I do not believe that this is impossible to achieve.

It is exceedingly important not to liquidate their problem since it is the spearhead of the entire Palestinian affair as a whole. But it is equally important for the refugees to become an efficient and influential force so that they may become a Palestinian Arab power. Let us recall once more that the Jews also constructed camps for the refugees they took in, but in these camps they worked, they trained for jobs, they lived and produced.

This is the proposal I am putting forward.

I will allow myself to return to one point. The problem of settling the land, of forming an attachment to it and of turning it into a powerful base, may appear to be of secondary importance, not pointing to a clear and rapid solution. But then, there are no easy, decisive, and rapid solutions for any of the world's really great problems. Nevertheless, in the course of time a new influential and unalterable situation can be created through initiatives, decisions and actions.

Israel is keenly aware of this problem; that is why she has always based her actions accordingly. Therefore, right after seizing any parcel of land she sets out to establish a settlement there. That is – a populated, productive fighting unit organically attached to the soil; in other words, it sets out rapidly to create a new demographic, geographic and political reality.

This is how the Israelis have been acting for almost a century, ever since the first Jewish immigrants began to arrive in Palestine. And that is how they acted only a few days ago when they began to set up new settlements near Jerusalem.

Two Years Later

By Abba Eban*

'He who does not remember the past is doomed to repeat it'
– Santayana

It was both an end and a beginning. The end was of the Israeli decade between the Sinai Campaign and the Six Day War. In all Jewish history there are probably no ten consecutive years of richer achievement. They were restless times – spirited, inventive, turbulent, with energy shooting off in all directions. As they rolled on, Israel seemed to lose its earlier vulnerability; the national structure took on a solid look. The population had risen sharply and the rate of economic expansion had few parallels anywhere. Israel's agriculture knew many triumphs; indeed, its talent for profusion stirred the hope of other nations in a famine-stricken world. The industrial apparatus also became more elaborate and diverse. Many in the world drew confidence from the fact that a small people could, by exertion and example, rise to respected levels in social progress, democratic vitality, scientific research and the humane arts. Israel's flag flew in a hundred capitals – and with special pride in those places where formal diplomacy was enhanced by a practical role in development. It was clear that the official Arab view of Israel as a dark conspiracy, a rapacious colonial adventure or a transient crusade had been rejected by the opinion and sentiment of mankind. Much in Israel was still imperfect, lacking outer form and inner harmony. But by 1967 there was an air of permanence. And the Defence Forces, at their highest pitch of ardour and efficiency, were the shield of all that had been patiently accumulated in the pioneering decades.

History works not in logic or precision but in irony. It was Israel's very stability that brought about the disruption of the Middle Eastern security system. For as Arab leaders watched the course of events they must have been seized by an urgent

*Reprinted with special permission from the *Jerusalem Post* magazine, 6 June 1969.

sense of 'now or never'. Unless the hated 'reality' were challenged at once might it not soon be too strong ever to be uprooted? The haunting question-mark over Israel's existence was beginning to fade away. It seemed that peace might grow out of the sheer habit and attrition of established conditions growing daily more entrenched. It was therefore in a mood of desperation that the summit conferences improvised their policies for keeping peace at bay. They could still rely on two elements to work a disruptive course, even when the military balance seemed to discourage confrontation. Terrorist attacks with their irredentist ideology would keep the wounds open and the fever high; and Soviet policy gave militant Arab nationalism a strong incentive for not regarding anything as finally settled. It was getting late – but there was still a gambler's chance.

The dice were thrown at Bir Gafgafa on 22 May 1967. In that unforgotten speech Nasser spoke his resolve to have his victory against Israel – 'with or without war'. In any case the 'hopes and assumptions' of 1957 together with the agreements of 1949 were swept away, leaving Arab–Israel relations in a juridical vacuum which is still unfilled.

The armistice epoch is now the possession of history and nothing of it can ever be revived. We are more aware of how the two decades ended than of what had been enacted before the end. The fact that a chapter of history is concluded does not mean that it leaves no lessons behind. What Israel achieved in resistance, development, growth and self-expression in her first twenty years stand before us to be analysed and understood.

Those achievements sprang from a highly condensed vitality. They were the work of a close-knit community with a strong internal solidarity, whose culture, social ideals, historic memories and national identity were held uniquely to itself, undiluted by anything outside which could weaken their primary force. There was, above all, a Jewish power of decision about how things should be fashioned and what levels should be attained. There was no major dispersion of energies. The burdens of Jewish destiny were, in all truth, heavy enough; but there

was no illusion that we could carry them on shoulders addition-
ally laden with other burdens outside the Jewish scope. The
diversities in Jewish society were tense; at one stage they
seemed to hold the nation's union in jeopardy. But they were
never aggravated by an attempt to cope with a million Arab
'problems' in conditions of revolt. Everything in Israel's
achievement for twenty years was owed to its Jewish character.
The institutional pattern, the economic structure, the social
fabric, the intellectual and technological momentum, the historic pride, the spiritual vision, the ardent loyalties, and, by virtue of these, the capacity of defence, were all made possible
by an atomically compressed Jewish vitality. Israel was strong
because she governed herself – and herself alone. It was a victorious exercise in self-determination with full knowledge that
in the 1960s the capacity to determine oneself excludes the
capacity to determine others.

The eruption of energies in Israel's first two decades had
been made possible by the political decisions of the period following the Second World War. There was a lucid choice in favour of exercising a power of Jewish decision and creativity
within a broad but limited area, rather than of having access
to a broader area in which, however, a Jewish power of decision and creativity would at best be diluted and at worst flooded
out of existence. Our territorial conceptions were closely related to the need for immediate statehood and the unconditional
conservation of Jewish identity. We therefore sought the most
spacious and secure house of which we could realistically expect to be the masters. We refused to elevate the size of the
house above the need for mastery of it. Thus the exigencies of
space and security were brought into harmony with the national, cultural and social ends which lay at the root of our
destiny. An adequate geography was one part of our statehood;
the other part, no less decisive, was the particular human cohesion which we were striving to re-assert.

It is only recently that we have noticed a tendency to regard
our country's territorial configuration as a lonely and supreme
criterion, ignoring the parallel problems of its human composition, its spiritual ethos, its Jewish singularity, and its poignan

but undying passion for peace. We have even lived to see an article in a Hebrew newspaper extolling the virtues of colonialism; pointing out that this manly pursuit has admittedly dwindled in Europe but now enjoys a lease of life in Mongolia, Tibet and Sinkiang, and hinting as broadly as possible that Israel's 'manifest destiny' may be at hand, while her belated part of the white man's burden remains to be fulfilled under the guise of restoring Zion. The writer's conclusion is that a nation's 'provincial confinement of space does injury to the universal human conception'! ('Colonization is at its Height': E. Livneh *Ha'aretz*, 3 June 1969). One could leave this absurdity in its place as evidence of a shallow pseudo-intellectualism. The point is that it could not have been written or published a few years ago except by a professional humorist with a gift for parody. It illustrates the derangement that we shall incur if our territorial and security conceptions are isolated from the broader framework of national purpose.

What we have to change are the political, juridical and territorial conditions which created Israel's danger – not the intense Jewish cohesion which enabled her to surmount it.

The infirmities which brought the collapse of the armistice system will rise to the surface of our memory whenever the first days of June come around. It is not necessary for Israelis to use many words to recall to one another the full horror which loomed before us two years ago. There are sounds and visions which will never leave us: the 250,000 Arab soldiers crushing us into a corner from south, and north, and east; the 15,000 tanks with spearheads a few hours, sometimes a few minutes, from our homes; the neighbouring airfields with their load of death designed for precisely determined targets; the careful labour of eight decades about to be engulfed in a kind of Mongol massacre; the piratical blockade which cut us off from half the world, and choked the passage through which 90 per cent of our vital fuel came; the exultant voices on the air waves proclaiming war and announcing our destruction; the operation orders in Arab army headquarters describing how our men, women and children were to be torn to bits; the frenzied mobs in Arab streets, exultant with the imminent prospect of blood and spoils; and the cool, wicked voices across the southern frontier, calmly declaring that Israel's destruction was at hand.

Does anyone expect us to forget that picture? It is the point of reference for everything that we now do and say. Our policy can be simply phrased: never to return to the political anarchy and territorial vulnerability from which we have emerged. For the dangers that faced us were felt by Israel, and by much of the world opinion, against a special background of Jewish memories. Dark recollections crowd in upon us whenever we think about the implication of defeat. The issue was not only military occupation but physical massacre. After all, much in Jewish history is too terrible to be believed; but nothing is too terrible to have happened. Thus with the reaction on 5 June, our history celebrated one of its sharpest transitions.

The moment will linger and shine in the national memory for ever, the unforgettable hour of truth that will move Israel to its ultimate generation.

When we set out for the international arena on the morrow of the war, the national decision was not to manoeuvre tactically, but to take a stand on principle. We would identify the factors which had brought about the collapse of the armistice regime; and from the diagnosis the remedy would flow in total consistency.

First, the pre-1967 situation was fragile and eccentric in its juridical and political structure. The 1949 agreements and the 'hopes and expectations' of 1957 were temporary and hedged in with every kind of political reservation. They did not commit their Arab signatories to the ideological necessity of proclaiming the end of the conflict. And since the 1957 arrangements were announced in a way that liberated Egypt from responsibility, Cairo's honour and permanent interest were never engaged.

It follows that the new peace settlement must be expressed in normal ties which leave no room for doubt that the signa tories are totally committed to each other's sovereignty. The conception of negotiated peace treaties is mainly important fo:

its effect on Arab ideologies. These are often more decisive than Arab facts. The form and content of the peace must be such as would require Egyptian and Jordanian leaders, on the morrow of signature, to begin the long, hard process of detoxification. They would have to tell their people that a great historic conflict is now resolved, and that Arab nationalism is reconciled to a sovereign and distinctly Jewish state, as part of the history, the reality and the destiny of the Middle East. There is no reason why they should say this about any 'arrangement' that is not freely negotiated and contractually signed.

Second, a peace negotiation must provide an opportunity for determining agreed and secure boundaries. Prime Minister Golda Meir has pointed out that if the boundaries are to be agreed, they cannot be identical with the present cease-fire lines. If we add her vehement opposition, and that of her predecessor, to the idea of a State of Israel in which the power of Jewish majority and decision is not eternally and totally assured, we get a picture of the degree in which the territorial problem is still open. It is not true that Israel's security could rest exclusively on the nature of the peace and need not have any topographical or territorial implications. The 4 June lines were never agreed as final boundaries, as is clear from the relevant provisions of the 1949 agreements. But no less decisive is the fact that they were not 'secure boundaries', as the events of May–June 1967 dramatically proved. A secure boundary for Israel is one that can be defended without the agonizing need of pre-emptive action. The previous lines, with their topographical disadvantage in the north, the south-west and the east, involved such comprehensive Arab proximity to every settled area and population of Israel that whenever a tripartite Arab concentration was concerted, Israel's choice was to await the slaughter or to strike at the concentrations of Arab air and armour before they could be brought to action against her. Moreover, the ability to cut off Israel's water in the north and to obstruct southern maritime passage gave Arab states the convenient opportunity of creating situations which would lay the tactical military initiative on Israel's shoulders. There is, of course, little to be said for the doctrine which I heard in Paris on 24 May 1967: 'The aggressor is he who shoots the first bullet.' The nature of aggression is far more lucidly illuminated by the French historian Taine a century ago. He said, simply: 'The aggressor is he who makes war inevitable.' There is an uncanny link between this definition and the statements of Nasser and Haykal in the last week of May announcing: 'We have made it inevitable for Israel either to be choked to death or to be smashed in an attempt to overcome our military concentrations.' Since the echoes of Arab hostility will not soon die away and Arab preponderance of land and population is inexorable, Israel's right to defensible boundaries is a dictate not only of national survival, but of deep international interest.

Third, mankind learned a stark lesson in May–June 1967 about the inherent fragility of the external factors on which Israel was sometimes urged to rely for her security. It is possible that the startling weakness of deterrent guarantees and of the United Nations peace-keeping role has significance across the whole range of international life. For Israel the message rings out clear and loud. The powers recoiled from the exercise of their commitments, some in direct flight, others after sincere but impotent attempts to honour that which they had promised a decade ago. In the UN's role, the salient fact is not the instant withdrawal of UN troops to make Sinai safe for belligerency. Far more significant is the fiasco staged in the Security Council between 24 May and 3 June. With all the elements of a war looming before it, the Council heard several of its members reflect on whether they should have been summoned from their vacation resorts at all. Eventually, there was a fragmented debate of such impotence and frivolity as to mock Israel's peril and the hopes invested by small nations in a dream of an international security system. Even a mild call to Egypt to abstain temporarily from the exercise of blockade lay beyond the Security Council's will and power. In the history of international institutions there is no more disturbing a document than the record of the Security Council's proceedings during the two weeks before hostilities began. International apathy comes a close second to Arab belligerence and Soviet incitement amongst the parent causes of the June 1967 war. The factors which make for great power disengagement and for the debility of the UN peace-keeping function have not changed in the past two years. Accordingly, the peace that we seek must rest for its sanction and fulfilment not on the illusory prospect of external intervention but on equilibrium of power and rights in the Middle East itself. Peace treaties, secure boundaries and a locally guaranteed peace structure are nothing but the corollary of the 1967 war.

In order to have time and opportunity for expounding these three principles it was first necessary to achieve a defensive success. The fear and likelihood were that international pressures would again compel us to surrender our security assets without opportunity to translate them into permanent peace. I recall the traumatic conviction with which much of Israeli opinion expected this result. There was more at work here than a national tendency, fed by experience, to expect disaster at every stage of the road. The fear that we should face a call for withdrawal without peace was nourished by strong rationality. First there was the memory of 1956–7. Then there was the general bias in recent international relations to accompany cease-fires with an immediate return to the point from which the conflict had erupted. Finally there was the sheer weight and strength of the forces arrayed against us. The Arab world exceeds Israel in every attribute of strength except in military power. It surpasses us in area, population, the multiplicity of representation in international organs, the influence derived from oil and the sheer strategic weight of a sub-continental expanse. All this would be formidable enough even if it were not enhanced by a blind identification of the Soviet world with whatever Arab nationalism chooses to say. In Arabic literature and journalism, I discern a stunned astonishment at the failure to translate this superiority into an effective lever for Israel's removal from the cease-fire lines.

So much is said and written in sensitive reaction to criticism of Israel's posture that our nation has lost awareness of a fundamental success in its diplomatic and information struggle. Our central political and juridical principles are widely supported and little contested. From the moment that the Security Council refused, for the first time since the end of the Second World War, to accompany a cease-fire with a request for withdrawal to previous lines, we have seen a steady reinforcement of certain basic political attitudes. That there can be no withdrawal of forces from cease-fire lines, except on the establishment of peace; that this peace must directly and formally engage the honour and interest of Arab states; that in due time there must be direct negotiation and formal signature; and that the Middle East must at last have secure and recognized boundaries which are not identical with previous armistice or cease-fire lines – all these ideas are not isolated Israeli obsessions. They represent a central current in international thought. To be exhorted by governments and peoples across the world not to move without peace has been for me an impressive experience, in comparison with the contrary doctrine to which we had to listen eleven years ago.

Our dialogue with the United States, however frank in acknowledgement of divergencies, must, in justice, include a recollection of America's pioneering role in advancing these ideas and clinging to them against heavy challenge. This role in turn would never have unfolded without the political phase which preceded the 5 June hostilities. On this point Ambassador Rabin has spoken with perception:

I should point out one outstanding achievement of the period of waiting. One of the factors in the delay was the political consideration. Israel gave a number of states time: firstly the US to prove that it was not possible – by political means – to prevent Egyptian belligerence. I do not mean a delay of 48–72 hours, but to a greater number of days. The discussions of the Security Council during that period proved that the UN was not capable of bringing about a change in the situation that had been created at that time. The efforts of the state that had guaranteed freedom of passage after the Sinai Campaign to implement their undertakings were unsuccessful.

This feeling of failure on the part of the free world exercised a great influence upon the resolute attitude to prevent the inclusion of the withdrawal of the Israel Defence Forces as part of the UN cease-fire decision.

The complete absence of the inclusion of the withdrawal as part of the cease-fire decision spared Israel difficult and severe political struggles. [Emphasis mine.]

It was the strength of the Israel Defence Forces alone that routed the Arab forces and established new defensive lines from Suez in the south, the Jordan in the east, and the Golan Heights in the north.

The political result of the waiting was one of the factors that made it possible to continue to maintain these defence lines as long as the Arab states are not prepared for peace. Today, among other factors, because of the waiting, we are capable of maintaining the best defensive lines for Israel that could have been sketched in the Middle East, without any decision or pressure for withdrawal. and with many states, headed by the US, prepared to continue to assist us and increase the arming of Israel. [Emphasis mine.] Address in Tel Aviv, 3 March 1969.

We enter the third year of our political struggle with our political fortifications intact. It is a rare and unexpected achievement. It owes much to the unity and strength of the national will. It is fortified by a genuine belief that the Middle East is ripe for an adventure in innovation, and not for a repetition of past instabilities. And it is directly anchored in the decision of the Israel government, in June 1967, to define peace and security as its central goals, to which all other issues including territorial changes would be strictly adapted. The result is that Israel's policy, in its major expression, has been at work within an international consensus.

It is not only that time has been gained and security preserved. The value of time lies in its potentiality of influence on the Arab mind. Our strategy is to convince the Arab governments that the ice will not thaw except under the warm wind of a direct, substantive, detailed dialogue on peace. They are still gripped by a nostalgic hope that a solution short of peace and mutual recognition will make its appearance from outside. The candidates for an externally fashioned solution change. The General Assembly, regular and special, the Security Council, and Ambassador Jarring have all done their work; and nothing on the ground is altered. The dream now focuses, unrealistically, on the hope that the four permanent members of the Security

Council do not mean what they say and will both formulate
and 'impose' a solution which will leave Arab governments
uncommitted to a final renunciation of conflict.

For many centuries it was a habit of the Middle East to have
its destiny fashioned outside itself. The real sources of interest
and decision lay far away. In the meantime, two parallel changes have come about. Local sources of choice and decision have
arisen through the transition of the Middle East from tutelage
to sovereignty. And the traditional factors which governed the
life of the region are in course of disengagement. There is nothing here for which anybody outside will risk his life and blood.
The Middle East is no longer a crossroad on the way to Eastern
empires. Its territory is not needed for bases now that seaborne
power holds the field. Oil seeks its markets so ardently as to
lose its capacity for pressure. And the centenary of the Suez
Canal finds it closed to traffic with no apocalyptic effect on the
world economy. Moreover, the powers are not in the police
mood of the fifties. When they say that they have no interest
or capacity to impose settlements there is every reason for taking them at their word.

Our business is to inculcate in the Arab heart a mood compounded of despair and hope : despair of changing the cease-
fire lines without peace – and hope that a peace negotiation
will bring Israel's interests into harmony with Arab security,
peace and honour. This involves something more than obdur-
acy in maintaining the cease-fire lines until peace. It also
requires that the ambition of peace should not lose its credibility; and that the pursuit of it should be constant, irrespective
of its actual prospect. Passive imagery such as that of 'waiting
for the telephone to ring' does not fit the problem itself. Nor
does it reflect the fact that, in Mr Allon's words, 'peace with
concessions is preferable to the present situation'. When all
comes to be written the world will be impressed by the range
and versatility of Israel's attempts to explore the possibility
of a free, unpredjudiced negotiation. These will not cease, and
will not be confined to any single channel of exploration. The
world community can help by respecting the autonomous responsibility of the governments at issue. This principle

was well stated by the Indian Foreign Minister five years ago:

> My final appeal is to realize that the differences between India and Pakistan can be solved only by those two countries; and that there is more chance of a settlement if there is no intervention by third parties. No superimposed solution will do any good.
>
> If the Council is interested in the maintenance of peace it should avoid any solution superimposed upon the two countries, or intervention in any talks or discussions we might have with each other.

Since Israel's responsibility is great there is much importance in the expression and formulation of its views. The balance between the maintenance of the cease-fire until peace and the willingness to change them when peace comes has been under challenge from the territorial fundamentalists within our gates. This challenge towers over all the other factors which have complicated Israel's posture in world opinion.

There is no doubt where the central current of Israeli policy lies. It was sketched clearly by Prime Minister Golda Meir when she said in the Knesset a few weeks ago: 'We have said: agreed boundaries. This is because we want peace. Every child knows that agreed boundaries are not the lines which we now hold.' More specifically, Defence Minister Dayan said to our party Secretariat: 'There is no serious opinion here which does not admit that in return for true peace we would pay a high price in territory. I have not heard any serious suggestion that we should make a million more Arabs Israeli citizens. On the contrary there is a general consensus that we should preserve the Jewishness of the state.' (14.11.68).

The view that peace includes territorial compromise and the maintenance of Israel's particular identity was not questioned during the early summer of 1967. There have since been attempts to evade this logic by appeals to historic emotion; and by the concept of a 'Palestinian' settlement leaving our present security positions intact. Both are illusory.

All my sentiment and conviction lead me to attach great weight to Israel's historic connexions with this land. If I have spoken little on this point, it is because of a reluctance to bring faith into the service of political controversy; there is nothing less edifying than the spectacle of politicians waving Bibles at each other. After many hours over many years spent in the contemplation of our historic experience I have publicly confessed my belief that 'it is impossible to understand and therefore to explain the current Jewish reality without a constant probing of ancient roots'.

The issue is not drawn between those who cherish and those who belittle the historic legacy. It lies between different interpretations of what that legacy means. There are those who have convinced themselves that Israel's gift to history lies in a special principle of cartography, without specifying exactly which map is to be sanctified. There are others of us who revere the associations which the soil yields up from the past to the present, but who deem the historic promise to include other balancing factors including peace ('Seek ye peace and pursue it') and the morality of neighbourliness. What passes my understanding are articles and speeches on historic rights which ignore the Hebrew ideal of peace and Jewish identity.

The Jewish mind has never conceived a more dynamic or transcendent notion than that of peace. To say, for example, that the soil of Jenin has meant more in Israel's history than the idea of international peace is to betray a grossly unhistoric bias. While Divine promise gives us a right to the Land of Israel, it does not inhibit us from a partial exercise of that right in the name of higher ends, such as peace and the preservation of our unique and particular peoplehood. To challenge the government's policy on historic grounds is not faith, but heresy – and ignorance. That is why the central current of Israeli opinion, with vast support in the Jewish world, has declined to foreclose the prospect of a negotiated peace, replacing ceasefire lines by agreed and improved territorial boundaries, ensuring an improved security and the maintenance of a Jewish power of decision and control. A state could not exist with nearly half of its own citizens opposed to its aims, alienated from its culture, and supported in their dissension by millions in neighbouring lands. Here we should listen to a lucid Arab voice. The words are of Cecil Hourani (*Encounter*, November 1967):

If the Israeli government accepts the Arabs within the territories she controls as full Israeli citizens, with equal civil and political rights, the concept of Israel which has hitherto been incorporated into her laws will have to be changed. Israel will no longer be a Jewish state. It will become a Jewish–Arab state in which nationality will be a function of residence or citizenship. Israel, in other words, as she has been since 1948, will no longer exist, and Palestine, with Arabs and Jews living together, will have been restored.

'Israel, in other words, will no longer exist.' This is the pathos of our history. There is a constant fight for identity, and, sometimes, a suicidal instinct for losing it by our own decision.

The only course is to promote an intimate link with the Palestinian Arabs without now closing the probability that they have a future separate from ours. Much can be done in the provision of services, livelihood, investment, economic stimulation, commerce and ordinary, plain human encounter. But this is no substitute for the larger vision of peace with the whole Arab world. We should pursue our work in the administered areas with rationality, with paternalism and in a clear understanding of the limitations inherent in the task. If they wish to develop a representative body within the law this should not be impeded. There is no value in gimmick analogies like that of Quebec. After all, Quebec does not consist of 10 million people surrounded by another 50 million of their compatriots, all of whom have been nourished in the belief that Canada of 20 millions beyond Quebec ought to be wiped out. The truth is that we have no escape from the uniqueness which we are here to assert and express. And as observers of the Palestinian scene we cannot forget that whenever the Palestinian Arabs have had a chance of proclaiming their separate identity they have preferred to merge their lot into a broader Arab context.

We shall do well to stay faithful to the policies, formulation and, above all, the moods of June 1967, even if public opinion has shifted to another emphasis. The business of democratic leadership is not to follow all stray movements of opinion, but to take the right decisions in the hope of winning public understanding of them, sooner or later. If a political leader decides to keep his ear permanently fixed to the ground, his posture will lack elegance and flexibility of movement.

The memory of June is war, but its inner meaning is peace. Peace will swallow everything – the war and its echoes; the graves that have been dug and the tears that have been shed because of them; the hatreds that have been raised, the wrongs that have been endured – and the inexpressible hopes that have been kindled.

A Soldier Reflects on Peace Hopes

By Moshe Dayan*

At this course, people learn how to make war. But on this occasion, if I may, I should like to discuss the other side of the picture – the question of peace between us and the Arabs, or, more precisely, the problematics of peace. In a brief address, obviously, it is impossible to treat the subject exhaustively, and I, at all events, am not capable of doing so. I shall therefore merely try to cast some light on the subject.

I have chosen Dr Arthur Ruppin as one personality who casts light on the subject. He came to Israel for the first time in 1907, was expelled 'forever' by the Turkish Governor Jemal Pasha, and came back to the country after the English conquest, this time really forever.

Two unique elements are involved, if we wish to present the problem through the eyes of Dr Ruppin. The first is the period in which he lived. From 1920 to 1942, Dr Ruppin was one of the architects of the Zionist venture, the 'father of Zionist settlement'. This was the inter-war era, a concentrated period of twenty successive years, whose distance from us lends itself to evaluation and review. At the same time, the period is not quite so distant that its links with the present day are severed. From this standpoint of distance on the one hand, and links on

---

*Text of an address by General M. Dayan to a graduating class at the Israel Army Staff and Command College (*Jerusalem Post*, 27 September 1968).

the other, it might perhaps be proper to pinpoint 1936 as the focal year of the period. This was the year of the riots, which raged thirty years before the Six Day War.

Not only was the period unique, but perhaps the man him self more so. Not the man as a typical representative of the period, but Dr Ruppin with his special qualities, which permitted him to see things with greater clarity, depth and honesty than many other men of his day.

Dr Ruppin was a humanist by nature, a man of conscience, and when he encountered the 'Arab question', he wanted to be persuaded that Zionism could be fulfilled without detriment to the Arabs of Palestine. In his education and schooling alike, he was a scientist and he studied things not only through their concrete expression, but also through the forecast of their future development and transformation. Above all, Ruppin was a man of action: 'For the Jews of Europe,' he wrote in his diary, 'Zionism is a religion, but for me it means action.' And in the 'Arab question', he did not look for appropriate formulas but for practical solutions. Moreover, since his life was utterly dedicated to Jewish settlement in Israel, he inevitably saw the 'Arab question' as it was reflected through settlement. The ground he had his feet on was Zionist fulfilment, and he was only prepared to turn his gaze towards what was capable of achievement, without quitting this basic posture.

I cannot conclude my remarks about Ruppin the man, without including a paragraph from Berl Katznelson's eulogy of him:

From generation to generation we see the thirty-six righteous men, whom we depict in the form of drawers of water, foresters or peasants. It would never occur to us to seek one of these thirty-six righteous men on some congress platform, in an office, in a university chair, or among public figures. I would not have used this figure of speech, had I considered it an exaggeration. Ruppin embodied unique characteristics which we associate solely with the thirty-six righteous men. He was modest without being self-effacing. He was not infected by the taint of power. Even the great publicity which he enjoyed from time to time in the course of his functions left him unspoiled.

I do not think it would be too outrageous of me to assume that most of the people here have not read the three volumes of Dr Arthur Ruppin's autobiography. I shall therefore permit myself, in the following, to quote relevant extracts from this diary of his.

Ruppin was put in charge of Zionist settlement in Israel in 1920, after the First World War. He obviously anticipated that, with the collapse of the Ottoman Empire, the wave of national liberation would also reach the Arab countries, and the Palestine Arabs as well. In the first days of his work he may perhaps have not realized the implications of this development for Zionism. But in 1923, three years after taking over his functions, not only did the 'Arab question' reveal itself to him, but he also discovered that his predecessors had overlooked it.

At this period, in 1923, Ruppin underwent the first phase in his approach to the 'Arab question'. He not only recognized the existence of the problem but even diagnosed a solution, namely the merging and integration of the Jews among the peoples of the Middle East. Although he was already nearing his fifties, his criticism of others, and his confidence in himself, are steeped in the spirit of youth. In 1923 he wrote in his diary:

Herzl's conception was naïve, and can be explained by the fact that he failed utterly to understand the conditions among the peoples of the Orient, and create, along with our brethren of the same race – the Arabs (and the Armenians) – a new Near East cultural community. More than ever before, it appears to me, Zionism can only find its justification in the racial association of the Jews with the peoples of the Near East. I am currently gathering material for a book about the Jews, whose basic premise will be the racial issue. I propose to include pictures of the ancient Oriental peoples, and of the modern populations, and to portray types which were to be found in the past, as well as in the present, among the group of nations of Syria and Asia Minor. I intend to show that those very same types are still to be found among present-day Jewry.

Ruppin understood that this approach implied a fundamental change in the Zionist concept, but he was not deterred by this fact. 'Zionism will last', he wrote, 'only if it is given a radic-

ally different scientific basis.' The need to set Zionist fulfilment
on a scientific foundation, the aspiration to find in Zionism
some justification *vis-à-vis* the Palestine Arabs, and the need to
lay down realistic answers based on a knowledge of local conditions – these principles are an integral part of Ruppin's nature.
He clung to them later too, even when he discovered that the
question was more complicated than it appeared at first, and
required other solutions.

Ruppin did not hold on for very long to this idea of integration among the Arab peoples. As soon as he got to know realities better, he sensed that the common racial origins of Israelis
and Arabs, and the resemblance between the Jewish nose and
the Armenian nose, did not constitute an adequate basis on
which to construct a 'new Near East cultural community'. In
1925 Ruppin arrived at the second phase of the 'Arab question'
– the bi-national phase.

During his bi-national state phase, which coincided with his
adherence to the Brit Shalom Movement, which he founded in
1926 and left after differences with his fellow-members in 1929,
Ruppin believed that Eretz Israel ought to be a common state
for two nations. The Jews and the Arabs, in other words, should
continue their existence as different and separate peoples, and
not merge into a 'new cultural community' – but at the same
time they should maintain one single state, a bi-national state.

At this point, two things should be stressed. First, as Ruppin
grew more and more immersed in his Zionist work and increased in stature, his awareness of the need to ensure the further independent continuation of the Jewish community was
profound. He believed that this could be attained, if the aims of
Zionism were realized. 'World history knows no laws, not even
the laws of reasonableness. There is therefore no sense in pre-
dicting the future. This is also the answer to those who claim to
"prove" that Zionism has no future.' (1932). The second thing
is that he saw the essence of Zionism as persistent and expanding immigration and settlement. He regarded these as 'essential
conditions', and did not diverge from them even when he feared
there might be a contradiction between Zionism and the 'Arab
question'.

As early as 1928, in fact, inner doubts of this sort troubled him.

In that conversation it became clear how difficult it is to realize Zionism and still bring it continually into line with the demands of general ethics. I was well and truly depressed. Will Zionism indeed deteriorate into a pointless chauvinism? Is there in fact no way of assigning, in Israel, a sphere of activity to a growing number of Jews, without oppressing the Arabs? I see a special difficulty in the restricted land area. Surely the day is not far off, when no more unoccupied land will be available and the settlement of a Jew will automatically lead to the dispossession of an Arab *fellah*? What will happen then?

The idea of the bi-national state was supposed to reply to three problems. The first problem was that of nationality. Each people would preserve its own nationality. The second problem was to prevent the Jews dominating the Arabs, and vice versa. 'Under the aegis of the League of Nations, Eretz Israel must become a state in which Jews and Arabs live side by side, as two nations with equal rights. Neither shall be dominant, and neither shall be enslaved.' On the third problem, that of Jewish immigration and the dispossession of the Arabs, Ruppin wrote : 'Just as it is the right of the Arabs to remain in the country, so is it the right of the Jews to immigrate thereto.' (1929).

This phase, like its predecessor, was a revolutionary one. Here again, as before, Ruppin believed that points of difference could be ironed out objectively speaking, but in order to achieve this other mistakes must not be repeated. 'We want to extricate ourselves from the error which was prevalent in Europe for 100 years, and which caused the World War – namely that only one nation can rule in one state.'

As regards the abstract formulation, the bi-national state may have provided the answer for Ruppin to the question of how Arabs and Jews would live in common. But as he came to know realities better, he discovered more and more difficulties, and Ruppin, with his intellectual integrity, did not allow generalizations to obscure factual truth.

I am therefore convinced that a number of serious conflicts of interest exist between the Jews and the Arabs. For the time being

I do not see how these conflicts can be resolved in such a way as to allow the Jews the possibility of free immigration, and free cultural and economic development – things which are essential conditions for Zionism – and in such a way that the interests of the Arabs should not be impaired, on the other hand. [1928].

Ruppin knew, moreover, that the idea of the bi-national state was merely an ideological point of departure, an indication of framework within whose bounds he hoped it would be possible to solve the problem. 'In the course of debates within the Brit Shalom Movement, we formulated the concept that the solution must necessarily lie within a bi-national state ... even the bi-national state, obviously, gave a general reply to the problem, and it was my intention to make use of the Brit Shalom further, as a means of clarifying decisive questions, which would emerge from this general answer.' (1936).

And the questions, in fact, still remain: 'The "conflicts of interest" were of a substantive nature.' There was the question of land. 'On every site where we purchase land and where we settle people, the present cultivators will inevitably be dispossessed.' Thus he wrote about immigration: 'Since our immigrants, for the vast majority, are people without means, the possibility should not be ruled out that these immigrants would take away the livelihood of the Arabs.' Then there was the different standard of living and other factors.

But the main difficulty stemmed from the fact that the Arabs simply did not want the Jews to come to Eretz Israel. Every solution – including the establishment of a bi-national state – faced the alternative of either making allowances for the views and desires of the Arabs, and putting an end to Zionism, or carrying on with immigration, land purchase and settlement, while denying the right of the Arabs of Palestine to determine the future of the country. Any solution, or arrangement, which would be contingent on the agreement of the Arabs, or on the introduction of a democratic constitution whereby decision on questions at issue would be taken by a majority (an Arab majority naturally) – this implied the cessation of immigration, and of Jewish economic development.

Ruppin understood this, and in his letter to Hans John (30 May 1928) he wrote:

During our last conversation, you pointed out quite rightly that all the Arabs of Eretz Israel oppose the Zionist movement, and until we are capable of suggesting a satisfactory solution to the conflict of interests they will carry on being our antagonists. If, under these circumstances, a constitution worthy of the name were granted, it would stand to reason that the Arab would make use of all the rights assured them by the constitution, to prevent, as a majority, all economic progress on the part of the Jewish minority. The meaning of this would be, quite simply, the end of the Zionist movement.

The crux of the problem, therefore, lies in the impossibility of arriving at agreement and cooperation with the Arabs. But, at this stage, Ruppin still believed that it was possible to find the 'redeeming formula', which would serve as a bridge for understanding between Arabs and Jews. And so he founded the Brit Shalom Movement.

As time went on, the 'Arab question' did not become any less grave, but in fact worsened. In 1936 Ruppin needed to find a solution for it, no less than he did in 1923, and in fact more. He saw this as a vital necessity, not just to resolve the conflict with the Arabs, but also in order to put relations with himself and with his conscience into proper order. But was there a way of squaring the circle? Did the magic formula exist, to reach agreement with the Arabs, without thereby ceding the fundamentals of Zionism?

I was at odds with the other members of the Brit Shalom, in my appraisal of the prospects of reaching an agreement with the Arabs. In this respect, the Brit members displayed great optimism. They thought that economic advantages, and certain political guarantees, would in themselves be calculated to persuade the Arabs to accept the Jewish national home. There was nothing new in this concept. It was, in fact, just a continuation of the false approach towards the Arabs, which had prevailed in the Zionist movement from its beginning. Nobody ever imagined, beforehand, that those very same Arabs who during the days of Turkish oppression were prepared with equanimity to accept year by year a few hundred meek Jews who lived on *halluka* charity, would struggle by force against tens or hundreds of thousands of strong, straight-backed Zionists at a time when the country was under a free British administration. The 'peaceful infiltration', which they hoped for so much, proved in reality to be a deceptive illusion. If we could learn any lesson from the history of the world in recent decades, this lesson would be that the political posture of nations is not dependent on considerations of good sense, but on instincts. All the economic advantages, and all the logical considerations, will not move the Arabs to give up the control of Eretz Israel in favour of the Jews, after they consider it was handed to them, or to share this control with the Jews, as long as the Arabs constitute the decisive majority in Eretz Israel. I gave expression to these ideas in a letter to Dr Jacobson, 3 December 1931, when I wrote: What we can get today from the Arabs – we don't need. What we need – we can't get.

The year 1936 brought Ruppin to the third phase of his approach to the 'Arab question'. He ceased believing in the possibility of persuading the Arabs to agree to cooperate. No 'legal formula', no 'political guarantees', no 'economic advantages' and no 'negotiations' would bring the Arabs to consent to the Jews' return to Zion. This was undoubtedly due not only to the cumulative failures of attempts at dialogues with the Arab leaders, but also to the fact that the Arabs' anti-Zionist political stand grew a great deal more outspoken, and found expression in bloody outbreaks of violence, especially during the 1936 riots.

What next? What are the conclusions? After sixteen years of trial and inner doubts, Ruppin demolished his own entire ideological structure. He had long since abandoned the Brit Shalom Movement. He was perhaps disappointed, he was certainly wiser, but he did not despair, on any account:

Nowadays, I personally am in a mood of calm and dispassion. I have formulated the following theory for myself: It is only natural, and inevitable, that Arab opposition to Jewish immigration should find an outlet from time to time in outbreaks of this sort. It is our destiny to be in a state of continual warfare with the Arabs, and there is no other alternative but that lives should be lost. This situation may well be undesirable, but such is the reality. If we want to continue our work in Eretz Israel, against the desires of the Arabs – then we shall be compelled to take such loss of life into consideration!

As regards his own conscience, and as regards his self-recounting, Ruppin was calm and dispassionate. He had formulated a theory for himself, and it satisfied him. But what of the practical aspect?

And what ought to be done in order to reduce or remove tensions between the two peoples, since after all, this tension cannot continue interminably? To my mind, no negotiations with the Arabs today can help us move forward, since the Arabs still hope to be able to get rid of us, over our heads ... not negotiations, but the development of Eretz Israel, as we increase our ratio of the population, and strengthen our economic power, can lead to a lessening of tension. When the time comes, and the Arabs realize that it is not a question of negotiations, in which they are asked to grant us something which we do not yet have, but of conceding the existence of a reality, then the weight of facts will lead to a lessening of tension.

To create the facts: immigration, settlement, economic development and so forth. In these activities, Ruppin sees not only the fulfilment of Jewish longings. Once translated into facts, they will also convince the Arabs to stop fighting against us. 'We must increase our strength and our numbers, until we reach parity with the Arabs. The life or death of the Zionist movement will depend on this. . . . Perhaps a bitter truth, but it is the truth with a capital T.' (1936). 'The weight of facts – the increase of our strength and numbers will lead to a lessening of tension with the Arabs. When will we reach that stage? Within five to ten years.' (1936). In this timetable, things like the policy of Hitler, the World War and the end of the Mandate were not taken into account.

Ruppin's heart-searching over the path to agreement with the Arabs had thus come full circle. The fulfilment of Zionism embodied the solution to the 'Arab question'. Does this mean that Ruppin realized he was wrong, while his colleagues in the leadership, whom he called 'naïve' and 'ignorant of the Arab problem', were correct? Not at all. The prevalent point of view held that the 'Arab question' should be left alone, and it would find its own solution thanks to the prosperity, the development, the progress and the culture which the Jews would bring to the

Arabs of the country. Ruppin, on the other hand, stopped deal-ing with the 'Arab question', because he realized that the Arabs would not agree to Zionism, *in spite of* all these things.

In the years that followed, developments were determined as a result of factors unconnected with the pattern of relation-ships between the 'Arab question' and Zionist fulfilment. Never-theless, I should like to quote Ruppin's point of view on two more issues: the Peel Commission's partition proposal, and the White Paper. They are of interest for the subject of this lecture – if not directly, then indirectly.

Apart from Ruppin, the British Empire too was in a quandary in those years, over the question of Arabs and Jews in Eretz Israel. The solution it proposed (the Peel Commission, 1939) was partition – not integration, not a bi-national state, and not cooperation. This means the establishment of separate states for Jews and Arabs. The Jewish state was assigned an area of some 5,000 sq.km. To give some idea of the proportion, the state of Israel, today, has an area of 20,250 sq.km., in other words four times as large, while the area within the present cease-fire lines is 88,000 sq.km., eighteen times larger than the area of the 'Jew-ish state' in the Peel Commission's proposals.

On 1 August 1937 Ruppin wrote:

After studying the partition proposal, I have come to the conclu-sion that we shall not be able to absorb the 300,000 Arabs in it. Since it will be impossible to get them to leave of their own accord, it is essential that the Jewish state should have other boundaries, inside of which not 300,000 but at the most 100,000 Arabs, would remain. I have put my 'personal' plan for the new Jewish State in writing. According to this plan, the area will be reduced from 5 million to 1.5 million dunams.

It should be recalled that in those days there were 363,000 Jews in Eretz Israel, and the 100,000 Arabs whom Ruppin was ready to absorb in the Jewish state would have been equivalent to 750,000 Arabs, absorbed by the Jewish state we have today.

During the Zionist Congress in Zurich, Ruppin brought to the Zionist Executive his proposal to give up two thirds of the area proposed by the Royal Commission, and to establish a midget Jewish state on an area of 1.5 million dunams. After the Executive meeting he wrote in his diary: 'I explained my ideas to him [Weizmann]. I did not feel they made a great impression ...' (1937). We may disagree with Ruppin's conclusion, but we cannot accuse him of not having learnt the bitter lesson of life side-by-side with the Arabs.

And finally – the White Paper:

The White Paper was eventually published yesterday. It contains no surprise.... I do not know why, but this document irritates me far less than it irritates all the other Jews. Is it because I have grown old, and my senses are dulled? Or perhaps it is because I no longer believe in policies on paper? This White Paper is a direct function of a specific political set-up (a united Arab front, England's fear of the Arabs) and it will be just as short-lived as this political set-up. [1939].

Chief of staff, officers and guests: I trust you will forgive me for having spoken at length. In other circumstances, I would have been able to end at this point. But in the present forum and in these days, in surveying the development of Ruppin's ideas on the Arab question, I do not want to avoid making a number of concrete observations.

Firstly about what Ruppin called 'political set-up'. When he said that the White Paper was the production of a political set-up, and that this would leave nothing of the White Paper when it vanished, he was perfectly correct. Ruppin understood this, not because old age had dulled his senses, but because he had amassed wisdom during his years of work. His view of the White Paper was the result of his understanding, and not of dull senses.

Between then and now, the political set-up has in fact changed entirely. A Jewish state has been established, with close to three million inhabitants. We have been victorious in three wars. We have an army whose strength should not be underestimated, and a people standing behind it, investing huge sums of money to aid our economy. Second, the dimensions have changed. When Ruppin thought in terms of Arabs, he meant the Palestine Arabs. When we talk about Arabs nowdays, we mean the Arab states. Not only that, but these states are also supported by the world's second greatest power – the Soviet Union.

Dimensions have changed in the 'demographic question' in terms of the size of our own population as well as that of the Palestine Arabs. Geographically, too, there have been changes in the areas settled by us, as well as the areas occupied by our forces today.

Third, the facts are no longer the same. Ruppin was wrong to hope that, by creating facts, tensions between us and the Arabs would be lessened. What greater 'creation of facts' could there be than the establishment of the state, the concentration of 2.5 million Jews there, and the victories in three wars? But despite this, do the Arabs today agree to sign a peace agreement with us? The facts have been created, but the tension is no less than it was before.

Here I shall permit myself to add one observation. We see the facts which we ourselves create, but everybody who believes that facts are decisive in this issue, must remember that the Arabs, too, could well point to facts – their large and steadily increasing numbers, their influence in the world, the oil resources at their disposal, and so forth. In other words, everybody who adheres to the formula whereby the facts we create will bring the other side to accept us, can just as well point to significant facts on the Arab side the moment he steps into the Arabs' shoes.

At any rate, if we return to Ruppin's forecasts, the facts he hoped for, as regards the increase in strength and numbers, did come to pass. But I fear that they have not yet convinced the Arabs to accept us, or our political existence, to regard us as an acceptable neighbour state with equal rights. Perhaps Ruppin's error on this point stemmed from the fact that he thought in rational categories, whereas Arab opposition stems from emotions.

Fourth, there is his letter to Jacobson of 12 April 1931, about the prospects of an agreement with the Arabs, in which he said : 'What we can get today from the Arabs, we don't need. What we need – we can't get.' This definition sounds to me very up-to-date, when I sometimes read that today the Arabs are offering us the 1947 partition plans

And finally, today too, unfortunately, a year after the war, and despite the fact that we are standing on the Suez Canal and on the River Jordan, in Gaza and in Nablus; despite all our efforts – including a willingness for far-reaching concessions – to bring the Arabs to the peace table, the things which Ruppin said thirty-two years ago still seem sound. It was during the 1936 riots that he wrote:

> The Arabs do not agree to our venture. If we want to continue our work in Eretz Israel against their desires, there is no alternative but that lives should be lost. It is our destiny to be in a state of continual warfare with the Arabs. This situation may well be undesirable, but such is the reality.

Annexation and Democracy

By Yehoshua Arieli*

My subject today is democracy and the problem of the occupied territories. I will commence by saying that more than one year and a half has elapsed since the war; the peace that was expected at the close of the war hasn't come and the prospects of obtaining it seem to be decreasing. This change in the prospects of peace and of the perspective in general has also led to changes in attitudes towards the occupied territories. It actually seemed at one time that the policies conducted particularly in Sumaria and Judea held hopes of creating some kind of normalization. Today, things look different, but then it appeared as if the policy of open bridges would help maintain the status quo without harming too much the national sentiments of the population of these territories.

The same thing happened as far as Sinai is concerned. It can be said that the Sinai Peninsula has become a permanent element in not only military, but also, to some extent, economic planning. As far as the Sinai Peninsula is concerned, here too there seems to be a growing impression that occupation will be maintained for a long time. The formula which the National Unity government adopted a year and half ago of holding on

*Reprinted by special permission from *New Outlook*, July 1969.

to the territories until a negotiated peace has been achieved, has for all practical purposes turned into an excuse not to state the terms and aims of the peace and at the same time not to define clearly the aims and methods in the occupied territories, in the fear that any definition concerning either peace or the territories would lead to breaking up the coalition and the beginning of a domestic struggle that all sides, of course, want to avoid.

It is therefore not surprising that in this present, what seems to be interim and undefined period, there is a growing tendency, of indeterminate strength, to believe that it is to Israel's advantage to hold on as long as possible, or for ever, to the status quo. This view has been explicitly formulated by the group that has made it its ideology: the Movement for a Greater Israel. I am convinced that if the views of this group, or of those knowingly or not close to it, were adopted as policy by the government, they would have led us to the edge of the abyss and threatened the very existence of the state of Israel. They would destroy our democracy, damage our souls and create a fanatic and retrogressive society in Israel, culturally and morally. Indeed, you have to be either a demagogue or very naïve to say that the path to peace is a short one and that we are sure to find it. There is, however, a tremendous difference between policies that are imposed upon us by the force of reality and those we choose for ourselves as desirable. The partisans of annexation and of including the territories within the state of Israel as an aim and goal of policy, bar the way to any other solution and are prepared to endanger both peace and security for an aim which may have various justifications, into which I won't go here.

The question that arises is, therefore, what would happen – and I shall speak only of the domestic aspects – if we really carried out the policy of permanently including the territories formally, or even informally, within the borders of the State of Israel.

I see the danger in three fields: in that of the political regime, of society, and of personal and collective attitudes. The famous Spanish-American philosopher, George Santayana, once said that anyone who isn't prepared to learn from history will have to repeat it. Those who love their country and are concerned over its fate must look at the problems not from the aspect of the present situation or of our desires, but historically, and ask, what will happen, how will our society develop in the supposed new situation of annexing the territories. Implementing a programme of that kind would lead to immediate changes in two fields : in our international status and in the composition of the society that for practical purposes would be under the jurisdiction of the state of Israel; in other words, the national composition of our population. As I have already pointed out, the state of Israel has so far defined its position in keeping with international practice, that is that a settlement reached with the signing of a peace treaty would include the return of the occupied territories to a full or at least great extent.

However, if, in one way or another, we were to begin actually to annex the territories and to ignore the fact that we were only in an interim situation, our international situation would change radically. It could be assumed – and today after the illusions that certain circles cultivated concerning America have proven false it is even clearer – that theoretical or practical policies of annexation would have left us in a situation of international isolation, and facing not only a UN condemnation but the danger of perhaps being expelled from the UN or of the application of sanctions. If we assume that for domestic reasons the United States would not have wanted to participate, these sanctions would be made the responsibility of other countries who were ready to apply them, and we would thereby become a country under siege.

I do not want to prophesy whether the state of Israel would be ready to enter into that situation or could hold out in such a situation. For the sake of argument I will assume that we could hold out in a situation of siege and total isolation, the way Rhodesia is actually doing. In many ways, though, of course the situation isn't the same. Our geo-political environment is unlike that of Rhodesia. We don't have the tremendous support of a great and rich country like South Africa, nor do the new nations of Africa resemble the Arab world. But let us assume for a moment that we could succeed in holding out in such a situation. There is no doubt that for a state under siege the permanent condition of life is one of war as a natural state of affairs, of being permanently preoccupied with fighting for its very existence. Both society and government would have to reorganize themselves on the basis of a permanent state of emergency. All the economic and human resources would be permanently mobilized to maintain the state's existence and security; the planning and control of manpower resources and economic factors would be concentrated in the hands of an emergency authority. In such conditions no country can allow itself the luxury of party politics or of using the country's resources for the wasteful ways of a working democracy. Actually a kind of unity would have to be established that would not permit any deviations or outlays that were not related to the emergency situation. In this situation, the state cannot be dependent upon a public opinion which may not always support it and will have to guide public opinion and impose on it those views that fit in with what the government thinks necessary for the emergency.

In such a situation the society would also adopt the hierarchical structure of the army command in which the borders between civil and military fields would tend to disappear and in which a new ruling bureaucratic, technological, military and managerial élite would be formed, no longer dependent upon institutions and processes based on the democratic procedure of elections, representation and public control. A state of emergency demands internal cohesion and cannot afford freedom of expression. Censorship and public indoctrination would become necessary to maintain the state of emergency.

We can also assume that the Arab population of the territories would intensify its resistance and terror if this situation became a permanent one for it. The authorities would therefore have to apply increasingly harsh measures of repression leading to a further vicious circle of terror and repression. Concomitantly with the society's adaptation to the state of emergency politically and socially, a process of psychological adaptation would also have to take place. It is impossible to maintain a situation of war under conditions of emergency and fear for an extended time, without the individual's developing defence mechanisms making it possible to withstand the tension of continuing danger and strain.

This last need creates a tendency to reject any criticism coming from the outside and to develop a fanatic nationalism and self-righteousness, refusing to consider any alternatives or to listen to the voice of doubt. A value system will come into being centred completely around the values and norms of national cohesion and national identification. There would also come into being a strange combination of narrow-minded tribalism and fanatic, historic nationalism. That is the kind of combination that exists today in South Africa and which, to some extent, has always been present in situations like those described above.

Ultimately we would be driven into a situation that the American sociologist, Harold Lasswell, has called the 'garrison state'. This is not a new phenomenon; it has appeared in history at various times and in similar situations. The Spartan community was like that, as were the states established by the feudal warrior-classes in the Middle Ages, the Turkish Mongols at certain times, Sweden at the beginning of the eighteenth and France in the nineteenth centuries. As for the twentieth century, I shall only recall Japan and South Africa, and, to a certain degree, Soviet Russia.

I have just spoken of the problems implied by international isolation which could be a result of adopting decisions in keeping with the views of our maximalist movement. However, even if we assume, for the sake of argument, that we won't have to face that kind of situation, that we won't be isolated, that we will find persons or groups or countries to help us out of the siege, the question still remains : What will our situation be like politically and socially from the standpoint of the relations between the Arab minority and ourselves if we absorb the large Arab minority of the occupied territories into our midst?

There is no doubt that if we add the Arabs of the West Bank and Gaza to our present Arab citizens, we are talking about one and a quarter million inhabitants today. If we assume that the Arab natural increase and our natural increase plus immigration remain more or less stable, it is not hard to see that within a short time the Arab minority will grow to about 40 per cent. How will a state with a 40 per cent Arab minority be able to maintain and develop its institutions and unique democratic character?

Among the members of the Greater Israel Movement, and its knowing and unknowing supporters, there are some who argue that it would be possible to grant immediate civil rights to the large minority on condition that the state forgo its national and Zionist character. I have no debate with these people since it is clear that giving up the state's mission puts the situation of the Arabs in a new light, though I doubt whether the Arab side, for its part, would be prepared to give up its own national character. My argument, however, is with those circles who, in the name of Jewish history, of the historic rights of the Jewish people, of Israel's security as a Jewish state, want to annex this minority and thereby, with their own hands, destroy the character of our society as both a Jewish society and a democratic one.

We, therefore, have to ask what would happen if, as we would be obliged to do, we granted equal civil rights to this large Arab minority. From this standpoint, the state of Israel is undoubtedly not like other countries. There are countries, especially in the West, and my example is the United States, where both nationality and citizenship are defined in general and universal terms. That is – both citizens and the state are defined in inclusive terms permitting any person to become a citizen and identify himself with the state. The definition of citizens may either be historical or universal as in the United States and to some lesser extent in the enlightened democracies of Europe.

The situation in Israel is different. Without going into evaluations or into details, Israel is the national state *par excellence*. It is the classic antithesis to American democracy from the viewpoint of national character. The state of Israel's uniqueness lies first and foremost in the simple fact that it was formed and exists in order to solve the problem of the Jewish people as a whole, which is dispersed the world over and which can return to its land if it wants. What is more, this state's function is not limited, as in most of the countries existing today, to those problems deriving from the existing population within its borders. The state's functions are transcendental – that is, go beyond the borders of the state and beyond the given present to the future and to the people as a whole, in order to solve its problem.

It is clear now that for this kind of state and nationalism the possibilities of non-Jewish identification are limited. Even when the non-Jew has full rights, can identify with the society as one maintaining law and security, supplying services and the possibilities of livelihood and personal development, he can only if he is a Zionist at heart identify himself with the transcendental aims of the state. This is true too for the Arab community living in the country who are citizens of Israel and whom we consider full citizens. Though this minority never fled or was caused to flee from the country, has lived and chosen to live with us from the very beginning, has developed with the state of Israel itself, improved its situation and found many common points of contact with the state, there is still no doubt that this minority has been torn in its hearts and in its loyalties.

However, there is a considerable difference between the situation of the Arab citizens of Israel and the large minority we are adding to them, on whom we are imposing citizenship against its will, which has been educated in blind hatred for twenty years, has gone through the suffering of the refugee camps and therefore justly or unjustly looked upon this country as an expropriator. In practice, we can assume that this minority would never be ready to accept citizenship, and if it accepted it with its 40 per cent minority, would form an irredentist movement destroying the democratic structure of the country and compelling us against our will to move from a situation of equality and equal citizenship to increasing repression and all that involved.

I therefore don't assume that that would be the path w would take. It is much more reasonable to assume that thos supporting this aim are actually talking of what they call encouraging emigration or a transition period without civil rights. It is clear that as long as this encouragement of emigration is left to natural trends, it will not succeed. The Arabs have learnt the lesson that it doesn't pay to leave this country if there is no need. This encouragement would, therefore, have to adopt other methods, which would only intensify the hatred of the refugees and worsen their situation immeasurably, or compel us to go over to a situation of open discrimination.

It is clear that a situation of complete discrimination would bring us back to the same situation that I spoke of when I spoke of the results of international isolation. It would put us into a situation where the state would have to deny to one part of its population its essential rights. It would have to differentiate between the one community and the other, and here I would like to quote Abraham Lincoln, changing only one word, that: a democratic government cannot remain for a long time half democratic and half oppressive. It must change and become either the one or the other. I have no doubt what would happen to us. We would have to adapt ourselves to a state that was unwillingly turning into a police state, to a government whose need to maintain a special class with the responsibility for repression would affect its own mentality. We would have lost our souls for some additional territory.

I have drawn for you here the two results that seem to me to be inevitable if we make the inclusion of the Arab community and the annexation of territory an end in itself rather than a temporary problem which we have to solve. Finally I would like to point out that in these circles – which to my sorrow include persons who grew up in the labour movement and were educated to socialism – we find developing a kind of nationalist and mythological mentality which prepares them psychologically and intellectually for a situation in which one part of the state would become a ruling people and the other part a people without rights and without self-determination.

I don't say that these attitudes are held today by a large part of the Jewish community. On the contrary, I am sure that their part is small, though it is very influential and vocal especially in the mass media. But I would like to warn ourselves not to allow ourselves to drift, against our will and by endless improvisations, into a position and situation that will force us into roles and activities we would abhor and avoid by all means if we had a choice.

Sartre Looks at the Middle East Again*

A.S.: Now, more than a year after the Six Day War, would you like to tell me your position on this question?

J.-P.S.: I think that the Six Day War was only one battle and that the conflict is continuing today in a different form. Consequently, the real problem is that of negotiating in order to establish a peace. It is clear that the six days which temporarily gave Israel a victory but did not settle anything are, on the contrary, the origin of a war which may last for years before it reaches a solution.

A.S.: It seems to me that today there is a certain tendency to look at history from an almost manichaeistic point of view, that is – that there are peoples who are, *en bloc*, thought to be anti-imperialistic and other peoples who are condemned *en bloc* as 'imperialistic'. Marxism, on the contrary, teaches us that there are only classes that can be pro-imperialistic and classes that are anti-imperialistic. The opinion that a good part of the Left has had of Israel is the following: that Israel is a pro-imperialistic state, the spearhead of American imperialism in the Middle East. What do you think of this simplification of the facts of the situation?

J.-P.S.: First of all, I think that manichaeism is one of the greatest dangers of our epoch, of the thought of our epoch. It is our affair, as intellectuals, precisely because we write and

*This interview between Arturo Schwartz and Jean-Paul Sartre was originally written for the *Quaderni del Medio Oriente* of Milan which Mr Schwartz edits. Reprinted with special permission from *New Outlook*, Vol. 12, No 3.

speak, to condemn this manichaeism. In the case of the Israeli-Arab conflict, there is not total justice on one side or the other, but we have to understand both sides completely. When the Arabs say, for example, that Israel is the bridgehead of American imperialism, that doesn't mean very much for me. What seems to me to be much more important is that the Israeli economy is not built to function alone. The economy of a country like Israel should be entirely centred in the Middle East, but in reality it is an economy that is half that of a developed country, half that of an undeveloped one. In its trade with the capitalist and industrialized countries, Israel generally supplies fruits, vegetables or flowers; its economy cannot be maintained sufficiently by this kind of production and foreign trade, nor even by polishing diamonds. Evidently, on the contrary, the economy must be expanded and diversified. You know that Israel, which lived for a long time on the war reparations paid by the Germans, suffered a terrible crisis, when I was there, because these reparations came to an end. In addition, the Israelis need the money given by the pro-Israeli Jews of New York and the United States. That is a supplement and not the essential, but without that addition, there would be a catastrophe.

It is completely absurd to consider Israel the spearhead of American imperialism, but it is a definite fact that Israel presently needs the support of those American Jews. We must also understand that, in Israel's present situation, it is they who supply the arms, who are aiding her, who – in effect – mean something for this country. Israel often finds herself in a situation where the country and the country's press approve of measures taken by the Americans which intellectuals – the Left, for example – cannot approve. I recall, for example, that shortly after the Six Day War some of my Israeli friends who belong to the Peace Movement made a demonstration against the war in Vietnam; they were booed by part of the public. That is to say – there is a kind of sympathy for the Americans and, more particularly, for the Jewish population there. That is something that is absolutely real, in the same way that in every case that I have been able to read their papers – on the Athens affair or other matters of that kind, for example – the press – except for the very minimal extreme left-wing – has been almost entirely in agreement with the imperialist positions.

However, I do not at all think that means Israel is the spearhead of American imperialism. The fact is simply that today the Arabs have put Israel in a position where she is condemned – militarily and economically – to depend not on the governments of the imperialist states but on the Jewish minorities of these same states, who to a large extent support the politics of these states. I held a meeting on Vietnam in Tel Aviv. I was listened to but I felt the very strong resistance of the public when I attacked the war. So you see how we must distinguish between what people can be made to be and what they are.

In any case, to consider Israel a creature of the United States is absurd. Simply put – there is a kind of alignment that comes from the structure itself.

On the other hand, in the same way, those who claim that the Arabs started the war, that they are criminals, forget to consider the situation of the Palestinians, the absolutely insufferable situation of the Palestinians. They also forget that the Arabs, from the beginning, have been led by British manoeuvres to take a negative attitude towards Israel, which has persisted since 1948, when an idiotic war was provoked. I say idiotic not only because it did not have much sense from the political point of view, but it had even less from the military viewpoint. The Arabs were pushed into a defeat and they have never digested this first debacle. In addition, at the same time, there was an immense population of refugees – the Palestinians – whom I saw in Gaza. They represent a permanent humiliation for the Arabs. It is said, quite wrongly, that the Arabs maintain these unfortunates in their misery in order to show them to visitors. That is not true. There are certainly people who profit from this situation, but it is impossible, for a list of reasons which it would take too long to explain, for an economy like Egypt's to absorb all of the people who are in the camps and to integrate them in the working and active population. When you see the standard of living of an Egyptian *fellah*, it is clear that

Egypt cannot support all these people and give them work. In the same way, when we condemn the Arabs we always forget the war of 1956: Suez; or, we should say, that Israel was allied to the imperialist powers. Consequently, as you see, my judgement on both sides is extremely moderate.

I understand Israel today very well. I understand that kind of presentiment, almost of death, that you find very much among the young people and even the older ones, who say: if we lose a single battle, the state will disappear, consequently we will fight to the last. I even understand the excesses of the Israeli right; I deplore them profoundly but I have succeeded a little in understanding from within how these people could have come to this by a kind of despair – a despair that is linked to pride and to their victories, but still despair. I can equally understand how the Arabs, who have been humiliated many times by the Israeli victories, who were the victims of a real Israeli aggression in 1956, have confounded imperialism and the presence of Israel. We are now in a period of passion on both sides. An enormous amount of time is needed to achieve something, to change mentalities. To say that Israel is imperialistic and that the Arabs, among whom there are completely feudal countries, are socialist states, is a really crude idea. But it is also quite true, however, that in certain Arab countries a Left is trying to do something and there is, therefore, a movement that is constantly defeated and beaten down but is trying to do something a little more progressive, a little more social. At the same time, it is certain that the course of events has led Israel, on the contrary, to give a larger and larger part to the capitalist sector, to the market economy, in a country which started by being socialist. Here there are two tendencies which, if you like, are opposed, while the Arab Left, though it won't take shape tomorrow, certainly exists and is trying to go ahead.

That is why I say to you that for me it is absolutely impossible at the present to do anything else but to try, perpetually, to tell the first: 'They are not imperialists; they are the victims of imperialism,' and the second: 'They are not simply militarists, it is not because of religious or militarist reasons that this business has taken place, but really for profound reasons.'

The unity of the Arab world is really something impossible to achieve – we see that; but it would be desirable. If that unity existed, it might reasonably have the effect of making the relations between Israel and the Arabs less tense, because the only means the Arabs have today, with the structures of their societies so diverse, of being jointed together, is to say, 'We want the death of Israel.' If these societies found themselves on a more homogeneous level they would probably find other, more positive reasons to help each other, for example, by social and economic ties. They would not have the special need for this negative tool – the enemy. It is striking that some Israelis laugh out loud when you tell them of Nasser's efforts – which I have seen myself – to raise the standard of living of his people; but inversely I have heard Egyptian Marxists supporting the theory that is absolutely contrary to Marxism, that there cannot be an Israeli left; though it is quite evident that the class struggle exists in Israel as it does elsewhere and that consequently there are the elements of a Left.

We are today in the midst of passion and I really don't see the possibility, except for the long range, of succeeding in uncapping these bombs of passion . . .

A.S.: We spoke at the beginning of a tendency manifested in the political philosophies of many countries – the tendency to manichaeism. There is also another tendency which is becoming more and more prevalent; this has to do with the systematic falsification of history, also linked to the total reversal of values, for the manipulation of public opinion. . . . Don't you think that this reversal of values, this systematic falsification of history is also being shown by some papers that speak of the aggression conducted by the Arab states in 1948 against the state of Israel as an Israeli aggression against the Arabs. We have all read the articles in the Polish *Trybunu Ludu* and in many, many other papers of the Communist parties both in power and not in power, who today, at a distance of twenty years, are trying to present Israel as the aggressor in 1948. After all, we know very well that, on the one hand, Israel owes her existence to a UN decision that was supported, among the rest, by the Soviet

Union and the Popular Democracies, and on the other, that the Arab League states lent themselves on this occasion to the manoeuvres of British imperialism which provoked the 1948 aggression in order to return through the window after being chased out of the door. In 1948, then, unequivocally, the imperialist forces played the proto-fascist and clerical Arab card against a secular and anti-imperialist Israel.

J.-P.S.: As for the Middle East, you are right; it is certain that it is absolutely mad to attribute the role of aggressor in 1948 to Israel. I would simply remark, continuing to oppose manichaeism, that in Israel herself, except for the extreme Left, the events of 1956 are pictured as a just reaction to the attacks that actually took place at that time, when in actuality it was a clear matter of a concerted attack, together with the imperialist powers who were seeking something completely different, to occupy the Suez Canal. We thus find the same tendency in Israel.

As a matter of fact, I don't know of any real democracy. It might have been born in Czechoslovakia. Today they are trying to strangle it. But, with her very stratified parties, with the Histadrut also stratified, we cannot consider Israel as setting an example of democracy. Of course, there is the experience of the kibbutz, that is a very fine thing. But I don't think that an Israeli citizen has much more of an opportunity of being informed and of choosing than we have in our countries. On other levels there is great force in Israel – for example, the situation of the women – or the powerful desire of people to know and understand. And then don't forget that the Arabs within Israel are also second-class citizens. They certainly are not mistreated – or, rather, they weren't. Now the situation is terribly tense – but they weren't being maltreated when I was there. But lands have been taken away, there have been evictions, there are work difficulties, the impossibility of going higher than the status of building worker, and since there was a building crisis just at the time when I was there, there was a large reflux of Arabs to their villages when they had no more land to cultivate. In addition, for many of them there are the passes: they cannot move around without permission. Finally, in any case, a minority is a minority: it can vote as much as it wants, it will remain a minority if it is a minority; that isn't the fault of the Israelis, that's the way it is. In reality, Israel's basic problem can be posed in the following terms: must Israel, as the Israelis themselves say, remain a state apart, or consider itself a state like all the others? That is to say: there are the Jews; they have been persecuted, they have something among them – as I have always found among all the Jews I have seen in Europe – this is, a kind of heritage of permanent persecution and which is their great value. If it is thus, then the state of Israel must be an example, we have to demand more from this state than from others. Or you can say that Israel is like any other state, it is no longer a matter of Jews in Israel, but of Israel, and then we consider it as it is, and we must admit it has the same faults as the other states.

A.S.: We have spoken of the wars of 1948 and 1956 but let's go on to what happened last June; there, too, the Left found itself divided. On one side, they said that Israel was the aggressor, and on the other, that it was a case of legitimate defence, Israel having been actually threatened with annihilation. All the steps that were taken during the weeks preceding the June war seem to show that. It was a matter of a self-defence reflex, which made all the Israeli population fight with the courage of despair and unanimously support the government. We found the same unanimity during the Czechoslovak crisis when the whole population showed solidarity with the leadership and unanimously condemned the Soviet aggression. What is your point of view in this respect? Do you think that last year Israel defended herself in order to ensure her survival, or that Israel was the aggressor?

J.-P.S.: Do you know what they call that journal that comes out in English?

A.S.: *New Outlook*.

J.-P.S.: That's it, have you read the translation there, because I haven't read it in the original in Egyptian, of an article by Haykal in which eight days, I think, before 6 June, before the outbreak of hostilities, he said, 'Make no mistake, it is war. Israel is compelled to attack.' It is compelled, he said, not only economically but psychologically; however, the reason is not so important, but it is certain that in *Al Ahram*, at the time when the Gulf of Aqaba was blockaded, Haykal wrote: 'Israel has to attack; in other words, we have put her in a position which will oblige her to attack ...'

A.S.: Nasser, also, in other words, said the same thing. After having blockaded the Gulf of Aqaba, he declared, 'Now we leave to Israel the choice between dying by slow strangulation or dying by being massacred by us rapidly.'

J.-P.S.: In my view, however, that does not mean that Nasser wanted the war. I think that that declaration was mainly supposed to tell the Syrians: 'We are going as far as possible, but you know there is going to be a war.' I cannot admit that the Nasser I saw and the one who attacked are the same person; in other words, I think that when he acted and talked as he did at that time, Nasser was the victim of his great idea of pan-Arabism, of pan-Islamism. In this, I think he was manoeuvred by the Syrians, but at the same time I think he was aware of this, because his position as the leader, the leader who wants to be the head of the Arab world, always compels him to seem violent; he has already been doing that with great ease for years. Nasser's politics have always consisted, in sum, of being violent in words, but of inclining towards negotiations, towards a diplomatic showdown. That is what led him to war this time, because it was too strong. However, in any case, all that I want to say is that for me Israel was not the aggressor. Israel actually could not do anything else at that time, but fight back ...

A.S.: I am completely in agreement with you in your analysis and I would add another consideration. I would maybe go a little further and say that it is very probable that the Israelis and the Arab states were both caught in an imperialist trap. American imperialism had every interest in a conflict in the Middle East in order to detract attention from Vietnam and Soviet imperialism had every interest in a defeat for the Arab states a defeat that they knew was absolutely certain – in

The Israel–Arab Reader

order to be able to fulfil the old dream of the Tsars of having warm-water bases. Don't you think that we can admit, therefore, that the Middle Eastern conflict was mainly provoked by the rivalry between Soviet and American imperialisms?

J.-P.S.: On that point I am completely in agreement; even more in agreement since we find ourselves once more in very different circumstances, in a similar conflict – the Soviets and the English in Nigeria and Biafra, in order to serve the same interests; in this case, too, we have a kind of complicity. In the Israeli affair, we have a Soviet–American complicity, an objective one, of course, but unquestionable. The role of the Soviets in the Middle East and especially in the Arab world seemed to me very repulsive because they incited the Arabs, not only by giving them arms so that they could win a war, something which, strictly speaking, might be a moral crime, but politically excusable, but they incited them so that they would lose. Now, having lost, they are in their hands. Without this defeat, Soviet technicians today would not be on the spot – that is, along the Suez Canal, in the Egyptian artillery, etc. It is quite clear that it was a trap in which both the Arabs and the Israelis allowed themselves to be taken. The desire to keep some hot spots here and there comes from the same strategy. I am convinced of that; consequently the roles of the two great imperialisms in this affair seem to me absolutely criminal.

A.S.: It is clear that some Arab countries are governed by military groups which are today objectively anti-imperialist. But don't you think that their anti-imperialism is purely opportunistic, that at the desired moment they will go back to the bourgeoisie and to the American imperialist circles?

J.-P.S.: No, I don't think so, but I would say that I don't know the Arab world well enough to speak in general. I know Egypt very little : I have spoken a little with Egyptians. I don't have the impression that the honest men I have seen in all the levels of responsibility would like to ally themselves again with American imperialism because I believe that they have attained some consciousness. What happened with the construction of the Aswan Dam taught the leaders of the Left, or, at least the progressives, the price they had to pay for the alliance with the

United States. What seems to me more serious is the fact that in all the countries the counter-revolutionary forces are very far from being strangled. They are even within the governments and consequently we can admit the possibility of the situation being reversed. Given a bourgeoisie which only asks one thing – an alliance with the United States – it is extremely possible; it can happen from one day to the next. Basically, however, no matter how paradoxical that may seem, Egypt's dictatorial elements are also anti-imperialist, with something of a progressive depth. But there are also men in the army, as we have also seen, who preferred a defeat so that they could succeed in allying with the Americans.

A.S. : What do you think are the conditions that could assure peace in the Middle East ?

J.-P.S. : In my opinion, there is at the present time no practical perspective of a thaw. That does not mean that there may not be tomorrow, or the day after, but I feel that today all that we can say, abstractly, is this. By what conditions, in another climate, can we envisage a peace that would permit a real class struggle to be established? I think those conditions are the following : the full right of Palestinian society also to recover a sovereignty recognized by the Israelis, the evacuation of all the regions occupied by the Israelis, though almost certainly some frontier rectifications would have to be made. It is still very dangerous; when you see the Heights of Golan over Lake Kinneret it isn't possible. But I don't see why patriotic or religious reasons are interjected; I don't at all know why the Israelis should keep Jerusalem, for example; why Jerusalem shouldn't be made a completely neutral zone and simply given to the four or five most eminent religious representatives, under UN protection. At the same time – in addition – but that is another problem – there must be equality for Arab and Israeli citizens. But naturally all that must be accompanied by absolute recognition of Israel's sovereignty. But all that, for the present, as you understand, is abstract and utopian; the situation is changing every day, for the worse ...

A.S.: Going back to reality and the perspective of a real

socialist revolution in the Middle East which needs the revolutionary union of the exploited – Arabs and Israelis . . .

J.-P.S.: We could conceive, for example, that this war, like many others, could lead to revolution. Very often revolutions have been engendered by war and not by peace. In other words, we could very well conceive of a series of defeats and economic catastrophes on both sides which could, on both sides, lead to a revolt; that would be a really revolutionary revolt. But we are very far from that at the present and, like you, I would infinitely more prefer peace ultimately creating the conditions for a real class struggle, a real revolution, but we can also conceive of what you have just said. In any case, what is sure, also, for the present, is that I don't see any possibility of creating conditions favourable for peace in the immediate future. I don't see any because as I have told you, and I understand both very well, the Israelis have a strong presentiment of death and the idea that they will fight to the end; the Arabs also have a deep and justified feeling of humiliation and the same desire to fight to the end. We are in a sea of passion. You must understand that I, of course, am not a psychologist, but emotions also count when they reflect a certain social and economic situation.

Finally, there is one more thing I would like to say: for peace, granted that we are obviously on the utopian level, there would have to be not only all that I have said, but, in addition to the recognition of Israel's sovereignty, steps taken by both sides to achieve the integration of the Israeli economy in the Middle East. That would be a Middle East economy and not the centrifugal one, finding its resources in foreign countries, which is also one of the great reasons for Arab hostility. We would have to conceive of an economy whose technical capital, for a time in any case, would come from the Israeli engineers who would try to supply such elements to the neighbouring countries. But we are imagining a change, aren't we? It is, however, only on this basis that a stable peace can be established and, at the same time, the true depths of what we call the class struggle uncovered.

A.S.: In your essay, 'Reflections on the Jewish Question', you say that it would be a lazy solution to wait for the future revolution to take care of liquidating the 'Jewish question'. What other solution do you envisage now – Zionism?

J.-P.S.: I would say that – that the questions are mixed together, aren't they? Nothing frightens the Arabs more than Zionism, because they consider it to mean that Israel has to grow larger and, therefore, to take territories. That isn't what Israel says she wants to do, but it is clear that if we consider that most of the Jews are still outside Israel today, if the ideal desired by Israel is to have them all come back to Israel, then there won't be enough to feed everybody, except by territorial annexations. On the other hand, I can plainly see the reasons for the hostility of the socialist, or so-called socialist, countries towards Zionism. That is something else, completely, and is fundamentally because of the desire to establish Jewish communities in socialist countries, which are jealous of their sovereignty, as communities of dual affiliation – that is, belonging to their countries and at the same time, being able to choose to go to Israel, and thus not quite like the other citizens. In my opinion, nothing could be more clumsy; it means encouraging anti-Semitism. If a Soviet or Rumanian citizen, even now only too much tempted by anti-Semitism, does not have the right to leave the country except under very specific circumstances, while a Rumanian Jew, on the contrary, can call himself both Rumanian and Israeli, according to his choice, the non-Jew will think both that these people are more favoured than he is, and also that they are non-loyal. At the same time the government looks on them with hostility, saying that from the moment they choose or can choose Israel, they are not socialists. Whether they are wrong or right I don't know, but what I am sure of is that this kind of Zionist activity is a very serious thing. I would think that we would have to recognize Israel's right, as a sovereign state, to accept all the Jews who may want to come to her, but that she should not make militant Zionist policies abroad.

In other words, if some Jew is persecuted, no matter where, or even if he isn't persecuted, but simply wants to go to Israel, he can go there and become an Israeli citizen with full rights. But it is another thing to send teams of specialists to make propaganda in order to bring Jews to Israel. I say this even more clearly because in my opinion Zionism has already passed, for the good reason that now, if there will be new crisis of anti-Semitism, and I don't think there will be any (people haven't been cured of their anti-Semitism, but I believe that the idea of a violent anti-Semitism which would make the situation of the Jews intolerable cannot exist in the foreseeable future), I think that the Jews of the Diaspora will prefer to stay where they are. The American Jews give large sums to Israel; they go there from time to time; some of them insist on eating kosher there, though at home they eat what they like, but it amuses them – it is picturesque. But they are much too americanized, they like the American life too much. All, or almost all, the French Jews who could have come to Israel – I know them, I saw them in Israel; they are the people I understand very well, who were shocked by French attitudes between 1940 and 1945; that attitude wasn't uglier than that of other Western countries but it was ugly enough, wasn't it? Well, all those Jews are already in Israel.

On the other hand, I see a new generation being born. At the time of the war, the Leftist of my age, or a little over fifty, either hesitated or justified Israel; but, on the contrary, people of twenty or twenty-one, twenty-three – the socialist, trotsky-ites, the communists, independently of their political positions – that is an age when one thinks independently of the positions of the parties to which one belongs – were very radically anti-Israel. That was not at all because they considered Israel imperialist – no, they said that, afterwards – I think it was something internal, a certain kind of integration in a country, while fighting, as they think, for the revolution to eventually take place in their country. I don't know if it is the same thing in Italy, but that is the way it is amongst us. Therefore, for me, Zionism is dead. Under these conditions, I wonder why Israel fights for its Zionist positions. I often ask Simha Flapan – why are you Zionists?

A.S.: We could sum up by saying that Zionism, which at a certain time played a role that we need not hesitate to say was progressive, since it was a movement of national liberation that decided the renaissance of the Jewish people, today has a reactionary role. History gives many examples of movements which were progressive at the start and reactionary later. The bourgeoisie in 1889 was a revolutionary class. We could say that Zionism's *raison d'être* no longer is justified; and, even more, by surviving itself, it borrows all the faults of those things that want to survive despite the events. Zionism today is developing as a chauvinism that can only be very dangerous since its intransigence threatens the very existence of the state it helped to create.

J.-P.S.: I think so: because Zionism was an advanced conception in an epoch when the powers were colonialists and when, until lately, the whole world was colonialist. It was impregnated with colonialism from the start. I don't think Israel is a colonizing country; all I want to say is that the atmosphere in which Zionism was a progressive force was one in which it was considered natural to take a piece of territory and to establish oneself in some large, underdeveloped country, etc. What they did, actually, at that time, everything that was done, was completely normal. The drama was in the fact that there was an awakening of Arab consciousness. So we are wrong about these men who have worked with their hands from the beginning, when we treat them as *colons*. But the best answer would be precisely to declare that Zionism no longer existed: Zionism has contributed to creating our state; we are here; there are certain elements of the Zionist ideology of which we no longer approve; we appreciate its beginnings, but except for that, it is finished. In addition, it is no longer effective. Only one thing can be done, and that is to say that when someone is a Zionist, he is not a Leftist. That is the argument of all the Arabs: that if someone is Zionist, he isn't Leftist, because he wants a state built on race – an argument that could equally, in some way, be turned against them. But I think that would be an answer.

That is also utopian because I have the impression that the Israelis still have a very great attachment to Zionist practice, even if it is no longer valid. They don't want to resign themselves to liquidating it. I am thinking of the curious fashion in which Israelis speak to Jews who aren't in Israel; it is always curious, with a little bit of reserve and hostility: 'Why, why aren't you here?' I am thinking of Lanzmann, for example, they like him a lot, he has been among them in Israel, but finally they ask him, 'Why aren't you here?'

I very well understand the point of view of some of them. For example, I have a young friend there, thirty at most. He is a remarkable person, a Frenchman who is in a kibbutz. It is very evident that he came there shocked: his grandfather and grandmother were killed by the Nazis, and when he came back he found that anti-Semitism had survived all that, that the anti-Semites had seen the massacre of the Jews and remained anti-Semites. He was very young; he had very deep hatred for all those people. He left in order not to have anything to do with them. When he thinks of Jews in France – if they are sixty years old, good, they are like his parents, he tolerates that because they are old – but the others, he thinks, have understood nothing. How can a thirty-year-old Jew live in France after all he has seen? We feel all the deep emotional past resting on real structures. It is because of that we can't hope for Zionism to disappear from one day to the next. But all that does not prevent us from having the courage to say that Israel's sovereignty includes the right of all Jews, if they desire, to go to Israel and become Israeli citizens. At the same time, it implies that they won't make propaganda in order to bring the citizens of other countries to Israel.

The Great Powers, the Arabs and the Israelis

By Bernard Lewis*

I

During the months that followed the Arab–Israeli war of June 1967, the view gradually gained ground in the West that the Arab defeat represented a considerable Russian victory. Some more imaginative observers argued that the Russians had de

*Reprinted by special permission from *Foreign Affairs*, July 1969 Copyright by the Council on Foreign Relations, Inc., New York

liberately engineered both the war and the defeat in order to achieve this result; others, without going as far as to ascribe conscious purpose, nevertheless agreed that, by increasing the hostility of the Arabs to the West and their dependence on the Soviet Union, the crisis, the war and their aftermath had greatly strengthened the Soviet political and strategic position in the Middle East and correspondingly weakened that of the United States. Observers and commentators spoke with mounting anxiety about the growth of Soviet influence in the area and the threat which it offered to the interests of the free world.

More recent developments have suggested that this mood of dejection, like the vicarious euphoria which followed immediately after the Israeli military victory, is misplaced or at least exaggerated. The situation in the Arab lands and the attitude of their peoples and even governments are more complex and less one-sided than might appear. The Soviet government has been sufficiently dissatisfied with the position to make repeated attempts – and with growing urgency – to change it. The latest of these is the four-power talks to devise, and possibly apply, a solution to the Arab–Israeli conflict.

The Israeli reaction to this proposal was predictably hostile. Of the four governments concerned, two appear to be firmly committed to the Arab cause, the other two are seen in Israel as practising a kind of unilateral evenhandedness. This was exemplified in the debate at the Security Council over Israeli–Arab clashes at the very moment when the four-power talks were beginning. The United States and Britain wanted to condemn both sides; the Soviet Union, followed by France, insisted on condemning Israel only. In the Israeli view, a bench consisting of two impartial judges and two hostile advocates is unlikely to arrive at a balanced judgement. More immediately relevant is the Israeli conviction that any compromise likely to be reached among the four powers would be at Israel's expense. The November Resolution did indeed require concessions from both sides – but the Israeli concession, being territorial and strategic, could be reversed only by another victory in war, while the Arab concession, being diplomatic, could be reversed by a simple declaration. To Israel, the sacrifices and the risks seemed unequal.

Israeli opposition to the four-power talks was manifest from the start. Such talks, they argued, were foredoomed to failure, and in the meantime their effect was to paralyse the Jarring mission and encourage Arab recalcitrance. Israeli spokesmen were at pains to show that the fear of an explosion and a nuclear confrontation, which had impelled the West to agree to the talks in the first place, was greatly exaggerated. The Middle East, they said, was not at peace – but it was not at war either, and there was no immediate danger requiring precipitate action.

Arab leaders took an obliquely opposite view of the four powers, but seemed to share the Israeli assumption that an agreed settlement would be to Israel's disadvantage. The Arabs, like the Israelis, made it clear that they would not submit to an imposed settlement; they appeared, however, to expect that an agreement, if reached, would be such that no imposition would be necessary on their side. Their attitude to the talks was therefore much more hopeful than that of the Israelis, and became more so as Israel fears visibly mounted. Arab governments agreed that the situation was explosive, and did what they could to emphasize and exemplify this point.

The really crucial attitude is of course that of the Soviet Union. The talks were begun on a Russian initiative; their outcome will depend largely on what Russia is willing and able to do. It is therefore important to examine the causes and purposes – the two are not identical – of the Russian approach.

In part, no doubt, the Soviet government – in this as in other initiatives – has sought a propaganda advantage. Even if the talks came to nothing, they could still serve the useful purpose of accentuating the polarization of the Middle East; they could identify the United States more firmly with Israel in Arab eyes, and thus improve the waning image of the Soviets. But propaganda is clearly not the only purpose. The Soviets are visibly concerned about their position in the Middle East – and about more than their image. The timing of the Soviet initiative – between American administrations – could be tactical, with a view to catching the other side at a disadvantage. It could also reflect a sense of urgency – a desire to seize the earliest possible opportunity to avert a serious danger to Russian interests.

II

Broadly, there are two views of the Russian position in the Middle East, which can be expressed in extreme form as follows.

According to one view, the Russians have during the last two years achieved an immense success – the fulfilment of the centuries-old dream of the Tsars. They have won great political influence in the Arab lands – dominant in some, powerful in others, threatening even in those countries that are still more or less in the Western camp. Russia is now an established Mediterranean power, with friendly ports on the eastern and southern shores, and is reaching across the land bridges to Asia and Africa.

A diametrically opposite view is expressed in the saying that the Middle East is Russia's Vietnam. According to this interpretation, Russia was unwittingly sucked in on the losing side, with a perilous and endless commitment, in an undertaking of great risk, high cost and dubious results. There is a further parallel in that the Russian involvement in the Middle East appears to be highly, even symbolically, unpopular with such public opinion as can be discerned in Russia and her East European satellites. This is indirectly confirmed by the charges of Zionism levelled against liberals and reformists in Czechoslovakia, Russia and elsewhere, and by the effort and energy devoted in Communist domestic propaganda to discrediting Israel.

A critical assessment of the Russian position shows both gains and losses. In several Arab states, the regimes in power have become dependent on Russian support, though whether against the enemies or against the people of their countries is not always clear. Soviet power in the Mediterranean, though no doubt of limited military effectiveness in the event of a major great-power clash, is of considerable political value in the rather Victorian style of imperial diplomacy currently pursued by the Russians.

Two substantial gains have already been achieved. With a Soviet fleet in the Mediterranean, a Western intervention such as that of 1958, when American marines landed in Lebanon and British troops in Jordan, is no longer possible. That is to say, such a landing would not now be possible for either side, and this represents a net Soviet gain. A second Soviet gain is the ability to exercise additional pressure on Turkey and Iran, which can now be threatened from the south as well as the north. To achieve this result may well have been the original purpose of the whole Soviet operation in the Arab lands; it is still a major objective of Soviet policy, and one which is being pursued with some success.

These Soviet gains have, however, been counterbalanced by serious losses. While the advance of Soviet power has been accelerated in the Mediterranean area, it has been virtually arrested in the southern half of the Middle East, in the countries bordering on the Red Sea, the Persian Gulf and the Indian Ocean. In May 1967 the prospects for a southward expansion of Soviet influence seemed excellent. In Somalia, the Soviets were already strongly entrenched and were encouraging Somali irredentist claims against both Ethiopia and Kenya. In southern Arabia, British rule was coming to an end, and there was no reason to doubt that it would be followed by a regime closely linked with Cairo and thus also with Moscow. With the coast from Hodeida to Aden under their control, the Egyptians would not have needed to trouble themselves with the Yemeni interior. With the Suez Canal and Aden at its disposal, the Soviet Navy would soon have established supremacy in the Red Sea, and the regimes on both shores would have been due for realignment or replacement. The way was open to further penetration in southern and eastern Arabia, and especially in the Gulf, where Iraq was already in the revolutionary camp and Iran could be isolated and threatened at its weakest point.

All this was stopped by the June war. With the closure of the Canal, Soviet naval activity east of Suez was severely limited; the Egyptians withdrew from the Yemen, and the ripe plum of Aden fell to the ground and was not picked. The Somalis, deeply discouraged by the Soviet failure to help the Arabs, decided that irredentism with Soviet support was unsafe, and, since war was not practicable, they proceeded with unusual logic to make peace. In the Gulf, in Arabia and in North Africa, the conservative forces rallied, and the Arab monarchs were even able to impose a halt in subversion on an Egyptian government that was now financially dependent on them.[1]

Even in the Mediterranean area, the Soviet posture is not as comfortable as it might have seemed. Without the Suez Canal, without air-transit rights across Turkey or Iran, without contiguous land access and the possibility of moving troops over the border as in Czechoslovakia, the Soviet position remains precarious and exposed. Politically, too, Soviet influence is a diminishing asset. The Russians have now become heavily involved in the Arab lands, and are thus losing what was previously their main psychological advantage, remoteness. Like Nazi Germany in the past, Soviet Russia at first appeared to the Arabs as an almost mythical champion of their cause – the enemy of their enemies, the mighty power that would defeat and destroy them. Unlike the Nazis, the Russians arrived and revealed themselves to their admirers – with the inevitable disillusionment. Instead of Westerners, it was now Russians who appeared in the roles of experts, advisers, technicians and teachers; and it was Russians who suffered and inflicted all the innumerable irritations and exasperations that are inseparable from these roles. At closer quarters, the Russians and their methods began to look suspiciously familiar. Other powers in the past had used the same combination – the expert, the engineer, the concessionaire and the missionary on the one hand, with the fleet and the flag on the other. The concessionaires used different methods, and the missionaries brought a different message, but they still worked with the same pattern of native princes, native clients and native converts to maintain and extend their authority.

No one loves protectors, still less protectors who do not protect. The Russian failure to help the Arabs in war or save them

1. Unlike earlier similar agreements with the West, the truce in radio propaganda reached with the three monarchs seems to have been effective. One possible reason is that the Saudis, Kuwaits and Libyans themselves understand Arabic, and do not need to rely on translated abstracts.

in peace could no longer be concealed, and there were growing signs of impatience with the Soviet combination of hectoring and inefficiency. The invasion of Czechoslovakia brought a new shock. Arab governments in general felt obliged to support or at least excuse the Soviet action, and some spokesmen even went so far as to rejoice that the Soviets had now demonstrated their readiness and ability to defy the world and occupy a country in a few hours. This, it was said, was how they could deal with Israel, when the time came. More perceptive Arabs, however, were deeply alarmed by the Czechoslovak affair and the memories of Hungary which it evoked. This kind of action, they observed, was taken by the Soviets, not against their enemies, but against their allies. It was a profoundly disturbing thought.

Some Soviet strategists would no doubt prefer to maintain, rather than solve, the Palestine problem. As long as it exists, Russia will be able to outbid America in hostility to Israel, and will therefore be better placed to win Arab support. This is an advantage to the Soviet Union, and an embarrassment to the United States, in those Arab countries that are still neutral or pro-Western. There are, however, signs of another and more disillusioned Soviet approach to the Middle East, and of a growing consciousness of the hazards of Middle Eastern adventure.

The Russians are of course well aware of the decline in their popularity, and of the wistful glances now being cast towards the West. There are also other considerations which may well cause them anxiety. The Russian involvement in the Arab lands is better than the American predicament in Vietnam, in that there is no loss of life – that is, of course, of Russian life. But it is worse in two important respects, the one economic, the other political. The immense cost of the Vietnam operation can still be borne out of the vast surplus of the American economy, causing only minor dislocation at home; the cost of the Russian adventure in the Middle East has to be met by a Soviet public that is still short of many basic consumer goods and becoming increasingly resentful of such deprivation.

Perhaps the most serious aspect of the situation, from the point of view of the Soviets, is the political danger to which they are exposed. This danger takes two forms. On the one hand, their political ascendancy in some of the Arab states, without effective air and military support, remains precarious, and can be terminated by internal political action. Recent developments in Syria and Iraq indicate a desire in those countries to extricate themselves from too close a connexion with Russia. Still more alarming is the possibility of another war and another Arab defeat. The Russian commitment to the revolutionary Arab states appears open-ended. By precipitate action on the part of regimes with which they are associated but which they do not control, the Russians might again be forced to choose between humiliation and confrontation. It is not a pleasing prospect, and one can well understand the Soviet anxiety to escape from a situation in which such a choice might be forced on them.

Soviet interests and purposes in the Middle East have changed since the time of the first Soviet penetration into the Arab world. In those days, the West was still predominant in the area, and was therefore interested in stability ; the Russians were outside, and consequently interested in disruption. Today, with Soviet influence predominant in part of the area, their interest in stability in that part may outweigh their interest in disruption in the remainder. Stability could enable them to consolidate and exploit the position they have gained, and perhaps in time extend it. The most immediate advantages they would gain would be the use of the Suez Canal, with the consequent extension of their influence east of Suez, and release from the constant danger of involvement in another military defeat. There might even be some advantage to the Soviet Union in the resumption by the United States of a certain role in Arab affairs. It would no doubt be too much to hope for a return to an earlier phase, when the United States shared in the cost of maintaining a Soviet satellite, but some sharing of the cost and odium of supporting the existing regimes might not be altogether unwelcome.

III

In the West there have been, broadly speaking, two opinions on the whole question of the four-power talks, each with its own characteristic judgements and forms of expression. According

to one, there is in the Middle East an 'explosive situation' which
needs to be 'de-fused' before it detonates into a nuclear confrontation. Both East and West, it is believed, recognize this danger, and are prepared to offer some sacrifices in order to avert
it. By negotiation and compromise the powers could devise a
reasonable formula of settlement, and could then induce (the
word 'impose' is, in Anglo-American usage, unacceptable) their
respective protégés to accept it.

According to the second view, the danger of an unintended
confrontation is remote, and there is in consequence no real
willingness to make the kind of sacrifices that might produce
a great-power agreement. Even if there were, the great powers
could not make good their undertakings, since they cannot compel their protégés to act against what they regard as their
vital interests.

Supporters of the first view argue that in any case initiative
is better than drift. The attempt is worth making, and even if
it fails the position is no worse than before. Critics of the four-
power talks point out that the mere proposal to hold such talks
brought an immediate worsening of the situation along the
cease-fire lines, and that the progress of the talks has been accompanied by mounting tension and violence, designed specifically to influence them. When the talks, as is inevitable, fail to
produce any substantial result, the situation, it is argued, will
be worse than before. The parties to the dispute will have worked themselves into new and more intransigent military and
political attitudes; the great powers will have further diminished
their own credit and authority – their ability to inspire respect
or fear in their own protégés or those of their opponents.

Three main points are at issue: the danger of a nuclear confrontation, the possibility of a Russo-American compromise,
and the ability of the superpowers to impose a solution on Israel
and the Arabs.

The danger of a confrontation exists wherever the interests
and spheres of influence of the two superpowers meet – in East
Asia, South-east Asia, the Mediterranean, Germany, even the
Caribbean. It has, however, much decreased since the Cuban
missile crisis and the resulting awareness on both sides of the

risks involved. If ever a confrontation in the Middle East seemed likely, it was in the summer of 1967, when an uncontrolled political and military crisis threatened to involve both super-powers. Both refused to become involved, and each signalled its refusal clearly to the other. Since then the risks and possibilities of the situation are better understood, and the chances of a confrontation by accident – a collision in the dark – correspondingly reduced. There remains the possibility of a confrontation by choice. This would, as things are now, have to be Russia's choice, since in the event of another local war it would almost certainly be the Arabs, not Israel, who would need to be rescued. One of the present aims of Russian policy is to avoid the need to make such a choice; another aim, which could be either complementary or alternative, is to change the present situation in the Middle East in such a way as to transfer the burden of choice to the other side, i.e. to the United States. Such a transfer would, however, only be possible, if at all, with American assistance, which is hardly likely to be forthcoming.

Both the United States and the Soviet Union are seen as the patrons of their respective protégés – Israel and the revolutionary Arab states. Both superpowers may at times yearn audibly for release from this uncomfortable and compromising relationship, but there is little prospect of either of them being able to achieve it in present circumstances. The world sees them as protectors, and judges them by the effectiveness of their protection. If they falter or fail, even those who benefit by their failure will despise them and be confirmed in the wisdom of their own choice of patron. Neither patron can afford to be seen as faithless, unreliable or inept; but equally neither can afford to appear too obviously ruthless and overbearing, selfishly subordinating its protégés' interests to its own.

One of the Soviet Union's purposes is to restore confidence – among the Arabs and elsewhere – in its effectiveness and reliability as a patron. This can be achieved only by giving its protégés effective support. Another is to escape from its present dilemma in the Middle East. This could be achieved either by extricating itself from its commitments, or by transforming the situation in such a way that it would be able to meet these commitments with relative ease and safety. The first would be damaging to Russia's influence with its Arab clients, or to those clients' influence with their own peoples; the second could involve very great risks. The Soviet government's assessment of those risks, and consequent choice of direction, will be decisively affected by the content and expression of American policy.

IV

In the English-speaking countries we still feel a strong inner compulsion to act, in great matters, in accordance with moral principles, or at least to persuade ourselves that we are so doing. When obliged by circumstances to have dealings with the adversary, we feel a corresponding compulsion to see him as something other and better than what he is, and thus morally to justify our dealings with him. This can be dangerous. It may be necessary to negotiate and compromise with the Soviet government. It would be very foolish to cherish delusions as to the nature and purposes of Soviet power.

It is possible, but not likely, that the four-power talks will end in open disagreement. It is possible, but still less likely, that they will produce a workable settlement, acceptable to both parties. The most probable result is some amplification of the November Resolution, perhaps even including the outlines of a general settlement of specific issues, such as frontiers, refugees and navigation, but leaving the details of application and the methods of implementation to the Arabs and Israelis. If, in spite of their differences, the four powers manage to agree on a detailed settlement, and, what is more important, on the manner and sequence of its implementation – what then? There would still be the problem of persuading Israel and the Arab states to comply effectively with its provisions; and the chances are that any settlement likely to be accepted by the four powers would be rejected by one or all of the parties to the dispute. One of the facts of the present international order is the ability of even the smallest countries to defy the great powers in what they regard as matters of vital national interest. There are no doubt powerful means of persuasion at the disposal of the Russians in Cairo and Damascus and the Americans in Jerusalem, but it would be politically difficult, if not impossible, to use them. The two superpowers have to consider the effects of such pressure on neutrals, allies, clients – even, in varying measure, on their own domestic opinion. Neither the Israelis nor the Arabs have much reason to rely on the United Nations for the protection of their vital interests; neither can be wholly confident that its patron would come to the rescue in any conflict with a purely local enemy. Both therefore would be reluctant to accept any sacrifices which might weaken their position, politically or militarily, in the event of another local war.

The two major problems of the area – the East–West rivalry and the Arab–Israeli conflict – would remain. The two are not necessarily connected, and the West has usually tried to keep them separate. The Soviet Union, on the other hand, has tried to combine them in order to maximize anti-Western feeling and to exploit its advantage in hostility to Israel. But the Russians, too, may begin to recognize the dangers of this policy and to see the merits of some measure of disengagement.

If there is indeed a danger of nuclear confrontation in the Middle East, it would be enormously increased by a guaranteed settlement, which would involve the guarantors in every border incident. It might, however, be reduced by a limited and agreed disengagement. This could not be general, since the powers have vital interests in the area apart from the Arab–Israeli conflict; it could not be unilateral, since this would merely mean the victory and domination of the other side. But all four powers might well find some advantage in achieving that measure of détente which lies in their own hands, i.e. by separating the Arab–Israeli conflict in their own mutual relations, and reducing it to the relative harmlessness, to world peace, of the Cyprus and Kashmir disputes.

At the present stage, the Arab–Israeli conflict is virtually insoluble. In Arab eyes, an Israeli solution would mean submission to intolerable injustice and humiliation; in Israeli eyes, an Arab solution would mean the immediate or slightly deferred extinction of the state and society. In time there will no doubt be some changes of outlook and assessment on both sides, and a possibility of compromise may then arise. (For example, the

replacement of Zionism and pan-Arabism by Israel and
Egyptian patriotism would make an accommodation much
easier. But this is still very problematic.) Meanwhile there is
little that the great powers can do.

That little should not, however, be neglected. The imagery of
gunpowder and explosion that is often used with reference to
the Middle East is somewhat misleading. The Arab–Israeli crisis
is not so much explosive as inflamed, not a bomb to be defused
but a fever to be isolated and cooled. To this end the powers
could make some contribution by administering poultices instead of irritants. They could restrict the entry of weapons into
the area – equitably and by agreement; they could call a mora-
torium on their own probing and propaganda, which spread
infection and raise the temperature; they might even agree to
a cease-fire in public debate, and thereby give the patient some
relief from the glare of publicity and the passion and posturing
that it evokes. These things would not solve the Palestine problem, but they would bring the time of solution perceptibly
nearer.

Such a policy would of course require a degree of restraint
from the superpowers which may well prove unattainable. The
failure of either is the failure of both. And in the meantime,
with or without such a disengagement, the larger problem of
their political and strategic confrontation across the Middle
East would remain. Here it would be well to recall that the
Arab–Israeli conflict, for all its importance and the attention it
receives, is not the only issue in the region, nor the most decisive in the real relationship between the great powers. If the
object of Western policy is to prevent Soviet domination of the
Middle East, then it would be wise to devote rather more attention to the southern and eastern waters, where the intrusion
of the Soviet naval and air power would transform the whole
balance of strength in Asia and Africa, and above all to Turkey and Iran, the guardians of the northern approaches.

Soviet Global Policy and the Middle East

By Uri Ra'anan*

I suppose it is something of a truism to say that the Soviet regime, with all its global commitments, usually gives first priority to questions which affect its domestic power base, and that, of course, means the USSR itself and the dependent countries of Eastern Europe. However, this does not imply that developments elsewhere in the international sphere cannot and do not have such a profound effect on the Soviet empire as to become – indirectly – of the greatest importance to the Kremlin. There is some cause for believing that, during the last few years, certain events in the so-called Third World, including the Middle East, have had precisely such an effect on Moscow; this effect has been felt particularly in what must be regarded as the Achilles' Heel of Soviet power, namely Eastern Europe. The result has been that the Kremlin has reacted disproportionately – with a certain amount of hysteria – to events which, in themselves, need not have been of tremendous concern to the Russians.

To understand the causal relationship which is involved, one has to re-examine the premises on which Soviet international strategy has been based ever since the end of the Khrushchev period and the beginning of the Brezhnev-Kosygin era. Shortly after Khrushchev was otherthrown, the central organs of the Soviet Communist Party and the Soviet state came out with a series of policy definitions which may be translated into plain language, more or less as follows:

(a) That the USSR is obliged by the consequences of the thermonuclear stalemate to go on avoiding an armed confrontation with the West;

(b) That this has many disadvantages but also provides a breathing spell during which some of Russia's major economic and power deficiencies might be overcome and the rest of the bloc might be consolidated, politically, economically and

*Reprinted with special permission from *Midstream*, May 1969.

militarily, so as to repair some of the ravages of 'polycentrism' and of the Sino-Soviet split;

(c) That, at the same time, this would leave the Kremlin free to continue with semi-covert attempts to change the psychological and political balance in the Third World, while, of course, always taking good care to avoid a possible Western reaction (by keeping Soviet interference at a very low visibility level and by insisting that whatever may be happening in Afro-Asia is merely the result of internal or 'domestic' developments). Consequently, Moscow would be able to give limited and indirect support to the so-called 'national liberation movement' against colonial or pro-Western governments, while, at the same time, also wooing those of the independent Afro-Asian rulers who cherish radical and anti-Western sentiments and among whom the Castros of the future might be found. (That is, of course, always presuming that Castros are necessarily an asset for the Soviet Union.)

This global blueprint of political strategy was intimately linked to a new ideological formulation which had emerged in Khrushchev's day and which, to all intents and purposes, has come to replace the old concept of a world Communist movement; I am referring to the slogan of a tripartite alliance between 'the socialist camp, the proletarian parties of the West, and the national liberation movement'. The third member of this triple alliance, the 'national liberation movement', was to be represented not so much by guerrillas fighting in the bush as by militant and anti-Western dictators who ruled certain selected countries in sub-Saharan Africa, in the Middle East and in South-east Asia. Some six or seven of these rulers, including those of Ghana, Guinea, Mali, Congo (Brazzaville), Algeria, the UAR and Syria, were suddenly hailed in Moscow as 'revolutionary democrats'; they were said to have adopted a 'non-capitalist path' which would eventually lead towards socialism, and their one-party regimes were invited to participate as honorary associates at gatherings which had previously been purely Communist functions. For instance, the ruling parties of Ghana, Guinea and Mali were invited as guests to the 22nd

Congress of the Soviet Communist Party as early as 1961, and additional invitations were extended to the Algerian FLN and to Egypt's Arab Socialist Union to the 23rd Communist Party Congress in 1966. In this manner, countries which are really well outside the immediate Eurasian heartland of the Soviet camp were granted a type of client or 'protected' status.

This was a very significant development which received most serious underpinning – it was enshrined in holy writ, so to speak – with the appearance of the definitive second edition of the volume on Soviet 'Military Strategy', which was edited by Marshal Sokolovsky and other members of the Soviet General Staff. In this basic statement of its purposes and functions, the Red Army not only committed itself to act as a shield over every country of the 'camp' itself, that is every formally Communist regime, but, in a sense, also extended its protection over the new 'revolutionary democratic' regimes of Africa and Asia by stressing that 'an aggressive local war against one of the non-socialist countries that affects the basic interests' of the Soviet Union would be among the cases which would 'obviously lead to a new world war'.

To all intents and purposes, this amounted to a new 'doctrine of irreversibility'; in fact, the Hungarian leader, Kádár, recently has used this very term. In other words, the thermonuclear stalemate was deemed to constitute a guarantee that no change of status would occur in countries which belong, formally speaking, to the Eastern or Western camps; however, in the Third World, by acting very cautiously and circuitously, Moscow would still be able to add new candidate members to its bloc and, once it had declared them to belong to this category, they too would be protected by the global stalemate against a reversal of status.

Of course, one could argue that this Soviet approach was, in a sense, naïve, since it did not rest on a requisite measure of power. The air and maritime approaches to Africa–Asia continued and continue today to be dominated by the West or, to be precise, by the US Sixth and Seventh Fleets. Probably owing to Khrushchev's rather simplistic attitude towards the essential ingredients of an air and sea striking force, the Soviet Union, much to the chagrin of its military factions, only belatedly took steps to establish a physical presence outside its own immediate perimeter. It should be remembered that the keel of the first Soviet helicopter carrier was only laid in 1962–3, the Marine Corps (or 'Maritime Infantry') was only reactivated late in 1964, and Soviet aircraft carriers continue to be conspicuous by their absence. Clearly, therefore, the 'doctrine of irreversibility' was based far less on the physical ability of the Soviet Union to deter the West than on its success in psychological warfare – in other words, its power to bluff the West. That the Soviet posture actually rested on feet of clay should have been painfully apparent after the Cuban Missile Crisis; but, strangely enough, the prestige sop which was thrown out to Khrushchev by the Kennedy administration, namely the so-called 'guarantee' not to invade Cuba or to overthrow the Castro regime, helped to obscure one of the main lessons of the Soviet fiasco. Khrushchev could argue – and did argue – that, whatever had been the fate of the Soviet missiles themselves, Moscow had successfully secured Western acquiescence in the doctrine that, once a country and a regime – even in the Western hemisphere – had acquired associate status in the Communist 'camp', the West was obliged to refrain from action to reverse this development.

It must be remembered, however, that it was not only the West which had to be deterred by the new Soviet posture. The peoples of Eastern Europe, as well as of the new Afro-Asian 'revolutionary democracies', also had to be convinced of the determination and the capacity of the Soviet leadership to act ruthlessly against developments within those countries and without, which might change their political status quo. This was by no means an easy task, since, as we have noted, the Soviet Union lacked a ready striking force, equal to the US Sixth and Seventh Fleets, through which it could bring its power to bear in Africa and Asia. In Eastern Europe, on the other hand, where Soviet forces were present, it was not feasible for Moscow to stage a Hungarian-type invasion once a month just to demonstrate that Soviet determination remained undiminished. As a result the Russians regarded it as essential both in Afro-Asia and in Eastern Europe to 'put up a front' which would be sufficiently stern and bold to be convincing to clients and associates – always hoping, of course, that Soviet power would not actually be put to the test. Above all, it was vitally important that nothing should occur in either of the two areas concerned, Eastern Europe and Afro-Asia, which would place in serious doubt the credibility of the Soviet commitment to implement the new 'doctrine of irreversibility'. For Soviet credibility to be seriously jeopardized, one of the following contingencies had to arise in Moscow's client states:

(a) The overthrow of a regime and its replacement by a neutral or pro-Western government;

(b) An attack upon the territory of such a state without effective Soviet counter measures;

(c) Loss of territory by such a state.

A series of events of this type was bound to confront the Kremlin with a 'credibility gap' of almost unbridgeable proportions. The sad fact, from the point of view of the Brezhnev regime, is that, since 1965, *all* of these unpleasant contingencies have actually arisen, in a series of what must be regarded as unparalleled setbacks for the Soviet protectors of some twenty Communist and 'revolutionary democratic' states.

As far as the first contingency is concerned, the regimes of the 'revolutionary democrats' ruling Ghana, Congo (Brazzaville) and Mali have been overthrown, practically without a struggle, and replaced by governments which are far less friendly to the Soviet Union – with Moscow unable to play any significant part whatsoever at the decisive moment. The pro-Soviet 'revolutionary democrat' who was ruling Algeria, Ben Bella, was similarly removed, much to the dismay both of the Soviet Union and the Italian and French Communist Parties. Admittedly, in this particular case, Ben Bella's successor has since then resumed a fairly close relationship with the Soviet Union. In Indonesia, the militantly Leftist regime of Sukarno was toppled and the Indonesian Communist Party was decimated by the Indonesian Army, which was largely equipped with Soviet weapons. Although Moscow probably was disinclined to mourn either Sukarno or Aidit, both of whom had been pro-Chinese, nevertheless the massacre of Communists is a very embarrassing event for a state which claims to be the heart and centre of the International Communist Movement. The fact remains that, after spending almost two billion dollars in military and economic aid, the Soviet Union at the vital moment, was able to exert no leverage at all.

As for contingency B – attack upon the territory of a country aligned with the USSR – there is, of course, the notorious case of a Communist country, a full member of the 'Socialist camp', supposedly protected by the shield of the Red Army, which was bombed with impunity for almost three years by Western planes, with Moscow apparently incapable of taking effective counter-measures. (The reference is, of course, to Vietnam.) The only action the Russians did take, apart from purely propagandistic steps, was to send a very limited amount of military equipment to Vietnam, which, incidentally, is of lower quality than the weapons previously dispatched to non-Communist regimes in the Middle East. Thus, the Vietnamese had to make do with the MiG-17, when the Iraqis and Egyptians had long since received the MiG-21.

Finally, contingency C, loss of territory by clients of the USSR: two regimes of 'revolutionary democrats' in the Middle East, that is, the Nasser regime in the UAR and the Ba'ath regime in Syria, were humiliatingly defeated in battle, their armies and air forces were almost annihilated and they lost sizeable stretches of territory in the process. Yet the Soviet Union did not lift a finger to rescue them, but instead rushed to the 'Hot Line' to assure the United States that Moscow was not about to become involved; subsequently, the Russians accepted a cease-fire which did not include a clause for the withdrawal of Israel troops from the Sinai Peninsula or the Golan Heights. Of course, as in the case of the Cuban Missile Crisis, the Soviets have since then found a way to console themselves; they allege that they have, at any rate, been successful in 'saving' the 'revolutionary democratic' regimes in Cairo and in Damascus. However, this is surely a somewhat hollow 'victory', since the 'enemy', in this particular case, had not been trying to overthrow the Damascus and Cairo regimes at all, but merely to liquidate the military threat posed by the Egyptian and Syrian armies. It is an old adage in international affairs that, if you cannot score a positive gain, then you must ascribe to your enemy objectives which he does not really have and then claim you have, at any rate, defeated those aims.

To sum up: in a period of three to four years, the Brezhnev regime had saddled its 'doctrine of irreversibility' with a 'credibility gap' of vast proportions. In some four or five 'revolutionary democracies', the Leftist regime has been overthrown, while two others have lost a war and considerable stretches of territory, without Soviet protection proving to be of the slightest value in either of these contingencies. What is even worse, a member of the Communist camp could be bombed and strafed without deriving any meaningful benefit from the Red Army's shield.

Thus, there is no question but that the Kremlin must be deeply conscious of the cumulative effect of all these debacles, and the almost hysterical reaction of Soviet and East European leaders to the Six Day War in the Middle East indicates that this is, indeed, the case. Many observers wondered at the time why an event in an area which, after all, is well outside the confines of the Soviet empire, should have provoked repeated emergency summit gatherings of Communist leaders. The truth is, as we shall see, that they were far less anxious about the Middle East as such, than they were about the growing impact of repeated Soviet setbacks on the situation in Eastern Europe itself.

At this point, the Kremlin resorted to a new formulation in order to attribute its setbacks not to its own shortcomings but rather to a change in the 'enemy's' tactics. Shortly after the Six Day War, the theoretical organ of the Italian Party, *Rinascita*, published a revealing statement, which claimed that the US had abandoned containment and had reverted to a policy of 'rolling back' Soviet influence, in order to change the global balance, support pro-Western governments, and overthrow pro-Soviet regimes. The very use of the phrase 'roll back' amounts practically to an admission of a series of setbacks; what makes this particular statement highly significant is the fact that, shortly before the article appeared, an Italian Communist delegation had been to see Boris Ponomarev, who is the Secretary of the Soviet Communist Party's Central Committee in charge of relations with Communist parties outside the bloc. It appears that this particular phrase had emanated from him, so that there is some reason for thinking that the Kremlin is, indeed, anxious about the cumulative effect of this 'roll back', especially on the Soviet empire itself.

It is not possible here to present detailed documentation for this view, but two illustrations may suffice to show that it is supported by the 'facts of life' in Eastern Europe.

In the beginning of 1967, a Hungarian magazine (*Elet es Irodalom*) published the results of an opinion poll of Hungarian students on questions of both domestic and international concern. The author of the article revealed that he was 'taken aback' by the answers and he quoted some respondents as saying 'in a brutal way' that 'many people have already interfered in the Vietnamese war and if Hungary too interferes on the side of the Soviet Union, the Americans would include us in the bombing as well'. There could hardly be a better illustration of the low opinion which Soviet behaviour in Vietnam has created throughout Eastern Europe of the protective value of the Soviet 'shield'. In case there was any doubt about this conclusion, the author of the article proceeded to quote other students as saying that, in such an eventuality, 'no nation would fight on Hungary's behalf'. It must be realized that this prevalent impression of the Soviet Union as an unreliable power in case of need carried with it an even graver implication from the Kremlin's point of view, namely that Russia's own determination to apply her power, even in her own interests, could no longer be taken very seriously.

A second example concerns the 1967 Middle East war, and the effect on Eastern Europe of what was clearly regarded as an unmitigated Soviet debacle. It now emerges that this became a convenient symbol or battleflag in the fight against Soviet domination of Eastern Europe. In the heyday of Czech liberalism, in April of 1968, Prague Radio's well-known lady commentator, Vera Stovickova, made some highly significant revelations concerning this point. Hinting broadly at the outside pressure which had forced Czechoslovakia into an extremely one-sided posture during the Middle East war, she stated :

In our country last year, the old leadership [that is the Novotny regime] adopted an extreme standpoint, without taking into consideration the true state of affairs, and forced it in an utterly undemocratic manner upon the public. Resistance to this policy thus became first, the struggle for the right to a just viewing of the Arab–Israel conflict, and second, it became a part of the struggle for democratization, against the dictating of views by those in power. [She left little doubt that this meant Moscow as well as Novotny.] And so in our country we arrived at the extraordinary situation in which one's attitude to the war in the Middle East became the criterion for one's attitude to the internal crisis.... Diplomatic workers, journalists and politicians, as a whole, split up: on the one side there stood ... those who actually believed only in the Holy War of the Arabs, as well as those who were waiting upon the men in power, as usual; and on the other side there stood ... those who believed only in the Holy War of Israelis as well as those who insisted on the right to an objective standpoint. My choice in those times when I could not write the objective truth ... was silence on the subject.

Thus we have a clear indication that members of the élite itself – diplomats, journalists and politicians – were utilizing the Six Day War as a symbol both of the struggle against Soviet hegemony and of the fact that Soviet power and influence could be successfully defied. This, incidentally, may be the reason why the Soviet campaign against 'Zionism' in Eastern Europe has been conducted so ferociously of late. This is, apparently, not only an attack upon a single religious and ethnic group, although *that* is the case as well, but this shows that Moscow has caught on to the fact that this particular Soviet setback in the Middle East was gladly seized upon as a symbol of liberal and autonomist circles in Eastern Europe, and they, too, are being attacked under the name of 'Zionism'. It is, of course, well known that certain Polish Air Force officers gleefully drank to the health of the victors in the Six Day War as a way of expressing their true opinion of the Soviet Union. None of the officers concerned is believed to have been Jewish, and some may well have been anti-Semitic – yet, paradoxically, they are among the people who are now being attacked as 'Zionists'!

Soviet action in Czechoslovakia only becomes fully comprehensible when viewed against the background of the cumulative effect on Eastern Europe of the series of global setbacks which have been outlined here and of the Soviet 'credibility gap' which has been created as a result of these debacles.

As Moscow saw it, the 'roll back' was real enough and serious enough, even if it was not really the result of a new policy by the 'imperialists', but rather the outcome of a measurable gap between Soviet pretensions and Soviet power. One faction in the Kremlin is believed to have felt that if, after Cuba, Ghana, Algeria, Indonesia, the bombing of North Vietnam and the Middle Eastern setback, Moscow permitted Prague to glide away with impunity, the USSR would become a laughing-stock and would never again be taken seriously in Eastern Europe and elsewhere.

Thus the June 1967 war was a disaster from the Soviet point of view – not only because it led to the destruction of more than one billion dollars' worth of Soviet equipment and the annihilation of Soviet-trained armies, as well as an undermining of the prestige of the pro-Soviet regimes, but also because a chain of cause-and-effect relationships linked this defeat with the Soviet debacle in Prague.

Yet, in spite of this, some Western commentators seem to labour under the belief that, since the 1967 war, the Soviets have, in some mysterious way, been able to turn disaster into glorious victory; that Moscow, in fact, has come up with what to me seems to be a very unpromising recipe, namely, 'in order to win, start by losing one war'. We are told that there has been complete 'polarization' in the Middle East, meaning presumably that the Soviet Union is left alone with one party in the Arab–Israel conflict, and the US with the other party. This state of affairs is supposed to be wonderful for the Kremlin, because it allegedly gives it 'a predominant influence over the region'. Of course, this presupposes that Cairo, Damascus and Algiers are the whole of the Middle East and it leaves out such 'minor and unimportant details' as Turkey, Iran, Israel, Cyprus, Ethiopia

Tunisia, Lebanon, Libya and Morocco to mention only a few. Moreover, from what sovietologists can gather, Moscow is by *no means* overjoyed with this 'polarization'. Since Stalin, Soviet leaders have always liked to ask, and correctly so, 'how many divisions do our friends have?' Unlike some Western commentators, the Kremlin is only too conscious of the fact that 'polarization' leaves it in lonely splendour with thrice-defeated regimes, whose armies all the Soviet hardware and training of fourteen years have not been able to turn into fighting machines, whereas the US is left 'merely' with the strongest and nationally most cohesive military powers in the region, Turkey, Iran and Israel. Seen from Moscow, this does not at all look like a promising equation.

Of course, there *are* the famous three Soviet naval squadrons with their facilities in Syrian, Egyptian and Algerian harbours, but I would hope that this development might be viewed with a little common sense. First of all, Soviet naval vessels have been utilizing such facilities ever since 1965 – in the case of Egypt, i.e. prior to the June 1967 war and not as a result of that war. In the second place, the whole aim of the Red Mediterranean Navy is to become self-contained – independent of vulnerable shore facilities, so that the latter, at most, are of temporary value. Finally, the Soviet Mediterranean squadrons have no aircraft carriers: they contain merely one helicopter carrier, their shore-based facilities are immobile and therefore very vulnerable, their dock and repair facilities are totally inadequate to their number, they have few landing craft, and probably only about one battalion of marines. However, even if they were completely equal or superior to the Sixth Fleet, which is simply not the case, this would not mean a great deal for the Kremlin. After all, there can be no battle in isolation between the Soviet Mediterranean Navy and the US Sixth Fleet. An attack by Soviet vessels on US ships in the Mediterranean is the beginning of a thermonuclear war. Thus, it is not too relevant what the local strength of the Soviet Navy really is. In purely military terms, it is the global thermonuclear balance which matters. In other words, as long as the US Sixth Fleet is there, the Soviet squadrons constitute little more than a psychological weapon. Thus, the most publicized advantage which the Kremlin has allegedly gained because of so-called Middle Eastern 'polarization' is dubious at best.

However, the disadvantages of 'polarization' are only too real, as Moscow realizes very well. In order to understand this, we have to review the antecedents of the June 1967 war. We should recall that this was the accidental result of a somewhat mismanaged operation by one of the departments of the Soviet KGB, the notorious Disinformation Department of the late General Agoyansk. It will be recalled that the Egyptians, who had come to rely almost entirely on Soviet intelligence in Israel, were informed by Moscow that the Israelis were allegedly massing for an attack on Syria and that only an Egyptian mobilization in the Sinai Peninsula could save Damascus. The Egyptian War Minister, Badran, later revealed during his trial that the Egyptians had discovered, too late, that the Soviet allegations had been 'a mere hallucination'.

In fact, what the Russians had intended to do was merely to repeat their old hoary ploy, which dates back all the way to 1957 – manufacturing a phony 'invasion danger' and then posing as the 'saviours' of the Damascus regime. They felt assured that there would be no actual war, because they believed that UNEF would remain as a buffer between Egypt and Israel, at least in the vital Straits of Tiran. They overlooked one minor detail, and that was the possible reaction of the Secretary-General of the United Nations. U Thant, as will be recalled, instead of following the procedures which were clearly set out for such a contingency in a memorandum left by his predecessor Hammarskjöld, namely to employ delaying tactics, abruptly withdrew UN Forces after Egypt's mobilization. Thus, Nasser was unexpectedly left in sole possession of the Straits of Tiran, whereupon he promptly declared a blockade of Israel vessels, a step which Israel had warned for ten years would constitute a *casus belli*. In other words, Soviet Intelligence, by overlooking this possibility, helped to bring about a war disastrous to the Arab countries.

The subsequent purges in Moscow were partially due to this bungled operation. Arab bitterness towards Moscow following the disaster was almost entirely the result of the feeling that Soviet misinformation had been responsible. Thus Moscow was left, rather apologetically, face to face with the bitter and humiliated losers of the June war, who kept badgering the Kremlin to do something in order to make up for its sins in 1967. Specifically this meant that Russia should, if necessary, stage a military confrontation with the West in order to regain territories which Egypt and Syria were quite unable to regain for themselves.

Needless to say, Moscow did not have the slightest intention of doing anything of the kind. Moreover, 'polarization' also meant that if Cairo continued cutting its ties with the West, the USSR might eventually have to feed and to provide entirely for an isolated Egypt, at a daily cost of several million dollars (which would be worse than five Cubas) – or face the eventual overthrow of its client, the Nasser regime. The Russians have enjoyed these prospects so little that, far from encouraging 'polarization', they are believed to have told Nasser repeatedly to keep some ties with the West: 'Don't rely on us for economic aid – try again to get some from the West – don't ask *us* to get back the Sinai Peninsula for you – why don't you turn to the Americans?'

The Soviets did, in fact, want to keep the Nasser regime in power and see it regain lost territories, since these territories constitute a living symbol and a perpetual reminder of the Soviet 'credibility gap', which has been described. However, they wanted to achieve this aim at no cost to themselves. Consequently they came up with the brilliant idea of permitting the US to pull the chestnuts out of the fire for them – that, of course requiring another campaign of the 'disinformation' type. In this particular case, a new war scare was started, except that now it was not the Israelis, but the Egyptians who were supposed to be girding for the fray. In spite of the fact that Nasser's army is at least eighteen months from battle readiness, as he himself has repeatedly indicated, a credulous world was informed that the Egyptian leader was hovering on the brink of the abyss, that Gromyko had rushed to Cairo to restrain Nasser but was only just managing to do so, and that he might lose his grip over

Nasser – *unless* the West rushed to accept the Soviet plan for the Middle East, namely, force the Israelis to withdraw to the pre-June 1967 situation.

In that eventuality, of course, the Kremlin, at no cost or danger to itself, would be able to save the now somewhat shaky Egyptian regime, prove to the Middle East that reliance on the Soviet Union had, in the end, borne fruit and regained lost land, thus closing the 'credibility gap' which has been plaguing the Soviet leadership.

On the surface, it seems hardly credible that the West should be so naïve as to buy such a suggestion – although after seeing some of the Western reactions to the Soviet ploy, one wonders whether the Russians had not perhaps calculated correctly after all. Just how little intelligence the West is credited with can be seen from a special broadcast to North America which was made by the Soviet expert on Egypt, Georgi Mirsky, on 7 February 1969. The Middle Eastern situation, he said, was 'dangerous now and of course war can break out at any moment, but if war can break out at any moment, it can only be because the US takes a very equivocal position. If America really brings pressure upon Israel, then this could help the cause of peace. I believe the time has come for America to bring this kind of pressure to bear upon Israel. This is a very dangerous situation.' The pressure presumably refers to forcing the Israelis to withdraw from vital strategic areas without a peace treaty and without any real security (which seems somewhat more like a prescription for war than for peace). However, the picture conjured up by Mr Mirsky is very interesting and also a little strange since, according to him, there is no real clash between US and Soviet interests, but rather both are threatened by a gigantic third superpower – which numbers two and a half million inhabitants.

The question arises whether, under these circumstances, any useful purpose can be served by discussing the Middle East with the Russians. The answer to this question can be yes only if it is realized clearly just what Moscow is attempting to do, and if, as a result, talks are directed to a somewhat different goal. What would be worth discussing is not the imposition of an entirely one-sided and totally unrealistic 'solution' – but rather the institutionalization of a tacit agreement between the two superpowers, which has existed, *de facto*, since June 1967. A US – Soviet agreement on the Middle East can only be bilateral, that is to say, it can only cover the actions of the two superpowers themselves, but it cannot be multilateral; it cannot cover the actions of third parties. The Middle East is not an international protectorate and its people are not satellites; moreover, the US and Soviet aims in the region are far from compatible at this stage. What could be usefully discussed, therefore, is not an Arab–Israel settlement which has no meaning or future unless it is freely, wholeheartedly and permanently reached between the parties themselves, but ways of ensuring that conflict in the area remains limited and does not involve the outside world. I believe this can be done with relative ease, since, in any case, the superpowers have been acting on parallel lines in this particular respect.

There could be talks on a possible US–Soviet understanding along the following lines :

1. That neither side will directly intervene in the region, provided the other party refrains from doing so. This would mean that neither troops, 'volunteers', 'advisers', pilots and vessels from either side would participate in Middle Eastern battles.

2. That any renewed fighting in the area should be limited to five or six days at the most, through a Security Council cease-fire order – as happened in all previous Middle Eastern wars. This poses no particular problem, since none of the armies concerned has the necessary material and reserves for a very prolonged war.

3. Finally, the superpowers shall try to bring about a cease-fire the moment there is danger that vital Middle East ern population centres might be destroyed or conquered (Cairo, Alexandria, Tel Aviv, Jerusalem). This too should not be particularly difficult, because the Egyptians now do not have the strength to reach the Israel centres and the Israelis have no particular incentive to reach the Egyptian centres, since they could not conceivably occupy areas with tens of millions of inhabitants.

An understanding on these three points could thus lead the two great powers to assuring that a Middle Eastern conflict would neither spread nor wreak irreparable damage. I don't believe that such a US–Soviet agreement could or should involve the question of arms supplies to the region. The Soviets basically have nothing to offer their Middle Eastern friends except arms, and therefore they would either refuse to agree to a limitation pact or they would renege on it – or they would accept only a cut-off date which would give all advantages to their allies, and leave the other side defenceless. Therefore, an arms limitation agreement is a utopian concept. Nor is it necessarily desirable, for, cut off from outside supplies, the combatants would themselves go in for research and development and would squander more – not fewer – resources on military expenditures.

A US–Soviet understanding along the lines suggested – to 'unharness', as it were, the Middle Eastern conflict from the global contest – would leave the local peoples to work out their own destiny, now in conflict, but hopefully later in peace. But this cannot be achieved by a unilateral US disengagement, which would merely remove all restraint on Soviet actions in the region. The Sixth Fleet will have to stay there as a standing reminder to the USSR that neither superpower will permit the other to intervene.

A Selective Bibliography

Zionism

Alex Bein: *Theodor Herzl*, Philadelphia, 1940.

Adolf Boehm: *Die zionistische Bewegung.* 2 vols. Berlin and Jerusalem, 1935/37.

Israel Cohen: *The Zionist Movement.* New York, 1946.

Benjamin Halpern: *The Idea of a Jewish State.* Cambridge, Mass., 1961.

Arthur Herzberg (ed.): *The Zionist Idea. A Historical Analysis and Reader.* New York, 1960.

Leonard Stein: *The Balfour Declaration.* London, 1961.

Chaim Weizmann: *Trial and Error.* New York, 1949.

Arabism and the Arab World

George Antonius: *The Arab Awakening.* Philadelphia, 1939; London, 1946.

Erskine B. Childers: *The Road to Suez: A Study of Western-Arab Relations.* London, 1962.

Charles D. Cremeans: *The Arabs and the World.* New York, 1963.

Sami Hadawi: *Bitter Harvest, Palestine 1914–1967.* New York, 1967.

Slyvia Haim (ed.): *Arab Nationalism. An Anthology.* Berkeley, 1962.

Kemal H. Karpat (ed.): *Political and Social Thought in the Contemporary Middle East.* New York, 1968.

Tom Little: *Modern Egypt.* New York, 1967.

Gamal Abdel Nasser: *The Philosophy of the Revolution.* Cairo, 1964.

Mohammed Neguib: *Egypt's Destiny*. London, 1955.

H. Z. Nuseibeh: *The Ideas of Arab Nationalism*. Princeton, 1956.

Maxime Rodinson: *Israel and the Arabs*. London, 1968.

Fayez Sayegh: *Arab Unity: Hope and Fulfilment*. New York, 1958.

Keith Wheelock: *Nasser's New Egypt*. New York, 1960.

Palestine

Esco Foundation for Palestine: *Palestine: A study of Jewish, Arab and British policies*. 2 vols. New Haven, 1947.

Paul L. Hanna: *British Policy in Palestine*. New York, 1942.

J C. Hurewitz: *The Struggle for Palestine*. New York, 1950.

John Marlowe: *The Seat of Pilate. An Account of the Palestine Mandate*. London, 1959.

Royal Commission on Palestine: *Palestine Royal Commission Report*. London, 1937.

Sir Ronald Storrs: *Memoirs. (Orientations)*. New York, 1937.

A survey of Palestine. (3 vols.) Government Printing Office. Jerusalem, 1945–6.

Christopher Sykes: *Crossroads to Israel. Palestine from Balfour to Bevin*. London, 1965.

Israel

David Ben Gurion: *Rebirth and Destiny of Israel*. New York, 1954.

— *Years of Challenge*. London, 1963.

Marver H. Bernstein: *The Politics of Israel: The First Decade of Statehood*. Princeton, 1957.

Abba Eban: *Voice of Israel*. New York, 1957.

Walter Eytan: *The First Ten Years. A Diplomatic History of Israel*. New York, 1958.

Leonard Fine: *Politics in Israel*. Boston, 1967.

Don Peretz: *Israel and the Palestine Arabs*. Washington, 1958.

Terence Prittie: *Israel, Miracle in the Desert*. London, 1967.
Nadav Safran: *The United States and Israel*. Cambridge, Mass., 1963.

The Three Wars

E. L. M. Burns: *Between Arab and Israeli*, New York, 1962.
Winston S. Churchill and Randolph S. Churchill: *The Six Day War*. London, 1967.
Rony E. Gabbay: *A Political Study of the Arab–Jewish Conflict: the Refugee Problem*. Paris, 1959.
Robert Henriques: *One Hundred Hours to Suez. An Account of Israel's Campaign in the Sinai Peninsula*. London, 1957.
David Kimche and Dan Bawly: *The Sandstorm: The Arab–Israeli War of 1967*. London, 1968.
Jon and David Kimche: *Both Sides of the Hill*. New York, 1960.
Walter Laqueur: *The Road to Jerusalem. The Origins of the Arab–Israeli Conflict*. New York, 1968.
Netanel Lorch: *The Edge of the Sword. Israel's War of Independence 1947–49*. New York, 1961.
Terence Robertson: *Crisis. The Inside Story of the Suez Conspiracy*. London, 1965.
Hugh Thomas: *The Suez Affair*. London, 1970.
Constantine Zurayk: *The Meaning of the Disaster*. Beirut, 1956.

Other Books

Lukasz Hirszowicz: *The Third Reich and the Arab East*. London, 1966.
Charles Issawi: *Egypt in Revolution. An Economic Analysis*. New York, 1963.
Malcolm Kerr: *The Arab Cold War 1958–1964*. London, 1965.
Walter Laqueur (ed.): *The Middle East in Transition*. New York, 1958.
Bernard Lewis: *The Middle East and the West*. New York, 1964.
Patrick Seale: *The Struggle for Syria*. London, 1965.